The Designer's Guide
to VHDL

The Designer's Guide to VHDL

Peter J. Ashenden

THE UNIVERSITY OF ADELAIDE

Morgan Kaufmann Publishers, Inc.

San Francisco, California

Sponsoring Editor	Bruce M. Spatz
Production Manager	Yonie Overton
Senior Production Editor	Cheri Palmer
Editorial Assistant	Jane Elliott
Cover Design	Carron Design
Text Design	Rebecca Evans & Associates
Copyeditor	Gary Morris
Proofreader	Jennifer McClain
Printer	Edwards Brothers, Inc.

Figure 18-8 (p. 512) and Appendix B (pp. 512–624) reprinted from IEEE Std 1076-1993
"IEEE Standard VHDL Language Reference Manual," Copyright © 1994 by the Institute of
Electrical and Electronic Engineers, Inc. Appendix C (pp. 625–628) reprinted from IEEE Std
1164-1993 "IEEE Standard Multivalue Logic System for VHDL Model Interoperability
(Std_logic_1164)," Copyright © 1993 by the Institute of Electrical and Electronic Engineers,
Inc. The IEEE disclaims any responsibility or liability resulting from the placement and use in
the described manner. Information is reprinted with the permission of the IEEE.

Morgan Kaufmann Publishers, Inc.
Editorial and Sales Office
340 Pine Street, Sixth Floor
San Francisco, CA 94104-3205
USA

Telephone	415/392-2665
Facsimile	415/982-2665
Internet	mkp@mkp.com
Web site	http://www.mkp.com

01   9

Library of Congress Cataloging-in-Publication Data

Ashenden, Peter J.
    The designer's guide to VHDL / Peter J. Ashenden
       p.   cm.
    Includes bibliographical references and index.
    ISBN 1-55860-270-4 (pbk.)
    1. VHDL (Computer hardware description language) 2. Electronic
digital computers—computer simulation.   I. Title
TK7888.3.A863   1995
621.39'2—dc20   95-33228
                              CIP

To my wife Katrina

Foreword

by Paul Menchini
Research Triangle Park, North Carolina

Digital electronic systems are increasing exponentially in their complexity over time. This fact, coupled with decreasing product lifetimes and increasing reliability requirements, has forced designers to dramatically increase their productivity and the quality of their designs.

VHDL was developed in response to these trends. Borrowing complexity management and error detection techniques from the software engineering world, VHDL was developed to eliminate irrelevant detail, allow technology-independent description, catch errors earlier, and promote portable and interoperable models from the gate to the system level.

In response, EDA tools have been designed to take an ever-greater share of the burden from designers. A single representation medium can now drive design processes from specification down to detailed digital design.

Originally developed as the United States Department of Defense's standard hardware description language (HDL), VHDL has evolved through two additional rounds of IEEE standardization into one of the two preeminent HDLs in use throughout the world. Continued development in the areas of detailed timing models, synthesis directives, analog capabilities, and so forth mean the VHDL will continue to provide the expressive facilities needed by state-of-the-art designs well into the next century. New tools leveraging on VHDL's precise definition continue to be introduced and offer increased simulation performance, increased synthesis capabilities, and entirely new capabiliites, such as the formal verification of the functional equivalence of models.

Because VHDL uses concepts not commonly found in hardware description, designers approaching VHDL for the first time need a sure guide to the features using these concepts. One of the few books on VHDL that does not rely heavily on experience with programming languages, *A Designer's Guide to VHDL* is ideal for the nonprogrammer wishing to learn VHDL.

This book explores in detail the latest version of VHDL, VHDL-93 (IEEE Std. 1076–1993). Assuming no prior knowledge of VHDL, Professor Ashenden walks the reader through VHDL, first addressing simple modeling issues, then moving on to the more complex. As VHDL contains many features, the reader is greatly aided by the inclusion of four fully worked case studies. These case studies put VHDL's features in context and show how they work in concert to model digital systems of varying levels of complexity and varying levels of detail.

Appendices cover the use of VHDL in synthesis, as well as other standards built upon the VHDL framework. As an aid to the experienced user of VHDL, other appendices contain syntax summaries and a list of differences from the initial IEEE standard, IEEE Std. 1076–1987.

Welcome to VHDL!

Contents

Preface

VHDL is a language for describing digital electronic systems. It arose out of the United States government's Very High Speed Integrated Circuits (VHSIC) program. In the course of this program, it became clear that there was a need for a standard language for describing the structure and function of integrated circuits (ICs). Hence the VHSIC Hardware Description Language (VHDL) was developed. It was subsequently developed further under the auspices of the Institute of Electrical and Electronic Engineers (IEEE) and adopted in the form of the IEEE Standard 1076 *Standard VHDL Language Reference Manual* in 1987.

Like all IEEE standards, the VHDL standard is subject to review every five years. Comments and suggestions from users of the 1987 standard were analyzed by the IEEE working group responsible for VHDL, and in 1992 a revised version of the standard was proposed. This was eventually adopted in 1993. This book describes the 1993 version of VHDL, often referred to as VHDL-93.

VHDL is designed to fill a number of needs in the design process. First, it allows description of the structure of a system, that is, how it is decomposed into subsystems and how those subsystems are interconnected. Second, it allows the specification of the function of a system using familiar programming language forms. Third, as a result, it allows the design of a system to be simulated before being manufactured, so that designers can quickly compare alternatives and test for correctness without the delay and expense of hardware prototyping. Fourth, it allows the detailed structure of a design to be synthesized from a more abstract specification, allowing designers to concentrate on more strategic design decisions and reducing time to market.

This book presents a structured guide to the modeling facilities offered by the VHDL language, showing how they can be used for the design of digital systems. The book does not purport to teach digital design, since that topic is large enough by itself to warrant several textbooks covering its various aspects. Instead, the book assumes that the reader has at least a basic grasp of digital design concepts, such as might be gained from a first course in digital design in an engineering degree program. Some exposure to computer programming and to concepts of computer organization will also be beneficial. This book is suitable for use in an introductory or intermediate-level course in digital or computer design. It will also serve practicing engineers who need to acquire VHDL fluency as part of their changing job requirements.

Structure of the Book

The Designer's Guide to VHDL is organized so that it can be read linearly from front to back. This path offers a graduated development, with each chapter building on ideas introduced in the preceding chapters. Each chapter introduces a number of related concepts or language facilities and illustrates each one with examples. Scattered throughout the book are four case studies, which bring together preceding material in the form of extended worked examples.

Chapter 1 introduces the idea of a hardware description language and outlines the reasons for its use and the benefits that ensue. It then proceeds to introduce the basic concepts underlying VHDL, so that they can serve as a basis for examples in subsequent chapters. The next three chapters cover the aspects of VHDL that are most like conventional programming languages. These may be used to describe the behavior of a system in algorithmic terms. Chapter 2 explains the basic type system of the language and introduces the scalar data types. Chapter 3 describes the sequential control structures, and Chapter 4 covers composite data structures used to represent collections of data elements.

In Chapter 5, the main facilities of VHDL used for modeling hardware are covered in detail. These include facilities for modeling the basic behavioral elements in a design, the signals that interconnect them and the hierarchical structure of the design. The combination of facilities described in these early chapters is sufficient for many modeling tasks, so Chapter 6 brings them together in the first case study, in which a multiplier/accumulator circuit is designed.

The next group of chapters extends this basic set of facilities with language features that make modeling of large systems more tractable. Chapter 7 introduces procedures and functions, which can be used to encapsulate behavioral aspects of a design. Chapter 8 introduces the package as a means of collecting together related parts of a design or of creating modules that can be reused in a number of designs. Chapter 9 then covers aliases as a way of managing the large number of names that arise in a large model. The material in this group of chapters is brought together in the next case study in Chapter 10, in which a package of binary arithmetic operations is developed.

The third group of chapters covers advanced modeling features in VHDL. Chapter 11 deals with the important topic of resolved signals, and Chapter 12 describes generic constants as a means of parameterizing the behavior and structure of a design. While these language facilities form the basis of many real-world models, their treatment in this book is left to this late chapter. Experience has shown that the ideas can be difficult to understand without a solid foundation in the more basic language aspects. Chapter 13 deals with the topics of component instantiation and configuration. These features are also important in large real-world models, but they can be difficult to understand. Hence this book introduces structural modeling through the mechanism of direct instantiation in earlier chapters and leaves the more general case of component instantiation and configuration until this later chapter. In Chapter 14, generated regular structures are covered. Chapter 15 brings the material in this group of chapters together in the third case study, in which a register-transfer-level model of a CPU is described.

The fourth group of chapters covers language facilities generally used for system-level modeling. Chapter 16 is a detailed treatment of the related topics of guarded signals and blocks. Chapter 17 introduces the notion of access types (or pointers) and uses them to develop linked data structures. This leads to a discussion of abstract data types as a means of managing the complexity associated with linked data structures. Chapter 18 covers the language facilities for input and output using files, including binary files and text files. Chapter 19 is a case study in which a queuing network model of a computer system is developed.

The final pair of chapters draws the tour of VHDL to a close by covering the remaining language facilities. Chapter 20 describes the attribute mechanism as a means of annotating a design with additional information. Chapter 21 is a miscellany of advanced topics not covered in the previous chapters.

Whereas a complete reading of this book provides a complete coverage of the language, there are several shorter paths through the material. Some suggested minimal paths for readers with different requirements are as follows.

- For an introductory course in digital modeling using VHDL: Chapters 1 to 5, 7, 8, 11 and 12, plus the case study in Chapter 6. Chapters 9 and 10 may be included if time permits.

- For a more advanced course: add Chapters 13 and 14, and as much of the case study in Chapter 15 as time permits.

- For readers proficient in using conventional programming languages: treat Chapters 2 to 4 as review.

- For readers with some previous introductory-level background in VHDL: treat Chapters 1 to 4 as review.

Each chapter in the book is followed by a set of exercises designed to help the reader develop understanding of the material. Where an exercise relates to a particular topic described in the chapter, the section number is included in square brackets. An approximate "difficulty" rating is also provided, expressed using the following symbols:

❶ quiz-style exercise, testing basic understanding

❷ basic modeling exercise—10 minutes to half an hour effort

❸ advanced modeling exercise—half to two hours effort

❹ modeling project—half a day or more effort

Answers for the first category of exercises are provided in Appendix G. The remaining categories involve developing VHDL models. Readers are encouraged to test correctness of their models by running them on a VHDL simulator. This is a much more effective learning exercise than comparing paper models with paper solutions.

One pervasive theme running through the presentation in this book is that modeling a system using a hardware description language is essentially a software design exercise. This implies that good software engineering practice should be applied. Hence the treatment in this book draws directly from experience in software engineering. There are numerous hints and techniques from small-scale and large-scale software engineering presented throughout the book, with the sincere intention that they might be of use to readers.

Resources for Help and Information

While this book attempts to be comprehensive in its coverage of VHDL, there will no doubt be questions that it does not answer. For these, the reader will need to seek other resources. A valuable source of experience and advice, often overlooked, is one's colleagues, either at the workplace or in user groups. User groups generally hold regular meetings that either formally or informally include a time for questions and answers. Many also run computer bulletin board systems with discussion groups for problem solving. There are a number of VHDL user groups around the world, many operating under the auspices of the VHDL International organization. The part of the organization for VHDL users is the VHDL International Users' Forum. It sponsors conferences, design contests and other activities. The contact address is

VIUF (VHDL International Users' Forum)
407 Chester Street
Menlo Park, CA 94025

Phone: 415 / 329-0578

Fax: 415 / 324-3150

E-mail: viuf–info@vhdl.org

The administrative arm of the organization can be contacted at

VI (VHDL International)
3140 De La Cruz Blvd., Suite 200
Santa Clara, CA 95054-2046

Phone: 408 / 492-9806

Fax: 408 / 434-7977

E-mail: vi–info@vhdl.org

VIUF also maintains an on-line information service, the *VHDL International Users' Forum Internet Services* (VIIS) server. It is accessible via the World-Wide Web, using the URL:

http://vhdl.org

The home page contains pointers to repositories maintained by several VHDL standards groups and user groups.

Readers who have access to the Usenet electronic news network will find the news group comp.lang.vhdl a valuable resource. This discussion group is a source of announcements, sample models, questions and answers and useful software. Participants include VHDL users and people actively involved in the language standard working group and in VHDL tool development. The "frequently asked questions" (FAQ) file for this group is a mine of useful pointers to books, products and other information. It is archived on the VIIS server mentioned above.

One resource that must be mentioned is the IEEE Standard 1076–1993 *Standard VHDL Language Reference Manual*, sometimes referred to as the "VHDL Bible." It is the authoritative source of information about VHDL. However, since it is a definitional document, not a tutorial, it is written in a complex legalistic style. This makes it very difficult to use to answer the usual questions that arise when writing VHDL models.

It should only be used once you are somewhat familiar with VHDL. It can be ordered from the IEEE at the following address, and quoting the publication number SH16840.

Ask*IEEE
Attn: Manager, Document Delivery
P. O. Box 4327
Burlingame, CA 94011-4327

Phone: 800 / 949-IEEE (within US and Canada)
        415 / 259-5040 (outside US and Canada)

Fax: 415 / 259-5045

E-mail: askieee@ieee.org

Readers who are interested in the VHDL subset for synthesis developed by the European VHDL Synthesis Working Group (EVSWG), mentioned in Appendix A, should contact Eugenio Villar (e-mail: villar@bree.unican.es) for information. The EVSWG maintains an e-mail mailing list at the address evswg@bree.unican.es. Readers should contact the list manager, Fran Llacer, at llacer@bree.unican.es to be included on the mailing list.

This book contains numerous examples of VHDL models that may also serve as a resource for resolving questions. The VHDL source code for these examples and the case studies, as well as other related information, is available for on-line access on the World-Wide Web, using the URL:

http://www.mkp.com/books_catalog/1–55860–270–4.asp

Although I have been careful to avoid errors in the example code, there are no doubt some that I have missed. I would be pleased to hear about them, so that I can correct them in the on-line code and in future printings of this book. Errata and general comments can be e-mailed to me at

petera@cs.adelaide.edu.au

Acknowledgements

The seeds for this book go back to 1990 when I developed a brief set of notes, *The VHDL Cookbook*, for my computer architecture class at the University of Adelaide. At the time, there were few books on VHDL available, so I made my booklet available for on-line access. News of its availability spread quickly around the world, and within days, my e-mail in-box was bursting. At the time of writing this, over four years later, I still regularly receive messages about the *Cookbook*. Many of the respondents urged me to write a full textbook version. With that encouragement, I embarked upon the exercise that led to this book. I am grateful to the many engineers, students and teachers around the world who gave me that impetus. I hope that this book will go some way towards meeting their needs.

When I embarked upon writing, I was not aware of the amount of effort that would be required. Thanks are due to my colleagues at the University of Adelaide for advice and support over the last three years. Thanks also to Philip Wilsey and his postgraduate students at the University of Cincinnati for providing a lively and stimulating working environment during my sabbatical visit there in 1993. The book came along in leaps and bounds during that time.

Given the number of example models in this book, it was important that they be thoroughly checked. Model Technology, Inc., kindly donated use of their V–System analyzer and simulator for this purpose. I gratefully acknowledge this contribution and thank them for their timely responses to my frequent questions.

I would particularly like to thank Bruce Spatz and his enthusiastic staff at Morgan Kaufmann Publishers for their patience and encouragement, despite continued slippages in the completion date. Many thanks to Cheri Palmer, the Production Editor, for her efforts in expediting the final stages in the sprint to the finish line. Thanks are also due to the reviewers: Poras Balsara of University of Texas, Paul Menchini of Menchini & Associates, David Pitts of GTE Labs and University of Lowell, and Philip Wilsey of University of Cincinnati. Their insight and helpful comments were the source of much improvement in the writing and presentation. In particular, I am indebted to Paul for his meticulous markup of my draft—*mille grazie*, Paul! Also, thanks very much to David Bishop for his valuable contribution, Appendix A, on synthesis. I am sure David's practical hints will be more useful to readers than any theoretical dissertation I could have written.

Lastly, I would like to thank my wife Katrina, to whom this book is dedicated. I used to think that authors dedicating their books to their partners was somewhat contrived, if not downright corny! However, now that I've been through the exercise, I understand the value of a partner's understanding, encouragement and support. Katrina has been more than generous with these, and has suffered my late nights and frequent ill-humor with much forbearance. I am deeply grateful.

Fundamental Concepts

In this introductory chapter, we describe what we mean by digital system modeling and see why modeling and simulation are an important part of the design process. We see how the hardware description language VHDL can be used to model digital systems, and introduce some of the basic concepts underlying the language. We complete this chapter with a description of the basic lexical and syntactic elements of the language, to form a basis for the detailed descriptions of language features that follow in later chapters.

1.1   Modeling Digital Systems

If we are to discuss the topic of modeling digital systems, we first need to agree on what a digital system is. Different engineers would come up with different definitions, depending on their background and the field in which they were working. Some may consider a single VLSI circuit to be a self-contained digital system. Others might take a larger view and think of a complete computer, packaged in a cabinet with peripheral controllers and other interfaces.

For the purposes of this book, we include any digital circuit that processes or stores information as a digital system. We thus consider both the system as a whole and the various parts from which it is constructed. Thus our discussions cover a range of systems from the low-level gates that make up the components to the top-level functional units.

If we are to encompass this range of views of digital systems, we must recognize the complexity with which we are dealing. It is not humanly possible to comprehend such complex systems in their entirety. We need to find methods of dealing with the complexity, so that we can, with some degree of confidence, design components and systems that meet their requirements.

The most important way of meeting this challenge is to adopt a systematic methodology of design. If we start with a requirements document for the system, we can design an abstract structure that meets the requirements. We can then decompose this structure into a collection of components that interact to perform the same function. Each of these components can in turn be decomposed until we get to a level where we have some ready-made, primitive components that perform a required function. The result of this process is a hierarchically composed system, built from the primitive elements.

The advantage of this methodology is that each subsystem can be designed independently of others. When we use a subsystem, we can think of it as an abstraction rather than having to consider its detailed composition. So at any particular stage in the design process, we only need to pay attention to the small amount of information relevant to the current focus of design. We are saved from being overwhelmed by masses of detail.

We use the term *model* to mean our understanding of a system. The model represents that information which is relevant and abstracts away from irrelevant detail. The implication of this is that there may be several models of the same system, since different information is relevant in different contexts. One kind of model might concentrate on representing the function of the system, whereas another kind might represent the way in which the system is composed of subsystems. We will come back to this idea in more detail in the next section.

There are a number of important motivations for formalizing this idea of a model. First, when a digital system is needed, the requirements of the system must be specified. The job of the engineers is to design a system that meets these requirements. To do that, they must be given an understanding of the requirements, hopefully in a way that leaves them free to explore alternative implementations and to choose the best according to some criteria. One of the problems that often arises is that requirements are incompletely and ambiguously spelled out, and the customer and the design engineers disagree on what is meant by the requirements document. This problem can be avoided by using a formal model to communicate requirements.

A second reason for using formal models is to communicate understanding of the function of a system to a user. The designer cannot always predict every possible way in which a system may be used, and so is not able to enumerate all possible behaviors. If the designer provides a model, the user can check it against any given set of inputs and determine how the system behaves in that context. Thus a formal model is an invaluable tool for documenting a system.

A third motivation for modeling is to allow testing and verification of a design using simulation. If we start with a requirements model that defines the behavior of a system, we can simulate the behavior using test inputs and note the resultant outputs of the system. According to our design methodology, we can then design a circuit from subsystems, each with its own model of behavior. We can simulate this composite system with the same test inputs and compare the outputs with those of the previous simulation. If they are the same, we know that the composite system meets the requirements for the cases tested. Otherwise we know that some revision of the design is needed. We can continue this process until we reach the bottom level in our design hierarchy, where the components are real devices whose behavior we know. Subsequently, when the design is manufactured, the test inputs and outputs from simulation can be used to verify that the physical circuit functions correctly. This approach to testing and verification of course assumes that the test inputs cover all of the circumstances in which the final circuit will be used. The issue of test coverage is a complex problem in itself and is an active area of research.

A fourth motivation for modeling is to allow formal verification of the correctness of a design. Formal verification requires a mathematical statement of the required function of a system. This statement may be expressed in the notation of a formal logic system, such as temporal logic. Formal verification also requires a mathematical definition of the meaning of the modeling language or notation used to describe a design. The process of verification involves application of the rules of inference of the logic system to prove that the design implies the required function. While formal verification is not yet in everyday use, it is an active area of research. There have already been significant demonstrations of formal verification techniques in real design projects, and the promise for the future is bright.

One final, but equally important, motivation for modeling is to allow automatic synthesis of circuits. If we can formally specify the function required of a system, it is in theory possible to translate that specification into a circuit that performs the function. The advantage of this approach is that the human cost of design is reduced, and engineers are free to explore alternatives rather than being bogged down in design detail. Also, there is less scope for errors being introduced into a design and not being detected. If we automate the translation from specification to implementation, we can be more confident that the resulting circuit is correct.

The unifying factor behind all of these arguments is that we want to achieve maximum reliability in the design process for minimum cost and design time. We need to ensure that requirements are clearly specified and understood, that subsystems are used correctly and that designs meet the requirements. A major contributor to excessive cost is having to revise a design after manufacture to correct errors. By avoiding errors, and by providing better tools for the design process, costs and delays can be contained.

1.2   Domains and Levels of Modeling

In the previous section, we mentioned that there may be different models of a system, each focussing on different aspects. We can classify these models into three domains: *function*, *structure* and *geometry*. The functional domain is concerned with the operations performed by the system. In a sense, this is the most abstract domain of description, since it does not indicate how the function is implemented. The structural domain deals with how the system is composed of interconnected subsystems. The geometric domain deals with how the system is laid out in physical space.

Each of these domains can also be divided into levels of abstraction. At the top level, we consider an overview of function, structure or geometry, and at lower levels we introduce successively finer detail. Figure 1-1 (devised by Gajski and Kuhn, see reference [6]) represents the domains on three independent axes, and represents the levels of abstraction by the concentric circles crossing each of the axes.

FIGURE 1-1

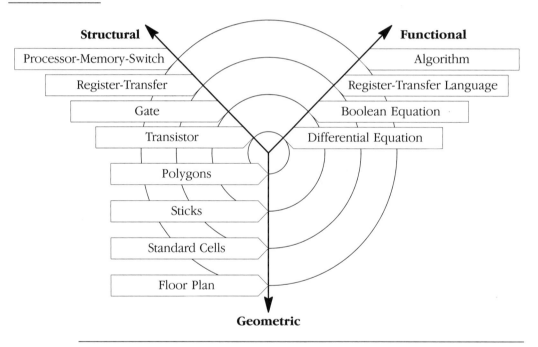

Domains and levels of abstraction. The radial axes show the three different domains of modeling. The concentric rings show the levels of abstraction, with the more abstract levels on the outside and more detailed levels towards the center.

Let us look at this classification in more detail, showing how at each level we can create models in each domain. As an example, we consider a single-chip microcontroller system used as the controller for some measurement instrument, with data input connections and some form of display outputs.

At the most abstract level, the function of the entire system may be described in terms of an algorithm, much like an algorithm for a computer program. This level of functional modeling is often called *behavioral modeling*, a term we shall adopt when presenting abstract descriptions of a system's function. A possible algorithm for our instrument controller is shown in Figure 1-2. This model describes how the controller repeatedly scans each data input and writes a scaled display of the input value.

FIGURE 1-2

```
loop
    for each data input loop
        read the value on this input;
        scale the value using the current scale factor for this input;
        convert the scaled value to a decimal string;
        write the string to the display output corresponding to this input;
    end loop;
    wait for 10 ms;
end loop;
```

An algorithm for a measurement instrument controller.

At this top level of abstraction, the structure of a system may be described as an interconnection of such components as processors, memories and input/output devices. This level is sometimes called the Processor Memory Switch (PMS) level, named after the notation used by Bell and Newell (see reference [2]). Figure 1-3 shows a structural model of the instrument controller drawn using this notation. It consists of a processor connected via a switch to a memory component and to controllers for the data inputs and display outputs.

FIGURE 1-3

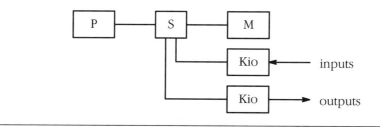

A PMS model of the controller structure. It is constructed from a processor (P), a memory (M), an interconnection switch (S) and two input/output controllers (Kio).

In the geometric domain at this top level of abstraction, a system to be implemented as a VLSI circuit may be modeled using a floor plan. This shows how the components described in the structural model are arranged on the silicon die. Figure 1-4 shows a possible floor plan for the instrument controller chip. There are analogous geometric descriptions for systems integrated in other media. For example, a personal computer system might be modeled at the top level in the geometric domain by an assembly diagram showing the positions of the motherboard and plug-in expansion boards in the desktop cabinet.

The next level of abstraction in modeling, depicted by the second ring in Figure 1-1, describes the system in terms of units of data storage and transformation. In the structur-

FIGURE 1-4

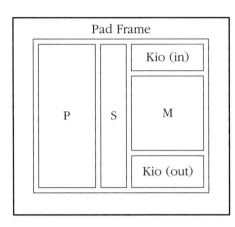

A floor plan model of the controller geometry.

FIGURE 1-5

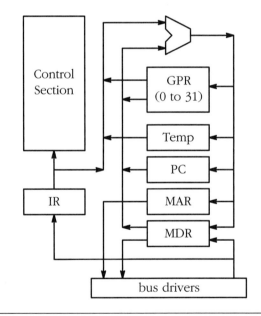

A register-transfer-level structural model of the controller processor. It consists of a general purpose register (GPR) file, registers for the program counter (PC), memory address (MAR), memory data (MDR), temporary values (Temp) and fetched instructions (IR), an arithmetic unit, bus drivers and the control section.

al domain, this is often called the *register-transfer* level, composed of a *data path* and a *control section*. The data path contains data storage registers, and data is transferred between them through transformation units. The control section sequences operation of the data path components. For example, a register-transfer-level structural model of the processor in our controller is shown in Figure 1-5.

In the functional domain, a *register-transfer language* (RTL) is often used to specify the operation of a system at this level. Storage of data is represented using register variables, and transformations are represented by arithmetic and logical operators. For example, an RTL model for the processor in our example controller might include the following description:

```
MAR ← PC,  memory_read ← 1
PC ← PC + 1
wait until ready = 1
IR ← memory_data
memory_read ← 0
```

This section of the model describes the operations involved in fetching an instruction from memory. The contents of the PC register are transferred to the memory address register, and the **memory_read** signal is asserted. Then the value from the PC register is transformed (incremented in this case) and transferred back to the PC register. When the **ready** input from the memory is asserted, the value on the memory data input is transferred to the instruction register. Finally, the **memory_read** signal is negated.

In the geometric domain, the kind of model used depends on the physical medium. In our example, standard library cells might be used to implement the registers and data transformation units, and these must be placed in the areas allocated in the chip floor plan.

The third level of abstraction shown in Figure 1-1 is the conventional logic level. At this level, structure is modeled using interconnections of gates, and function is modeled by Boolean equations or truth tables. In the physical medium of a custom integrated circuit, geometry may be modeled using a virtual grid, or "sticks," notation.

At the most detailed level of abstraction, we can model structure using individual transistors, function using the differential equations that relate voltage and current in the circuit, and geometry using polygons for each mask layer of an integrated circuit. Most designers do not need to work at this detailed level, as design tools are available to automate translation from a higher level.

1.3   Modeling Languages

In the previous section, we saw that different kinds of models can be devised to represent the various levels of function, structure and physical arrangement of a system. There are also different ways of expressing these models, depending on the use made of the model.

As an example, consider the ways in which a structural model may be expressed. One common form is a circuit schematic. Graphical symbols are used to represent subsystems, and instances of these are connected using lines that represent wires. This graphical form is generally the one preferred by designers. However, the same structural information can be represented textually in the form of a net list.

When we move into the functional domain, we usually see textual notations used for modeling. Some of these are intended for use as specification languages, to meet the need for describing the operation of a system without indicating how it might be implemented. These notations are usually based on formal mathematical methods, such as temporal logic or abstract state machines. Other notations are intended for simulating the system for test and verification purposes and are typically based on conventional programming languages. Yet other notations are oriented towards hardware synthesis and usually have a more restricted set of modeling facilities, since some programming language constructs are difficult to translate into hardware.

The purpose of this book is to describe the modeling language VHDL. VHDL includes facilities for describing structure and function at a number of levels, from the most abstract down to the gate level. It also provides an attribute mechanism that can be used to annotate a model with information in the geometric domain. VHDL is intended, among other things, as a modeling language for specification and simulation. We can also use it for hardware synthesis if we restrict ourselves to a subset that can be automatically translated into hardware.

1.4   VHDL Modeling Concepts

In the previous section, we looked at the three domains of modeling: function, structure and geometry. In this section, we look at the basic modeling concepts in each of these domains and introduce the corresponding VHDL elements for describing them. This will provide a feel for VHDL and a basis from which to work in later chapters. As an example, we look at ways of describing a four-bit register, shown in Figure 1-6.

FIGURE 1-6

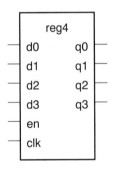

A four-bit register module. The register is named reg4 *and has six inputs,* d0, d1, d2, d3, en *and* clk, *and four outputs,* q0, q1, q2 *and* q3.

FIGURE 1-7

```
entity reg4 is
    port ( d0, d1, d2, d3, en, clk : in bit;
           q0, q1, q2, q3 : out  bit );
end entity reg4;
```

A VHDL entity description of a four-bit register.

Using VHDL terminology, we call the module **reg4** a design *entity*, and the inputs and outputs are *ports*. Figure 1-7 shows a VHDL description of the interface to this entity. This is an example of an *entity declaration*. It introduces a name for the entity and lists the input and output ports, specifying that they carry bit values ('0' or '1') into and out of the entity. From this we see that an entity declaration describes the external view of the entity.

Elements of Behavior

In VHDL, a description of the internal implementation of an entity is called an *architecture body* of the entity. There may be a number of different architecture bodies of the one interface to an entity, corresponding to alternative implementations that perform the same function. We can write a *behavioral* architecture body of an entity, which describes the function in an abstract way. Such an architecture body includes only *process statements*, which are collections of actions to be executed in sequence. These actions are called *sequential statements* and are much like the kinds of statements we see in a conventional programming language. The types of actions that can be performed include evaluating expressions, assigning values to variables, conditional execution, repeated execution and subprogram calls. In addition, there is a sequential statement that is unique to hardware modeling languages, the *signal assignment* statement. This is similar to variable assignment, except that it causes the value on a signal to be updated at some future time.

To illustrate these ideas, let us look at a behavioral architecture body for the reg4 entity, shown in Figure 1-8. In this architecture body, the part after the first **begin** keyword includes one process statement, which describes how the register behaves. It starts with the process name, **storage**, and finishes with the keywords **end process**.

The process statement defines a sequence of actions that are to take place when the system is simulated. These actions control how the values on the entity's ports change over time, that is, they control the behavior of the entity. This process can modify the values of the entity's ports using signal assignment statements.

FIGURE 1-8

```
architecture behav of reg4 is
begin

    storage : process is
        variable stored_d0, stored_d1, stored_d2, stored_d3 : bit;
    begin
        if en = '1' and clk = '1' then
            stored_d0 := d0;
            stored_d1 := d1;
            stored_d2 := d2;
            stored_d3 := d3;
        end if;
        q0 <= stored_d0 after 5 ns;
        q1 <= stored_d1 after 5 ns;
        q2 <= stored_d2 after 5 ns;
        q3 <= stored_d3 after 5 ns;
        wait on d0, d1, d2, d3, en, clk;
    end process storage;

end architecture behav;
```

A behavioral architecture body of the reg4 *entity.*

The way this process works is as follows. When the simulation is started, the signal values are set to '0', and the process is activated. The process's variables (listed after the keyword **variable**) are initialized to '0', then the statements are executed in order. The first statement is a condition that tests whether the values of the en and clk signals are both '1'. If they are, the statements between the keywords **then** and **end if** are executed, updating the process's variables using the values on the input signals. After the conditional if statement, there are four signal assignment statements that cause the output signals to be updated 5 ns later.

When all of these statements in the process have been executed, the process reaches the *wait statement* and *suspends*, that is, it becomes inactive. It stays suspended until one of the signals to which it is *sensitive* changes value. In this case, the process is sensitive to the signals d0, d1, d2, d3, en and clk, since they are listed in the wait statement. When one of these changes value, the process is resumed. The statements are executed again, starting from the keyword **begin**, and the cycle repeats. Notice that while the process is suspended, the values in the process's variables are not lost. This is how the process can represent the state of a system.

Elements of Structure

An alternative way of describing the implementation of an entity is to specify how it is composed of subsystems. We can give a structural description of the entity's implementation. An architecture body that is composed only of interconnected subsystems is called a *structural* architecture body. Figure 1-9 shows how the reg4 entity might be composed of latches and gates. If we are to describe this in VHDL, we will need entity declarations and architecture bodies for the subsystems, shown in Figure 1-10.

Figure 1-11 is a VHDL architecture body declaration that describes the structure shown in Figure 1-9. The *signal declaration*, before the keyword **begin**, defines the internal signals of the architecture. In this example, the signal int_clk is declared to carry a bit value ('0' or '1'). In general, VHDL signals can be declared to carry arbitrarily complex values. Within the architecture body the ports of the entity are also treated as signals.

In the second part of the architecture body, a number of *component instances* are created, representing the subsystems from which the reg4 entity is composed. Each component instance is a copy of the entity representing the subsystem, using the corresponding basic architecture body. (The name work refers to the current working library, in which all of the entity and architecture body descriptions are assumed to be held.)

The *port map* specifies the connection of the ports of each component instance to signals within the enclosing architecture body. For example, bit0, an instance of the d_latch entity, has its port d connected to the signal d0, its port clk connected to the signal int_clk and its port q connected to the signal q0.

Mixed Structural and Behavioral Models

Models need not be purely structural or purely behavioral. Often it is useful to specify a model with some parts composed of interconnected component instances, and other parts described using processes. We use signals as the means of joining component instances and processes. A signal can be associated with a port of a component instance and can also be assigned to or read in a process.

FIGURE 1-9

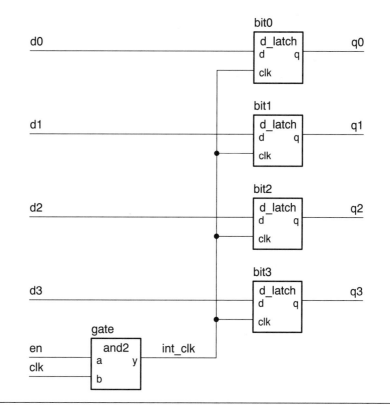

A structural composition of the reg4 *entity.*

FIGURE 1-10

```
entity d_latch is
    port ( d, clk : in bit;  q : out bit );
end d_latch;

architecture basic of d_latch is
begin
    latch_behavior : process is
    begin
        if clk = '1' then
            q <= d after 2 ns;
        end if;
        wait on clk, d;
    end process latch_behavior;
end architecture basic;
```

(continued on page 12)

(continued from page 11)

```
entity and2 is
    port ( a, b : in bit;  y : out bit );
end and2;

architecture basic of and2 is
begin
    and2_behavior : process is
    begin
        y <= a and b after 2 ns;
        wait on a, b;
    end process and2_behavior;
end architecture basic;
```

Entity declarations and architecture bodies for D-flipflop and two-input and gate.

FIGURE 1-11

```
architecture struct of reg4 is
    signal int_clk : bit;
begin
    bit0 : entity work.d_latch(basic)
        port map (d0, int_clk, q0);
    bit1 : entity work.d_latch(basic)
        port map (d1, int_clk, q1);
    bit2 : entity work.d_latch(basic)
        port map (d2, int_clk, q2);
    bit3 : entity work.d_latch(basic)
        port map (d3, int_clk, q3);
    gate : entity work.and2(basic)
        port map (en, clk, int_clk);
end architecture struct;
```

A VHDL structural architecture body of the reg4 *entity.*

We can write such a hybrid model by including both component instance and process statements in the body of an architecture. These statements are collectively called *concurrent statements*, since the corresponding processes all execute concurrently when the model is simulated. An outline of such a model is shown in Figure 1-12. This model describes a multiplier consisting of a data path and a control section. The data path is described structurally, using a number of component instances. The control section is described behaviorally, using a process that assigns to the control signals for the data path.

Test Benches

In our introductory discussion, we mentioned testing through simulation as an important motivation for modeling. We often test a VHDL model using an enclosing model

FIGURE 1-12

```
entity multiplier is
    port ( clk, reset : in bit;
            multiplicand, multiplier : in integer;
            product : out integer );
end entity multiplier;
```

\- -

```
architecture mixed of multiplier is
    signal partial_product, full_product : integer;
    signal arith_control, result_en, mult_bit, mult_load : bit;
begin -- mixed
    arith_unit : entity work.shift_adder(behavior)
        port map ( addend => multiplicand, augend => full_product,
                sum => partial_product,
                add_control => arith_control);
    result : entity work.reg(behavior)
        port map ( d => partial_product, q => full_product,
                en => result_en, reset => reset);
    multiplier_sr : entity work.shift_reg(behavior)
        port map ( d => multiplier, q => mult_bit,
                load => mult_load, clk => clk);
    product <= full_product;
    control_section : process is
        -- variable declarations for control_section
        -- . . .
    begin -- control section
        -- sequential statements to assign values to control signals
        -- . . .
        wait on clk, reset;
    end process control_section;
end architecture mixed;
```

An outline of a mixed structural and behavioral model of a multiplier.

called a *test bench*. The name comes from the analogy with a real hardware test bench, on which a device under test is stimulated with signal generators and observed with signal probes. A VHDL test bench consists of an architecture body containing an instance of the component to be tested and processes that generate sequences of values on signals connected to the component instance. The architecture body may also contain processes that test that the component instance produces the expected values on its output signals. Alternatively, we may use the monitoring facilities of a simulator to observe the outputs.

A test bench model for the behavioral implementation of the **reg4** register is shown in Figure 1-13. The entity declaration has no port list, since the test bench is entirely self-contained. The architecture body contains signals that are connected to the input and output ports of the component instance **dut**, the device under test. The process labeled **stimulus** provides a sequence of test values on the input signals by performing signal assignment statements, interspersed with wait statements. Each wait statement specifies a 20 ns pause during which the register device determines its output values. We can use a simulator to observe the values on the signals **q0** to **q3** to verify that the register operates correctly. When all of the stimulus values have been applied, the stimulus process waits indefinitely, thus completing the simulation.

FIGURE 1-13

```
entity test_bench is
end entity test_bench;

_____

architecture test_reg4 of test_bench is
    signal d0, d1, d2, d3, en, clk, q0, q1, q2, q3 : bit;
begin
    dut : entity work.reg4(behav)
        port map ( d0, d1, d2, d3, en, clk, q0, q1, q2, q3 );
    stimulus : process is
    begin
        d0 <= '1';  d1 <= '1';  d2 <= '1';  d3 <= '1';
        en <= '0';  clk <= '0';
        wait for 20 ns;
        en <= '1';  wait for 20 ns;
        clk <= '1';  wait for 20 ns;
        d0 <= '0';  d1 <= '0';  d2 <= '0';  d3 <= '0';  wait for 20 ns;
        en <= '0';  wait for 20 ns;
        . . .
        wait;
    end process stimulus;
end architecture test_reg4;
```

A VHDL test bench for the **reg4** *register model.*

Analysis, Elaboration and Execution

One of the main reasons for writing a model of a system is to enable us to simulate it. This involves three stages: *analysis, elaboration* and *execution*. Analysis and elaboration are also required in preparation for other uses of the model, such as logic synthesis.

In the first stage, analysis, the VHDL description of a system is checked for various kinds of errors. Like most programming languages, VHDL has rigidly defined *syntax* and *semantics*. The syntax is the set of grammatical rules that govern how a model is written. The rules of semantics govern the meaning of a program. For example, it makes sense to perform an addition operation on two numbers but not on two processes.

During the analysis phase, the VHDL description is examined, and syntactic and static semantic errors are located. The whole model of a system need not be analyzed at once. Instead, it is possible to analyze *design units*, such as entity and architecture body declarations, separately. If the analyzer finds no errors in a design unit, it creates an intermediate representation of the unit and stores it in a library. The exact mechanism varies between VHDL tools.

The second stage in simulating a model, elaboration, is the act of working through the design hierarchy and creating all of the objects defined in declarations. The ultimate product of design elaboration is a collection of signals and processes, with each process possibly containing variables. A model must be reducible to a collection of signals and processes in order to simulate it.

We can see how elaboration achieves this reduction by starting at the top level of a model, namely, an entity, and choosing an architecture of the entity to simulate. The architecture comprises signals, processes and component instances. Each component instance is a copy of an entity and an architecture that also comprises signals, processes and component instances. Instances of those signals and processes are created, corresponding to the component instance, and then the elaboration operation is repeated for the sub-component instances. Ultimately, a component instance is reached that is a copy of an entity with a purely behavioral architecture, containing only processes. This corresponds to a primitive component for the level of design being simulated. Figure 1-14 shows how elaboration proceeds for the structural architecture body of the **reg4** entity. As each instance of a process is created, its variables are created and given initial values. We can think of each process instance as corresponding to one instance of a component.

The third stage of simulation is the execution of the model. The passage of time is simulated in discrete steps, depending on when events occur. Hence the term *discrete event simulation* is used. At some simulation time, a process may be stimulated by changing the value on a signal to which it is sensitive. The process is resumed and may schedule new values to be given to signals at some later simulated time. This is called *scheduling a transaction* on that signal. If the new value is different from the previous value on the signal, an *event* occurs, and other processes sensitive to the signal may be resumed.

The simulation starts with an *initialization phase*, followed by repetitive execution of a *simulation cycle*. During the initialization phase, each signal is given an initial value, depending on its type. The simulation time is set to zero, then each process instance is activated and its sequential statements executed. Usually, a process will include a signal assignment statement to schedule a transaction on a signal at some later simulation time. Execution of a process continues until it reaches a wait statement, which causes the process to be suspended.

During the simulation cycle, the simulation time is first advanced to the next time at which a transaction on a signal has been scheduled. Second, all the transactions scheduled for that time are performed. This may cause some events to occur on some signals. Third, all processes that are sensitive to those events are resumed and are allowed to continue until they reach a wait statement and suspend. Again, the processes usually execute signal assignments to schedule further transactions on signals. When all the processes have suspended again, the simulation cycle is repeated. When the simulation gets to the stage where there are no further transactions scheduled, it stops, since the simulation is then complete.

FIGURE 1-14

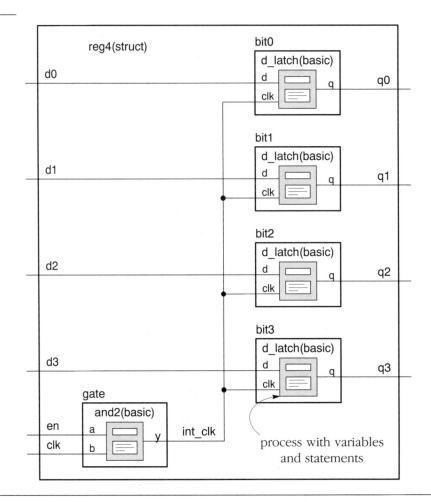

The elaboration of the **reg4** *entity using the structural architecture body. Each instance of the* **d_latch** *and* **and2** *entities is replaced with the contents of the corresponding* **basic** *architecture. These each consist of a process with its variables and statements.*

1.5 Learning a New Language: Lexical Elements and Syntax

When we learn a new natural language, such as Greek, Chinese or English, we start by learning the alphabet of symbols used in the language, then form these symbols into words. Next, we learn the way to put the words together to form sentences, and learn the meaning of these combinations of words. We reach fluency in a language when we can easily express what we need to say using correctly formed sentences.

The same ideas apply when we need to learn a new special-purpose language, such as VHDL for describing digital systems. We can borrow a few terms from language theory to describe what we need to learn. First, we need to learn the alphabet with which the language is written. The VHDL alphabet consists of all of the characters in the ISO eight-bit character set. This includes uppercase and lowercase letters (including letters with diacritical marks, such as à, ä, and so forth), digits 0 to 9, punctuation and other special characters. Second, we need to learn the *lexical elements* of the language. In VHDL, these are the identifiers, reserved words, special symbols and literals. Third, we need to learn the *syntax* of the language. This is the grammar that determines what combinations of lexical elements make up legal VHDL descriptions. Fourth, we need to learn the *semantics*, or meaning, of VHDL descriptions. It is the semantics that allow a collection of symbols to describe a digital design. Fifth, we need to learn how to develop our own VHDL descriptions to describe a design we are working with. This is the creative part of modeling, and fluency in this part will greatly enhance our design skills.

In the remainder of this chapter, we describe the lexical elements used in VHDL and introduce the notation we use to describe the syntax rules. Then in subsequent chapters, we introduce the different facilities available in the language. For each of these, we show the syntax rules, describe the corresponding semantics and give examples of how they are used to model particular parts of a digital system. We also include some exercises at the end of each chapter to provide practice in the fifth stage of learning described above.

VHDL-87

VHDL-87 uses the ASCII character set, rather than the full ISO character set. ASCII is a subset of the ISO character set, consisting of just the first 128 characters. This includes all of the unaccented letters, but excludes letters with diacritical marks.

Lexical Elements

In the following section, we discuss the lexical elements of VHDL: *comments*, *identifiers*, *reserved words*, *special symbols*, *numbers*, *characters*, *strings* and *bit strings*.

Comments

When we are writing a hardware model in VHDL, it is important to annotate the code with comments. The reason for doing this is to help readers understand the structure and logic behind the model. It is important to realize that although we only write a model once, it may subsequently be read and modified many times, both by its author and by other engineers. Any assistance we can give to understanding the model is worth the effort.

A VHDL model consists of a number of lines of text. A comment can be added to a line by writing two dashes together, followed by the comment text. For example:

> *. . . a line of VHDL description . . .*   *-- a descriptive comment*

The comment extends from the two dashes to the end of the line and may include any text we wish, since it is not formally part of the VHDL model. The code of a model can include blank lines and lines that only contain comments, starting with two dashes. We can write long comments on successive lines, each starting with two dashes, for example:

-- The following code models
-- the control section of the system
. . . some VHDL code . . .

Identifiers

Identifiers are used to name items in a VHDL model. It is good practice to use names that indicate the purpose of the item, so VHDL allows names to be arbitrarily long. However, there are some rules about how identifiers may be formed. A basic identifier

- may only contain alphabetic letters ('A' to 'Z' and 'a' to 'z'), decimal digits ('0' to '9') and the underline character ('_');
- must start with an alphabetic letter;
- may not end with an underline character; and
- may not include two successive underline characters.

Some examples of valid basic identifiers are

A   X0   counter   Next_Value   generate_read_cycle

Some examples of invalid basic identifiers are

last@value   *-- contains an illegal character for an identifier*
5bit_counter   *-- starts with a non-alphabetic character*
_A0   *-- starts with an underline*
A0_   *-- ends with an underline*
clock__pulse   *-- two successive underlines*

Note that the case of letters is not considered significant, so the identifiers **cat** and **Cat** are the same. Underline characters in identifiers are significant, so **This_Name** and **ThisName** are different identifiers.

In addition to the basic identifiers, VHDL allows *extended identifiers*, which can contain any sequence of characters. Extended identifiers are included to allow communication between computer-aided engineering tools for processing VHDL descriptions and other tools that use different rules for identifiers. An extended identifier is written by enclosing the characters of the identifier between '\' characters. For example:

\data bus\ \global.clock\ \923\ \d#1\ \start__\

If we need to include a '\' character in an extended identifier, we do so by doubling the character, for example:

\A:\\name\   *-- contains a '\' between the ':' and the 'n'*

Note that the case of letters is significant in extended identifiers and that all extended identifiers are distinct from all basic identifiers. So the following are all distinct identifiers:

name \name\ \Name\ \NAME\

VHDL-87

VHDL-87 only allows basic identifiers, not extended identifiers. The rules for forming basic identifiers are the same as those for VHDL-93.

Reserved Words

Some identifiers, called reserved words or keywords, are reserved for special use in VHDL. They are used to denote specific constructs that form a model, so we cannot use them as identifiers for items we define. The full list of reserved words is shown in Figure 1-15. Often, when a VHDL program is typeset, reserved words are printed in boldface. This convention is followed in this book.

FIGURE 1-15

abs	**entity**	**next**	**select**
access	**exit**	**nor**	**severity**
after	**file**	**not**	**signal**
alias	**for**	**null**	**shared**
all	**function**	**of**	**sla**
and		**on**	**sll**
architecture	**generate**	**open**	**sra**
array	**generic**	**or**	**srl**
assert	**group**	**others**	**subtype**
attribute	**guarded**	**out**	**then**
begin	**if**	**package**	**to**
block	**impure**	**port**	**transport**
body	**in**	**postponed**	**type**
buffer	**inertial**	**procedure**	**unaffected**
bus	**inout**	**process**	**units**
case	**is**	**pure**	**until**
component	**label**	**range**	**use**
configuration	**library**	**record**	**variable**
constant	**linkage**	**register**	
disconnect	**literal**	**reject**	**wait**
downto	**loop**	**rem**	**when**
else	**map**	**report**	**while**
elsif	**mod**	**return**	**with**
end	**nand**	**rol**	**xnor**
	new	**ror**	**xor**

VHDL-87

The following identifiers are not used as reserved words in VHDL-87. They may be used as identifiers for other purposes, although it is not advisable to do so, as this may cause difficulties in porting the models to VHDL-93.

group	postponed	ror	sra
impure	pure	shared	srl
inertial	reject	sla	unaffected
literal	rol	sll	xnor

Special Symbols

VHDL uses a number of special symbols to denote operators, to delimit parts of language constructs and as punctuation. Some of these special symbols consist of just one character. They are

    & ' ( ) * + , – . / : ; < = > |

Other special symbols consist of pairs of characters. The two characters must be typed next to each other, with no intervening space. These symbols are

    => ** := /= >= <= <>

Numbers

There are two forms of numbers that can be written in VHDL code: *integer literals* and *real literals*. An integer literal simply represents a whole number and consists of digits without a decimal point. Real literals, on the other hand, can represent fractional numbers. They always include a decimal point, which is preceded by at least one digit and followed by at least one digit. Real literals represent an approximation to real numbers.
    Some examples of decimal integer literals are

    23 0 146

Note that –10, for example, is not an integer literal. It is actually a combination of a negation operator and the integer literal 10.
    Some examples of real literals are

    23.1 0.0 3.14159

    Both integer and real literals can also use exponential notation, in which the number is followed by the letter 'E' or 'e', and an exponent value. This indicates a power of 10 by which the number is multiplied. For integer literals, the exponent must not be negative, whereas for real literals, it may be either positive or negative. Some examples of integer literals using exponential notation are

    46E5 1E+12 19e00

Some examples of real literals using exponential notation are

    1.234E09 98.6E+21 34.0e–08

    Integer and real literals may also be expressed in a base other than base 10. In fact, the base can be any integer between 2 and 16. To do this, we write the number surrounded by sharp characters ('#'), preceded by the base. For bases greater than 10, the letters 'A' through 'F' (or 'a' through 'f') are used to represent the digits 10 through 15. For example, several ways of writing the value 253 are as follows:

    2#11111101# 16#FD# 16#0fd# 8#0375#

Similarly, the value 0.5 can be represented as

    2#0.100#   8#0.4#   12#0.6#

Note that in all these cases, the base itself is expressed in *decimal*.

Based literals can also use exponential notation. In this case, the exponent, expressed in decimal, is appended to the based number after the closing sharp character. The exponent represents the power of the base by which the number is multiplied. For example, the number 1024 could be represented by the integer literals:

    2#1#E10   16#4#E2   10#1024#E+00

Finally, as an aid to readability of long numbers, we can include underline characters as separators between digits. The rules for including underline characters are similar to those for identifiers; that is, they may not appear at the beginning or end of a number, nor may two appear in succession. Some examples are

    123_456   3.141_592_6   2#1111_1100_0000_0000#

Characters

A character literal can be written in VHDL code by enclosing it in single quotation marks. Any of the printable characters in the standard character set (including a space character) can be written in this way. Some examples are

    'A'   -- uppercase letter
    'z'   -- lowercase letter
    ','   -- the punctuation character comma
    '"'   -- the punctuation character single quote
    ' '   -- the separator character space

Strings

A string literal represents a sequence of characters and is written by enclosing the characters in double quotation marks. The string may include any number of characters (including zero), but it must fit entirely on one line. Some examples are

    "A string"
    "We can include any printing characters (e.g., &%@^*) in a string!!"
    "00001111ZZZZ"
    ""   -- empty string

If we need to include a double quotation mark character in a string, we write two double quotation mark characters together. The pair is interpreted as just one character in the string. For example:

    "A string in a string: ""A string"". "

If we need to write a string that is longer than will fit on one line, we can use the concatenation operator (&) to join two substrings together. (This operator is discussed in Chapter 4.) For example:

    "If a string will not fit on one line, "
    & "then we can break it into parts on separate lines."

Bit Strings

VHDL includes values that represent bits (binary digits), which can be either '0' or '1'. A bit-string literal represents a sequence of these bit values. It is represented by a string of digits, enclosed by double quotation marks and preceded by a character that specifies the base of the digits. The base specifier can be one of the following:

- B for binary,
- O for octal (base 8), and
- X for hexadecimal (base 16).

For example, some bit-string literals specified in binary are

    B"0100011"   B"10"   b"1111_0010_0001"   B""

Notice that we can include underline characters in bit-string literals to separate adjacent digits. The underline characters do not affect the meaning of the literal; they simply make the literal more readable. The base specifier can be in uppercase or lowercase. The last of the examples above denotes an empty bit string.

If the base specifier is octal, the digits '0' through '7' can be used. Each digit represents exactly three bits in the sequence. Some examples are

    O"372"   *-- equivalent to B"011_111_010"*
    o"00"   *-- equivalent to B"000_000"*

If the base specifier is hexadecimal, the digits '0' through '9' and 'A' through 'F' or 'a' through 'f' (representing 10 through 15) can be used. In hexadecimal, each digit represents exactly four bits. Some examples are

    X"FA"   *-- equivalent to B"1111_1010"*
    x"0d"   *-- equivalent to B"0000_1101"*

Notice that O"372" is not the same as X"FA", since the former is a sequence of nine bits, whereas the latter is a sequence of eight bits.

Syntax Descriptions

In the remainder of this book, we describe rules of syntax using a notation based on the Extended Backus-Naur Form (EBNF). These rules govern how we may combine lexical elements to form valid VHDL descriptions. It is useful to have a good working knowledge of the syntax rules, since VHDL analyzers expect valid VHDL descriptions as input. The error messages they otherwise produce may in some cases appear cryptic if we are unaware of the syntax rules.

The idea behind EBNF is to divide the language into *syntactic categories*. For each syntactic category we write a rule that describes how to build a VHDL clause of that category by combining lexical elements and clauses of other categories. These rules are analogous to the rules of English grammar. For example, there are rules that describe a sentence in terms of a subject and a predicate, and that describe a predicate in terms of a verb and an object phrase. In the rules for English grammar, "sentence", "subject", "predicate", and so on, are the syntactic categories.

In EBNF, we write a rule with the syntactic category we are defining on the left of a "⇐" sign (read as "is defined to be"), and a pattern on the right. The simplest kind of pattern is a collection of items in sequence, for example:

variable_assignment ⇐ target := expression ;

This rule indicates that a VHDL clause in the category "variable_assignment" is defined to be a clause in the category "target", followed by the symbol ":=", followed by a clause in the category "expression", followed by the symbol ";". To find out whether the VHDL clause

d0 := 25 + 6;

is syntactically valid, we would have to check the rules for "target" and "expression". As it happens, "d0" and "25 + 6" are valid subclauses, so the whole clause conforms to the pattern in the rule and is thus a valid variable assignment. On the other hand, the clause

25 fred := x **if** := .

cannot possibly be a valid variable assignment, since it doesn't match the pattern on the right side of the rule.

The next kind of rule to consider is one that allows for an optional component in a clause. We indicate the optional part by enclosing it between the symbols "〚" and "〛". For example:

function_call ⇐ name 〚 (association_list) 〛

This indicates that a function call consists of a name that may be followed by an association list in parentheses. Note the use of the outline symbols for writing the pattern in the rule, as opposed to the normal solid symbols that are lexical elements of VHDL.

In many rules, we need to specify that a clause is optional, but if present, it may be repeated as many times as needed. For example, in this simplified rule for a process statement:

process_statement ⇐
    process is
       { process_declarative_item }
    begin
       { sequential_statement }
    end process ;

the curly braces specify that a process may include zero or more process declarative items and zero or more sequential statements. A case that arises frequently in the rules of VHDL is a pattern consisting of some category followed by zero or more repetitions of that category. In this case, we use dots within the braces to represent the repeated category, rather than writing it out again in full. For example, the rule

```
case_statement ⇐
    case expression is
        case_statement_alternative
        { ∘∘∘ }
    end case ;
```

indicates that a case statement must contain at least one case statement alternative, but
may contain an arbitrary number of additional case statement alternatives as required.
If there is a sequence of categories and symbols preceding the braces, the dots represent
only the last element of the sequence. Thus, in the example above, the dots represent
only the case statement alternative, not the sequence "**case** expression **is** case_state-
ment_alternative".

We also use the dots notation where a list of one or more repetitions of a clause
is required, but some delimiter symbol is needed between repetitions. For example,
the rule

identifier_list ⇐ identifier { , ∘∘∘ }

specifies that an identifier list consists of one or more identifiers, and that if there is more
than one, they are separated by comma symbols. Note that the dots always represent
a repetition of the category immediately preceding the left brace symbol. Thus, in the
above rule, it is the identifier that is repeated, not the comma.

Many syntax rules allow a category to be composed of one of a number of alternatives. One way to represent this is to have a number of separate rules for the category,
one for each alternative. However, it is often more convenient to combine alternatives
using the "|" symbol. For example, the rule

mode ⇐ **in** | **out** | **inout**

specifies that the category "mode" can be formed from a clause consisting of one of the
reserved words chosen from the alternatives listed.

The final notation we use in our syntax rules is parenthetic grouping, using the symbols "(" and ")". These simply serve to group part of a pattern, so that we can avoid
any ambiguity that might otherwise arise. For example, the inclusion of parentheses
in the rule

term ⇐ factor { (* | / | **mod** | **rem**) factor }

makes it clear that a factor may be followed by one of the operator symbols, and then
another factor. Without the parentheses, the rule would be

term ⇐ factor { * | / | **mod** | **rem** factor }

indicating that a factor may be followed by one of the operators *, / or **mod** alone, or
by the operator **rem** and then another factor. This is certainly not what is intended.
The reason for this incorrect interpretation is that there is a *precedence*, or order of
priority, in the EBNF notation we are using. In the absence of parentheses, a sequence
of pattern components following one after the other is considered as a group with
higher precedence than components separated by "|" symbols.

This EBNF notation is sufficient to describe the complete grammar of VHDL. However, there are often further constraints on a VHDL description that relate to the meaning

of the lexical elements used. For example, a description specifying connection of a signal to a named object that identifies a component instead of a port is incorrect, even though it may conform to the syntax rules. To avoid such problems, many rules include additional information relating to the meaning of a language feature. For example, the rule shown above describing how a function call is formed is augmented thus:

function_call ⟸ *function*_name 〚 (*parameter*_association_list) 〛

The italicized prefix on a syntactic category in the pattern simply provides semantic information. This rule indicates that the name cannot be just any name, but must be the name of a function. Similarly, the association list must describe the parameters supplied to the function. (We will describe the meaning of functions and parameters in a later chapter.) The semantic information is for our benefit as designers reading the rule, to help us understand the intended semantics. So far as the syntax is concerned, the rule is equivalent to the original rule without the italicized parts.

In the following chapters, we will introduce each new feature of VHDL by describing its syntax using EBNF rules, and then we will describe the meaning and use of the feature through examples. In many cases, we will start with a simplified version of the syntax to make the description easier to learn and come back to the full details in a later chapter. For reference, Appendix E contains a complete listing of VHDL syntax in EBNF notation.

Exercises

1. [❶ 1.4] Briefly outline the purposes of the following VHDL modeling constructs: entity declaration, behavioral architecture body, structural architecture body, process statement, signal assignment statement and port map.

2. [❶ 1.5] Comment symbols are often used to make lines of a model temporarily ineffective. The symbol is added at the front of the line, turning the line into a comment. The comment symbol can be simply removed to reactivate the statement. The following process statement includes a line to assign a value to a test signal, to help debug the model. Modify the process to make the assignment ineffective.

```
apply_transform : process is
begin
    d_out <= transform(d_in) after 200 ps;
    debug_test <= transform(d_in);
    wait on enable, d_in;
end process apply_transform;
```

3. [❶ 1.5] Which of the following are valid VHDL basic identifiers? Which are reserved words? Of the invalid identifiers, why are they invalid?

last_item   prev item   value–1   buffer

element#5   _control   93_999   entry_

4. [❶ 1.5] Rewrite the following decimal literals as hexadecimal literals.

1   34   256.0   0.5

5. [❶ 1.5] What decimal numbers are represented by the following literals?

    8#14#   2#1000_0100#   16#2C#

    2.5E5   2#1#E15   2#0.101#

6. [❶ 1.5] What is the difference between the literals 16#23DF# and X"23DF"?

7. [❶ 1.5] Express the following octal and hexadecimal bit strings as binary bit-string literals.

    O"747"   O"377"   O"1_345"

    X"F2"   X"0014"   X"0000_0001"

8. [❷ 1.4] Write an entity declaration and a behavioral architecture body for a two-input multiplexer, with input ports a, b and sel and an output port z. If the sel input is '0', the value of a should be copied to z, otherwise the value of b should be copied to z. Write a test bench for the multiplexer model, and test it using a VHDL simulator.

9. [❷ 1.4] Write an entity declaration and a structural architecture body for a four-bit-wide multiplexer, using instances of the two-bit multiplexer from Exercise 8. The input ports are a0, a1, a2, a3, b0, b1, b2, b3 and sel, and the output ports are z0, z1, z2 and z3. When sel is '0', the inputs a0 to a3 are copied to the outputs, otherwise the inputs b0 to b3 are copied to the outputs. Write a test bench for the multiplexer model, and test it using a VHDL simulator.

Scalar Data Types and Operations

The concept of type is very important when describing data in a VHDL model. The type of a data object defines the set of values that the object can assume, as well as the set of operations that can be performed on those values. A scalar type consists of single, indivisible values. In this chapter we look at the basic scalar types provided by VHDL and see how they can be used to define data objects that model the internal state of a module.

2.1   Constants and Variables

An *object* is a named item in a VHDL model that has a value of a specified type. There are four classes of objects: constants, variables, signals and files. In this chapter, we look at constants and variables; signals are described fully in Chapter 5, and files in Chapter 18. Constants and variables are objects in which data can be stored for use in a model. The difference between them is that the value of a constant cannot be changed after it is created, whereas a variable's value can be changed as many times as necessary using variable assignment statements.

Constant and Variable Declarations

Both constants and variables need to be declared before they can be used in a model. A *declaration* simply introduces the name of the object, defines its type and may give it an initial value. The syntax rule for a constant declaration is

> constant_declaration ⇐
>   **constant** identifier { , ... } : subtype_indication [:= expression] ;

The identifiers listed are the names of the constants being defined (one per name), and the subtype indication specifies the type of all of the constants. We look at ways of specifying the type in detail in subsequent sections of this chapter. The optional part shown in the syntax rule is an expression that specifies the value that each constant assumes. This part can only be omitted in certain cases that we discuss in Chapter 8. Until then, we always include it in examples. Here are some examples of constant declarations:

> **constant** number_of_bytes : integer := 4;
> **constant** number_of_bits : integer := 8 * number_of_bytes;
> **constant** e : real := 2.718281828;
> **constant** prop_delay : time := 3 ns;
> **constant** size_limit, count_limit : integer := 255;

The reason for using a constant is to have a name and an explicitly defined type for a value, rather than just writing the value as a literal. This makes the model more intelligible to the reader, since the name and type convey much more information about the intended use of the object than the literal value alone. Furthermore, if we need to change the value as the model evolves, we only need to update the declaration. This is much easier and more reliable than trying to find and update all instances of a literal value throughout a model. It is good practice to use constants rather than writing literal values within a model.

The form of a variable declaration is similar to a constant declaration. The syntax rule is

> variable_declaration ⇐
>   **variable** identifier { , ... } : subtype_indication [:= expression] ;

Here also the initialization expression is optional. If we omit it, the default initial value assumed by the variable when it is created depends on the type. For scalar types, the default initial value is the leftmost value of the type. For example, for integers it is the smallest representable integer. Some examples of variable declarations are

```
variable index : integer := 0;
variable sum, average, largest : real;
variable start, finish : time := 0 ns;
```

If we include more than one identifier in a variable declaration, it is the same as having separate declarations for each identifier. For example, the last declaration above is the same as the two declarations

```
variable start : time := 0 ns;
variable finish : time := 0 ns;
```

This is not normally significant unless the initialization expression is such that it potentially produces different values on two successive evaluations. The only time this may occur is if the initialization expression contains a call to a function with side effects (see Chapter 7).

Constant and variable declarations can appear in a number of places in a VHDL model, including in the declaration parts of processes. In this case, the declared object can be used only within the process. One restriction on where a variable declaration may occur is that it may not be placed so that the variable would be accessible to more than one process. This is to prevent the strange effects that might otherwise occur if the processes were to modify the variable in indeterminate order. The exception to this rule is if a variable is declared specially as a *shared* variable. We will leave discussion of shared variables until Chapter 21.

EXAMPLE

Figure 2-1 outlines an architecture body that shows how constant and variable declarations may be included in a VHDL model.

FIGURE 2-1

```
architecture sample of ent is
    constant pi : real := 3.14159;
begin
    process is
        variable counter : integer;
    begin
        . . .        -- statements using pi and counter
    end process;
end architecture sample;
```

An architecture body showing declarations of a constant pi *and a variable* counter.

Variable Assignment

Once a variable has been declared, its value can be modified by an assignment statement. The syntax of a variable assignment statement is given by the rule

variable_assignment_statement ⇐ ⟦ label : ⟧ name := expression ;

The optional label provides a means of identifying the assignment statement. We will discuss reasons for labeling statements in Chapter 20. Until then, we will simply omit the label in our examples. The name in a variable assignment statement identifies the variable to be changed, and the expression is evaluated to produce the new value. The type of this value must match the type of the variable. The full details of how an expression is formed are covered in the rest of this chapter. For now, just think of expressions as the usual combinations of identifiers and literals with operators. Here are some examples of assignment statements:

```
program_counter := 0;
index := index + 1;
```

The first assignment sets the value of the variable **program_counter** to zero, overwriting any previous value. The second example increments the value of **index** by one.

It is important to note the difference between a variable assignment statement, shown here, and a signal assignment statement, introduced in Chapter 1. A variable assignment immediately overwrites the variable with a new value. A signal assignment, on the other hand, schedules a new value to be applied to a signal at some later time. We will return to signal assignments in Chapter 5. Because of the significant difference between the two kinds of assignment, VHDL uses distinct symbols: ":=" for variable assignment and "<=" for signal assignment.

VHDL-87

Variable assignment statements may not be labeled in VHDL-87.

2.2   Scalar Types

The notion of *type* is very important in VHDL. We say that VHDL is a *strongly typed* language, meaning that every object may only assume values of its nominated type. Furthermore, the definition of each operation includes the types of values to which the operation may be applied. The aim of strong typing is to allow detection of errors at an early stage of the design process, namely, when a model is analyzed.

In this section, we show how a new type is declared. We then show how to define different *scalar* types. A scalar type is one whose values are indivisible. In Chapter 4 we will show how to declare types whose values are composed of collections of element values.

Type Declarations

We introduce new types into a VHDL model by using type declarations. The declaration names a type and specifies which values may be stored in objects of the type. The syntax rule for a type declaration is

type_declaration ⇐ **type** identifier **is** type_definition ;

One important point to note is that if two types are declared separately with identical type definitions, they are nevertheless distinct and incompatible types. For example, if we have two type declarations:

> **type** apples **is range** 0 **to** 100;
> **type** oranges **is range** 0 **to** 100;

we may not assign a value of type apples to a variable of type oranges, since they are of different types.

An important use of types is to specify the allowed values for ports of an entity. In the examples in Chapter 1, we saw the type name bit used to specify that ports may take only the values '0' and '1'. If we define our own types for ports, the type names must be declared in a *package*, so that they are visible in the entity declaration. We will describe packages in more detail in Chapter 8; we introduce them here to enable us to write entity declarations using types of our own devising. For example, suppose we wish to define an adder entity that adds small integers in the range 0 to 255. We write a package containing the type declaration, as follows:

> **package** int_types **is**
>
> > **type** small_int **is range** 0 **to** 255;
>
> **end package** int_types;

This defines a package named int_types, which provides the type named small_int. The package is a separate design unit and is analyzed before any entity declaration that needs to use the type it provides. We can use the type by preceding an entity declaration with a *use clause*, for example:

> **use** work.int_types.**all**;
>
> **entity** small_adder **is**
> > **port** (a, b : **in** small_int; s : **out** small_int);
> **end entity** small_adder;

When we discuss packages in Chapter 8, we will explain the precise meaning of use clauses such as this. For now, we treat it as "magic" needed to declare types for use in entity declarations.

Integer Types

In VHDL, integer types have values that are whole numbers. An example of an integer type is the predefined type integer, which includes all the whole numbers representable on a particular host computer. The language standard requires that the type integer include at least the numbers $-2,147,483,647$ to $+2,147,483,647$ ($-2^{31}+1$ to $+2^{31}-1$), but VHDL implementations may extend the range.

We can define a new integer type using a range-constraint type definition. The simplified syntax rule for an integer type definition is

> integer_type_definition $\Leftarrow$
> > **range** simple_expression (**to** ∥ **downto**) simple_expression

which defines the set of integers between (and including) the values given by the two expressions. The expressions must evaluate to integer values. If we use the keyword **to**, we are defining an *ascending range*, in which values are ordered from the smallest on the left to the largest on the right. On the other hand, using the keyword **downto** defines a *descending range*, in which values are ordered left to right from largest to smallest. The reasons for distinguishing between ascending and descending ranges will become clear later.

EXAMPLE

Here are two integer type declarations:

type day_of_month **is range** 0 **to** 31;
type year **is range** 0 **to** 2100;

These two types are quite distinct, even though they include some values in common. Thus if we declare variables of these types:

variable today : day_of_month := 9;
variable start_year : year := 1987;

it would be illegal to make the assignment:

start_year := today;

Even though the number 9 is a member of the type **year**, in context it is treated as being of type **day_of_month**, which is incompatible with type **year**. This type rule helps us to avoid inadvertently mixing numbers that represent different kinds of things.

If we wish to use an arithmetic expression to specify the bounds of the range, the values used in the expression must be *locally static*, that is, they must be known when the model is analyzed. For example, we can use constant values in an expression as part of a range definition:

constant number_of_bits : integer := 32;
type bit_index **is range** 0 **to** number_of_bits − 1;

The operations that can be performed on values of integer types include the familiar arithmetic operations:

+	addition, or identity
−	subtraction, or negation
*	multiplication
/	division
mod	modulo
rem	remainder
abs	absolute value
**	exponentiation

The result of an operation is an integer of the same type as the operand or operands. For the binary operators (those that take two operands), the operands must be of the same type. The right operand of the exponentiation operator must be a non-negative integer.

The identity and negation operators are unary, meaning that they only take a single, right operand. The result of the identity operator is its operand unchanged, while the negation operator produces zero minus the operand. So, for example, the following all produce the same result:

A + (–B),   A – (+B),   A – B

The division operator produces an integer that is the result of dividing, with any fractional part truncated towards zero. The remainder operator is defined such that the relation

A = (A / B) * B + (A **rem** B)

is satisfied. The result of **A rem B** is the remainder left over from division of **A** by **B**. It has the same sign as **A** and has absolute value less than the absolute value of **B**. For example:

5 **rem** 3 = 2,   (–5) **rem** 3 = –2,   5 **rem** (–3) = 2,   (–5) **rem** (–3) = –2

Note that in these expressions, the parentheses are required by the grammar of VHDL. The two operators, **rem** and negation, may not be written side by side. The modulo operator conforms to the mathematical definition satisfying the relation

A = B * N + (A **mod** B)   – – for some integer N

The result of **A mod B** has the same sign as **B** and has absolute value less than the absolute value of **B**. For example:

5 **mod** 3 = 2,   (–5) **mod** 3 = 1,   5 **mod** (–3) = –1,   (–5) **mod** (–3) = –2

When a variable is declared to be of an integer type, the default initial value is the leftmost value in the range of the type. For ascending ranges, this will be the least value, and for descending ranges, it will be the greatest value. If we have these declarations:

```
type set_index_range is range 21 downto 11;
type mode_pos_range is range 5 to 7;
variable set_index : set_index_range;
variable mode_pos : mode_pos_range;
```

the initial value of **set_index** is 21, and that of **mode_pos** is 5. The initial value of a variable of type integer is –2,147,483,647 or less, since this type is predefined as an ascending range that must include –2,147,483,647.

Floating-Point Types

Floating-point types in VHDL are used to represent real numbers. Mathematically speaking, there is an infinite number of real numbers within any interval, so it is not possible to represent real numbers exactly on a computer. Hence floating-point types are only an approximation to real numbers. The term "floating point" refers to the fact that they are represented using a mantissa part and an exponent part. This is similar to the way in which we represent numbers in scientific notation.

There is a predefined floating-point type called **real**, which includes at least the range –1.0E+38 to +1.0E+38, with at least six decimal digits of precision. This corresponds to the IEEE standard 32-bit representation commonly used for floating-point numbers. Some implementations of VHDL may extend this range and may provide higher precision.

We define a new floating-point type using a range-constraint type definition. The simplified syntax rule for a floating-point type definition is

floating_type_definition ⇐
    range simple_expression (**to** ‖ **downto**) simple_expression

This is similar to the way in which an integer type is declared, except that the bounds must evaluate to floating-point numbers. Some examples of floating-point type declarations are

type input_level **is range** −10.0 **to** +10.0;
type probability **is range** 0.0 **to** 1.0;

The operations that can be performed on floating-point values include the arithmetic operations addition and identity (+), subtraction and negation (−), multiplication (*), division (/), absolute value (**abs**) and exponentiation (**). The result of an operation is of the same floating-point type as the operand or operands. For the binary operators (those that take two operands), the operands must be of the same type. The exception is that the right operand of the exponentiation operator must be an integer. The identity and negation operators are unary (meaning that they only take a single, right operand).

Variables that are declared to be of a floating-point type have a default initial value that is the leftmost value in the range of the type. So if we declare a variable to be of the type input_level shown above:

variable input_A : input_level;

its initial value is −10.0.

Physical Types

The remaining numeric types in VHDL are physical types. They are used to represent real-world physical quantities, such as length, mass, time and current. The definition of a physical type includes the *primary unit* of measure and may also include some *secondary units*, which are integral multiples of the primary unit. The simplified syntax rule for a physical type definition is

physical_type_definition ⇐
    range simple_expression (**to** ‖ **downto**) simple_expression
        units
            identifier ;
            { identifier = physical_literal ; }
        end units ⟦ identifier ⟧

This is like an integer type definition, but with the units definition part added. The primary unit (the first identifier after the **units** keyword) is the smallest unit that is represented. We may then define a number of secondary units, as we shall see in a moment. The range specifies the multiples of the primary unit that are included in the type. If the identifier is included at the end of the units definition part, it must repeat the name of the type being defined.

EXAMPLE

Here is a declaration of a physical type representing electrical resistance:

type resistance **is range** 0 **to** 1E9
   units
      ohm;
   end units resistance;

Literal values of this type are written as a numeric literal followed by the unit name, for example:

5 ohm 22 ohm 471_000 ohm

Notice that we must include a space before the unit name. Also, if the number is the literal 1, it can be omitted, leaving just the unit name. So the following two literals represent the same value:

ohm 1 ohm

Note that values such as –5 ohm and 1E16 ohm are not included in the type **resistance**, since the values –5 and 1E16 lie outside of the range of the type.

Now that we have seen how to write physical literals, we can look at how to specify secondary units in a physical type declaration. We do this by indicating how many primary units comprise a secondary unit. Our declaration for the resistance type can now be extended:

type resistance **is range** 0 **to** 1E9
   units
      ohm;
      kohm = 1000 ohm;
      Mohm = 1000 kohm;
   end units resistance;

Notice that once one secondary unit is defined, it can be used to specify further secondary units. Of course, the secondary units do not have to be powers of 10 times the primary unit; however, the multiplier must be an integer. For example, a physical type for length might be declared as

type length **is range** 0 **to** 1E9
   units
      um;   *—— primary unit: micron*
      mm = 1000 um; *—— metric units*
      m = 1000 mm;
      mil = 254 um;   *—— imperial units*
      inch = 1000 mil;
   end units length;

We can write physical literals of this type using the secondary units, for example:

23 mm 450 mil 9 inch

When we write physical literals, we can write non-integral multiples of primary or secondary units. If the value we write is not an exact multiple of the primary unit, it is rounded down to the nearest multiple. For example, we might write the following literals of type **length**, each of which represents the same value:

   0.1 inch   2.54 mm   2.540528 mm

The last of these is rounded down to **2540 um**, since the primary unit for **length** is **um**. If we write the physical literal **6.8 um**, it is rounded down to the value **6 um**.

   Many of the arithmetic operators can be applied to physical types, but with some restrictions. The addition, subtraction, identity and negation operators can be applied to values of physical types, in which case they yield results that are of the same type as the operand or operands. A value of a physical type can be multiplied by an integer or a floating-point number to yield a value of the same physical type, for example:

   5 mm * 6 = 30 mm

   A value of a physical type can be divided by an integer or floating-point number to yield a value of the same physical type. Furthermore, two values of the same physical type can be divided to yield an integer, for example:

   18 kohm / 2.0 = 9 kohm,   33 kohm / 22 ohm = 1500

   Finally, the **abs** operator may be applied to a value of a physical type to yield a value of the same type, for example:

   abs 2 foot = 2 foot,   **abs** (–2 foot) = 2 foot

   The restrictions make sense when we consider that physical types represent actual physical quantities, and arithmetic should be done so as to produce results of the correct dimensions. It doesn't make sense to multiply two lengths together to yield a length; the result should logically be an area. So VHDL does not allow direct multiplication of two physical types. Instead, we must convert the values to abstract integers to do the calculation, then convert the result back to the final physical type. (See the discussion of the 'pos and 'val attributes in Section 2.4.)

   A variable that is declared to be of a physical type has a default initial value that is the leftmost value in the range of the type. For example, the default initial values for the types declared above are **0 ohm** for **resistance** and **0 um** for **length**.

VHDL-87

   A physical type definition in VHDL-87 may not repeat the type name after the keywords **end units**.

Time

The predefined physical type **time** is very important in VHDL, as it is used extensively to specify delays. Its definition is

```
type time is range implementation defined
    units
        fs;
        ps = 1000 fs;
        ns = 1000 ps;
        us = 1000 ns;
        ms = 1000 us;
        sec = 1000 ms;
        min = 60 sec;
        hr = 60 min;
    end units;
```

By default, the primary unit **fs** is the *resolution limit* used when a model is simulated. Time values smaller than the resolution limit are rounded down to zero units. A simulator may allow us to select a secondary unit of **time** as the resolution limit. In this case, the unit of all physical literals of type **time** in the model must not be less than the resolution limit. When the model is executed, the resolution limit is used to determine the precision with which time values are represented. The reason for allowing reduced precision in this way is to allow a greater range of time values to be represented. This may allow a model to be simulated for a longer period of simulation time.

Enumeration Types

Often when writing models of hardware at an abstract level, it is useful to use a set of names for the encoded values of some signals, rather than committing to a bit-level encoding straightaway. VHDL *enumeration types* allow us to do this. For example, suppose we are modeling a processor, and we want to define names for the function codes for the arithmetic unit. A suitable type declaration is

type alu_function **is** (disable, pass, add, subtract, multiply, divide);

Such a type is called an *enumeration*, because the literal values used are enumerated in a list. The syntax rule for enumeration type definitions in general is

enumeration_type_definition ⇐
    ((identifier ‖ character_literal) { , ... })

There must be at least one value in the type, and each value may be either an identifier, as in the above example, or a character literal. An example of this latter case is

type octal_digit **is** ('0', '1', '2', '3', '4', '5', '6', '7');

Given the above two type declarations, we could declare variables:

variable alu_op : alu_function;
variable last_digit : octal_digit := '0';

and make assignments to them:

alu_op := subtract;
last_digit := '7';

Different enumeration types may include the same identifier as a literal (called *over-loading*), so the context of use must make it clear which type is meant. To illustrate this, consider the following declarations:

```
type logic_level is (unknown, low, undriven, high);
variable control : logic_level;
type water_level is (dangerously_low, low, ok);
variable water_sensor : water_level;
```

Here, the literal **low** is overloaded, since it is a member of both types. However, the assignments

```
control := low;
water_sensor := low;
```

are both acceptable, since the types of the variables are sufficient to determine which **low** is being referred to.

When a variable of an enumeration type is declared, the default initial value is the leftmost element in the enumeration list. So **unknown** is the default initial value for type logic_level, and **dangerously_low** is that for type water_level.

There are three predefined enumeration types defined as

```
type severity_level is (note, warning, error, failure);
type file_open_status is (open_ok, status_error, name_error, mode_error);
type file_open_kind is (read_mode, write_mode, append_mode);
```

The type **severity_level** is used in assertion statements, which we will discuss in Chapter 3, and the types file_open_status and file_open_kind are used for file operations, which we will discuss in Chapter 18. For the remainder of this section, we look at the other predefined enumeration types and the operations applicable to them.

VHDL-87

The types file_open_status and file_open_kind are not predefined in VHDL-87.

Characters

In Chapter 1 we saw how to write literal character values. These values are members of the predefined enumeration type **character**, which includes all of the characters in the ISO eight-bit character set. The type definition is shown in Figure 2-2. Note that this type is an example of an enumeration type containing a mixture of identifiers and character literals as elements.

The first 128 characters in this enumeration are the ASCII characters, which form a subset of the ISO character set. The identifiers from **nul** to **usp** and **del** are the non-printable ASCII control characters. Characters **c128** to **c159** do not have any standard names, so VHDL just gives them nondescript names based on their position in the character set. The character at position 160 is a non-breaking space character, distinct from the ordinary space character, and the character at position 173 is a soft hyphen.

To illustrate the use of the **character** type, we declare variables as follows:

```
variable cmd_char, terminator : character;
```

FIGURE 2-2

```
type character is (
    nul,    soh,    stx,    etx,    eot,    enq,    ack,    bel,
    bs,     ht,     lf,     vt,     ff,     cr,     so,     si,
    dle,    dc1,    dc2,    dc3,    dc4,    nak,    syn,    etb,
    can,    em,     sub,    esc,    fsp,    gsp,    rsp,    usp,
    ' ',    '!',    '"',    '#',    '$',    '%',    '&',    ''',
    '(',    ')',    '*',    '+',    ',',    '-',    '.',    '/',
    '0',    '1',    '2',    '3',    '4',    '5',    '6',    '7',
    '8',    '9',    ':',    ';',    '<',    '=',    '>',    '?',
    '@',    'A',    'B',    'C',    'D',    'E',    'F',    'G',
    'H',    'I',    'J',    'K',    'L',    'M',    'N',    'O',
    'P',    'Q',    'R',    'S',    'T',    'U',    'V',    'W',
    'X',    'Y',    'Z',    '[',    '\',    ']',    '^',    '_',
    '`',    'a',    'b',    'c',    'd',    'e',    'f',    'g',
    'h',    'i',    'j',    'k',    'l',    'm',    'n',    'o',
    'p',    'q',    'r',    's',    't',    'u',    'v',    'w',
    'x',    'y',    'z',    '{',    '|',    '}',    '~',    del,
    c128,   c129,   c130,   c131,   c132,   c133,   c134,   c135,
    c136,   c137,   c138,   c139,   c140,   c141,   c142,   c143,
    c144,   c145,   c146,   c147,   c148,   c149,   c150,   c151,
    c152,   c153,   c154,   c155,   c156,   c157,   c158,   c159,
    ' ',    '¡',    '¢',    '£',    '¤',    '¥',    '¦',    '§'
    '¨',    '©',    'ª',    '«',    '¬',    '',    '®',    '¯'
    '°',    '±',    '²',    '³',    '´',    'µ',    '¶',    '·',
    ' ',    '¹',    'º',    '»',    '¼',    '½',    '¾',    '¿',
    'À',    'Á',    'Â',    'Ã',    'Ä',    'Å',    'Æ',    'Ç',
    'È',    'É',    'Ê',    'Ë',    'Ì',    'Í',    'Î',    'Ï',
    'Ð',    'Ñ',    'Ò',    'Ó',    'Ô',    'Õ',    'Ö',    '×',
    'Ø',    'Ù',    'Ú',    'Û',    'Ü',    'Ý',    'Þ',    'ß',
    'à',    'á',    'â',    'ã',    'ä',    'å',    'æ',    'ç',
    'è',    'é',    'ê',    'ë',    'ì',    'í',    'î',    'ï',
    'ð',    'ñ',    'ò',    'ó',    'ô',    'õ',    'ö',    '÷',
    'ø',    'ù',    'ú',    'û',    'ü',    'ý',    'þ',    'ÿ');
```

The definition of the predefined enumeration type character.

and then make the assignments

```
cmd_char := 'P';
terminator := cr;
```

VHDL-87

Since VHDL-87 uses the ASCII character set, the predefined type **character** includes only the first 128 characters shown in Figure 2-2.

Booleans

One of the most important predefined enumeration types in VHDL is the type boolean, defined as

type boolean **is** (false, true);

This type is used to represent condition values, which can control execution of a behavioral model. There are a number of operators that we can apply to values of different types to yield Boolean values, namely, the relational and logical operators. The relational operators equality ("=") and inequality ("/=") can be applied to operands of any type (except files), including the composite types that we will see later in this chapter. The operands must both be of the same type, and the result is a Boolean value. For example, the expressions

123 = 123,   'A' = 'A',   7 ns = 7 ns

all yield the value **true**, and the expressions

123 = 456,   'A' = 'z',   7 ns = 2 us

yield the value **false**.

The relational operators that test ordering are the less-than ("<"), less-than-or-equal-to ("<="), greater-than (">") and greater-than-or-equal-to (">=") operators. These can only be applied to values of types that are ordered, including all of the scalar types described in this chapter. As with the equality and inequality operators, the operands must be of the same type, and the result is a Boolean value. For example, the expressions

123 < 456,   789 ps <= 789 ps,   '1' > '0'

all result in **true**, and the expressions

96 >= 102,   2 us < 4 ns,   'X' < 'X'

all result in **false**.

The logical operators **and, or, nand, nor, xor, xnor** and **not** take operands that must be Boolean values, and they produce Boolean results. Figure 2-3 shows the results produced by the binary logical operators. The result of the **not** operator is **true** if the operand is **false**, and **false** if the operand is **true**.

FIGURE 2-3

A	B	A **and** B	A **nand** B	A **or** B	A **nor** B	A **xor** B	A **xnor** B
false	false	false	true	false	true	false	true
false	true	false	true	true	false	true	false
true	false	false	true	true	false	true	false
true	true	true	false	true	false	false	true

The truth table for binary logical operators.

The operators **and, or, nand** and **nor** are called "short-circuit" operators, as they only evaluate the right operand if the left operand does not determine the result. For example, if the left operand of the **and** operator is false, we know that the result is false, so we do not need to consider the other operand. This is useful where the left operand is a test that guards against the right operand causing an error. Consider the expression

(b /= 0) **and** (a/b > 1)

If b were zero and we evaluated the right-hand operand, we would cause an error due to dividing by zero. However, because **and** is a short-circuit operator, if b were zero the left-hand operand would evaluate to false, so the right-hand operand would not be evaluated. For the **nand** operator, the right-hand operand is similarly not evaluated if the left-hand is false. For **or** and **nor**, the right-hand operand is not evaluated if the left-hand is true.

VHDL-87

The logical operator **xnor** is not provided in VHDL-87.

Bits

Since VHDL is used to model digital systems, it is useful to have a data type to represent bit values. The predefined enumeration type **bit** serves this purpose. It is defined as

type bit **is** ('0', '1');

Notice that the characters '0' and '1' are overloaded, since they are members of both **bit** and **character**. Where '0' or '1' occurs in a model, the context is used to determine which type is being used.

The logical operators that we mentioned for Boolean values can also be applied to values of type **bit**, and they produce results of type **bit**. The value '0' corresponds to false, and '1' corresponds to true. So, for example:

'0' **and** '1' = '0',   '1' **xor** '1' = '0'

The operands must still be of the same type as each other. Thus it is not legal to write

'0' **and** true

The difference between the types **boolean** and **bit** is that **boolean** values are used to model abstract conditions, whereas **bit** values are used to model hardware logic levels. Thus, '0' represents a low logic level and '1' represents a high logic level. The logical operators, when applied to **bit** values, are defined in terms of positive logic, with '0' representing the negated state and '1' representing the asserted state. If we need to deal with negative logic, we need to take care when writing logical expressions to get the correct logic sense. For example, if write_enable_n, select_reg_n and write_reg_n are negative logic bit variables, we perform the assignment

write_reg_n := **not** (**not** write_enable_n **and not** select_reg_n);

The variable write_reg_n is asserted ('0') only if write_enable_n is asserted and select_reg_n is asserted. Otherwise it is negated ('1').

Standard Logic

Since VHDL is designed for modeling digital hardware, it is necessary to include types to represent digitally encoded values. The predefined type **bit** shown above can be used for this in more abstract models, where we are not concerned about the details of electrical signals. However, as we refine our models to include more detail, we need to take account of the electrical properties when representing signals. There are many ways we can define data types to do this, but the IEEE has standardized one way in a package called **std_logic_1164**. The full details of the package are included in Appendix C. One of the types defined in this package is an enumeration type called **std_ulogic**, defined as

```
type std_ulogic is ( 'U',      -- Uninitialized
                     'X',      -- Forcing unknown
                     '0',      -- Forcing zero
                     '1',      -- Forcing one
                     'Z',      -- High impedance
                     'W',      -- Weak unknown
                     'L',      -- Weak zero
                     'H',      -- Weak one
                     '-' );    -- Don't care
```

This type can be used to represent signals driven by active drivers (forcing strength), resistive drivers such as pull-ups and pull-downs (weak strength) or three-state drivers including a high-impedance state. Each kind of driver may drive a "zero", "one" or "unknown" value. An "unknown" value is driven by a model when it is unable to determine whether the signal should be "zero" or "one". For example, the output of an and-gate is unknown when its inputs are driven by high-impedance drivers. In addition to these values, the leftmost value in the type represents an "uninitialized" value. If we declare signals of **std_ulogic** type, by default they take on 'U' as their initial value. If a model tries to operate on this value instead of a real logic value, we have detected a design error in that the system being modeled does not start up properly. The final value in **std_ulogic** is a "don't care" value. This is sometimes used by logic synthesis tools, and may also be used when defining test vectors, to denote that the value of a signal to be compared with a test vector is not important.

Even though the type **std_ulogic** and the other types defined in the **std_logic_1164** package are not actually built into the VHDL language, we can write models as though they were, with a little bit of preparation. For now, we describe some "magic" to include at the beginning of a model that uses the package; we explain the details in Chapter 8. If we include the line

library ieee; **use** ieee.std_logic_1164.**all**;

preceding each entity or architecture body that uses the package, we can write models as though the types were built into the language.

With this preparation in hand, we can now create constants, variables and signals of type **std_ulogic**. As well as assigning values of the type, we can also use the logical operators **and**, **or**, **not**, and so on. Each of these operates on **std_ulogic** values and returns a **std_ulogic** result of 'U', 'X', '0' or '1'. The operators are "optimistic," in that if they can determine a '0' or '1' result despite inputs being unknown, they do so. Otherwise they return 'X' or 'U'. For example '0' **and** 'Z' returns '0', since one input to an and-gate being '0' always causes the output to be '0', regardless of the other input.

2.3   Type Classification

In the preceding sections we have looked at the scalar types provided in VHDL. Figure 2-4 illustrates the relationships between these types, the predefined scalar types and the types we look at in later chapters.

FIGURE 2-4

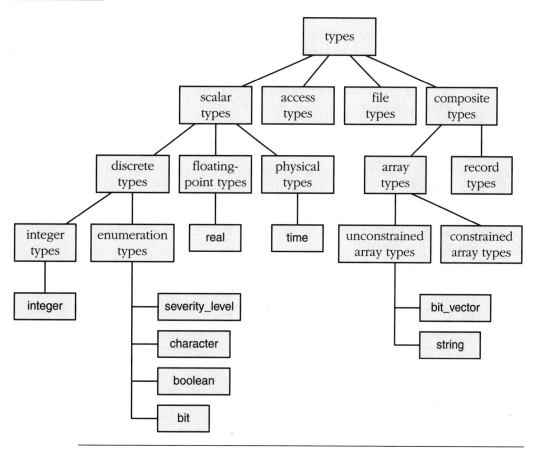

A classification of VHDL types.

The scalar types are all those composed of individual values that are ordered. Integer and floating-point types are ordered on the number line. Physical types are ordered by the number of base units in each value. Enumeration types are ordered by their declaration. The discrete types are those that represent discrete sets of values and comprise the integer types and enumeration types. Floating-point and physical types are not discrete, as they approximate a continuum of values.

Subtypes

In Section 2.2 we saw how to declare a type, which defines a set of values. Often a model contains objects that should only take on a restricted range of the complete set of values. We can represent such objects by declaring a *subtype*, which defines a restricted set of values from a *base type*. The condition that determines which values are in the subtype is called a *constraint*. Using a subtype declaration makes clear our intention about which values are valid and makes it possible to check that invalid values are not used. The simplified syntax rules for a subtype declaration are

> subtype_declaration ⇐ **subtype** identifier **is** subtype_indication ;
>
> subtype_indication ⇐
>   name 〚 **range** simple_expression (**to** ‖ **downto**) simple_expression 〛

We will look at more advanced forms of subtype indications in later chapters. The subtype declaration defines the identifier as a subtype of the named base type, with the range constraint restricting the values for the subtype. The constraint is optional, which means that it is possible to have a subtype that includes all of the values of the base type.

EXAMPLE

Here is a declaration that defines a subtype of integer:

subtype small_int **is** integer **range** –128 **to** 127;

Values of small_int are constrained to be within the range –128 to 127. If we declare some variables:

variable deviation : small_int;
variable adjustment : integer;

we can use them in calculations:

deviation := deviation + adjustment;

Note that in this case, we can mix the subtype and base type values in the addition to produce a value of type integer, but the result must be within the range –128 to 127 for the assignment to succeed. If it is not, an error will be signaled when the variable is assigned. All of the operations that are applicable to the base type can also be used on values of a subtype. The operations produce values of the base type rather than the subtype. However, the assignment operation will not assign a value to a variable of a subtype if the value does not meet the constraint.

Another point to note is that if a base type is a range of one direction (ascending or descending), and a subtype is specified with a range constraint of the opposite direction, it is the subtype specification that counts. For example, the predefined type integer is an ascending range. If we declare a subtype as

subtype bit_index **is** integer **range** 31 **downto** 0;

this subtype is a descending range.

The VHDL standard includes two predefined integer subtypes, defined as

subtype natural **is** integer **range** 0 **to** *highest integer*;
subtype positive **is** integer **range** 1 **to** *highest integer*;

Where the logic of a design indicates that a number should not be negative, it is good style to use one of these subtypes rather than the base type **integer**. In this way, we can detect any design errors that incorrectly cause negative numbers to be produced. There is also a predefined subtype of the physical type **time**, defined as

subtype delay_length **is** time **range** 0 fs **to** *highest time*;

This subtype should be used wherever a non-negative time delay is required.

VHDL-87
_____

The subtype **delay_length** is not predefined in VHDL-87.

_____

Type Qualification

Sometimes it is not clear from the context what the type of a particular value is. In the case of overloaded enumeration literals, it may be necessary to specify explicitly which type is meant. We can do this using *type qualification*, which consists of writing the type name followed by a single quote character, then an expression enclosed in parentheses. For example, given the enumeration types

type logic_level **is** (unknown, low, undriven, high);
type system_state **is** (unknown, ready, busy);

we can distinguish between the common literal values by writing

logic_level'(unknown),   system_state'(unknown)

Type qualification can also be used to narrow a value down to a particular subtype of a base type. For example, if we define a subtype of logic_level

subtype valid_level **is** logic_level **range** low **to** high;

we can explicitly specify a value of either the type or the subtype

logic_level'(high),   valid_level'(high)

Of course, it is an error if the expression being qualified is not of the type or subtype specified.

Type Conversion

When we introduced the arithmetic operators in previous sections, we stated that the operands must be of the same type. This precludes mixing integer and floating-point values in arithmetic expressions. Where we need to do mixed arithmetic, we can use *type conversions* to convert between integer and floating-point values. The form of a type conversion is the name of the type we want to convert to, followed by a value in parentheses. For example, to convert between the types **integer** and **real**, we could write real(123),   integer(3.6)

Converting an integer to a floating-point value is simply a change in representation, although some loss of precision may occur. Converting from a floating-point value to an integer involves rounding to the nearest integer. Numeric type conversions are not the only conversion allowed. In general, we can convert between any closely related types. Other examples of closely related types are certain array types, discussed in Chapter 4.

One thing to watch out for is the distinction between type qualification and type conversion. The former simply states the type of a value, whereas the latter changes the value, possibly to a different type. One way to remember this distinction is to think of "*qu*ote for *qu*alification."

2.4   Attributes of Scalar Types

A type defines a set of values and a set of applicable operations. There is also a predefined set of *attributes* that are used to give information about the values included in the type. Attributes are written by following the type name with a quote mark (') and the attribute name. The value of an attribute can be used in calculations in a model. We now look at some of the attributes defined for the types we have discussed in this chapter.

First, there are a number of attributes that are applicable to all scalar types and provide information about the range of values in the type. If we let T stand for any scalar type or subtype, x stand for a value of that type and s stand for a string value, the attributes are

T'left	first (leftmost) value in T
T'right	last (rightmost) value in T
T'low	least value in T
T'high	greatest value in T
T'ascending	true if T is an ascending range, false otherwise
T'image(x)	a string representing the value of x
T'value(s)	the value in T that is represented by s

The string produced by the 'image attribute is a correctly formed literal according to the rules shown in Chapter 1. The strings allowed in the 'value attribute must follow those rules and may include leading or trailing spaces. These two attributes are useful for input and output in a model, as we will see when we come to that topic.

EXAMPLE

To illustrate the attributes listed above, we include some declarations from previous examples:

```
type resistance is range 0 to 1E9
    units
        ohm;
        kohm = 1000 ohm;
```

          Mohm = 1000 kohm;
      end units resistance;

type set_index_range **is range** 21 **downto** 11;

type logic_level **is** (unknown, low, undriven, high);

For these types:

```
resistance'left = 0 ohm
resistance'right = 1E9 ohm
resistance'low = 0 ohm
resistance'high = 1E9 ohm
resistance'ascending = true
resistance'image(2 kohm) = "2000 ohm"
resistance'value("5 Mohm") = 5_000_000 ohm

set_index_range'left = 21
set_index_range'right = 11
set_index_range'low = 11
set_index_range'high = 21
set_index_range'ascending = false
set_index_range'image(14) = "14"
set_index_range'value("20") = 20

logic_level'left = unknown
logic_level'right = high
logic_level'low = unknown
logic_level'high = high
logic_level'ascending = true
logic_level'image(undriven) = "undriven"
logic_level'value("Low") = low
```

Next, there are attributes that are applicable to just discrete and physical types. For any such type T, a value x of that type and an integer n, the attributes are

T'pos(x)	position number of x in T
T'val(n)	value in T at position n
T'succ(x)	value in T at position one greater than that of x
T'pred(x)	value in T at position one less than that of x
T'leftof(x)	value in T at position one to the left of x
T'rightof(x)	value in T at position one to the right of x

For enumeration types, the position numbers start at zero for the first element listed and increase by one for each element to the right. So, for the type logic_level shown above, some attribute values are

```
logic_level'pos(unknown) = 0
logic_level'val(3) = high
logic_level'succ(unknown) = low
logic_level'pred(undriven) = low
```

For integer types, the position number is the same as the integer value, but the type of the position number is a special anonymous type called *universal integer*. This is the same type as that of integer literals and, where necessary, is implicitly converted to any other declared integer type. For physical types, the position number is the integer number of base units in the physical value. For example:

```
time'pos(4 ns) = 4_000_000
```

since the base unit is **fs**.

EXAMPLE

We can use the 'pos and 'val attributes in combination to perform mixed-dimensional arithmetic with physical types, producing a result of the correct dimensionality. Suppose we define physical types to represent length and area, as follows:

```
type length is range integer'low to integer'high
    units
        mm;
    end units length;
type area is range integer'low to integer'high
    units
        square_mm;
    end units area;
```

and variables of these types:

```
variable L1, L2 : length;
variable A : area;
```

The restrictions on multiplying values of physical types prevents us from writing something like

```
A := L1 * L2;    -- this is incorrect
```

To achieve the correct result, we can convert the length values to abstract integers using the 'pos attribute, then convert the result of the multiplication to an area value using 'val, as follows:

```
A := area'val( length'pos(L1) * length'pos(L2) );
```

Note that in this example, we do not need to include a scale factor in the multiplication, since the base unit of **area** is the square of the base unit of **length**.

For ascending ranges, T'succ(x) and T'rightof(x) produce the same value, and T'pred(x) and T'leftof(x) produce the same value. For descending ranges, T'pred(x) and T'rightof(x) produce the same value, and T'succ(x) and T'leftof(x) produce the same value. For all ranges, T'succ(T'high), T'pred(T'low), T'rightof(T'right) and T'leftof(T'left) cause an error to occur.

The last attribute we introduce here is T'base. For any subtype T, this attribute produces the base type of T. The only context in which this attribute may be used is as the prefix of another attribute. For example, if we have the declarations

```
type opcode is (nop, load, store, add, subtract, negate, branch, halt);
subtype arith_op is opcode range add to negate;
```

then

```
arith_op'base'left = nop
arith_op'base'succ(negate) = branch
```

VHDL-87

The attributes 'ascending, 'image and 'value are not provided in VHDL-87.

2.5 Expressions and Operators

In Section 2.1 we showed how the value resulting from evaluation of an expression can be assigned to a variable. In this section, we summarize the rules governing expressions. We can think of an expression as being a formula that specifies how to compute a value. As such, it consists of primary values combined with operators. The precise syntax rules for writing expressions are shown in Appendix E. The primary values that can be used in expressions include

- literal values,
- identifiers representing data objects (constants, variables, and so on),
- attributes that yield values,
- qualified expressions,
- type-converted expressions, and
- expressions in parentheses.

We have seen examples of these in this chapter and in Chapter 1. For reference, all of the operators and the types they can be applied to are summarized in Figure 2-5. We will discuss array operators in Chapter 4.

The operators in this table are grouped by precedence, with ******, **abs** and **not** having highest precedence and the logical operators lowest. This means that if an expression contains a combination of operators, those with highest precedence are applied first. Parentheses can be used to alter the order of evaluation, or for clarity.

VHDL-87

The shift operators (**sll**, **srl**, **sla**, **sra**, **rol** and **ror**) and the **xnor** operator are not provided in VHDL-87.

FIGURE 2-5

Operator	Operation	Left operand type	Right operand type	Result type
**	exponentiation	integer or floating-point	integer	same as left operand
abs	absolute value		numeric	same as operand
not	negation		bit, boolean or 1-D array of bit or boolean	same as operand
*	multiplication	integer or floating-point	same as left operand	same as operands
		physical	integer or floating-point	same as left operand
		integer or floating-point	physical	same as right operand
/	division	integer or floating-point	same as left operand	same as operands
		physical	integer or floating-point	same as left operand
		physical	same as left operand	universal integer
mod	modulo	integer	same as left operand	same as operands
rem	remainder	integer	same as left operand	same as operands
+	identity		numeric	same as operand
−	negation		numeric	same as operand
+	addition	numeric	same as left operand	same as operands
−	subtraction	numeric	same as left operand	same as operands
&	concatenation	1-D array	same as left operand	same as operands
		1-D array	element type of left operand	same as left operand
		element type of right operand	1-D array	same as right operand
		element type of result	element type of result	1-D array
sll	shift-left logical	1-D array of bit or boolean	integer	same as left operand
srl	shift-right logical			
sla	shift-left arithmetic			
sra	shift-right arithmetic			
rol	rotate left			
ror	rotate right			

Operator	Operation	Left operand type	Right operand type	Result type
=	equality	any except file	same as left operand	boolean
/=	inequality			
<	less than	scalar or 1-D array	same as left operand	boolean
<=	less than or equal	of any discrete type		
>	greater than			
>=	greater than or equal			
and	logical and	bit, boolean	same as left operand	same as operands
or	logical or	or 1-D array of		
nand	negated logical and	bit or boolean		
nor	negated logical or			
xor	exclusive or			
xnor	negated exclusive or			

VHDL operators in order of precedence, from most-binding to least-binding.

Exercises

1. [❶ 2.1] Write constant declarations for the number of bits in a 32-bit word and for the number π (3.14159).

2. [❶ 2.1] Write variable declarations for a counter, initialized to 0; a status flag used to indicate whether a module is busy; and a standard-logic value used to store a temporary result.

3. [❶ 2.1] Given the declarations in Exercise 2, write variable assignment statements to increment the counter, to set the status flag to indicate the module is busy and to indicate a weak unknown temporary result.

4. [❶ 2.2] Write a package declaration containing type declarations for small non-negative integers representable in eight bits; fractional numbers between −1.0 and +1.0; electrical currents, with units of nA, μA, mA and A; and traffic light colors.

5. [❶ 2.4] Given the subtype declarations

    subtype pulse_range **is** time **range** 1 ms **to** 100 ms;
    subtype word_index **is** integer **range** 31 **downto** 0;

    what are the values of 'left, 'right, 'low, 'high and 'ascending attributes of each of these subtypes?

6. [● 2.4] Given the type declaration

    type state **is** (off, standby, active1, active2);

    what are the values of

    state'pos(standby)   state'val(2)
    state'succ(active2)   state'pred(active1)
    state'leftof(off)   state'rightof(off)

7. [● 2.5] For each of the following expressions, indicate whether they are syntactical-ly correct, and if so, determine the resulting value.

    2 * 3 + 6 / 4   3 + −4
    "cat" & character'('0')   true **and** x **and not** y **or** z
    B"101110" **sll** 3   B"100010" **sra** 2 & X"2C"

8. [❷ 2.1] Write a counter model with a clock input clk of type **bit**, and an output q of type **integer**. The behavioral architecture body should contain a process that de-clares a count variable initialized to zero. The process should wait for changes on clk. When clk changes to '1', the process should increment the count and assign its value to the output port.

9. [❷ 2.2] Write a model that represents a simple ALU with integer inputs and output, and a function select input of type **bit**. If the function select is '0', the ALU output should be the sum of the inputs; otherwise the output should be the difference of the inputs.

10. [❷ 2.2] Write a model for a digital integrator that has a clock input of type **bit** and data input and output each of type **real**. The integrator maintains the sum of succes-sive data input values. When the clock input changes from '0' to '1', the integrator should add the current data input to the sum and provide the new sum on the out-put.

11. [❷ 2.2] Following is a process that generates a regular clock signal.

    ```
    clock_gen : process is
    begin
        clk <= '1';  wait for 10 ns;
        clk <= '0';  wait for 10 ns;
    end process clock_gen;
    ```

    Use this as the basis for experiments to determine how your simulator behaves with different settings for the resolution limit. Try setting the resolution limit to 1 ns (the default for many simulators), 1 ps and 1 μs.

12. [❷ 2.2] Write a model for a tristate buffer using the standard-logic type for its data and enable inputs and its data output. If the enable input is '0' or 'L', the output should be 'Z'. If the enable input is '1' or 'H' and the data input is '0' or 'L', the output should be '0'. If the enable input is '1' or 'H' and the data input is '1' or 'H', the output should be '1'. In all other cases, the output should be 'X'.

Sequential Statements

In the previous chapter we saw how to represent the internal state of models using VHDL data types. In this chapter we look at how that data may be manipulated within processes. This is done using *sequential statements*, so called because they are executed in sequence. We have already seen one of the basic sequential statements, the variable assignment statement, when we were looking at data types and objects. The statements we look at in this chapter deal with controlling actions within a model, hence they are often called *control structures*. They allow selection between alternative courses of action as well as repetition of actions.

3.1 If Statements

In many models, the behavior depends on a set of conditions that may or may not hold true during the course of simulation. We can use an *if statement* to express this behavior. The syntax rule for an if statement is

> if_statement ⟸
>   ⟦ *if*_label : ⟧
>   **if** *boolean*_expression **then**
>   { sequential_statement }
>   { **elsif** *boolean*_expression **then**
>   { sequential_statement } }
>   ⟦ **else**
>   { sequential_statement } ⟧
>   **end if** ⟦ *if*_label ⟧ ;

At first sight, this may appear somewhat complicated, so we start with some simple examples and work up to examples showing the general case. The label may be used to identify the if statement. We will discuss labeled statements in Chapter 20. A simple example of an if statement is

```
if en = '1' then
    stored_value := data_in;
end if;
```

The expression after the keyword **if** is the condition that is used to control whether or not the statement after the keyword **then** is executed. If the condition evaluates to true, the statement is executed. In this example, if the value of the object **en** is '1', the assignment is made; otherwise it is skipped. We can also specify actions to be performed if the condition is false. For example:

```
if sel = 0 then
    result <= input_0;  -- executed if sel = 0
else
    result <= input_1;  -- executed if sel /= 0
end if;
```

Here, as the comments indicate, the first signal assignment statement is executed if the condition is true, and the second signal assignment statement is executed if the condition is false.

In many models, we may need to check a number of different conditions and execute a different sequence of statements for each case. We can construct a more elaborate form of if statement to do this, for example:

```
if mode = immediate then
    operand := immed_operand;
elsif opcode = load or opcode = add or opcode = subtract then
    operand := memory_operand;
else
    operand := address_operand;
end if;
```

In this example, the first condition is evaluated, and if true, the statement after the first **then** keyword is executed. If the first condition is false, the second condition is evaluated, and if it evaluates to true, the statement after the second **then** keyword is executed. If the second condition is false, the statement after the **else** keyword is executed.

In general, we can construct an if statement with any number of **elsif** clauses (including none), and we may include or omit the **else** clause. Execution of the if statement starts by evaluating the first condition. If it is false, successive conditions are evaluated, in order, until one is found to be true, in which case the corresponding statements are executed. If none of the conditions is true, and we have included an **else** clause, the statements after the **else** keyword are executed.

We are not restricted to just one statement in each part of the if statement. This is illustrated by the following if statement:

```
if opcode = halt_opcode then
    PC := effective_address;
    executing := false;
    halt_indicator <= true;
end if;
```

If the condition is true, all three statements are executed, one after another. On the other hand, if the condition is false, none of the statements are executed. Furthermore, each statement contained in an if statement can be any sequential statement. This means we can nest if statements, for example:

```
if phase = wash then
    if cycle_select = delicate_cycle then
        agitator_speed <= slow;
    else
        agitator_speed <= fast;
    end if;
    agitator_on <= true;
end if;
```

In this example, the condition **phase = wash** is first evaluated, and if true, the nested if statement and the following signal assignment statement are executed. Thus the assignment **agitator_speed <= slow** is executed only if both conditions evaluate to true, and the assignment **agitator_speed <= fast** is executed only if the first condition is true and the second condition is false.

EXAMPLE

Let us develop a behavioral model for a simple heater thermostat. The device can be modeled as an entity with two integer inputs, one that specifies the desired temperature and another that is connected to a thermometer, and one Boolean output that turns a heater on and off. The thermostat turns the heater on if the measured temperature falls below two degrees less than the desired temperature, and turns the heater off if the measured temperature rises above two degrees greater than the desired temperature. Figure 3-1 shows the entity and architecture bodies for the thermostat. The entity declaration defines the input and output ports.

FIGURE 3-1

```
entity thermostat is
    port ( desired_temp, actual_temp : in integer;
            heater_on : out boolean );
end entity thermostat;

_____

architecture example of thermostat is
begin
    controller : process (desired_temp, actual_temp) is
    begin
        if actual_temp < desired_temp – 2 then
            heater_on <= true;
        elsif actual_temp > desired_temp + 2 then
            heater_on <= false;
        end if;
    end process controller;
end architecture example;
```

An entity and architecture body for a heater thermostat.

Since it is a behavioral model, the architecture body contains only a process statement that implements the required behavior. The process statement includes a *sensitivity list* after the keyword **process**. This is a list of signals to which the process is sensitive. When any of these signals change value, the process resumes and executes the sequential statements. After it has executed the last statement, the process suspends again. In this example, the process is sensitive to changes on either of the input ports. Thus, if we adjust the desired temperature, or if the measured temperature from the thermometer varies, the process is resumed. The body of the process contains an if statement that compares the actual temperature with the desired temperature. If the actual temperature is too low, the process executes the first signal assignment to turn the heater on. If the actual temperature is too high, the process executes the second signal assignment to turn the heater off. If the actual temperature is within the range, the state of the heater is not changed, since there is no **else** clause in the if statement.

VHDL-87

If statements may not be labeled in VHDL-87.

3.2 Case Statements

If we have a model in which the behavior is to depend on the value of a single expression, we can use a *case statement*. The syntax rules are as follows:

case_statement ⟸
    〚 *case*_label : 〛
    case expression **is**
        (**when** choices => 〔 sequential_statement 〕)
        〔 ... 〕
    end case 〚 *case*_label 〛 ;

choices ⟸ (simple_expression ‖ discrete_range ‖ **others**) 〔 ‖ ... 〕

The label may be used to identify the case statement. We will discuss labeled statements in Chapter 20. We start with some simple examples of case statements and build up from them. First, suppose we are modeling an arithmetic/logic unit, with a control input, func, declared to be of the enumeration type:

type alu_func **is** (pass1, pass2, add, subtract);

We could describe the behavior using a case statement:

```
case func is
    when pass1 =>
        result := operand1;
    when pass2 =>
        result := operand2;
    when add =>
        result := operand1 + operand2;
    when subtract =>
        result := operand1 – operand2;
end case;
```

At the head of this case statement is the *selector expression*, between the keywords **case** and **is**. In this example it is a simple expression consisting of just a primary value. The value of this expression is used to select which statements to execute. The body of the case statement consists of a series of *alternatives*, each starting with the keyword **when**, followed by one or more *choices* and a sequence of statements. The choices are values that are compared with the value of the selector expression. There must be exactly one choice for each possible value of the selector expression. The case statement finds the alternative with the same choice value as the selector expression and executes the statements in that alternative. In this example, the choices are all simple expressions of type alu_func. If the value of func is pass1, the statement result := operand1 is executed; if the value is pass2, the statement result := operand2 is executed; and so on.

A case statement bears some similarity to an if statement in that they both select among alternative groups of sequential statements. The difference lies in how the statements to be executed are chosen. We saw in the previous section that an if statement evaluates successive Boolean conditions in turn until one is found to be true. The group of statements corresponding to that condition is then executed. A case statement, on the other hand, evaluates a single selector expression to derive a selector value. This value is then compared with the choice values in the case statement alternatives to determine which statement to execute. An if statement provides a more general mechanism for selecting between alternatives, since the conditions can be arbitrarily complex Boolean expressions. However, case statements are an important and useful modeling mechanism, as the examples in this section show.

The selector expression of a case statement must result in a value of a discrete type, or a one-dimensional array of character elements, such as a character string or bit string (see Chapter 4). Thus, we can have a case statement that selects an alternative based on an integer value. If we assume index_mode and instruction_register are declared as

subtype index_mode **is** integer **range** 0 **to** 3;

variable instruction_register : integer **range** 0 **to** 2**16 − 1;

then we can write a case statement that uses a value of this type:

```
case index_mode'((instruction_register / 2**12) rem 2**2) is
    when 0 =>
        index_value := 0;
    when 1 =>
        index_value := accumulator_A;
    when 2 =>
        index_value := accumulator_B;
    when 3 =>
        index_value := index_register;
end case;
```

Notice that in this example, we use a qualified expression in the selector expression. If we had omitted this, the result of the expression would have been **integer**, and we would have had to include alternatives to cover all possible integer values. The type qualification avoids this need by limiting the possible values of the expression.

Another rule to remember is that the type of each choice must be the same as the type resulting from the selector expression. Thus in the above example, it is illegal to include an alternative such as

```
when 'a' => ...          --illegal!
```

since the choice listed cannot be an integer. Such a choice does not make sense, since it can never match a value of type **integer**.

We can include more than one choice in each alternative by writing the choices separated by the "|" symbol. For example, if the type **opcodes** is declared as

```
type opcodes is
    (nop, add, subtract, load, store, jump, jumpsub, branch, halt);
```

we could write an alternative including three of these values as choices:

```
when load | add | subtract =>
    operand := memory_operand;
```

If we have a number of alternatives in a case statement and we want to include an alternative to handle all possible values of the selector expression not mentioned in previous alternatives, we can use the special choice **others**. For example, if the variable opcode is a variable of type opcodes, declared above, we can write

```
case opcode is
    when load | add | subtract =>
        operand := memory_operand;
    when store | jump | jumpsub | branch =>
        operand := address_operand;
    when others =>
        operand := 0;
end case;
```

In this example, if the value of operand is anything other than the choices listed in the first and second alternatives, the last alternative is selected. There may only be one alternative that uses the **others** choice, and if it is included, it must be the last alternative in the case statement. An alternative that includes the **others** choice may not include any other choices. Note that, if all of the possible values of the selector expression are covered by previous choices, we may still include the **others** choice, but it can never be matched.

The remaining form of choice that we have not yet mentioned is a *discrete range*, specified by these simplified syntax rules:

discrete_range ⇐
    *discrete*_subtype_indication
    ‖ simple_expression (**to** ‖ **downto**) simple_expression

subtype_indication ⇐
    type_mark
        ⟦ **range** simple_expression (**to** ‖ **downto**) simple_expression ⟧

These forms allow us to specify a range of values in a case statement alternative. If the value of the selector expression matches any of the values in the range, the statements in the alternative are executed. The simplest way to specify a discrete range is just to write the left and right bounds of the range, separated by a direction keyword. For example, the case statement above could be rewritten as

```
case opcode is
    when add to load =>
        operand := memory_operand;
    when branch downto store =>
        operand := address_operand;
    when others =>
        operand := 0;
end case;
```

Another way of specifying a discrete range is to use the name of a discrete type, and possibly a range constraint to narrow down the values to a subset of the type. For example, if we declare a subtype of opcodes as

```
subtype control_transfer_opcodes is opcodes range jump to branch;
```

we can rewrite the second alternative as

when control_transfer_opcodes | store =>
    operand := address_operand;

Note that we may only use a discrete range as a choice if the selector expression is of a discrete type. We may not use a discrete range if the selector expression is of an array type, such as a bit-vector type. If we specify a range by writing the bounds and a direction, the direction has no significance except to identify the contents of the range.

An important point to note about the choices in a case statement is that they must all be written using *locally static* values. This means that the values of the choices must be determined during the analysis phase of design processing. All of the above examples satisfy this requirement. To give an example of a case statement that fails this requirement, suppose we have an integer variable **N**, declared as

variable N : integer := 1;

If we wrote the case statement

case *expression* **is**   *-- example of an illegal case statement*
    when N | N+1 => . . .
    when N+2 **to** N+5 => . . .
    when others => . . .
end case;

the values of the choices depend on the value of the variable **N**. Since this might change during the course of execution, these choices are not locally static. Hence the case statement as written is illegal. On the other hand, if we had declared **C** to be a constant integer, for example with the declaration

constant C : integer := 1;

then we could legally write the case statement

case *expression* **is**
    when C | C+1 => . . .
    when C+2 **to** C+5 => . . .
    when others => . . .
end case;

This is legal, since we can determine, by analyzing the model, that the first alternative includes choices 1 and 2, the second includes numbers between 3 and 6 and the third covers all other possible values of the expression.

The previous examples all show only one statement in each alternative. As with the if statement, we can write an arbitrary number of sequential statements of any kind in each alternative. This includes writing nested case statements, if statements or any other form of sequential statements in the alternatives.

Although the preceding rules governing case statements may seem complex, in practice there are just a few things to remember, namely:

- all possible values of the selector expression must be covered by one and only one choice,
- the values in the choices must be locally static, and

- if the **others** choice is used it must be in the last alternative and must be the only choice in that alternative.

EXAMPLE

We can write a behavioral model of a multiplexer with a select input **sel**; four data inputs **d0**, **d1**, **d2** and **d3**; and a data output **z**. The data inputs and outputs are of the IEEE standard-logic type, and the select input is of type **sel_range**, which we assume to be declared elsewhere as

type sel_range **is range** 0 **to** 3;

We show in Chapter 8, when we discuss packages, how we define a type for use in an entity declaration. The entity declaration defining the ports and a behavioral architecture body are shown in Figure 3-2. The architecture body contains just a process declaration. Since the output of the multiplexer must change if any of the data or select inputs change, the process must be sensitive to all of the inputs. It makes use of a case statement to select which of the data inputs is to be assigned to the data output.

FIGURE 3-2

```
library ieee;  use ieee.std_logic_1164.all;
entity mux4 is
    port ( sel : in sel_range;
           d0, d1, d2, d3 : in std_ulogic;
           z : out std_ulogic );
end entity mux4;

------------------------------------------------

architecture demo of mux4 is
begin
    out_select : process (sel, d0, d1, d2, d3) is
    begin
        case sel is
            when 0 =>
                z <= d0;
            when 1 =>
                z <= d1;
            when 2 =>
                z <= d2;
            when 3 =>
                z <= d3;
        end case;
    end process out_select;
end architecture demo;
```

An entity and architecture body for a four-input multiplexer.

VHDL-87

Case statements may not be labeled in VHDL-87.

3.3 Null Statements

Sometimes when writing models we need to state that when some condition arises, no action is to be performed. This need often arises when we use case statements, since we must include an alternative for every possible value of the selector expression. Rather than just leaving the statement part of an alternative blank, we can use a *null statement* to state explicitly that nothing is to be done. The syntax rule for the null statement is simply

> null_statement ⇐ ⟦ label : ⟧ **null** ;

The optional label serves to identify the statement. We discuss labeled statements in Chapter 20. A simple, unlabeled null statement is

> **null**;

An example of its use in a case statement is

```
case opcode is
    when add =>
        Acc := Acc + operand;
    when subtract =>
        Acc := Acc – operand;
    when nop =>
        null;
end case;
```

We can use a null statement in any place where a sequential statement is required, not just in a case statement alternative. A null statement may be used during the development phase of model writing. If we know, for example, that we will need an entity as part of a system, but we are not yet in a position to write a detailed model for it, we can write a behavioral model that does nothing. Such a model just includes a process with a null statement in its body:

```
control_section : process ( sensitivity-list ) is
begin
    null;
end process control_section;
```

Note that the process must include the sensitivity list, for reasons that are explained in Chapter 5.

VHDL-87

Null statements may not be labeled in VHDL-87.

3.4 Loop Statements

Often we need to write a sequence of statements that is to be repeatedly executed. We use a *loop statement* to express this behavior. There are several different forms of loop statements in VHDL; the simplest is a loop that repeats a sequence of statements indefinitely, often called an *infinite loop*. The syntax rule for this kind of loop is

loop_statement ⇐
    ⟦ *loop*_label : ⟧
    loop
        { sequential_statement }
    end loop ⟦ *loop*_label ⟧ ;

In most computer programming languages, an infinite loop is not desirable, since it means that the program never terminates. However, when we are modeling digital systems, an infinite loop can be useful, since many hardware devices repeatedly perform the same function until we turn off the power. Typically a model for such a system includes a loop statement in a process body; the loop, in turn, contains a wait statement.

EXAMPLE

Figure 3-3 is a model for a counter that starts from zero and increments on each clock transition from '0' to '1'. When the counter reaches 15, it wraps back to zero on the next clock transition. The architecture body for the counter contains a process that first initializes the **count** output to zero, then repeatedly waits for a clock transition before incrementing the count value.

FIGURE 3-3

```
entity counter is
    port ( clk : in bit;  count : out natural );
end entity counter;
```

```
architecture behavior of counter is
begin
    incrementer : process is
        variable count_value : natural := 0;
    begin
        count <= count_value;
        loop
            wait until clk = '1';
            count_value := (count_value + 1) mod 16;
            count <= count_value;
        end loop;
    end process incrementer;
end architecture behavior;
```

An entity and architecture body for a counter.

The wait statement in this example causes the process to suspend in the middle of the loop. When the clk signal changes from '0' to '1', the process resumes and updates the count value and the **count** output. The loop is then repeated starting with the wait statement, so the process suspends again.

Another point to note in passing is that the process statement does not include a sensitivity list. This is because it includes a wait statement. A process may contain either a sensitivity list or wait statements, but not both. We will return to this in detail in Chapter 5.

Exit Statements

In the previous example, the loop repeatedly executes the enclosed statements, with no way of stopping. Usually we need to exit the loop when some condition arises. We can use an *exit statement* to exit a loop. The syntax rule is

exit_statement ⇐
    〖 label : 〗 **exit** 〖 *loop*_label 〗 〖 **when** *boolean*_expression 〗 ;

The optional label at the start of the exit statement serves to identify the statement. We discuss labeled statements in Chapter 20. The simplest form of exit statement is just

    exit;

When this statement is executed, any remaining statements in the loop are skipped, and control is transferred to the statement after the **end loop** keywords. So in a loop we can write

    if *condition* **then**
        exit;
    end if;

where *condition* is a Boolean expression. Since this is perhaps the most common use of the exit statement, VHDL provides a shorthand way of writing it, using the **when** clause. We use an exit statement with the **when** clause in a loop of the form

    loop
        . . .
        exit when *condition*;
        . . .
    end loop;
    . . .   *-- control transferred to here*
             -- when condition becomes true within the loop

EXAMPLE

We now revise the previous counter model to include a **reset** input that, when '1', causes the **count** output to be reset to zero. The output stays at zero as long as the **reset** input is '1' and resumes counting on the next clock transition after **reset** changes to '0'. The revised entity declaration, shown in Figure 3-4, includes the new input port.

FIGURE 3-4

```
entity counter is
    port ( clk, reset : in bit;  count : out natural );
end entity counter;

_____

architecture behavior of counter is
begin
    incrementer : process is
        variable count_value : natural := 0;
    begin
        count <= count_value;
        loop
            loop
                wait until clk = '1' or reset = '1';
                exit when reset = '1';
                count_value := (count_value + 1) mod 16;
                count <= count_value;
            end loop;
            -- at this point, reset = '1'
            count_value := 0;
            count <= count_value;
            wait until reset = '0';
        end loop;
    end process incrementer;
end architecture behavior;
```

An entity and architecture body of the revised counter, including a reset *input.*

The architecture body is revised by nesting the loop inside another loop statement and adding the **reset** signal to the original wait statement. The inner loop performs the same function as before, except that when **reset** changes to '1', the process is resumed, and the exit statement causes the inner loop to be terminated. Control is transferred to the statement just after the end of the inner loop. As the comment indicates, we know that this point can only be reached when **reset** is '1'. The count value and **count** outputs are reset, and the process then waits for **reset** to return to '0'. While it is suspended at this point, any changes on the clock input are ignored. When **reset** changes to '0', the process resumes, and the outer loop repeats.

This example also illustrates another important point. When we have nested loop statements, with an exit statement inside the inner loop, the exit statement causes control to be transferred out of the inner loop only, not the outer loop. By default, an exit statement transfers control out of the immediately enclosing loop.

In some cases, we may wish to transfer control out of an inner loop and also a containing loop. We can do this by labeling the outer loop and using the label in the exit statement. We can write

> loop_name : **loop**
>
>   . . .
>
>   **exit** loop_name;
>
>   . . .
>
> **end loop** loop_name ;

This labels the loop with the name loop_name, so that we can indicate which loop to exit in the exit statement. The loop label can be any valid identifier. The exit statement referring to this label can be located within nested loop statements.

To illustrate how loops can be nested, labeled and exited, let us consider the following statements:

> outer : **loop**
>
>   . . .
>
>   inner : **loop**
>
>   . . .
>
>   **exit** outer **when** *condition-1*;   *-- exit 1*
>
>   . . .
>
>   **exit when** *condition-2*;   *-- exit 2*
>
>   . . .
>
>   **end loop** inner;
>
>   . . .   *-- target A*
>
>   **exit** outer **when** *condition-3*;   *-- exit 3*
>
>   . . .
>
> **end loop** outer;
>
>   . . .   *-- target B*

This example contains two loop statements, one labeled inner nested inside another labeled outer. The first exit statement, tagged with the comment exit 1, transfers control to the statement tagged target B if its condition is true. The second exit statement, tagged exit 2, transfers control to target A. Since it does not refer to a label, it only exits the immediately enclosing loop statement, namely, loop inner. Finally, the exit statement tagged exit 3 transfers control to target B.

VHDL-87

Exit statements may not be labeled in VHDL-87.

Next Statements

Another kind of statement that we can use to control the execution of loops is the *next statement*. When this statement is executed, the current iteration of the loop is completed without executing any further statements, and the next iteration is begun. The syntax rule is

next_statement ⇐
     〚 label : 〛 **next** 〚 *loop*_label 〛 〚 **when** *boolean*_expression 〛 ;

The optional label at the start of the next statement serves to identify the statement. We discuss labeled statements in Chapter 20. A next statement is very similar in form to an exit statement, the difference being the keyword **next** instead of **exit**. The simplest form of next statement is

next;

which starts the next iteration of the immediately enclosing loop. We can also include a condition to test before completing the iteration:

next when *condition*;

and we can include a loop label to indicate for which loop to complete the iteration:

next *loop-label*;

or:

next *loop-label* **when** *condition*;

A next statement that exits the immediately enclosing loop can be easily rewritten as an equivalent loop with an if statement replacing the next statement. For example, the following two loops are equivalent:

loop	**loop**
statement-1;	*statement-1*;
next when *condition*;	**if not** *condition* **then**
statement-2;	*statement-2*;
end loop;	**end if**;
	end loop;

However, nested labeled loops that contain next statements referring to outer loops cannot be so easily rewritten. As a matter of style, if we find ourselves about to write such a collection of loops and next statements, it's probably time to think more carefully about what we are trying to express. If we check the logic of the model, we may be able to find a simpler formulation of loop statements. Complicated loop/next structures can be confusing, making the model hard to read and understand.

VHDL-87

Next statements may not be labeled in VHDL-87.

While Loops

We can augment the basic loop statement introduced previously to form a *while loop*, which tests a condition before each iteration. If the condition is true, iteration proceeds. If it is false, the loop is terminated. The syntax rule for a while loop is

```
loop_statement ⇐
    ⟦ loop_label : ⟧
    while condition loop
        { sequential_statement }
    end loop ⟦ loop_label ⟧ ;
```

The only difference between this form and the basic loop statement is that we have added the keyword **while** and the condition before the **loop** keyword. All of the things we said about the basic loop statement also apply to a while loop. We can write any sequential statements in the body of the loop, including exit and next statements, and we can label the loop by writing the label before the **while** keyword.

There are three important points to note about while loops. The first point is that the condition is tested before each iteration of the loop, including the first iteration. This means that if the condition is false before we start the loop, it is terminated immediately, with no iterations being executed. For example, given the while loop

```
while index > 0 loop
    . . .        -- statement A: do something with index
end loop;
    . . .        -- statement B
```

if we can demonstrate that index is not greater than zero before the loop is started, then we know that the statements inside the loop will not be executed, and control will be transferred straight to statement B.

The second point is that in the absence of exit statements within a while loop, the loop terminates only when the condition becomes false. Thus, we know that the negation of the condition must hold when control reaches the statement after the loop. Similarly, in the absence of next statements within a while loop, the loop performs an iteration only when the condition is true. Thus, we know that the condition holds when we start the statements in the loop body. In the above example, we know that index must be greater then zero when we execute the statement tagged statement A, and also that index must be less than or equal to zero when we reach statement B. This knowledge can help us reason about the correctness of the model we are writing.

The third point is that when we write the statements inside the body of a while loop, we must make sure that the condition will eventually become false, or that an exit statement will eventually exit the loop. Otherwise the while loop will never terminate. Presumably, if we had intended to write an infinite loop, we would have used a simple loop statement.

EXAMPLE

We can develop a model for an entity cos that might be used as part of a specialized signal processing system. The entity has one input, theta, which is a real number representing an angle in radians, and one output, result, representing the cosine function of the value of theta. We can use the relation

$$\cos \theta = 1 - \frac{\theta^2}{2!} + \frac{\theta^4}{4!} - \frac{\theta^6}{6!} + \cdots$$

by adding successive terms of the series until the terms become smaller than one millionth of the result. The entity and architecture body declarations are shown in Figure 3-5.

FIGURE 3-5

```
entity cos is
    port ( theta : in real;  result : out real );
end entity cos;

_____

architecture series of cos is
begin
    summation : process (theta) is
        variable sum, term : real;
        variable n : natural;
    begin
        sum := 1.0;
        term := 1.0;
        n := 0;
        while abs term > abs (sum / 1.0E6) loop
            n := n + 2;
            term := (–term) * theta**2 / real(((n–1) * n));
            sum := sum + term;
        end loop;
        result <= sum;
    end process summation;
end architecture series;
```

An entity and architecture body for a cosine module.

The architecture body consists of a process that is sensitive to changes in the input signal **theta**. Initially, the variables **sum** and **term** are set to 1.0, representing the first term in the series. The variable **n** starts at 0 for the first term. The cosine function is computed using a while loop that increments **n** by two and uses it to calculate the next term based on the previous term. Iteration proceeds as long as the last term computed is larger in magnitude than one millionth of the sum. When the last term falls below this threshold, the while loop is terminated. We can determine that the loop will terminate, since the values of successive terms in the series get progressively smaller. This is because the factorial function grows at a greater rate than the exponential function.

For Loops

Another way we can augment the basic loop statement is the *for loop*. A for loop includes a specification of how many times the body of the loop is to be executed. The syntax rule for a for loop is

loop_statement ⇐
    ⟦ *loop*_label : ⟧
    for identifier **in** discrete_range **loop**
        { sequential_statement }
    end loop ⟦ *loop*_label ⟧ ;

We saw on page 59 that a discrete range can be of the form

simple_expression (**to** ∥ **downto**) simple_expression

representing all the values between the left and right bounds, inclusive. The identifier is called the *loop parameter*, and for each iteration of the loop, it takes on successive values of the discrete range, starting from the left element. For example, in this for loop:

    for count_value **in** 0 **to** 127 **loop**
        count_out <= count_value;
        wait for 5 ns;
    end loop;

the identifier count_value takes on the values 0, 1, 2 and so on, and for each value, the assignment and wait statements are executed. Thus the signal count_out will be assigned values 0, 1, 2 and so on, up to 127, at 5 ns intervals.

We also saw that a discrete range can be specified using a discrete type or subtype name, possibly further constrained to a subset of values by a range constraint. For example, if we have the enumeration type

    type controller_state **is** (initial, idle, active, error);

we can write a for loop that iterates over each of the values in the type

    for state **in** controller_state **loop**

       . . .

    end loop;

Within the sequence of statements in the for loop body, the loop parameter is a constant whose type is the base type of the discrete range. This means we can use its value by including it in an expression, but we cannot make assignments to it. Unlike other constants, we do not need to declare it. Instead, the loop parameter is implicitly declared over the for loop. It only exists when the loop is executing, and not before or after it. For example, the following process statement shows how not to use the loop parameter:

    erroneous : **process is**
        variable i, j : integer;
    begin
        i := loop_param;   *-- error!*
        for loop_param **in** 1 **to** 10 **loop**
            loop_param := 5;   *-- error!*
        end loop;
        j := loop_param;   *-- error!*
    end process erroneous;

The assignments to i and j are illegal since the loop parameter is defined neither before nor after the loop. The assignment within the loop body is illegal because loop_param is a constant and thus may not be modified.

A consequence of the way the loop parameter is defined is that it *hides* any object of the same name defined outside the loop. For example, in this process:

```
hiding_example : process is
    variable a, b : integer;
begin
    a := 10;
    for a in 0 to 7 loop
        b := a;
    end loop;
    -- a = 10, and b = 7
    . . .
end process hiding_example;
```

the variable a is initially assigned the value 10, and then the for loop is executed, creating a loop parameter also called a. Within the loop, the assignment to b uses the loop parameter, so the final value of b after the last iteration is 7. After the loop, the loop parameter no longer exists, so if we use the name a, we are referring to the variable object, whose value is still 10.

As we mentioned above, the for loop iterates with the loop parameter assuming successive values from the discrete range starting from the leftmost value. An important point to note is that if we specify a null range, the for loop body does not execute at all. A null range can arise if we specify an ascending range with the left bound greater than the right bound, or a descending range with the left bound less than the right bound. For example, the for loop

```
for i in 10 to 1 loop
    . . .
end loop;
```

completes immediately, without executing the enclosed statements. If we really want the loop to iterate with i taking values 10, 9, 8 and so on, we should write

```
for i in 10 downto 1 loop
    . . .
end loop;
```

One final thing to note about for loops is that, like basic loop statements, they can enclose arbitrary sequential statements, including next and exit statements, and we can label a for loop by writing the label before the **for** keyword.

EXAMPLE

We now rewrite the cosine model in Figure 3-5 to calculate the result by summing the first 10 terms of the series. The entity declaration is unchanged. The revised architecture body, shown in Figure 3-6, consists of a process that uses a for loop instead of a while loop. As before, the variables sum and term are set to 1.0, representing the first term in the series. The variable n is replaced by the for

FIGURE 3-6

```
architecture fixed_length_series of cos is
begin
    summation : process (theta) is
        variable sum, term : real;
    begin
        sum := 1.0;
        term := 1.0;
        for n in 1 to 9 loop
            term := (–term) * theta**2 / real(((2*n–1) * 2*n));
            sum := sum + term;
        end loop;
        result <= sum;
    end process summation;
end architecture fixed_length_series;
```

The revised architecture body for the cosine module.

loop parameter. The loop iterates nine times, calculating the remaining nine terms of the series.

Summary of Loop Statements

The preceding sections describe the various forms of loop statements in detail. It is worth summarizing this information in one place, to show the few basic points to remember. First, the syntax rule for all loop statements is

loop_statement ⟸
    ⟦ *loop*_label : ⟧
    ⟦ **while** condition ∥ **for** identifier **in** discrete_range ⟧ **loop**
        { sequential_statement }
    end loop ⟦ *loop*_label ⟧ ;

Second, in the absence of exit and next statements, the while loop iterates as long as the condition is true, and the for loop iterates with the loop parameter assuming successive values from the discrete range. If the condition in a while loop is initially false, or if the discrete range in a for loop is a null range, then no iterations occur.

Third, the loop parameter in a for loop cannot be explicitly declared, and it is a constant within the loop body. It also shadows any other object of the same name declared outside the loop.

Finally, an exit statement can be used to terminate any loop, and a next statement can be used to complete the current iteration and commence the next iteration. These statements can refer to loop labels to terminate or complete iteration for an outer level of a nested set of loops.

3.5   Assertion and Report Statements

One of the reasons for writing models of computer systems is to verify that a design functions correctly. We can partially test a model by applying sample inputs and checking that the outputs meet our expectations. If they do not, we are then faced with the task of determining what went wrong inside the design. This task can be made easier using *assertion statements* that check that expected conditions are met within the model. An assertion statement is a sequential statement, so it can be included anywhere in a process body. The full syntax rule for an assertion statement is

assertion_statement ⇐
    〚 label : 〛 **assert** *boolean*_expression
        〚 **report** expression 〛 〚 **severity** expression 〛 ;

The optional label allows us to identify the assertion statement. We will discuss labeled statements in Chapter 20. The simplest form of assertion statement just includes the keyword **assert** followed by a condition expression that we expect to be true when the assertion statement is executed. If the condition is not met, we say that an *assertion violation* has occurred. If an assertion violation arises during simulation of a model, the simulator reports the fact. During synthesis, the condition in an assertion statement may be interpreted as a condition that the synthesizer may assume to be true. During formal verification, the condition may be interpreted as a condition to be proven by the verifier. For example, if we write

    assert initial_value <= max_value;

and initial_value is larger than max_value when the statement is executed during simulation, the simulator will let us know. During synthesis, the synthesizer may assume that initial_value <= max_value and optimize the circuit based on that information. During formal verification, the verifier may attempt to prove that initial_value <= max_value for all possible input stimuli and execution paths leading to the assertion statement.

If we have a number of assertion statements throughout a model, it is useful to know which assertion is violated. We can get the simulator to provide extra information by including a **report** clause in an assertion statement, for example:

    assert initial_value <= max_value
      report "initial value too large";

The string that we provide is used to form part of the assertion violation message. We can write any expression in the report clause provided it yields a string value, for example:

    assert current_character >= '0' **and** current_character <= '9'
      report "Input number " & input_string & " contains a non–digit";

Here the message is derived by concatenating three string values together.

In Section 2.2 on page 38, we mentioned a predefined enumeration type **severity_level**, defined as

    type severity_level **is** (note, warning, error, failure);

We can include a value of this type in a **severity** clause of an assertion statement. This value indicates the degree to which the violation of the assertion affects operation of the model. The value note can be used to pass informative messages out from a simulation, for example:

```
assert free_memory >= low_water_limit
    report "low on memory, about to start garbage collect"
    severity note;
```

The severity level warning can be used if an unusual situation arises in which the model can continue to execute, but may produce unusual results, for example:

```
assert packet_length /= 0
    report "empty network packet received"
    severity warning;
```

We can use the severity level error to indicate that something has definitely gone wrong and that corrective action should be taken, for example:

```
assert clock_pulse_width >= min_clock_width
    severity error;
```

Finally, the value failure can be used if we detect an inconsistency that should never arise, for example:

```
assert (last_position – first_position + 1) = number_of_entries
    report "inconsistency in buffer model"
    severity failure;
```

We have seen that we can write an assertion statement with either or both of a **report** clause and a **severity** clause. If both are present, the syntax rule shows us that the report clause must come first. If we omit the **report** clause, the default string in the error message is "Assertion violation." If we omit the **severity** clause, the default value is error. The severity value is usually used by a simulator to determine whether or not to continue execution after an assertion violation. Most simulators allow the user to specify a severity threshold, beyond which execution is stopped.

Usually, failure of an assertion means either that the entity is being used incorrectly as part of a larger design or that the model for the entity has been incorrectly written. We illustrate both cases.

EXAMPLE

A set/reset (SR) flipflop has two inputs, S and R, and an output Q. When S is '1', the output is set to '1', and when R is '1', the output is reset to '0'. However, S and R may not both be '1' at the same time. If they are, the output value is not specified. Figure 3-7 is a behavioral model for an SR flipflop that includes a check for this illegal condition.

The architecture body contains a process sensitive to the S and R inputs. Within the process body we write an assertion statement that requires that S and R not both be '1'. If both are '1', the assertion is violated, so the simulator writes an "Assertion violation" message with severity error. If execution continues after the violated assertion, the value '1' will first be assigned to Q, followed by the value

FIGURE 3-7

```
entity SR_flipflop is
    port ( S, R : in bit;  Q : out bit );
end entity SR_flipflop;

------------------------------------------------

architecture checking of SR_flipflop is
begin
    set_reset : process (S, R) is
    begin
        assert S = '1' nand R = '1';
        if S = '1' then
            Q <= '1';
        end if;
        if R = '1' then
            Q <= '0';
        end if;
    end process set_reset;
end architecture checking;
```

An entity and architecture body for a set/reset flipflop, including a check for correct usage.

'0'. The resulting value is '0'. This is allowed, since the state of **Q** was not specified for this illegal condition, so we are at liberty to choose any value. If the assertion is not violated, then at most one of the following if statements is executed, correctly modeling the behavior of the SR flipflop.

EXAMPLE

To illustrate the use of an assertion statement as a "sanity check," let us look at a model, shown in Figure 3-8, for an entity that has three integer inputs, **a**, **b** and **c**, and produces an integer output **z** that is the largest of its inputs.

The architecture body is written using a process containing nested if statements. For this example we have introduced an "accidental" error into the model. If we simulate this model and put the values **a** = 7, **b** = 3 and **c** = 9 on the ports of this entity, we expect that the value of **result**, and hence the output port, is 9. The assertion states that the value of **result** must be greater than or equal to all of the inputs. However, our coding error causes the value 7 to be assigned to **result**, and so the assertion is violated. This violation causes us to examine our model more closely, and correct the error.

FIGURE 3-8

```
entity max3 is
    port ( a, b, c : in integer;  z : out integer );
end entity max3;
```

(continued on page 76)

(continued from page 75)

```
architecture check_error of max3 is
begin
    maximizer : process (a, b, c)
        variable result : integer;
    begin
        if a > b then
            if a > c then
                result := a;
            else
                result := a;  -- Oops!  Should be: result := c;
            end if;
        elsif  b > c then
            result := b;
        else
            result := c;
        end if;
        assert result >= a and result >= b and result >= c
            report "inconsistent result for maximum"
            severity failure;
        z <= result;
    end process maximizer;
end architecture check_error;
```

_____

An entity and architecture body for a maximum selector module, including a check for a correctly generated result.

═══

Another important use for assertion statements is in checking timing constraints that apply to a model. For example, most clocked devices require that the clock pulse be longer than some minimum duration. We can use the predefined primary "**now**" in an expression to calculate durations. We return to "**now**" in a later chapter. Suffice it to say that it yields the current simulation time when it is evaluated.

EXAMPLE
─────────

An edge-triggered register has a data input and a data output of type **real** and a clock input of type **bit**. When the clock changes from '0' to '1', the data input is sampled, stored and transmitted through to the output. Let us suppose that the clock input must remain at '1' for at least 5 ns. Figure 3-9 is a model for this register, including a check for legal clock pulse width.

The architecture body contains a process that is sensitive to changes on the clock input. When the clock changes from '0' to '1', the input is stored, and the current simulation time is recorded in the variable **pulse_start**. When the clock changes from '1' to '0', the difference between **pulse_start** and the current simulation time is checked by the assertion statement.

FIGURE 3-9

```
entity edge_triggered_register is
    port ( clock : in bit;
            d_in : in real;  d_out : out real );
end entity edge_triggered_register;

_____

architecture check_timing of edge_triggered_register is
begin
    store_and_check : process (clock) is
        variable stored_value : real;
        variable pulse_start : time;
    begin
        case clock is
            when '1' =>
                pulse_start := now;
                stored_value := d_in;
                d_out <= stored_value;
            when '0' =>
                assert now = 0 ns or (now – pulse_start) >= 5 ns
                    report "clock pulse too short";
        end case;
    end process store_and_check;
end architecture check_timing;
```

An entity and architecture body for an edge-triggered register, including a timing check for correct pulse width on the clock input.

VHDL-87

Assertion statements may not be labeled in VHDL-87.

VHDL also provides us with a *report statement*, which is similar to an assertion statement. The syntax rule for the report statement shows this similarity:

report_statement ⇐
    ⟦ label : ⟧ **report** expression ⟦ **severity** expression ⟧ ;

The differences are that there is no condition, and if the severity level is not specified, the default is **note**. Indeed, the report statement can be thought of as an assertion statement in which the condition is the value **false** and the severity is **note**, hence it always produces the message. One way in which the report statement is useful is as a means of including "trace writes" in a model as an aid to debugging.

EXAMPLE

Suppose we are writing a complex model and we are not sure that we have got the logic quite right. We can use report statements to get the processes in the model to write out messages, so that we can see when they are activated and what they are doing. An example process is

```
transmit_element : process (transmit_data) is
    . . .           -- variable declarations
begin
    report "transmit_element: data = "
                & data_type'image(transmit_data);

    . . .
end process transmit_element;
```

VHDL-87

Report statements are not provided in VHDL-87. We achieve the same effect by writing an assertion statement with the condition "**false**" and a severity level of note. For example, the VHDL-93 report statement

```
report "Initialization complete";
```

can be written in VHDL-87 as

```
assert false
    report "Initialization complete" severity note;
```

Exercises

1. [❶ 3.1] Write an if statement that sets a variable **odd** to '1' if an integer n is odd, or to '0' if it is even.

2. [❶ 3.1] Write an if statement that, given the year of today's date in the variable **year**, sets the variable **days_in_February** to the number of days in February. A year is a leap year if it is divisible by four, except for years that are divisible by 100.

3. [❶ 3.2] Write a case statement that strips the strength information from a standard-logic variable x. If x is '0' or 'L', set it to '0'. If x is '1' or 'H', set it to '1'. If x is 'X', 'W', 'Z', 'U' or '–', set it to 'X'. (This is the conversion performed by the standard-logic function to_X01.)

4. [❶ 3.2] Write a case statement that sets an integer variable **character_class** to 1 if the character variable ch contains a letter, to 2 if it contains a digit, to 3 if it contains some other printable character or to 4 if it contains a non-printable character. Note that the VHDL character set contains accented letters, as shown in Figure 2-2 on page 39.

5. [❶ 3.4] Write a loop statement that samples a bit input d when a clock input clk changes to '1'. So long as d is '0', the loop continues executing. When d is '1', the loop exits.

6. [❶ 3.4] Write a while loop that calculates the exponential function of x to an accuracy of one part in 10^4 by summing terms of the following series:

$$e^x = 1 + \frac{x}{1} + \frac{x^2}{2!} + \frac{x^3}{3!} + \frac{x^4}{4!} + \cdots$$

7. [❶ 3.4] Write a for loop that calculates the exponential function of x by summing the first eight terms of the series.

8. [❶ 3.5] Write an assertion statement that expresses the requirement that a flipflop's two outputs, q and q_n, of type **std_ulogic**, are complementary.

9. [❶ 3.5] We can use report statements in VHDL to achieve the same effect as using "trace writes" in software programming languages, to report a message when part of the model is executed. Insert a report statement in the model of Figure 3-4 to cause a trace message when the counter is reset.

10. [❷ 3.1] Develop a behavioral model for a limiter with three integer inputs, **data_in**, **lower** and **upper**; an integer output, **data_out**; and a bit output, **out_of_limits**. The **data_out** output follows **data_in** so long as it is between **lower** and **upper**. If **data_in** is less than **lower**, **data_out** is limited to **lower**. If **data_in** is greater than **upper**, **data_out** is limited to **upper**. The **out_of_limit** output indicates when **data_out** is limited.

11. [❷ 3.2] Develop a model for a floating-point arithmetic unit with data inputs x and y, data output z and function code input of an enumerated type with values **add**, **sub**, **mult**, **div** and **recip**. Function code **add** produces addition, **sub** produces subtraction of y from x, **mult** produces multiplication, **div** produces division of x by y and **recip** produces reciprocal of y.

12. [❷ 3.4] Write a model for a counter with an output port of type **natural**, initially set to 15. When the **clk** input changes to '1', the counter decrements by one. After counting down to zero, the counter wraps back to 15 on the next clock edge.

13. [❷ 3.4] Modify the counter of Exercise 12 to include an asynchronous load input and a data input. When the load input is '1', the counter is preset to the data input value. When the load input changes back to '0', the counter continues counting down from the preset value.

14. [❷ 3.4] Develop a model of an averaging module that calculates the average of batches of 16 real numbers. The module has clock and data inputs and a data output. The module accepts the next input number when the clock changes to '1'. After 16 numbers have been accepted, the module places their average on the output port, then repeats the process for the next batch.

15. [❷ 3.5] Write a model that causes assertion violations with different severity levels. Experiment with your simulator to determine its behavior when an assertion violation occurs. See if you can specify a severity threshold above which it stops execution.

Composite Data Types and Operations

Now that we have seen the basic data types and sequential operations from which the behavioral part of a VHDL model is formed, it is time to look at composite data types. We first mentioned them in the classification of data types in Chapter 2. Composite data objects consist of related collections of data elements in the form of either an *array* or a *record*. We can treat an object of a composite type as a single object or manipulate its constituent elements individually. In this chapter, we see how to define composite types and how to manipulate them using operators and sequential statements.

4.1 Arrays

An *array* consists of a collection of values, all of which are of the same type as each other. The position of each element in an array is given by a scalar value called its *index*. To create an array object in a model, we first define an array type in a type declaration. The syntax rule for an array type definition is

array_type_definition ⇐
    array (discrete_range { , ... }) **of** *element*_subtype_indication

This defines an array type by specifying one or more index ranges (the list of discrete ranges) and the element type or subtype. Recall from previous chapters that a discrete range is a subset of values from a discrete type (an integer or enumeration type), and that it can be specified as shown by the simplified syntax rule

discrete_range ⇐
    *discrete*_subtype_indication
    ⏐ simple_expression (**to** ⏐ **downto**) simple_expression

Recall also that a subtype indication can be just the name of a previously declared type (a type mark), and can include a range constraint to limit the set of values from that type, as shown by the simplified rule

subtype_indication ⇐
    type_mark ⟦ **range** simple_expression (**to** ⏐ **downto**) simple_expression ⟧

We illustrate these rules for defining arrays with a series of examples. We start with single-dimensional arrays, in which there is just one index range. Here is a simple example to start off with, showing the declaration of an array type to represent words of data:

type word **is array** (0 **to** 31) **of** bit;

Each element is a bit, and the elements are indexed from 0 up to 31. An alternative declaration of a word type, more appropriate for "little-endian" systems, is

type word **is array** (31 **downto** 0) **of** bit;

The difference here is that index values start at 31 for the leftmost element in values of this type and continue down to 0 for the rightmost. The index values of an array do not have to be numeric. For example, given this declaration of an enumeration type:

type controller_state **is** (initial, idle, active, error);

we could then declare an array as follows:

type state_counts **is array** (idle **to** error) **of** natural;

This kind of array type declaration relies on the type of the index range being clear from the context. If there were more than one enumeration type with values **idle** and **error**, it would not be clear which one to use for the index type. To make it clear, we can use the alternative form for specifying the index range, in which we name the index type and include a range constraint. The previous example could be rewritten as

type state_counts **is**
    array (controller_state **range** idle **to** error) **of** natural;

If we need an array element for every value in an index type, we need only name the index type in the array declaration without specifying the range. For example:

subtype coeff_ram_address **is** integer **range** 0 **to** 63;
type coeff_array **is array** (coeff_ram_address) **of** real;

Once we have declared an array type, we can define objects of that type, including constants, variables and signals. For example, using the types declared above, we can declare variables as follows:

variable buffer_register, data_register : word;
variable counters : state_counts;
variable coeff : coeff_array;

Each of these objects consists of the collection of elements described by the corresponding type declaration. An individual element can be used in an expression or as the target of an assignment by referring to the array object and supplying an index value, for example:

coeff(0) := 0.0;

If active is a variable of type controller_state, we can write

counters(active) := counters(active) + 1;

An array object can also be used as a single composite object. For example, the assignment

data_register := buffer_register;

copies all of the elements of the array buffer_register into the corresponding elements of the array data_register.

EXAMPLE

Figure 4-1 is a model for a memory that stores 64 real-number coefficients, initialized to 0.0. We assume the type coeff_ram_address is previously declared as above. The architecture body contains a process with an array variable representing the coefficient storage. When the process starts, it initializes the array using a for loop. It then repetitively waits for any of the input ports to change. When rd is '1', the array is indexed using the address value to read a coefficient. When wr is '1', the address value is used to select which coefficient to change.

FIGURE 4-1

entity coeff_ram **is**
    port (rd, wr : **in** bit; addr : **in** coeff_ram_address;
            d_in : **in** real; d_out : **out** real);
end entity coeff_ram;

(continued on page 84)

(continued from page 83)

```
architecture abstract of coeff_ram is
begin
    memory : process is
        type coeff_array is array (coeff_ram_address) of real;
        variable coeff : coeff_array;
    begin
        for index in coeff_ram_address loop
            coeff(index) := 0.0;
        end loop;
        loop
            wait on rd, wr, addr, d_in;
            if rd = '1' then
                d_out <= coeff(addr);
            end if;
            if wr = '1' then
                coeff(addr) := d_in;
            end if;
        end loop;
    end process memory;
end architecture abstract;
```

An entity and architecture body for a memory module that stores real-number coefficients. The memory storage is implemented using an array.

Multidimensional Arrays

VHDL also allows us to create multidimensional arrays, for example, to represent matrices or tables indexed by more than one value. A multidimensional array type is declared by specifying a list of index ranges, as shown by the syntax rule on page 82. For example, we might include the following type declarations in a model for a finite-state machine:

```
type symbol is ('a', 't', 'd', 'h', digit, cr, error);
type state is range 0 to 6;

type transition_matrix is array (state, symbol) of state;
```

Each index range can be specified as shown above for single-dimensional arrays. The index ranges for each dimension need not all be from the same type, nor have the same direction. An object of a multidimensional array type is indexed by writing a list of index values to select an element. For example, if we have a variable declared as

```
variable transition_table : transition_matrix;
```

we can index it as follows:

```
transition_table(5, 'd');
```

EXAMPLE

In three-dimensional graphics, a point in space may be represented using a three-element vector [x, y, z] of coordinates. Transformations, such as scaling, rotation and reflection, may be done by multiplying a vector by a 3 × 3 transformation matrix to get a new vector representing the transformed point. We can write VHDL type declarations for points and transformation matrices:

```
type point is array (1 to 3) of real;
type matrix is array (1 to 3, 1 to 3) of real;
```

We can use these types to declare point variables p and q and a matrix variable transform:

```
variable p, q : point;
variable transform : matrix;
```

The transformation can be applied to the point p to produce a result in q with the following statements:

```
for i in 1 to 3 loop
    q(i) := 0.0;
    for j in 1 to 3 loop
        q(i) := q(i) + transform(i, j) * p(j);
    end loop;
end loop;
```

Array Aggregates

We have seen how we can write literal values of scalar types. Often we also need to write literal array values, for example, to initialize a variable or constant of an array type. We can do this using a VHDL construct called an array *aggregate*, according to the syntax rule

aggregate ⇐ ((⟦ choices => ⟧ expression) { , ... })

Let us look first at the form of aggregate without the choices part. It simply consists of a list of the elements enclosed in parentheses, for example:

```
type point is array (1 to 3) of real;
constant origin : point := (0.0, 0.0, 0.0);
variable view_point : point := (10.0, 20.0, 0.0);
```

This form of array aggregate uses *positional association* to determine which value in the list corresponds to which element of the array. The first value is the element with the leftmost index, the second is the next index to the right, and so on, up to the last value, which is the element with the rightmost index. There must be a one-to-one correspondence between values in the aggregate and elements in the array.

An alternative form of aggregate uses *named association*, in which the index value for each element is written explicitly using the choices part shown in the syntax rule. The choices may be specified in exactly the same way as those in alternatives of a case statement, discussed in Chapter 3. As a reminder, here is the syntax rule for choices:

choices ⇐ (simple_expression ‖ discrete_range ‖ **others**) { | ∘∘∘ }

For example, the variable declaration and initialization could be rewritten as

variable view_point : point := (1 => 10.0, 2 => 20.0, 3 => 0.0);

The main advantage of named association is that it gives us more flexibility in writing aggregates for larger arrays. To illustrate this, let us return to the coefficient memory described above. The type declaration was

type coeff_array **is array** (coeff_ram_address) **of** real;

Suppose we want to declare the coefficient variable, initialize the first few locations to some non-zero value and initialize the remainder to zero. Following are a number of ways of writing aggregates that all have the same effect:

variable coeff : coeff_array := (0 => 1.6, 1 => 2.3, 2 => 1.6, 3 **to** 63 => 0.0);

Here we are using a range specification to initialize the bulk of the array value to zero.

variable coeff : coeff_array := (0 => 1.6, 1 => 2.3, 2 => 1.6, **others** => 0.0);

The keyword **others** stands for any index value that has not been previously mentioned in the aggregate. If the keyword **others** is used, it must be the last choice in the aggregate.

variable coeff : coeff_array := (0 | 2 => 1.6, 1 => 2.3, **others** => 0.0);

The "|" symbol can be used to separate a list of index values, for which all elements have the same value.

Note that we may not mix positional and named association in an array aggregate, except for the use of an **others** choice in the final postion. Thus, the following aggregate is illegal:

variable coeff : coeff_array := (1.6, 2.3, 2 => 1.6, **others** => 0.0);   *-- illegal*

We can also use aggregates to write multidimensional array values. In this case, we treat the array as though it were an array of arrays, writing an array aggregate for each of the leftmost index values first.

EXAMPLE

We can use a two-dimensional array to represent the transition matrix of a finite-state machine (FSM) that interprets simple modem commands. A command must consist of the string "atd" followed by a string of digits and a cr character, or the string "ath" followed by cr. The state transition diagram is shown in Figure 4-2. The symbol "other" represents a character other than 'a', 't', 'd', 'h', a digit or cr. An outline of a process that implements the FSM is shown in Figure 4-3.

The type declarations for **symbol** and **state** represent the command symbols and the states for the FSM. The transition matrix, next_state, is a two-dimensional array constant indexed by the state and symbol type. An element at position (i, j) in this matrix indicates the next state the FSM should move to when it is in state i and the next input symbol is j. The matrix is initialized according to the transition diagram. The process uses the current_state variable and successive input symbols

FIGURE 4-2

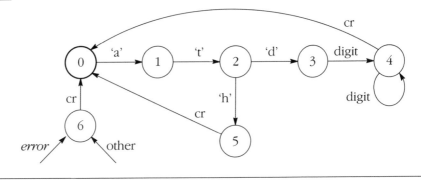

The state transition diagram for a modem command finite-state machine. State 0 is the initial state. The machine returns to this state after recognizing a correct command. State 6 is the error state, to which the machine goes if it detects an illegal or unexpected character.

FIGURE 4-3

```
modem_controller : process is
        type symbol is ('a', 't', 'd', 'h', digit, cr, other);
        type symbol_string is array (1 to 20) of symbol;
        type state is range 0 to 6;
        type transition_matrix is array (state, symbol) of state;

        constant next_state : transition_matrix :=
            ( 0 => ('a' => 1, others => 6),
              1 => ('t' => 2, others => 6),
              2 => ('d' => 3, 'h' => 5, others => 6),
              3 => (digit => 4, others => 6),
              4 => (digit => 4, cr => 0, others => 6),
              5 => (cr => 0, others => 6),
              6 => (cr => 0, others => 6) );
        variable command : symbol_string;
        variable current_state : state := 0;
begin
        . . .
        for index in 1 to 20 loop
            current_state := next_state( current_state, command(index) );
            case current_state is
                . . .
            end case;
        end loop;
        . . .
end process modem_controller;
```

An outline of a process that implements the finite-state machine to accept a modem command.

as indices into the transition matrix to determine the next state. For each transition, it performs some action based on the new state. The actions are implemented within the case statement.

Another place in which we may use an aggregate is the target of a variable assignment or a signal assignment. The full syntax rule for a variable assignment statement is

variable_assignment_statement ⇐
    ⟦ label : ⟧ (name ‖ aggregate) := expression ;

If the target is an aggregate, it must contain a variable name at each element position. Furthermore, expression on the right-hand side of the assignment must produce a composite value of the same type as the target aggregate. Each element of the right-hand side is assigned to the corresponding variable in the target aggregate. The full syntax rule for a signal assignment also allows the target to be in the form of an aggregate, with each element being a signal name. We can use assignments of this form to split a composite value among a number of scalar signals. For example, if we have a variable flag_reg, which is a four-element bit vector, we can perform the following signal assignment to four signals of type bit:

    (z_flag, n_flag, v_flag, c_flag) <= flag_reg;

Since the right-hand side is a bit vector, the target is taken as a bit-vector aggregate. The leftmost element of flag_reg is assigned to z_flag, the second element of flag_reg is assigned to n_flag, and so on. This form of multiple assignment is much more compact to write than four separate assignment statements.

Array Attributes

In Chapter 2 we saw that attributes could be used to refer to information about scalar types. There are also attributes applicable to array types; they refer to information about the index ranges. Array attributes can also be applied to array objects, such as constants, variables and signals, to refer to information about the types of the objects. Given some array type or object A, and an integer N between 1 and the number of dimensions of A, VHDL defines the following attributes:

A'left(N)	Left bound of index range of dimension N of A
A'right(N)	Right bound of index range of dimension N of A
A'low(N)	Lower bound of index range of dimension N of A
A'high(N)	Upper bound of index range of dimension N of A
A'range(N)	Index range of dimension N of A
A'reverse_range(N)	Reverse of index range of dimension N of A
A'length(N)	Length of index range of dimension N of A
A'ascending(N)	true if index range of dimension N of A is an ascending range, false otherwise

For example, given the array declaration

type A **is array** (1 **to** 4, 31 **downto** 0) **of** boolean;

some attribute values are

A'left(1) = 1   A'low(1) = 1
A'right(2) = 0   A'high(2) = 31
A'range(1) is 1 **to** 4   A'reverse_range(2) is 0 **to** 31
A'length(1) = 4   A'length(2) = 32
A'ascending(1) = true   A'ascending(2) = false

For all of these attributes, to refer to the first dimension (or if there is only one dimension), we can omit the dimension number in parentheses, for example:

A'low = 1   A'length = 4

In the next section, we see how these array attributes may be used to deal with array ports. We will also see, in Chapter 7, how they may be used with subprogram parameters that are arrays. Another major use is in writing for loops to iterate over elements of an array. For example, given an array variable **free_map** that is an array of bits, we can write a for loop to count the number of '1' bits without knowing the actual size of the array:

```
count := 0;
for index in free_map'range loop
    if free_map(index) = '1' then
        count := count + 1;
    end if;
end loop;
```

The 'range and 'reverse_range attributes can be used in any place in a VHDL model where a range specification is required, as an alternative to specifying the left and right bounds and the range direction. Thus, we may use the attributes in type and subtype definitions, in subtype constraints, in for loop parameter specifications, in case statement choices and so on. The advantage of taking this approach is that we can specify the size of the array in one place in the model and in all other places use array attributes. If we need to change the array size later for some reason, we need only change the model in one place.

VHDL-87

The array attribute 'ascending is not provided in VHDL-87.

4.2 Unconstrained Array Types

The array types we have seen so far in this section are called *constrained* arrays, since the type definition constrains index values to be within a specific range. VHDL also allows us to define *unconstrained* array types, in which we just indicate the type of the index values, without specifying bounds. An unconstrained array type definition is described by the alternate syntax rule

array_type_definition ⇐
    array ((type_mark **range** <>) { , ... })
        of *element*_subtype_indication

The symbol "<>", often called "box," can be thought of as a placeholder for the index range, to be filled in later when the type is used. An example of an unconstrained array type declaration is

    type sample **is array** (natural **range** <>) **of** integer;

An important point to understand about unconstrained array types is that when we declare an object of such a type, we need to provide a constraint that specifies the index bounds. We can do this in several ways. One way is to provide the constraint when an object is created, for example:

    variable short_sample_buf : sample(0 **to** 63);

This indicates that index values for the variable short_sample are natural numbers in the ascending range 0 to 63. Another way to specify the constraint is to declare a subtype of the unconstrained array type. Objects can then be created using this subtype, for example:

    subtype long_sample **is** sample(0 **to** 255);
    variable new_sample_buf, old_sample_buf : long_sample;

These are both examples of a new form of subtype indication that we have not yet seen. The syntax rule is

    subtype_indication ⇐ type_mark ⟦ (discrete_range { , ... }) ⟧

The type mark is the name of the unconstrained array type, and the discrete range specifications constrain the index type to a subset of values used to index array elements. Each discrete range must be of the same type as the corresponding index type.

When we declare a constant of an unconstrained array type, there is a third way in which we can provide a constraint. We can infer it from the expression used to initialize the constant. If the initialization expression is an array aggregate written using named association, the index values in the aggregate imply the index range of the constant. For example, in the constant declaration

    constant lookup_table : sample := (1 => 23, 3 => –16, 2 => 100, 4 => 11);

the index range is 1 to 4.

If the expression is an aggregate using positional association, the index value of the first element is assumed to be the leftmost value in the array subtype. For example, in the constant declaration

    constant beep_sample : sample := (127, 63, 0, –63, –127, –63, 0, 63);

the index range is 0 to 7, since the index subtype is **natural**. The index direction is ascending, since **natural** is defined to be an ascending range.

Strings

VHDL provides a predefined unconstrained array type called **string**, declared as

    type string **is array** (positive **range** <>) **of** character;

In principle the index range for a constrained string may be either an ascending or descending range, with any positive integers for the index bounds. However, most applications simply use an ascending range starting from 1. For example:

    constant LCD_display_len : positive := 20;
    subtype LCD_display_string **is** string(1 **to** LCD_display_len);
    variable LCD_display : LCD_display_string := (**others** => ' ');

Bit Vectors

VHDL also provides a predefined unconstrained array type called **bit_vector**, declared as

    type bit_vector **is array** (natural **range** <>) **of** bit;

This type can be used to represent words of data at the architectural level of modeling. For example, subtypes for representing bytes of data in a little-endian processor might be declared as

    subtype byte **is** bit_vector(7 **downto** 0);

Alternatively, we can supply the constraint when an object is declared, as in the following:

    variable channel_busy_register : bit_vector(1 **to** 4);

Standard-Logic Arrays

The standard-logic package std_logic_1164 provides an unconstrained array type for vectors of standard-logic values. It is declared as

    type std_ulogic_vector **is array** (natural **range** <>) **of** std_ulogic;

This type can be used in a way similar to bit vectors, but provides more detail in representing the electrical levels used in a design. We can define subtypes of the standard-logic vector type, for example:

    subtype std_ulogic_word **is** std_ulogic_vector(0 **to** 31);

Or we can directly create an object of the standard-logic vector type:

    signal csr_offset : std_ulogic_vector(2 **downto** 1);

String and Bit-String Literals

In Chapter 1, we saw that a string literal may be used to write a value representing a sequence of characters. We can use a string literal in place of an array aggregate for a value of type **string**. For example, we can initialize a string constant as follows:

    constant ready_message : string := "Ready   ";

We can also use string literals for any other one-dimensional array type whose elements are of an enumeration type that includes characters. The IEEE standard-logic array type std_ulogic_vector is an example. Thus we could declare and initialize a variable as follows:

    variable current_test : std_ulogic_vector(0 **to** 13) := "ZZZZZZZZZZ----";

In Chapter 1 we also saw bit-string literals as a way of writing a sequence of bit values. Bit strings can be used in place of array aggregates to write values of bit-vector types. For example, the variable channel_busy_register defined above may be initialized with an assignment:

    channel_busy_register := b"0000";

We can also use bit-string literals for other one-dimensional array types whose elements are of an enumeration type that includes the characters '0' and '1'. Each character in the bit-string literal represents one, three or four successive elements of the array value, depending on whether the base specified in the literal is binary, octal or hexadecimal. Again, using std_ulogic_vector as an example type, we can write a constant declaration using a bit-string literal:

    constant all_ones : std_ulogic_vector(15 **downto** 0) := X"FFFF";

VHDL-87

Bit-string literals may only be used as literals for array types in which the elements are of type **bit**. The predefined type bit_vector is such a type. However, the standard-logic type std_ulogic_vector is not. We may use string literals for array types such as std_ulogic_vector.

Unconstrained Array Ports

An important use of an unconstrained array type is to specify the type of an array port. This use allows us to write an entity interface in a general way, so that it can connect to array signals of any size or with any range of index values. When we instantiate the entity, the index bounds of the array signal connected to the port are used as the bounds of the port.

EXAMPLE

Suppose we wish to model a family of and gates, each with a different number of inputs. We declare the entity interface as shown in Figure 4-4. The input port is of the unconstrained type bit_vector. The architecture body includes a process that is sensitive to changes on the input port. When any element changes, the process performs a logical and operation across the input array. It uses the 'range attribute to determine the index range of the array, since the index range is not known until the entity is instantiated.

FIGURE 4-4

```
entity and_multiple is
    port ( i : in bit_vector;  y : out bit );
end entity and_multiple;

_____

architecture behavioral of and_multiple is
begin
    and_reducer : process ( i ) is
        variable result : bit;
    begin
        result := '1';
        for index in i'range loop
            result := result and i(index);
        end loop;
        y <= result;
    end process and_reducer;
end architecture behavioral;
```

An entity and architecture body for an and gate with an unconstrained array input port.

To illustrate the use of the multiple-input gate entity, suppose we have the following signals:

```
signal count_value : bit_vector(7 downto 0);
signal terminal_count : bit;
```

We instantiate the entity, connecting its input port to the bit-vector signal:

```
tc_gate : entity work.and_multiple(behavioral)
    port map ( i => count_value, y => terminal_count);
```

For this instance, the input port is constrained by the index range of the signal. The instance acts as an eight-input and gate.

4.3 Array Operations and Referencing

Although an array is a collection of values, much of the time we operate on arrays one element at a time, using the operators described in Chapter 2. However, if we are working with one-dimensional arrays of scalar values, we can use some of the operators to operate on whole arrays, combining elements in a pairwise fashion.

First, the logical operators (**and**, **or**, **nand**, **nor**, **xor** and **xnor**) can be applied to two one-dimensional arrays of bit or Boolean elements. The operands must be of the same length and type, and the result is computed by applying the operator to matching elements from each array to produce an array of the same length. Elements are matched starting from the leftmost position in each array. An element at a given position from the left in one array is matched with the element at the same position from the left in the other array. The operator **not** can also be applied to a single array of bit or Boolean elements, with the result being an array of the same length and type as the operand. The following declarations and statements illustrate this use of logical operators when applied to bit vectors:

```
subtype pixel_row is bit_vector (0 to 15);
variable current_row, mask : pixel_row;

current_row := current_row and not mask;
current_row := current_row xor X"FFFF";
```

Second, the shift operators introduced in Chapter 2 (**sll**, **srl**, **sla**, **sra**, **rol** and **ror**) can be used with a one-dimensional array of bit or Boolean values as the left operand and an integer value as the right operand. A shift-left logical operation shifts the elements in the array n places to the left (n being the right operand), filling in the vacated positions with '0' or **false** and discarding the leftmost n elements. If n is negative, the elements are instead shifted to the right. Some examples are

```
B"10001010" sll 3  =  B"01010000"      B"10001010" sll −2  =  B"00100010"
```

The shift-right logical operation similarly shifts elements n positions to the right for positive n, or to the left for negative n, for example:

```
B"10010111" srl 2  =  B"00100101"      B"10010111" srl −6  =  B"11000000"
```

The next two shift operations, shift-left arithmetic and shift-right arithmetic, operate similarly, but instead of filling vacated positions with '0' or **false**, they fill them with a copy of the element at the end being vacated, for example:

```
B"01001011" sra 3  =  B"00001001"      B"10010111" sra 3  =  B"11110010"
B"00001100" sla 2  =  B"00110000"      B"00010001" sla 2  =  B"01000111"
```

As with the logical shifts, if n is negative, the shifts work in the opposite direction, for example:

```
B"00010001" sra −2  =  B"01000111"
B"00110000" sla −2  =  B"00001100"
```

A rotate-left operation moves the elements of the array n places to the left, transferring the n elements from the left end of the array around to the vacated positions at the right end. A rotate-right operation does the same, but in the opposite direction.

As with the shift operations, a negative right argument reverses the direction of rotation. Some examples are

B"10010011" **rol** 1 = B"00100111"   B"10010011" **ror** 1 = B"11001001"

Relational operators form the third group of operations that can be applied to one-dimensional arrays. The array elements can be of any discrete type. The two operands need not be of the same length, so long as they have the same element type. The way these operators work can be most easily seen when they are applied to strings of characters, in which case they are compared according to case-sensitive dictionary ordering.

To see how dictionary comparison can be generalized to one-dimensional arrays of other element types, let us consider the "<" operator applied to two arrays a and b. If both a and b have length 0, a < b is false. If a has length 0, and b has non-zero length, then a < b. Alternatively, if both a and b have non-zero length, then a < b if a(1) < b(1), or if a(1) = b(1) and the rest of a < the rest of b. In the remaining case, where a has non-zero length and b has length 0, a < b is false. Comparison using the other relational operators is performed analogously.

The one remaining operator that can be applied to one-dimensional arrays is the concatenation operator (&), which joins two array values end to end. For example, when applied to bit vectors, it produces a new bit vector with length equal to the sum of the lengths of the two operands. Thus, b"0000" & b"1111" produces b"0000_1111".

The concatenation operator can be applied to two operands, one of which is an array and the other of which is a single scalar element. It can also be applied to two scalar values to produce an array of length 2. Some examples are

"abc" & 'd' = "abcd"
'w' & "xyz" = "wxyz"
'a' & 'b' = "ab"

VHDL-87

The logical operator **xnor** and the shift operators **sll**, **srl**, **sla**, **sra**, **rol** and **ror** are not provided in VHDL-87.

Array Slices

Often we want to refer to a contiguous subset of elements of an array, but not the whole array. We can do this using *slice* notation, in which we specify the left and right index values of part of an array object. For example, given arrays a1 and a2 declared as follows:

type array1 **is array** (1 **to** 100) **of** integer;
type array2 **is array** (100 **downto** 1) **of** integer;

variable a1 : array1;
variable a2 : array2;

we can refer to the array slice a1 (11 **to** 20), which is an array of 10 elements having the indices 11 to 20. Similarly, the slice a2(50 **downto** 41) is an array of 10 elements but with a descending index range. Note that the slices a1(10 **to** 1) and a2(1 **downto** 10) are *null* slices, since the index ranges specified are null. Furthermore, the ranges specified in the slice must have the same direction as the original array. Thus we may not legally write a1(10 **downto** 1) or a2(1 **to** 10).

EXAMPLE

Figure 4-5 is a behavioral model for a byte-swapper that has one input port and one output port, each of which is a bit vector of subtype **halfword**, declared as follows:

    subtype halfword **is** bit_vector(0 **to** 15);

The process in the architecture body swaps the two bytes of input with each other. It shows how the slice notation can be used for signal array objects in signal assignment statements.

FIGURE 4-5

```
entity byte_swap is
    port ( input : in halfword;  output : out halfword );
end entity byte_swap;

----------------------------------------------------

architecture behavior of byte_swap is
begin
    swap : process (input)
    begin
        output(8 to 15) <= input(0 to 7);
        output(0 to 7) <= input(8 to 15);
    end process swap;
end architecture behavior;
```

An entity and architecture body for a byte-swapper module.

VHDL-87

In VHDL-87, the range specified in a slice may have the opposite direction to that of the index range of the array. In this case, the slice is a null slice.

Array Type Conversions

In Chapter 2 we introduced the idea of type conversion of a numeric value to another value of a closely related type. A value of an array type can also be converted to a value of another array type, provided both array types have the same element type, the same number of dimensions and index types that can be type converted. The type conversion simply produces a new array value of the specified type, with each index converted to the value in the corresponding position of the new type's index range.

To illustrate the idea of type-converting array values, suppose we have the following declarations in a model:

```
subtype name is string(1 to 20);
type display_string is array (integer range 0 to 19) of character;

variable item_name : name;
variable display : display_string;
```

We cannot directly assign the value of **item_name** to **display**, since the types are different. However, we can using a type conversion:

```
display := display_string(item_name);
```

This produces a new array, with the left element having index 0 and the right element having index 19, which is compatible with the assignment target.

A common case in which we do not need a type conversion is the assigment of an array value of one subtype to an array object of a different subtype of the same base type. This occurs where the index ranges of the target and the operand have different bounds or directions. VHDL automatically includes an implicit subtype conversion in the assignment. For example, given the subtypes and variables declared thus:

```
subtype big_endian_upper_halfword is bit_vector(0 to 15);
subtype little_endian_upper_halfword is bit_vector(31 downto 16);

variable big : big_endian_upper_halfword;
variable little : little_endian_upper_halfword;
```

we could make the following assignments without including explicit type conversions:

```
big := little;
little := big;
```

4.4   Records

In this section, we discuss the second class of composite types, *records*. A record is a composite value comprising elements that may be of different types from one another. Each element is identified by a name, which is unique within the record. This name is used to select the element from the record value. The syntax rule for a record type definition is

```
record_type_definition ⇐
    record
        ( identifier { , ... } : subtype_indication ; )
        { ... }
    end record [ identifier ]
```

Each of the names in the identifier lists declares an element of the indicated type or subtype. Recall that the curly brackets in the syntax rule indicate that the enclosed part may be repeated indefinitely. Thus, we can include several elements of different types within the record. The identifier at the end of the record type definition, if included, must repeat the name of the record type.

VHDL-87

The record type name may not be included at the end of a record type definition in VHDL-87.

The following is an example record type declaration and variable declarations using the record type:

```
type time_stamp is record
        seconds : integer range 0 to 59;
        minutes : integer range 0 to 59;
        hours : integer range 0 to 23;
    end record time_stamp;
variable sample_time, current_time : time_stamp;
```

Whole record values can be assigned using assignment statements, for example:

```
sample_time := current_time;
```

We can also refer to an individual element in a record using a *selected name*, for example:

```
sample_hour := sample_time.hours;
```

In the expression on the right of the assignment symbol, the prefix before the dot names the record value, and the suffix after the dot selects the element from the record. A selected name can also be used on the left side of an assignment to identify a record element to be modified, for example:

```
current_time.seconds := clock mod 60;
```

EXAMPLE

In the early stages of designing a new instruction set for a CPU, we don't want to commit to an encoding of opcodes and operands within an instruction word. Instead we use a record type to represent the components of an instruction. We illustrate this in Figure 4-6, an outline of a system-level behavioral model of a CPU and memory that uses record types to represent instructions and data.

FIGURE 4-6

```
architecture system_level of computer is
    type opcodes is (add, sub, addu, subu, jmp, breq, brne, ld, st, . . . );
    type reg_number is range 0 to 31;
    constant r0 : reg_number := 0;  constant r1 : reg_number := 1;  . . .

    type instruction is record
            opcode : opcodes;
            source_reg1, source_reg2, dest_reg : reg_number;
            displacement : integer;
        end record instruction;
```

```
        type word is record
                instr : instruction;
                data : bit_vector(31 downto 0);
            end record word;

    signal address : natural;
    signal read_word, write_word : word;
    signal mem_read, mem_write : bit := '0';
    signal mem_ready : bit := '0';

begin

    cpu : process is
        variable instr_reg : instruction;
        variable PC : natural;
        . . .        -- other declarations for register file, etc.
    begin
        address <= PC;
        mem_read <= '1';
        wait until mem_ready = '1';
        instr_reg := read_word.instr;
        mem_read <= '0';
        PC := PC + 4;
        case instr_reg.opcode is        -- execute the instruction
            . . .
        end case;
    end process cpu;

    memory : process is
        type memory_array is array (0 to 2**14 – 1) of word;
        variable store : memory_array :=
            ( 0  => ( ( ld, r0, r0, r2, 40 ), X"00000000" ),
              1  => ( ( breq, r2, r0, r0, 5 ), X"00000000" ),
              . . .
              40 => ( ( nop, r0, r0, r0, 0 ), X"FFFFFFFE"),
              others => ( ( nop, r0, r0, r0, 0 ), X"00000000") );
    begin
        . . .
    end process memory;
end architecture system_level;
```

An outline of a behavioral architecture body for a computer system comprising a CPU and a memory, using record values to represent instructions and data values.

The record type **instruction** represents the information to be included in each instruction of a program and includes the opcode, source and destination register numbers and a displacement. The record type **word** represents a word stored in memory. Since a word might represent an instruction or data, elements are included in the record for both possibilities. Unlike many conventional programming languages, VHDL does not provide variant parts in record values. The record type **word** illustrates how composite data values can include elements that are themselves composite values, provided the included elements are of a constrained subtype. The signals in the model are used for the address, data and control connections between the CPU and the memory.

Within the CPU process the variable **instr_reg** represents the instruction register containing the current instruction to be executed. The process fetches a word from memory and copies the instruction element from the record into the instruction register. It then uses the opcode field of the value to determine how to execute the instruction.

The memory process contains a variable that is an array of word records representing the memory storage. The array is initialized with a program and data. Words representing instructions are initialized with a record aggregate containing an instruction record aggregate and a bit vector, which is ignored. Similarly, words representing data are initialized with an aggregate containing an instruction aggregate, which is ignored, and the bit vector of data.

Record Aggregates

We can use a record aggregate to write a literal value of a record type—for example, to initialize a record variable or constant. Using a record aggregate is analogous to using an array aggregate for writing a literal value of an array type (see page 85). A record aggregate is formed by writing a list of the elements enclosed in parentheses. An aggregate using positional association lists the elements in the same order as they appear in the record type declaration. For example, given the record type **time_stamp** shown above, we can initialize a constant as follows:

constant midday : time_stamp := (0, 0, 12);

We can also use named association, in which we identify each element in the aggregate by its name. The order of elements identified using named association does not affect the aggregate value. The example above could be rewritten as

constant midday : time_stamp := (hours => 12, minutes => 0, seconds => 0);

Unlike array aggregates, we can mix positional and named association in record aggregates, provided all of the named elements follow any positional elements. We can also use the symbols "|" and **others** when writing choices. Here are some more examples, using the types **instruction** and **time_stamp** declared above:

```
constant nop_instr : instruction :=
        ( opcode => addu,
          source_reg1 | source_reg2 | dest_reg => 0,
          displacement => 0 );
```

variable latest_event : time_stamp := (**others** => 0); *-- initially midnight*

Note that unlike array aggregates, we can't use a range of values to identify elements in a record aggregate, since the elements are identified by names, not indexed by a discrete range.

Exercises

1. [❶ 4.1] Write an array type declaration for an array of 30 integers, and a variable declaration for a variable of the type. Write a for loop to calculate the average of the array elements.

2. [❶ 4.1] Write an array type declaration for an array of bit values, indexed by standard-logic values. Then write a declaration for a constant, **std_ulogic_to_bit**, of this type, that maps standard-logic values to the corresponding bit value. (Assume unknown values map to '0'.) Given a standard-logic vector **v1** and a bit-vector variable **v2**, both indexed from 0 to 15, write a for loop that uses the constant **std_ulogic_to_bit** to map the standard-logic vector to the bit vector.

3. [❶ 4.1] The data on a diskette is arranged in 18 sectors per track, 80 tracks per side and two sides per diskette. A computer system maintains a map of free sectors. Write a three-dimensional array type declaration to represent such a map, with a '1' element representing a free sector and a '0' element representing an occupied sector. Write a set of nested for loops to scan a variable of this type to find the location of the first free sector.

4. [❶ 4.2] Write a declaration for a subtype of **std_ulogic_vector**, representing a byte. Declare a constant of this subtype, with each element having the value 'Z'.

5. [❶ 4.2] Write a for loop to count the number of '1' elements in a bit-vector variable **v**.

6. [❶ 4.3] An eight-bit vector **v1** representing a two's-complement binary integer can be sign-extended into a 32-bit vector **v2** by copying it to the leftmost eight positions of **v2**, then performing an arithmetic right shift to move the eight bits to the rightmost eight positions. Write variable assignment statements that use slicing and shift operations to express this procedure.

7. [❶ 4.4] Write a record type declaration for a test stimulus record containing a stimulus bit vector of three bits, a delay value and an expected response bit vector of eight bits.

8. [❷ 4.1] Develop a model for a register file that stores 16 words of 32 bits each. The register file has data input and output ports, each of which is a 32-bit word; read-address and write-address ports, each of which is an integer in the range 0 to 15; and a write-enable port of type **bit**. The data output port reflects the content of the location whose address is given by the read-address port. When the write-enable port is '1', the input data is written to the register file at the location whose address is given by the write-address port.

9. [❷ 4.1] Develop a model for a priority encoder with a 16-element bit-vector input port, an output port of type **natural** that encodes the index of the leftmost '1' value in the input and an output of type **bit** that indicates whether any input elements are '1'.

10. [❷ 4.2] Write a package that declares an unconstrained array type whose elements are integers. Use the type in an entity declaration for a module that finds the maximum of a set of numbers. The entity has an input port of the unconstrained array type and an integer output. Develop a behavioral architecture body for the entity. How should the module behave if the actual array associated with the input port is empty (i.e., of zero length)?

11. [❷ 4.2/4.3] Develop a model for a general and-or-invert gate, with two standard-logic vector input ports a and b and a standard-logic output port y. The output of the gate is $\overline{a_0.b_0 + a_1.b_1 + \cdots + a_{n-1}.b_{n-1}}$.

12. [❷ 4.4] Develop a model of a 3-to-8 decoder and a test bench to exercise the decoder. In the test bench, declare the record type that you wrote for Exercise 7 and a constant array of test record values. Initialize the array to a set of test vectors for the decoder, and use the vectors to perform the test.

Basic Modeling Constructs

The description of a module in a digital system can be divided into two facets: the external view and the internal view. The external view describes the interface to the module, including the number and types of inputs and outputs. The internal view describes how the module implements its function. In VHDL, we can separate the description of a module into an *entity declaration*, which describes the external interface, and one or more *architecture bodies*, which describe alternative internal implementations. These were introduced in Chapter 1 and are discussed in detail in this chapter. We also look at how a design is processed in preparation for simulation or synthesis.

5.1 Entity Declarations

Let us first examine the syntax rules for an entity declaration and then show some examples. We start with a simplified description of entity declarations and move on to a full description later in this chapter. The syntax rules for this simplified form of entity declaration are

> entity_declaration ⇐
>   **entity** identifier **is**
>   [**port** (*port*_interface_list) ;]
>   { entity_declarative_item }
>   **end** [**entity**] [identifier] ;
> interface_list ⇐
>   (identifier { , ... } : [mode] subtype_indication
>   [:= expression]) { ; ... }
> mode ⇐ **in** | **out** | **inout**

The identifier in an entity declaration names the module so that it can be referred to later. If the identifier is included at the end of the declaration, it must repeat the name of the entity. The port clause names each of the *ports*, which together form the interface to the entity. We can think of ports as being analogous to the pins of a circuit; they are the means by which information is fed into and out of the circuit. In VHDL, each port of an entity has a *type*, which specifies the kind of information that can be communicated, and a *mode*, which specifies whether information flows into or out from the entity through the port. These aspects of type and direction are in keeping with the strong typing philosophy of VHDL, which helps us avoid erroneous circuit descriptions. A simple example of an entity declaration is

```
entity adder is
    port ( a : in word;
           b : in word;
           sum : out word );
end entity adder;
```

This example describes an entity named **adder**, with two input ports and one output port, all of type **word**, which we assume is defined elsewhere. We can list the ports in any order; we do not have to put inputs before outputs. Also, we can include a list of ports of the same mode and type instead of writing them out individually. Thus the above declaration could equally well be written as follows:

```
entity adder is
    port ( a, b : in word;
           sum : out word );
end entity adder;
```

In this example we have seen input and output ports. We can also have bidirectional ports, with mode **inout**. These can be used to model devices that alternately sense and drive data through a pin. Such models must deal with the possibility of more than one connected device driving a given signal at the same time. VHDL provides a mechanism for this, *signal resolution*, which we will return to in Chapter 11.

The similarity between the description of a port in an entity declaration and the declaration of a variable may be apparent. This similarity is not coincidental, and we can extend the analogy by specifying a default value on a port description, for example:

```
entity and_or_inv is
    port ( a1, a2, b1, b2 : in bit := '1';
            y : out bit );
end entity and_or_inv;
```

The default value, in this case the '1' on the input ports, indicates the value each port should assume if it is left unconnected in an enclosing model. We can think of it as describing the value that the port "floats to." On the other hand, if the port is used, the default value is ignored. We say more about use of default values when we look at the execution of a model.

Another point to note about entity declarations is that the port clause is optional. So we can write an entity declaration such as

```
entity top_level is
end entity top_level;
```

which describes a completely self-contained module. As the name in this example implies, this kind of module usually represents the top level of a design hierarchy.

Finally, if we return to the first syntax rule on page 104, we see that we can include declarations of items within an entity declaration. These include declarations of constants, types, signals and other kinds of items that we will see later in this chapter. The items can be used in all architecture bodies corresponding to the entity. Thus, it makes sense to include declarations that are relevant to the entity and all possible implementations. Anything that is part of only one particular implementation should instead be declared within the corresponding architecture body.

EXAMPLE

Suppose we are designing an embedded controller using a microprocessor with a program stored in a read-only memory (ROM). The program to be stored in the ROM is fixed, but we still need to model the ROM at different levels of detail. We can include declarations that describe the program in the entity declaration for the ROM, as shown in Figure 5-1. These declarations are not directly accessible to a user of the ROM entity, but serve to document the contents of the ROM. Each architecture body corresponding to the entity can use the constant **program** to initialize whatever structure it uses internally to implement the ROM.

FIGURE 5-1

```
entity program_ROM is
    port ( address : in std_ulogic_vector(14 downto 0);
            data : out std_ulogic_vector(7 downto 0);
            enable : in std_ulogic );
```

(continued on page 106)

(continued from page 105)

```
            subtype instruction_byte is bit_vector(7 downto 0);
            type program_array is array (0 to 2**14 – 1) of instruction_byte;
            constant program : program_array
                := ( X"32", X"3F", X"03",    -- LDA  $3F03
                     X"71", X"23",           -- BLT  $23
                     . . .
                   );
end entity program_ROM;
```

An entity declaration for a ROM, including declarations that describe the program contained in it.

VHDL-87

The keyword **entity** may not be included at the end of an entity declaration in VHDL-87.

5.2 Architecture Bodies

The internal operation of a module is described by an architecture body. An architecture body generally applies some operations to values on input ports, generating values to be assigned to output ports. The operations can be described either by processes, which contain sequential statements operating on values, or by a collection of components representing sub-circuits. Where the operation requires generation of intermediate values, these can be described using *signals*, analogous to the internal wires of a module. The syntax rule for architecture bodies shows the general outline:

```
architecture_body ⇐
    architecture identifier of entity_name is
        { block_declarative_item }
    begin
        { concurrent_statement }
    end [ architecture ] [ identifier ] ;
```

The identifier names this particular architecture body, and the entity name specifies which module has its operation described by this architecture body. If the identifier is included at the end of the architecture body, it must repeat the name of the architecture body. There may be several different architecture bodies corresponding to a single entity, each describing an alternative way of implementing the module's operation. The block declarative items in an architecture body are declarations needed to implement the operations. The items may include type and constant declarations, signal declarations and other kinds of declarations that we will look at in later chapters.

VHDL-87

The keyword **architecture** may not be included at the end of an architecture body in VHDL-87.

Concurrent Statements

The *concurrent statements* in an architecture body describe the module's operation. One form of concurrent statement, which we have already seen, is a process statement. Putting this together with the rule for writing architecture bodies, we can look at a simple example of an architecture body corresponding to the **adder** entity on page 104:

```
architecture abstract of adder is
begin
    add_a_b : process (a, b) is
    begin
        sum <= a + b;
    end process add_a_b;
end architecture abstract;
```

The architecture body is named **abstract**, and it contains a process **add_a_b**, which describes the operation of the entity. The process assumes that the operator "+" is defined for the type **word**, the type of **a** and **b**. We will see in Chapter 7 how such a definition may be written. We could also envisage additional architecture bodies describing the adder in different ways, provided they all conform to the external interface laid down by the entity declaration.

We have looked at processes first because they are the most fundamental form of concurrent statement. All other forms can ultimately be reduced to one or more processes. Concurrent statements are so called because conceptually they can be activated and perform their actions together, that is, concurrently. Contrast this with the sequential statements inside a process, which are executed one after another. Concurrency is useful for modeling the way real circuits behave. If we have two gates whose inputs change, each evaluates its new output independently of the other. There is no inherent sequencing governing the order in which they are evaluated. We look at process statements in more detail in Section 5.3. Then, in Section 5.4, we look at another form of concurrent statement, the component instantiation statement, used to describe how a module is composed of interconnected sub-modules.

Signal Declarations

When we need to provide internal signals in an architecture body, we must define them using *signal declarations*. The syntax for a signal declaration is very similar to that for a variable declaration:

```
signal_declaration ⇐
    signal identifier { , ... } : subtype_indication [ := expression ] ;
```

This declaration simply names each signal, specifies its type and optionally includes an initial value for all signals declared by the declaration.

EXAMPLE

Figure 5-2 is an example of an architecture body for the entity **and_or_inv**, defined on page 105. The architecture body includes declarations of some signals
that are internal to the architecture body. They can be used by processes within
the architecture body but are not accessible outside, since a user of the module
need not be concerned with the internal details of its implementation. Values are
assigned to signals using signal assignment statements within processes. Signals
can be sensed by processes to read their values.

FIGURE 5-2

```
architecture primitive of and_or_inv is
    signal and_a, and_b : bit;
    signal or_a_b : bit;
begin
    and_gate_a : process (a1, a2) is
    begin
        and_a <= a1 and a2;
    end process and_gate_a;
    and_gate_b : process (b1, b2) is
    begin
        and_b <= b1 and b2;
    end process and_gate_b;
    or_gate : process (and_a, and_b) is
    begin
        or_a_b <= and_a or and_b;
    end process or_gate;
    inv : process (or_a_b) is
    begin
        y <= not or_a_b;
    end process inv;
end architecture primitive;
```

*An architecture body corresponding to the **and_or_inv** entity shown on page 105.*

An important point illustrated by this example is that the ports of the entity are also
visible to processes inside the architecture body and are used in the same way as signals. This corresponds to our view of ports as external pins of a circuit: from the internal point of view, a pin is just a wire with an external connection. So it makes sense
for VHDL to treat ports like signals inside an architecture of the entity.

5.3   Behavioral Descriptions

At the most fundamental level, the behavior of a module is described by signal assignment statements within processes. We can think of a process as the basic unit of behavioral description. A process is executed in response to changes of values of signals

and uses the present values of signals it reads to determine new values for other signals. A signal assignment is a sequential statement and thus can only appear within a process. In this section, we look in detail at the interaction between signals and processes.

Signal Assignment

In all of the examples we have looked at so far, we have used a simple form of signal assignment statement. Each assignment just provides a new value for a signal. The value is determined by evaluating an expression, the result of which must match the type of the signal. What we have not yet addressed is the issue of timing: when does the signal take on the new value? This is fundamental to modeling hardware, in which events occur over time. First, let us look at the syntax for a basic signal assignment statement in a process:

> signal_assignment_statement ⇐
>   ⟦ label : ⟧ name <= ⟦ delay_mechanism ⟧ waveform ;
> waveform ⇐ (*value*_expression ⟦ **after** *time*_expression ⟧) { , ₒₒₒ }

The optional label allows us to identify the statement. We will discuss labeled statements in Chapter 20. The syntax rules tell us that we can specify a delay mechanism, which we come to soon, and one or more waveform elements, each consisting of a new value and an optional delay time. It is these delay times in a signal assignment that allow us to specify when the new value should be applied. For example, consider the following assignment:

> y <= **not** or_a_b **after** 5 ns;

This specifies that the signal **y** is to take on the new value at a time 5 ns later than that at which the statement executes. The delay can be read in one of two ways, depending on whether the model is being used purely for its descriptive value or for simulation. In the first case, the delay can be considered in an abstract sense as a specification of the module's propagation delay: whenever the input changes, the output is updated 5 ns later. In the second case, it can be considered in an operational sense, with reference to a host machine simulating operation of the module by executing the model. Thus if the above assignment is executed at time 250 ns, and or_a_b has the value '1' at that time, then the signal **y** will take on the value '0' at time 255 ns. Note that the statement itself executes in zero modeled time.

The time dimension referred to when the model is executed is *simulation time*, that is, the time in which the circuit being modeled is deemed to operate. This is distinct from real execution time on the host machine running a simulation. We measure simulation time starting from zero at the start of execution and increasing in discrete steps as events occur in the model. Not surprisingly, this technique is called *discrete event simulation*. A discrete event simulator must have a simulation time clock, and when a signal assignment statement is executed, the delay specified is added to the current simulation time to determine when the new value is to be applied to the signal. We say that the signal assignment schedules a *transaction* for the signal, where the transaction consists of the new value and the simulation time at which it is to be applied. When simulation time advances to the time at which a transaction is scheduled, the signal is updated with the new value. We say that the signal is *active* during that simulation cycle. If the new value is different from the old value it replaces on a signal, we say an *event* occurs on the signal. The importance of this distinction is that processes respond to events on signals, not to transactions.

The syntax rules for signal assignments show that we can schedule a number of transactions for a signal, to be applied after different delays. For example, a clock driver process might execute the following assignment to generate the next two edges of a clock signal (assuming T_pw is a constant that represents the clock pulse width):

    clk <= '1' **after** T_pw, '0' **after** 2*T_pw;

If this statement is executed at simulation time 50 ns and T_pw has the value 10 ns, one transaction is scheduled for time 60 ns to set clk to '1', and a second transaction is scheduled for time 70 ns to set clk to '0'. If we assume that clk has the value '0' when the assignment is executed, both transactions produce events on clk.

This signal assignment statement shows that when more than one transaction is included, the delays are all measured from the current time, not the time in the previous element. Furthermore, the transactions in the list must have strictly increasing delays, so that the list reads in the order that the values will be applied to the signal.

EXAMPLE

We can write a process declaration for a clock generator using the above signal assignment statement to generate a symmetrical clock signal with pulse width T_pw. The difficulty is to get the process to execute regularly every clock cycle. One way to do this is by making it resume whenever the clock changes and scheduling the next two transitions when it changes to '0'. This approach is shown in Figure 5-3.

FIGURE 5-3

```
clock_gen : process (clk) is
begin
    if clk = '0' then
        clk <= '1' after T_pw, '0' after 2*T_pw;
    end if;
end process clock_gen;
```

A process that generates a symmetric clock waveform.

Since a process is the basic unit of a behavioral description, it makes intuitive sense to be allowed to include more than one signal assignment statement for a given signal within a single process. We can think of this as describing the different ways in which a signal's value can be generated by the process at different times.

EXAMPLE

We can write a process that models a two-input multiplexer as shown in Figure 5-4. The value of the **sel** port is used to select which signal assignment to execute to determine the output value.

FIGURE 5-4

```
mux : process (a, b, sel) is
begin
    case sel is
        when '0' =>
            z <= a after prop_delay;
        when '1' =>
            z <= b after prop_delay;
    end case;
end process mux;
```

A process that models a two-input multiplexer.

We say that a process defines a *driver* for a signal if and only if it contains at least one signal assignment statement for the signal. So this example defines a driver for the signal **z**. If a process contains signal assignment statements for several signals, it defines drivers for each of those signals. A driver is a *source* for a signal in that it provides values to be applied to the signal. An important rule to remember is that for normal signals, there may only be one source. This means that we cannot write two different processes each containing signal assignment statements for the one signal. If we want to model such things as buses or wired-or signals, we must use a special kind of signal called a *resolved signal*, which we will discuss in Chapter 11.

VHDL-87

Signal assignment statements may not be labeled in VHDL-87.

Signal Attributes

In Chapter 2 we introduced the idea of attributes of types, which give information about allowed values for the types. Then, in Chapter 4, we saw how we could use attributes of array objects to get information about their index ranges. We can also refer to attributes of signals to find information about their history of transactions and events. Given a signal **S**, and a value **T** of type **time**, VHDL defines the following attributes:

S'delayed(T)	A signal that takes on the same values as **S** but is delayed by time **T**.
S'stable(T)	A Boolean signal that is true if there has been no event on **S** in the time interval **T** up to the current time, otherwise false.

S'quiet(T)	A Boolean signal that is true if there has been no transaction on S in the time interval T up to the current time, otherwise false.
S'transaction	A signal of type **bit** that changes value from '0' to '1' or vice versa each time there is a transaction on S.
S'event	True if there is an event on S in the current simulation cycle, false otherwise.
S'active	True if there is a transaction on S in the current simulation cycle, false otherwise.
S'last_event	The time interval since the last event on S.
S'last_active	The time interval since the last transaction on S.
S'last_value	The value of S just before the last event on S.

The first three attributes take an optional time parameter. If we omit the parameter, the value 0 fs is assumed. These attributes are often used in checking the timing behavior within a model. For example, we can verify that a signal **d** meets a minimum setup time requirement of **Tsu** before a rising edge on a clock **clk** of type std_ulogic as follows:

```
if clk'event and (clk = '1' or clk = 'H')
          and (clk'last_value = '0' or clk'last_value = 'L') then
    assert d'last_event >= Tsu
        report "Timing error: d changed within setup time of clk";
end if;
```

Similarly, we might check that the pulse width of a clock signal input to a module doesn't exceed a maximum frequency by testing its pulse width:

```
assert (not clk'event) or clk'delayed'last_event >= Tpw_clk
    report "Clock frequency too high";
```

Note that we test the time since the last event on a delayed version of the clock signal. When there is currently an event on a signal, the 'last_event attribute returns the value 0 fs. In this case, we determine the time since the previous event by applying the 'last_event attribute to the signal delayed by 0 fs. We can think of this as being an infinitesimal delay. We will return to this idea later in this chapter, in our discussion of delta delays.

EXAMPLE
───────────

We can use a similar test for the rising edge of a clock signal to model an edge-triggered module, such as a flipflop. The flipflop should load the value of its **D** input on a rising edge of **clk**, but asynchronously clear the outputs whenever **clr** is '1'. The entity declaration and a behavioral architecture body are shown in Figure 5-5.

If the flipflop did not have the asynchronous clear input, the model could have used a simple wait statement such as

```
wait until clk = '1';
```

to trigger on a rising edge. However, with the clear input present, the process must be sensitive to changes on both clk and clr at any time. Hence it uses the 'event attribute to distinguish between clk changing to '1' and clr going back to '0' while clk is stable at '1'.

FIGURE 5-5

```
entity edge_triggered_Dff is
    port ( D : in bit;  clk : in bit;  clr : in bit;
            Q : out bit );
end entity edge_triggered_Dff;

_____

architecture behavioral of edge_triggered_Dff is
begin
    state_change : process (clk, clr) is
    begin
        if clr = '1' then
            Q <= '0' after 2 ns;
        elsif clk'event and clk = '1' then
            Q <= D after 2 ns;
        end if;
    end process state_change;
end architecture behavioral;
```

An entity and architecture body for an edge-triggered flipflop, using the 'event *attribute to check for changes on the* clk *signal.*

VHDL-87

In VHDL-87, the 'last_value attribute for a composite signal returns the aggregate of last values for each of the scalar elements of the signal. For example, suppose a bit-vector signal s initially has the value B"00" and changes to B"01" and then B"11" in successive events. After the last event, the result of s'last_value is B"00" in VHDL-87. In VHDL-93 it is B"01", since that is the last value of the entire composite signal.

Wait Statements

Now that we have seen how to change the values of signals over time, the next step in behavioral modeling is to specify when processes respond to changes in signal values. This is done using *wait statements*. A wait statement is a sequential statement with the following syntax rule:

wait_statement ⇐
    〚 label : 〛 **wait** 〚 **on** *signal*_name 〚 , ... 〛 〛
                        〚 **until** *boolean*_expression 〛
                        〚 **for** *time*_expression 〛 ;

The optional label allows us to identify the statement. We will discuss labeled statements in Chapter 20. The purpose of the wait statement is to cause the process that executes the statement to suspend execution. The *sensitivity* clause, *condition* clause and *timeout* clause specify when the process is subsequently to resume execution. We can include any combination of these clauses, or we may omit all three. Let us go through each clause and describe what it specifies.

The sensitivity clause, starting with the word **on**, allows us to specify a list of signals to which the process responds. If we just include a sensitivity clause in a wait statement, the process will resume whenever any one of the listed signals changes value, that is, whenever an event occurs on any of the signals. This style of wait statement is useful in a process that models a block of combinatorial logic, since any change on the inputs may result in new output values; for example:

```
half_add : process is
begin
    sum <= a xor b after T_pd;
    carry <= a and b after T_pd;
    wait on a, b;
end process half_add;
```

The process starts execution by generating values for **sum** and **carry** based on the initial values of **a** and **b**, then suspends on the wait statement until either **a** or **b** (or both) change values. When that happens, the process resumes and starts execution from the top.

This form of process is so common in modeling digital systems that VHDL provides the shorthand notation that we have seen in many examples in preceding chapters. A process with a sensitivity list in its heading is exactly equivalent to a process with a wait statement at the end, containing a sensitivity clause naming the signals in the sensitivity list. So the **half_add** process above could be rewritten as

```
half_add : process (a, b) is
begin
    sum <= a xor b after T_pd;
    carry <= a and b after T_pd;
end process half_add;
```

EXAMPLE

Let us return to the model of a two-input multiplexer shown in Figure 5-4. The process in that model is sensitive to all three input signals. This means that it will resume on changes on either data input, even though only one of them is selected at any time. If we are concerned about this slight lack of efficiency in simulation, we can write the process differently, using wait statements to be more selective about the signals to which the process is sensitive each time it suspends. The revised model is shown in Figure 5-6. In this model, when input **a** is selected, the process only waits for changes on the select input and on **a**. Any changes on **b** are ignored. Similarly, if **b** is selected, the process waits for changes on **sel** and on **b**, ignoring changes on **a**.

FIGURE 5-6

```
entity mux2 is
    port ( a, b, sel : in bit;
            z : out bit );
end entity mux2;
```

```
architecture behavioral of mux2 is
    constant prop_delay : time := 2 ns;
begin
    slick_mux : process is
    begin
        case sel is
            when '0' =>
                z <= a after prop_delay;
                wait on sel, a;
            when '1' =>
                z <= b after prop_delay;
                wait on sel, b;
        end case;
    end process slick_mux;
end architecture behavioral;
```

An entity and architecture body for a multiplexer that avoids being resumed in response to changes on the input signal that is not currently selected.

The condition clause in a wait statement, starting with the word **until**, allows us to specify a condition that must be true for the process to resume. For example, the wait statement

wait until clk = '1';

causes the executing process to suspend until the value of the signal clk changes to '1'. The condition expression is tested while the process is suspended to determine whether to resume the process. A consequence of this is that even if the condition is true when the wait statement is executed, the process will still suspend until the appropriate signals change and cause the condition to be true again. If the wait statement doesn't include a sensitivity clause, the condition is tested whenever an event occurs on any of the signals mentioned in the condition.

EXAMPLE

The clock generator process from the example on page 110 can be rewritten using a wait statement with a condition clause, as shown in Figure 5-7. Each time the process executes the wait statement, clk has the value '0'. However, the process still suspends, and the condition is tested each time there is an event on clk. When clk changes to '1', nothing happens, but when it changes to '0' again, the process resumes and schedules transactions for the next cycle.

FIGURE 5-7

```
clock_gen : process is
begin
    clk <= '1' after T_pw, '0' after 2*T_pw;
    wait until clk = '0';
end process clock_gen;
```

The revised clock generator process.

If a wait statement includes a sensitivity clause as well as a condition clause, the condition is only tested when an event occurs on any of the signals in the sensitivity clause. For example, if a process suspends on the following wait statement:

wait on clk **until** reset = '0';

the condition is tested on each change in the value of **clk**, regardless of any changes on **reset**.

The timeout clause in a wait statement, starting with the word **for**, allows us to specify a maximum interval of simulation time for which the process should be suspended. If we also include a sensitivity or condition clause, these may cause the process to be resumed earlier. For example, the wait statement

wait until trigger = '1' **for** 1 ms;

causes the executing process to suspend until **trigger** changes to '1', or until 1 ms of simulation time has elapsed, whichever comes first. If we just include a timeout clause by itself in a wait statement, the process will suspend for the time given.

EXAMPLE

We can rewrite the clock generator process from the example on page 110 yet again, this time using a wait statement with a timeout clause, as shown in Figure 5-8. In this case we specify the clock period as the timeout, after which the process is to be resumed.

FIGURE 5-8

```
clock_gen : process is
begin
    clk <= '1' after T_pw, '0' after 2*T_pw;
    wait for 2*T_pw;
end process clock_gen;
```

A third version of the clock generator process.

If we refer back to the syntax rule for a wait statement shown on page 113, we note that it is legal to write

wait;

This form causes the executing process to suspend for the remainder of the simulation. Although this may at first seem a strange thing to want to do, in practice it is quite useful. One place where it is used is in a process whose purpose is to generate stimuli for a simulation. Such a process should generate a sequence of transactions on signals connected to other parts of a model and then stop. For example, the process

```
test_gen : process is
begin
    test0 <= '0' after 10 ns, '1' after 20 ns, '0' after 30 ns, '1' after 40 ns;
    test1 <= '0' after 10 ns, '1' after 30 ns;
    wait;
end process test_gen;
```

generates all four possible combinations of values on the signals test0 and test1. If the final wait statement were omitted, the process would cycle forever, repeating the signal assignment statements without suspending, and the simulation would make no progress.

VHDL-87
___

Wait statements may not be labeled in VHDL-87.

___

Delta Delays

Let us now return to the topic of delays in signal assignments. In many of the example signal assigments in previous chapters, we omitted the delay part of waveform elements. This is equivalent to specifying a delay of 0 fs. The value is to be applied to the signal at the current simulation time. However, it is important to note that the signal value does not change as soon as the signal assignment statement is executed. Rather, the assignment schedules a transaction for the signal, which is applied after the process suspends. Thus the process does not see the effect of the assignment until the next time it resumes, even if this is at the same simulation time. For this reason, a delay of 0 fs in a signal assignment is called a *delta delay*.

To understand why delta delays work in this way, it is necessary to review the simulation cycle, introduced in Chapter 1 on page 15. Recall that the simulation cycle consists of two phases: a signal update phase followed by a process execution phase. In the signal update phase, simulation time is advanced to the time of the earliest scheduled transaction, and the values in all transactions scheduled for this time are applied to their corresponding signals. This may cause events to occur on some signals. In the process execution phase, all processes that respond to these events are resumed and execute until they suspend again on wait statements. The simulator then repeats the simulation cycle.

Let us now consider what happens when a process executes a signal assignment statement with delta delay, for example:

```
data <= X"00";
```

Suppose this is executed at simulation time *t* during the process execution phase of the current simulation cycle. The effect of the assignment is to schedule a transaction to put the value X"00" on **data** at time *t*. The transaction is not applied immediately, since the simulator is in the process execution phase. Hence the process continues executing, with **data** unchanged. When all processes have suspended, the simulator starts the next simulation cycle and updates the simulation time. Since the earliest transaction is now at time *t*, simulation time remains unchanged. The simulator now applies the value X"00" in the scheduled transaction to **data**, then resumes any processes that respond to the new value.

Writing a model with delta delays is useful when we are working at a high level of abstraction and are not yet concerned with detailed timing. If all we are interested in is describing the order in which operations take place, delta delays provide a means of ignoring the complications of timing. We have seen this in many of the examples in previous chapters. However, we should note a common pitfall encountered by most beginner VHDL designers when using delta delays: they forget that the process does not see the effect of the assignment immediately. For example, we might write a process that includes the following statements:

```
s <= '1';
. . .
if s = '1' then . . .
```

and expect the process to execute the if statement assuming **s** has the value '1'. We would then spend fruitless hours debugging our model until we remembered that **s** still has its old value until the next simulation cycle, after the process has suspended.

EXAMPLE

Figure 5-9 is an outline of an abstract model of a computer system. The CPU and memory are connected with address and data signals. They synchronize their operation with the **mem_read** and **mem_write** control signals and the **mem_ready** status signal. No delays are specified in the signal assignment statements, so synchronization occurs over a number of delta delay cycles, as shown in Figure 5-10.

FIGURE 5-9

```
architecture abstract of computer_system is
    subtype word is bit_vector(31 downto 0);
    signal address : natural;
    signal read_data, write_data : word;
    signal mem_read, mem_write : bit := '0';
    signal mem_ready : bit := '0';
begin
```

```
cpu : process is
    variable instr_reg : word;
    variable PC : natural;
    . . .          -- other declarations
begin
    loop
        address <= PC;
        mem_read <= '1';
        wait until mem_ready = '1';
        instr_reg := read_data;
        mem_read <= '0';
        wait until mem_ready = '0';
        PC := PC + 4;
        . . .          -- execute the instruction
    end loop;
end process cpu;

memory : process is
    type memory_array is array (0 to 2**14 – 1) of word;
    variable store : memory_array := (
        . . .
        );
begin
    wait until mem_read = '1' or mem_write = '1';
    if mem_read = '1' then
        read_data <= store( address / 4 );
        mem_ready <= '1';
        wait until mem_read = '0';
        mem_ready <= '0';
    else
        . . .          -- perform write access
    end if;
end process memory;
end architecture abstract;
```

An outline of an abstract model for a computer system, consisting of a CPU and a memory. The processes use delta delays to synchronize communication, rather than modeling timing of bus transactions in detail.

When the simulation starts, the CPU process begins executing its statements and the memory suspends. The CPU schedules transactions to assign the next instruction address to the **address** signal and the value '1' to the **mem_read** signal, then suspends. In the next simulation cycle, these signals are updated and the memory process resumes, since it is waiting for an event on **mem_read**. The memory process schedules the data on the **read_data** signal and the value '1' on **mem_ready**, then suspends. In the third cycle, these signals are updated and the CPU process resumes. It schedules the value '0' on **mem_read** and suspends. Then, in the fourth cycle, **mem_read** is updated and the memory process is resumed, scheduling the value '0' on **mem_ready** to complete the handshake. Finally, on the fifth cycle, **mem_ready** is updated and the CPU process resumes and executes the fetched instruction.

FIGURE 5-10

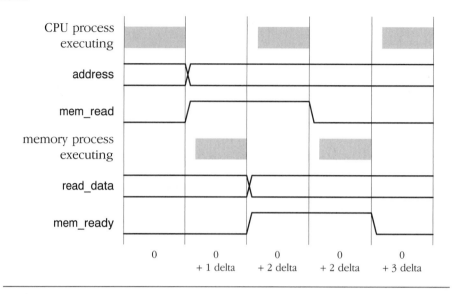

Synchronization over successive delta cycles in a simulation of a read operation between the CPU and memory shown in Figure 5-9.

Transport and Inertial Delay Mechanisms

So far in our discussion of signal assignments, we have implicitly assumed that there were no pending transactions scheduled for a signal when a signal assignment statement was executed. In many models, particularly at higher levels of abstraction, this will be the case. If, on the other hand, there are pending transactions, the new transactions are merged with them in a way that depends on the *delay mechanism* used in the signal assignment statement. This is an optional part of the signal assignment syntax shown on page 109. The syntax rule for the delay mechanism is

delay_mechanism ⇐ **transport** ⟦ [**reject** *time*_expression] **inertial**

A signal assignment with the delay mechanism part omitted is equivalent to specifying **inertial**. We look at the *transport* delay mechanism first, since it is simpler, and then return to the *inertial* delay mechanism.

We use the transport delay mechanism when we are modeling an ideal device with infinite frequency response, in which any input pulse, no matter how short, produces an output pulse. An example of such a device is an ideal transmission line, which transmits all input changes delayed by some amount. A process to model a transmission line with delay 500 ps is

```
transmission_line : process (line_in) is
begin
    line_out <= transport line_in after 500 ps;
end process transmission_line;
```

In this model the output follows any changes in the input, but delayed by 500 ps. If the input changes twice or more within a period shorter than 500 ps, the scheduled transactions are simply queued by the driver until the simulation time at which they are to be applied, as shown in Figure 5-11.

FIGURE 5-11

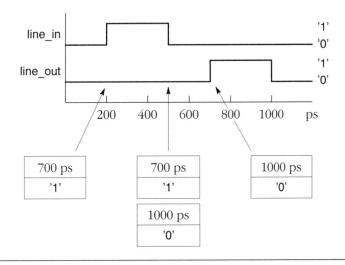

Transactions queued by a driver using transport delay. At time 200 ps the input changes, and a transaction is scheduled for 700 ps. At time 500 ps, the input changes again, and another transaction is scheduled for 1000 ps. This is queued by the driver behind the earlier transaction. When simulation time reaches 700 ps, the first transaction is applied, and the second transaction remains queued. Finally, simulation time reaches 1000 ps, and the final transaction is applied, leaving the driver queue empty.

In this example, each new transaction that is generated by a signal assignment statement is scheduled for a simulation time that is later than the pending transactions queued by the driver. The situation gets a little more complex when variable delays are used, since we can schedule a transaction for an earlier time than a pending transaction. The semantics of the transport delay mechanism specify that if there are pending transactions on a driver that are scheduled for a time later than or equal to a new transaction, those later transactions are deleted.

EXAMPLE

Figure 5-12 is a process that describes the behavior of an asymmetric delay element, with different delay times for rising and falling transitions. The delay for rising transitions is 800 ps and for falling transitions 500 ps. If we apply an input pulse of only 200 ps duration, we would expect the output not to change, since the delayed falling transition should "overtake" the delayed rising transition. If we were simply to add each transition to the driver queue when a signal assignment statement is executed, we would not get this behavior. However, the semantics of the transport delay mechanism produce the desired behavior, as Figure 5-13 shows.

FIGURE 5-12

```
asym_delay : process (a) is
    constant Tpd_01 : time := 800 ps;
    constant Tpd_10 : time := 500 ps;
begin
    if a = '1' then
        z <= transport a after Tpd_01;
    else  -- a = '0'
        z <= transport a after Tpd_10;
    end if;
end process asym_delay;
```

A process that describes a delay element with asymmetric delays for rising and falling transitions.

FIGURE 5-13

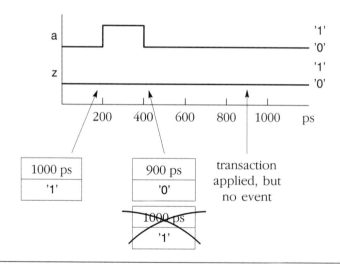

Transactions in a driver using asymmetric transport delay. At time 200 ps the input changes, and a transaction is scheduled for 1000 ps. At time 400 ps, the input changes again, and another transaction is scheduled for 900 ps. Since this is earlier than the pending transaction at 1000 ps, the pending transaction is deleted. When simulation time reaches 900 ps, the remaining transaction is applied, but since the value is '0', no event occurs on the signal.

Most real electronic circuits don't have infinite frequency response, so it is not appropriate to model them using transport delay. In real devices, changing the values of internal nodes and outputs involves moving electronic charge around in the presence of capacitance, inductance and resistance. This gives the device some inertia; it tends to stay in the same state unless we force it by applying inputs for a sufficiently long duration. This is why VHDL includes the inertial delay mechanism, to allow us to model devices that reject input pulses too short to overcome their inertia. Inertial delay is the mechanism used by default in a signal assignment, or we can specify it explicitly by including the word **inertial**.

To explain how inertial delay works, let us first consider a model in which all the signal assignments for a given signal use the same delay value, say 3 ns, as in the following inverter model:

```
inv : process (a) is
begin
    y <= inertial not a after 3 ns;
end process inv;
```

So long as input events occur more than 3 ns apart, this model does not present any problems. Each time a signal assignment is executed, there are no pending transactions, so a new transaction is scheduled, and the output changes value 3 ns later. However, if an input changes less than 3 ns after the previous change, this represents a pulse less than the propagation delay of the device, so it should be rejected. This behavior is shown at the top of Figure 5-14. In a simple model such as this, we can interpret inertial delay as saying if a signal assignment would produce an output pulse shorter than the propagation delay, then the output pulse does not happen.

FIGURE 5-14

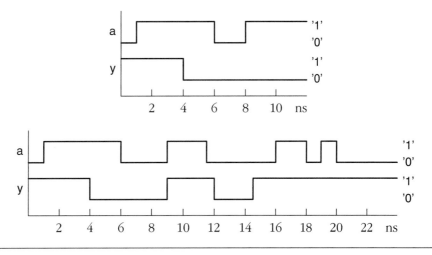

Results of signal assignments using the inertial delay mechanism. In the top waveform, an inertial delay of 3 ns is specified. The input change at time 1 ns is reflected in the output at time 4 ns. The pulse from 6 to 8 ns is less than the propagation delay, so it doesn't affect the output. In the bottom waveform, an inertial delay of 3 ns and a pulse rejection limit of 2 ns are specified. The input changes at 1, 6, 9 and 11.5 ns are all reflected in the output, since they occur greater than 2 ns apart. However, the subsequent input pulses are less than or equal to the pulse rejection limit in length, and so do not affect the output.

Next, let us extend this model by specifying a pulse rejection limit, after the word **reject** in the signal assignment:

```
inv : process (a) is
begin
    y <= reject 2 ns inertial not a after 3 ns;
end process inv;
```

We can interpret this as saying if a signal assignment would produce an output pulse shorter than (or equal to) the pulse rejection limit, the output pulse does not happen. In this simple model, so long as input changes occur more than 2 ns apart, they produce output changes 3 ns later, as shown at the bottom of Figure 5-14. Note that the pulse rejection limit specified must be between 0 fs and the delay specified in the signal assignment. Omitting a pulse rejection limit is the same as specifying a limit equal to the delay, and specifying a limit of 0 fs is the same as specifying transport delay.

Now let us look at the full story of inertial delay, allowing for varying the delay time and pulse rejection limit in different signal assignments applied to the same signal. As with transport delay, the situation becomes more complex, and it is best to describe it in terms of deleting transactions from the driver. Those who are unlikely to be writing models that deal with timing at this level of detail may wish to move on to the next section.

An inertially delayed signal assignment involves examining the pending transactions on a driver when adding a new transaction. Suppose a signal assignment schedules a new transaction for time t_{new}, with a pulse rejection limit of t_r. First, any pending transactions scheduled for a time later than or equal to t_{new} are deleted, just as they are when transport delay is used. Then the new transaction is added to the driver. Second, any pending transactions scheduled in the interval $t_{new} - t_r$ to t_{new} are examined. If there is a run of consecutive transactions immediately preceding the new transaction with the same value as the new transaction, they are kept in the driver. All other transactions in the interval are deleted.

An example will make this clearer. Suppose a driver for signal **s** contains pending transactions as shown at the top of Figure 5-15, and the process containing the driver executes the following signal assignment statement at time 10 ns:

s <= **reject** 5 ns **inertial** '1' **after** 8 ns;

The pending transactions after this assignment are shown at the bottom of Figure 5-15.

FIGURE 5-15

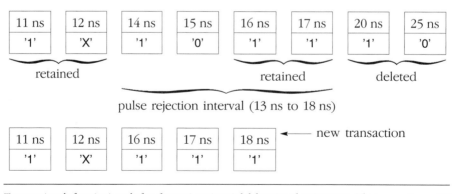

Transactions before (top) and after (bottom) an inertial delay signal assignment. The transactions at 20 and 25 ns are deleted because they are scheduled for later than the new transaction. Those at 11 and 12 ns are retained because they fall before the pulse rejection interval. The transactions at 16 and 17 ns fall within the rejection interval, but they form a run leading up to the new transaction, with the same value as the new transaction; hence they are also retained. The other transactions in the rejection interval are deleted.

One final point to note about specifying the delay mechanism in a signal assignment statement is that if a number of waveform elements are included, the specified mechanism only applies to the first element. All the subsequent elements schedule transactions using transport delay. Since the delays for multiple waveform elements must be in ascending order, this means that all of the transactions after the first are just added to the driver transaction queue in the order written.

EXAMPLE

A detailed model of a two-input and gate is shown in Figure 5-16. When a change on either of the input signals results in a change scheduled for the output, the **delay** process determines the propagation delay to be used. On a rising output transition, spikes of less than 400 ps are rejected, and on a falling or unknown transition, spikes of less than 300 ps are rejected. Note that the result of the **and** operator, when applied to standard-logic values, is always 'U', 'X', '0' or '1'. Hence the **delay** process need not compare result with 'H' or 'L' when testing for rising or falling transitions.

FIGURE 5-16

```
library ieee;  use ieee.std_logic_1164.all;

entity and2 is
    port ( a, b : in std_ulogic;  y : out std_ulogic );
end entity and2;

-------------------------------------------------------------

architecture detailed_delay of and2 is

    signal result : std_ulogic;

begin

    gate : process (a, b) is
    begin
        result <= a and b;
    end process gate;

    delay : process (result) is
    begin
        if result = '1' then
            y <= reject 400 ps inertial '1' after 1.5 ns;
        elsif result = '0' then
            y <= reject 300 ps inertial '0' after 1.2 ns;
        else
            y <= reject 300 ps inertial 'X' after 500 ps;
        end if;
    end process delay;

end architecture detailed_delay;
```

An entity and architecture body for a two-input and gate. The process gate *implements the logical function of the entity, and the process* delay *implements its detailed timing characteristics using inertially delayed signal assignments. A delay of 1.5 ns is used for rising transitions, 1.2 ns for falling transitions.*

VHDL-87

VHDL-87 does not allow specification of the pulse rejection limit in a delay mechanism. The syntax rule in VHDL-87 is

delay_mechanism ⇐ **transport**

If the delay mechanism is omitted, inertial delay is used, with a pulse rejection limit equal to the delay specified in the waveform element.

Process Statements

We have been using processes quite extensively in examples in this and previous chapters, so we have seen most of the details of how they are written and used. To summarize, let us now look at the formal syntax for a process statement and review process operation. The syntax rule is

process_statement ⇐
    [*process*_label :]
    process [(*signal*_name { , ⚬⚬⚬ })] [**is**]
        { process_declarative_item }
    begin
        { sequential_statement }
    end process [*process*_label] ;

Recall that a process statement is a concurrent statement that can be included in an architecture body to implement all or part of the behavior of a module. The process label identifies the process. While it is optional, it is a good idea to include a label on each process. A label makes it easier to debug a simulation of a system, since most simulators provide a way of identifying a process by its label. Most simulators also generate a default name for a process if we omit the label in the process statement. Having identified a process, we can examine the contents of its variables or set breakpoints at statements within the process.

The declarative items in a process statement may include constant, type and variable declarations, as well as other declarations that we will come to later. Note that ordinary variables may only be declared within process statements, not outside of them. The variables are used to represent the state of the process, as we have seen in the examples. The sequential statements that form the process body may include any of those that we introduced in Chapter 3, plus signal assignment and wait statements. When a process is activated during simulation, it starts executing from the first sequential statement and continues until it reaches the last. It then starts again from the first. This would be an infinite loop, with no progress being made in the simulation, if it were not for the inclusion of wait statements, which suspend process execution until some relevant event occurs. Wait statements are the only statements that take more than zero simulation time to execute. It is only through the execution of wait statements that simulation time advances.

A process may include a sensitivity list in parentheses after the keyword **process**. The sensitivity list identifies a set of signals that the process monitors for events. If the sensitivity list is omitted, the process should include one or more wait statements. On the other hand, if the sensitivity list is included, then the process body cannot include any wait statements. Instead, there is an implicit wait statement, just before the **end process** keywords, that includes the signals listed in the sensitivity list as signals in an **on** clause.

VHDL-87

The keyword **is** may not be included in the header of a process statement in VHDL-87.

Concurrent Signal Assignment Statements

The form of process statement that we have been using is the basis for all behavioral modeling in VHDL, but for simple cases, it can be a little cumbersome and verbose. For this reason, VHDL provides us with some useful shorthand notations for *functional* modeling, that is, behavioral modeling in which the operation to be described is a simple combinatorial transformation of inputs to an output. We look at the basic form of two of these statements, *concurrent signal assignment* statements, which are concurrent statements that are essentially signal assignments. Unlike ordinary signal assignments, concurrent signal assignment statements can be included in the statement part of an architecture body. The syntax rule is

> concurrent_signal_assignment_statement ⇐
> ⟦ label : ⟧ conditional_signal_assignment
> | ⟦ label : ⟧ selected_signal_assignment

which tells us that the two forms are called a *conditional signal assignment* and a *selected signal assignment*. Each of them may include a label, which serves exactly the same purpose as a label on a process statement: it allows the statement to be identified by name during simulation or synthesis.

Conditional Signal Assignment Statements

The conditional signal assignment statement is a shorthand for a collection of ordinary signal assignments contained in an if statement, which is in turn contained in a process statement. The simplified syntax rule for a conditional signal assignment is

> conditional_signal_assignment ⇐
> name <= ⟦ delay_mechanism ⟧
> { waveform **when** *boolean*_expression **else** }
> waveform ⟦ **when** *boolean*_expression ⟧ ;

The conditional signal assignment allows us to specify which of a number of waveforms should be assigned to a signal depending on the values of some conditions. Let us look at some examples and show how each conditional signal assignment can be transformed into an equivalent process statement. First, the top statement in Figure 5-17 is a functional description of a multiplexer, with four data inputs (d0, d1, d2 and d3), two select inputs (sel0 and sel1) and a data output (z). All of these signals are of type bit. This statement has exactly the same meaning as the process statement shown at the bottom of Figure 5-17.

FIGURE 5-17

```
zmux : z <= d0 when sel1 = '0' and sel0 = '0' else
            d1 when sel1 = '0' and sel0 = '1' else
            d2 when sel1 = '1' and sel0 = '0' else
            d3 when sel1 = '1' and sel0 = '1';
```

```
zmux : process is
begin
    if sel1 = '0' and sel0 = '0' then
        z <= d0;
    elsif sel1 = '0' and sel0 = '1' then
        z <= d1;
    elsif sel1 = '1' and sel0 = '0' then
        z <= d2;
    elsif sel1 = '1' and sel0 = '1' then
        z <= d3;
    end if;
    wait on d0, d1, d2, d3, sel0, sel1;
end process zmux;
```

Top: a functional model of a multiplexer, using a conditional signal assignment statement. Bottom: the equivalent process statement.

The advantage of the conditional signal assignment form over the equivalent process is clearly evident from this example. The simple combinatorial transformation is obvious to the reader, uncluttered by the details of the process mechanism. This is not to say that processes are a bad thing, rather that in simple cases, we would rather hide that detail to make the model clearer. Looking at the equivalent process shows us something important about the conditional signal assignment statement, namely, that it is sensitive to all of the signals mentioned in the waveforms and the conditions. So whenever any of these change value, the conditional assignment is reevaluated and a new transaction scheduled on the driver for the target signal.

If we look more closely at the multiplexer model, we note that the last condition is redundant, since the signals sel0 and sel1 are of type bit. If none of the previous conditions are true, the signal should always be assigned the last waveform. So we can rewrite the example as shown in Figure 5-18.

FIGURE 5-18

```
zmux : z <= d0 when sel1 = '0' and sel0 = '0' else
            d1 when sel1 = '0' and sel0 = '1' else
            d2 when sel1 = '1' and sel0 = '0' else
            d3;
```

```
zmux : process is
begin
    if sel1 = '0' and sel0 = '0' then
        z <= d0;
    elsif sel1 = '0' and sel0 = '1' then
        z <= d1;
    elsif sel1 = '1' and sel0 = '0' then
        z <= d2;
    else
        z <= d3;
    end if;
    wait on d0, d1, d2, d3, sel0, sel1;
end process zmux;
```

A revised functional model for the multiplexer, with its equivalent process statement.

A very common case in function modeling is to write a conditional signal assignment with no conditions, as in the following example:

```
PC_incr : next_PC <= PC + 4 after 5 ns;
```

At first sight this appears to be an ordinary sequential signal assignment statement, which by rights ought to be inside a process body. However, if we look at the syntax rule for a concurrent signal assignment, we note that this can in fact be recognized as such if all of the optional parts except the label are omitted. In this case, the equivalent process statement is

```
PC_incr : process is
begin
    next_PC <= PC + 4 after 5 ns;
    wait on PC;
end process PC_incr;
```

Another case that sometimes arises when writing functional models is the need for a process that schedules an initial set of transactions and then does nothing more for the remainder of the simulation. An example is the generation of a reset signal. One way of doing this is as follows:

```
reset_gen : reset <= '1', '0' after 200 ns when extended_reset else
                     '1', '0' after 50 ns;
```

The thing to note here is that there are no signals named in any of the waveforms or the conditions (assuming that extended_reset is a constant). This means that the statement is executed once when simulation starts, schedules two transactions on reset and remains quiescent thereafter. The equivalent process is

```
reset_gen : process is
begin
    if extended_reset then
        reset <= '1', '0' after 200 ns;
```

```
        else
                reset <= '1', '0' after 50 ns;
        end if;
        wait;
    end process reset_gen;
```

Since there are no signals involved, the wait statement has no sensitivity clause. Thus after the if statement has executed, the process suspends forever.

If we include a delay mechanism specification in a conditional signal assignment statement, it is used whichever waveform is chosen. So we might rewrite the model for the asymmetric delay element shown in Figure 5-12 as

```
asym_delay : z <= transport a after Tpd_01 when a = '1' else
                                    a after Tpd_10;
```

One problem with conditional signal assignments, as we have described them so far, is that they always assign a new value to a signal. Sometimes we may not want to change the value of a signal, or more specifically, we may not want to schedule any new transactions on the signal. We can use the keyword **unaffected** instead of a normal waveform for these cases, as shown at the top of Figure 5-19.

FIGURE 5-19
_____

```
        scheduler :
            request <= first_priority_request after scheduling_delay
                            when priority_waiting and server_status = ready else
                        first_normal_request after scheduling_delay
                            when not priority_waiting and server_status = ready else
                        unaffected
                            when server_status = busy else
                        reset_request after scheduling_delay;
```
_____
```
        scheduler : process is
        begin
            if priority_waiting and server_status = ready then
                request <= first_priority_request after scheduling_delay;
            elsif not priority_waiting and server_status = ready then
                request <= first_normal_request after scheduling_delay;
            elsif server_status = busy then
                null;
            else
                request <= reset_request after scheduling_delay;
            end if;
            wait on first_priority_request, priority_waiting, server_status,
                        first_normal_request, reset_request;
        end process scheduler;
```
_____

*Top: a conditional signal assignment statement showing use of the **unaffected** waveform. Bottom: the equivalent process statement.*

The effect of the **unaffected** waveform is to include a null statement in the equivalent process, causing it to bypass scheduling a transaction when the corresponding condition is true. (Recall that the effect of the null sequential statement is to do nothing.) So the example at the top of Figure 5-19 is equivalent to the process shown at the bottom. Note that we can only use **unaffected** in a concurrent signal assignment, not in a sequential signal assignment.

VHDL-87

In VHDL-87 the syntax rule for a conditional signal assignment statement is

conditional_signal_assignment ⇐
    name <= ⟦ **transport** ⟧
            { waveform **when** *boolean*_expression **else** }
            waveform ;

The delay mechanism is restricted to the keyword **transport**. The final waveform may not be conditional. Furthermore, we may not use the keyword **unaffected**. If the required behavior cannot be expressed with these restrictions, we must write a full process statement instead of a conditional signal assignment statement.

Selected Signal Assignment Statements

The selected signal assignment statement is similar in many ways to the conditional signal assignment statement. It, too, is a shorthand for a number of ordinary signal assignments embedded in a process. But for a selected signal assignment, the equivalent process contains a case statement instead of an if statement. The simplified syntax rule is

selected_signal_assignment ⇐
    with expression **select**
        name <= ⟦ delay_mechanism ⟧
            { waveform **when** choices , }
            waveform **when** choices ;

This statement allows us to choose between a number of waveforms to be assigned to a signal depending on the value of an expression. As an example, let us consider the selected signal assignment shown at the top of Figure 5-20. This has the same meaning as the process statement containing a case statement shown at the bottom of Figure 5-20.

A selected signal assignment statement is sensitive to all of the signals in the selector expression and in the waveforms. This means that the selected signal assignment in Figure 5-20 is sensitive to b and will resume if b changes value, even if the value of alu_function is alu_pass_a.

An important point to note about a selected signal assignment statement is that the case statement in the equivalent process must be legal according to all of the rules that we described in Chapter 3. This means that every possible value for the selector expression must be accounted for in one of the choices, that no value is included in more than one choice and so on.

FIGURE 5-20

```
alu : with alu_function select
        result <=  a + b after Tpd      when alu_add | alu_add_unsigned,
                   a – b after Tpd      when alu_sub | alu_sub_unsigned,
                   a and b after Tpd  when alu_and,
                   a or b after Tpd    when alu_or,
                   a after Tpd          when alu_pass_a;
```

```
alu : process is
begin
    case alu_function is
        when alu_add | alu_add_unsigned =>  result <= a + b after Tpd;
        when alu_sub | alu_sub_unsigned =>  result <= a – b after Tpd;
        when alu_and                    =>  result <= a and b after Tpd;
        when alu_or                     =>  result <= a or b after Tpd;
        when alu_pass_a                 =>  result <= a after Tpd;
    end case;
    wait on alu_function, a, b;
end process alu;
```

Top: a selected signal assignment. Bottom: its equivalent process statement.

Apart from the difference in the equivalent process, the selected signal assignment is similar to the conditional assignment. Thus the special waveform **unaffected** can be used to specify that no assignment take place for some values of the selector expression. Also, if a delay mechanism is specified in the statement, that mechanism is used on each sequential signal assignment within the equivalent process.

EXAMPLE

We can use a selected signal assignment to express a combinatorial logic function in truth-table form. Figure 5-21 shows an entity declaration and an architecture body for a full adder. The selected signal assignment statement has, as its selector expression, a bit vector formed by aggregating the input signals. The choices list all possible values of inputs, and for each, the values for the c_out and s outputs are given.

FIGURE 5-21

```
entity full_adder is
    port ( a, b, c_in : bit;  s, c_out : out bit );
end entity full_adder;
```

```
architecture truth_table of full_adder is
begin
    with bit_vector'(a, b, c_in) select
        (c_out, s) <= bit_vector'("00") when "000",
                      bit_vector'("01") when "001",
```

```
                    bit_vector'("01") when "010",
                    bit_vector'("10") when "011",
                    bit_vector'("01") when "100",
                    bit_vector'("10") when "101",
                    bit_vector'("10") when "110",
                    bit_vector'("11") when "111";
  end architecture truth_table;
```

An entity declaration and functional architecture body for a full adder.

This example illustrates the most common use of aggregate targets in signal assignments. Note that the type qualification is required in the selector expression to specify the type of the aggregate. The type qualification is needed in the output values to distinguish the bit-vector string literals from character string literals.

VHDL-87

In VHDL-87, the delay mechanism is restricted to the keyword **transport**, as discussed on page 126. Furthermore, the keyword **unaffected** may not be used. If the required behavior cannot be expressed without using the keyword **unaffected**, we must write a full process statement instead of a selected signal assignment statement.

Concurrent Assertion Statements

VHDL provides another shorthand process notation, the *concurrent assertion statement*, which can be used in behavioral modeling. As its name implies, a concurrent assertion statement represents a process whose body contains an ordinary sequential assertion statement. The syntax rule is

concurrent_assertion_statement ⇐
    ⟦ label : ⟧
    assert *boolean*_expression
        ⟦ **report** expression ⟧ ⟦ **severity** expression ⟧ ;

This syntax appears to be exactly the same as that for a sequential assertion statement, but the difference is that it may appear as a concurrent statement. The optional label on the statement serves the same purpose as that on a process statement: to provide a way of referring to the statement during simulation or synthesis. The process equivalent to a concurrent assertion contains a sequential assertion with the same condition, report clause and severity clause. The sequential assertion is then followed by a wait statement whose sensitivity list includes the signals mentioned in the condition expression. Thus the effect of the concurrent assertion statement is to check that the condition holds true each time any of the signals mentioned in the condition change value. Concurrent assertions provide a very compact and useful way of including timing and correctness checks in a model.

EXAMPLE

We can use concurrent assertion statements to check for correct use of a set/reset flipflop, with two inputs s and r and two outputs q and q_n, all of type bit. The requirement for use is that s and r are not both '1' at the same time. The entity and architecture body are shown in Figure 5-22.

FIGURE 5-22

```
entity S_R_flipflop is
    port ( s, r : in bit;  q, q_n : out bit );
end entity S_R_flipflop;
------------------------------------------------------

architecture functional of S_R_flipflop is
begin
    q <= '1' when s = '1' else
            '0' when r = '1';
    q_n <= '0' when s = '1' else
            '1' when r = '1';
    check : assert not (s = '1' and r = '1')
                    report "Incorrect use of S_R_flip_flop: s and r both '1'";
end architecture functional;
```

An entity and architecture body for a set/reset flipflop, including a concurrent assertion statement to check for correct usage.

The first and second concurrent statements implement the functionality of the model. The third checks for correct use and is resumed when either s or r changes value, since these are the signals mentioned in the Boolean condition. If both of the signals are '1', an assertion violation is reported. The equivalent process for the concurrent assertion is

```
check : process is
begin
    assert not (s = '1' and r = '1')
        report "Incorrect use of S_R_flip_flop: s and r both '1'";
    wait on s, r;
end process check;
```

Entities and Passive Processes

We complete this section on behavioral modeling by returning to declarations of entities. We can include certain kinds of concurrent statements in an entity declaration, to monitor use and operation of the entity. The extended syntax rule for an entity declaration that shows this is

entity_declaration ⇐
    entity identifier **is**
        ⟦ **port** (*port*_interface_list) ; ⟧
        { entity_declarative_item }
    ⟦ **begin**
        { concurrent_assertion_statement
        ∥ *passive*_concurrent_procedure_call_statement
        ∥ *passive*_process_statement } ⟧
    end ⟦ **entity** ⟧ ⟦ identifier ⟧ ;

The concurrent statements included in an entity declaration must be *passive*, that is, they may not affect the operation of the entity in any way. A concurrent assertion statement meets this requirement, since it simply tests a condition whenever events occur on signals to which it is sensitive. A process statement is passive if it contains no signal assignment statements or calls to procedures containing signal assignment statements. Such a process can be used to trace events that occur on the entity's inputs. We will describe the remaining alternative, concurrent procedure call statements, when we discuss procedures in Chapter 7. A concurrent procedure call is passive if the procedure called contains no signal assignment statements or calls to procedures containing signal assignment statements.

EXAMPLE

We can rewrite the entity declaration for the set/reset flipflop of Figure 5-22 as shown in Figure 5-23. If we do this, the check is included for every possible implementation of the flipflop and does not need to be included in the corresponding architecture bodies.

FIGURE 5-23

```
entity S_R_flipflop is
    port ( s, r : in bit;  q, q_n : out bit );
begin
    check : assert not (s = '1' and r = '1')
                    report "Incorrect use of S_R_flip_flop: s and r both '1'";
end entity S_R_flipflop;
```

The revised entity declaration for the set/reset flipflop, including the concurrent assertion statement to check for correct usage.

EXAMPLE

Figure 5-24 shows an entity declaration for a read-only memory (ROM). It includes a passive process, **trace_reads**, that is sensitive to changes on the **enable** port. When the value of the port changes to '1', the process reports a message tracing the time and address of the read operation. The process does not affect

FIGURE 5-24

```
entity ROM is
    port ( address : in natural;
            data : out bit_vector(0 to 7);
            enable : in bit );
begin
    trace_reads : process (enable) is
    begin
        if enable = '1' then
            report "ROM read at time " & time'image(now)
                    & " from address " & natural'image(address);
        end if;
    end process trace_reads;
end entity ROM;
```

An entity declaration for a ROM, including a passive process for tracing read operations.

the course of the simulation in any way, since it does not include any signal assignments.

5.4   Structural Descriptions

A structural description of a system is expressed in terms of subsystems interconnected by signals. Each subsystem may in turn be composed of an interconnection of sub-subsystems, and so on, until we finally reach a level consisting of primitive components, described purely in terms of their behavior. Thus the top-level system can be thought of as having a hierarchical structure. In this section, we look at how to write structural architecture bodies to express this hierarchical organization.

Component Instantiation and Port Maps

We have seen earlier in this chapter that the concurrent statements in an architecture body describe an implementation of an entity interface. In order to write a structural implementation, we must use a concurrent statement called a *component instantiation* statement, the simplest form of which is governed by the syntax rule

component_instantiation_statement ⇐
   *instantiation*_label :
        entity *entity*_name ⟦ (*architecture*_identifier) ⟧
            ⟦ **port map** (port_association_list) ⟧ ;

This form of component instantiation statement performs *direct instantiation* of an entity. We can think of component instantiation as creating a copy of the named entity, with the corresponding architecture body substituted for the component instance. The port map specifies which ports of the entity are connected to which signals in the enclosing architecture body. The simplified syntax rule for a port association list is

port_association_list ⇐
 ([*port*_name =>] (*signal*_name ‖ expression ‖ **open**)) { , ... }

Each element in the association list associates one port of the entity either with one signal of the enclosing architecture body or with the value of an expression, or leaves the port unassociated, as indicated by the keyword **open**.

Let us look at some examples to illustrate component instantiation statements and the association of ports with signals. Suppose we have an entity declared as

```
entity DRAM_controller is
    port ( rd, wr, mem : in bit;
              ras, cas, we, ready : out bit );
end entity DRAM_controller;
```

and a corresponding architecture called fpld. We might create an instance of this entity as follows:

```
main_mem_controller : entity work.DRAM_controller(fpld)
    port map ( cpu_rd, cpu_wr, cpu_mem,
                  mem_ras, mem_cas, mem_we, cpu_rdy );
```

In this example, the name **work** refers to the current working library in which entities and architecture bodies are stored. We return to the topic of libraries in the next section. The port map of this example lists the signals in the enclosing architecture body to which the ports of the copy of the entity are connected. *Positional association* is used: each signal listed in the port map is connected to the port at the same position in the entity declaration. So the signal **cpu_rd** is connected to the port **rd**, the signal **cpu_wr** is connected to the port **wr** and so on.

One of the problems with positional association is that it is not immediately clear which signals are being connected to which ports. Someone reading the description must refer to the entity declaration to check the order of the ports in the entity interface. A better way of writing a component instantiation statement is to use *named association*, as shown in the following example:

```
main_mem_controller : entity work.DRAM_controller(fpld)
    port map ( rd => cpu_rd, wr => cpu_wr,
                  mem => cpu_mem, ready => cpu_rdy,
                  ras => mem_ras, cas => mem_cas, we => mem_we );
```

Here, each port is explicitly named along with the signal to which it is connected. The order in which the connections are listed is immaterial. The advantage of this approach is that it is immediately obvious to the reader how the entity is connected into the structure of the enclosing architecture body.

In the preceding example we have explicitly named the architecture body to be used corresponding to the entity instantiated. However, the syntax rule for component instantiation statements shows this to be optional. If we wish, we can omit the specification of the architecture body, in which case the one to be used may be chosen when the overall model is processed for simulation, synthesis or some other purpose. At that time, if no other choice is specified, the most recently analyzed architecture body is selected. We return to the topic of analyzing models in the next section.

EXAMPLE

In Figure 5-5 we looked at a behavioral model of an edge-triggered flipflop. We can use the flipflop as the basis of a four-bit edge-triggered register. Figure 5-25 shows the entity declaration and a structural architecture body.

FIGURE 5-25

```
entity reg4 is
    port ( clk, clr, d0, d1, d2, d3 : in bit;
           q0, q1, q2, q3 : out bit );
end entity reg4;
```

```
architecture struct of reg4 is
begin
    bit0 : entity work.edge_triggered_Dff(behavioral)
        port map (d0, clk, clr, q0);
    bit1 : entity work.edge_triggered_Dff(behavioral)
        port map (d1, clk, clr, q1);
    bit2 : entity work.edge_triggered_Dff(behavioral)
        port map (d2, clk, clr, q2);
    bit3 : entity work.edge_triggered_Dff(behavioral)
        port map (d3, clk, clr, q3);
end architecture struct;
```

An entity and structural architecture body for a four-bit edge-triggered register, with an asynchronous clear input.

We can use the register entity, along with other entities, as part of a structural architecture for the two-digit decimal counter represented by the schematic of Figure 5-26. Suppose a digit is represented as a bit vector of length four, described by the subtype declaration

subtype digit **is** bit_vector(3 **downto** 0);

Figure 5-27 shows the entity declaration for the counter, along with an outline of the structural architecture body. This example illustrates a number of important points about component instances and port maps. First, the two component instances val0_reg and val1_reg are both instances of the same entity/architecture pair. This means that two distinct copies of the architecture **struct** of **reg4** are created, one for each of the component instances. We return to this point when we discuss the topic of elaboration in the next section. Second, in each of the port maps, ports of the entity being instantiated are associated with separate elements of array signals. This is allowed, since a signal that is of a composite type, such as an array, can be treated as a collection of signals, one per element. Third, some of the signals connected to the component instances are signals declared within the enclosing architecture body, **registered**, whereas the **clk** signal is a port of the entity **reg4**. This again illustrates the point that within an architecture body, the ports of the corresponding entity are treated as signals.

FIGURE 5-26

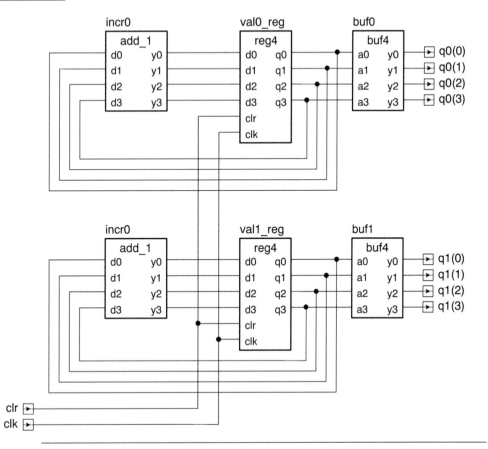

A schematic for a two-digit counter using the reg4 *entity.*

FIGURE 5-27

```
entity counter is
    port ( clk, clr : in bit;  q0, q1 : out digit );
end entity counter;

------------------------------------------------------

architecture registered of counter is
    signal current_val0, current_val1, next_val0, next_val1 : digit;
begin
    val0_reg : entity work.reg4(struct)
        port map ( d0 => next_val0(0), d1 => next_val0(1),
                   d2 => next_val0(2), d3 => next_val0(3),
                   q0 => current_val0(0), q1 => current_val0(1),
                   q2 => current_val0(2), q3 => current_val0(3),
                   clk => clk, clr => clr );
```

(continued on page 140)

(continued from page 139)

```
            val1_reg : entity work.reg4(struct)
                port map ( d0 => next_val1(0), d1 => next_val1(1),
                           d2 => next_val1(2), d3 => next_val1(3),
                           q0 => current_val1(0), q1 => current_val1(1),
                           q2 => current_val1(2), q3 => current_val1(3),
                           clk => clk, clr => clr );
        incr0 : entity work.add_1(boolean_eqn) . . .;

        incr1 : entity work.add_1(boolean_eqn) . . .;

        buf0 : entity work.buf4(basic) . . .;

        buf1 : entity work.buf4(basic) . . .;

    end architecture registered;
```

An entity declaration of a two-digit decimal counter, with an outline of an architecture body using the
reg4 entity.

We saw in the above example that we can associate separate ports of an instance with individual elements of an actual signal of a composite type, such as an array or record type. If an instance has a composite port, we can write associations the other way around, that is, we can associate separate actual signals with individual elements of the port. This is sometimes called *subelement association*. For example, if the instance DMA_buffer has a port **status** of type FIFO_status, declared as

```
type FIFO_status is record
        nearly_full, nearly_empty, full, empty : bit;
    end record FIFO_status;
```

we could associate a signal with each element of the port as follows:

```
DMA_buffer : entity work.FIFO
        port map ( . . ., status.nearly_full => start_flush,
                         status.nearly_empty => end_flush,
                         status.full => DMA_buffer_full,
                         status.empty => DMA_buffer_empty, . . . );
```

This illustrates two important points about subelement association. First, all elements of the composite port must be associated with an actual signal. We cannot associate some elements and leave the rest unassociated. Second, all of the associations for a particular port must be grouped together in the association list, without any associations for other ports among them.

We can use subelement association for ports of an array type by writing an indexed element name on the left side of an association. Furthermore, we can associate a slice of the port with an actual signal that is a one-dimensional array, as the following example shows.

EXAMPLE
___

Suppose we have a register entity, declared as shown at the top of Figure 5-28. The ports d and q are arrays of bits. The architecture body for a microprocessor, outlined at the bottom of Figure 5-28, instantiates this entity as the program status register (PSR). Individual bits within the register represent condition and interrupt flags, and the field from bit 6 down to bit 4 represents the current interrupt priority level.

FIGURE 5-28
___

```
entity reg is
    port ( d : in bit_vector(7 downto 0);
            q : out bit_vector(7 downto 0);
            clk : in bit );
end entity reg;

_____

architecture RTL of microprocessor is
    signal interrupt_req : bit;
    signal interrupt_level : bit_vector(2 downto 0);
    signal carry_flag, negative_flag, overflow_flag, zero_flag : bit;
    signal program_status : bit_vector(7 downto 0);
    signal clk_PSR : bit;
    . . .
begin
    PSR : entity work.reg
        port map ( d(7) => interrupt_req,
                    d(6 downto 4) => interrupt_level,
                    d(3) => carry_flag,    d(2) => negative_flag,
                    d(1) => overflow_flag, d(0) => zero_flag,
                    q => program_status,
                    clk => clk_PSR );

    . . .
end architecture RTL;
```

An entity declaration for a register with array type ports, and an outline of an architecture body that instantiates the entity. The port map includes subelement associations with individual elements and a slice of the d port.

In the port map of the instance, subelement association is used for the input port d to connect individual elements of the port with separate actual signals of the architecture. A slice of the port is connected to the interrupt_level signal. The output port q, on the other hand, is associated in whole with the bit-vector signal program_status.

___

We may also use subelement association for a port that is of an unconstrained array type. The index bounds of the port are determined by the least and greatest index values used in the association list, and the index range direction is determined by the port type. For example, suppose we declare an and gate entity:

```
entity and_gate is
    port ( i : in bit_vector;  y : out bit );
end entity and_gate;
```

and a number of signals:

```
signal serial_select, write_en, bus_clk, serial_wr : bit;
```

We can instantiate the entity as a three-input and gate:

```
serial_write_gate : entity work.and_gate
    port map ( i(1) => serial_select,
               i(2) => write_en,
               i(3) => bus_clk,
               y => serial_wr );
```

Since the input port i is unconstrained, the index values in the subelement associations determine the index bounds for this instance. The least value is one and the greatest value is three. The port type is bit_vector, which has an ascending index range. Thus, the index range for the port in the instance is an ascending range from one to three.

The syntax rule for a port association list shows that a port of a component instance may be associated with an expression instead of a signal. In this case, the value of the expression is used as a constant value for the port throughout the simulation. If real hardware is synthesized from the model, the port of the component instance would be tied to a fixed value determined by the expression. Association with an expression is useful when we have an entity provided as part of a library, but we do not need to use all of the functionality provided by the entity. When associating a port with an expression, the value of the expression must be *globally static*, that is, we must be able to determine the value from constants defined when the model is elaborated. So, for example, the expression must not include references to any signals.

EXAMPLE

Given a four-input multiplexer described by the entity declaration

```
entity mux4 is
    port ( i0, i1, i2, i3, sel0, sel1 : in bit;
           z : out bit );
end entity mux4;
```

we can use it as a two-input multiplexer by instantiating it as follows:

```
a_mux : entity work.mux4
    port map ( sel0 => select_line, i0 => line0, i1 => line1,
               z => result_line,
               sel1 => '0', i2 => '1', i3 => '1' );
```

For this component instance, the high-order select bit is fixed at '0', ensuring that only one of line0 or line1 is passed to the output. We have also followed the practice, recommended for many logic families, of tying unused inputs to a fixed value, in this case '1'.

Some entities may be designed to allow inputs to be left open by specifying a default value for a port. When the entity is instantiated, we can specify that a port is to be left open by using the keyword **open** in the port association list, as shown in the syntax rule on page 137.

EXAMPLE

The and_or_inv entity declaration on page 105 includes a default value of '1' for each of its input ports, as again shown here:

```
entity and_or_inv is
    port ( a1, a2, b1, b2 : in bit := '1';
           y : out bit );
end entity and_or_inv;
```

We can write a component instantiation to perform the function **not ((A and** B) **or** C) using this entity as follows:

```
f_cell : entity work.and_or_inv
    port map ( a1 => A, a2 => B, b1 => C, b2 => open, y => F );
```

The port **b2** is left open, so it assumes the default value '1' specified in the entity declaration.

There is some similarity between specifying a default value for an input port and associating an input port with an expression. In both cases the expression must be globally static (that is, we must be able to determine its value when the model is elaborated). The difference is that a default value is only used if the port is left open when the entity is instantiated, whereas association with an expression specifies that the expression value is to be used to drive the port for the entire simulation or life of the component instance. If a port is declared with a default value and then associated with an expression, the expression value is used, overriding the default value.

Output and bidirectional ports may also be left unassociated using the **open** keyword, provided they are not of an unconstrained array type. If a port of mode **out** is left open, any value driven by the entity is ignored. If a port of mode **inout** is left open, the value used internally by the entity (the *effective value*) is the value that it drives on to the port.

A final point to make about unassociated ports is that we can simply omit a port from a port association list to specify that it remain open. So, given an entity declared as follows:

```
entity and3 is
    port ( a, b, c : in bit := '1';
           z, not_z : out bit );
end entity and3;
```

the component instantiation

>   g1 : **entity** work.and3 **port map** (a => s1, b => s2, not_z => ctrl1);

has the same meaning as

>   g1 : **entity** work.and3 **port map** (a => s1, b => s2, not_z => ctrl1,
>   c => **open**, z => **open**);

The difference is that the second version makes it clear that the unused ports are deliberately left open, rather than being accidentally overlooked in the design process. This is useful information for someone reading the model.

VHDL-87

VHDL-87 does not allow direct instantiation. Instead, we must declare a *component* with a similar interface to the entity, instantiate the component and *bind* each component instance to the entity and an associated architecture body. Component declarations and binding are described in Chapter 13.

VHDL-87 does not allow association of an expression with a port in a port map. However, we can achieve a similar effect by declaring a signal, initializing it to the value of the expression and associating the signal with the port. For example, if we declare two signals

>   **signal** tied_0 : bit := '0';
>   **signal** tied_1 : bit := '1';

we can rewrite the port map shown on page 142 as

>   **port map** (sel0 => select_line, i0 => line0, i1 => line1,
>   z => result_line,
>   sel1 => tied_0, i2 => tied_1, i3 => tied_1);

5.5   Design Processing

Now that we have seen how a design may be described in terms of entities, architectures, component instantiations, signals and processes, it is time to take a practical view. A VHDL description of a design is usually used to simulate the design and perhaps to synthesize the hardware. This involves processing the description using computer-based tools to create a simulation program to run or a hardware net-list to build. Both simulation and synthesis require two preparatory steps: analysis and elaboration. Simulation then involves executing the elaborated model, whereas synthesis involves creating a net-list of primitive circuit elements that perform the same function as the elaborated model. In this section, we look at the analysis, elaboration and execution operations introduced in Chapter 1. We will leave a discussion of synthesis to Appendix A.

Analysis

The first step in processing a design is to analyze the VHDL descriptions. A correct description must conform to the rules of syntax and semantics that we have discussed at length. An *analyzer* is a tool that verifies this. If a description fails to meet a rule, the analyzer provides a message indicating the location of the problem and which rule was broken. We can then correct the error and retry the analysis. Another task performed by the analyzer in most VHDL systems is to translate the description into an internal form more easily processed by the remaining tools. Whether such a translation is done or not, the analyzer places each successfully analyzed description into a *design library*.

A complete VHDL description usually consists of a number of entity declarations and their corresponding architecture bodies. Each of these is called a *design unit*. Organizing a design as a hierarchy of modules, rather than as one large flat design, is good engineering practice. It makes the description much easier to understand and manage.

The analyzer analyzes each design unit separately and places the internal form into the library as a *library unit*. If a unit being analyzed uses another unit, the analyzer extracts information about the other unit from the library, to check that the unit is used correctly. For example, if an architecture body instantiates an entity, the analyzer needs to check the number, type and mode of ports of the entity to make sure it is instantiated correctly. To do this, it requires that the entity be previously analyzed and stored in the library. Thus, we see that there are dependency relations between library units in a complete description that enforce an order of analysis of the original design units.

To clarify this point, we divide design units into *primary units*, which include entity declarations, and *secondary units*, which include architecture bodies. There are other kinds of design units in each class, which we come to in later chapters. A primary unit defines the external view or interface to a module, whereas a secondary unit describes an implementation of the module. Thus the secondary unit depends on the corresponding primary unit and must be analyzed after the primary unit has been analyzed. In addition, a library unit may draw upon the facilities defined in some other primary unit, as in the case of an architecture body instantiating some other entity. In this case, there is a further dependency between the secondary unit and the referenced primary unit. Thus we may build up a network of dependencies of units upon primary units. Analysis must be done in such an order that a unit is analyzed before any of its dependents. Furthermore, whenever we change and reanalyze a primary unit, all of the dependent units must also be reanalyzed. Note, however, that there is no way in which any unit can be dependent upon a secondary unit; that is what makes a secondary unit secondary. This may seem rather complicated, and indeed, in a large design, the dependency relations can form a complex network. For this reason, most VHDL systems include tools to manage the dependencies, automatically reanalyzing units where necessary to ensure that an outdated unit is never used.

EXAMPLE
_____

The structural architecture of the **counter** module, described on page 140, leads to the network of dependencies shown in Figure 5-29. One possible order of compilation for this set of design units is

entity edge_triggered_Dff
architecture behav of edge_triggered_Dff

FIGURE 5-29

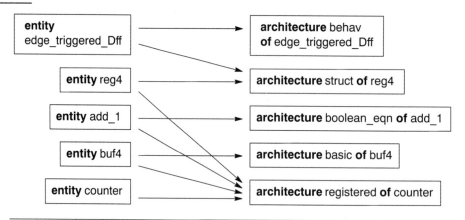

The dependency network for the counter *module. The arrows point from a primary unit to a dependent secondary unit.*

entity reg4
architecture struct of reg4

entity add_1
architecture boolean_eqn of add_1

entity buf4
architecture basic of buf

entity counter
architecture registered of counter

In this order, each primary unit is analyzed immediately before its corresponding secondary unit, and each primary unit is analyzed before any secondary unit that instantiates it. This is not the only possible order. Another alternative is to analyze all of the entity declarations first, then analyze the architecture bodies in arbitrary order.

Design Libraries, Library Clauses and Use Clauses

So far, we have not actually said what a design library is, other than that it is where library units are stored. Indeed, this is all that is defined by the VHDL language specification, since to go further is to enter into the domain of the host operating system under which the VHDL tools are run. Some systems may use a database to store analyzed units, whereas others may simply use a directory in the host file system as the design library. The documentation for each VHDL tool suite indicates what we need to know about how the suite deals with design libraries.

A VHDL tool suite must also provide some means of using a number of separate design libraries. When a design is analyzed, we nominate one of the libraries as the *working library*, and the analyzed design is stored in this library. We use the special library name **work** in our VHDL models to refer to the current working library. We have seen examples of this in this chapter's component instantiation statements, in which a previously analyzed entity is instantiated in an architecture body.

If we need to access library units stored in other libraries, we refer to the libraries as *resource libraries*. We do this by including a *library clause* immediately preceding a design unit that accesses the resource libraries. The syntax rule for a library clause is

library_clause $\Leftarrow$ **library** identifier $\{$, ... $\}$;

The identifiers are used by the analyzer and the host operating system to locate the design libraries, so that the units contained in them can be used in the description being analyzed. The exact way that the identifiers are used varies between different tool suites and is not defined by the VHDL language specification. Note that we do not need to include the library name **work** in a library clause; the current working library is automatically available.

EXAMPLE

Suppose we are working on part of a large design project code-named Wasp, and we are using standard cell parts supplied by Widget Designs, Inc. Our system administrator has loaded the design library for the Widget cells in a directory called /local/widget/cells in our workstation file system, and our project leader has set up another design library in /projects/wasp/lib for some in-house cells we need to use. We consult the manual for our VHDL analyzer and use operating system commands to set up the appropriate mapping from the identifiers **widget_cells** and **wasp_lib** to these library directories. We can then instantiate entities from these libraries, along with entities we have previously analyzed, into our own working library, as shown in Figure 5-30.

FIGURE 5-30

```
library widget_cells, wasp_lib;
architecture cell_based of filter is
    -- declaration of signals, etc
    . . .
begin
    clk_pad : entity wasp_lib.in_pad
        port map ( i => clk, z => filter_clk );
    accum : entity widget_cells.reg32
        port map ( en => accum_en, clk => filter_clk, d => sum,
                   q => result );
    alu : entity work.adder
        port map ( a => alu_op1, b => alu_op2, y => sum, c => carry );
    -- other component instantiations
    . . .
end architecture cell_based;
```

An outline of a library unit referring to entities from the resource libraries widget_cells *and* wasp_lib.

If we need to make frequent reference to library units from a design library, we can include a *use clause* in our model to avoid having to write the library name each time. The simplified syntax rules are

use_clause ⇐ **use** selected_name { , ... } ;

selected_name ⇐ name . (identifier ‖ **all**)

If we include a use clause with a library name as the prefix of the selected name (preceding the dot), and a library unit name from the library as the suffix (after the dot), the library unit is made *directly visible*. This means that subsequent references in the model to the library unit need not prefix the library unit name with the library name. For example, we might precede the architecture body in the previous example with the following library and use clauses:

library widget_cells, wasp_lib;

use widget_cells.reg32;

This makes **reg32** directly visible within the architecture body, so we can omit the library name when referring to it in component instantiations; for example:

accum : **entity** reg32
    port map (en => accum_en, clk => filter_clk, d => sum,
                q => result);

If we include the keyword **all** in a use clause, all of the library units within the named library are made directly visible. For example, if we wanted to make all of the Wasp project library units directly visible, we might precede a library unit with the use clause:

use wasp_lib.**all**;

Care should be taken when using this form of use clause with several libraries at once. If two libraries contain library units with the same name, VHDL avoids ambiguity by making neither of them directly visible. The solution is either to use the full selected name to refer to the particular library unit required, or to include in use clauses only those library units really needed in a model.

Use clauses can also be included to make names from packages directly visible. We will return to this idea when we discuss packages in detail in Chapter 8.

Elaboration

Once all of the units in a design hierarchy have been analyzed, the design hierarchy can be *elaborated*. The effect of elaboration is to "flesh out" the hierarchy, producing a collection of processes interconnected by *nets*. This is done by substituting the contents of an architecture body for every instantiation of its corresponding entity. Each net in the elaborated design consists of a signal and the ports of the substituted architecture bodies to which the signal is connected. (Recall that a port of an entity is treated as a signal within a corresponding architecture body.) Let us outline how elaboration proceeds, illustrating it step by step with an example.

Elaboration is a recursive operation, started at the topmost entity in a design hierarchy. We use the **counter** example from page 140 as our topmost entity. The first step is to create the ports of the entity. Next, an architecture body corresponding to the entity is chosen. If we do not explicitly specify which architecture body to choose, the most recently analyzed architecture body is used. For this illustration, we use the architecture **registered**. This architecture body is then elaborated, first by creating any signals that it declares, then by elaborating each of the concurrent statements in its body. Figure 5-31 shows the **counter** design with the signals created.

FIGURE 5-31

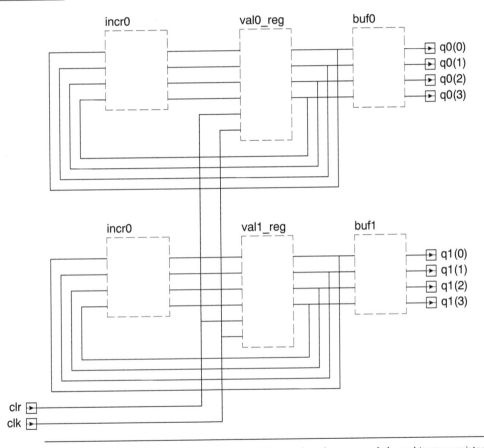

The first stage of elaboration of the counter *entity. The ports have been created, the architecture* registered *selected and the signals of the architecture created.*

The concurrent statements in this architecture are all component instantiation statements. Each of them is elaborated by creating new instances of the ports specified by the instantiated entity and joining them into the nets represented by the signals with which they are associated. Then the internal structure of the specified architecture body of the instantiated entity is copied in place of the component instance, as shown in Figure 5-32. The architectures substituted for the instances of the **add_1** and **buf4** entities are both behavioral, consisting of processes that read the input ports and make assignments to the output ports. Hence elaboration is complete for these architectures. However, the architecture **struct**, substituted for each of the instances of **reg4**, contains

FIGURE 5-32

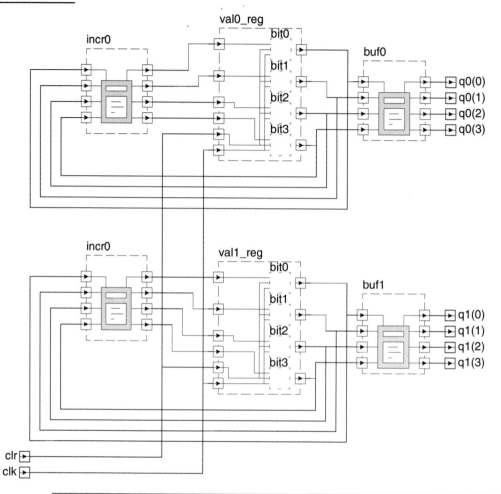

The counter design further elaborated. Behavioral architectures, consisting of just processes, have been substituted for instances of the **add_1** *and* **buf4** *entities. A structural architecture has been substituted for each instance of the* **reg4** *entity.*

further signals and component instances. Hence they are elaborated in turn, producing the structure shown in Figure 5-33 for each instance. We have now reached a stage where we have a collection of nets comprising signals and ports, and processes that sense and drive the nets.

Each process statement in the design is elaborated by creating new instances of the variables it declares and by creating a driver for each of the signals for which it has signal assignment statements. The drivers are joined to the nets containing the signals they drive. For example, the **storage** process within **bit0** of **val0_reg** has a driver for the port **q**, which is part of the net based on the signal current_val0(0).

Once all of the component instances and all of the resulting processes have been elaborated, elaboration of the design hierarchy is complete. We now have a fully

FIGURE 5-33

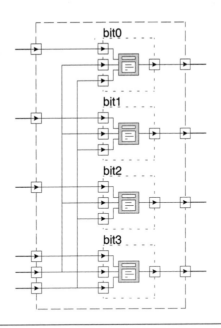

A register within the counter structure elaborated down to architectures that consist only of processes and signals.

fleshed-out version of the design, consisting of a number of process instances and a number of nets connecting them. Note that there are several distinct instances of some of the processes, one for each use of an entity containing the process, and each process instance has its own distinct version of the process variables. Each net in the elaborated design consists of a signal, a collection of ports associated with it and a driver within a process instance.

Execution

Now that we have an elaborated design hierarchy, we can execute it to simulate operation of the system it describes. Much of our previous discussion of VHDL statements was in terms of what happens when they are executed, so we do not go over statement execution again here. Instead, we concentrate on the simulation algorithm introduced in Chapter 1.

Recall that the simulation algorithm consists of an initialization phase followed by a repeated simulation cycle. The simulator keeps a clock to measure out the passage of simulation time. In the initialization phase, the simulation time is set to zero. Each driver is initialized to drive its signal with the initial value declared for the signal or the default value for the signal if no initial value was declared. Next, each of the process instances in the design is started and executes the sequential statements in its body. We usually write a model so that at least some of these initial statements schedule some transactions to get the simulation under way, then suspend by executing a wait statement. When all of the process instances have suspended, initialization is complete and the simulator can start the first simulation cycle.

At the beginning of a simulation cycle, there may be a number of drivers with transactions scheduled on them and a number of process instances that have scheduled timeouts. The first step in the simulation cycle is to advance the simulation time clock to the earliest time at which a transaction or process timeout has been scheduled. Second, all of the transactions scheduled for this time are performed, updating the corresponding signals and possibly causing events on those signals. Third, all process instances that are sensitive to any of these events are resumed. In addition, process instances whose timeout expires at the current simulation time are resumed during this step. All of these processes execute their sequential statements, possibly scheduling more transactions or timeouts, and eventually suspend again by executing wait statements. When they have all suspended, the simulation cycle is done and the next cycle can start. If there are no more transactions or timeouts scheduled, or if simulation time reaches **time'high** (the largest representable time value), the simulation is complete.

Describing the operation of a simulator in this way is a little like setting a play in a theatre without any seats—nobody is there to watch it, so what's the point! In reality, a simulator is part of a suite of VHDL tools and provides us with various means to control and monitor the progress of the simulation. Typical simulators allow us to step through the model one line at a time or to set breakpoints, causing the simulation to stop when a line of the model is executed or a signal is assigned a particular value. They usually provide commands to display the value of signals or variables. Many simulators also provide a graphical waveform display of the history of signal values similar to a logic analyzer display, and allow storage and subsequent redisplay of the history for later analysis. It is these facilities that make the simulation useful. Unfortunately, since there is a great deal of variation between the facilities provided by different simulators, it is not practical to go into any detail in this book. Simulator vendors usually provide training documentation and lab courses that explain how to use the facilities provided by their products.

Exercises

1. [❶ 5.1] Write an entity declaration for a lookup table ROM modeled at an abstract level. The ROM has an address input of type **lookup_index**, which is an integer range from 0 to 31, and a data output of type **real**. Include declarations within the declarative part of the entity to define the ROM contents, initialized to numbers of your choice.

2. [❶ 5.3] Trace the transactions applied to the signal **s** in the following process. At what times is the signal active, and at what times does an event occur on it?

```
process is
begin
    s <= 'Z', '0' after 10 ns,  '1' after 30 ns;
    wait for 50 ns;
    s <= '1' after 5 ns; 'H' after 15 ns;
    wait for 50 ns;
    s <= 'Z';
    wait;
end process;
```

3. [❶ 5.3] Given the assignments to the signal s made by the process in Exercise 2, trace the values of the signals s'delayed(5 ns), s'stable(5 ns), s'quiet(5 ns) and s'transaction. What are the values of s'last_event, s'last_active and s'last_value at time 60 ns?

4. [❶ 5.3] Write a wait statement that suspends a process until a signal s changes from '1' to '0' while an enable signal en is '1'.

5. [❶ 5.3] Write a wait statement that suspends a process until a signal ready changes to '1' or until a maximum of 5 ms has elapsed.

6. [❶ 5.3] Suppose the signal s currently has the value '0'. What is the value of the Boolean variables v1 and v2 after execution of the following statements within a process?

```
s <= '1';
v1 := s = '1';
wait on s;
v2 := s = '1';
```

7. [❶ 5.3] Trace the transactions scheduled on the driver for z by the following statements, and show the values taken on by z during simulation.

```
z <= transport '1' after 6 ns;
wait for 3 ns;
z <= transport '0' after 4 ns;
wait for 5 ns;
z <= transport '1' after 6 ns;
wait for 1 ns;
z <= transport '0' after 4 ns;
```

8. [❶ 5.3] Trace the transactions scheduled on the driver for x by the following statements, and show the values taken on by x during simulation. Assume x initially has the value zero.

```
x <= reject 5 ns inertial 1 after 7 ns, 23 after 9 ns, 5 after 10 ns,
                 23 after 12 ns, –5 after 15 ns;
wait for 6 ns;
x <= reject 5 ns inertial 23 after 7 ns;
```

9. [❶ 5.3] Write the equivalent process for the conditional signal assignment statement

```
mux_logic :
     z <= a and not b after 5 ns when enable = '1' and sel = '0' else
          x or y after 6 ns when enable = '1' and sel = '1' else
          '0' after 4 ns;
```

10. [❶ 5.3] Write the equivalent process for the selected signal assignment statement

```
with bit_vector'(s, r) select
     q <= unaffected when "00",
          '0' when "01",
          '1' when "10" | "11";
```

11. [❶ 5.3] Write a concurrent assertion statement that verifies that the time between changes of a clock signal, clk, is at least T_pw_clk.

12. [❶ 5.4] Write component instantiation statements to model the structure shown by the following schematic diagram. Assume that the entity ttl_74x74 and the corresponding architecture basic have been analyzed into the library work.

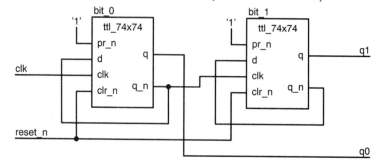

13. [❶ 5.4] Sketch a schematic diagram of the structure modeled by the following component instantiation statements.

```
decode_1 : entity work.ttl_74x138(basic)
   port map ( c => a(2), b => a(1), a => a(0),
              g1 => a(3), g2a_n => sel_n, g2b_n => '0',
              y7_n => en_n(15), y6_n => en_n(14),
              y5_n => en_n(13), y4_n => en_n(12),
              y3_n => en_n(11), y2_n => en_n(10),
              y1_n => en_n(9), y0_n => en_n(8) );

decode_0 : entity work.ttl_74x138(basic)
   port map ( c => a(2), b => a(1), a => a(0),
              g1 => '1', g2a_n => sel_n, g2b_n => a(3),
              y7_n => en_n(7), y6_n => en_n(6),
              y5_n => en_n(5), y4_n => en_n(4),
              y3_n => en_n(3), y2_n => en_n(2),
              y1_n => en_n(1), y0_n => en_n(0) );
```

14. [❶ 5.5] The example on page 145 shows one possible order of analysis of the design units in the counter of Figure 5-29. Show two other possible orders of analysis.

15. [❶ 5.5] Write a context clause that makes the resource libraries company_lib and project_lib accessible and that makes directly visible the entities in_pad and out_pad from company_lib and all entities from project_lib.

16. [❷ 5.3] Develop a behavioral model for a four-input multiplexer, with ports of type bit and a propagation delay from data or select input to data output of 4.5 ns. You should declare a constant for the propagation delay, rather than writing it as a literal in signal assignments in the model.

17. [❷ 5.3] Develop a behavioral model for a negative-edge-triggered four-bit counter with asynchronous parallel load inputs. The entity declaration is

```
entity counter is
   port ( clk_n, load_en : in std_ulogic;
          d : in std_ulogic_vector(3 downto 0);
          q : out std_ulogic_vector(3 downto 0) );
end entity counter;
```

18. [❷ 5.3] Develop a behavioral model for a D-latch with a clock-to-output propagation delay of 3 ns and a data-to-output propagation delay of 4 ns.

19. [❷ 5.3] Develop a behavioral model for an edge-triggered flipflop that includes tests to verify the following timing constraints: data setup time of 3 ns, data hold time of 2 ns and minimum clock pulse width of 5 ns.

20. [❷ 5.3] Develop a model of an adder whose interface is specified by the following entity declaration:

```
entity adder is
    port ( a, b : in integer;  s : out integer );
end entity adder;
```

For each pair of integers that arrive on the inputs, the adder produces their sum on the output. Note that successive integers on each input may have the same value, so the adder must respond to transactions rather than to events. While integers in a pair may arrive in the inputs at different times, you may assume that neither value of the following pair will arrive until both values of the first pair have arrived. The adder should produce the sum only when both input values of a pair have arrived.

21. [❷ 5.3] Develop a behavioral model for a two-input Muller-C element, with two input ports and one output, all of type **bit**. The inputs and outputs are initially '0'. When both inputs are '1', the output changes to '1'. It stays '1' until both inputs are '0', at which time it changes back to '0'. Your model should have a propagation delay for rising output transitions of 3.5 ns, and for falling output transitions of 2.5 ns.

22. [❷ 5.3] The following process statement models a producer of data:

```
producer : process is
    variable next_data : natural := 0;
begin
    data <= next_data;  next_data := next_data + 1;
    data_ready <= '1';
    wait until data_ack = '1';
    data read <= '0';
    wait until data_ack = '0';
end process producer;
```

The process uses a four-phase handshaking protocol to synchronize data transfer with a consumer process. Develop a process statement to model the consumer. It, too, should use delta delays in the handshaking protocol. Include the process statements in a test-bench architecture body, and experiment with your simulator to see how it deals with models that use delta delays.

23. [❷ 5.3] Develop a behavioral model for a multitap delay line, with the following interface:

```
entity delay_line is
    port ( input : in std_ulogic;  output : out std_ulogic_vector );
end entity delay_line;
```

Each element of the output port is a delayed version of the input. The delay to the leftmost output element is 5 ns, to the next element is 10 ns and so on. The delay to the rightmost element is 5 ns times the length of the output port. Assume the delay line acts as an ideal transmission line.

24. [❷ 5.3] Develop a functional model using conditional signal assignment statements of an address decoder for a microcomputer system. The decoder has an address input port of type **natural** and a number of active-low select outputs, each activated when the address is within a given range. The outputs and their corresponding ranges are

ROM_sel_n	16#0000# to 16#3FFF#
RAM_sel_n	16#4000# to 16#5FFF#
PIO_sel_n	16#8000# to 16#8FFF#
SIO_sel_n	16#9000# to 16#9FFF#
INT_sel_n	16#F000# to 16#FFFF#

25. [❷ 5.3] Develop a functional model of a BCD-to-seven-segment decoder for a light-emitting diode (LED) display. The decoder has a four-bit input that encodes a numeric digit between 0 and 9. There are seven outputs indexed from 'a' to 'g', corresponding to the seven segments of the LED display as shown in the margin. An output bit being '1' causes the corresponding segment to illuminate. For each input digit, the decoder activates the appropriate combination of segment outputs to form the displayed representation of the digit. For example, for the input "0010", which encodes the digit 2, the output is "1101101". Your model should use a selected signal assignment statement to describe the decoder function in truth-table form.

26. [❷ 5.3] Write an entity declaration for a four-bit counter with an asynchronous reset input. Include a process in the entity declaration that measures the duration of each reset pulse and reports the duration at the end of each pulse.

27. [❷ 5.4] Develop a structural model of an eight-bit odd-parity checker using instances of an exclusive-or gate entity. The parity checker has eight inputs, i0 to i7, and an output, p, all of type **std_ulogic**. The logic equation describing the parity checker is

$$P = ((I_0 \oplus I_1) \oplus (I_2 \oplus I_3)) \oplus ((I_4 \oplus I_5) \oplus (I_6 \oplus I_7))$$

28. [❸ 5.4] Develop a structural model of a 14-bit counter with parallel load inputs, using instances of the four-bit counter described in Exercise 17. Ensure that any unused inputs are properly connected to a constant driving value.

29. [❸ 5.3] Develop a behavioral model for a D-latch with tristate output. The entity declaration is

```
entity d_latch is
    port ( latch_en, out_en, d : in std_ulogic;  q : out std_ulogic );
end entity d_latch;
```

When latch_en is asserted, data from the d input enters the latch. When latch_en is negated, the latch maintains the stored value. When out_en is asserted, data passes through to the output. When out_en is negated, the output has the value 'Z' (high-impedance). The propagation delay from latch_en to q is 3 ns and from d to q is 4 ns. The delay from out_en asserted to q active is 2 ns and from out_en negated to q high-impedance is 5 ns.

30. [❸ 5.3] Develop a functional model of a four-bit carry-look-ahead adder. The adder has two four-bit data inputs, a(3 **downto** 0) and b(3 **downto** 0), a four-bit data output, s(3 **downto** 0), a carry input, c_in, a carry output, c_out, a carry generate output, g and a carry propagate output, p. The adder is described by the logic equations and associated propagation delays:

$$S_i = A_i \oplus B_i \oplus C_{i-1} \quad \text{(delay is 5 ns)}$$
$$G_i = A_i \, B_i \quad \text{(delay is 2 ns)}$$
$$P_i = A_i + B_i \quad \text{(delay is 3 ns)}$$
$$C_i = G_i + P_i \, C_{i-1} = G_i + P_i \, G_{i-1} + P_i \, P_{i-1} \, G_{i-2} + \ldots + P_i \, P_{i-1} \ldots P_0 \, C_{-1}$$
$$\text{(delay is 5 ns)}$$
$$G = G_3 + P_3 \, G_2 + P_3 \, P_2 \, G_1 + P_3 \, P_2 \, P_1 \, G_0 \quad \text{(delay is 5 ns)}$$
$$P = P_3 \, P_2 \, P_1 \, P_0 \quad \text{(delay is 3 ns)}$$

where the G_i are the intermediate carry generate signals, the P_i are the intermediate carry propagate signals and the C_i are the intermediate carry signals. C_{-1} is c_in and C_3 is c_out. Your model should use the expanded equation to calculate the intermediate carries, which are then used to calculate the sums.

31. [❸ 5.3] Develop a behavioral model for a four-input arbiter with the following entity interface:

```
entity arbiter is
    port ( request : in bit_vector(0 to 3);
           acknowledge : out bit_vector(0 to 3) );
end entity arbiter;
```

The arbiter should use a round-robin discipline for responding to requests. Augment the entity declaration by including a concurrent assertion statement that verifies that no more than one acknowledgement is issued at once and that an acknowledgement is only issued to a requesting client.

32. [❸ 5.3] Write an entity declaration for a 7474 positive edge-triggered JK-flipflop with asynchronous active-low preset and clear inputs, and Q and $\overline{Q}$ outputs. Include concurrent assertion statements and passive processes as necessary in the entity declaration to verify that

- the preset and clear inputs are not activated simultaneously,
- the setup time of 6 ns from the J and K inputs to the rising clock edge is observed,
- the hold time of 2 ns for the J and K inputs after the rising clock edge is observed, and
- the minimum pulse width of 5 ns on each of the clock, preset and clear inputs is observed.

Write a behavioral architecture body for the flipflop and a test bench that exercises the statements in the entity declaration.

33. [❸ 5.4] Define entity interfaces for a microprocessor, a ROM, a RAM, a parallel I/O controller, a serial I/O controller, an interrupt controller and a clock generator. Use instances of these entities and an instance of the address decoder described in Exercise 24 to develop a structural model of a microcomputer system.

34. [❸ 5.4] Develop a structural model of a 16-bit carry-look-ahead adder, using instances of the four-bit adder described in Exercise 30. You will need to develop a carry-look-ahead generator with the following interface:

    entity carry_look_ahead_generator **is**
        port (p0, p1, p2, p3, g0, g1, g2, g3 : **in** bit;
              c_in : **in** bit; c1, c2, c3 : **out** bit);
    end entity carry_look_ahead_generator

    The carry-look-ahead generator is connected to the four-bit adders as follows:

    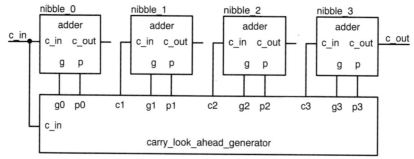

    It calculates the carry output signals using the generate, propagate and carry inputs in the same way that the four-bit counters calculate their internal carry signals.

35. [❹ 5.3] Develop a behavioral model for a household burglar alarm. The alarm has inputs for eight sensors, each of which is normally '0'. When an intruder is detected, one of the sensors changes to '1'. There is an additional input from a key-switch and an output to a siren. When the key-switch input is '0', the alarm is disabled and the siren output is '0'. When the key-switch input changes to '1', there is a 30 s delay before the alarm is enabled. Once enabled, detection of an intruder starts another 30 s delay, after which time the siren output is set to '1'. If the key-switch input changes back to '0', the alarm is immediately disabled.

36. [❹ 5.3] In his book *Structured Computer Organization*, Tanenbaum describes the use of a Hamming code for error detection and correction of 16-bit data ([12], pages 44–48). Develop behavioral models for a Hamming code generator and for an error detector and corrector. Devise a test bench that allows you to introduce single-bit errors into the encoded data, to verify that the error corrector works properly.

37. [❹ 5.3] Develop a behavioral model of a 4K × 8-bit serial-input/output RAM. The device has a chip-enable input ce, a serial clock clk, a data input d_in and a data output d_out. When ce is '1', the data input is sampled on 23 successive rising clock edges to form the 23 bits of a command string. A string of the form

    "1 A_{11} A_{10} ... A_0 0 1 D_7 D_6 ... D_0"

    is a write command, in which the bits A_i are the address and the bits D_j are the data to be written. A string of the form

    "1 A_{11} A_{10} ... A_0 1 1 $X X X X X X X X$"

    is a read command, in which the bits denoted by X are ignored. The RAM produces the successive bits of read data synchronously with the last eight rising clock edges of the command.

38. [❹ 5.3/5.4] Develop a model of a device to count the number of cars in a parking lot. The lot has a gate through which only one car at a time may enter or leave. There are two pairs, labeled A and B, each comprising a LED and a photodetector, mounted on the gate as shown in the following diagram:

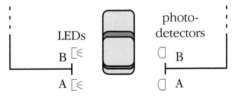

Each detector produces a '1' output when a car obscures the corresponding LED. When a car enters the yard, the front of the car obscures LED A, then LED B. When the car has advanced sufficiently, LED A becomes visible again, followed by LED B. The process is reversed for a car leaving the lot. Note that a car may partially enter or leave the lot and then reverse.

Your model should include a clocked finite-state machine (FSM) with two inputs, one from each detector, and increment and decrement outputs that pulse to '1' for one clock cycle when a car has totally entered or left the lot. The FSM outputs should drive a three-digit chain of BCD up/down counters, whose outputs are connected to seven-segment decoders.

Case Study: A Pipelined Multiplier Accumulator

Now that we have covered the basic modeling facilities provided by VHDL, we work through our first case study, the design of a pipelined multiplier accumulator (MAC) for a stream of complex numbers. Many digital signal processing algorithms, such as digital demodulation, filtering and equalization, make use of MACs. We use this design exercise to bring together concepts and techniques introduced in previous chapters.

6.1 Algorithm Outline

A complex MAC operates on two sequences of complex numbers, $\{x_i\}$ and $\{y_i\}$. The MAC multiplies corresponding elements of the sequences and accumulates the sum of the products. The result is

$$\sum_{i=1}^{N} x_i\, y_i$$

where N is the length of the sequences. Each complex number is represented in Cartesian form, consisting of a real and an imaginary part. If we are given two complex numbers x and y, their product is a complex number p, calculated as follows:

$$p\_real = x\_real \times y\_real - x\_imag \times y\_imag$$

$$p\_imag = x\_real \times y\_imag + x\_imag \times y\_real$$

The sum of x and y is a complex number s calculated as follows:

$$s\_real = x\_real + y\_real$$

$$s\_imag = x\_imag + y\_imag$$

Our MAC calculates its result by taking successive pairs of complex numbers, one each from the two input sequences, forming their complex product and adding it to an accumulator register. The accumulator is initially cleared to zero and is reset after each pair of sequences has been processed.

If we count the operations required for each pair of input numbers, we see that the MAC must perform four multiplications to form partial products, then a subtraction and an addition to form the full product and finally two additions to accumulate the result. This is shown diagrammatically at the top of Figure 6-1. Since the operations must be performed in this order, the time taken to complete processing one pair of inputs is the sum of the delays for the three steps. In a high-performance digital signal processing application, this delay may cause the bandwidth of the system to be reduced below a required minimum.

We can avoid the delay by *pipelining* the MAC, that is, organizing it like an assembly line, as shown at the bottom of Figure 6-1. The first pair of input numbers is stored in the input register on the first clock edge. During the first clock cycle, the multipliers calculate the partial products, while the system prepares the next pair of inputs. On the second clock edge, the partial products are stored in the first pipeline register, and the next pair of inputs is entered into the input register. During the second clock cycle, the subtracter and adder produce the full product for the first input pair, the multipliers produce the partial products for the second input pair and the system prepares the third input pair. On the third clock edge, these are stored, respectively, in the second pipeline register, the first pipeline register and the input register. Then in the third clock cycle, the adders accumulate the product of the first pair with the previous sum, and the preceding stages operate on the second and third pairs, while the system prepares the fourth pair. The sum in the accumulator is updated on the fourth clock edge. Thus, three clock cycles after the first pair of numbers was entered into the input latch, the sum including this pair is available at the output of the MAC. Thereafter, successive

FIGURE 6-1

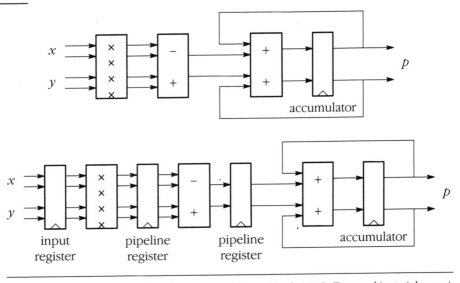

Dataflow diagrams showing order of operations performed by the MAC. Top: combinatorial organization. Bottom: pipelined organization.

sums are available each clock cycle. The advantage of this approach is that the clock period can be reduced to the slowest of the pipeline stages, rather than the total of their delays.

One detail we have yet to consider is initializing and restarting the pipeline. We need to do this to accumulate sums of products of a number of input sequences, one after another. The simplest approach is to include a "clear" input to the accumulator register that forces its content to zero on the next clock edge. For each pair of sequences to be multiplied and accumulated, we start entering numbers into the input registers on successive clock edges. Then, two clock cycles after we have entered the first pair of numbers, we assert the clear input. This causes the accumulator to reset at the same time as the product of the first pair of numbers reaches the second pipeline register. On the following cycle, this product will be added to the zero value forced into the accumulator. After the last pair in the input sequences has been entered, we must wait three clock cycles until the final sum appears at the output of the MAC. We must separate successive input sequences by at least one idle cycle and reset the accumulator between summations.

The final issue in this outline of the MAC algorithm is the representation of the data. We use a 16-bit, two's-complement, fixed-point binary representation. Each of the real and imaginary parts of the two complex inputs and the complex output of the MAC uses the format shown in Figure 6-2. Bit 15 is the sign bit, and the binary point is assumed to be between bits 15 and 14. Using this format, we can represent numbers in the range −1 (inclusive) to +1 (exclusive), with a resolution of 2^{-15}. This raises the possibility of overflow occurring while summing a sequence of numbers, so we include an overflow status signal in our design. Overflow can occur in two cases. First, intermediate partial sums may fall outside of the range −1 to +1. We can reduce the likelihood of this happening by expanding the range used to represent intermediate

FIGURE 6-2

bit index	15	14	13	12	11	10	9	8	7	6	5	4	3	2	1	0
bit weight	-2^0	2^{-1}	2^{-2}	2^{-3}	2^{-4}	2^{-5}	2^{-6}	2^{-7}	2^{-8}	2^{-9}	2^{-10}	2^{-11}	2^{-12}	2^{-13}	2^{-14}	2^{-15}

The format of a 16-bit, two's-complement, fixed-point binary number.

results to –16 to +16. However, if an intermediate sum falls outside of the expanded range, the summation for the entire sequence is in error, so the overflow signal must be set. It remains set until the accumulator is cleared, indicating the end of the summation.

The second overflow case occurs if the final sum falls outside the range of values representable by the MAC output. This may be a transient condition, since a subsequent product, when added to the sum, may bring the sum back in range. We assert the overflow signal only during a cycle in which the final sum is out of range, rather than latching the overflow until the end of summation.

MAC Entity Declaration

Now that we have described the requirements and the algorithm to be performed by the MAC, we can specify its interface. This is defined by the entity declaration shown in Figure 6-3. The clk port is used to synchronize operation of the MAC. All data transfers into registers in the pipeline are done on the rising edge (from '0' to '1') of this signal. The clr port causes the accumulator registers to be cleared to zero and the overflow condition to be reset. The ports x_real, x_imag, y_real and y_imag are the real and imaginary parts of the two input data sequences. These input ports, as well as the clr port, are sampled synchronously on the rising edge of the clk signal. The ports s_real and s_imag are the real and imaginary parts of the accumulated sum, and the ovf port is the overflow flag, set as described above. These output ports become valid after each rising edge of the clk signal.

FIGURE 6-3

```
library ieee;  use ieee.std_logic_1164.all;
entity mac is
    port ( clk, clr : in std_ulogic;
           x_real : in std_ulogic_vector(15 downto 0);
           x_imag : in std_ulogic_vector(15 downto 0);
           y_real : in std_ulogic_vector(15 downto 0);
           y_imag : in std_ulogic_vector(15 downto 0);
           s_real : out std_ulogic_vector(15 downto 0);
           s_imag : out std_ulogic_vector(15 downto 0);
           ovf : out std_ulogic );
end entity mac;
```

An entity declaration for the MAC.

6.2 A Behavioral Model

Our first implementation of the MAC is a behavioral model. This model allows us to focus on the algorithm without being distracted by other details at this early stage of the design. When we have the behavioral model working, we will be able to use it to generate test data for more detailed implementations. Our behavioral model is expressed as an architecture body, containing a single process that implements the MAC algorithm described in Section 6.1.

Note that the algorithm as described involves performing arithmetic on binary vectors representing fixed-point numbers. We can avoid this by converting the input data to VHDL's predefined floating-point type **real**, performing the calculations using the predefined arithmetic operators, then converting the results back to binary vectors. Note that this approach may lead to slightly different results from the ultimate implementation using binary fixed-point representation, due to the difference in precision between the two representations. We should bear this in mind when comparing the output of the behavioral model with the models we develop later, and ignore any small discrepancies. We convert between the two representations in our behavioral model using two entities, since we have learned in previous chapters how to declare and instantiate entities. (In Chapter 7 we will see how we can use function subprograms to do the conversions.)

The entity and architecture body for the converter from fixed-point binary representation to floating-point representation are shown in Figure 6-4. The process in the architecture body is sensitive to the input vector. Whenever the vector changes value, the process first converts it from the **std_ulogic_vector** type to a bit vector in the variable **temp**, using the conversion function **to_bitvector** defined in the IEEE standard-logic package. The process then treats the bit vector as a signed binary number and converts it to an integer in the variable **int_result**. The leftmost bit in the number is the sign bit and has a weight of -2^{15}. The remaining bits have positive weights from 2^{14} down to 2^0. The process computes the final result by converting the integer to the predefined **real** type and scaling it into the range -1 to $+1$. This final value is assigned to the output port **r**, with delta delay.

FIGURE 6-4

```
library ieee;  use ieee.std_logic_1164.all;

entity to_fp is
    port ( vec : in std_ulogic_vector(15 downto 0);
           r : out real );
end entity to_fp;

– – – – – – – – – – – – – – – – – – – – – – – – – – – – – – – – – – – – – – – –

architecture behavioral of to_fp is
begin

    behavior : process (vec) is

        variable temp : bit_vector(vec'range);
        variable negative : boolean;
        variable int_result : integer;
```

(continued on page 166)

(continued from page 165)

```
      begin
          temp := to_bitvector(vec);
          negative := temp(temp'left) = '1';
          if negative then
              temp := not temp;
          end if;
          int_result := 0;
          for index in vec'range loop    -- sign bit of temp = '0'
              int_result := int_result * 2 + bit'pos(temp(index));
          end loop;
          if negative then
              int_result := (−int_result) − 1;
          end if;
          -- convert to floating point and scale to [−1, +1)
          r <= real(int_result) / real(2**15);
      end process behavior;
  end architecture behavioral;
```

An entity and architecture body for the converter from fixed-point to floating-point representation.

The entity and architecture body for the converter from floating-point to fixed-point representation are shown in Figure 6-5. The process in the architecture body is sensitive to changes in the floating-point input port. The number is assumed to lie in the range −1.0 (inclusive) to +1.0 (exclusive). If it is outside of this range, the entity will not convert the number correctly, since it cannot be represented in the fixed-point format used. When the number changes, the new value is scaled to an integer in the range -2^{15} to $+2^{15}-1$ in the variable **temp**. This is then converted into signed binary form in the standard-logic vector **result** and then assigned to the output with delta delay. Note the way in which bit values are derived from the integer value in **temp**. In each iteration of the for loop, the expression "**temp rem 2**" returns an integer, 0 or 1, representing the least-significant bit of **temp**. Since 0 is the position number of the bit value '0' and 1 is the position number of the bit value '1', we can use the **bit'val** attribute to convert the integer to a value of type **bit**. We then convert that bit value to a standard-logic value using the conversion function **to_X01**. Lastly, we divide **temp** by two to move the next most-significant bit to the least-significant bit position, in preparation for the next iteration of the loop.

FIGURE 6-5

```
      library ieee;  use ieee.std_logic_1164.all;

      entity to_vector is
          port ( r : in real;
                  vec : out std_ulogic_vector(15 downto 0) );
      end entity to_vector;
```

```
architecture behavioral of to_vector is
begin
    behavior : process (r) is
        variable temp : integer range –2**15 to 2**15 – 1;
        variable negative : boolean;
        variable result : std_ulogic_vector(vec'range);
    begin
        -- scale to [-2**15, +2**15) and convert to integer
        if r * real(2**15) < real(–2**15) then
            temp := –2**15;
        elsif r * real(2**15) >= real(2**15 – 1) then
            temp := 2**15 – 1;
        else
            temp := integer(r * real(2**15));
        end if;
        negative := temp < 0;
        if negative then
            temp := –(temp + 1);
        end if;
        result := (others => '0');
        for index in result'reverse_range loop
            result(index) := to_X01(bit'val(temp rem 2));
            temp := temp / 2;
            exit when temp = 0;
        end loop;
        if negative then
            result := not result;
            result(result'left) := '1';
        end if;
        vec <= result;
    end process behavior;
end architecture behavioral;
```

An entity and architecture body for the converter from floating-point to fixed-point representation.

The behavioral architecture body for the MAC is shown in Figure 6-6. The constant Tpd_clk_out represents the propagation delay from a rising clock edge to a change on the data and overflow output ports. The signals declared in the architecture are the floating-point representations of the data input and output ports. The inputs are converted to floating point using instances of the to_fp entity. The results calculated by the model on fp_s_real and fp_s_imag are converted back to fixed point using instances of to_vector.

The process **behavior** implements the MAC algorithm. The variables of type **real** declared in the process represent the pipeline registers described in Section 6.1. The two Boolean variables represent the overflow conditions arising from the accumulators. The process is sensitive to the **clk** signal and performs a new calculation on each rising edge. It works from the output end of the pipeline back towards the input end to avoid overwriting intermediate results from the previous clock cycle before they have been used in the current cycle.

FIGURE 6-6

```
architecture behavioral of mac is
    constant Tpd_clk_out : time := 3 ns;
    signal fp_x_real, fp_x_imag,
           fp_y_real, fp_y_imag,
           fp_s_real, fp_s_imag : real := 0.0;
begin
    x_real_converter : entity work.to_fp(behavioral)
        port map ( x_real, fp_x_real );
    x_imag_converter : entity work.to_fp(behavioral)
        port map ( x_imag, fp_x_imag );
    y_real_converter : entity work.to_fp(behavioral)
        port map ( y_real, fp_y_real );
    y_imag_converter : entity work.to_fp(behavioral)
        port map ( y_imag, fp_y_imag );
    behavior : process (clk) is
        variable input_x_real, input_x_imag, input_y_real, input_y_imag : real := 0.0;
        variable real_part_product_1, real_part_product_2,
                 imag_part_product_1, imag_part_product_2 : real := 0.0;
        variable real_product, imag_product : real := 0.0;
        variable real_sum, imag_sum : real := 0.0;
        variable real_accumulator_ovf, imag_accumulator_ovf : boolean := false;

        type boolean_to_stdulogic_table is array (boolean) of std_ulogic;
        constant boolean_to_stdulogic : boolean_to_stdulogic_table
                    := (false => '0', true => '1');
    begin
        if rising_edge(clk) then
            -- work from the end of the pipeline back to the start, so as
            -- not to overwrite previous results in pipeline registers before
            -- they are used

            -- update accumulator and generate outputs
            if To_X01 (clr) = '1' then
                real_sum := 0.0;
                real_accumulator_ovf := false;
                imag_sum := 0.0;
                imag_accumulator_ovf := false;
            else
                real_sum := real_product + real_sum;
                real_accumulator_ovf := real_accumulator_ovf
                                    or real_sum < -16.0
                                    or real_sum >= +16.0;
                imag_sum := imag_product + imag_sum;
                imag_accumulator_ovf := imag_accumulator_ovf
                                    or imag_sum < -16.0
                                    or imag_sum >= +16.0;
            end if;
```

```
                    fp_s_real <= real_sum after Tpd_clk_out;
                    fp_s_imag <= imag_sum after Tpd_clk_out;
                    ovf <= boolean_to_stdulogic(
                                    real_accumulator_ovf or imag_accumulator_ovf
                                    or real_sum < –1.0 or real_sum >= +1.0
                                    or imag_sum < –1.0 or imag_sum >= +1.0 )
                                after Tpd_clk_out;
                    –– update product registers using partial products
                    real_product := real_part_product_1 – real_part_product_2;
                    imag_product := imag_part_product_1 + imag_part_product_2;

                    –– update partial product registers using latched inputs
                    real_part_product_1 := input_x_real * input_y_real;
                    real_part_product_2 := input_x_imag * input_y_imag;
                    imag_part_product_1 := input_x_real * input_y_imag;
                    imag_part_product_2 := input_x_imag * input_y_real;

                    –– update input registers using MAC inputs
                    input_x_real := fp_x_real;
                    input_x_imag := fp_x_imag;
                    input_y_real := fp_y_real;
                    input_y_imag := fp_y_imag;
                end if;
            end process behavior;

        s_real_converter : entity work.to_vector(behavioral)
            port map ( fp_s_real, s_real );

        s_imag_converter : entity work.to_vector(behavioral)
            port map ( fp_s_imag, s_imag );

    end architecture behavioral;
```

A behavioral architecture body for the MAC.

The process first calculates the new sum and overflow status. If the clr input is '1', both the accumulator and overflow variables are reset. Otherwise the process accumulates a new complex sum, based on the previous complex sum and the contents of the product registers, and stores it in the accumulator register variables. It also determines whether the results are within the range –16.0 to +16.0 and sets the overflow register variables accordingly. The output data signals are assigned the new contents of the accumulators, and the overflow signal is set if either of the overflow register variables is set, or if either of the data outputs falls outside the range –1.0 to +1.0. Next, the process updates the product register variables, using the previously calculated partial products. It then updates the partial products using the previously stored input values and finally stores the new input data values in the input register variables.

Testing the Behavioral Model

We can test the behavioral model of the MAC by instantiating it in a test-bench model that generates stimulus values on signals connected to the MAC inputs. The entity declaration and architecture body for the test bench are shown in Figure 6-7. The entity has no ports, since it is completely self-contained. The architecture body contains sig-

FIGURE 6-7

```vhdl
entity mac_test is
end entity mac_test;

-------------------------------------------------------------

library ieee;  use ieee.std_logic_1164.all;
architecture bench_behavioral of mac_test is
    signal clk, clr, ovf : std_ulogic := '0';
    signal x_real, x_imag,
           y_real, y_imag,
           s_real, s_imag : std_ulogic_vector(15 downto 0);
    type complex is record
            re, im : real;
        end record;
    signal x, y, s : complex := (0.0, 0.0);
    constant Tpw_clk : time := 50 ns;
begin
    x_real_converter : entity work.to_vector(behavioral) port map (x.re, x_real);
    x_imag_converter : entity work.to_vector(behavioral) port map (x.im, x_imag);
    y_real_converter : entity work.to_vector(behavioral) port map (y.re, y_real);
    y_imag_converter : entity work.to_vector(behavioral) port map (y.im, y_imag);
    dut : entity work.mac(behavioral)
        port map ( clk, clr,
                    x_real, x_imag, y_real, y_imag, s_real, s_imag,
                    ovf );
    s_real_converter : entity work.to_fp(behavioral) port map (s_real, s.re);
    s_imag_converter : entity work.to_fp(behavioral) port map (s_imag, s.im);
    clock_gen : process is
    begin
        clk <= '1' after Tpw_clk, '0' after 2 * Tpw_clk;
        wait for 2 * Tpw_clk;
    end process clock_gen;
    stimulus : process is
    begin
        -- first sequence
                                          clr <= '1';  wait until clk = '0';
        x <= (+0.5, +0.5);  y <= (+0.5, +0.5);  clr <= '1';  wait until clk = '0';
        x <= (+0.2, +0.2);  y <= (+0.2, +0.2);  clr <= '1';  wait until clk = '0';
        x <= (+0.1, -0.1);  y <= (+0.1, +0.1);  clr <= '1';  wait until clk = '0';
        x <= (+0.1, -0.1);  y <= (+0.1, +0.1);  clr <= '0';  wait until clk = '0';
        -- should be (0.4, 0.58) when it falls out the other end
                                          clr <= '0';  wait until clk = '0';
        x <= (+0.5, +0.5);  y <= (+0.5, +0.5);  clr <= '0';  wait until clk = '0';
        x <= (+0.5, +0.5);  y <= (+0.1, +0.1);  clr <= '0';  wait until clk = '0';
        x <= (+0.5, +0.5);  y <= (+0.5, +0.5);  clr <= '1';  wait until clk = '0';
        x <= (-0.5, +0.5);  y <= (-0.5, +0.5);  clr <= '0';  wait until clk = '0';
                                          clr <= '0';  wait until clk = '0';
```

```
                                                         clr <= '0';  wait until clk = '0';
                                                         clr <= '0';  wait until clk = '0';
                                                         clr <= '1';  wait until clk = '0';

            wait;
          end process stimulus;
      end architecture bench_behavioral;
```

A test bench for the behavioral model of the MAC.

nals that are connected to the input and output ports of the MAC "device under test." In order to simplify the task of writing complex values in the test bench, we use a record type to represent complex numbers. The type **complex** contains two elements of type **real**, representing the two parts of a complex number. The signals **x**, **y** and **s** in the test bench are used for the inputs and outputs of the MAC. Instances of the **to_vector** and **to_fp** entities are used to convert between the floating-point parts of the complex numbers and the binary-vector representations used by the MAC. The constant **Tpw_clk** is used to determine the pulse width for the high and low phases of the clock signal, generated by the process **clock_gen**.

Stimulus values for the MAC are provided by the process labeled **stimulus**. During the first four clock cycles, the process keeps the **clr** input active. This clears the accumulator registers while the MAC pipeline starts operation. The stimulus process sets up new complex number data each clock cycle. These enter the pipeline in sequence, and, after a delay due to the pipeline latency, the accumulated sums start appearing on the outputs. Figure 6-8 shows the timing of calculations performed on this first sequence. The final result we should expect is the complex number (0.04, 0.58). The result shown in Figure 6-8 is slightly different, due to the reduced precision of the 16-bit fixed-point number representation.

After the result from the first sequence has progressed through to the MAC output, the stimulus process clears the accumulator to prepare it to start accumulating results for the second sequence. This sequence is designed to test the overflow output of the MAC. The sum of the first three pairs produces a number that lies outside of the range −1.0 to +1.0, so we would expect the **ovf** output to be '1' when that sum reaches the output. However, addition of the product of the next pair brings the accumulated sum back into range, so we would expect **ovf** to revert to '0'. This behavior is shown in Figure 6-9, which continues the timing shown in Figure 6-8.

The stimulus values, or *test vectors,* used to test the MAC model in this example are synthetically generated by the model designer. While such vectors are useful for small-scale testing, they do not provide high test coverage. There may be errors in the model that are not revealed by the small number of vectors. As the famous computer scientist Nicklaus Wirth commented, "Testing can reveal the presence of bugs, not their absence." We can gain more confidence in the model by providing significantly larger sets of test vectors. One approach is to use a pseudo-random number generator to generate long streams of test vectors. (We will show an example of a random number generator in Chapter 19.) Another approach is to create files of test vectors. A test bench can read such files to stimulate the model under test. We will discuss the use of files in VHDL in Chapter 18.

FIGURE 6-8

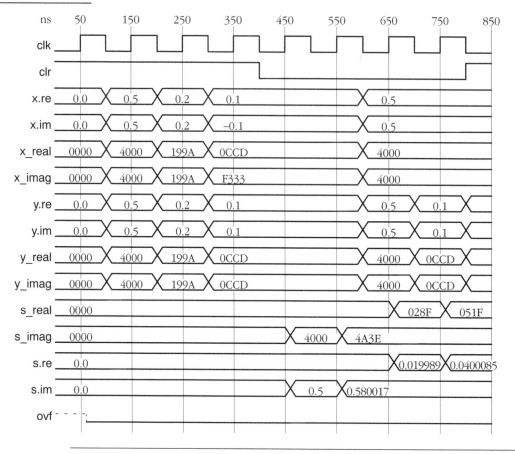

The timing of MAC operation on the first sequence in the test bench.

6.3   A Register-Transfer-Level Model

We now turn to a register-transfer-level implementation of the MAC, based on the pipe-line diagram shown in Figure 6-1. A more detailed diagram of the MAC at the register-transfer level is shown in Figure 6-10. The real and imaginary parts of the two complex inputs are stored in the first set of pipeline registers. The multipliers use the stored values to produce the four partial products. Since the input values are 16-bit fixed-point numbers between −1.0 inclusive and +1.0 exclusive, the partial products are 32-bit fixed-point numbers between −1.0 and +1.0 inclusive, represented as shown in Figure 6-11. The partial products are stored in the second set of pipeline registers. The subtracter and adder use these values to produce the full 33-bit products in the range −2.0 to +2.0 inclusive. However, only 20 bits of the products are stored in the next set of pipeline registers. The least-significant 13 bits are truncated. This still leaves two extra bits beyond the final precision required for the MAC outputs, in order to re-duce the effect of rounding errors during accumulation of the sums. The accumulator

FIGURE 6-9

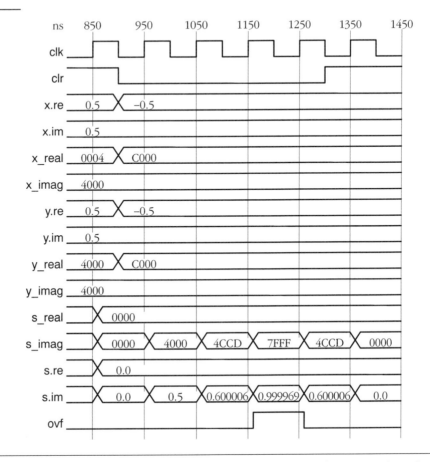

Continued timing of MAC operation on the second sequence in the test bench.

adders use an extended range, −16.0 inclusive to +16.0 exclusive, so the pipelined products must be sign-extended by two bits before being added into the previously accumulated sums. The adders also produce overflow status outputs, which are used to set flipflops that record the overflow condition for a sequence of inputs. Finally, the accumulated sums are reduced to 16 bits at the MAC output. The least-significant two bits are truncated and bits 17 to 20 are discarded. The overflow logic must check that these discarded bits are all the same as the sign bit; otherwise the result is outside the range −1.0 to +1.0, and overflow has occurred.

Modules in the Register-Transfer-Level Model

We now look at models for each of the modules used in the register-transfer-level MAC design. First, Figure 6-12 shows a description of the pipeline register module. The register has a clock input port, **clk**, and stores a copy of the input data on each rising edge of the clock. Note that the data input and output ports are of the unconstrained array type **std_ulogic_vector**. This allows us to use the same module for registers of dif-

FIGURE 6-10

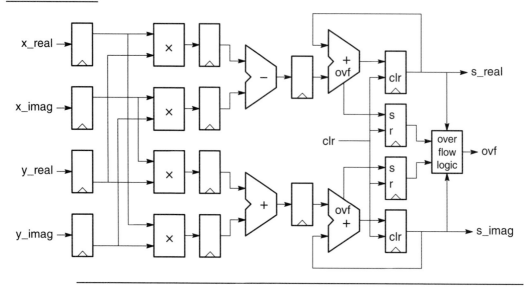

The register-transfer-level organization of the MAC.

FIGURE 6-11

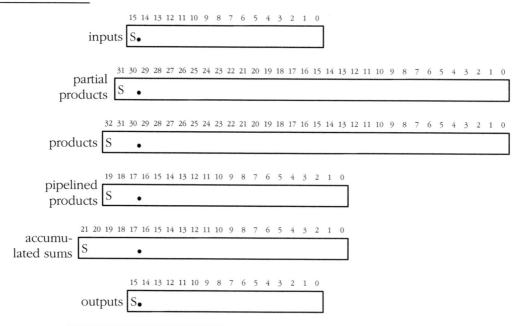

The format of fixed-point intermediate results within the MAC, showing the positions of the sign bits (S) and the binary points.

FIGURE 6-12

```
library ieee;  use ieee.std_logic_1164.all;

entity reg is
    port ( clk : in std_ulogic;
              d : in std_ulogic_vector;
              q : out std_ulogic_vector );
end entity reg;
```

```
architecture behavioral of reg is
begin

    behavior : process (clk) is
    begin
        if rising_edge(clk) then
            q <= d;
        end if;
    end process behavior;

end architecture behavioral;
```

An entity and architecture body for a pipeline register.

ferent widths. The actual width of each register is determined by the width of the actual input and output signals connected to the register. The behavioral architecture body for the register module contains a single process that is sensitive to changes on the **clk** port. The process uses the **rising_edge** operation provided by the IEEE standard-logic package to test whether the change is from a '0' state to a '1' state. If so, the process updates its output using the input data.

The next module to look at is the multiplier, shown in Figure 6-13. The behavioral architecture body contains a process that is sensitive to the two inputs, **a** and **b**. Whenever either of these inputs changes, the process computes their product using a long multiplication algorithm based on the usual "paper and pencil" method used for decimal arithmetic. The multiplication is performed on the absolute values of the operands, so the process first sets the variable **negative_result** for use later in adjusting the sign of the result. If one of the inputs is negative and the other positive, the result is negative. If both inputs are negative or both positive, the result is positive. The process then tests whether each number is negative (indicated by the sign bit being '1'), and if so, negates it by complementing and adding one. Next, the multiplication of the values is performed. The result is initialized to zero. For each bit in the multiplier (**op2**), if the bit is '1', the multiplicand is added into the result. The addition is performed with a slice of the result, at an offset that depends on the position of the multiplier bit. Finally, the result is negated if required by complementing and adding one, and is assigned to the output.

FIGURE 6-13

```vhdl
library ieee;  use ieee.std_logic_1164.all;
entity multiplier is
    port ( a, b : in std_ulogic_vector(15 downto 0);
           p : out std_ulogic_vector(31 downto 0) );
end entity multiplier;

-------------------------------------------------------

architecture behavioral of multiplier is
begin
    behavior : process (a, b) is
        constant Tpd_in_out : time := 40 ns;
        variable negative_result  : boolean;
        variable op1 : std_ulogic_vector(15 downto 0);
        variable op2 : std_ulogic_vector(15 downto 0);
        variable result : std_ulogic_vector(31 downto 0);
        variable carry_in, carry : std_ulogic;
    begin
        op1 := to_X01(a);
        op2 := to_X01(b);
        -- make both operands positive, remembering sign of result
        negative_result := (op1(15) = '1') xor (op2(15) = '1');
        if (op1(15) = '1') then
            carry := '1';
            for index in 0 to 15 loop
                carry_in := carry;
                carry := carry_in and not op1(index);
                op1(index) := not op1(index) xor carry_in;
            end loop;
        end if;
        if (op2(15) = '1') then
            carry := '1';
            for index in 0 to 15 loop
                carry_in := carry;
                carry := carry_in and not op2(index);
                op2(index) := not op2(index) xor carry_in;
            end loop;
        end if;
        -- do long multiplication
        result := (others => '0');
        for count in 0 to 15 loop
            carry := '0';
            if (op2(count) = '1') then
                for index in 0 to 15 loop
                    carry_in := carry;
                    carry := (result(index+count) and op1(index))
                            or (carry_in and (result(index+count) xor op1(index)));
                    result(index+count) := result(index+count) xor op1(index)
                                                                xor carry_in;
                end loop;
```

```
                result(count+16) := carry;
            end if;
        end loop;
        -- result now contains unsigned product, with binary point
        -- between bits 30 and 29.  assign output with sign adjusted.
        if negative_result then
            carry := '1';
            for index in 0 to 31 loop
                carry_in := carry;
                carry := carry_in and not result(index);
                result(index) := not result(index) xor carry_in;
            end loop;
        end if;
        p <= result after Tpd_in_out;
    end process behavior;

end architecture behavioral;
```

An entity and architecture body for the multiplier module.

The next part of the MAC pipeline is the stage that adds and subtracts the pipelined partial products. We can implement the adder and the subtracter with a single module that can be set to perform either operation, since the two operations are very closely related. Figure 6-14 shows the entity declaration and architecture body for the adder/subtracter module. The ports a and b are the data inputs, and s is the sum or difference. The format of these data ports is shown in Figure 6-11. The mode input port determines which operation the module performs. If it is '0', the module adds a and b, whereas if it is '1', the module subtracts b from a.

FIGURE 6-14

```
library ieee;  use ieee.std_logic_1164.all;

entity product_adder_subtracter is
    port ( mode : in std_ulogic;
           a, b : in std_ulogic_vector(31 downto 0);
           s : out std_ulogic_vector(32 downto 0) );
end entity product_adder_subtracter;

----------------------------------------------------------------

architecture behavioral of product_adder_subtracter is
begin

    behavior : process (a, b) is

        constant Tpd_in_out : time := 3 ns;
        variable op2 : std_ulogic_vector(b'range);
        variable carry_in : std_ulogic;
        variable carry_out : std_ulogic;
```

(continued on page 178)

(continued from page 177)

```
begin
    carry_out := To_X01(mode);
    if To_X01(mode) = '1' then
        op2 := not b;
    else
        op2 := b;
    end if;
    for index in 0 to 31 loop
        carry_in := carry_out;  -- of previous bit
        s(index) <= a(index) xor op2(index) xor carry_in after Tpd_in_out;
        carry_out := (a(index) and op2(index))
                            or (carry_in and (a(index) xor op2(index)));
    end loop;
    s(32) <= a(31) xor op2(31) xor carry_out after Tpd_in_out;
    end process behavior;

end architecture behavioral;
```

An entity and architecture body for the adder/subtracter module.

The architecture body contains a single process, sensitive to the inputs. When any of them changes, the process calculates a new output value. If **mode** is '0', the process performs a binary addition of the two operands. The carry into the least-significant position is set to '0'. If mode is '1', the process adds the negation of the second operand. It does this by complementing the second operand and initializing the carry into the least-significant position to '1' (the value of the **mode** input). The for loop in the process performs the addition one bit at a time, for all 32 bits of the operands. The most-significant bit of the result, bit 32, is formed by repeating the addition of the most-significant bits of the operands, but using the carry out of the 32-bit addition. This achieves the same effect as sign-extending the operands to 33 bits.

The full products formed by the MAC pipeline are next added into the previously accumulated sum with another pair of adder modules. These are smaller than the product adder and subtracter but have an additional overflow output. The entity and architecture body for the accumulator adder module are shown in Figure 6-15. The process in the architecture body performs addition using the same algorithm as that used by the product adder/subtracter. Since the result vector is the same size as the input vector, the sum may not be representable in the given number of bits. This condition is detected when the carry from bit 20 to the sign bit differs from the carry produced by adding the sign bits. The **xor** operator is used to perform this inequality test to produce the value for the overflow output.

The results produced by the accumulator adders are stored in the accumulator registers. These are similar to the pipeline registers but have an additional input used to clear the register to zero. The entity and architecture body are shown in Figure 6-16. If the **clr** input is '1' on a rising edge of **clk**, the register is cleared. If clr is '0' on the rising clock edge, new data is stored.

FIGURE 6-15

```
library ieee;  use ieee.std_logic_1164.all;
entity accumulator_adder is
    port ( a, b : in std_ulogic_vector(21 downto 0);
           s : out std_ulogic_vector(21 downto 0);
           ovf : out std_ulogic );
end entity accumulator_adder;
```

```
architecture behavioral of accumulator_adder is
begin
    behavior : process (a, b) is
        constant Tpd_in_out : time := 3 ns;
        variable carry_in : std_ulogic;
        variable carry_out : std_ulogic := '0';
    begin
        for index in 0 to 21 loop
            carry_in := carry_out;  -- of previous bit
            s(index) <= a(index) xor b(index) xor carry_in after Tpd_in_out;
            carry_out := (a(index) and b(index))
                            or (carry_in and (a(index) xor b(index)));
        end loop;
        ovf <= carry_out xor carry_in after Tpd_in_out;  -- ovf is carry_out /= carry_in
    end process behavior;
end architecture behavioral;
```

An entity and architecture body for the accumulator adder module.

FIGURE 6-16

```
library ieee;  use ieee.std_logic_1164.all;
entity accumulator_reg is
    port ( clk : in std_ulogic;
           clr : in std_ulogic;
           d : in std_ulogic_vector(21 downto 0);
           q : out std_ulogic_vector(21 downto 0) );
end entity accumulator_reg;
```

```
architecture behavioral of accumulator_reg is
begin
    behavior : process (clk) is
        constant Tpd_clk_out : time := 3 ns;
    begin
        if rising_edge(clk) then
            if To_X01(clr) = '1' then
                q <= (others => '0') after Tpd_clk_out;
```

(continued on page 180)

(continued from page 179)

```
            else
                q <= d after Tpd_clk_out;
            end if;
        end if;
    end process behavior;
end architecture behavioral;
```

An entity and architecture body for the accumulator register.

The overflow flags from the accumulators are used to set a pair of flipflops, one for each of the real and imaginary parts of the sum. The set/reset flipflop module used for this purpose is described by the entity and behavioral architecture body shown in Figure 6-17. On each rising edge of the clock input, the process in the architecture body tests the clr and set inputs. If clr is '1', the flipflop output is cleared to '0'. Otherwise, if set is '1', the output is set to '1'. If neither input is '1', the flipflop state is unchanged.

FIGURE 6-17

```
library ieee;  use ieee.std_logic_1164.all;

entity synch_sr_ff is
    port ( clk : in std_ulogic;
           set, clr : in std_ulogic;
           q : out std_ulogic );
end entity synch_sr_ff;

--------------------------------------------------------

architecture behavioral of synch_sr_ff is
begin

    behavior : process (clk) is

        constant Tpd_clk_out : time := 3 ns;

    begin
        if rising_edge(clk) then
            if To_X01(clr) = '1' then
                q <= '0' after Tpd_clk_out;
            elsif To_X01(set) = '1' then
                q <= '1' after Tpd_clk_out;
            end if;
        end if;
    end process behavior;
end architecture behavioral;
```

An entity and architecture body for the set/reset flipflop module.

The final module in the MAC is the block of logic that determines the overflow output, ovf. The entity declaration and a functional architecture body for this module are shown in Figure 6-18. The inputs are the latched overflow status flags from the accumulator adders and the sign bits and significant bits to the left of the binary points in the accumulator registers. The architecture body contains a single concurrent signal assignment statement to determine the value of the output port ovf. The output is set to '1' if either of the latched status flags is '1' or if either of the accumulator register values is outside of the range −1.0 inclusive to +1.0 exclusive. The latter condition is tested by comparing the sign bit of each value (bit 21) with the pre-decimal significant bits. If any of the pre-decimal bits are different from the sign bit, the value is out of range. The inequality tests are performed using the **xor** operator defined in the IEEE standard-logic package.

FIGURE 6-18

```
library ieee;  use ieee.std_logic_1164.all;

entity overflow_logic is
    port ( real_accumulator_ovf, imag_accumulator_ovf : in std_ulogic;
           real_sum, imag_sum : std_ulogic_vector(21 downto 17);
           ovf : out std_ulogic );
end entity overflow_logic;

— — — — — — — — — — — — — — — — — — — — — — — — — — — — — — — — — —

architecture behavioral of overflow_logic is

    constant Tpd_in_out : time := 3 ns;

begin
    ovf <= real_accumulator_ovf or imag_accumulator_ovf
                or ( real_sum(21) xor real_sum(20) )
                or ( real_sum(21) xor real_sum(19) )
                or ( real_sum(21) xor real_sum(18) )
                or ( real_sum(21) xor real_sum(17) )
                or ( imag_sum(21) xor imag_sum(20) )
                or ( imag_sum(21) xor imag_sum(19) )
                or ( imag_sum(21) xor imag_sum(18) )
                or ( imag_sum(21) xor imag_sum(17) ) after Tpd_in_out;

end architecture behavioral;
```

An entity and architecture body for the overflow logic block.

The Register-Transfer-Level Architecture Body

Now that we have seen descriptions of each of the modules used in the MAC, we can assemble them into a register-transfer-level structural model based on Figure 6-10. The architecture body is shown in Figure 6-19. The signals declared in the architecture body represent the values calculated by each pipeline stage and the outputs of the pipeline registers. The first four instances of the reg entity represent the input pipeline registers connected to the real and imaginary data input ports. These are followed by instances of the multiplier entity, which are used to form the partial products according to the formulas given in Section 6.1. The partial products are then stored in the second set of pipeline registers, represented by the next four instances of the reg entity. Next, the model includes two instances of the product_adder_subtracter entity. The first of these has its mode port tied to '1', causing it to subtract its inputs to form the real part of the product. The other instance has its mode input tied to '0', causing it to add its inputs for the imaginary part. The real and imaginary parts of the product are both 32 bits; however, only the most-significant 20 bits of each are stored in the third set of pipeline registers, represented by the next two instances of the **reg** entity. Following them are the two instances of the **accumulator_adder** entity, which add the two parts of the product to the previously accumulated sums. The inputs to these adders are 22 bits, so the products must be sign-extended by two bits. This is done by connecting the sign bit of each product part in parallel to the three most-significant input bits of the adder. The outputs from the adders are stored in the accumulator registers, represented by the two instances of the **accumulator_reg** entity. These registers differ from the other pipeline registers in that they can be cleared to zero by activating their **clr** inputs, which are connected to the **clr** input of the MAC. The overflow status signals from the accumulators are latched in the two instances of the **synch_sr_ff** entity. The status signals are used to set the flipflops, and the **clr** input to the MAC is used to reset them. The outputs of the accumulator registers, reduced in size to 16 bits each, are used to drive the real and imaginary data outputs of the MAC. The latched accumulator overflow status signals and the five most-significant bits of each data output are connected to the instance of the **overflow_logic** entity, which determines the value of the MAC **ovf** port.

FIGURE 6-19

```
architecture rtl of mac is
    signal pipelined_x_real,
           pipelined_x_imag,
           pipelined_y_real,
           pipelined_y_imag : std_ulogic_vector(15 downto 0);
    signal real_part_product_1,
           real_part_product_2,
           imag_part_product_1,
           imag_part_product_2 : std_ulogic_vector(31 downto 0);
    signal pipelined_real_part_product_1,
           pipelined_real_part_product_2,
           pipelined_imag_part_product_1,
           pipelined_imag_part_product_2 : std_ulogic_vector(31 downto 0);
    signal real_product,
           imag_product : std_ulogic_vector(32 downto 0);
    signal pipelined_real_product,
           pipelined_imag_product : std_ulogic_vector(19 downto 0);
    signal real_sum,
           imag_sum : std_ulogic_vector(21 downto 0);
    signal real_accumulator_ovf,
           imag_accumulator_ovf : std_ulogic;
    signal pipelined_real_sum,
           pipelined_imag_sum : std_ulogic_vector(21 downto 0);
    signal pipelined_real_accumulator_ovf,
           pipelined_imag_accumulator_ovf : std_ulogic;
begin
```

```
x_real_input_reg : entity work.reg(behavioral)
    port map ( clk => clk, d => x_real, q => pipelined_x_real );
x_imag_input_reg : entity work.reg(behavioral)
    port map ( clk => clk, d => x_imag, q => pipelined_x_imag );
y_real_input_reg : entity work.reg(behavioral)
    port map ( clk => clk, d => y_real, q => pipelined_y_real );
y_imag_input_reg : entity work.reg(behavioral)
    port map ( clk => clk, d => y_imag, q => pipelined_y_imag );
real_mult_1 : entity work.multiplier(behavioral)
    port map ( a => pipelined_x_real, b => pipelined_y_real,
               p => real_part_product_1 );
real_mult_2 : entity work.multiplier(behavioral)
    port map ( a => pipelined_x_imag, b => pipelined_y_imag,
               p => real_part_product_2 );
imag_mult_1 : entity work.multiplier(behavioral)
    port map ( a => pipelined_x_real, b => pipelined_y_imag,
               p => imag_part_product_1 );
imag_mult_2 : entity work.multiplier(behavioral)
    port map ( a => pipelined_x_imag, b => pipelined_y_real,
               p => imag_part_product_2 );
real_part_product_reg_1 : entity work.reg(behavioral)
    port map ( clk => clk, d => real_part_product_1,
               q => pipelined_real_part_product_1 );
real_part_product_reg_2 : entity work.reg(behavioral)
    port map ( clk => clk, d => real_part_product_2,
               q => pipelined_real_part_product_2 );
imag_part_product_reg_1 : entity work.reg(behavioral)
    port map ( clk => clk, d => imag_part_product_1,
               q => pipelined_imag_part_product_1 );
imag_part_product_reg_2 : entity work.reg(behavioral)
    port map ( clk => clk, d => imag_part_product_2,
               q => pipelined_imag_part_product_2 );
real_product_subtracter : entity work.product_adder_subtracter(behavioral)
    port map ( mode => '1',
               a => pipelined_real_part_product_1,
               b => pipelined_real_part_product_2,
               s => real_product );
imag_product_adder : entity work.product_adder_subtracter(behavioral)
    port map ( mode => '0',
               a => pipelined_imag_part_product_1,
               b => pipelined_imag_part_product_2,
               s => imag_product );
real_product_reg : entity work.reg(behavioral)
    port map ( clk => clk,
               d => real_product(32 downto 13),
               q => pipelined_real_product );
```

(continued on page 184)

(continued from page 183)

```
            imag_product_reg : entity work.reg(behavioral)
                port map ( clk => clk,
                            d => imag_product(32 downto 13),
                            q => pipelined_imag_product );
            real_accumulator : entity work.accumulator_adder(behavioral)
                port map ( a(19 downto 0) => pipelined_real_product(19 downto 0),
                            a(20) => pipelined_real_product(19),
                            a(21) => pipelined_real_product(19),
                            b => pipelined_real_sum,
                            s => real_sum,
                            ovf => real_accumulator_ovf );
            imag_accumulator : entity work.accumulator_adder(behavioral)
                port map ( a(19 downto 0) => pipelined_imag_product(19 downto 0),
                            a(20) => pipelined_imag_product(19),
                            a(21) => pipelined_imag_product(19),
                            b => pipelined_imag_sum,
                            s => imag_sum,
                            ovf => imag_accumulator_ovf );
            real_accumulator_reg : entity work.accumulator_reg(behavioral)
                port map ( clk => clk, clr => clr,
                            d => real_sum,  q => pipelined_real_sum );
            imag_accumulator_reg : entity work.accumulator_reg(behavioral)
                port map ( clk => clk, clr => clr,
                            d => imag_sum,  q => pipelined_imag_sum );
            real_accumulator_ovf_reg : entity work.synch_sr_ff(behavioral)
                port map ( clk => clk,
                            set => real_accumulator_ovf, clr => clr,
                            q => pipelined_real_accumulator_ovf );
            imag_accumulator_ovf_reg : entity work.synch_sr_ff(behavioral)
                port map ( clk => clk,
                            set => imag_accumulator_ovf, clr => clr,
                            q => pipelined_imag_accumulator_ovf );
            s_real <= pipelined_real_sum(21) & pipelined_real_sum(16 downto 2);
            s_imag <= pipelined_imag_sum(21) & pipelined_imag_sum(16 downto 2);
            result_overflow_logic : entity work.overflow_logic(behavioral)
                port map ( real_accumulator_ovf => pipelined_real_accumulator_ovf,
                            imag_accumulator_ovf => pipelined_imag_accumulator_ovf,
                            real_sum => pipelined_real_sum(21 downto 17),
                            imag_sum => pipelined_imag_sum(21 downto 17),
                            ovf => ovf );
    end architecture rtl;
```

A register-transfer-level structural architecture body for the MAC.

Testing the Register-Transfer-Level Model

We could test the register-transfer-level model of the MAC using the same test bench that we used for the behavioral model. This would simply involve replacing the component instance dut, as follows:

```
dut : entity work.mac(rtl)
        port map (clk, clr, x_real, x_imag, y_real, y_imag, s_real, s_imag, ovf );
```

We could then simulate the test bench and manually compare the results with those produced by the behavioral model. However, a better approach is to modify the test bench to include instances of each of the behavioral and register-transfer-level models, as shown in Figure 6-20. The revised test bench stimulates the two instances with the same input data and automatically compares the results they produce. The clock generator and stimulus processes are the same as those in the previous test bench. The additional process, verifier, is resumed midway through each clock cycle, after the outputs from each of the MAC devices has had time to stabilize. The process first verifies that the two devices produce the same overflow status outputs. Then, if both device outputs have not overflowed, the process compares the complex outputs of the two devices, to verify that they are within a single bit of being equal. Note that since we are comparing real numbers, we must compare the values in this way. Since the behavioral model calculates its result using the predefined floating-point type real, and the MAC calculates its result using fixed-point numbers with less precision than real, we should expect the actual results to differ slightly. This difference comes about due to the different round-off errors introduced by the different methods of calculation. If we were to use the equality operator ("=") to compare the results, the test would certainly fail.

FIGURE 6-20

```
library ieee;  use ieee.std_logic_1164.all;
architecture bench_verify of mac_test is
    signal clk, clr, behavioral_ovf, rtl_ovf : std_ulogic := '0';
    signal x_real, x_imag,
            y_real, y_imag,
            behavioral_s_real, behavioral_s_imag,
            rtl_s_real, rtl_s_imag : std_ulogic_vector(15 downto 0);
    type complex is record
            re, im : real;
        end record;
    signal x, y, behavioral_s, rtl_s : complex := (0.0, 0.0);
    constant Tpw_clk : time := 50 ns;
begin
    x_real_converter : entity work.to_vector(behavioral) port map (x.re, x_real);
    x_imag_converter : entity work.to_vector(behavioral) port map (x.im, x_imag);
    y_real_converter : entity work.to_vector(behavioral) port map (y.re, y_real);
    y_imag_converter : entity work.to_vector(behavioral) port map (y.im, y_imag);
```

(continued on page 186)

(continued from page 185)

```
        dut_behavioral : entity work.mac(behavioral)
            port map ( clk, clr,
                        x_real, x_imag, y_real, y_imag,
                        behavioral_s_real, behavioral_s_imag, behavioral_ovf );
        dut_rtl : entity work.mac(rtl)
            port map ( clk, clr,
                        x_real, x_imag, y_real, y_imag,
                        rtl_s_real, rtl_s_imag, rtl_ovf );
        behavioral_s_real_converter :
            entity work.to_fp(behavioral) port map (behavioral_s_real, behavioral_s.re);
        behavioral_s_imag_converter :
            entity work.to_fp(behavioral) port map (behavioral_s_imag, behavioral_s.im);
        rtl_s_real_converter :
            entity work.to_fp(behavioral) port map (rtl_s_real, rtl_s.re);
        rtl_s_imag_converter :
            entity work.to_fp(behavioral) port map (rtl_s_imag, rtl_s.im);
        clock_gen : process is
        begin
            . . .         -- as in previous test bench
        end process clock_gen;
        stimulus : process is
        begin
            . . .         -- as in previous test bench
        end process stimulus;
        verifier : process
            constant epsilon : real := 4.0E-5;  -- 1-bit error in 15-bit mantissa
        begin
            wait until clk = '0';
            assert behavioral_ovf = rtl_ovf
                report "Overflow flags differ" severity error;
            if behavioral_ovf = '0' and rtl_ovf = '0' then
                assert abs (behavioral_s.re - rtl_s.re) < epsilon
                    report "Real sums differ" severity error;
                assert abs (behavioral_s.im - rtl_s.im) < epsilon
                    report "Imag sums differ" severity error;
            end if;
        end process verifier;
end architecture bench_verify;
```

A test bench that compares outputs of the behavioral and register-transfer-level implementations of the MAC.

Exercises

1. [❶ 6.2] In the behavioral model of the pipelined MAC, results for each stage are computed starting with the last stage and working forward. Show why it would be incorrect to work from the first stage to the last stage.

2. [❶ 6.2] Devise a sequence of input values for the MAC that cause the sum in the accumulator to overflow.

3. [❶ 6.2] Trace the values of the variables in the process **behavior** in the behavioral MAC model during each clock cycle for the first sequence generated by the test bench of Figure 6-7.

4. [❶ 6.3] For each of the fixed-point formats shown in Figure 6-11, show how the values +0.5 and −0.5 are represented.

5. [❸ 6.1/6.2] Develop a behavioral model of a non-pipelined MAC, based on the data-flow diagram at the top of Figure 6-1. Adapt the test bench of Figure 6-7 to test your model.

6. [❹] A polynomial function of degree n is

$$p(x) = a_0 + a_1x + a_2x^2 + \cdots + a_nx^n$$

where x is the input variable. We can rewrite the polynomial as

$$p(x) = a_0 + x \, (a_1 + x \, (a_2 + x \, (... \, (a_{n-1} + x \, a_n)...)))$$

We can evaluate a polynomial in the order implied by this form using n pipeline stages. The first stage evaluates $a_{n-1} + x \, a_n$ and passes the result and the value of x to the second stage. The second stage multiplies the previous result by x, adds a_{n-2} and passes this result and x to the third stage. The remaining stages continue in like manner.

Develop a behavioral model of a pipelined polynomial evaluator that evaluates polynomials of degree 3. The entity interface is

```
entity polynomial is
    port ( clk, mode, clr : in bit;
           coeff_addr : in bit_vector(1 downto 0);
           x : in bit_vector(15 downto 0);
           p : out bit_vector(15 downto 0);
           ovf : out bit );
end entity polynomial;
```

The **mode** input is used to load coefficient values into internal registers. When **mode** is '1', the value on the **x** input is loaded into the register selected by the **coeff_addr** inputs. When **x** is '0', the **x** input is used as the next data value for which the polynomial is to be calculated. The **clr** input is used to clear the internal pipeline registers. The **x** input and the **p** output both encode fixed-point values, with the binary point implied between bits 11 and 10. Thus, values in the range −16.0 inclusive to +16.0 exclusive can be represented. The same range is used in the internal pipeline registers. If a calculation in any stage overflows, an overflow flag is propagated through the remainder of the pipeline and presented at the **ovf** output.

Test your model by using it to evaluate the following polynomial functions:

$$e^x \approx 1 + x + \frac{x^2}{2} + \frac{x^3}{6}$$

$$\cos x \approx 1 - \frac{x^2}{2}$$

Refine your model to the register-transfer level, defining entities for the required multipliers, adders, registers and logic blocks.

7. [❹] Develop a behavioral model for a two-stage pipelined floating-point multiplier. The two operands and the result are in IEEE single-precision format. The first stage of the pipeline multiplies the mantissas, subtracts the biases from the exponents and adds the unbiased exponents. The second stage normalizes the result and adds the bias to the result exponent. Write a test bench to test your model, comparing its results with those calculated using VHDL's predefined floating-point multiplication operation. Next, refine your pipelined multiplier to the register-transfer level, defining entities for the required multipliers, adders, registers and logic blocks. Do not worry about infinities, NaNs, denormals or rounding according to the IEEE standard. You may wish to add provisions for these aspects of IEEE floating-point arithmetic as an extension to the exercise.

Subprograms

When we write complex behavioral models it is useful to divide the code into sections, each dealing with a relatively self-contained part of the behavior. VHDL provides a *subprogram* facility to let us do this. In this chapter, we look at the two kinds of subprograms: *procedures* and *functions*. The difference between the two is that a procedure encapsulates a collection of sequential statements that are executed for their effect, whereas a function encapsulates a collection of statements that compute a result. Thus a procedure is a generalization of a statement, whereas a function is a generalization of an expression.

7.1   Procedures

We start our discussion of subprograms with procedures. There are two aspects to using procedures in a model: first the procedure is declared, then elsewhere the procedure is *called*. The syntax rule for a procedure declaration is

subprogram_body ⇐
    procedure identifier ⟦ (*parameter*_interface_list) ⟧ **is**
        { subprogram_declarative_part }
    begin
        { sequential_statement }
    end ⟦ **procedure** ⟧ ⟦ identifier ⟧ ;

For now we will just look at procedures without the parameter list part; we will come back to parameters in the next section.

The *identifier* in a procedure declaration names the procedure. The name may be repeated at the end of the procedure declaration. The sequential statements in the body of a procedure implement the algorithm that the procedure is to perform and can include any of the sequential statements that we have seen in previous chapters. A procedure can declare items in its declarative part for use in the statements in the procedure body. The declarations can include types, subtypes, constants, variables and nested subprogram declarations. The items declared are not accessible outside of the procedure; we say they are *local* to the procedure.

EXAMPLE

Figure 7-1 is a declaration for a procedure that calculates an average of a collection of data values stored in an array called **samples** and assigns the result to a variable called **average**. This procedure has a local variable **total** for accumulating the sum of array elements. Unlike variables in processes, procedure local variables are created anew and initialized each time the procedure is called.

FIGURE 7-1

```
procedure average_samples is
    variable total : real := 0.0;
begin
    assert samples'length > 0 severity failure;
    for index in samples'range loop
        total := total + samples(index);
    end loop;
    average := total / real(samples'length);
end procedure average_samples;
```

A declaration for a procedure to average a number of values.

The actions of a procedure are invoked by a *procedure call* statement, which is yet another VHDL sequential statement. A procedure with no parameters is called simply by writing its name, as shown by the syntax rule

procedure_call_statement ⟸ ⟦ label : ⟧ *procedure_*name ;

The optional label allows us to identify the procedure call statement. We will discuss labeled statements in Chapter 20. As an example, we might include the following statement in a process:

average_samples;

The effect of this statement is to invoke the procedure **average_samples**. This involves creating and initializing a new instance of the local variable **total**, then executing the statements in the body of the procedure. When the last statement in the procedure is completed, we say the procedure *returns*; that is, the thread of control of statement execution returns to the process from which the procedure was called, and the next statement in the process after the call is executed.

We can write a procedure declaration in the declarative part of an architecture body or a process. We can also declare procedures within other procedures, but we will leave that until a later section. If a procedure is included in an architecture body's declarative part, it can be called from within any of the processes in the architecture body. On the other hand, declaring a procedure within a process hides it away from use by other processes.

EXAMPLE

The outline in Figure 7-2 illustrates a procedure defined within a process. The procedure **do_arith_op** encapsulates an algorithm for arithmetic operations on two values, producing a result and a flag indicating whether the result is zero. It has a variable **result**, which it uses within the sequential statements that implement the algorithm. The statements also use the signals and other objects declared in the architecture body. The process **alu** invokes **do_arith_op** with a procedure call statement. The advantage of separating the statements for arithmetic operations into a procedure in this example is that it simplifies the body of the **alu** process.

FIGURE 7-2

```
architecture rtl of control_processor is
    type func_code is (add, subtract);
    signal op1, op2, dest : integer;
    signal Z_flag : boolean;
    signal func : func_code;
    . . .
begin
```

(continued on page 192)

(continued from page 191)

```
alu : process is
    procedure do_arith_op is
        variable result : integer;
    begin
        case func is
            when add =>
                result := op1 + op2;
            when subtract =>
                result := op1 – op2;
        end case;
        dest  <=  result after Tpd;
        Z_flag  <=  result = 0 after Tpd;
    end procedure do_arith_op;
begin
    . . .
    do_arith_op;
    . . .
end process alu;

. . .

end architecture rtl;
```

An outline of an architecture body with a process containing a procedure. The procedure encapsulates part of the behavior of the process and is invoked by the procedure call statement within the process.

Another important use of procedures arises when some action needs to be performed several times at different places in a model. Instead of writing several copies of the statements to perform the action, the statements can be encapsulated in a procedure, which is then called from each place.

EXAMPLE

Figure 7-3 shows an outline of a process taken from a behavioral model of a CPU. The process fetches instructions from memory and interprets them. Since the actions required to fetch an instruction and to fetch a data word are identical, the process encapsulates them in a procedure, **read_memory**. The procedure copies the address from the memory address register to the address bus, sets the memory read signal to '1', then activates the memory request signal. When the memory responds, the procedure copies the data from the data bus signal to the memory data register and acknowledges to the memory by setting the request signal back to '0'. When the memory has completed its operation, the procedure returns.

The procedure is called in two places within the process. First, it is called to fetch an instruction. The process copies the program counter into the memory address register and calls the procedure. When the procedure returns, the process copies the data from the memory data register, placed there by the procedure, to the instruction register. The second call to the procedure takes place when a "load

FIGURE 7-3 _____

```
instruction_interpreter : process is
    variable mem_address_reg, mem_data_reg,
             prog_counter, instr_reg, accumulator, index_reg : word;
    . . .
    procedure read_memory is
    begin
        address_bus <= mem_address_reg;
        mem_read <= '1';
        mem_request <= '1';
        wait until mem_ready = '1';
        mem_data_reg := data_bus_in;
        mem_request <= '0';
        wait until mem_ready = '0';
    end procedure read_memory;
begin
    . . .        -- initialization
    loop
        -- fetch next instruction
        mem_address_reg := prog_counter;
        read_memory;                         -- call procedure
        instr_reg := mem_data_reg;
        . . .
        case opcode is
            . . .
            when load_mem =>
                mem_address_reg := index_reg + displacement;
                read_memory;                 -- call procedure
                accumulator := mem_data_reg;
            . . .
        end case;
    end loop;
end process instruction_interpreter;
```

An outline of an instruction interpreter process from a CPU model. The procedure read_memory *is called from two places.*

memory" instruction is executed. The process sets the memory address register using the values of the index register and some displacement, then calls the memory read procedure to perform the read operation. When it returns, the process copies the data to the accumulator.

Since a procedure call is a form of sequential statement and a procedure body implements an algorithm using sequential statements, there is no reason why one procedure cannot call another procedure. In this case, control is passed from the calling procedure to the called procedure to execute its statements. When the called procedure returns, the calling procedure carries on executing statements until it returns to its caller.

EXAMPLE

The process outlined in Figure 7-4 is a control sequencer for a register-transfer-level model of a CPU. It sequences the activation of control signals with a two-phase clock on signals **phase1** and **phase2**. The process contains two procedures, **control_write_back** and **control_arith_op**, that encapsulate parts of the control algorithm. The process calls **control_arith_op** when an arithmetic operation must be performed. This procedure sequences the control signals for the source and destination operand registers in the data path. It then calls **control_write_back**, which sequences the control signals for the register file in the data path, to write the value from the destination register. When this procedure is completed, it returns to the first procedure, which then returns to the process.

FIGURE 7-4

```
control_sequencer : process is
    procedure control_write_back is
    begin
        wait until phase1 = '1';
        reg_file_write_en <= '1';
        wait until phase2 = '0';
        reg_file_write_en <= '0';
    end procedure control_write_back;

    procedure control_arith_op is
    begin
        wait until phase1 = '1';
        A_reg_out_en <= '1';
        B_reg_out_en <= '1';
        wait until phase1 = '0';
        A_reg_out_en <= '0';
        B_reg_out_en <= '0';
        wait until phase2 = '1';
        C_reg_load_en <= '1';
        wait until phase2 = '0';
        C_reg_load_en <= '0';
        control_write_back;              -- call procedure
    end procedure control_arith_op;

    . . .

begin
    . . .
    control_arith_op;                    -- call procedure
    . . .
end process control_sequencer;
```

An outline of a control sequencer processor for a register-transfer-level model of a CPU. The process contains procedures that encapsulate parts of the control algorithm. The process calls these procedures, which may in turn call other procedures.

VHDL-87

The keyword **procedure** may not be included at the end of a procedure declaration in VHDL-87. Procedure call statements may not be labeled in VHDL-87.

Return Statement in a Procedure

In all of the examples above, the procedures completed execution of the statements in their bodies before returning. Sometimes it is useful to be able to return from the middle of a procedure, for example, as a way of handling an exceptional condition. We can do this using a *return* statement, described by the simplified syntax rule

return_statement ⇐ ⟦ label : ⟧ **return** ;

The optional label allows us to identify the return statement. We will discuss labeled statements in Chapter 20. The effect of the return statement, when executed in a procedure, is that the procedure is immediately terminated and control is transferred back to the caller.

EXAMPLE

Figure 7-5 is a revised version of the instruction interpreter process from Figure 7-3. The procedure to read from memory is revised to check for the reset signal becoming active during a read operation. If it does, the procedure returns immediately, aborting the operation in progress. The process then exits the fetch/ execute loop and starts the process body again, reinitializing its state and output signals.

FIGURE 7-5

```
instruction_interpreter : process is
    . . .
    procedure read_memory is
    begin
        address_bus <= mem_address_reg;
        mem_read <= '1';
        mem_request <= '1';
        wait until mem_ready = '1' or reset = '1';
        if reset = '1' then
            return;
        end if;
        mem_data_reg := data_bus_in;
        mem_request <= '0';
        wait until mem_ready = '0';
    end procedure read_memory;
```

(continued on page 196)

(continued from page 195)

```
begin
    . . .        -- initialization
    loop
        . . .
        read_memory;
        exit when reset = '1';
        . . .
    end loop;
end process instruction_interpreter;
```

A revised instruction interpreter process. The read memory procedure now checks for the reset signal becoming active.

VHDL-87

Return statements may not be labeled in VHDL-87.

7.2   Procedure Parameters

Now that we have looked at the basics of procedures, we will discuss procedures that include parameters. A *parameterized procedure* is much more general in that it can perform its algorithm using different data objects or values each time it is called. The idea is that the caller passes parameters to the procedure as part of the procedure call, and the procedure then executes its statements using the parameters.

When we write a parameterized procedure, we include information in the *parameter interface list* (or *parameter list*, for short) about the parameters to be passed to the procedure. The syntax rule for a procedure declaration on page 190 shows where the parameter list fits in. Following is the syntax rule for a parameter list:

interface_list ⇐
    (⟦ **constant** ‖ **variable** ‖ **signal** ⟧
      identifier { , ₒₒₒ } : ⟦ mode ⟧ subtype_indication
                      ⟦ := *static*_expression ⟧) { ; ₒₒₒ }

mode ⇐ **in** ‖ **out** ‖ **inout**

As we can see, it is similar to the port interface list used in declaring entities. This similarity is not coincidental, since they both specify information about objects upon which the user and the implementation must agree. In the case of a procedure, the user is the caller of the procedure, and the implementation is the body of statements within the procedure. The objects defined in the parameter list are called the *formal parameters* of the procedure. We can think of them as placeholders that stand for the *actual parameters*, which are to be supplied by the caller when it calls the procedure. Since the syntax rule for a parameter list is quite complex, let us start with some simple examples and work up from them.

EXAMPLE

First, let's rewrite the procedure **do_arith_op**, from Figure 7-2 on page 191, so that the function code is passed as a parameter. The new version is shown in Figure 7-6. In the parameter interface list we have identified one formal parameter named **op**. This name is used in the statements in the procedure to refer to the value that will be passed as an actual parameter when the procedure is called. The mode of the formal parameter is **in**, indicating that it is used to pass information into the procedure from the caller. This means that the statements in the procedure can use the value but cannot modify it. In the parameter list we have specified the type of the parameter as **func_code**. This indicates that the operations performed on the value in the statements must be appropriate for a value of this type, and that the caller may only pass a value of this type as an actual parameter.

FIGURE 7-6

```
procedure do_arith_op ( op : in func_code ) is
    variable result : integer;
begin
    case op is
        when add =>
            result := op1 + op2;
        when subtract =>
            result := op1 – op2;
    end case;
    dest  <=  result after Tpd;
    Z_flag  <=  result = 0 after Tpd;
end procedure do_arith_op;
```

A procedure to perform an arithmetic operation, parameterized by the kind of operation.

Now that we have parameterized the procedure, we can call it from different places passing different function codes each time. For example, a call at one place might be

    do_arith_op (add);

The procedure call simply includes the actual parameter value in parentheses. In this case we pass the literal value **add** as the actual parameter. At another place in the model we might pass the value of the signal **func** shown in the model on page 191:

    do_arith_op (func);

In this example, we have specified the mode of the formal parameter as **in**. Note that the syntax rule for a parameter list indicates that the mode is an optional part. If we leave it out, mode **in** is assumed, so we could have written the procedure as

    procedure do_arith_op (op : func_code) **is** . . .

While this is equally correct, it's not a bad idea to include the mode specification for **in** parameters, to make our intention explicitly clear.

The syntax rule for a parameter list also shows us that we can specify the *class* of a formal parameter, namely, whether it is a constant, a variable or a signal within the procedure. If the mode of the parameter is **in**, the class is assumed to be *constant*, since a constant is an object that cannot be updated by assignment. It is just a quirk of VHDL that we can specify both **constant** and **in**, even though to do so is redundant. Usually we simply leave out the keyword **constant**, relying on the mode to make our intentions clear. (The exceptions are parameters of access types, discussed in Chapter 17, and file types, discussed in Chapter 18.) For an **in** mode constant-class parameter, we write an expression as the actual parameter. The value of this expression must be of the type specified in the parameter list. The value is passed to the procedure for use in the statements in its body.

Let us now turn to formal parameters of mode **out**. Such a parameter lets us transfer information out from the procedure back to the caller. Here is an example, before we delve into the details.

EXAMPLE

The procedure in Figure 7-7 performs addition of two unsigned numbers represented as bit vectors of type word32, which we assume is defined elsewhere. The procedure has two **in** mode parameters **a** and **b**, allowing the caller to pass two bit-vector values. The procedure uses these values to calculate the sum and overflow flag. Within the procedure, the two **out** mode parameters, result and overflow, appear as variables. The procedure performs variable assignments to update their values, thus transferring information back to the caller.

FIGURE 7-7

```
procedure addu ( a, b : in word32;
                 result : out word32;  overflow : out boolean ) is
    variable sum : word32;
    variable carry : bit := '0';
begin
    for index in sum'reverse_range loop
        sum(index) := a(index) xor b(index) xor carry;
        carry := ( a(index) and b(index) ) or ( carry and ( a(index) xor b(index) ) );
    end loop;
    result := sum;    overflow := carry = '1';
end procedure addu;
```

A procedure to add two bit vectors representing unsigned integers.

A call to this procedure may appear as follows:

```
variable PC, next_PC : word32;
variable overflow_flag : boolean;
    . . .
```

addu (PC, X"0000_0004", next_PC, overflow_flag);

In this procedure call statement, the first two actual parameters are expressions, whose values are passed in through the formal parameters **a** and **b**. The third and fourth actual parameters are the names of variables. When the procedure returns, the values assigned by the procedure to the formal parameters result and overflow are used to update the variables next_PC and overflow_flag.

In the above example, the **out** mode parameters are of the class *variable*. Since this class is assumed for **out** parameters, we usually leave out the class specification **variable**, although it may be included if we wish to state the class explicitly. We will come back to signal-class parameters in a moment. The mode **out** indicates that the only way the procedure may use the formal parameters is to update them by variable assignment to transfer information back to the caller. It may not read the parameter values, as it can with **in** mode parameters. For an **out** mode, variable-class parameter, the caller must supply a variable as an actual parameter. Both the actual parameter and the value returned must be of the type specified in the parameter list.

The third mode we can specify for formal parameters is **inout**, which is a combination of **in** and **out** modes. It is used for objects that are to be both read and updated by a procedure. As with **out** parameters, they are assumed to be of class variable if the class is not explicitly stated. For **inout** mode variable parameters, the caller supplies a variable as an actual parameter. The value of this variable is used to initialize the formal parameter, which may then be used in the statements of the procedure. The procedure may also perform variable assignments to update the formal parameter. When the procedure returns, the value of the formal parameter is copied back to the actual parameter variable, transferring information back to the caller.

EXAMPLE

The procedure in Figure 7-8 negates a number represented as a bit vector, using the "complement and add one" method. Since **a** is an **inout** mode parameter, we can refer to its value in expressions in the procedure body. (This differs from

FIGURE 7-8

```
procedure negate ( a : inout word32 ) is
    variable carry_in : bit := '1';
    variable carry_out : bit;
begin
    a := not a;
    for index in a'reverse_range loop
        carry_out := a(index) and carry_in;
        a(index) := a(index) xor carry_in;
        carry_in := carry_out;
    end loop;
end procedure negate;
```

A procedure to negate an integer represented by a bit vector.

the parameter **result** in the **addu** procedure of the previous example.) We might include the following call to this procedure in a model:

> **variable** op1 : word32;
>
> . . .
>
> negate (op1);

This uses the value of **op1** to initialize the formal parameter **a**. The procedure body is then executed, updating **a**, and when it returns, the final value of **a** is copied back into **op1**.

Signal Parameters

The third class of object that we can specify for formal parameters is *signal*, which indicates that the algorithm performed by the procedure involves a signal passed by the caller. A signal parameter can be of any of the modes **in**, **out** or **inout**. The way that signal parameters work is somewhat different from constant and variable parameters, so it is worth spending a bit of time understanding them.

When a caller passes a signal as a parameter of mode **in**, instead of passing the value of the signal, it passes the signal object itself. Any reference to the formal parameter within the procedure is exactly like a reference to the actual signal itself. A consequence of this is that if the procedure executes a wait statement, the signal value may be different after the wait statement completes and the procedure resumes. This behavior differs from that of constant parameters of mode **in**, which have the same value for the whole of the procedure.

EXAMPLE

Suppose we wish to model the receiver part of a network interface. It receives fixed-length packets of data on the signal rx_data. The data is synchronized with changes, from '0' to '1', of the clock signal rx_clock. Figure 7-9 is an outline of part of the model.

FIGURE 7-9

```
architecture behavioral of receiver is
    . . .        -- type declarations, etc
    signal recovered_data : bit;
    signal recovered_clock : bit;
    . . .
    procedure receive_packet ( signal rx_data : in bit;
                               signal rx_clock : in bit;
                               data_buffer : out packet_array ) is
    begin
        for index in packet_index_range loop
            wait until rx_clock = '1';
            data_buffer(index) := rx_data;
        end loop;
    end procedure receive_packet;
```

```
begin
    packet_assembler : process is
        variable packet : packet_array;
    begin
        . . .
        receive_packet ( recovered_data, recovered_clock, packet );
        . . .
    end process packet_assembler;
    . . .
end architecture behavioral;
```

An outline of a model of a network receiver, including a procedure with signal parameters of mode **in***.*

During execution of the model, the process **packet_assembler** calls the procedure **receive_packet**, passing the signals **recovered_data** and **recovered_clock** as actual parameters. We can think of the procedure as executing "on behalf of" the process. When it reaches the wait statement, it is really the calling process that suspends. The wait statement mentions **rx_clock**, and since this stands for **recovered_clock**, the process is sensitive to changes on **recovered_clock** while it is suspended. Each time it resumes, it reads the current value of **rx_data** (which represents the actual signal **recovered_data**) and stores it in an element of the array parameter **data_buffer**.

Now let's look at signal parameters of mode **out**. In this case, the caller must name a signal as the actual parameter, and the procedure is passed a reference to the driver for the signal. When the procedure performs a signal assignment statement on the formal parameter, the transactions are scheduled on the driver for the actual signal parameter. In Chapter 5, we said that a process that contains a signal assignment statement contains a driver for the target signal, and that an ordinary signal may only have one driver. When such a signal is passed as an actual **out** mode parameter, there is still only the one driver. We can think of the signal assignments within the procedure as being performed on behalf of the process that calls the procedure.

EXAMPLE

Figure 7-10 is an outline of an architecture body for a signal generator. The procedure **generate_pulse_train** has **in** mode constant parameters that specify the characteristics of a pulse train and an **out** mode signal parameter on which it generates the required pulse train. The process **raw_signal_generator** calls the procedure, supplying **raw_signal** as the actual signal parameter for **s**. A reference to the driver for **raw_signal** is passed to the procedure, and transactions are generated on it.

An incidental point to note is the way we have specified the actual value for the **separation** parameter in the procedure call. This ensures that the sum of the **width** and **separation** values is exactly equal to **period**, even if **period** is not an even multiple of the time resolution limit. This illustrates an approach sometimes called

FIGURE 7-10

```
library ieee;  use ieee.std_logic_1164.all;
architecture top_level of signal_generator is
    signal raw_signal : std_ulogic;
    . . .
    procedure generate_pulse_train ( width, separation : in delay_length;
                                     number : in natural;
                                     signal s : out std_ulogic ) is
    begin
        for count in 1 to number loop
            s <= '1', '0' after width;
            wait for width + separation;
        end loop;
    end procedure generate_pulse_train;
begin
    raw_signal_generator : process is
    begin
        . . .
        generate_pulse_train ( width => period / 2,
                               separation => period – period / 2,
                               number => pulse_count,
                               s => raw_signal );
        . . .
    end process raw_signal_generator;
    . . .
end architecture top_level;
```

An outline of a model for a signal generator, including a pulse generator procedure with an **out** *mode signal parameter.*

"defensive programming," in which we try to ensure that the model works correctly in all possible circumstances.

As with variable-class parameters, we can also have a signal-class parameter of mode **inout**. When the procedure is called, both the signal and a reference to its driver are passed to the procedure. The statements within it can read the signal value, include it in sensitivity lists in wait statements, query its attributes and schedule transactions using signal assignment statements.

A final point to note about signal parameters relates to procedures declared immediately within an architecture body. The target of any signal assignment statements within such a procedure must be a signal parameter, rather than a direct reference to a signal declared in the enclosing architecture body. The reason for this restriction is that the procedure may be called by more than one process within the architecture body. Each process that performs assignments on a signal has a driver for the signal. Without the restriction, we would not be able to tell easily by looking at the model where the drivers for the signal were located. The restriction makes the model more comprehensible and hence easier to maintain.

Default Values

The one remaining part of a procedure parameter list that we have yet to discuss is the optional default value expression, shown in the syntax rule on page 196. Note that we can only specify a default value for a formal parameter of mode **in**, and the parameter must be of the class constant or variable. If we include a default value in a parameter specification, we have the option of omitting an actual value when the procedure is called. We can either use the keyword **open** in place of an actual parameter value, or, if the actual value would be at the end of the parameter list, simply leave it out. If we omit an actual value, the default value is used instead.

EXAMPLE

Figure 7-11 is a procedure that increments an unsigned integer represented as a bit vector. The amount to increment by is specified by the second parameter, which has a default value of the bit-vector representation of 1.

FIGURE 7-11

```
procedure increment ( a : inout word32;  by : in word32 := X"0000_0001" ) is
    variable sum : word32;
    variable carry : bit := '0';
begin
    for index in a'reverse_range loop
        sum(index) := a(index) xor by(index) xor carry;
        carry := ( a(index) and by(index) ) or ( carry and ( a(index) xor by(index) ) );
    end loop;
    a := sum;
end procedure increment;
```

A procedure to increment a bit vector representing an unsigned integer.

If we have a variable count declared to be of type word32, we can call the procedure to increment it by 4, as follows:

increment(count, X"0000_0004");

If we want to increment the variable by 1, we can make use of the default value for the second parameter and call the procedure without specifying an actual value to increment by, as follows:

increment(count);

This call is equivalent to

increment(count, by => **open**);

Unconstrained Array Parameters

In Chapter 4 we described unconstrained array types, in which the index range of the array was left unspecified using the "box" ("<>") notation. For such a type, we constrain the index bounds when we create an object, such as a variable or a signal. Another use of an unconstrained array type is as the type of a formal parameter to procedure. This use allows us to write a procedure in a general way, so that it can operate on array values of any size or with any range of index values. When we call the procedure and provide a constrained array as the actual parameter, the index bounds of the actual array are used as the bounds of the formal array parameter. Let us look at an example to show how unconstrained array parameters work.

EXAMPLE

Figure 7-12 is a procedure that finds the index of the first bit set to '1' in a bit vector. The formal parameter v is of type bit_vector, which is an unconstrained array type. Note that in writing this procedure, we do not explicitly refer to the index bounds of the formal parameter v, since they are not known. Instead, we use the 'range attribute.

FIGURE 7-12

```
procedure find_first_set ( v : in bit_vector;
                           found : out boolean;
                           first_set_index : out natural ) is
begin
    for index in v'range loop
        if v(index) = '1' then
            found := true;
            first_set_index := index;
            return;
        end if;
    end loop;
    found := false;
end procedure find_first_set;
```

A procedure to find the first set bit in a bit vector.

When the procedure is executed, the formal parameters stand for the actual parameters provided by the caller. So if we call this procedure as follows:

```
variable int_req : bit_vector (7 downto 0);
variable top_priority : natural;
variable int_pending : boolean;
. . .

find_first_set ( int_req, int_pending, top_priority );
```

v'range returns the range 7 **downto** 0, which is used to ensure that the loop parameter index iterates over the correct index values for v. If we make a different call:

```
variable free_block_map : bit_vector(0 to block_count−1);
variable first_free_block : natural;
variable free_block_found : boolean;
    . . .
find_first_set ( free_block_map, free_block_found, first_free_block );
```

v'range returns the index range of the array **free_block_map**, since that is the actual parameter corresponding to **v**.

When we have formal parameters that are of array types, either constrained or unconstrained, we can use any of the array attributes mentioned in Chapter 4 to refer to the index bounds and range of the actual parameters. We can use the attribute values to define new local constants or variables whose index bounds and ranges depend on those of the parameters. The local objects are created anew each time the procedure is called.

EXAMPLE

The procedure in Figure 7-13 has two bit-vector parameters, which it assumes represent signed integer values in two's-complement form. It performs an arithmetic comparison of the numbers. It operates by taking temporary copies of each of the bit-vector parameters, inverting the sign bits and performing a lexical comparison using the built-in "<" operator. This is equivalent to an arithmetic comparison of the original numbers. Note that the temporary variables are declared to be of the same size as the parameters by using the 'range attribute, and the sign bits (the leftmost bits) are indexed using the 'left attribute.

FIGURE 7-13

```
procedure bv_lt ( bv1, bv2 : in bit_vector;  result : out boolean ) is
    variable tmp1 : bit_vector(bv1'range) := bv1;
    variable tmp2 : bit_vector(bv2'range) := bv2;
begin
    tmp1(tmp1'left) := not tmp1(tmp1'left);
    tmp2(tmp2'left) := not tmp2(tmp2'left);
    result :=  tmp1 < tmp2;
end procedure bv_lt;
```

A procedure to compare two bit vectors representing two's-complement signed integers.

Summary of Procedure Parameters

Let us now summarize all that we have seen in specifying and using parameters for procedures. The syntax rule on page 196 shows that we can specify five aspects of each formal parameter. First, we may specify the class of object, which determines how the formal parameter appears within the procedure, namely, as a constant, a variable or a signal. Second, we give a name to the formal parameter so that it can be referred to in the procedure body. Third, we may specify the mode, **in**, **out** or **inout**, which determines the direction in which information is passed between the caller and the procedure, and hence whether the procedure can read or assign to the formal parameter. Fourth, we must specify the type or subtype of the formal parameter, which restricts the type of actual parameters that can be provided by the caller. This is important as a means of preventing inadvertent misuse of the procedure. Fifth, we may include a default value, giving a value to be used if the caller does not provide an actual parameter. These five aspects clearly define the interface between the procedure and its callers, allowing us to partition a complex behavioral model into sections and concentrate on each section without being distracted by other details.

Once we have encapsulated some operations in a procedure, we can then call that procedure from different parts of a model, providing actual parameters to specialize the operation at each call. The syntax rule for a procedure call is

> procedure_call_statement ⇐
>   〚 label : 〛 *procedure*_name 〚 (*parameter*_association_list) 〛 ;

This is a sequential statement, and so it may be used in a process or inside of another subprogram body. If the procedure has formal parameters, the call can specify actual parameters to associate with the formal parameters. The actual associated with a constant-class formal is the value of an expression. The actual associated with a variable-class formal must be a variable, and the actual associated with a signal-class formal must be a signal. The simplified syntax rule for the parameter association list is

> *parameter*_association_list ⇐
>   (〚 *parameter*_name => 〛
>   expression ‖ *signal*_name ‖ *variable*_name ‖ **open**) { , ... }

This is in fact the same syntax rule that applies to port maps in component instantiations, seen in Chapter 5. Most of what we said there also applies to procedure parameter association lists. For example, we can use positional association in the procedure call by providing one actual parameter for each formal parameter in the order listed in the procedure declaration. Alternatively, we can use named association by identifying explicitly which formal corresponds to which actual parameter in the call. In this case, the parameters can be in any order. Also, we can use a mix of positional and named association, provided all of the positional parameters come first in the call.

EXAMPLE

Suppose we have a procedure declared as

procedure p (f1 : **in** t1; f2 : **in** t2; f3 : **out** t3; f4 : **in** t4 := v4) **is**
begin
    . . .
end procedure p;

We could call this procedure, providing actual parameters in a number of ways, including

```
p ( val1, val2, var3, val4 );
p ( f1 => val1, f2 => val2, f4 => val4, f3 => var3 );
p ( val1, val2, f4 => open, f3 => var3 );
p ( val1, val2, var3 );
```

7.3   Concurrent Procedure Call Statements

In Chapter 5 we saw that VHDL provides concurrent signal assignment statements and concurrent assertions as shorthand notations for commonly used kinds of processes. Now that we have looked at procedures and procedure call statements, we can introduce another shorthand notation, the *concurrent procedure call statement*. As its name implies, it is short for a process whose body contains a sequential procedure call statement. The syntax rule is

concurrent_procedure_call_statement ⇐
    [label :] *procedure*_name [(*parameter*_association_list)] ;

This looks identical to an ordinary sequential procedure call, but the difference is that it appears as a concurrent statement, rather than as a sequential statement. A concurrent procedure call is exactly equivalent to a process that contains a sequential procedure call to the same procedure with the same actual parameters. For example, a concurrent procedure call of the form

```
call_proc : p ( s1, s2, val1 );
```

where s1 and s2 are signals and val1 is a constant, is equivalent to the process

```
call_proc : process is
begin
    p ( s1, s2, val1 );
    wait on s1, s2;
end process call_proc;
```

This also shows that the equivalent process contains a wait statement, whose sensitivity clause includes the signals mentioned in the actual parameter list. This is useful, since it results in the procedure being called again whenever the signal values change. Note that only signals associated with **in** mode or **inout** mode parameters are included in the sensitivity list. It would not make sense to include signals associated with **out** mode parameters, since the procedure never reads them but only assigns to them.

EXAMPLE

We can write a procedure that checks setup timing of a data signal with respect to a clock signal, as shown in Figure 7-14. When the procedure is called, it tests to see if there is a rising edge on the clock signal, and if so, checks that the data signal has not changed within the setup time interval. We can invoke this procedure using a concurrent procedure call, for example:

```
check_ready_setup : check_setup ( data => ready, clock => phi2,
                                   Tsu => Tsu_rdy_clk );
```

FIGURE 7-14

```
procedure check_setup ( signal data, clock : in bit;
                        constant Tsu : in time ) is
begin
    if clock'event and clock = '1' then
        assert data'last_event >= Tsu
            report "setup time violation" severity error;
    end if;
end procedure check_setup;
```

A procedure to check setup timing of a data signal.

The procedure is called whenever either of the signals in the actual parameter list, **ready** or phi2, changes value. When the procedure returns, the concurrent procedure call statement suspends until the next event on either signal. The advantage of using a concurrent procedure call like this is twofold. First, we can write a suite of commonly used checking procedures and reuse them whenever we need to include a check in a model. This is potentially a great improvement in productivity. Second, the statement that invokes the check is more compact and readily understandable than the equivalent process written in-line.

Another point to note about concurrent procedure calls is that if there are no signals associated with **in** mode or **inout** mode parameters, the wait statement in the equivalent process does not have a sensitivity clause. If the procedure ever returns, the process suspends indefinitely. This may be useful if we only want the procedure to be called once at startup time. On the other hand, we may write the procedure so that it never returns. If we include wait statements within a loop in the procedure, it behaves somewhat like a process itself. The advantage of this is that we can declare a procedure that performs some commonly needed behavior and then invoke one or more instances of it using concurrent procedure call statements.

EXAMPLE

The procedure in Figure 7-15 generates a periodic clock waveform on a signal passed as a parameter. The **in** mode constant parameters specify the shape of a clock waveform. The procedure waits for the initial phase delay, then loops indefinitely, scheduling a new rising and falling transition on the clock signal parameter on each iteration. It never returns to its caller. We can use this procedure to generate a two-phase non-overlapping pair of clock signals, as follows:

```
signal phi1, phi2 : std_ulogic := '0';
. . .

gen_phi1 : generate_clock ( phi1, Tperiod => 50 ns,
                            Tpulse => 20 ns, Tphase => 0 ns );

gen_phi2 : generate_clock ( phi2, Tperiod => 50 ns,
                            Tpulse => 20 ns, Tphase => 25 ns );
```

FIGURE 7-15

```
procedure generate_clock ( signal clk : out std_ulogic;
                           constant Tperiod, Tpulse, Tphase : in time ) is
begin
    wait for Tphase;
    loop
        clk <= '1', '0' after Tpulse;
        wait for Tperiod;
    end loop;
end procedure generate_clock;
```

A procedure that generates a clock waveform on a signal.

Each of these calls represents a process that calls the procedure, which then executes the clock generation loop on behalf of its parent process. The advantage of this approach is that we only had to write the loop once in a general-purpose procedure. Also, we have made the model more compact and understandable.

7.4 Functions

Let us now turn our attention to the second kind of subprogram in VHDL: *functions*. We can think of a function as a generalization of expressions. The expressions that we described in Chapter 2 combined values with operators to produce new values. A function is a way of defining a new operation that can be used in expressions. We define how the new operation works by writing a collection of sequential statements that calculate the result. The syntax rule for a function declaration is very similar to that for a procedure declaration:

subprogram_body ⇐
  〚 **pure** ∥ **impure** 〛
  function identifier
     〚 (*parameter*_interface_list) 〛 **return** type_mark **is**
   { subprogram_declarative_item }
  begin
   { sequential_statement }
  end 〚 **function** 〛 〚 identifier 〛 ;

The identifier in the declaration names the function. It may be repeated at the end of the declaration. Unlike a procedure subprogram, a function calculates and returns a result that can be used in an expression. The function declaration specifies the type of the result after the keyword **return**. The parameter list of a function takes the same form as that for a procedure, with two restrictions. First, the parameters of a function may not be of the class variable. If the class is not explicitly mentioned, it is assumed to be constant. Second, the mode of each parameter must be **in**. If the mode is not explicitly specified, it is assumed to be **in**. We come to the reasons for these restrictions in a moment. Like a procedure, a function can declare local items in its declarative part for use in the statements in the function body.

A function passes the result of its computation back to its caller using a return statement, given by the syntax rule

return_statement ⇐ ⟦ label : ⟧ **return** expression ;

The optional label allows us to identify the return statement. We will discuss labeled statements in Chapter 20. The form described by this syntax rule differs from the return statement in a procedure subprogram in that it includes an expression to provide the function result. Furthermore, a function must include at least one return statement of this form, and possibly more. The first to be executed causes the function to complete and return its result to the caller. A function cannot simply run into the end of the function body, since to do so would not provide a way of specifying a result to pass back to the caller.

A function call looks exactly like a procedure call. The syntax rule is

function_call ⇐ *function*_name ⟦ (*parameter*_association_list) ⟧

The difference is that a function call is part of an expression, rather than being a sequential statement on its own, like a procedure call.

EXAMPLE

Figure 7-16 is a simple function that calculates whether a value is within given bounds and returns a result limited to those bounds. A call to this function might be included in a variable assignment statement, as follows:

```
new_temperature := limit ( current_temperature + increment,
                           10, 100 );
```

In this statement, the expression on the right-hand side of the assignment consists of just the function call, and the result returned is assigned to the variable **new_temperature**. However, we might also use the result of a function call in further computation, for example:

```
new_motor_speed := old_motor_speed
                      + scale_factor * limit ( error, –10, +10 );
```

FIGURE 7-16

```
function limit ( value, min, max : integer ) return integer is
begin
    if value > max then
        return max;
    elsif value < min then
        return min;
    else
        return value;
    end if;
end function limit;
```

A function to limit a value to specified bounds.

EXAMPLE

The function in Figure 7-17 determines the number represented in binary by a bit-vector value. The algorithm scans the bit vector from the most-significant end. For each bit, it multiplies the previously accumulated value by two and then adds in the integer value of the bit. The accumulated value is then used as the result of the function, passed back to the caller by the return statement.

FIGURE 7-17

```
function bv_to_natural ( bv : in bit_vector ) return natural is
    variable result : natural := 0;
begin
    for index in bv'range loop
        result := result * 2 + bit'pos(bv(index));
    end loop;
    return result;
end function bv_to_natural;
```

A function that converts the binary representation of an unsigned number to a numeric value.

As an example of using this function, consider a model for a read-only memory, which represents the stored data as an array of bit vectors, as follows:

```
type rom_array is array (natural range 0 to rom_size–1)
                of bit_vector(0 to word_size–1);
variable rom_data : rom_array;
```

If the model has an address port that is a bit vector, we can use the function to convert the address to a natural value to index the ROM data array, as follows:

```
data <= rom_data ( bv_to_natural(address) ) after Taccess;
```

VHDL-87

The keyword **function** may not be included at the end of a function declaration in VHDL-87. Return statements may not be labeled in VHDL-87.

Functional Modeling

In Chapter 5 we looked at concurrent signal assignment statements for functional modeling of designs. We can use functions in VHDL to help us write functional models more expressively by defining a function that encapsulates the data transformation to be performed and then calling the function in a concurrent signal assignment statement. For example, given a declaration of a function to add two bit vectors:

```
function bv_add ( bv1, bv2 : in bit_vector ) return bit_vector is
begin
    . . .
end function bv_add;
```

and signals declared in an architecture body:

> **signal** source1, source2, sum : bit_vector(0 **to** 31);

we can write a concurrent signal assignment statement as follows:

> adder : sum <= bv_add(source1, source2) **after** T_delay_adder;

Pure and Impure Functions

Let us now return to the reason for the restrictions on the class and mode of function formal parameters stated above. These restrictions are in keeping with our idea that a function is a generalized form of operator. If we pass the same values to an operator, such as the addition operator, in different expressions, we expect the operator to return the same result each time. By restricting the formal parameters of a function in the way described above, we go part of the way to ensuring the same property for function calls. One additional restriction we need to make is that the function may not refer to any variables or signals declared by its parents, that is, by any process, subprogram or architecture body in which the function declaration is nested. Otherwise the variables or signals might change values between calls to the function, thus influencing the result of the function. We call a function that makes no such reference a *pure* function. We can explicitly declare a function to be pure by including the keyword **pure** in its definition, as shown by the syntax rule on page 209. If we leave it out, the function is assumed to be pure. Both of the above examples of function declarations are pure functions.

On the other hand, we may deliberately relax the restriction about a function referencing its parents' variables or signals by including the keyword **impure** in the function declaration. This is a warning to any caller of the function that it might produce different results on different calls, even when passed the same actual parameter values.

EXAMPLE

Many network protocols require a sequence number in the packet header so that they can handle packets getting out of order during transmission. We can use an impure function to generate sequence numbers when creating packets in a behavioral model of a network interface. Figure 7-18 is an outline of a process that represents the output side of the network interface.

In this model, the process has a variable **next_seq_number**, used by the function **generate_seq_number** to determine the return value each time it is called. The function has the side effect of incrementing this variable, thus changing the value to be returned on the next call. Because of the reference to the variable in the function's parent, the function must be declared to be impure. The advantage of writing the function this way lies in the expressive power of its call. The function call is simply part of an expression, in this case yielding an element in a record aggregate of type **pkt_header**. Writing it this way makes the process body more compact and easily understandable.

FIGURE 7-18

```
network_driver : process is
    constant seq_modulo : natural := 2**5;
    subtype seq_number is natural range 0 to seq_modulo-1;
    variable next_seq_number : seq_number := 0;
    . . .
    impure function generate_seq_number return seq_number is
        variable number : seq_number;
    begin
        number := next_seq_number;
        next_seq_number := (next_seq_number + 1) mod seq_modulo;
        return number;
    end function generate_seq_number;
begin  -- network_driver
    . . .
    new_header := pkt_header'( dest => target_host_id,
                               src => my_host_id,
                               pkt_type => control_pkt,
                               seq => generate_seq_number );

    . . .
end process network_driver;
```

An outline of a network driver process, including an impure function to calculate sequence numbers for network packets.

The Function Now

VHDL provides a predefined function, now, that returns the current simulation time when it is called. It is defined as

impure function now **return** delay_length;

It is defined to be an impure function because it returns a different value when called at different times during the course of a simulation. Recall that the type delay_length is a predefined subtype of the physical type time, constrained to non-negative time values. The function now is often used to check that the inputs to a model obey the required timing constraints.

EXAMPLE

Figure 7-19 is a process that checks the clock and data inputs of an edge-triggered flipflop for adherence to the minimum hold time constraint, Thold_d_clk. When the clock signal changes to '1', the process saves the current simulation time in the variable last_clk_edge_time. When the data input changes, the process tests whether the current simulation time has advanced beyond the time of the last clock edge by at least the minimum hold time, and reports an error if it has not.

FIGURE 7-19

```
hold_time_checker : process ( clk, d ) is
    variable last_clk_edge_time : time := 0 fs;
begin
    if clk'event and clk = '1' then
        last_clk_edge_time := now;
    end if;
    if d'event then
        assert now – last_clk_edge_time >= Thold_d_clk
            report "hold time violation";
    end if;
end process hold_time_checker;
```

A process that checks for data hold time after clock rising edges for an edge-triggered flipflop.

VHDL-87

The function **now** returns a value of type **time** in VHDL-87, since the subtype delay_length is not predefined in VHDL-87.

7.5 Overloading

When we are writing subprograms, it is a good idea to choose names for our subprograms that indicate what operations they perform, to make it easier for a reader to understand our models. This raises the question of how to name two subprograms that perform the same kind of operation but on parameters of different types. For example, we might wish to write two procedures to increment variables holding numeric values, but in some cases the values are represented as type **integer**, and in other cases they are represented using type **bit_vector**. Ideally, since both procedures perform the same operation, we would like to give them the same name, such as **increment**. But if we did that, would we be able to tell them apart when we wanted to call them? Recall that VHDL strictly enforces the type rules, so we have to refer to the right procedure depending on the type of the variable we wish to increment.

Fortunately, VHDL allows us to define subprograms in this way, using a technique called *overloading* of subprogram names. We can define two distinct subprograms with the same name but with different numbers or types of formal parameters. When we call one of them, the number and types of the actual parameters we supply in the call are used to determine which subprogram to invoke. It is the context of the call that determines how to resolve the apparent ambiguity. We have already seen overloading applied to identifiers used as literals in enumeration types (see Chapter 2). We saw that if two enumeration types included the same identifier, the context of use in a model is used to determine which type is meant.

The precise rules used to disambiguate a subprogram call when the subprogram name is overloaded are quite complex, so we will not enumerate them all here. Fortunately, they are sufficiently complete to sort out most situations that arise in practice.

Instead, we look at some examples to show how overloading of procedures and functions works in straightforward cases. First, here are some procedure outlines for the increment operation described above:

procedure increment (a : **inout** integer; n : **in** integer := 1) **is** . . .

procedure increment (a : **inout** bit_vector; n : **in** bit_vector := B"1") **is** . . .

procedure increment (a : **inout** bit_vector; n : **in** integer := 1) **is** . . .

Suppose we also have some variables declared as follows:

variable count_int : integer := 2;
variable count_bv : bit_vector (15 **downto** 0) := X"0002";

If we write a procedure call using count_int as the first actual parameter, it is clear that we are referring to the first procedure, since it is the only one whose first formal parameter is an integer. Both of the following calls can be disambiguated in this way:

increment (count_int, 2);
increment (count_int);

Similarly, both of the next two calls can be sorted out:

increment (count_bv, X"0002");
increment (count_bv, 1);

The first call refers to the second procedure, since the actual parameters are both bit vectors. Similarly, the second call refers to the third procedure, since the actual parameters are a bit vector and an integer. Problems arise, however, if we try to make a call as follows:

increment (count_bv);

This could equally well be a call to either the second or the third procedure, both of which have default values for the second formal parameter. Since it is not possible to determine which procedure is meant, a VHDL analyzer rejects such a call as an error.

Overloading Operator Symbols

When we introduced function subprograms in Section 7.4, we described them as a generalization of operators used in expressions, such as "+", "–", **and, or** and so on. Looking at this the other way around, we could say that the predefined operators are specialized functions, with a convenient notation for calling them. In fact, this is exactly what they are. Furthermore, since each of the operators can be applied to values of various types, we see that the functions they represent are overloaded, so the types of the operands determine the particular version of each operator used in an expression.

Given that we can define our own types in VHDL, it would be convenient if we could extend the predefined operators to work with these types. For example, if we are using bit vectors to model integers using two's-complement notation, we would like to use the addition operator to add two bit vectors in this form. Fortunately, VHDL provides a way for us to define new functions using the operator symbols as names. Our bit-vector addition function can be declared as

```
function "+" ( left, right : in bit_vector ) return bit_vector is
begin
      . . .
end function "+";
```

We can then call this function using the infix "+" operator with bit-vector operands, for example:

```
variable addr_reg : bit_vector(31 downto 0);
. . .
addr_reg := addr_reg + X"0000_0004";
```

Operators denoted by reserved words can be overloaded in the same way. For example, we can declare a bit-vector absolute-value function as

```
function "abs" ( right : in bit_vector ) return bit_vector is
begin
      . . .
end function "abs";
```

We can use this operator with a bit-vector operand, for example:

```
variable accumulator : bit_vector(31 downto 0);
. . .
accumulator := abs accumulator;
```

We can overload any of the operator symbols shown in Figure 2-5 on page 50. One important point to note, however, is that overloaded versions of the logical operators **and**, **nand**, **or** and **nor** are not evaluated in the short-circuit manner described in Chapter 2. For any type of operands other than **bit** and **boolean**, both operands are evaluated first, then passed to the function.

EXAMPLE

The std_logic_1164 package defines functions for logical operators applied to values of type std_ulogic and std_ulogic_vector. We can use them in functional models to write Boolean equations that represent the behavior of a design. For example, Figure 7-20 describes a block of logic that controls an input/output register in a microcontroller system. The architecture body describes the behavior in terms of Boolean equations. Its concurrent signal assignment statements use the logical operators **and** and **not**, referring to the overloaded functions defined in the std_logic_1164 package.

FIGURE 7-20

```
library ieee;  use ieee.std_logic_1164.all;
entity reg_ctrl is
    port ( reg_addr_decoded, rd, wr, io_en, cpu_clk : in std_ulogic;
           reg_rd, reg_wr : out std_ulogic );
end entity reg_ctrl;
```

```
architecture bool_eqn of reg_ctrl is
begin
      rd_ctrl : reg_rd <= reg_addr_decoded and rd and io_en;
      rw_ctrl : reg_wr <= reg_addr_decoded and wr and io_en
                                             and not cpu_clk;
end architecture bool_eqn;
```

An entity and architecture body for a logic block that controls operation of a register.

VHDL-87

Since VHDL-87 does not provide the shift operators **sll**, **srl**, **sla**, **sra**, **rol**, and **ror** and the logical operator **xnor**, they cannot be used as operator symbols.

7.6 Visibility of Declarations

The last topic we need to discuss in relation to subprograms is the use of names de-clared within a model. We have seen that names of types, constants, variables and other items defined in a subprogram can be used in that subprogram. Also, in the case of procedures and impure functions, names declared in an enclosing process, subpro-gram or architecture body can also be used. The question we must answer is: What are the limits of use of each name?

To answer this question, we introduce the idea of the *visibility* of a declaration, which is the region of the text of a model in which it is possible to refer to the declared name. We have seen that architecture bodies, processes and subprograms are each divided into two parts: a declarative part and a body of statements. A name declared in a declarative part is visible from the end of the declaration itself down to the end of the corresponding statement part. Within this area we can refer to the declared name. Before the declaration, within it and beyond the end of the statement part, we cannot refer to the name because it is not visible.

EXAMPLE

Figure 7-21 shows an outline of an architecture body of a model. It contains a number of declarations, including some procedure declarations. The visibility of each of the declarations is indicated. The first item to be declared is the type t; its visibility extends to the end of the architecture body. Thus it can be referred in other declarations, such as the variable declarations. The second declaration is the signal s; its visibility likewise extends to the end of the architecture body. So the assignment within procedure p1 is valid. The third and final declaration in the declarative part of the architecture body is that of the procedure p1, whose visibility extends to the end of the architecture body, allowing it to be called in either of the processes. It includes a local variable, v1, whose visibility extends only to the end of p1. This means it can be referred to in p1, as shown in the signal assignment statement, but neither process can refer to it.

FIGURE 7-21

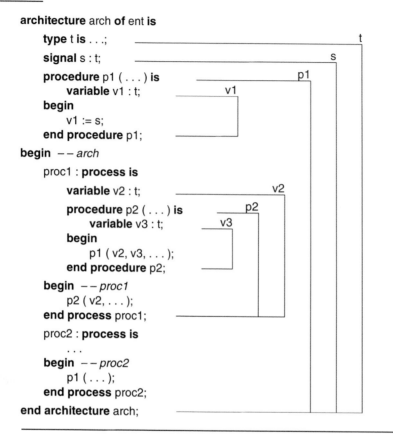

```
architecture arch of ent is
    type t is . . .;
    signal s : t;
    procedure p1 ( . . . ) is
        variable v1 : t;
    begin
        v1 := s;
    end procedure p1;
begin  -- arch
    proc1 : process is
        variable v2 : t;
        procedure p2 ( . . . ) is
            variable v3 : t;
        begin
            p1 ( v2, v3, . . . );
        end procedure p2;
    begin  -- proc1
        p2 ( v2, . . . );
    end process proc1;
    proc2 : process is
        . . .
    begin  -- proc2
        p1 ( . . . );
    end process proc2;
end architecture arch;
```

An outline of an architecture body, showing the visibility of declared names within it.

In the statement part of the architecture body, we have two process statements, **proc1** and **proc2**. The first includes a local variable declaration, v2, whose visibility extends to the end of the process body. Hence we can refer to v2 in the process body and in the procedure p2 declared within the process. The visibility of **p2** likewise extends to the end of the body of **proc1**, allowing us to call p2 within proc1. The procedure p2 includes a local variable declaration, v3, whose visibility extends to the end of the statement part of p2. Hence we can refer to v3 in the statement part of **p2**. However, we cannot refer to v3 in the statement part of **proc1**, since it is not visible in that part of the model.

Finally, we come to the second process, **proc2**. The only items we can refer to here are those declared in the architecture body declarative part, namely, t, s and p1. We cannot call the procedure p2 within proc2, since it is local to proc1.

One point we mentioned earlier about subprograms but did not go into in detail was that we can include nested subprogram declarations within the declarative part of a subprogram. This means we can have local procedures and functions within a procedure or a function. In such cases, the simple rule for the visibility of a declaration still applies, so any items declared within an outer procedure before the declaration of a nested procedure can be referred to inside the nested procedure.

EXAMPLE

Figure 7-22 is an outline of an architecture of a cache memory for a computer system. The entity interface includes ports named mem_addr, mem_ready, mem_ack and mem_data_in. The process behavior contains a procedure, read_block, which reads a block of data from main memory on a cache miss. It has the local variables memory_address_reg and memory_data_reg. Nested inside of this procedure is another procedure, read_memory_word, which reads a single word of data from memory. It uses the value placed in memory_address_reg by the outer procedure and leaves the data read from memory in memory_data_reg.

FIGURE 7-22

```
architecture behavioral of cache is
begin
    behavior : process is

        . . .

        procedure read_block ( start_address : natural;  entry : out cache_block ) is
            variable memory_address_reg : natural;
            variable memory_data_reg : word;

            procedure read_memory_word is
            begin
                mem_addr <= memory_address_reg;  mem_read <= '1';
                wait until mem_ack = '1';
                memory_data_reg := mem_data_in;  mem_read <= '0';
                wait until mem_ack = '0';
            end procedure read_memory_word;

        begin  -- read_block
            for offset in 0 to block_size – 1 loop
                memory_address_reg := start_address + offset;
                read_memory_word;
                entry(offset) := memory_data_reg;
            end loop;
        end procedure read_block;

    begin  -- behavior

        . . .

        read_block ( miss_base_address, data_store(entry_index) );

        . . .

    end process behavior;
end architecture behavioral;
```

An outline of a behavioral architecture of a cache memory.

Now let us consider a model in which we have one subprogram nested inside of another, and each declares an item with the same name as the other, as shown in Figure 7-23. Here, the first variable v is visible within all of the procedure p2 and the statement body of p1. However, because p2 declares its own local variable called v, the variable belonging to p1 is not *directly visible* where p2's v is visible. We say the inner variable declaration *hides* the outer declaration, since it declares the same name. Hence the addition within p2 applies to the local variable v of p2 and does not affect the variable v of p1. If we need to refer to an item that is visible but hidden, we can use a selected name. For example, within p2 in Figure 7-23, we can use the name p1.v to refer to the variable v declared in p1. Although the outer declaration is not directly visible, it is *visible by selection*.

FIGURE 7-23

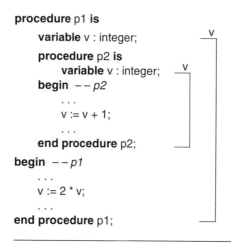

```
procedure p1 is
    variable v : integer;                          v
    procedure p2 is
         variable v : integer;        v
    begin  ––p2
        . . .
        v := v + 1;
        . . .
    end procedure p2;
begin  ––p1
    . . .
    v := 2 * v;
    . . .
end procedure p1;
```

Nested procedures showing hiding of names. The declaration of v in p2 hides the variable v declared in p1.

The idea of hiding is not restricted to variable declarations within nested procedures. Indeed, it applies in any case where we have one declarative part nested within another, and an item is declared with the same name in each declarative part in such a way that the rules for resolving overloaded names are unable to distinguish between them. The advantage of having inner declarations hide outer declarations, as opposed to the alternative of simply disallowing an inner declaration with the same name, is that it allows us to write local procedures and processes without having to know the names of all items declared at outer levels. This is certainly beneficial when writing large models. In practice, if we are reading a model and need to check the use of a name in a statement against its declaration, we only need to look at successively enclosing declarative parts until we find a declaration of the name, and that is the declaration that applies.

Exercises

1. [❶ 7.2] Write parameter specifications for the following constant-class parameters:
   * an integer, operand1,
   * a bit vector, tag, indexed from 31 down to 16, and
   * a Boolean, trace, with default value false.

2. [❶ 7.2] Write parameter specifications for the following variable-class parameters:
   * a real number, average, used to pass data back from a procedure, and
   * a string, identifier, modified by a procedure.

3. [❶ 7.2] Write parameter specifications for the following signal-class parameters:
   * a bit signal, clk, to be assigned to by a procedure, and
   * an unconstrained standard-logic vector signal, data_in, whose value is to be read by a procedure.

4. [❶ 7.2] Given the following procedure declaration:

   procedure stimulate (**signal** target : **out** bit_vector;
                         delay : **in** delay_length := 1 ns;
                         cycles : **in** natural := 1) **is** . . .

   write procedure calls using a signal **s** as the actual parameter for target and using the following values for the other parameters:
   * delay = 5 ns, cycles = 3,
   * delay = 10 ns, cycles = 1, and
   * delay = 1 ns, cycles = 15.

5. [❶ 7.3] Suppose we have a procedure declared as

   procedure shuffle_bytes (**signal** d_in : **in** std_ulogic_vector(0 **to** 15);
                             signal d_out : **out** std_ulogic_vector(0 **to** 15);
                             signal shuffle_control : **in** std_ulogic;
                             prop_delay : delay_length) **is** . . .

   Write the equivalent process for the following concurrent procedure call:

   swapper : shuffle_bytes (ext_data, int_data, swap_control, Tpd_swap);

6. [❶ 7.4] Suppose we have a function declared as

   function approx_log_2 (a : **in** bit_vector) **return** positive **is** . . .

   that calculates the minimum number of bits needed to represent a binary-encoded number. Write a variable assignment statement that calculates the minimum number of bits needed to represent the product of two numbers in the variables multiplicand and multiplier, as assigns the result to the variable product_size.

7. [❶ 7.4] Write an assertion statement that verifies that the current simulation time has not exceeded 20 ms.

8. [❶ 7.5] Given the declarations of the three procedures named increment and the variables count_int and count_bv shown on page 215, which of the three procedures, if any, is referred to by each of the following procedure calls?

```
increment ( count_bv, –1 );
increment ( count_int );
increment ( count_int, B"1" );
increment ( count_bv, 16#10# );
```

9. [❶ 7.6] Show the parts of the following model in which each of the declared items is visible:

   architecture behavioral **of** computer system **is**

       signal internal_data : bit_vector(31 **downto** 0);

       interpreter : **process is**

           variable opcode : bit_vector(5 **downto** 0);

           procedure do_write **is**
             variable aligned_address : natural;
           begin
             . . .
           end procedure do_write;

       begin
         . . .
       end process interpreter;

   end architecture behavioral;

10. [❷ 7.1] Write a procedure that calculates the sum of squares of elements of an array variable **deviations**. The elements are real numbers. Your procedure should store the result in a real variable **sum_of_squares**.

11. [❷ 7.1] Write a procedure that generates a 1 μs pulse every 20 μs on a signal **syn_clk**. When the signal **reset** changes to '1', the procedure should immediately set **syn_clk** to '0' and return.

12. [❷ 7.2] Write a procedure called **align_address** that aligns a binary encoded address in a bit-vector variable parameter. The procedure has a second parameter that indicates the alignment size. If the size is 1, the address is unchanged. If the size is 2, the address is rounded to a multiple of 2 by clearing the least-significant bit. If the size is 4, two bits are cleared, and if the size is 8, three bits are cleared. The default alignment size is 4.

13. [❷ 7.2/7.3] Write a procedure that checks the hold time of a data signal with respect to rising edges of a clock signal. Both signals are of the IEEE standard-logic type. The signals and the hold time are parameters of the procedure. The procedure is invoked by a concurrent procedure call.

14. [❷ 7.2/7.3] Write a procedure, to be invoked by a concurrent procedure call, that assigns successive natural numbers to a signal at regular intervals. The signal and the interval between numbers are parameters of the procedure.

15. [❷ 7.4] Write a function, **weaken**, that maps a standard-logic value to the same value, but with weak drive strength. Thus, '0' and 'L' are mapped to 'L', '1' and 'H' are mapped to 'H', 'X' and 'W' are mapped to 'W' and all other values are unchanged.

16. [❷ 7.4] Write a function, returning a Boolean result, that tests whether a standard-logic signal currently has a valid edge. A valid edge is defined to be a transition from '0' or 'L' to '1' or 'H' or vice versa. Other transitions, such as 'X' to '1', are not valid.

17. [❷ 7.4] Write two functions, one to find the maximum value in an array of integers and the other to find the minimum value.

18. [❷ 7.5] Write overloaded versions of the logical operators to operate on integer operands. The operators should treat the value 0 as logical falsehood and any non-zero value as logical truth.

19. [❸ 7.2] Write a procedure called **scan_results** with an **in** mode bit-vector signal parameter **results**, and **out** mode variable parameters **majority_value** of type bit, **majority_count** of type natural and **tie** of type boolean. The procedure counts the occurrences of '0' and '1' values in **results**. It sets **majority_value** to the most frequently occurring value, **majority_count** to the number of occurrences and **tie** to true if there are an equal number of occurrences of '0' and '1'.

20. [❸ 7.2/7.3] Write a procedure that stimulates a bit-vector signal passed as a parameter. The procedure assigns to the signal a sequence of all possible bit-vector values. The first value is assigned to the signal immediately, then subsequent values are assigned at intervals specified by a second parameter. After the last value is assigned, the procedure returns.

21. [❸ 7.2/7.3] Write a passive procedure that checks that setup and hold times for a data signal with respect to rising edges of a clock signal are observed. The signals and the setup and hold times are parameters of the procedure. Include a concurrent procedure call to the procedure in the statement part of a D-flipflop entity.

22. [❸ 7.4] Write a function that calculates the cosine of a real number, using the series

$$\cos \theta = 1 - \frac{\theta^2}{2!} + \frac{\theta^4}{4!} - \frac{\theta^6}{6!} + \cdots$$

Next, write a second function that returns a cosine table of the following type:

    type table **is array** (0 **to** 1023) **of** real;

Element i of the table has the value $\cos i\pi/2048$. Finally, develop a behavioral model of a cosine lookup ROM. The architecture body should include a constant of type **table**, initialized using a call to the second function.

23. [❸ 7.4/7.5] Write functions, overloading the "*", "+" and "–" operators, to perform multiplication, addition and subtraction of fixed-point binary numbers. Your functions should use the data formats and algorithms found in the **multiplier** and **product_adder_subtracter** entities in Chapter 6. Use the functions in concurrent assignment statements in a functional model of a complex multiplier, with the following entity interface:

```
entity complex_multiplier is
    port ( x_real, x_imag,
           y_real, y_imag : in std_ulogic_vector(15 downto 0);
           p_real, p_imag : out std_ulogic_vector(32 downto 0) );
end entity complex_multiplier;
```

Packages and Use Clauses

Packages in VHDL provide an important way of organizing the data and subprograms declared in a model. In this chapter, we describe the basics of packages and show how they may be used. We also look at one of the predefined packages, which includes all of the predefined types and operators available in VHDL.

8.1   Package Declarations

A VHDL package is simply a way of grouping a collection of related declarations that serve a common purpose. They might be a set of subprograms that provide operations on a particular type of data, or they might just be the set of declarations needed to model a particular design. The important thing is that they can be collected together into a separate design unit that can be worked on independently and reused in different parts of a model.

Another important aspect of packages is that they separate the external view of the items they declare from the implementation of those items. The external view is specified in a *package declaration*, whereas the implementation is defined in a separate *package body*. We will look at package declaration first and return to the package body shortly.

The syntax rule for writing a package declaration is

package_declaration ⇐
    package identifier **is**
        { package_declarative_item }
    end [**package**] [identifier] ;

The identifier provides a name for the package, which we can use elsewhere in a model to refer to the package. Inside the package declaration we write a collection of declarations, including type, subtype, constant, signal and subprogram declarations, as well as several other kinds of declarations that we see in later chapters. These are the declarations that are provided to the users of the package. The advantage of placing them in a package is that they do not clutter up other parts of a model, and they can be shared within and between models without having to rewrite them. Figure 8-1 is a simple example of a package declaration.

FIGURE 8-1

```
package cpu_types is
    constant word_size : positive := 16;
    constant address_size : positive := 24;

    subtype word is bit_vector(word_size – 1 downto 0);
    subtype address is bit_vector(address_size – 1 downto 0);

    type status_value is ( halted, idle, fetch, mem_read, mem_write,
                           io_read, io_write, int_ack );
end package cpu_types;
```

A package that declares some useful constants and types for a CPU model.

VHDL-87

The keyword **package** may not be included at the end of a package declaration in VHDL-87.

A package is another form of design unit, along with entity declarations and architecture bodies. It is separately analyzed and is placed into the working library as a library unit by the analyzer. From there, other library units can refer to an item declared in the package using the *selected name* of the item. The selected name is formed by writing the library name, then the package name and then the name of the item, all separated by dots; for example:

work.cpu_types.status_value

EXAMPLE

Suppose the **cpu_types** package, shown in Figure 8-1, has been analyzed and placed into the **work** library. We might make use of the declared items when modeling an address decoder to go with a CPU. The entity declaration and architecture body of the decoder are shown in Figure 8-2.

FIGURE 8-2

```
entity address_decoder is
    port ( addr : in work.cpu_types.address;
           status : in work.cpu_types.status_value;
           mem_sel, int_sel, io_sel : out bit );
end entity address_decoder;
```

––

```
architecture functional of address_decoder is
    constant mem_low : work.cpu_types.address := X"000000";
    constant mem_high : work.cpu_types.address := X"EFFFFF";
    constant io_low : work.cpu_types.address := X"F00000";
    constant io_high : work.cpu_types.address := X"FFFFFF";
begin
    mem_decoder :
        mem_sel <=
            '1' when ( work.cpu_types."="(status, work.cpu_types.fetch)
                       or work.cpu_types."="(status, work.cpu_types.mem_read)
                       or work.cpu_types."="(status, work.cpu_types.mem_write) )
                     and addr >= mem_low and addr <= mem_high else
            '0';
    int_decoder :
        int_sel <= '1' when work.cpu_types."="(status, work.cpu_types.int_ack) else
                   '0';
    io_decoder :
        io_sel <=
            '1' when ( work.cpu_types."="(status, work.cpu_types.io_read)
                       or work.cpu_types."="(status, work.cpu_types.io_write) )
                     and addr >= io_low and addr <= io_high else
            '0';
end architecture functional;
```

An entity and architecture body for an address decoder, using items declared in the cpu_types *package.*

Note that we have to use selected names to refer to the subtype **address**, the type **status_value**, the enumeration literals of **status_value** and the implicitly declared "=" operator, defined in the package **cpu_types**. This is because they are not directly visible within the entity declaration and architecture body. We will see later in this chapter how a use clause can help us avoid long selected names. If we needed to type-qualify the enumeration literals, we would use selected names for both the type name and the literal name; for example:

```
work.cpu_types.status_value'(work.cpu_types.fetch)
```

We have seen that a package, when analyzed, is placed into the working library. Items in the package can be accessed by other library units using selected names starting with **work**. However, if we are writing a package of generally useful declarations, we may wish to place them into a different library, such as a project library, where they can be accessed by other designers. Different VHDL tool suites provide different ways of specifying the library into which a library unit is placed. We must consult the documentation for a particular product to find out what to do. However, once the package has been included in a resource library, we can refer to items declared in it using selected names, starting with the resource library name. As an example, we might consider the IEEE standard-logic package, which must be placed in a resource library called **ieee**. We can refer to the types declared in that package, for example:

variable stored_state : ieee.std_logic_1164.std_ulogic;

One kind of declaration we can include in a package declaration is a signal declaration. This gives us a way of defining a signal, such as a master clock or reset signal, that is global to a whole design, instead of being restricted to a single architecture body. Any module that needs to refer to the global signal simply names it using the selected name as described above. This avoids the clutter of having to specify the signal as a port in each entity that uses it, making the model a little less complex. However, it does mean that a module can affect the overall behavior of a system by means other than through its ports, namely, by assigning to global signals. This effectively means that part of the module's interface is implicit, rather than being specified in the port map of the entity. As a matter of style, global signals declared in packages should be used sparingly, and their use should be clearly documented with comments in the model.

EXAMPLE

The package shown in Figure 8-3 declares two clock signals for use within an integrated circuit design for an input/output interface controller. The top-level architecture of the controller circuit is outlined in Figure 8-4. The instance of the **phase_locked_clock_gen** entity uses the **ref_clock** port of the circuit to generate the two-phase clock waveforms on the global clock signals. The architecture also includes an instance of an entity that sequences bus operations using the bus control signals and generates internal register control signals. The architecture body for the sequencer is outlined in Figure 8-5. It creates an instance of a register entity and connects the global clock signals to its clock input ports.

FIGURE 8-3

```
library ieee;  use ieee.std_logic_1164.all;
package clock_pkg is
    constant Tpw : delay_length := 4 ns;
    signal clock_phase1, clock_phase2 : std_ulogic;
end package clock_pkg;
```

A package that declares global clock signals.

FIGURE 8-4

```
library ieee;  use ieee.std_logic_1164.all;
entity io_controller is
    port ( ref_clock : in std_ulogic; . . . );
end entity io_controller;
```
- -
```
architecture top_level of io_controller is

    . . .

begin
    internal_clock_gen : entity work.phase_locked_clock_gen(std_cell)
        port map ( reference => ref_clock,
                    phi1 => work.clock_pkg.clock_phase1,
                    phi2 => work.clock_pkg.clock_phase2 );
    the_bus_sequencer : entity work.bus_sequencer(fsm)
        port map ( rd, wr, sel, width, burst, addr(1 downto 0), ready,
                    control_reg_wr, status_reg_rd, data_fifo_wr, data_fifo_rd,
                    . . . );

    . . .

end architecture top_level;
```

An outline of the entity and architecture body for the input/output controller integrated circuit. The architecture body uses the master clock signals.

FIGURE 8-5

```
architecture fsm of bus_sequencer is
    -- This architecture implements the sequencer as a finite state machine.
    -- NOTE: it uses the clock signals from clock_pkg to synchronize the fsm.
    signal next_state_vector : . . .;
begin
    bus_sequencer_state_register : entity work.state_register(std_cell)
        port map ( phi1 => work.clock_pkg.clock_phase1,
                   phi2 => work.clock_pkg.clock_phase2,
                   next_state => next_state_vector,
                   . . . );
    . . .
end architecture fsm;
```

An outline of the architecture body for the bus sequencer of the input/output controller circuit.

Subprograms in Package Declarations

Another kind of declaration that may be included in a package declaration is a subprogram declaration—either a procedure or a function declaration. This ability allows us to write subprograms that implement useful operations and to call them from a number of different modules. An important use of this feature is to declare subprograms that operate on values of a type declared by the package. This gives us a way of conceptually extending VHDL with new types and operations, so-called *abstract data types*, a topic we return to in a later chapter.

An important aspect of declaring a subprogram in a package declaration is that we only write the header of the subprogram, that is, the part that includes the name and the interface list defining the parameters (and result type for functions). We leave out the body of the subprogram. The reason for this is that the package declaration, as we mentioned earlier, provides only the external view of the items it declares, leaving the implementation of the items to the package body. For items such as types and signals, the complete definition is needed in the external view. However, for subprograms, we need only know the information contained in the header to be able to call the subprogram. As users of a subprogram, we need not be concerned with how it achieves its effect or calculates its result. This is an example of a general principle called *information hiding*: making an interface visible but hiding the details of implementation. To illustrate this idea, suppose we have a package declaration that defines a bit-vector subtype:

```
subtype word32 is bit_vector(31 downto 0);
```

We can include in the package a procedure to do addition on **word32** values that represent signed integers. The procedure declaration in the package declaration is

```
procedure add ( a, b : in word32;
                result : out word32;  overflow : out boolean );
```

Note that we do not include the keyword **is** or any of the local declarations or statements needed to perform the addition. These are deferred to the package body. All we include is the description of the formal parameters of the procedure. Similarly, we might include a function to perform an arithmetic comparison of two **word32** values:

> **function** "<" (a, b : **in** word32) **return** boolean;

Again, we omit the local declarations and statements, simply specifying the formal parameters and the result type of the function.

Constants in Package Declarations

Just as we can apply the principle of information hiding to subprograms declared in a package, we can also apply it to constants declared in a package. The external view of a constant is just its name and type. We need to know these in order to use it, but we do not actually need to know its value. This may seem strange at first, but if we recall that the idea of introducing constant declarations in the first place was to avoid scattering literal values throughout a model, it makes more sense. We defer specifying the value of a constant declared in a package by omitting the initialization expression, for example:

> **constant** max_buffer_size : positive;

This defines the constant to be a positive integer value. However, since we cannot see the actual value, we are not tempted to write the value as an integer literal in a model that uses the package. The specification of the actual value is deferred to the package body, where it is not visible to a model that uses the package. Given the above deferred constant in a package declaration, the corresponding package body must include the full constant declaration, for example:

> **constant** max_buffer_size : positive := 4096;

Note that we do not have to defer the value in a constant declaration—it is optional.

EXAMPLE

We can extend the package specification from Figure 8-1, declaring useful types for a CPU model, by including declarations related to opcode processing. The revised package is shown in Figure 8-6. It includes a subtype that represents an opcode value, a function to extract an opcode from an instruction word and a number of constants representing the opcodes for different instructions.

Figure 8-7 shows a behavioral model of a CPU that uses these declarations. The instruction set interpreter process declares a variable of the **opcode** type and uses the **extract_opcode** function to extract the bits representing the opcode from the fetched instruction word. It then uses the constants from the package as choices in a case statement to decode and execute the instruction specified by the opcode.

FIGURE 8-6

```
package cpu_types is
    constant word_size : positive := 16;
    constant address_size : positive := 24;

    subtype word is bit_vector(word_size – 1 downto 0);
    subtype address is bit_vector(address_size – 1 downto 0);

    type status_value is ( halted, idle, fetch, mem_read, mem_write,
                           io_read, io_write, int_ack );

    subtype opcode is bit_vector(5 downto 0);

    function extract_opcode ( instr_word : word ) return opcode;

    constant op_nop : opcode := "000000";
    constant op_breq : opcode := "000001";
    constant op_brne : opcode := "000010";
    constant op_add : opcode := "000011";   . . .
end package cpu_types;
```

A revised version of the package used in a CPU model.

FIGURE 8-7

```
architecture behavioral of cpu is
begin
    interpreter : process is
            variable instr_reg : work.cpu_types.word;
            variable instr_opcode : work.cpu_types.opcode;
    begin
        . . .         -- initialize
        loop
            . . .          -- fetch instruction
            instr_opcode := work.cpu_types.extract_opcode ( instr_reg );
            case instr_opcode is
                when work.cpu_types.op_nop => null;
                when work.cpu_types.op_breq => . . .
                . . .
            end case;
        end loop;
    end process interpreter;
end architecture behavioral;
```

An outline of a CPU model that uses items declared in the revised cpu_types *package.*

Note that since the constants are used as choices in the case statement, they must be locally static. If we had deferred the values of the constants to the package body, their value would not be known when the case statement was analyzed. This is why we included the constant values in the package declaration. In general, the value of a deferred constant is not locally static.

8.2 Package Bodies

Now that we have seen how to define the interface to a package, we can turn to the package body. Each package declaration that includes subprogram declarations or deferred constant declarations must have a corresponding package body to fill in the missing details. However, if a package declaration only includes other kinds of declarations, such as types, signals or fully specified constants, no package body is necessary. The syntax rule for a package body is similar to that for the interface, but with the inclusion of the keyword **body**:

> package_body ⇐
>   **package body** identifier **is**
>   { package_body_declarative_item }
>   **end** [**package body**] [identifier] ;

The items declared in a package body must include the full declarations of all subprograms defined in the corresponding package declaration. These full declarations must include the subprogram headers exactly as they are written in the package declaration, to ensure that the implementation *conforms* with the interface. This means that the names, types, modes and default values of each of the formal parameters must be repeated exactly. There are only two variations allowed. First, a numeric literal may be written differently, for example, in a different base, provided it has the same value. Second, a simple name consisting just of an identifier may be replaced by a selected name, provided it refers to the same item. While this conformance requirement might seem an imposition at first, in practice it is not. Any reasonable text editor used to create a VHDL model allows the header to be copied from the package declaration with little difficulty. Similarly, a deferred constant defined in a package declaration must have its value specified by repeating the declaration in the package body, this time filling in the initialization expression as in a full constant declaration.

In addition to the full declarations of items deferred from the package declaration, a package body may include declarations of additional types, subtypes, constants and subprograms. These items are used to implement the subprograms defined in the package declaration. Note that the items declared in the package declaration cannot be declared again in the body (apart from subprograms and deferred constants, as described above), since they are automatically visible in the body. Furthermore, the package body cannot include declarations of additional signals. Signal declarations may only be included in the interface declaration of a package.

EXAMPLE

Figure 8-8 shows outlines of a package declaration and a package body declaring overloaded versions of arithmetic operators for bit-vector values. The functions treat bit vectors as representing signed integers in binary form. Only the function headers are included in the package declaration. The package body contains the full function bodies. It also includes a function, **mult_unsigned**, not defined in the package declaration. It is used internally in the package body to implement the signed multiplication operator.

FIGURE 8-8

package bit_vector_signed_arithmetic **is**

    function "+" (bv1, bv2 : bit_vector) **return** bit_vector;

    function "–" (bv : bit_vector) **return** bit_vector;

    function "*" (bv1, bv2 : bit_vector) **return** bit_vector;

    . . .

end package bit_vector_signed_arithmetic;

---

package body bit_vector_signed_arithmetic **is**

    function "+" (bv1, bv2 : bit_vector) **return** bit_vector **is** . . .

    function "–" (bv : bit_vector) **return** bit_vector **is** . . .

    function mult_unsigned (bv1, bv2 : bit_vector) **return** bit_vector **is**

      . . .

    begin

      . . .

    end function mult_unsigned;

    function "*" (bv1, bv2 : bit_vector) **return** bit_vector **is**

    begin

      if bv1 (bv1'left) = '0' **and** bv2(bv2'left) = '0' **then**

        return mult_unsigned(bv1, bv2);

      elsif bv1 (bv1'left) = '0' **and** bv2(bv2'left) = '1' **then**

        return –mult_unsigned(bv1, –bv2);

      elsif bv1 (bv1'left) = '1' **and** bv2(bv2'left) = '0' **then**

        return –mult_unsigned(–bv1, bv2);

      else

        return mult_unsigned(–bv1, –bv2);

      end if;

    end function "*";

    . . .

end package body bit_vector_signed_arithmetic;

An outline of a package declaration and body that define signed arithmetic functions on integers represented as bit vectors.

VHDL-87

The keywords **package body** may not be included at the end of a package body in VHDL-87.

One final point to mention on the topic of packages relates to the order of analysis. We mentioned before that a package is a separate design unit that is analyzed separately from other design units, such as entity declarations and architecture bodies. In fact, a package declaration and its corresponding package body are each separate design units, hence they may be analyzed separately. A package declaration is a primary design unit, and a package body is a secondary design unit. The package body depends on information defined in the package declaration, so the declaration must be analyzed first. Furthermore, the declaration must be analyzed before any other design unit that refers to an item defined by the package. Once the declaration has been analyzed, it does not matter when the body is analyzed in relation to units that use the package, provided it is analyzed before the model is elaborated. In a large suite of models, the dependency relationships can get quite complex, and a correct order of analysis can be difficult to find. A good VHDL tool suite will provide some degree of automating this process by working out the dependency relationships and analyzing those units needed to build a particular target unit to simulate or synthesize.

8.3 Use Clauses

We have seen how we can refer to an item provided by a package by writing its selected name, for example, **work.cpu_types.status_value**. This name refers to the item **status_value** in the package **cpu_types** stored in the library **work**. If we need to refer to this object in many places in a model, having to write the library name and package name becomes tedious and can obscure the intent of the model. We saw in Chapter 5 that we can write a *use clause* to make a library unit directly visible in a model, allowing us to omit the library name when referring to the library unit. Since an analyzed package is a library unit, use clauses also apply to making packages directly visible. So we could precede a model with a use clause referring to the package defined in the example in Figure 8-1 on page 226:

use work.cpu_types;

This use clause allows us to write declarations in our model more simply, for example:

variable data_word : cpu_types.word;
variable next_address : cpu_types.address;

In fact, the use clause is more general than this usage indicates and allows us to make any name from a library or package directly visible. Let us look at the full syntax rule for a use clause, then discuss some of the possibilities.

use_clause ⇐ **use** selected_name { , … } ;

selected_name ⇐
    name . (identifier ‖ character_literal ‖ operator_symbol ‖ **all**)

The syntax rule for names, shown in Appendix E, includes the possibility of a name itself being either a selected name or a simple identifier. If we make these substitutions in the above syntax rule, we see that a selected name can be of the form

identifier . identifier . (identifier ‖ character_literal ‖ operator_symbol ‖ **all**)

One possibility is that the first identifier is a library name, and the second is the name of a package within the library. This form allows us to refer directly to items within a package without having to use the full selected name. For example, we can simplify the above declarations even further by rewriting the use clause as

use work.cpu_types.word, work.cpu_types.address;

The declarations can then be written as

variable data_word : word;
variable next_address : address;

We can place a use clause in any declarative part in a model. One way to think of a use clause is that it "imports" the names of the listed items into the part of the model containing the use clause, so that they can be used without writing the library or package name. The names become directly visible after the use clause, according to the same visibility rules that we discussed in Chapter 7.

The syntax rule for a use clause shows that we can write the keyword **all** instead of the name of a particular item to import from a package. This form is very useful, as it is a shorthand way of importing all of the names defined in the interface of a package. For example, if we are using the IEEE standard-logic package as the basis for the data types in a design, it is often convenient to import everything from the standard-logic package, including all of the overloaded operator definitions. We can do this with a use clause as follows:

use ieee.std_logic_1164.**all**;

This use clause means that the model imports all of the names defined in the package std_logic_1164 residing in the library **ieee**. This explains the "magic" that we have used in previous chapters when we needed to model data using the standard-logic types. The keyword **all** can be included for any package where we want to import all of the declarations from the package into a model.

EXAMPLE

Figure 8-9 is a revised version of the architecture body outlined in Figure 8-7 on page 232. It includes a use clause referring to items declared in the **cpu_types** package. This makes the rest of the model considerably less cluttered and easier to read. The use clause is included within the declarative part of the instruction set interpreter process. Thus the names "imported" from the package are directly visible in the rest of the declarative part and in the body of the process.

FIGURE 8-9

```
architecture behavioral of cpu is
begin
    interpreter : process is
        use work.cpu_types.all;
        variable instr_reg : word;
        variable instr_opcode : opcode;
    begin
        . . .        -- initialize
        loop
            . . .          -- fetch instruction
            instr_opcode := extract_opcode ( instr_reg );
            case instr_opcode is
                when op_nop => null;
```

```
                            when op_breq => . . .
                                  . . .
                          end case;
                        end loop;
                      end process interpreter;
                  end architecture behavioral;
```

A revised outline of a CPU model, including a use clause to refer to items from the cpu_types *package.*

One final point to clarify about use clauses before looking at an extended example is the way in which they may be included at the beginning of a design unit, as well as in declarative parts within a library unit. We have seen in Section 5.5 how we may include library and use clauses at the head of a design unit, such as an entity interface or architecture body. This area of a design unit is called its *context clause*. In fact, this is probably the most common place for including use clauses. The names imported here are made directly visible throughout the design unit. For example, if we want to use the IEEE standard-logic type std_ulogic in the declaration of an entity, we might write the design unit as follows:

```
library ieee;  use ieee.std_logic_1164.std_ulogic;

entity logic_block is
    port ( a, b : in std_ulogic;
              y, z : out std_ulogic );
end entity logic_block;
```

The library clause and the use clause together form the context clause for the entity declaration in this example. The library clause makes the contents of the library accessible to the model, and the use clause imports the type name std_ulogic declared in the package std_logic_1164 in the library ieee. By including the use clause in the context clause of the entity declaration, the std_ulogic type name is available when declaring the ports of the entity.

The names imported by a use clause in this way are made directly visible in the entire design unit after the use clause. In addition, if the design unit is a primary unit (such as an entity declaration or a package declaration), the visibility is extended to any corresponding secondary unit. Thus, if we include a use clause in the primary unit, we do not need to repeat it in the secondary unit, as the names are automatically visible there.

8.4 The Predefined Package Standard

In previous chapters, we have introduced numerous predefined types and operators. We can use them in our VHDL models without having to write type declarations or subprogram definitions for them. These predefined items all come from a special package called standard, located in a special design library called std. A full listing of the standard package is included for reference in Appendix B.

Because nearly every model we write needs to make use of the contents of this library and package, as well as the library **work**, VHDL includes an implicit context clause of the form

library std, work; **use** std.standard.**all**;

at the beginning of each design unit. Hence we can refer to the simple names of the predefined items without having to resort to their selected names. In the occasional case where we need to distinguish a reference to a predefined operator from an overloaded version, we can use a selected name, for example:

result := std.standard."<" (a, b);

EXAMPLE

A package that provides signed arithmetic operations on integers represented as bit vectors might include a relational operator, defined as shown in Figure 8-10. The function negates the sign bit of each operand, then compares the resultant bit vectors using the predefined relational operator from the package **standard**. The full selected name for the predefined operator is necessary to distinguish it from the function being defined. If the return expression were written as "tmp < tmp2", it would refer to the function in which it occurs, creating a circular definition.

FIGURE 8-10

```
function "<" ( a, b : bit_vector ) return boolean is
    variable tmp1 : bit_vector(a'range) := a;
    variable tmp2 : bit_vector(b'range) := b;
begin
    tmp1(tmp1'left) := not tmp1(tmp1'left);
    tmp2(tmp2'left) := not tmp2(tmp2'left);
    return std.standard."<" ( tmp1, tmp2 );
end function "<";
```

An operator function for comparing two bit vectors representing signed integers.

Exercises

1. [❶ 8.1] Write a package declaration for use in a model of an engine management system. The package contains declarations of a physical type, **engine_speed**, expressed in units of revolutions per minute (RPM); a constant, **peak_rpm**, with a value of 6000 RPM; and an enumeration type, **gear**, with values representing first, second, third, fourth and reverse gears. Assuming the package is analyzed and stored in the current working library, write selected names for each of the items declared in the package.

2. [❶ 8.1] Write a declaration for a procedure that increments an integer, as the procedure declaration would appear in a package declaration.

3. [❶ 8.1] Write a declaration for a function that tests whether an integer is odd, as the function declaration would appear in a package declaration.

4. [❶ 8.1] Write a deferred constant declaration for the real constant $e = 2.71828$.

5. [❶ 8.2] Is a package body required for the package declaration described in Exercise 1?

6. [❶ 8.3] Write a use clause that makes the **engine_speed** type from the package described in Exercise 1 directly visible.

7. [❶ 8.3] Write a context clause that makes a library **DSP_lib** accessible and that makes an entity **systolic_FFT** and all items declared in a package **DSP_types** in the library directly visible.

8. [❷ 8.1/8.2] Write a package declaration that includes a subtype declaration for the 16-bit fixed-point binary numbers used in the entity interface of the MAC of Chapter 6. The package declaration should also include conversion function declarations to convert between the fixed-point type and the predefined type **real**. Write a corresponding package body, using the algorithms in the architecture bodies of the **to_fp** and **to_vector** entities of Chapter 6 for the conversion functions.

9. [❷ 8.4] Integers can be represented in *signed magnitude* form, in which the leftmost bit represents the sign ('0' for non-negative, '1' for negative), and the remaining bits are the absolute value of the number, represented in binary. If we wish to compare bit vectors containing numbers in signed magnitude form, we cannot use the predefined relational operators directly. We must first transform each number as follows: if the number is negative, complement all bits; if the number is non-negative, complement only the sign bit. Write a comparison function, overloading the operator "<", to compare signed-magnitude bit vectors using this method.

10. [❸ 8.1/8.2] Develop a package declaration and body that provide operations for dealing with time-of-day values. The package defines a time-of-day value as a record containing hours, minutes and seconds since midnight and provides deferred constants representing midnight and midday. The operations provided by the package are

    • comparison ("<", ">", "<=" and ">="),

    • addition of a time-of-day value and a number of seconds to yield a time-of-day result, and

    • subtraction of two time-of-day values to yield a number-of-seconds result.

11. [❸ 8.1/8.2] Develop a package declaration and body to provide operations on character strings representing identifiers. An outline of the package declaration is

```
package identifier_pkg is

    subtype identifier is string(1 to 15);

    constant max_table_size : integer := 50;
    subtype table_index is integer range 1 to max_table_size;
    type table is array (table_index) of identifier;

    . . .

end package identifier_pkg;
```

The package also declares a procedure to convert alphabetic characters in a string to lowercase and a procedure to search for an occurrence of a given identifier in a table. The search procedure has two **out** mode parameters: a Boolean value indicating whether the sought string is in the table and a table_index value indicating its position, if present.

Aliases

Since the main purpose of a model written in VHDL is to describe a hardware design, it should be made as easy as possible to read and understand. In this chapter, we introduce *aliases* as a means of making a model clearer. As in everyday use, an alias is simply an alternate name for something. We see how we can use aliases in VHDL for both data objects and other kinds of items that do not represent data in a model.

9.1 Aliases for Data Objects

If we have a model that includes a data object, such as a constant, a variable, a signal or, as we see in a later chapter, a file, we can declare an alias for the object with an *alias declaration*. A simplified syntax rule for this is

alias_declaration ⇐ **alias** identifier **is** name ;

An alias declaration in this form simply defines an alternate identifier to refer to the named data object. We can refer to the object using the new identifier, treating it as being of the type specified in the original object's declaration. Operations we perform using the alias are actually applied to the original object. (The only exceptions are reading the 'simple_name, 'path_name and 'instance_name attributes and the attributes that provide information about the index ranges of an array. In these cases, the attributes refer to the alias name rather than the original object's name.)

EXAMPLE

One use of alias declarations is to define simple names for objects imported from packages. Suppose, for example, that we need to use objects from two different packages, alu_types and io_types, and that each declares a constant named data_width, possibly with different values. If we include use clauses for these packages in our model, as follows:

use work.alu_types.**all**, work.io_types.**all**;

neither of the versions of data_width becomes directly visible, since they have the same name. Hence we would have to refer to them as work.alu_types.data_width and work.io_types.data_width. However, we can avoid this long notation simply by introducing two alias declarations into our model, as shown in the architecture body outlined in Figure 9-1.

FIGURE 9-1

```
library ieee;  use ieee.std_logic_1164.all;
use work.alu_types.all, work.io_types.all;
architecture structural of controller_system is
    alias alu_data_width is work.alu_types.data_width;
    alias io_data_width is work.io_types.data_width;
    signal alu_in1, alu_in2,
        alu_result : std_logic_vector(0 to alu_data_width – 1);
    signal io_data : std_logic_vector(0 to io_data_width – 1);
    . . .
begin
    . . .
end architecture structural;
```

An outline of an architecture body that aliases objects imported from two packages.

As well as denoting a whole data object, an alias can denote a single element from a composite data object, such as a record or an array. We write the element name, including a record element selector or an array index, as the name to be aliased. For example, given the following declarations of types and a variable:

type register_array **is array** (0 **to** 15) **of** bit_vector(31 **downto** 0);

type register_set **is record**
   general_purpose_registers : register_array;
   program_counter : bit_vector(31 **downto** 0);
   program_status : bit_vector(31 **downto** 0);
  end record;

variable CPU_registers : register_set;

we can declare aliases for the record elements:

alias PSW **is** CPU_registers.program_status;
alias PC **is** CPU_registers.program_counter;
alias GPR **is** CPU_registers.general_purpose_registers;

We can also declare aliases for individual registers in the register array, for example:

alias SP **is** CPU_registers.general_purpose_registers(15);

The name that we are aliasing can itself be an alias. Hence the alias declaration for **SP** can be written using the alias name **GPR**:

alias SP **is** GPR(15);

An alias can also be used to denote a slice of a one-dimensional array. For example, given the above declaration for **CPU_registers**, we can declare an alias for part of the program status register:

alias interrupt_level **is** PSW(30 **downto** 26);

This declares interrupt_level to denote a bit vector, with indices from 30 down to 26, being part of the bit vector denoted by **PSW**. In general, if we declare an alias for an array slice in this way, the alias denotes an array with index range and direction determined by the slice.

In many cases, it would be convenient to use an alias to take a slightly different view of the array being aliased. For example, we would like to view the interrupt_level alias as a bit vector indexed from four down to zero. We can do this by using an extended form of alias declaration, described by the following syntax rule:

alias_declaration ⇐ **alias** identifier ⟦ : subtype_indication ⟧ **is** name ;

This shows that we can indicate the subtype for the alias. The subtype determines how we view the original object that the alias denotes. We can include a subtype indication in aliases for scalar objects, but the bounds and direction specified must be the same as those of the original object. Hence this only serves as a form of documentation, to restate the type information for the object. We can also include an unconstrained array type name as the alias subtype when aliasing an array object or slice. In this case the index bounds and direction come from the original object. However, when we declare an alias for an array or for an array slice, we can use the subtype indication to specify different index bounds and direction from the original object. The base type of the subtype indication must be the same as the base type of the original object. (This means that the subtype indication must refer to an array type with the same element and index types as the original object.) Furthermore, there must be the same number of elements in the alias subtype and the original object. Elements in the alias denote the corresponding elements in the actual object in left-to-right order. For example, if we were to declare the alias interrupt_level as follows:

alias interrupt_level : bit_vector(4 **downto** 0) **is** PSW(30 **downto** 26);

then interrupt_level(4) would denote PSW(30), interrupt_level(3) would denote PSW(29), and so on.

EXAMPLE

When we write subprograms that take parameters of unconstrained array types, the index bounds and direction of the parameter are not known until actual array objects are passed as arguments during a call. Without this knowledge, the body of the subprogram is difficult to write. For example, suppose we need to implement a function to perform addition on two bit vectors that represent two's-complement, signed integers. The function specification is

function "+" (bv1, bv2 : bit_vector) **return** bit_vector;

When the function is called it is possible that the first argument is indexed from 0 to 15, while the other argument is indexed from 31 down to 8. We must check that the arguments are of the same size and then index them in a loop running from the rightmost bit to the leftmost. The different ranges, directions and sizes make this difficult.

We can use aliases to make the task easier by viewing the objects as arrays with the same leftmost index and direction. The subprogram body is shown in Figure 9-2. The alias declarations create views of the bit-vector arguments, indexed from one up to their length. The function, after checking that the arguments are of the same length, can then use the same index values for corresponding elements of the two arguments and the result.

FIGURE 9-2

```
function "+" ( bv1, bv2 : bit_vector ) return bit_vector is
    alias norm1 : bit_vector(1 to bv1'length) is bv1;
    alias norm2 : bit_vector(1 to bv2'length) is bv2;
    variable result : bit_vector(1 to bv1'length);
    variable carry : bit := '0';
begin
    if bv1'length /= bv2'length then
        report "arguments of different length" severity failure;
    else
```

```
            for index in norm1'reverse_range loop
                result(index) := norm1(index) xor norm2(index) xor carry;
                carry := ( norm1(index) and norm2(index) )
                            or ( carry and ( norm1(index) or norm2(index) ) );
            end loop;
        end if;
        return result;
end function "+";
```

A function that performs addition on two bit vectors representing signed integers.

VHDL-87

An alias declaration in VHDL-87 must include a subtype indication.

9.2 Aliases for Non-Data Items

We saw in the previous section that we can declare aliases for data objects such as constants, variables and signals. We can also declare aliases for other named items that do not represent stored data, such as types, subprograms, packages, entities and so on. In fact, the only kinds of items for which we cannot declare aliases are labels, loop parameters and generate parameters (see Chapter 14). The syntax rule for alias declarations for non-data items is

alias_declaration ⇐
    alias (identifier ‖ character_literal ‖ operator_symbol)
        is name ⟦ signature ⟧ ;

We can use character literals as aliases for enumeration literals, and operator symbols as aliases for function subprograms. We will return to the optional signature part shortly.

If we define an alias for a type we can use the alias in any context where the original type name can be used. Furthermore, all of the predefined operations for values of the original type can be used without being declared. For example, if we define an alias:

alias binary_string **is** bit_vector;

we can declare objects to be of type **binary_string** and perform bit-vector operations on them; for example:

variable s1, s2 : binary_string(0 **to** 7);

. . .

s1 := s1 **and not** s2;

Declaring an alias for a type is different from declaring a new type. In the latter case, new overloaded versions of the operators would have to be declared. The alias, on the other hand, is simply another name for the existing type.

If we define an alias for an enumeration type, all of the enumeration literals of the original type are available for use. We do not need to define aliases for the literals, nor use fully selected names. For example, if a package system_types declares an enumeration type as follows:

    type system_status **is** (idle, active, overloaded);

and a model defines an alias for this type:

    alias status_type **is** work.system_types.system_status;

the model can simply refer to the literals **idle**, **active** and **overloaded**, instead of **work.system_types.overloaded** and so on. Similarly, if we declare an alias for a physical type, all of the unit names are available for use without aliasing or selection.

The optional signature part in an alias declaration is only used in aliases for subprograms and enumeration literals. These items can be overloaded, so it is possible that the name alone is not sufficient to identify which item is being aliased. The signature serves to identify one item uniquely. The syntax rule for a signature is

    signature $\Leftarrow$ [⟦ type_mark { , ... } ⟧ ⟦ **return** type_mark ⟧]

Note that the outer square bracket symbols ("[...]") are a required part of the signature, whereas the hollow square brackets ("⟦ ... ⟧") are part of the EBNF syntax and indicate optional parts of the signature.

When we declare an alias for a subprogram, the signature identifies which overloaded version of the subprogram name is aliased. The signature lists the types of each of the subprogram's parameters, in the same order that they appear in the subprogram's declaration. For example, if a package arithmetic_ops declares two procedures as follows:

    procedure increment (bv : **inout** bit_vector; by : **in** integer := 1);

    procedure increment (int : **inout** integer; by : **in** integer := 1);

we can declare aliases for the procedures as follows:

    alias bv_increment **is** work.arithmetic_ops.increment [bit_vector, integer];

    alias int_increment **is** work.arithmetic_ops.increment [integer, integer];

If the subprogram is a function, the signature also includes the type of the return value, after the keyword **return**. For example, we might alias the operator symbols "*", "+" and "−" to the bit operators **and**, **or** and **not**, as follows:

    alias "*" **is** "and" [bit, bit **return** bit];

    alias "+" **is** "or" [bit, bit **return** bit];

    alias "−" **is** "not" [bit **return** bit];

We would then be able to express Boolean equations using these operators. For example, given bit signals s, a, b and c, we could write

s <= a * b + (–a) * c;

If we wish to alias an individual literal of an enumeration type, we must deal with the possibility that the literal may belong to several different enumeration types. We can use a signature to distinguish one particular meaning by noting that an enumeration literal is equivalent to a function with no parameters that returns a value of the enumeration type. For example, when we write the enumeration literal '1', we can think of this as a call to a function with no parameters, returning a value of type bit. We can write an alias for this literal as follows:

alias high **is** std.standard.'1' [**return** bit];

The signature distinguishes the literal as being of type bit, rather than of any other character type. Note that a selected name is required for a character literal, since a character literal by itself is not a syntactically valid name.

EXAMPLE

One useful application of aliases for non-data items is to compose a package by collecting together a number of items declared in other packages. Figure 9-3 shows such a package for use in a DMA controller design. The package defines aliases for a number of types imported from the cpu_types package and for a function imported from a package that provides bit-vector arithmetic operations.

FIGURE 9-3

```
package DMA_controller_types_and_utilities is
    alias word is work.cpu_types.word;
    alias address is work.cpu_types.address;
    alias status_value is work.cpu_types.status_value;
    alias "+" is work.bit_vector_unsigned_arithmetic."+"
                    [ bit_vector, bit_vector return bit_vector ];

    . . .

end package DMA_controller_types_and_utilities;
```

A utility package for a DMA controller design, collecting together items imported from other packages.

The DMA controller architecture body outlined in Figure 9-4 imports the aliases from the utility package. The references to the names address and word denote the types originally defined in the package cpu_types, and the operator "+" denotes the bit-vector operator originally defined in the package bit_vector_unsigned_arithmetic.

FIGURE 9-4

```
architecture behavioral of DMA_controller is
    use work.DMA_controller_types_and_utilities.all;
begin
    behavior : process is
        variable address_reg0, address_reg1 : address;
        variable count_reg0, count_reg1 : word;
        . . .
    begin
        . . .
        address_reg0 := address_reg0 + X"0000_0004";
        . . .
    end process behavior;
end architecture behavioral;
```

An outline of the architecture body for the DMA controller that makes use of the aliases defined in the utility package.

VHDL-87
━━━━━━━━

VHDL-87 does not allow aliases for non-data items. Aliases may only be declared for data objects.

━━━

Exercises

1. [❶ 9.1] Given the following declarations:

    ```
    subtype byte is bit_vector(0 to 7);
    type data_array is array (0 to 31) of byte;
    type network_packet is record
            source, dest, flags : byte;
            payload : data_array;
            checksum : byte;
        end record network_packet;
    variable received_packet : network_packet;
    ```

    write alias declarations for the individual elements of the variable.

2. [❶ 9.1] The layout of information within the **flags** element of a network packet described in Exercise 1 is

0	1	2	3	4	5	6	7
AK	ACKNO			SEQNO			UD

    Write alias declarations for the individual fields of the **flags** element of the received_packet variable. The aliases for the ACKNO and SEQNO fields should view the fields as bit vectors indexed from two down to zero.

3. [❶ 9.2] Write an alias declaration that defines the name cons as an alias for the predefined operation "&" with a character left argument, a string right argument and a string result. Use the alias in a report statement that reports the string constructed from the value of the variable grade_char concatenated to the string "–grade".

4. [❷ 9.1] Develop a behavioral model of a bit-reversing module with the following entity interface:

```
entity reverser is
    port ( d_in : in std_ulogic_vector;
           d_out : out std_ulogic_vector );
end entity reverser;
```

When the entity is instantiated, the actual signals must be of the same length, but may differ in their index bounds and directions. The output is the input delayed by 500 ps using transport delay, and with the bits in reverse order from left to right.

Case Study: A Bit-Vector Arithmetic Package

10

We now come to our second case study, in which we develop a package of procedures and functions to perform arithmetic operations on bit vectors. The subprograms treat the bit vectors as binary-encoded integers. This case study draws on the facilities of VHDL described in the previous three chapters.

10.1 The Package Interface

VHDL provides certain predefined arithmetic operations, such as addition, subtraction, multiplication and division, on the predefined numeric types. However, while we may represent numbers with bit vectors by using a binary encoding, the language does not provide arithmetic operations for bit vectors. There are several alternative encoding schemes we may use to represent numbers, each with different interpretations of the bits within a vector. VHDL leaves the choice of representation to the designer. If we need to perform arithmetic operations on numbers represented as bit vectors, we must implement the operations according to the encoding we have chosen.

In this case study, we develop arithmetic operations for bit vectors that use conventional positional encoding to represent integers. We provide for both unsigned integers and signed integers using two's-complement representation. The bit-vector encodings for both number representations are shown in Figure 10-1. Each position in the bit vector has a corresponding weight, starting from 2^0 for the rightmost bit and increasing for positions further to the left. The difference between the two representations is that the weight of the leftmost bit is 2^{n-1} for unsigned numbers but -2^{n-1} for signed numbers. In this latter case, the leftmost bit is called the sign bit, since it is '1' for negative numbers and '0' for non-negative numbers. The integer represented by a given bit vector is determined by multiplying each bit by its corresponding weight and adding the products.

FIGURE 10-1

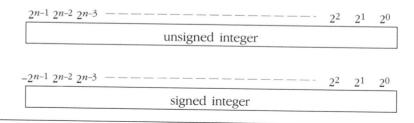

Bit-vector encodings for unsigned integers (top) and two's-complement signed integers (bottom). The symbol n *refers to the number of bits in the bit vector.*

Figure 10-2 shows the interface for our package of bit-vector arithmetic operations. The package contains declarations of a number of procedures and functions that implement the operations. The comment at the beginning of the package briefly describes the purpose of the package and outlines some constraints on how the procedures and functions should be used. It is good style to include a description such as this when writing a package interface. The requirement mentioned in this comment is that dyadic operations (those that take two operands) must be used with two bit vectors of the same length. Furthermore, the results returned by the operations, either as **out** mode parameters or as function results, must be of the same length as the operands. These requirements mean, for example, that we may add two 32-bit vectors and expect a 32-bit result. However, we may not add a 32-bit vector and a 16-bit vector, nor may we add two 32-bit vectors and expect a 33-bit result. While these restrictions may cause minor inconvenience in some applications, they considerably simplify the implementation of the operations, as we shall see in the next section.

The first group of operations provided by the package are a number of conversion functions that convert between numeric and bit-vector values. Conversions are included in both directions between the numeric type **natural** and unsigned binary vectors, and between the numeric type **integer** and signed binary vectors. The conversion functions that produce vector results have an additional parameter that indicates how long the result should be.

FIGURE 10-2

```
----------------------------------------------------------------

-- Bit-vector arithmetic package interface.

-- Does arithmetic and logical operations on bit vectors, treating them
-- as either unsigned or signed (two's complement) integers.  Leftmost bit
-- is most-significant or sign bit, rightmost bit is least-significant
-- bit.  Dyadic operations need the two arguments to be of the same
-- length; however, their index ranges and directions may differ.  Results
-- must be of the same length as the operands.

----------------------------------------------------------------

package bv_arithmetic is
    function bv_to_natural ( bv : in bit_vector ) return natural;
    function natural_to_bv ( nat : in natural;
                             length : in natural ) return bit_vector;
    function bv_to_integer ( bv : in bit_vector ) return integer;
    function integer_to_bv ( int : in integer;
                             length : in natural ) return bit_vector;
    procedure bv_add ( bv1, bv2 : in bit_vector;
                       bv_result : out bit_vector;
                       overflow : out boolean );
    function "+" ( bv1, bv2 : in bit_vector ) return bit_vector;
    procedure bv_sub ( bv1, bv2 : in bit_vector;
                       bv_result : out bit_vector;
                       overflow : out boolean );
    function "-" ( bv1, bv2 : in bit_vector ) return bit_vector;
    procedure bv_addu ( bv1, bv2 : in bit_vector;
                        bv_result : out bit_vector;
                        overflow : out boolean );
    function bv_addu ( bv1, bv2 : in bit_vector ) return bit_vector;
    procedure bv_subu ( bv1, bv2 : in bit_vector;
                        bv_result : out bit_vector;
                        overflow : out boolean );
    function bv_subu ( bv1, bv2 : in bit_vector ) return bit_vector;
```

(continued on page 254)

(continued from page 253)

```
        procedure bv_neg ( bv : in bit_vector;
                           bv_result : out bit_vector;
                           overflow : out boolean );
     function "–" ( bv : in bit_vector ) return bit_vector;
        procedure bv_mult ( bv1, bv2 : in bit_vector;
                           bv_result : out bit_vector;
                           overflow : out boolean );
     function "*" ( bv1, bv2 : in bit_vector ) return bit_vector;
        procedure bv_multu ( bv1, bv2 : in bit_vector;
                            bv_result : out bit_vector;
                            overflow : out boolean );
     function bv_multu ( bv1, bv2 : in bit_vector ) return bit_vector;
        procedure bv_div ( bv1, bv2 : in bit_vector;
                          bv_result : out bit_vector;
                          div_by_zero : out boolean;
                          overflow : out boolean );
     function "/" ( bv1, bv2 : in bit_vector ) return bit_vector;
        procedure bv_divu ( bv1, bv2 : in bit_vector;
                           bv_quotient : out bit_vector;
                           bv_remainder : out bit_vector;
                           div_by_zero : out boolean );
        procedure bv_divu ( bv1, bv2 : in bit_vector;
                           bv_quotient : out bit_vector;
                           div_by_zero : out boolean );
     function bv_divu ( bv1, bv2 : in bit_vector )  return bit_vector;
     function bv_lt ( bv1, bv2 : in bit_vector ) return boolean;
     function bv_le ( bv1, bv2 : in bit_vector ) return boolean;
     function bv_gt ( bv1, bv2 : in bit_vector ) return boolean;
     function bv_ge ( bv1, bv2 : in bit_vector ) return boolean;
     function bv_sext ( bv : in bit_vector;
                       length : in natural ) return bit_vector;
     function bv_zext ( bv : in bit_vector;
                       length : in natural ) return bit_vector;
   end package bv_arithmetic;
```

The interface for the bit-vector arithmetic package.

Second, the package includes several forms of addition, subtraction, multiplication and division operations. Operations are provided for signed and unsigned binary vectors. In each case, there are two forms of operation. The first form is a procedure that provides its results and status flags through **out** mode parameters. The status flags indicate whether the result is incorrect due to an arithmetic overflow or division by zero condition. There are two versions of the unsigned division procedure. One returns both the quotient and remainder, whereas the other returns just the quotient. The second form of each operation is a function that returns the result of the operation without indicating any exceptional conditions that may arise. These functions may be used if the occurrence of an exceptional condition is not of interest to the caller, or if the caller can guarantee that such a condition does not arise. The functions that operate on signed binary vectors are provided as overloaded versions of the familiar operator symbols "+", "–", "*" and "/". This means that we can use these operators to write expressions such as "a + b", where a and b are binary vector values.

The third group of operations included in the package are relational functions for comparing two signed binary vectors. We do not need to include functions to test for equality or inequality, since the predefined operators "=" and "/=" perform this test satisfactorily. Furthermore, we do not need to include relational functions for unsigned binary vectors. The predefined relational operators "<", "<=", ">" and ">=" compare bit vectors using lexical ordering. As it happens, this produces the same results as a numeric comparison of the numbers represented by the vectors, assuming unsigned representation. Hence the predefined operators can be used for this purpose.

The final group of operations in the package are the extension functions. Each operates on a binary vector and returns a binary vector of a different length, but representing the same integer value. The length of the result is specified by the second parameter of the function. In most uses of these functions, the result vector is longer than the original vector. The sign-extension function operates on signed vectors. Its result is formed by appending additional bits to the left and setting them to the same value as the sign bit of the original operand. The zero-extension function operates on unsigned binary vectors. It also appends bits to the left but simply sets them to '0'.

10.2 The Package Body

We now turn to the body of the bit-vector arithmetic package and see how the operations are implemented. Figure 10-3 outlines the package body. For each function and procedure defined in the package interface, there is a full implementation in the package body. The details of the parameter lists and return types are copied exactly from the package interface. We will not show the details of every operation in the package body, as there is much similarity between them. Instead, we will examine a representative collection and leave the rest as an exercise for the reader.

FIGURE 10-3

```
package body bv_arithmetic is

    -- Bodies of procedures and functions

    . . .

end package body bv_arithmetic;
```

An outline of the body of the bit-vector arithmetic package.

Figure 10-4 shows the implementation of the **bv_to_natural** conversion function, which converts a vector in unsigned binary representation to a numeric value. The algorithm used to perform the conversion is based on multiplying each bit in the bit

FIGURE 10-4

```
function bv_to_natural ( bv : in bit_vector ) return natural is
    variable result : natural := 0;
begin
    for index in bv'range loop
        result := result * 2 + bit'pos( bv(index) );
    end loop;
    return result;
end function bv_to_natural;
```

The implementation of the bv_to_natural *function.*

vector by its corresponding weight and accumulating the products. Given a bit vector $(b_{n-1}, b_{n-2}, \ldots, b_0)$ of length n, the numeric value it represents is

$$b_{n-1}2^{n-1} + b_{n-2}2^{n-2} + \cdots + b_0$$

We can factor out powers of two and rewrite this expression so that it does not involve exponentiation, as follows:

$$2 \times (\cdots (2 \times (2 \times (b_{n-1}) + b_{n-2}) + b_{n-3}) \cdots) + b_0$$

This is a commonly used optimization for evaluating polynomial expressions. The loop shown in Figure 10-4 evaluates the expression in this form, starting with the most-significant bit (the leftmost bit) of the parameter **bv** and working outwards to the least-significant bit. The sum is accumulated in the local variable **result**, which is initialized to 0. Hence, in the first iteration of the loop, multiplying **result** by 2 and adding the leftmost bit simply has the effect of setting it to the value of the leftmost bit, as required for the nested form of the polynomial expression. The numeric value of each bit is determined using the **pos** attribute of the type **bit**. For a '0' bit, this attribute has the value 0, and for a '1' bit it has the value 1. On completion of the loop, the accumulated value is returned as the function result.

One important point to note about this function is that if it is passed a vector representing a number larger than is representable in type **natural**, it fails. The multiplication step produces either an overflow error on the host machine running the simulation or an incorrect result without raising the overflow error. This behavior makes sense, since the result is not representable on the host machine. The function is safe provided it is passed vectors that represent numbers no larger than **natural'high**, which is guaranteed by the language standard to be at least 2,147,483,648.

The implementation of the **natural_to_bv** function is shown in Figure 10-5. The algorithm used to generate an unsigned binary vector from the numeric value is the inverse of that used in the previous function. The local variable **temp** is initialized to the numeric value to be converted and is repeatedly divided by two. The remainder of each division produces successive bits of the result, from least significant to most significant. These are stored in the local variable **result**, from right to left. The size of **result** is determined by the parameter **length**. When all bits of the vector have been calculated, the function returns **result**. Note that when we use this function, we must specify the

FIGURE 10-5

```
function natural_to_bv ( nat : in natural;
                        length : in natural ) return bit_vector is
    variable temp : natural := nat;
    variable result : bit_vector(length – 1 downto 0) := (others => '0');
begin
    for index in result'reverse_range loop
        result(index) := bit'val( temp rem 2 );
        temp := temp / 2;
        exit when temp = 0;
    end loop;
    return result;
end function natural_to_bv;
```

The implementation of the natural_to_bv *function.*

correct value for the length parameter, indicating the length of the vector we expect
the function to return. For example, if we were to call the function as follows:

```
reg(0 to 7) := natural_to_bv(counter, 16);
```

it would return a 16-element bit vector. The assignment to an eight-element bit vector
would then fail.

We now move on to the arithmetic operations provided by the package. The implementation of the **bv_add** procedure is shown in Figure 10-6. The procedure accepts
two bit vectors, **bv1** and **bv2**, representing two's-complement signed binary numbers,
and produces their sum in the bit vector **bv_result**. It also sets the Boolean parameter
overflow to indicate whether the sum is beyond the range that can be represented in
the result bit vector. The procedure expects **bv1**, **bv2** and **bv_result** all to be of the same
length and uses an assertion statement to verify that this is the case. The operands may,
however, have index ranges that start and end at different bounds or even have different directions. The procedure allows for this, treating the rightmost bit as the least significant and the leftmost bit as the sign bit. In order to simplify selection of corresponding bits from each operand during the addition algorithm, the procedure declares
aliases for the operands, **op1** and **op2**. Each alias has an index range starting from one
less than the length of the vector and descending to zero. The procedure also declares
a local bit-vector variable, result, in which it produces the sum. This vector also has
its index range descending to zero and has the same length as the **out** parameter bv_re-
sult. Once the procedure has verified that the operand and result parameters all have
the same length, it can use the same index values to select corresponding bits from
the operand aliases and the local result variable.

The addition algorithm starts from the least-significant bit position and works left-
wards. At each position, it uses the two operand bits and the carry in from the previous
position to generate the sum bit and the carry out to the next position. The **xor** operator
has the effect of adding bit values. Upon completion of the loop, the sum is used to
update the **bv_result** parameter, and the overflow status is calculated. At this stage,
carry_out is the carry out from the sign-bit position, and carry_in is the carry into the
sign-bit position. The addition has overflowed if these two carry values differ.

FIGURE 10-6

```
procedure bv_add ( bv1, bv2 : in bit_vector;
                        bv_result : out bit_vector;
                        overflow : out boolean ) is
    alias op1 : bit_vector(bv1'length − 1 downto 0) is bv1;
    alias op2 : bit_vector(bv2'length − 1 downto 0) is bv2;
    variable result : bit_vector(bv_result'length − 1 downto 0);
    variable carry_in : bit;
    variable carry_out : bit := '0';
begin
    if bv1'length /= bv2'length or bv1'length /= bv_result'length then
        report "bv_add: operands of different lengths"
        severity failure;
    else
        for index in result'reverse_range loop
            carry_in := carry_out;   −− of previous bit
            result(index) := op1(index) xor op2(index) xor carry_in;
            carry_out := (op1(index) and op2(index))
                            or (carry_in and (op1(index) xor op2(index)));
        end loop;
        bv_result := result;
        overflow := carry_out /= carry_in;
    end if;
end procedure bv_add;
```

The implementation of the bv_add *procedure.*

The next operation in the bit-vector arithmetic package is the overloaded operator "+", which performs signed addition on two vectors. The implementation of this function is identical to that of the **bv_add** procedure, except that the sum is returned as the function result, and the overflow status flag is not generated. The following two operations, **bv_sub** and the overloaded operator "−", are implemented similarly. The subtraction is performed by adding the negative of the second operand, calculated by complementing and adding one. This is done by initializing the carry into the least-significant position to '1' instead of '0' and by substituting **not** op2(index) for op2(index) in the loop. Following these operations are the unsigned addition and subtraction operations. Again, these are implemented similarly, but with the overflow condition determined by the carry out from the most-significant bit position.

Once we have defined the subtraction operation for signed binary vectors, we can use it to implement the negation operation. Figure 10-7 shows the implementation of **bv_neg**, a procedure that negates a binary vector and also returns an overflow status flag. It simply calls the **bv_sub** procedure to subtract the operand from zero, generating the result and the overflow flag. The constant **zero** is a bit vector of the same size as the operand, but with all bits set to '0'. The implementation of the overloaded unary operator "−" performs negation in the same way, but uses the overloaded subtraction operator that ignores overflow.

The next group of operations on which we focus is the set of multiplication operations. These are all implemented using the version for unsigned binary operands with

FIGURE 10-7

```
procedure bv_neg ( bv : in bit_vector;
                   bv_result : out bit_vector;
                   overflow : out boolean ) is
    constant zero : bit_vector(bv'range) := (others => '0');
begin
    bv_sub( zero, bv, bv_result, overflow );
end procedure bv_neg;
```

The implementation of the bv_neg *operation.*

FIGURE 10-8

```
procedure bv_multu ( bv1, bv2 : in bit_vector;
                     bv_result : out bit_vector;
                     overflow : out boolean ) is
    alias op1 : bit_vector(bv1'length − 1 downto 0) is bv1;
    alias op2 : bit_vector(bv2'length − 1 downto 0) is bv2;
    constant len : natural := bv1'length;
    constant accum_len : natural := len * 2;
    variable accum : bit_vector(accum_len − 1 downto 0) := (others => '0');
    constant zero : bit_vector(accum_len − 1 downto len):= (others => '0');
    variable addu_overflow : boolean;
begin
    if bv1'length /= bv2'length or bv1'length /= bv_result'length then
        report "bv_multu: operands of different lengths"
        severity failure;
    else
        for count in 0 to len − 1 loop
            if op2(count) = '1' then
                bv_addu( accum(count + len − 1 downto count), op1,
                         accum(count + len − 1 downto count), addu_overflow );
                accum(count + len) := bit'val(boolean'pos(addu_overflow));
            end if;
        end loop;
        bv_result := accum(len − 1 downto 0);
        overflow := accum(accum_len−1 downto len) /= zero;
    end if;
end procedure bv_multu;
```

The implementation of the bv_multu *procedure.*

overflow status, so we will describe it first. The procedure body is shown in Figure 10-8 and implements the operation using a binary long multiplication algorithm. Like the addition procedure described earlier, it expects its operand and result vector parameters to be of the same length and uses an assertion statement to verify this. It also declares aliases for the operands to simplify calculation of index values. The constant len represents the length of the operands. The procedure declares a local bit-vector variable accum, which is twice as long as the operands. It is used to accumulate partial products in the long multiplication algorithm, hence it is initialized to zero. The long multiplication is performed by the for loop in the procedure body. Each bit in the multiplier **op2** is tested in turn. If the bit is '1', the multiplicand **op1** is added into the accumulator, at a position determined by the position of the multiplier bit. If the bit is '0', the addition is skipped. The addition is performed using the unsigned binary vector addition procedure from the package. An overflow from the addition is treated as a carry into the next most-significant bit of the accumulator. The final result of the procedure is the least-significant half of the accumulated product. If any bits in the most-significant half of the product are '1', the product is larger than can be represented in the result vector. Thus the procedure sets the overflow flag if the most-significant half of the product is non-zero.

The multiplication procedure for signed binary vectors is shown in Figure 10-9. The procedure first examines the sign bits of the operands to determine the sign of the result. The result is negative if either operand is negative, but not if both are negative. The procedure stores the absolute values of the operands in the local variables **op1** and **op2**, using the overloaded unary negation operator to negate negative operands. It then uses the unsigned binary multiplication procedure to multiply the absolute values, giving the absolute value of the result. If the result should be negative, the procedure sets the result parameter to the negative of the calculated product. In this case, the overflow flag is set if the unsigned multiplication overflows or if the unsigned product is larger than the absolute value of the most negative representable integer. If the result should be non-negative, the result vector is set to the calculated product. The overflow flag is set if the unsigned multiplication overflows or if the unsigned product is larger than the most positive representable integer.

Next we come to the division operations. These are all based on the **bv_divu** procedure, which divides unsigned binary vectors, producing an unsigned result and a status flag for the "divide by zero" condition. This operation cannot result in overflow. The result can never be larger than the dividend (the first operand), since the divisor (the second operand) is an integer greater than or equal to one. The signed division operations work in an analogous manner to the signed multiplication operations. They perform the operation on the absolute values of the operands and adjust the sign of the result as necessary. The signed division operation can result in an overflow condition if the dividend is the most negative representable integer and the divisor is −1. Hence the version of the signed division operation that returns status information includes a parameter to return the overflow status.

The implementation of the unsigned division procedure, producing both the quotient and remainder, is shown in Figure 10-10. It is based on the non-restoring division algorithm, as described in Appendix A of Hennessy and Patterson [7] and Appendix I of Feldman and Retter [4]. The constant **len** is set to the length of the first operand vector. The procedure expects all operands to be of this length. The alias **dividend** denotes the first operand and has an index range descending to 0. The variable **divisor** is a copy of the second operand, extended in length by one bit. It is treated as an unsigned number. The local variable **quotient** is the same length as the operands and is used to accumulate successive quotient bits one at a time. The local variable **remainder** is a vector that is one bit longer than the operands and is treated as a signed number.

FIGURE 10-9

```
procedure bv_mult ( bv1, bv2 : in bit_vector;
                    bv_result : out bit_vector;
                    overflow : out boolean ) is
    variable negative_result : boolean;
    variable op1 : bit_vector(bv1'range) := bv1;
    variable op2 : bit_vector(bv2'range) := bv2;
    variable multu_result : bit_vector(bv1'range);
    variable multu_overflow : boolean;
    variable abs_min_int : bit_vector(bv1'range) := (others => '0');
begin
    if bv1'length /= bv2'length or bv1'length /= bv_result'length then
        report "bv_mult: operands of different lengths"
        severity failure;
    else
        abs_min_int(bv1'left) := '1';
        negative_result := (op1(op1'left) = '1') xor (op2(op2'left) = '1');
        if op1(op1'left) = '1' then
            op1 := - bv1;
        end if;
        if op2(op2'left) = '1' then
            op2 := - bv2;
        end if;
        bv_multu(op1, op2, multu_result, multu_overflow);
        if negative_result then
            overflow := multu_overflow or (multu_result > abs_min_int);
            bv_result := - multu_result;
        else
            overflow := multu_overflow or (multu_result(multu_result'left) = '1');
            bv_result := multu_result;
        end if;
    end if;
end procedure bv_mult;
```

The implementation of the bv_mult *procedure.*

The procedure checks that the two operand vectors and the two result vectors are all of the same length. Once it has established this, it uses len when calculating index values for all vectors. The procedure then tests whether the second operand is zero. If it is, the procedure sets the status flag div_by_zero to true and returns. Otherwise it proceeds with the division algorithm. This consists of a loop in which the sign of the remainder is first tested. If the remainder is positive, it is shifted left one place and the divisor is subtracted from it. If the remainder is negative, it is shifted left and the divisor is added to it. In both cases, the shift operation involves bringing the next bit of the dividend into the least-significant position of the remainder. The next bit of the quotient is the inverse of the sign bit of the resulting remainder. Upon completion of the loop, the remainder vector may still be negative. If it is, the procedure performs one final restoration by adding the divisor. The quotient and remainder vectors then

FIGURE 10-10 _____

```
procedure bv_divu ( bv1, bv2 : in bit_vector;
                    bv_quotient : out bit_vector;
                    bv_remainder : out bit_vector;
                    div_by_zero : out boolean ) is
    constant len : natural := bv1'length;
    constant zero_divisor : bit_vector(len–1 downto 0) := (others => '0');
    alias dividend : bit_vector(bv1'length–1 downto 0) is bv1;
    variable divisor : bit_vector(bv2'length downto 0) := '0' & bv2;
    variable quotient : bit_vector(len–1 downto 0);
    variable remainder : bit_vector(len downto 0) := (others => '0');
    variable ignore_overflow  : boolean;
begin
    if bv1'length /= bv2'length
        or bv1'length /= bv_quotient'length or bv1'length /= bv_remainder'length then
        report "bv_divu: operands of different lengths"
        severity failure;
    else
        -- check for zero divisor
        if bv2 = zero_divisor then
            div_by_zero := true;
            return;
        end if;
        -- perform division
        for iter in len–1 downto 0 loop
            if remainder(len) = '0' then
                remainder := remainder sll 1;
                remainder(0) := dividend(iter);
                bv_sub(remainder, divisor, remainder, ignore_overflow);
            else
                remainder := remainder sll 1;
                remainder(0) := dividend(iter);
                bv_add(remainder, divisor, remainder, ignore_overflow);
            end if;
            quotient(iter) := not remainder(len);
        end loop;
        if remainder(len) = '1' then
            bv_add(remainder, divisor, remainder, ignore_overflow);
        end if;
        bv_quotient := quotient;
        bv_remainder := remainder(len – 1 downto 0);
        div_by_zero := false;
    end if;
end procedure bv_divu;
```

The implementation of the bv_divu *procedure.*

contain the required results, so the procedure assigns them to the result parameters. It also sets the div_by_zero flag to false.

Following the arithmetic operators, we come to the relational operators on signed binary vectors. We look at the bv_lt function, shown in Figure 10-11. The remaining functions are implemented similarly. The bv_lt function expects its operands to be of the same length and verifies this using an assertion statement. The algorithm for comparing the vectors is based on some observations of two's-complement encoding. First, if we consider only non-negative numbers, we note that the binary codes start at "00...0" for the smallest number and increase to "01...1" for the largest. Thus the predefined lexical relation operator "<" performs the required comparison correctly. Second, if we consider only negative numbers, the binary codes start at "10...0" for the most negative number and increase to "11...1" for the least negative. Again the predefined operator "<" performs the required comparison. The problem with using this operator arises when we mix negative and non-negative numbers. The operator treats all negative numbers as greater than non-negative numbers, since negative numbers have the leftmost bit set to '1'. We can compensate for this by inverting the leftmost bit of each operand. If we do this, the transformed negative numbers have binary codes from "00...0" to "01...1", and the transformed non-negative numbers have codes from "10...0" to "11...1". A lexical comparison of these transformed codes then corresponds exactly to the required arithmetic comparison of the original vectors. The bv_lt function implements this algorithm. It copies the operand vectors into the local variables tmp1 and tmp2 and inverts their leftmost bits. It then returns the result of the predefined lexical comparison operator applied to tmp1 and tmp2.

FIGURE 10-11

```
function bv_lt ( bv1, bv2 : in bit_vector ) return boolean is
    variable tmp1 : bit_vector(bv1'range) := bv1;
    variable tmp2 : bit_vector(bv2'range) := bv2;
begin
    assert bv1'length = bv2'length
        report "bv_lt: operands of different lengths"
        severity failure;
    tmp1(tmp1'left) := not tmp1(tmp1'left);
    tmp2(tmp2'left) := not tmp2(tmp2'left);
    return tmp1 < tmp2;
end function bv_lt;
```

The implementation of the bv_lt *function.*

The final pair of operations in the package includes the functions bv_sext and bv_zext, each of which extends or truncates a binary vector, maintaining the same numeric value. The implementation of the sign-extension function is shown in Figure 10-12. This function, like many of the preceding operations, makes use of an alias for its operand to simplify index calculations. It declares a local variable, result, of the extended length required and sets each bit in it to the same value as the sign bit of the operand. The body of the function then overwrites the rightmost bits of this vector with a copy of the operand. Provided the extended length is greater than the

FIGURE 10-12

```
function bv_sext ( bv : in bit_vector;
                   length : in natural ) return bit_vector is
    alias bv_norm : bit_vector(bv'length – 1 downto 0) is bv;
    variable result : bit_vector(length – 1 downto 0) := (others => bv(bv'left));
    variable src_length : natural := bv'length;
begin
    if src_length > length then
        src_length := length;
    end if;
    result(src_length – 1 downto 0) := bv_norm(src_length – 1 downto 0);
    return result;
end function bv_sext;
```

The implementation of the **bv_sext** *function.*

source operand length, this has the effect of producing a vector whose leftmost bits are a replication of the operand sign bit. One property of the two's-complement representation used for signed numbers is that this form of extension preserves the numeric value represented by the vector. If the extended length is less than that of the operand, the function selects only the rightmost bits of the operand and copies them to the result vector. The number of bits selected in this case is determined by the extended length. The numeric value represented by the result is the same as that of the operand, provided none of the bits truncated from the operand were '0'.

The second extension function, **bv_zext**, is implemented identically to **bv_sext**, except that the result vector is initialized with all bits set to '0' instead of a copy of the operand sign bit.

10.3 An ALU Using the Arithmetic Package

To illustrate the use of the bit-vector arithmetic package, we look at a model of an arithmetic/logic unit (ALU) for the CPU of a computer. An extended version of this ALU forms part of a complete CPU model that we present as the next case study, in Chapter 15. For this illustration, we assume that the bit-vector arithmetic package has been analyzed and placed in a design library called **bv_utilities**. Figure 10-13 shows the entity declaration for the ALU. It makes use of a package, also shown in Figure 10-13, that defines a binary encoding for the ALU function select input. The data inputs and outputs are vectors of standard-logic values, representing signed or unsigned binary numbers. In addition, there are status output ports indicating a zero result, a negative result and an overflow arising from the operation performed.

Figure 10-14 shows a behavioral architecture for the ALU. It contains a process sensitive to changes on the data input ports and the function select input port. The process includes a use clause to import the names of operations defined in the bit-vector arithmetic package. When any of the inputs change value, the process converts the current data inputs from standard-logic vector values to bit vectors, using the conversion function **To_bitvector**, defined in the **std_logic_1164** package. If an input contains an unknown element, the conversion function maps it to the bit value '0'. The

FIGURE 10-13

```
library ieee;  use ieee.std_logic_1164.all;
package alu_types is
    subtype alu_func is std_ulogic_vector(3 downto 0);
    constant alu_add : alu_func := "0000";
    constant alu_addu : alu_func := "0001";
    constant alu_sub : alu_func := "0010";
    constant alu_subu : alu_func := "0011";
end package alu_types;
```

_____

```
library ieee;  use ieee.std_logic_1164.all;
use work.alu_types.all;
entity alu is
    port ( s1, s2 : in std_ulogic_vector;
           result : out std_ulogic_vector;
           func : in alu_func;
           zero, negative, overflow : out std_ulogic );
end entity alu;
```

A package providing declarations for use by the ALU model, and the entity declaration for the ALU.

process then uses the function select input to determine which operation to apply to the bit-vector values. Four cases are shown that involve signed and unsigned addition and subtraction. The operations are performed using the bit-vector arithmetic procedures, with the result being stored in the variable temp_result and the overflow status being stored in temp_overflow. The bit-vector result is converted back to the standard-logic vector type using the conversion function To_X01 and assigned to the ALU data output port. The bit-vector result is also tested to determine whether it is zero or represents a negative number and the status output ports set appropriately. Finally, the overflow status flag resulting from the arithmetic operation is converted and assigned to the overflow status port.

FIGURE 10-14

```
library bv_utilities;
architecture behavior of alu is
begin
    alu_op: process (s1, s2, func) is
        constant Tpd : delay_length := 10 ns;
        use bv_utilities.bv_arithmetic.all;
        variable bv_s1 : bit_vector(s1'range) := To_bitvector(s1);
        variable bv_s2 : bit_vector(s2'range) := To_bitvector(s2);
        variable temp_result : bit_vector(result'range);
        constant zero_result : bit_vector(result'range) := (others => '0');
        variable temp_overflow : boolean;
```

(continued on page 266)

(continued from page 265)

```
            type boolean_to_X01_table is array (boolean) of X01;
            constant boolean_to_X01 : boolean_to_X01_table
                            := ( false => '0', true => '1' );
        begin
            case func is
                when alu_add =>
                    bv_add(bv_s1, bv_s2, temp_result, temp_overflow);
                when alu_addu =>
                    bv_addu(bv_s1, bv_s2, temp_result, temp_overflow);
                when alu_sub =>
                    bv_sub(bv_s1, bv_s2, temp_result, temp_overflow);
                when alu_subu =>
                    bv_subu(bv_s1, bv_s2, temp_result, temp_overflow);
                when others =>
                    report "alu: illegal function code" severity error;
                    temp_result := X"0000_0000";
            end case;
            result <= To_X01(temp_result) after Tpd;
            zero <= boolean_to_X01(temp_result = zero_result) after Tpd;
            negative <= To_X01(temp_result(temp_result'left)) after Tpd;
            overflow <= boolean_to_X01(temp_overflow) after Tpd;
        end process alu_op;
    end architecture behavior;
```

A behavioral architecture of the ALU, using operations from the bit-vector arithmetic package.

Exercises

1. [❶ 10.1] A variable **PC** containing an unsigned binary number is declared as

    variable PC : bit_vector(31 **downto** 0);

    Write an assignment statement that uses operations from the bv_arithmetic package to increment **PC** by four, ignoring any overflow that may occur.

2. [❶ 10.1] Variables for a base address, a signed offset, a scale factor and an effective address are declared as

    variable base_address, effective_address : bit_vector(23 **downto** 0);
    variable offset : bit_vector(7 **downto** 0);
    variable scale_factor : positive **range** 1 **to** 8;

    Write an assignment statement that multiplies the offset by the scale factor, adds the product to the base address and assigns the result to the effective address.

3. [❸ 10.2] Complete the bv_arithmetic package body by writing the declarations of the subprograms omitted in this chapter. Develop a test bench that exercises each of the subprograms.

4. [❷ 10.3] Extend the ALU model to include signed and unsigned multiplication and division, and signed negation. You will need an additional status port to indicate the divide-by-zero condition.

5. [❸] Use the **bv_arithmetic** package to implement a similar package of arithmetic operations for binary numbers expressed as standard-logic vectors.

6. [❹] Develop a package of arithmetic operations for IEEE single-precision floating-point numbers represented as bit vectors. Your package should include addition, subtraction, multiplication, division and square-root operations, and conversion functions to convert between bit-vector and **real** values.

7. [❹] One approach to self-timed asynchronous circuit design is to represent each bit of information with two signals. One signal indicates the presence of a 0 bit, and the other indicates the presence of a 1 bit. If neither signal is asserted, no data is present. We can model this form of representation in VHDL using the declarations

```
type self_timed_bit is record
        zero, one : bit;
    end record self_timed_bit;
constant self_timed_no_data : self_timed_bit := ( zero => '0', one => '0');
constant self_timed_zero : self_timed_bit := ( zero => '1', one => '0');
constant self_timed_one : self_timed_bit := ( zero => '0', one => '1');
constant self_timed_illegal : self_timed_bit := ( zero => '1', one => '1');
```

Synchronization between modules is performed using a four-phase handshaking protocol. A module waits until data is present on all of its inputs, then performs its computation. When it no longer needs the input data, it asserts an acknowledge signal to the data source. (The acknowledge is a scalar bit, not a self-timed bit.) The source removes data from the input wires, and when all bits have returned to the no-data state, the module negates the acknowledge signal.

Develop a package for modeling asynchronous systems using this form of self-timed data. Your package should include declarations for signals carrying individual bits of data, vectors of bits and acknowledgements. You should provide procedures with signal parameters, for use in concurrent procedure calls, that implement arithmetic operations, storage registers and data-presence detectors. You should also include conversion functions to convert between self-timed data and conventional bit-vector data.

11

Resolved Signals

Throughout the previous chapters we have studiously avoided considering the case of multiple output ports connecting the one signal. The problem that arises in such a case is determining the final value of the signal when multiple sources drive it. In this chapter we discuss *resolved signals*, the mechanism provided by VHDL for modeling such cases.

11.1 Basic Resolved Signals

If we consider a real digital system with two outputs driving one signal, we can fairly readily determine the resulting value based on some analog circuit theory. The signal is driven to some intermediate state, depending on the drive capacities of the conflicting drivers. This intermediate state may or may not represent a valid logic state. Usually we only connect outputs in a design if at most one is active at a time, and the rest are in some high-impedance state. In this case, the resulting value should be the driving value of the single active output. In addition, we include some form of "pull-up" that determines the value of the signal when all outputs are inactive.

While this simple approach is satisfactory for some models, there are other cases where we need to go further. One of the reasons for simulating a model of a design is to detect errors such as multiple simultaneously active connected outputs. In this case, we need to extend the simple approach to detect such errors. Another problem arises when we are modeling at a higher level of abstraction and are using more complex types. We need to specify what, if anything, it means to connect multiple outputs of an enumeration type together.

The approach taken by VHDL is a very general one: the language requires the designer to specify precisely what value results from connecting multiple outputs. It does this through *resolved signals*, which are an extension of the basic signals we have used in previous chapters. A resolved signal includes in its definition a function, called the *resolution function*, that is used to calculate the final signal value from the values of all of its sources.

Let us see how this works by developing an example. We can model the values driven by a tristate output using a simple extension to the predefined type bit, for example:

```
type tri_state_logic is ('0', '1', 'Z');
```

The extra value, 'Z', is used by an output to indicate that it is in the high-impedance state. Next, we need to write a function that takes a collection of values of this type, representing the values driven by a number of outputs, and return the resulting value to be applied to the connected signal. For this example, we assume that at most one driver is active ('0' or '1') at a time and that the rest are all driving 'Z'. The difficulty with writing the function is that we should not restrict it to a fixed number of input values. We can avoid this by giving it a single parameter that is an unconstrained array of tri_state_logic values, defined by the type declaration

```
type tri_state_logic_array is array (integer range <>) of tri_state_logic;
```

The declaration of the resolution function is shown in Figure 11-1. The final step to making a resolved signal is to declare the signal, as follows:

```
signal s1 : resolve_tri_state_logic tri_state_logic;
```

This declaration is almost identical to a normal signal declaration, but with the addition of the resolution function name before the signal type. The signal still takes on values from the type tri_state_logic, but inclusion of a function name indicates that the signal is a resolved signal, with the named function acting as the resolution function. The fact that s1 is resolved means that we are allowed to have more than one

FIGURE 11-1

```
function resolve_tri_state_logic ( values : in tri_state_logic_array )
                            return tri_state_logic is
    variable result : tri_state_logic := 'Z';
begin
    for index in values'range loop
        if values(index) /= 'Z' then
            result := values(index);
        end if;
    end loop;
    return result;
end function resolve_tri_state_logic;
```

A resolution for resolving multiple values from tristate drivers.

source for it in the design. (Sources include drivers within processes and output ports of components associated with the signal.) When a transaction is scheduled for the signal, the value is not applied to the signal directly. Instead, the values of all sources connected to the signal, including the new value from the transaction, are formed into an array and passed to the resolution function. The result returned by the function is then applied to the signal as its new value.

Let us look at the syntax rule that describes the VHDL mechanism we have used in the above example. It is an extension of the rules for the subtype indication, which we first introduced in Chapters 2 and 4. The combined rule is

```
subtype_indication ⇐
    [ resolution_function_name ]
    type_mark
    [ range ( range_attribute_name
             ‖ simple_expression ( to ‖ downto ) simple_expression )
        ‖ ( discrete_range { , ... } ) ]
```

This rule shows that a subtype indication can optionally include the name of a function to be used as a resolution function. Given this new rule, we can include a resolution function name anywhere that we specify a type to be used for a signal. For example, we could write a separate subtype declaration that includes a resolution function name, defining a *resolved subtype*, then use this subtype to declare a number of resolved signals, as follows:

subtype resolved_logic **is** resolve_tri_state_logic tri_state_logic;

signal s2, s3 : resolved_logic;

The subtype resolved_logic is a resolved subtype of tri_state_logic, with resolve_tri_state_logic acting as the resolution function. The signals s2 and s3 are resolved signals of this subtype. Where a design makes extensive use of resolved signals, it is good practice to define resolved subtypes and use them to declare the signals and ports in the design.

The resolution function for a resolved signal is also invoked to initialize the signal. At the start of a simulation, the drivers for the signal are initialized to the expression included in the signal declaration, or to the default initial value for the signal type if no initialization expression is given. The resolution function is then invoked using these driver values to determine the initial value for the signal. In this way, the signal always has a properly resolved value, right from the start of the simulation.

Let us now return to the tristate logic type we introduced earlier. In the previous example, we assumed that at most one driver is '0' or '1' at a time. In a more realistic model, we need to deal with the possibility of driver conflicts, in which one source drives a resolved signal with the value '0' and another drives it with the value '1'. In some logic families, such driver conflicts cause an indeterminate signal value. We can represent this indeterminate state with a fourth value of the logic type, 'X', often called an *unknown* value. This gives us a complete and consistent *multivalued logic* type, which we can use to describe signal values in a design in more detail than we can using just bit values.

EXAMPLE

Figure 11-2 shows a package interface and the corresponding package body for the four-state multivalued logic type. The constant **resolution_table** is a lookup table used to determine the value resulting from two source contributions to a signal of the resolved logic type. The resolution function uses this table, indexing it with each element of the array passed to the function. If any source contributes 'X', or if there are two sources with conflicting '0' and '1' contributions, the result is 'X'. If one or more sources are '0' and the remainder 'Z', the result is '0'. Similarly, if one or more sources are '1' and the remainder 'Z', the result is '1'. If all sources are 'Z', the result is 'Z'. The lookup table is a compact way of representing this set of rules.

FIGURE 11-2

```
package MVL4 is
    type MVL4_ulogic is ('X', '0', '1', 'Z');  -- unresolved logic type
    type MVL4_ulogic_vector is array (natural range <>) of MVL4_ulogic;
    function resolve_MVL4 ( contribution : MVL4_ulogic_vector )
                        return MVL4_ulogic;
    subtype MVL4_logic is resolve_MVL4 MVL4_ulogic;
end package MVL4;

----------------------------------------------------------------

package body MVL4 is
    type table is array (MVL4_ulogic, MVL4_ulogic) of MVL4_ulogic;
    constant resolution_table : table :=
            --  'X'  '0'  '1'  'Z'
            --  -----------------
          ( (  'X', 'X', 'X', 'X' ),   -- 'X'
            (  'X', '0', 'X', '0' ),   -- '0'
            (  'X', 'X', '1', '1' ),   -- '1'
            (  'X', '0', '1', 'Z' ) ); -- 'Z'
```

```
        function resolve_MVL4 ( contribution : MVL4_ulogic_vector )
                         return MVL4_ulogic is
            variable result : MVL4_ulogic := 'Z';
        begin
            for index in contribution'range loop
                result := resolution_table(result, contribution(index));
            end loop;
            return result;
        end function resolve_MVL4;
    end package body MVL4;
```

A package interface and body for a four-state multivalued and resolved logic subtype.

We can use this package in a design for a tristate buffer. The entity declaration and a behavioral architecture body are shown in Figure 11-3. The buffer drives the value 'Z' on its output when it is disabled. It copies the input to the output when it is enabled and the input is a proper logic level ('0' or '1'). If either the input or the enable port is not a proper logic level, the buffer drives the unknown value on its output.

FIGURE 11-3

```
use work.MVL4.all;

entity tri_state_buffer is
    port ( a, enable : in MVL4_ulogic;  y : out MVL4_ulogic );
end entity tri_state_buffer;
```
_____

```
architecture behavioral of tri_state_buffer is
begin
    y <= 'Z' when enable = '0' else
         a   when enable = '1' and (a = '0' or a = '1') else
         'X';
end architecture behavioral;
```

An entity and behavioral architecture body for a tristate buffer.

Figure 11-4 shows the outline of an architecture body that uses the tristate buffer. The signal **selected_val** is a resolved signal of the multivalued logic type. It is driven by the two buffer output ports. The resolution function for the signal is used to determine the final value of the signal whenever a new transaction is applied to either of the buffer outputs.

FIGURE 11-4

```
use work.MVL4.all;
architecture gate_level of misc_logic is
    signal src1, src1_enable : MVL4_ulogic;
    signal src2, src2_enable : MVL4_ulogic;
    signal selected_val : MVL4_logic;
    . . .
begin
    src1_buffer : entity work.tri_state_buffer(behavioral)
        port map ( a => src1, enable => src1_enable, y => selected_val );
    src2_buffer : entity work.tri_state_buffer(behavioral)
        port map ( a => src2, enable => src2_enable, y => selected_val );

    . . .

end architecture gate_level;
```

An outline of an architecture body that uses the tristate buffer. The output ports of the two instances of the buffer form two sources for the resolved signal selected_val.

Composite Resolved Subtypes

The above examples have all shown resolved subtypes of scalar enumeration types. In fact, VHDL's resolution mechanism is more general. We can use it to define a resolved subtype of any type that we can legally use as the type of a signal. Thus, we can define resolved integer subtypes, resolved composite subtypes and others. In the latter case, the resolution function is passed an array of composite values and must determine the final composite value to be applied to the signal.

EXAMPLE

Figure 11-5 shows a package interface and body that define a resolved array subtype. Each element of an array value of this subtype can be 'X', '0', '1' or 'Z'. The unresolved type **uword** is a 32-element array of these values. The resolution function has an unconstrained array parameter consisting of elements of type **uword**. The function uses the lookup table to resolve corresponding elements from each of the contributing sources and produces a 32-element array result. The subtype **word** is the final resolved array subtype.

FIGURE 11-5

```
package words is
    type X01Z is ('X', '0', '1', 'Z');
    type uword is array (0 to 31) of X01Z;
    type uword_vector is array (natural range <>) of uword;
    function resolve_word ( contribution : uword_vector ) return uword;
    subtype word is resolve_word uword;
end package words;
```

```
------------------------------------------------------
package body words is
    type table is array (X01Z, X01Z) of X01Z;
    constant resolution_table : table :=
        --  'X'  '0'  '1'  'Z'
        --  -----------
        ( ( 'X', 'X', 'X', 'X' ),    -- 'X'
          ( 'X', '0', 'X', '0' ),    -- '0'
          ( 'X', 'X', '1', '1' ),    -- '1'
          ( 'X', '0', '1', 'Z' ) );  -- 'Z'
    function resolve_word ( contribution : uword_vector ) return uword is
        variable result : uword := (others => 'Z');
    begin
        for index in contribution'range loop
            for element in uword'range loop
                result(element) :=
                    resolution_table( result(element), contribution(index)(element) );
            end loop;
        end loop;
        return result;
    end function resolve_word;
end package body words;
```

A package interface and body for a resolved array subtype.

We can use these types to declare array ports in entity declarations and re-solved array signals with multiple sources. Figure 11-6 shows outlines of a CPU entity and a memory entity, which have bidirectional data ports of the unresolved array type. The architecture body for a computer system, also outlined in Figure 11-6, declares a signal of the resolved subtype and connects it to the data ports of the instances of the CPU and memory.

FIGURE 11-6

```
use work.words.all;

entity cpu is
    port ( address : out uword;  data : inout uword; . . . );
end entity cpu;
------------------------------------------------------
use work.words.all;

entity memory is
    port ( address : in uword;  data : inout uword; . . . );
end entity memory;
------------------------------------------------------
```

(continued on page 276)

(continued from page 275)

```
            architecture top_level of computer_system is
                use work.words.all;
                signal address : uword;
                signal data : word;
                . . .
        begin
                the_cpu : entity work.cpu(behavioral)
                    port map ( address, data, . . . );

                the_memory : entity work.memory(behavioral)
                    port map ( address, data, . . . );

                . . .

        end architecture top_level;
```

An outline of a CPU and memory entity with resolved array ports, and an architecture body for a computer system that uses the CPU and memory.

A resolved composite subtype works well provided every source for a resolved signal of the subtype is connected to every element of the signal. For the subtype shown in the example, every source must be a 32-element array and must connect to all 32 elements of the data signal. However, in a realistic computer system, sources are not always connected in this way. For example, we may wish to connect an eight-bit-wide device to the low-order eight bits of a 32-bit-wide data bus. We might attempt to express such a connection in a component instantiation statement, as follows:

```
boot_rom : entity work.ROM(behavioral)
    port map ( a => address, d => data(24 to 31), . . . );   -- illegal
```

If we add this statement to the architecture body in Figure 11-6, we have two sources for elements 0 to 23 of the data signal and three for elements 24 to 31. A problem arises when resolving the signal, since we are unable to construct an array containing the contributions from the sources. For this reason, VHDL does not allow us to write such a description; it is illegal.

The solution to this problem is to describe the data signal as an array of resolved elements, rather than as a resolved array of elements. We can declare an array type whose elements are values of the MVL4_logic type, shown in Figure 11-2. The array type declaration is

```
type MVL4_logic_vector is array (natural range <>) of MVL4_logic;
```

This approach has the added advantage that the array type is unconstrained, so we can use it to create signals of different widths, each element of which is resolved. An important point to note, however, is that the type MVL4_logic_vector is distinct from the type MVL4_ulogic_vector, since they are defined by separate type declarations. Neither is a subtype of the other. Hence we cannot legally associate a signal of type MVL4_logic_vector with a port of type MVL4_ulogic_vector, or a signal of type MVL4_ulogic_vector with a port of type MVL4_logic_vector. One solution is to identify all ports that may need to be associated with a signal of the resolved type and to declare them to be of the resolved type. This avoids the type mismatch that would otherwise occur. We illustrate this approach in the following example. Another solution is to use type conversions in the port maps. We will discuss type conversions in association lists in Chapter 21.

EXAMPLE

Let us assume that the type MVL4_logic_vector described above has been added to the package MVL4. Figure 11-7 shows entity declarations for a ROM entity and a single in-line memory module (SIMM), using the MVL4_logic_vector type for their data ports. The data port of the SIMM is 32 bits wide, whereas the data port of the ROM is parameterized by a generic constant.

FIGURE 11-7

```
use work.MVL4.all;
entity ROM is
    port ( a : in MVL4_ulogic_vector(15 downto 0);
            d : inout MVL4_logic_vector(7 downto 0);
            rd : in MVL4_ulogic );
end entity ROM;

– – – – – – – – – – – – – – – – – – – – – – – – – – – – – – – – – – – –

use work.MVL4.all;
entity SIMM is
    port ( a : in MVL4_ulogic_vector(9 downto 0);
            d : inout MVL4_logic_vector(31 downto 0);
            ras, cas, we, cs : in MVL4_ulogic );
end entity SIMM;

– – – – – – – – – – – – – – – – – – – – – – – – – – – – – – – – – – – –

architecture detailed of memory_subsystem is
    signal internal_data : MVL4_logic_vector(31 downto 0);
    . . .
begin
    boot_ROM : entity work.ROM(behavioral)
        port map ( a => internal_addr(15 downto 0),
                    d => internal_data(7 downto 0),
                    rd => ROM_select );
    main_mem : entity work.SIMM(behavioral)
        port map ( a => main_mem_addr, d => internal_data, . . . );

    . . .

end architecture detailed;
```

Entity declarations for memory modules whose data ports are arrays of resolved elements, and an outline of an architecture body that uses these entities.

Figure 11-7 also shows an outline of an architecture body that uses these two entities. It declares a signal, internal_data, of the MVL4_logic_vector type, representing 32 individually resolved elements. The SIMM entity is instantiated with its data port connected to all 32 internal data elements. The ROM entity is instantiated with the d_width generic constant set to eight, which constrains the data port of the instance to eight elements. These are connected to the rightmost eight elements of the internal data signal. When any of these elements is resolved, the resolution function is passed contributions from the corresponding elements of the SIMM and ROM data ports. When any of the remaining elements of the internal data signal are resolved, they have one less contribution, since they are not connected to any element of the ROM data port.

Summary of Resolved Subtypes

At this point, let us summarize the important points about resolved signals and their resolution functions. Resolved signals of resolved subtypes are the only means by which we may connect a number of sources together, since we need a resolution function to determine the final value of the signal or port from the contributing values. The resolution function must take a single parameter that is a one-dimensional unconstrained array of values of the signal type, and must return a value of the signal type. The index type of the array does not matter, so long as it contains enough index values for the largest possible collection of sources connected together. For example, an array type declared as follows is inadequate if the resolved signal has five sources:

```
type small_int is range 1 to 4;
type small_array is array (small_int range <>) of . . . ;
```

The resolution function must be a pure function; that is, it must not have any side effects. This requirement is a safety measure to ensure that the function always returns a predictable value for a given set of source values. Furthermore, since the source values may be passed in any order within the array, the function should be commutative; that is, its result should be independent of the order of the values. When the design is simulated, the resolution function is called whenever any of the resolved signal's sources is active. The function is passed an array of all of the current source values and the result it returns is used to update the signal value. When the design is synthesized, the resolution function specifies the way in which the synthesized hardware should combine values from multiple sources for a resolved signal.

11.2 IEEE Std_Logic_1164 Resolved Subtypes

In previous chapters we have used the IEEE standard multivalued logic package, std_logic_1164. We are now in a position to describe all of the items provided by the package, including the resolved subtypes and operators. The intent of the IEEE standard is that the multivalued logic subtypes defined in the package be used for models that must be interchanged between designers. The full package interface is included for reference in Appendix C. First, recall that the package provides the basic type std_ulogic, defined as

type std_ulogic **is** ('U', 'X', '0', '1', 'Z', 'W', 'L', 'H', '–');

and an array type std_ulogic_vector, defined as

type std_ulogic_vector **is array** (natural **range** <>) **of** std_ulogic;

We have not mentioned it before, but the "u" in "ulogic" stands for unresolved. These types serve as the basis for the declaration of the resolved subtype **std_logic**, defined as follows:

function resolved (s : std_ulogic_vector) **return** std_ulogic;

subtype std_logic **is** resolved std_ulogic;

The standard-logic package also declares an array type of standard-logic elements, analogous to the **bit_vector** type, for use in declaring array signals:

type std_logic_vector **is array** (natural **range** <>) **of** std_logic;

The IEEE standard recommends that models use the subtype **std_logic** and the type **std_logic_vector** instead of the unresolved types **std_ulogic** and **std_ulogic_vector**, even if a signal has only one source. The reason is that simulation vendors are expected to optimize simulation of models using the resolved subtype, but need not optimize use of the unresolved type. The disadvantage of this approach is that it prevents detection of erroneous designs in which multiple sources are inadvertently connected to a signal that should have only one source. Nevertheless, if we are to conform to the standard practice, we should use the resolved logic type. We will conform to the standard in the subsequent examples in this book.

The standard defines the resolution function **resolved** as shown in Figure 11-8. VHDL tools are allowed to provide built-in implementations of this function to improve performance. The function uses the constant **resolution_table** to resolve the driving values. If there is only one driving value, the function returns that value unchanged. If the function is passed an empty array, it returns the value 'Z'. (The circumstances under which a resolution function may be invoked with an empty array will be covered in Chapter 16.) The value of **resolution_table** shows exactly what is meant by "forcing" driving values ('X', '0' and '1') and "weak" driving values ('W', 'L' and 'H'). If one driver of a resolved signal drives a forcing value and another drives a weak value, the forcing value dominates. On the other hand, if both drivers drive different values with the same strength, the result is the unknown value of that strength ('X' or 'W'). The high-impedance value, 'Z', is dominated by forcing and weak values. If a "don't care" value ('–') is to be resolved with any other value, the result is the unknown value 'X'. The interpretation of the "don't care" value is that the model has not made a choice about its output state. Finally, if an "uninitialized" value ('U') is to be resolved with any other value, the result is 'U', indicating that the model has not properly initialized all outputs.

In addition to this multivalued logic subtype, the package **std_logic_1164** declares a number of subtypes for more restricted multivalued logic modeling. The subtype declarations are

subtype X01 **is** resolved std_ulogic **range** 'X' **to** '1';   *--('X', '0', '1')*
subtype X01Z **is** resolved std_ulogic **range** 'X' **to** 'Z';   *--('X', '0', '1', 'Z')*
subtype UX01 **is** resolved std_ulogic **range** 'U' **to** '1';   *--('U', 'X', '0', '1')*
subtype UX01Z **is** resolved std_ulogic **range** 'U' **to** 'Z'; *--('U', 'X', '0', '1', 'Z')*

FIGURE 11-8

```
type stdlogic_table is array (std_ulogic, std_ulogic) of std_ulogic;
constant resolution_table : stdlogic_table :=
    --  ----------------------------------
    --   'U',  'X',  '0',  '1',  'Z',  'W',  'L',  'H',  '-'
    --  ----------------------------------
    ( (  'U',  'U',  'U',  'U',  'U',  'U',  'U',  'U',  'U'  ),    --  'U'
      (  'U',  'X',  'X',  'X',  'X',  'X',  'X',  'X',  'X'  ),    --  'X'
      (  'U',  'X',  '0',  'X',  '0',  '0',  '0',  '0',  'X'  ),    --  '0'
      (  'U',  'X',  'X',  '1',  '1',  '1',  '1',  '1',  'X'  ),    --  '1'
      (  'U',  'X',  '0',  '1',  'Z',  'W',  'L',  'H',  'X'  ),    --  'Z'
      (  'U',  'X',  '0',  '1',  'W',  'W',  'W',  'W',  'X'  ),    --  'W'
      (  'U',  'X',  '0',  '1',  'L',  'W',  'L',  'W',  'X'  ),    --  'L'
      (  'U',  'X',  '0',  '1',  'H',  'W',  'W',  'H',  'X'  ),    --  'H'
      (  'U',  'X',  'X',  'X',  'X',  'X',  'X',  'X',  'X'  )     --  '-'
    );
function resolved ( s : std_ulogic_vector ) return std_ulogic is
    variable result : std_ulogic := 'Z';  -- weakest state default
begin
    if s'length = 1 then
        return s(s'low);
    else
        for i in s'range loop
            result := resolution_table(result, s(i));
        end loop;
    end if;
    return result;
end function resolved;
```

The definition of the resolution function resolved.

Each of these is a closed subtype; that is, the result of resolving values in each case is a value within the range of the subtype. The subtype **X01Z** corresponds to the type **MVL4** we introduced in Figure 11-2 on page 272.

The standard-logic package provides overloaded forms of the logical operators **and**, **nand**, **or**, **nor**, **xor**, **xnor** and **not** for standard-logic values and vectors, returning values in the range 'U', 'X', '0' or '1'. In addition, there are functions to convert between values of the full standard-logic type, the subtypes shown above and the predefined bit and bit-vector types. These are all listed in Appendix C.

VHDL-87

The VHDL-87 version of the standard-logic package does not provide the logical operator **xnor**, since **xnor** is not defined in VHDL-87.

11.3 Resolved Signals and Ports

In the previous discussion of resolved signals, we have limited ourselves to the simple case where a number of drivers or output ports of component instances drive a signal. Any input port connected to the resolved signal gets the final resolved value as the port value when a transaction is performed. We now look in more detail at the case of ports of mode **inout** being connected to a resolved signal. The question to answer here is, What value is seen by the input side of such a port? Is it the value driven by the component instance or the final value of the resolved signal connected to the port? In fact, it is the latter. An **inout** port models a connection in which the driver contributes to the associated signal's value, and the input side of the component senses the actual signal rather than using the driving value.

EXAMPLE

Some asynchronous bus protocols use a distributed synchronization mechanism based on a "wired-and" control signal. This is a single signal driven by each module using active-low open-collector or open-drain drivers and pulled up by the bus terminator. If a number of modules on the bus need to wait until all are ready to proceed with some operation, they use the control signal as follows. Initially, all modules drive the signal to the '0' state. When each is ready to proceed, it turns off its driver ('Z') and monitors the control signal. So long as any module is not yet ready, the signal remains at '0'. When all modules are ready, the bus terminator pulls the signal up to the '1' state. All modules sense this change and proceed with the operation.

Figure 11-9 shows an entity declaration for a bus module that has a port of the unresolved type **std_ulogic** for connection to such a synchronization control signal. The architecture body for a system comprising several such modules is also outlined. The control signal is pulled up by a concurrent signal assignment statement, which acts as a source with a constant driving value of 'H'. This is a value having a weak strength, which is overridden by any other source that drives '0'. It can pull the signal high only when all other sources drive 'Z'.

Figure 11-10 shows an outline of a behavioral architecture body for the bus module. Each instance initially drives its synchronization port with '0'. This value is passed up through the port and used as the contribution to the resolved signal from the entity instance. When an instance is ready to proceed with its operation, it changes its driving value to 'Z', modeling an open-collector or open-drain driver being turned off. The process then suspends until the value seen on the synchronization port changes to 'H'. If other instances are still driving '0', their contributions dominate, and the value of the signal stays '0'. When all other instances eventually change their contributions to 'Z', the value 'H' contributed by the pull-up statement dominates, and the value of the signal changes to 'H'. This value is passed back down through the ports of each instance, and the processes all resume.

FIGURE 11-9

```
library ieee;  use ieee.std_logic_1164.all;
entity bus_module is
    port ( synch : inout std_ulogic; . . . );
end entity bus_module;
```

```
architecture top_level of bus_based_system is
    signal synch_control : std_logic;
    . . .

begin

    synch_control_pull_up : synch_control <= 'H';
    bus_module_1 : entity work.bus_module(behavioral)
        port map ( synch => synch_control, . . . );
    bus_module_2 : entity work.bus_module(behavioral)
        port map ( synch => synch_control, . . . );

    . . .

end architecture top_level;
```

An entity declaration for a bus module that uses a "wired-and" synchronization signal, and an architecture body that instantiates the entity, connecting the synchronization port to a resolved signal.

FIGURE 11-10

```
architecture behavioral of bus_module is
begin
    behavior : process is
        . . .
    begin
        synch <= '0' after Tdelay_synch;
        . . .
        -- ready to start operation
        synch <= 'Z' after Tdelay_synch;
        wait until synch = 'H';
        -- proceed with operation
        . . .
    end process behavior;
end architecture behavioral;
```

An outline of a behavioral architecture body for a bus module, showing use of the synchronization control port.

Resolved Ports

Just as a signal declared with a signal declaration can be of a resolved subtype, so too can a port declared in an interface list of an entity. This is consistent with all that we have said about ports appearing just like signals to an architecture body. Thus if the architecture body contains a number of processes that must drive a port or a number of component instances that must connect outputs to a port, the port must be resolved. The final value driven by the resolved port is determined by resolving all of the sources within the architecture body. For example, we might declare an entity with a resolved port as follows:

```
library ieee;  use ieee.std_logic_1164.all;

entity IO_section is
    port ( data_ack : inout std_logic; . . . );
end entity IO_section;
```

The architecture body corresponding to this entity might instantiate a number of I/O controller components, each with their data acknowledge ports connected to the **data_ack** port of the entity. Each time any of the controllers updates its data acknowledge port, the standard-logic resolution function is invoked. It determines the driving value for the **data_ack** port by resolving the driving values from all controllers.

If it happens that the actual signal associated with a resolved port in an enclosing architecture body is itself a resolved signal, then the signal's resolution function will be called separately after the port's resolution function has determined the port's driving value. Note that the signal in the enclosing architecture body may use a different resolution function from the connected port, although in practice, most designs use the one function for resolution of all signals of a given subtype.

An extension of the above scenario is a design in which there are several levels of hierarchy, with a process nested at the deepest level generating a value to be passed out through resolved ports to a signal at the top level. At each level, a resolution function is called to determine the driving value of the port at that level. The value finally determined for the signal at the top level is called the *effective value* of the signal. It is passed back down the hierarchy of ports as the effective value of each **in** mode or **inout** mode port. This value is used on the input side of each port.

EXAMPLE

Figure 11-11 shows the hierarchical organization for a single-board computer system, consisting of a frame buffer for a video display, an input/output controller section, a CPU/memory section and a bus expansion block. These are all sources for the resolved data bus signal. The CPU/memory section in turn comprises a memory block and a CPU/cache block. Both of these act as sources for the data port, so it must be a resolved port. The cache has two sections, both of which act as sources for the data port of the CPU/cache block. Hence, this port must also be resolved.

Let us consider the case of one of the cache sections updating its data port. The new driving value is resolved with the current driving value from the other cache section to determine the driving value of the CPU/cache block data port. This result is then resolved with the current driving value of the memory block to determine the driving value of the CPU/memory section. Next, this driving value is resolved with the current driving values of the other top-level sections to determine the effective value of the data bus signal. The final step involves propagating this signal value back down the hierarchy for use as the effective value of each

FIGURE 11-11

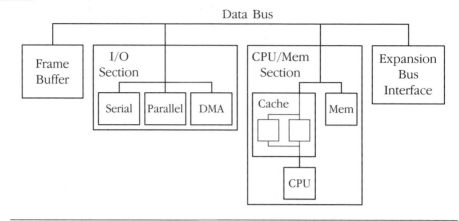

A hierarchical block diagram of a single-board computer system, showing the hierarchical connections of the resolved data bus ports to the data bus signal.

of the data ports. Thus, a module that reads the value of its data port will see the final resolved value of the data bus signal. This value is not necessarily the same as the driving value it contributes.

Driving Value Attribute

Since the value seen on a signal or on an **inout** mode port may be different from the value driven by a process, VHDL provides an attribute, 'driving_value, that allows the process to read the value it contributes to the prefix signal. For example, if a process has a driver for a resolved signal **s**, it may be driving **s** with the value 'Z' from a previously executed signal assignment statement, but the resolution function for **s** may have given it the value '0'. The process can refer to **s**'driving_value to retrieve the value 'Z'. Note that a process can only use this attribute to determine its own contribution to a signal; it cannot directly find out another process's contribution.

VHDL-87

The 'driving_value attribute is not provided in VHDL-87.

11.4 Resolved Signal Parameters

Let us now return to the topic of subprograms with signal parameters and see how they behave in the presence of resolved signals. Recall that when a procedure with an **out** mode signal parameter is called, the procedure is passed a reference to the caller's driver for the actual signal. Any signal assignment statements performed within the procedure body are actually performed on the caller's driver. If the actual signal parameter is a resolved signal, the values assigned by the procedure are used to resolve the signal value. No resolution takes place within the procedure. In fact, the procedure need not be aware that the actual signal is resolved.

In the case of an **in** mode signal parameter to a function or procedure, a reference to the actual signal parameter is passed when the subprogram is called, and the subprogram uses the actual value of the signal. If the signal is resolved, the subprogram sees the value determined after resolution. In the case of an **inout** signal parameter, a procedure is passed references to both the signal and its driver, and no resolution is performed internally to the procedure.

EXAMPLE

We can encapsulate the distributed synchronization protocol described in the example on page 281 in a set of procedures, each with a single signal parameter, as shown in Figure 11-12. Suppose a process uses a resolved signal **barrier** of subtype **std_logic** to synchronize with other processes. Figure 11-13 shows how the process might use the procedures to implement the protocol.

FIGURE 11-12

```
procedure init_synchronize ( signal synch : out std_logic ) is
begin
    synch <= '0';
end procedure init_synchronize;

procedure begin_synchronize ( signal synch : inout std_logic;
                              Tdelay : in delay_length := 0 fs ) is
begin
    synch <= 'Z' after Tdelay;
    wait until synch = 'H';
end procedure begin_synchronize;

procedure end_synchronize ( signal synch : inout std_logic;
                            Tdelay : in delay_length := 0 fs ) is
begin
    synch <= '0' after Tdelay;
    wait until synch = '0';
end procedure end_synchronize;
```

Three procedures that encapsulate the distributed synchronization operation.

The process has a driver for **barrier**, since the procedure calls associate the signal as an actual parameter with formal parameters of mode **out** and **inout**. A reference to this driver is passed to init_synchronize, which assigns the value '0' on behalf of the process. This value is used in the resolution of **barrier**. When the process is ready to start its synchronized operation, it calls begin_synchronize, passing references to its driver for **barrier** and to the actual signal itself. The procedure uses the driver to assign the value 'Z' on behalf of the process and then waits until the actual signal changes to 'H'. When the transaction on the driver matures, its value is resolved with other contributions from other processes and the result applied to the signal. This final value is used by the wait statement in the procedure to determine whether to resume the calling process. If the value is 'H', the process resumes,

FIGURE 11-13

```
synchronized_module : process is
    . . .
begin
    init_synchronize(barrier);
    . . .
    loop
        . . .
        begin_synchronize(barrier);
        . . .        -- perform operation, synchronized with other processes
        end_synchronize(barrier);
        . . .
    end loop;
end process synchronized_module;
```

An outline of a process that uses the distributed synchronization protocol procedures, with a resolved control signal barrier

the procedure returns to the caller and the operation goes ahead. When the process completes the operation, it calls **end_synchronize** to reset **barrier** back to '0'.

Exercises

1. [❶ 11.1] Suppose there are four drivers connected to a resolved signal that uses the resolution function shown in Figure 11-1 on page 271. What is the resolved value of the signal if the four drivers contribute these values:

   (a) 'Z', '1', 'Z', 'Z'?

   (b) '0', 'Z', 'Z, '0'?

   (c) 'Z', '1', 'Z', '0'?

2. [❶ 11.1] Rewrite the following resolved signal declaration as a subtype declaration followed by a signal declaration using the subtype.

   signal synch_control : wired_and tri_state_logic := '0';

3. [❶ 11.1] What is the initial value of the following signal of the type **MVL4_logic** defined in Figure 11-2 on page 272? How is that value derived?

   signal int_req : MVL4_logic;

4. [❶ 11.1] Does the result of the resolution function defined in Figure 11-2 on page 272 depend on the order of contributions from drivers in the array passed to the function?

5. [❶ 11.1] Suppose we define a resolved array subtype, **byte**, in the same way that the type **word** is defined in Figure 11-5 on page 274, but with eight elements in the array type instead of 32. We then declare a signal of type **byte** with three drivers. What is the resolved value of the signal if the three drivers contribute these values:

   (a) "ZZZZZZZZ", "ZZZZ0011", "ZZZZZZZZ"?

   (b) "XXXXZZZZ", "ZZZZZZZZ", "00000011"?

(c) "00110011", "ZZZZZZZZ", "ZZZZ1111"?

6. [❶ 11.1] Suppose a signal is declared as

   signal data_bus : MVL4_logic_vector(0 **to** 15);

   where **MVL4_logic_vector** is as described on page 276, and the following signal assignments are each executed in different processes:

   data_bus <= "ZZZZZZZZZZZZZZZZ";

   data_bus(0 to 7) <= "XXXXZZZZ";

   data_bus(8 to 15) <= "00111100";

   What is the resolved signal value after all of the transactions have been performed?

7. [❶ 11.2] Suppose there are four drivers connected to a signal of type **std_logic**. What is the resolved value of the signal if the four drivers contribute these values:

   (a) 'Z', '0', 'Z', 'H'?

   (b) 'H', 'Z', 'W', '0'?

   (c) 'Z', 'W', 'L', 'H'?

   (d) 'U', '0', 'Z', '1'?

   (e) 'Z', 'Z', 'Z', '–'?

8. [❶ 11.3] Below is a timing diagram for the system with two bus modules using the wired-and synchronization signal described in Figure 11-9 on page 282. The diagram shows the driving values contributed by each of the bus modules to the synch_control signal. Complete the diagram by drawing the resolved waveform for synch_control. Indicate the times at which each bus module proceeds with its internal operation, as described in Figure 11-10.

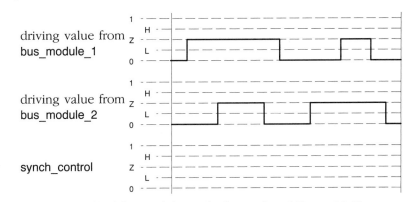

9. [❶ 11.3] Suppose all of the modules in the hierarchy of Figure 11-11 on page 284 use resolved ports for their data connections. If the Mem, Cache, Serial and DMA modules all update their data drivers in the same simulation cycle, how many times is the resolution function invoked to determine the final resolved values of the data signals?

10. [❶ 11.3] Suppose a process in a model drives a bidirectional port **synch_T** of type **std_logic**. Write a signal assignment statement that inverts the process's contribution to the port.

11. [❷ 11.1] Develop a model that includes two processes, each of which drives a signal of the type **MVL4_logic** described in Figure 11-2 on page 272. Experiment with your simulator to see if it allows you to trace the invocation and execution of the resolution function.

12. [❷ 11.2] Develop a model of an inverter with an open-collector output of type **std_logic**, and a model of a pull-up resistor that drives its single **std_logic** port with the value 'H'. Test the models in a test bench that connects the outputs of a number of inverter instances to a signal of type **std_logic**, pulled up with a resistor instance. Verify that the circuit implements the active-low wired-or operation.

13. [❷ 11.2] Develop a behavioral model of an eight-bit-wide bidirectional transceiver, such as the 74245 family of components. The transceiver has two bidirectional data ports, **a** and **b**, an active-low output-enable port, **oe_n**, and a direction port, **dir**. When **oe_n** is low and **dir** is low, data is received from **b** to **a**. When **oe_n** is low and **dir** is high, data is transmitted from **a** to **b**. When **oe_n** is high, both **a** and **b** are high impedance. Assume a propagation delay of 5 ns for all output changes.

14. [❷ 11.2] Many combinatorial logic functions can be implemented in integrated circuits using pass transistors acting as switches. While a pass transistor is, in principle, a bidirectional device, for many circuits it is sufficient to model it as a unidirectional device. Develop a model of a unidirectional pass transistor switch, with an input port, an output port and an enable port, all of type **std_logic**. When the enable input is 'H' or '1', the input value is passed to the output, but with weak drive strength. When the enable input is 'L' or '0', the output is high impedance. If the enable input is at an unknown level, the output is unknown, except that its drive strength is weak.

15. [❸ 11.2] Develop a behavioral model of a tristate buffer with data input, data output and enable ports, all of type **std_logic**. The propagation time from data input to data output when the buffer is enabled is 4 ns. The turn-on delay from the enable port is 3 ns, and the turn-off delay is 3.5 ns. Use the buffer and any other necessary gate models in a structural model of the eight-bit transceiver described in Exercise 13.

16. [❸ 11.2] Use the unidirectional pass transistor model of Exercise 14 in a structural model of a four-input multiplexer. The multiplexer has select inputs **s0** and **s1**. Pass transistors are used to construct the multiplexer as follows:

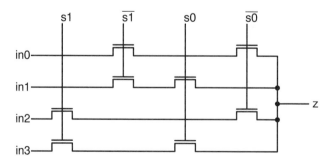

17. [❸ 11.2] Develop a model of a distributed priority arbiter for a shared bus in a multiprocessor computer system. Each bus requester has a request priority, R, between

0 and 31, with 0 indicating the most urgent request and 31 indicating no request. Priorities are binary-encoded using five-bit vectors, with bit 4 being the most-significant bit and bit 0 being the least-significant bit. The standard-logic values 'H' and '1' both represent the binary digit 1, and the standard-logic value '0' represents the binary digit 0. All requesters can drive and sense a five-bit arbitration bus, A, which is pulled up to 'H' by the bus terminator. The requesters each use A and their own priority to compute the minimum of all priorities by comparing the binary digits of priorities as follows. For each bit position i:

- if $(R_{4...i+1} = A_{4...i+1})$ and $(R_i = 0)$: drive A_i with '0' after T_{pd}
- if $(R_{4...i+1} \neq A_{4...i+1})$ or $(R_i = 1)$: drive A_i with 'Z' after T_{pd}

T_{pd} is the propagation delay between sensing a value on A and driving a resulting value on A. When the value on A has stabilized, it is the minimum of all request priorities. The requester with $R = A$ wins the arbitration. If you are not convinced that the distributed minimization scheme operates as required, trace its execution for various combinations of priority values.

18. [❹] Develop a behavioral model of a telephone keypad controller. The controller has outputs c1 to c3 and inputs r1 to r4, connected to the 12 switches of a touch-tone telephone as follows:

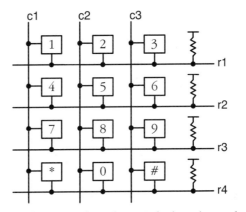

Each key in the keypad is a single-pole switch that shorts the row signal to the column signal when the key is pressed. Due to the mechanical construction of the switch, "switch bounce" occurs when the key is pressed. Several intermittent contacts are made between the signals over a period of up to 5 ms, before a sustained contact is made. Bounce also occurs when the key is released. Several intermittent contacts may occur over the same period before sustained release is achieved.

The keypad controller scans the keypad by setting each of the column signals to '0' in turn. While a given column signal is '0', the controller examines each of the row inputs. If a row input is 'H', the switch between the column and the row is open. If the row input is '0', the switch is closed. The entire keypad is scanned once every millisecond.

The controller generates a set of column outputs c1_out to c3_out and a set of row outputs r1_out to r4_out. A valid switch closure is indicated by exactly one column output and exactly one row output going to '1' at the same time. The controller filters out spurious switch closures due to switch bounce and ignores multiple concurrent switch closures.

19. [❹] The IEEE standard-logic type models two drive strengths: forcing and weak. This is insufficient to model detailed operation of circuits at the switch level. For example, in circuits that store a charge on the gate terminal of a MOS transistor, we need to distinguish the weaker capacitive drive strength of the stored value from the resistive strength of a value transmitted through a pass transistor. Develop a package that defines a resolved type similar to **std_logic**, with forcing, resistive and capacitive strengths for 0, 1 and unknown values.

20. [❹] Exercise 19 describes a logic type that incorporates three drive strengths. If we need to model switch level circuits in finer detail, we can extend the type to deal with an arbitrary number of drive strengths. Each time a signal is transmitted through a pass transistor, its drive strength is diminished. We can model this by representing a logic value as a record containing the bit value ('0', '1' or unknown) and an integer representing the strength. We use 0 to represent power-supply strength and a positive integer n to represent the strength of a signal after being transmitted through n pass transistors from the power supply. A normal driver has strength 1, to reflect the fact that it derives the driving value by turning on a transistor connected to one or the other power supply rail. (This scheme is described by Smith and Acosta in [10].)

    Develop a package that defines a resolved type based on this scheme. Include functions for separating the bit value and strength components of a combined value, for constructing a combined value from separate bit value and strength components and for weakening the strength component of a combined value. Use the package to model a pass transistor component. Then use the pass transistor in a model of an eight-input multiplexer similar to the four-input multiplexer of Exercise 16.

21. [❹] Self-timed asynchronous systems use handshaking to synchronize operation of interacting modules. In such systems, it is sometimes necessary to synchronize a number of modules at a *rendezvous*. Each module waits until all modules are ready to perform an operation. When all are ready, the operation commences. A scheme for rendezvous synchronization of a number of modules using three wired-and control signals was first proposed by Sutherland et al. for the TRIMOS-BUS [11] and was subsequently adopted for use in the arbitration protocol of the IEEE Futurebus [8].

    Develop a high-level model of a system that uses the three-wire synchronization scheme. You should include a package to support your model. The package should include a type definition for a record containing the three synchronization wires and a pair of procedures, one to wait for a rendezvous and another to leave the rendezvous after completion of the operation. The procedures should have a bidirectional signal parameter for the three-wire record and should determine the state of the synchronization protocol from the parameter value.

Generic Constants 12

The models that we have used as examples in preceding chapters all have fixed behavior and structure. In many respects, this is a limitation, and we would like to be able to write more general, or *generic*, models. VHDL provides us with a mechanism, called *generics*, for writing parameterized models. We discuss generics in this chapter and show how they may be used to write families of models with varying behavior and structure.

12.1 **Parameterizing Behavior**

We can write a generic entity by including a *generic interface list* in its declaration that defines the *formal generic constants* that parameterize the entity. The extended syntax rule for entity declarations including generics is

> entity_declaration ⇐
>   **entity** identifier **is**
>   ⟦ **generic** (*generic*_interface_list) ; ⟧
>   ⟦ **port** (*port*_interface_list) ; ⟧
>   { entity_declarative_item }
>   ⟦ **begin**
>   { concurrent_assertion_statement
>   ⎪ *passive*_concurrent_procedure_call_statement
>   ⎪ *passive*_process_statement } ⟧
>   **end** ⟦ **entity** ⟧ ⟦ identifier ⟧ ;

The difference between this and the simpler rule we have seen before is the inclusion of the optional generic interface list before the port interface list. The generic interface list is like any other interface list, but with the restriction that we can only include constant-class objects, which must be of mode **in**. Since these are the defaults for a generic interface list, we can use a simplified syntax rule:

> *generic*_interface_list ⇐
>   (identifier { , ... } : subtype_indication ⟦ := expression ⟧)
>   { ; ... }

A simple example of an entity declaration including a generic interface list is

```
entity and2 is
    generic ( Tpd : time );
    port ( a, b : in bit;  y : out bit );
end entity and2;
```

This entity includes one generic constant, Tpd, of the predefined type time. The value of this generic constant may be used within the entity statements and any architecture body corresponding to the entity. In this example the intention is that the generic constant specify the propagation delay for the module, so the value should be used in a signal assignment statement as the delay. An architecture body that does this is

```
architecture simple of and2 is
begin
    and2_function :
        y <= a and b after Tpd;
end architecture simple;
```

The visibility of a generic constant extends from the end of the generic interface list to the end of the entity declaration and extends into any architecture body corresponding to the entity declaration.

A generic constant is given an actual value when the entity is used in a component instantiation statement. We do this by including a *generic map*, as shown by the extended syntax rule for component instantiations:

component_instantiation_statement ⇐
    *instantiation*_label :
        entity *entity*_name 〚 (*architecture*_identifier) 〛
        〚 **generic map** (*generic*_association_list) 〛
        〚 **port map** (*port*_association_list) 〛 ;

The generic association list is like other forms of association lists, but since generic constants are always of class constant, the actual arguments we supply must be expressions. Thus the simplified syntax rule for a generic association list is

generic_association_list ⇐
    (〚 *generic*_name => 〛 (expression ‖ **open**)) { , ... }

To illustrate this, let us look at a component instantiation statement that uses the and2 entity shown above:

```
gate1 : entity work.and2(simple)
    generic map ( Tpd => 2 ns )
    port map ( a => sig1,  b => sig2,  y => sig_out );
```

The generic map specifies that this instance of the **and2** module uses the value 2 ns for the generic constant **Tpd**; that is, the instance has a propagation delay of 2 ns. We might include another component instantiation statement using **and2** in the same design but with a different actual value for **Tpd** in its generic map, for example:

```
gate2 : entity work.and2(simple)
    generic map ( Tpd => 3 ns )
    port map ( a => a1,  b => b1,  y => sig1 );
```

When the design is elaborated we have two processes, one corresponding to the instance **gate1** of **and2**, which uses the value 2 ns for **Tpd**, and another corresponding to the instance **gate2** of **and2**, which uses the value 3 ns.

EXAMPLE

As the syntax rule for the generic interface list shows, we may define a number of generic constants of different types and include default values for them. A more involved example is shown in Figure 12-1. In this example, the generic interface list includes a list of two generic constants that parameterize the propagation delay of the module and a Boolean generic constant, **debug**, with a default value of false. The intention of this last generic constant is to allow a design that instantiates this entity to activate some debugging operation. This operation might take the form of report statements within if statements that test the value of **debug**.

FIGURE 12-1

```
entity control_unit is
    generic ( Tpd_clk_out, Tpw_clk : delay_length;
            debug : boolean := false );
    port ( clk : in bit;
            ready : in bit;
            control1, control2 : out bit );
end entity control_unit;
```

An entity declaration for a block of sequential control logic, including generic constants that parameterize its behavior.

We have the same flexibility in writing a generic map as we have in other associa-tion lists. We can use positional association, named association or a combination of both. We can omit actual values for generic constants that have default expressions, or we may explicitly use the default value by writing the keyword **open** in the generic map. To illustrate these possibilities, here are three different ways of writing a generic map for the control_unit entity:

generic map (200 ps, 1500 ps, false)

generic map (Tpd_clk_out => 200 ps, Tpw_clk => 1500 ps)

generic map (200 ps, 1500 ps, debug => **open**)

EXAMPLE

Figure 12-2 shows the entity declaration and a behavioral architecture body for a D-flipflop. The model includes generic constants: **Tpd_clk_q** to specify the propagation delay from clock rising edge to output, **Tsu_d_clk** to specify the setup time of data before a clock edge and **Th_d_clk** to specify the hold time of data after a clock edge. The values of these generic constants are used in the architecture body.

FIGURE 12-2

```
entity D_flipflop is
    generic ( Tpd_clk_q, Tsu_d_clk, Th_d_clk : delay_length );
    port ( clk, d : in bit;  q : out bit );
end entity D_flipflop;
- - - - - - - - - - - - - - - - - - - - - - - - - - - - - - - - - - - - - - - - -
architecture basic of D_flipflop is
begin
    behavior : q <= d after Tpd_clk_q when clk = '1' and clk'event;
    check_setup : process is
    begin
        wait until clk = '1';
```

```
        assert d'last_event >= Tsu_d_clk
            report "setup violation";
    end process check_setup;

    check_hold : process is
    begin
        wait until clk'delayed(Th_d_clk) = '1';
        assert d'delayed'last_event >= Th_d_clk
            report "hold violation";
    end process check_hold;
end architecture basic;
```

An entity and architecture body for a D-flipflop. The entity declaration includes generic constants for specifying timing characteristics. These are used within the architecture body.

The entity might be instantiated as follows, with actual values specified in the generic map for the generic constants:

```
request_flipflop : entity work.D_flipflop(basic)
    generic map ( Tpd_clk_q => 4 ns,
                  Tsu_d_clk => 3 ns, Th_d_clk => 1 ns )
    port map ( clk => system_clock,
               d => request, q => request_pending );
```

12.2 Parameterizing Structure

The second main use of generic constants in entities is to parameterize their structure. We can use the value of a generic constant to specify the size of an array port. To see why this is useful, let us look at an entity declaration for a register. A register entity that uses an unconstrained array type for its input and output ports can be declared as

```
entity reg is
    port ( d : in bit_vector; q : out bit_vector; ... );
end entity reg;
```

While this is a perfectly legal entity declaration, it does not include the constraint that the input and output ports d and q should be of the same size. Thus we could write a component instantiation as follows:

```
signal small_data : bit_vector(0 to 7);
signal large_data : bit_vector(0 to 15);
. . .

problem_reg : entity work.reg
    port map ( d => small_data, q => large_data, . . . );
```

The model is analyzed and elaborated without the error being detected. It is only when the register tries to assign a small bit vector to a target bit vector of a larger size that the error is detected. We can avoid this problem by including a generic constant in the entity declaration to parameterize the size of the ports. We use the generic constant in constraints in the port declarations. To illustrate, here is the register entity declaration rewritten:

```
entity reg is
    generic ( width : positive );
    port ( d : in bit_vector(0 to width − 1);
           q : out bit_vector(0 to width − 1);
           . . . );
end entity reg;
```

In this declaration we require that the user of the register specify the desired port width for each instance. The entity then uses the width value as a constraint on both the input and output ports, rather than allowing their size to be determined by the signals associated with the ports. A component instantiation using this entity might appear as follows:

```
signal in_data, out_data : bit_vector(0 to bus_size − 1);

. . .

ok_reg : entity work.reg
    generic map ( width => bus_size )
    port map ( d => in_data,  q => out_data, . . . );
```

If the signals used as actual ports in the instantiation were of different sizes, the analyzer would signal the error early in the design process, making it easier to correct. As a matter of style, whenever the sizes of different array ports of an entity are related, generic constants should be considered to enforce the constraint.

EXAMPLE

A complete model for the register, including the entity declaration and an architecture body, is shown in Figure 12-3. The generic constant is used to constrain the widths of the data input and output ports in the entity declaration. It is also used in the architecture body to determine the size of the constant bit vector **zero**. This bit vector is the value assigned to the register output when it is reset, so it must be of the same size as the register port.

We can create instances of the register entity in a design, each possibly having different-sized ports. For example:

```
word_reg : entity work.reg(behavioral)
    generic map ( width => 32 )
    port map ( . . . );
```

creates an instance with 32-bit-wide ports. In the same design, we might include another instance, as follows:

```
subtype state_vector is bit_vector(1 to 5);

state_reg : entity work.reg(behavioral)
    generic map ( width => state_vector'length )
    port map ( . . . );
```

This register instance has five-bit-wide ports, wide enough to store values of the subtype state_vector.

FIGURE 12-3

```
entity reg is
    generic ( width : positive );
    port ( d : in  bit_vector(0 to width − 1);
           q : out  bit_vector(0 to width − 1);
           clk, reset : in bit );
end entity reg;
```

```
architecture behavioral of reg is
begin
    behavior : process (clk, reset) is
        constant zero : bit_vector(0 to width − 1) := (others => '0');
    begin
        if reset = '1' then
            q <= zero;
        elsif clk'event and clk = '1' then
            q <= d;
        end if;
    end process behavior;
end architecture behavioral;
```

An entity and architecture body for a register with parameterized port size.

Exercises

1. [❶ 12.1] Add to the following entity interface a generic clause defining generic constants Tpw_clk_h and Tpw_clk_l that specify the minimum clock pulse width timing. Both generic constants have a default value of 3 ns.

    ```
    entity flipflop is
        port ( clk, d : in bit;  q, q_n : out bit );
    end entity flipflop;
    ```

2. [❶ 12.1] Write a component instantiation statement that instantiates the following entity from the current working library. The actual value for the generic constant should be 10 ns, and the clk signal should be associated with a signal called master_clk.

    ```
    entity clock_generator is
        generic ( period : delay_length );
        port ( clk : out std_logic );
    end entity clock_generator;
    ```

3. [❶ 12.2] Following is an incomplete entity interface that uses a generic constant to specify the sizes of the standard-logic vector input and output ports. Complete the interface by filling in the types of the ports.

```
entity adder is
    generic ( data_length : positive );
    port ( a, b : in . . .;  sum : out . . . );
end entity adder;
```

4. [❶ 12.2] A system has an eight-bit data bus declared as

```
signal data_out : bit_vector(7 downto 0);
```

Write a component instantiation statement that instantiates the **reg** entity defined in Figure 12-3 to implement a four-bit control register. The register data input connects to the rightmost four bits of **data_out**, the clk input to io_write, the reset input to io_reset and the data output bits to control signals io_en, io_int_en, io_dir and io_mode.

5. [❷ 12.1] Develop a behavioral model of a D-latch with separate generic constants for specifying the following propagation delays:

- rising data input to rising data output,
- falling data input to falling data output,
- rising enable input to rising data output, and
- rising enable input to falling data output.

6. [❷ 12.1] Develop a behavioral model of a counter with output of type **natural** and clock and reset inputs of type **bit**. The counter has a Boolean generic constant, trace_reset. When this is true, the counter reports a trace message each time the reset input is activated.

7. [❷ 12.2] Develop a behavioral model of the adder described in Exercise 3. You may wish to use the operations provided by the **bv_arithmetic** package described in Chapter 10.

8. [❷ 12.2] Develop a behavioral model of a multiplexer with n select inputs, 2^n data inputs and one data output.

9. [❸] Develop a behavioral model of a RAM with generic constants governing the read access time, minimum write time, the address port width and the data port width.

Components
and Configurations

In Chapter 5 we saw how to write entity declarations and architecture bodies that describe the structure of a system. Within an architecture body, we can write component instantiation statements that describe instances of an entity and connect signals to the ports of the instances. This simple approach to building a hierarchical design works well if we know in advance all the details of the entities we want to use. However, that is not always the case, especially in a large design project. In this chapter we introduce an alternative way of describing the hierarchical structure of a design that affords significantly more flexibility at the cost of a little more effort in managing the design.

13.1 Components

The first thing we need to do to describe an interconnection of subsystems in a design is to describe the different kinds of components used. We have seen how to do this by writing entity declarations for each of the subsystems. Each entity declaration is a separate design unit and has corresponding architecture bodies that describe implementations. An alternative approach is to write *component declarations* in the declarative part of an architecture body or package interface. We can then create *instances* of the components within the statement part of the architecture body.

Component Declarations

A component declaration simply specifies the external interface to the component in terms of generic constants and ports. We do not need to describe any corresponding implementation, since all we are interested in is how the component is connected in the current level of the design hierarchy. This makes the architecture completely self-contained, since it does not depend on any other library units except its corresponding entity interface. Let us look at the syntax rule that governs how we write a component declaration.

```
component_declaration ⇐
    component identifier ⟦ is ⟧
        ⟦ generic ( generic_interface_list ) ; ⟧
        ⟦ port ( port_interface_list ) ; ⟧
    end component ⟦ identifier ⟧ ;
```

A simple example of a component declaration that follows this syntax rule is

```
component flipflop is
    generic ( Tprop, Tsetup, Thold : delay_length );
    port ( clk : in bit;  clr : in bit;  d : in bit;
           q : out bit );
end component flipflop;
```

This declaration defines a component type that represents a flipflop with clock, clear and data inputs, clk, clr and d, and a data output q. It also has generic constants for parameterizing the propagation delay, the data setup time and the data hold time.

Note the similarity between a component declaration and an entity declaration. This similarity is not accidental, since they both serve to define the external interface to a module. Although there is a very close relationship between components and entities, in fact they embody two different concepts. This may be a source of confusion to newcomers to VHDL. Nevertheless, the flexibility afforded by having the two different constructs is a powerful feature of VHDL, so we will work through it carefully in this section and try to make the distinction clear.

One way of thinking about the difference between an entity declaration and a component declaration is to think of the modules being defined as having different levels of "reality." An entity declaration defines a "real" module: something that ultimately will have a physical manifestation. For example, it may represent a circuit board in a rack, a packaged integrated circuit or a standard cell included in a piece of silicon. An entity declaration is a separate design unit that may be separately analyzed and placed into a design library. A component declaration, on the other hand, defines a "virtual," or "idealized," module that is included within an architecture body. It is as though we are saying, "For this architecture body, we assume there is a module as defined by this component declaration, since such a module meets our needs exactly." We specify the names, types and modes of the ports on the virtual module (the component) and proceed to lay out the structure of the design using this idealized view.

Of course, we do not make these assumptions about modules arbitrarily. One possibility is that we know what real modules are available and customize the virtual reality based on that knowledge. The advantage here is that the idealization cushions us from the irrelevant details of the real module, making the design easier to manage. Another possibility is that we are working "top down" and will later use the idealized module as the specification for a real module. Either way, eventually a link has to be made between an instance of a virtual component and a real entity so that the design can be constructed. In the rest of this section, we look at how to use components in an architecture body, then come back to the question of the binding between component instances and entities.

VHDL-87

The keyword **is** may not be included in the header of a component declaration, and the component name may not be repeated at the end of the declaration.

Component Instantiation

If a component declaration defines a kind of module, then a component instantiation specifies a usage of the module in a design. We have seen how we can instantiate an entity directly using a component instantiation statement within an architecture body. Let us now look at an alternative syntax rule that shows how we can instantiate a declared component:

component_instantiation_statement ⇐
    *instantiation*_label :
        [**component**] *component*_name
        [**generic map** (*generic*_association_list)]
        [**port map** (*port*_association_list)] ;

This syntax rule shows us that we may simply name a component declared in the architecture body and, if required, provide actual values for the generic constants and actual signals to connect to the ports. The label is required to identify the component instance.

EXAMPLE

We can construct a four-bit register using flipflops and an and gate, similar to the example in Chapter 5. The entity declaration is shown at the top of Figure 13-1. The architecture body describing the structure of this register uses the flipflop component shown on page 300. Note that all we have done here is

FIGURE 13-1

```
entity reg4 is
    port ( clk, clr : in bit;  d : in bit_vector(0 to 3);
            q : out bit_vector(0 to 3) );
end entity reg4;
```

```
architecture struct of reg4 is

    component flipflop is
        generic ( Tprop, Tsetup, Thold : delay_length );
        port ( clk : in bit;  clr : in bit;  d : in bit;
                q : out bit );
    end component flipflop;

begin

    bit0 : component flipflop
        generic map ( Tprop => 2 ns, Tsetup => 2 ns, Thold => 1 ns )
        port map ( clk => clk, clr => clr, d => d(0), q => q(0) );

    bit1 : component flipflop
        generic map ( Tprop => 2 ns, Tsetup => 2 ns, Thold => 1 ns )
        port map ( clk => clk, clr => clr, d => d(1), q => q(1) );

    bit2 : component flipflop
        generic map ( Tprop => 2 ns, Tsetup => 2 ns, Thold => 1 ns )
        port map ( clk => clk, clr => clr, d => d(2), q => q(2) );

    bit3 : component flipflop
        generic map ( Tprop => 2 ns, Tsetup => 2 ns, Thold => 1 ns )
        port map ( clk => clk, clr => clr, d => d(3), q => q(3) );

end architecture struct;
```

An entity declaration and architecture body for a register using a component declaration for a flipflop.

specify the structure of this level of the design hierarchy, without having indicated how the flipflop is implemented. We will see how that may be done in the remainder of this chapter.

VHDL-87

The keyword **component** may not be included in a component instantiation statement in VHDL-87. The keyword is allowed in VHDL-93 to distinguish between instantiation of a component and direct instantiation of an entity. In VHDL-87, the only form of component instantiaton statement provided is instantiation of a declared component.

Packaging Components

Let us now turn to the issue of design management for large projects and see how we can make management of large libraries of entities easier using packages and components. Usually, work on a large design is partitioned among several designers, each responsible for implementing one or more entities that are used in the complete system. Each entity may need to have some associated types defined in a utility package, so that entity ports can be declared using those types. When the entity is used, other designers will need component declarations to instantiate components that will eventually be bound to the entity. It makes good sense to include a component declaration in the utility package, along with the types and other related items. This means that users of the entity do not need to rewrite the declarations, thus avoiding a potential source of errors and misunderstanding.

EXAMPLE

Suppose we are responsible for designing a serial interface cell for a microcontroller circuit. We can write a package specification that defines the interface to be used in the rest of the design, as outlined in Figure 13-2. The component declaration in this package corresponds to our entity declaration for the serial interface, shown in Figure 13-3. When other designers working on integrating the entire circuit need to instantiate the serial interface, they only need to import the items in the package, rather than rewriting all of the declarations. Figure 13-4 shows an outline of a design that does this.

FIGURE 13-2

```
library ieee;  use ieee.std_logic_1164.all;
package serial_interface_defs is
    subtype reg_address_vector is std_logic_vector(1 downto 0);

    constant status_reg_address : reg_address_vector := B"00";
    constant control_reg_address : reg_address_vector := B"01";
    constant rx_data_register : reg_address_vector := B"10";
    constant tx_data_register : reg_address_vector := B"11";

    subtype data_vector is std_logic_vector(7 downto 0);

    . . .      -- other useful declarations

    component serial_interface is
        port ( clock_phi1, clock_phi2 : in std_logic;
            serial_select : in std_logic;
            reg_address : in reg_address_vector;
            data : inout data_vector;
            interrupt_request : out std_logic;
            rx_serial_data : in std_logic;
            tx_serial_data : out std_logic );
    end component serial_interface;
end package serial_interface_defs;
```

An outline of a package declaration containing useful definitions for a serial interface.

FIGURE 13-3

```
library ieee;  use ieee.std_logic_1164.all;
use work.serial_interface_defs.all;
entity serial_interface is
    port ( clock_phi1, clock_phi2 : in std_logic;
            serial_select : in std_logic;
            reg_address : in reg_address_vector;
            data : inout data_vector;
            interrupt_request : out std_logic;
            rx_serial_data : in std_logic;
            tx_serial_data : out std_logic );
end entity serial_interface;
```

An entity declaration for the serial interface.

FIGURE 13-4

```
library ieee;  use ieee.std_logic_1164.all;
architecture structure of microcontroller is
    use work.serial_interface_defs.serial_interface;
        . . .         -- declarations of other components, signals, etc
begin
    serial_a : component serial_interface
        port map ( clock_phi1 => buffered_phi1,
                    clock_phi2 => buffered_phi2,
                    serial_select => serial_a_select,
                    reg_address => internal_addr(1 downto 0),
                    data => internal_data_bus,
                    interrupt_request => serial_a_int_req,
                    rx_serial_data => rx_data_a,
                    tx_serial_data => tx_data_a );
        . . .       -- other component instances
end architecture structure;
```

An outline of an architecture body that uses the serial interface definitions package and instantiates the component defined in it.

13.2 Configuring Component Instances

Once we have described the structure of one level of a design using components and component instantiations, we still need to flesh out the hierarchical implementation for each component instance. We can do this by writing a *configuration declaration* for the design. In it, we specify which real entity interface and corresponding architecture body should be used for each of the component instances. This is called *binding* the component instances to design entities. Note that we do not specify any binding information for a component instantiation statement that directly instantiates an entity, since the entity and architecture body are specified explicitly in the component instantiation statement. Thus our discussion in this section only applies to instantiations of declared components.

Basic Configuration Declarations

We start by looking at a simplified set of syntax rules for configuration declarations, as the full set of rules is rather complicated. The simplest case arises when the entities to which component instances are bound are implemented with behavioral architectures. In this case, there is only one level of the hierarchy to flesh out. The simplified syntax rules are

configuration_declaration ⇐
    configuration identifier **of** *entity*_name **is**
        for *architecture*_name
            { **for** component_specification
                binding_indication ;
            end for ; }
        end for ;
      end ⟦ **configuration** ⟧ ⟦ identifier ⟧ ;
component_specification ⇐
    (*instantiation*_label { , ₀₀₀ } ‖ **others** ‖ **all**) : *component*_name
binding_indication ⇐ **use entity** *entity*_name ⟦ (*architecture*_identifier) ⟧

The identifier given in the configuration declaration identifies this particular specification for fleshing out the hierarchy of the named entity. There may be other configuration declarations, with different names, for the same entity. Within the configuration declaration we write the name of the particular architecture body to work with (included after the first **for** keyword), since there may be several corresponding to the entity. We then include the binding information for each component instance within the architecture body. The syntax rule shows that we can identify a component instance by its label and its component name, as used in the component instantiation in the architecture body. We bind it by specifying an entity name and a corresponding architecture body name. For example, we might bind instances bit0 and bit1 of the component flipflop as follows:

    for bit0, bit1 : flipflop
        use entity work.edge_triggered_Dff(basic);
    end for;

This indicates that the instances are each to be bound to the design entity edge_triggered_Dff, found in the current working library, and that the architecture body basic corresponding to that entity should be used as the implementation of the instances.

Note that since we can identify each component instance individually, we have the opportunity to bind different instances of a given component to different entity/ architecture pairs. After we have specified bindings for some of the instances in a design, we can use the keyword **others** to bind any remaining instances of a given component type to a given entity/architecture pair. Alternatively, if all instances of a particular component type are to have the same binding, we can use the keyword **all** instead of naming individual instances. The syntax rules also show that the architecture name corresponding to the entity is optional. If it is omitted, a default binding takes place when the design is elaborated for simulation or synthesis. The component instance is bound to whichever architecture body for the named entity has been most recently analyzed at the time of elaboration.

A configuration declaration is a primary design unit, and as such, may be separately analyzed and placed into the working design library as a library unit. If it contains sufficient binding information so that the full design hierarchy is fleshed out down to behavioral architectures, the configuration may be used as the target unit of a simulation. The design is elaborated by substituting instances of the specified architecture bodies for bound component instances in the way described in Section 5.5. The only difference is that when component declarations are instantiated, the configuration must be consulted to find the appropriate architecture body to substitute.

EXAMPLE

Let us look at a sample configuration declaration that binds the component instances in the four-bit register of Figure 13-1. Suppose we have a resource library for a project, star_lib, that contains the basic design entities that we need to use. Our configuration declaration might be written as shown in Figure 13-5.

FIGURE 13-5

```
library star_lib;
use star_lib.edge_triggered_Dff;

configuration reg4_gate_level of reg4 is
    for struct  -- architecture of reg4
        for bit0 : flipflop
            use entity edge_triggered_Dff(hi_fanout);
        end for;
        for others : flipflop
            use entity edge_triggered_Dff(basic);
        end for;
    end for;  -- end of architecture struct
end configuration reg4_gate_level;
```

A configuration declaration for a four-bit register model.

The library clause preceding the design unit is required to locate the resource library containing the entities we need. The use clause following it makes the entity names we require directly visible in the configuration declaration. The configuration is called reg4_gate_level and selects the architecture struct of the reg4 entity. Within this architecture, we single out the instance bit0 of the flipflop component and bind it to the entity edge_triggered_Dff with architecture hi_fanout. This shows how we can give special treatment to particular component instances when configuring bindings. We bind all remaining instances of the flipflop component to the edge_triggered_Dff entity using the basic architecture.

VHDL-87

The keyword **configuration** may not be included at the end of a configuration declaration in VHDL-87.

Configuring Multiple Levels of Hierarchy

In the previous section, we saw how to write a configuration declaration for a design in which the instantiated components are bound to behavioral architecture bodies. Most realistic designs, however, have deeper hierarchical structure. The components at the top level have architecture bodies that, in turn, contain component instances that must be configured. The architecture bodies bound to these second-level components may also contain component instances, and so on. In order to deal with configuring these more complex hierarchies, we need to use an alternative form of binding indication in the configuration declaration. The alternative syntax rule is

binding_indication ⇐ **use configuration** *configuration*_name

This form of binding indication for a component instance allows us to bind to a preconfigured entity/architecture pair simply by naming the configuration declaration for the entity. For example, a component instance of **reg4** with the label **flag_reg** might be bound in a configuration declaration as follows:

```
for flag_reg : reg4
    use configuration work.reg4_gate_level;
end for;
```

EXAMPLE

In Chapter 5 we looked at a two-digit decimal counter, implemented using four-bit registers. We assume that the type **digit** is defined as follows in a package named **counter_types**:

```
subtype digit is bit_vector(3 downto 0);
```

The entity declaration for **counter** is shown at the top of Figure 13-6. Now that we have seen how to use component declarations, we can rewrite the architecture body using component declarations for the registers, as shown at the bottom of Figure 13-6. We can configure this implementation of the counter with the configuration declaration shown in Figure 13-7. This configuration specifies that each instance of the **digit_register** component is bound using the information in the configuration declaration named **reg4_gate_level** in the current design library, shown in Figure 13-5. That configuration in turn specifies the entity to use (**reg4**), a corresponding architecture body (**struct**) and the bindings for each component instance in that architecture body. Thus the two configuration declarations combine to fully configure the design hierarchy down to the process level.

FIGURE 13-6

```
use work.counter_types.digit;

entity counter is
    port ( clk, clr : in bit;
            q0, q1 : out digit );
end entity counter;
```

```
architecture registered of counter is

    component digit_register is
        port ( clk, clr : in bit;
                d : in digit;
                q : out digit );
    end component digit_register;

    signal current_val0, current_val1, next_val0, next_val1 : digit;

begin

    val0_reg : component digit_register
        port map ( clk => clk, clr => clr, d => next_val0,
                    q => current_val0 );

    val1_reg : component digit_register
        port map ( clk => clk, clr => clr, d => next_val1,
                    q => current_val1 );

    -- other component instances
    . . .

end architecture registered;
```

An entity declaration and architecture body for a two-digit counter, using a component representing a four-bit register.

FIGURE 13-7

```
configuration counter_down_to_gate_level of counter is

    for registered

        for all : digit_register
            use configuration work.reg4_gate_level;
        end for;

        . . .        -- bindings for other component instances

    end for;  -- end of architecture registered

end configuration counter_down_to_gate_level;
```

A configuration declaration for the decimal counter.

The example above shows how we can use separate configuration declarations for each level of a design hierarchy. As a matter of style this is good practice, since it prevents the configuration declarations themselves from becoming too complex. The alternative approach is to configure an entity and its hierarchy fully within the one configuration declaration. We look at how this may be done, as some models from other designers may take this approach. While this approach is valid VHDL, we recommend the practice of splitting up the configuration information into separate configuration declarations corresponding to the entities used in the design hierarchy.

To see how to configure multiple levels within one declaration, we need to look at a more complex form of syntax rule for configuration declarations. In fact, we need to split the rule into two parts, so that we can write a recursive syntax rule.

configuration_declaration ⇐
    configuration identifier **of** *entity*_name **is**
        block_configuration
    end ⟦ **configuration** ⟧ ⟦ identifier ⟧ ;

block_configuration ⇐
    for *architecture*_name
        { **for** component_specification
            binding_indication ;
            ⟦ block_configuration ⟧
          end for ; }
    end for ;

The rule for a block configuration indicates how to write the configuration information for an architecture body and its inner component instances. (The reason for the name "block configuration" in the second rule is that it applies to block statements as well as architecture bodies. We discuss block statements in Chapter 16.) Note that we have included an extra part after the binding indication for a component instance. If the architecture that we bind to an instance also contains component instances, we can nest further configuration information for that architecture inside the enclosing block configuration.

EXAMPLE

We can write a configuration declaration equivalent to that in Figure 13-7 but containing all of the configuration information for the entire hierarchy, as shown in Figure 13-8. The difference between this configuration declaration and the one in Figure 13-7 is that the binding indication for instances of **digit_register** directly refers to the entity **reg4** and the architecture body **struct**, rather than using a separate configuration for the entity. The configuration then includes all of the binding information for component instances within **struct**. This relatively simple example shows how difficult it can be to read nested configuration declarations. Separate configuration declarations are easier to understand and provide more flexibility for managing alternative compositions of a design hierarchy.

FIGURE 13-8

```
library star_lib;
use star_lib.edge_triggered_Dff;
configuration full of counter is
    for registered  -- architecture of counter
        for all : digit_register
            use entity work.reg4(struct);
            for struct  -- architecture of reg4
                for bit0 : flipflop
                    use entity edge_triggered_Dff(hi_fanout);
                end for;
                for others : flipflop
                    use entity edge_triggered_Dff(basic);
                end for;
            end for;  -- end of architecture struct
        end for;
        . . .        -- bindings for other component instances
    end for;  -- end of architecture registered
end configuration full;
```

An alternate configuration declaration for the decimal counter.

Direct Instantiation of Configured Entities

As we have seen, a configuration declaration specifies the design hierarchy for a design
entity. We can make direct use of a fully configured design entity within an architecture
body by writing a component instantiation statement that directly names the configuration. The alternative syntax rule for component instantiation statements that expresses
this possibility is

```
component_instantiation_statement ⇐
    instantiation_label :
        configuration configuration_name
        〚 generic map ( generic_association_list ) 〛
        〚 port map ( port_association_list ) 〛 ;
```

The configuration named in the statement includes a specification of an entity and
a corresponding architecture body to use. We can include generic and port maps in
the component instantiation to provide actual values for any generic constants of the
entity and actual signals to connect to the ports of the entity. This is much like instantiating the entity directly, but with all of the configuration information for its implementation included.

EXAMPLE

Figure 13-9 shows an outline of an architecture body that directly instantiates the two-digit decimal counter entity. The component instantiation statement labeled **seconds** refers to the configuration **counter_down_to_gate_level**, shown in Figure 13-7. That configuration, in turn, specifies the counter entity and architecture to use.

FIGURE 13-9

```
architecture top_level of alarm_clock is

    use work.counter_types.digit;

    signal reset_to_midnight, seconds_clk : bit;
    signal seconds_units, seconds_tens : digit;
    . . .

begin

    seconds : configuration work.counter_down_to_gate_level
        port map ( clk => seconds_clk, clr => reset_to_midnight,
                   q0 => seconds_units, q1 => seconds_tens );

    . . .

end architecture top_level;
```

An outline of an architecture body that directly instantiates the configured decimal counter entity.

VHDL-87

VHDL-87 does not allow direct instantiation of configured entities. Instead, we must declare a component, instantiate the component, and write a separate configuration declaration that binds the instance to the configured entity.

Generic and Port Maps in Configurations

We now turn to a very powerful and important aspect of component configurations: the inclusion of generic maps and port maps in the binding indications. This facility provides a great deal of flexibility when binding component instances to design entities. However, the ideas behind the facility are somewhat difficult to grasp on first encounter, so we will work through them carefully. First, let us look at an extended syntax rule for a binding indication that shows how generic and port maps can be included:

```
binding_indication ⇐
    use ( entity entity_name [ ( architecture_identifier ) ]
        ‖ configuration configuration_name )
    [ generic map ( generic_association_list ) ]
    [ port map ( port_association_list ) ]
```

This rule indicates that after specifying the entity to which to bind (either directly or by naming a configuration), we may include a generic map or a port map or both. We show how this facility may be used by starting with some simple examples illustrating the more common uses. We then proceed to the general case.

One of the most important uses of this facility is to separate the specification of generic constants used for timing from the structure of a design. We can write component declarations in a structural description without including generic constants for timing. Later, when we bind each component instance to an entity in a configuration declaration, we can specify the timing values by supplying actual values for the generic constants of the bound entities.

EXAMPLE

Suppose we are designing an integrated circuit for a controller, and we wish to use the register whose entity declaration is shown in Figure 13-10. We can write a component declaration for the register without including the generic constants used for timing, as shown in the architecture body outlined in Figure 13-11. This component represents a virtual module that has all of the structural characteristics we need, but ignores timing. The component instantiation statement specifies a value for the port width generic constant, but does not specify any timing parameters.

FIGURE 13-10

```
library ieee;  use ieee.std_logic_1164.all;

entity reg is
    generic ( t_setup, t_hold, t_pd : delay_length;
              width : positive );
    port ( clock : in std_logic;
           data_in : in std_logic_vector(0 to width − 1);
           data_out : out std_logic_vector(0 to width − 1) );
end entity reg;
```

An entity declaration for a register, including generic constants for timing and port width.

FIGURE 13-11

```
architecture structural of controller is

    component reg is
        generic ( width : positive );
        port ( clock : in std_logic;
               data_in : in std_logic_vector(0 to width − 1);
               data_out : out std_logic_vector(0 to width − 1) );
    end component reg;

    . . .

begin
```

```
        state_reg : component reg
            generic map ( width => state_type'length )
            port map ( clock => clock_phase1,
                        data_in => next_state,
                        data_out => current_state );

    . . .

end architecture structural;
```

An outline of a structural architecture body of a controller design, using an idealized representation of the register module.

Since we are operating in the real world, we cannot ignore timing forever. Ultimately the values for the timing parameters will be determined from the physical layout of the integrated circuit. Meanwhile, during the design phase, we can use estimates for their values. When we write a configuration declaration for our design, we can configure the component instance as shown in Figure 13-12, supplying the estimates in a generic map. Note that we also need to specify a value for the width generic of the bound entity. In this example, we supply the value of the width generic of the component instance. We discuss this in more detail on page 315.

FIGURE 13-12

```
configuration controller_with_timing of controller is
    for structural
        for state_reg : reg
            use entity work.reg(gate_level)
            generic map ( t_setup => 200 ps, t_hold => 150 ps,
                            t_pd => 150 ps, width => width );
        end for;

        . . .

    end for;
end configuration controller_with_timing;
```

A configuration for the controller circuit, supplying values for the timing parameters of the register instance.

When we simulate the design, the estimated values for the generic constants are used by the real design entity to which the component instance is bound. Later, when the integrated circuit has been laid out, we can substitute, or *back annotate*, the actual timing values in the configuration declaration without having to modify the architecture body of the model. We can then resimulate to obtain test vectors for the circuit that take account of the real timing.

Another important use of generic and port maps in a configuration declaration arises when the entity to which we want to bind a component instance has different names for generic constants and ports. The maps in the binding indication can be used to make the link between component generics and ports on the one hand, and entity generics and ports on the other. Furthermore, the entity may have additional generics or ports beyond those of the component instance. In this case, the maps can be used to associate actual values or signals from the architecture body with the additional generics or ports.

EXAMPLE

Suppose we need to use a two-input-to-four-output decoder in a design, as shown in the outline of an architecture body in Figure 13-13. The component declaration for the decoder represents a virtual module that meets our needs exactly.

FIGURE 13-13

```
architecture structure of computer_system is
    component decoder_2_to_4 is
        generic ( prop_delay : delay_length );
        port ( in0, in1 : in bit;
                    out0, out1, out2, out3 : out bit );
    end component decoder_2_to_4;

    . . .

begin
    interface_decoder : component decoder_2_to_4
        generic map ( prop_delay => 4 ns )
        port map ( in0 => addr(4), in1 => addr(5),
                    out0 => interface_a_select, out1 => interface_b_select,
                    out2 => interface_c_select, out3 => interface_d_select );

    . . .

end architecture structure;
```

An outline of an architecture body for a computer system, using a four-output decoder component.

Now suppose we check in our library of entities for a real module to use for this instance and find a three-input-to-eight-output decoder. The entity declaration is shown in Figure 13-14. We could make use of this entity in our design if we could adapt to the different generic and port names and tie the unused ports to appropriate values. The configuration declaration in Figure 13-15 shows how this may be done. The generic map in the binding indication specifies the correspondence between entity generics and component generics. In this case, the component generic **prop_delay** is to be used for both entity generics. The port map in the binding indication similarly specifies which entity ports correspond to which component ports. Where the entity has extra ports, we can specify how those ports are to be connected. In this design, **s2** is tied to '0', **enable** is tied to '1' and the remaining ports are left unassociated (specified by the keyword **open**).

FIGURE 13-14

```
entity decoder_3_to_8 is
    generic ( Tpd_01, Tpd_10 : delay_length );
    port ( s0, s1, s2 : in bit;
            enable : in bit;
            y0, y1, y2, y3, y4, y5, y6, y7 : out bit );
end entity decoder_3_to_8;
```

An entity declaration for the real decoder module.

FIGURE 13-15

```
configuration computer_structure of computer_system is
    for structure
        for interface_decoder : decoder_2_to_4
            use entity work.decoder_3_to_8(basic)
            generic map ( Tpd_01 => prop_delay, Tpd_10 => prop_delay )
            port map ( s0 => in0, s1 => in1, s2 => '0',
                        enable => '1',
                        y0 => out0, y1 => out1, y2 => out2, y3 => out3,
                        y4 => open, y5 => open, y6 => open, y7 => open );
        end for;

        . . .

    end for;
end configuration computer_structure;
```

A configuration declaration for the computer system design, showing how the decoder component instance is bound to the real decoder entity.

The two preceding examples illustrate the most common uses of generic maps and port maps in configuration declarations. We now look at the general mechanism that underlies these examples, so that we can understand its use in more complex cases. We use the terms *local generics* and *local ports* to refer to the generics and ports of a component. Also, in keeping with previous discussions, we use the terms *formal generics* and *formal ports* to refer to the generics and ports of the entity to which the instance is bound.

When we write a component instantiation statement with a generic map and a port map, these maps associate actual values and signals with the *local* generics and ports of the component instance. Recall that the component is just a virtual module used as a template for a real module, so at this stage we have just made connections to the template. Next, we write a configuration declaration that binds the component instance to a real entity. The generic and port maps in the binding indication associate actual values and signals with the *formal* generics and ports of the entity. These actual values and signals may be the locals from the component instance, or they may be values and signals from the architecture body containing the component instance.

Figure 13-16 illustrates the mappings. It is this two-stage association mechanism that makes configurations so powerful in mapping a design to real modules.

Figure 13-16 shows that the actual values and signals supplied in the configuration declaration may be local generics or ports from the component instance. This is the case for the formal generics **Tpd_01** and **Tpd_10** and for the formal ports **s0**, **s1**, **y0**, **y1**, **y2** and **y3** in Figure 13-15. Every local generic and port of the component instance must be associated with a formal generic or port, respectively; otherwise the design is in error. The figure also shows that the configuration declaration may supply values or signals from the architecture body. Furthermore, they may be any other value or signal visible at the point of the component instantiation statement, such as the literals '0' and '1' shown in the example. Note that while it is legal to associate a signal in the architecture body with a formal port of the entity, it is not good practice to do so. This effectively modifies the structure of the circuit, making the overall design much more difficult to understand and manage. For example, in the configuration in Figure 13-15, had we associated the formal port **s2** with the signal **addr(6)** instead of the literal value '0', the operation of the circuit would be substantially altered.

FIGURE 13-16

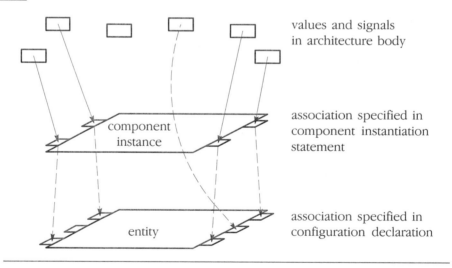

The generic and port maps in the component instantiation and the configuration declaration define a two-stage association. Values and signals in the architecture body are associated, via the local generics and ports, with the formal generics and ports of the bound entity.

The preceding examples show how we can use generic and port maps in binding indications to deal with differences between the component and the entity in the number and names of generics and ports. However, if the component and entity have similar interfaces, we can rely on a *default binding* rule. This rule is used automatically if we omit the generic map or the port map in a binding indication, as we did in the earlier examples in this section. The default rule causes each local generic or port of the component to be associated with a formal generic or port of the same name in the entity interface. If the entity interface includes further formal generics or ports, they remain open. If the entity does not include a formal with the same name as one of the locals, the design is in error. So, for example, if we declare a component as

```
component nand3 is
    port ( a, b, c : in bit := '1';  y : out bit );
end component nand3;
```

and instantiate it as

```
gate1 : component nand3
    port map ( a => s1, b => s2, c => open, y => s3 );
```

then attempt to bind to an entity declared as

```
entity nand2 is
    port ( a, b : in bit := '1';  y : out bit );
end entity nand2;
```

with a component configuration

```
for gate1 : nand3
    use entity work.nand2(basic);
end for;
```

an error occurs. The reason for the error is that there is no formal port named **c** to associate with the local port of that name. The default rule requires that such a correspondence be found, even though the local port is unconnected in the architecture body.

Deferred Component Binding

We have seen that we can specify the binding for a component instance either by naming an entity and a corresponding architecture body, or by naming a configuration. A third option is to leave the component instance unbound and to defer binding it until later in the design cycle. The syntax rule for a binding indication that expresses this option is

binding_indication ⇐ **use open**

If we use this form of binding indication to leave a component instance unbound, we cannot include a generic map or port map. This makes sense: since there is no entity, there are no formal generics or ports with which to associate actual values or signals.

A scenario in which we may wish to defer binding arises in complex designs that can be partially simulated before all subsystems are complete. We can write an architecture body for the system, including component declarations and instances as placeholders for the subsystems. Initially, we write a configuration declaration that defers bindings of the subsystems. Then, as the design of each subsystem is completed, the corresponding component configuration is updated to bind to the new entity. At intermediate stages it may be possible to simulate the system with some of the components unbound. The effect of the deferred bindings is simply to leave the corresponding ports unassociated when the design is elaborated. Thus the inputs to the unbound modules are not used, and the outputs remain undriven.

EXAMPLE

Figure 13-17 shows an outline of a structural architecture for a single-board computer system. The design includes all of the components needed to construct the system, including a CPU, main memory and a serial interface. However, if we have not yet designed an entity and architecture body for the serial interface, we cannot bind the component instance for the interface. Instead, we must leave it unbound, as shown in the configuration declaration in Figure 13-18. We can proceed to simulate the design, using the implementations of the CPU and main memory, provided we do not try to exercise the serial interface. If the processor were to try to access registers in the serial interface, it would get no response. Since there is no entity bound to the component instance representing the interface, there is nothing to drive the data or other signals connected to the instance.

FIGURE 13-17

```
architecture structural of single_board_computer is
    . . .        -- type and signal declarations
    component processor is
        port ( clk : in bit;  a_d : inout word; . . . );
    end component processor;
    component memory is
        port ( addr : in bit_vector(25 downto 0); . . . );
    end component memory;
    component serial_interface is
        port ( clk : in bit;  address : in bit_vector(3 downto 0); . . . );
    end component serial_interface;
begin
    cpu : component processor
        port map ( clk => sys_clk, a_d => cpu_a_d, . . . );
    main_memory : component memory
        port map ( addr => latched_addr(25 downto 0), . . . );
    serial_interface_a : component serial_interface
        port map ( clk => sys_clk, address => latched_addr(3 downto 0), . . . );
    . . .
end architecture structural;
```

An outline of an architecture body for a single-board computer, including component declarations and instances for the CPU, main memory and a serial interface controller.

FIGURE 13-18

```
library chips;
configuration intermediate of single_board_computer is
    for structural
```

```
        for cpu : processor
            use entity chips.XYZ3000_cpu(full_function)
            port map ( clock => clk, addr_data => a_d, . . . );
        end for;

        for main_memory : memory
            use entity work.memory_array(behavioral);
        end for;

        for all : serial_interface
            use open;
        end for;

        . . .

    end for;
end configuration intermediate;
```

A configuration declaration for the single-board computer, in which the serial interface is left unbound.

13.3 Configuration Specifications

We complete this chapter with a discussion of *configuration specifications*. These provide a way of including binding information for component instances in the same architecture body as the instances themselves, as opposed to separating the information out into a configuration declaration. In some respects, this language feature is a relic of VHDL-87, which did not allow direct instantiation of entities in an architecture body. In VHDL-93, if we know the interface of the entity and want to use it "as is," we can instantiate it directly, without having to write a corresponding component declaration. The main remaining use of configuration specifications is to bind a known entity to component instances in cases where our idealized module is different from the entity. Using a component declaration to describe the idealized module may make the design easier to understand. The syntax rule for a configuration specification is

```
configuration_specification ⇐
    for component_specification
        binding_indication ;
```

A configuration specification is similar to a component configuration without the keywords **end for**, so we need to take care not to confuse the two. The component specification and binding indication are written in exactly the same way in both cases. However, a configuration specification does not provide an opportunity to configure the internal structure of the architecture to which the component instance is bound. That must be done in a separate configuration declaration. If we write a configuration specification for a component instance, it must be included in the declarative part of the architecture body or block that directly contains the component instance.

The effect of a configuration specification in an architecture body is exactly the same as if the binding indication had been included in a configuration declaration. Thus, we can bind a component instance to a design entity, and we can specify the mapping between the local generics and ports of the component instance and the formal generics and ports of the entity.

EXAMPLE

Suppose we need to include a two-input nand gate in a model, but our library only provides a three-input nand gate, declared as

```
entity nand3 is
    port ( a, b, c : in bit;  y : out bit );
end entity nand3;
```

We can write our model using a component declaration to show that we really would prefer a two-input gate, and include a configuration specification to handle the difference in interfaces between the component instance and the entity. The architecture is shown in Figure 13-19.

FIGURE 13-19

```
library gate_lib;

architecture ideal of logic_block is

    component nand2 is
        port ( in1, in2 : in bit;  result : out bit );
    end component nand2;

    for all : nand2
        use entity gate_lib.nand3(behavioral)
        port map ( a => in1, b => in2, c => '1', y => result );
    . . .         – – other declarations

begin

    gate1 : component nand2
        port map ( in1 => s1, in2 => s2, result => s3 );

    . . .         – – other concurrent statements

end architecture ideal;
```

An outline of an architecture body that uses an idealized nand-gate component, and a configuration specification for the component instance.

Incremental Binding

We have now seen that there are two places where we can specify the mapping between the local generics and ports of a component instance and the formal generics and ports of the bound entity. The mappings can be specified either in a configuration specification or in a separate configuration declaration. We must now consider the possibility of having two binding indications for a given component instance, one in each of these places. VHDL does, in fact, allow this. The first binding indication, in the configuration specification in the architecture body, is called the *primary* binding indication. The second binding indication, in the configuration declaration, is called an *incremental* binding indication. The primary binding indication must at least specify the entity to which the instance is bound and may also include generic and port maps. If there is a primary binding indication, the incremental binding indication must not include an entity part. The full syntax rule for a binding indication allows for the entity part to be omitted in this case (see Appendix E). The incremental binding indication can also include generic and port maps, and the associations in them override those made in the primary binding indication, with some restrictions. We look at the various possibilities for this, with some examples.

The first possibility is that the primary binding indication for a component instance leaves some of the formal generics or ports of the entity unassociated. In this case, the incremental binding indication can "fill in the gaps" by associating actual values and signals with the unassociated generics and ports.

EXAMPLE

Figure 13-20 shows an architecture body for the control section of a processor, including a register component to store flag bits. The configuration specification binds the register component instance to the register entity shown in Figure 13-21. This entity has additional formal generics t_setup, t_hold and t_pd for timing parameters, and an additional port, reset_n. Since the component declaration does not include corresponding local generics and ports, and the configuration specification does not specify values or signals for the formal generics and ports, they are left open in the architecture body.

FIGURE 13-20

```
architecture structural of control_section is
    component reg is
        generic ( width : positive );
        port ( clk : in std_logic;
               d : in std_logic_vector(0 to width − 1);
               q : out std_logic_vector(0 to width − 1) );
    end component reg;

    for flag_reg : reg
        use entity work.reg(gate_level)
        port map ( clock => clk, data_in => d, data_out => q );

    . . .

begin
    flag_reg : component reg
        generic map ( width => 3 )
        port map ( clk => clock_phase1,
                   d(0) => zero_result, d(1) => neg_result,
                   d(2) => overflow_result,
                   q(0) => zero_flag, q(1) => neg_flag,
                   q(2) => overflow_flag );

    . . .

end architecture structural;
```

An architecture body of a processor control section, using an idealized representation of a register module. The configuration specification binds the component instance to the real register entity.

FIGURE 13-21

```
library ieee;  use ieee.std_logic_1164.all;
entity reg is
    generic ( t_setup, t_hold, t_pd : delay_length;
              width : positive );
    port ( clock : in std_logic;
           reset_n : in std_logic;
           data_in : in std_logic_vector(0 to width – 1);
           data_out : out std_logic_vector(0 to width – 1) );
end entity reg;
```

The entity declaration for the register used in the control section.

The configuration declaration for the design, shown in Figure 13-22, contains an incremental binding indication for the register component instance. It does not specify an entity/architecture pair, since that was specified in the primary binding indication. It does, however, include a generic map, filling in values for the formal generics that were left open by the primary binding indication. The generic map also associates the value of the local generic **width** with the formal generic **width**. The port map in the incremental binding indication associates the literal value '1' with the formal port reset_n.

FIGURE 13-22

```
configuration controller_with_timing of control_section is
    for structural
        for flag_reg : reg
            generic map ( t_setup => 200 ps, t_hold => 150 ps,
                          t_pd => 150 ps, width => width )
            port map ( reset_n => '1' );
        end for;

        . . .

    end for;
end configuration controller_with_timing;
```

A configuration for the controller circuit, supplying values for the timing parameters of the register instance.

The second possibility is that the primary binding indication associates actual values with the formal generics of the entity bound to the component instance. In this case, the incremental binding indication can include new associations for these formal generics, overriding the associations in the primary binding indication. This may be useful in the back-annotation stage of design processing. Estimates for values of generics controlling propagation delay can be included in the primary binding indication and the design simulated before doing physical layout. Later, when actual delay values have been calculated from the physical layout, they can be included in incremental binding indications in a configuration declaration without having to modify the architecture body in any way.

EXAMPLE

Figure 13-23 shows an outline of an architecture body for the interlock control logic of a pipelined processor. It declares a nor-gate component with a generic constant for the input port width, but with no generics for timing parameters. The architecture includes a configuration specification for the instance of the gate component, which binds it to a nor-gate entity that does include timing generics. The generic map in the configuration specification supplies estimates of the timing as actual values for the generics.

FIGURE 13-23

```
architecture detailed_timing of interlock_control is

    component nor_gate is
        generic ( input_width : positive );
        port ( input : in std_logic_vector(0 to input_width – 1);
               output : out std_logic );
    end component nor_gate;

    for ex_interlock_gate : nor_gate
        use entity cell_lib.nor_gate(primitive)
        generic map ( width => input_width,
                      Tpd01 => 250 ps, Tpd10 => 200 ps );  –– estimates

    . . .

begin

    ex_interlock_gate : component nor_gate
        generic map ( input_width => 2 )
        port map ( input(0) => reg_access_hazard,
                   input(1) => load_hazard,
                   output => stall_ex_n );

    . . .

end architecture detailed_timing;
```

An architecture body for the interlock control logic of a processor.

This model can be simulated with these estimates by configuring it as shown at the top of Figure 13-24. Since there is no further configuration information supplied for the nor-gate instance, the estimated timing values are used. After the design has been laid out and the real timing values have been determined, the configuration declaration can be updated as shown at the bottom of Figure 13-24. An incremental binding indication has been added, supplying the new values for the timing generics. When the design is simulated with this updated configuration, these new values override the estimates specified in the primary binding indication in the architecture body.

FIGURE 13-24

```
configuration interlock_control_with_estimates of interlock_control is
    for detailed_timing
    end for;

    . . .

end configuration interlock_control_with_estimates;
_____

configuration interlock_control_with_actual of interlock_control is
    for detailed_timing
        for ex_interlock_gate : nor_gate
            generic map ( Tpd01 => 320 ps, Tpd10 => 230 ps );
        end for;

        . . .

    end for;
end configuration interlock_control_with_actual;
```

Two versions of a configuration declaration for the interlock control logic.

The third possibility to consider is that the primary binding indication associates actual signals with the formal ports of the entity. In this case, the incremental binding indication cannot override the associations, since to do so would modify the structure of the design.

The final case that arises is one in which a component instantiation associates actual values and signals with local generics and ports, but the primary binding indication does not explictly associate actual values or signals with formal generics or ports of the same name. In this case, the default binding rule normally causes the local generics to be associated with formal generics of the same name and local ports to be associated with formal ports of the same name. However, we can preempt this default rule by supplying alternative associations for the formal generics and ports in the incremental binding indication.

EXAMPLE

Figure 13-25 outlines an architecture body for a block of miscellaneous logic. It includes a component declaration for a three-input nand gate and an instance of the component with an actual value supplied for a local timing generic. The primary binding indication binds the instance to a three-input nand gate entity, but does not specify the mappings between the local generic and ports and the formal generic and ports.

The configuration declaration for this design shown in Figure 13-26 overrides the default mapping. It supplies an actual value for the formal timing generic Tpd, instead of using the value of the local generic of that name. It maps the local port c onto the formal port a, and the local port a onto the formal port c. The local ports b and y map onto the formal ports of the same names.

FIGURE 13-25

```
architecture gate_level of misc_logic is
    component nand3 is
        generic ( Tpd : delay_length );
        port ( a, b, c : in bit;  y : out bit );
    end component nand3;

    for all : nand3
        use entity project_lib.nand3(basic);

    . . .

begin
    gate1 : component nand3
        generic map ( Tpd => 2 ns )
        port map ( a => sig1, b => sig2, c => sig3, y => out_sig );

    . . .

end architecture gate_level;
```

An architecture body for a block of logic.

FIGURE 13-26

```
configuration misc_logic_reconfigured of misc_logic is
    for gate_level
        for gate1 : nand3
            generic map ( Tpd => 1.6 ns )
            port map ( a => c, c => a, b => b, y => y );
        end for;
    end for;
end configuration misc_logic_reconfigured;
```

A configuration declaration for the logic block.

VHDL-87

VHDL-87 does not allow incremental binding. It is an error if a design includes both a configuration specification and a component configuration for a given component instance. If we expect to revise the associations in a generic map or port map of a configuration specification, we should omit the configuration specification and write the initial associations in the configuration declaration. Later, when we need to revise the associations, we can simply edit the configuration declaration without changing the architecture containing the component instance.

Exercises

1. [❶ 13.1] List some of the differences between an entity declaration and a component declaration.

2. [❶ 13.1] Write a component declaration for a binary magnitude comparitor, with two standard-logic vector data inputs, a and b, whose length is specified by a generic constant, and two standard-logic outputs indicating whether a = b and a < b. The component also includes a generic constant for the propagation delay.

3. [❶ 13.1] Write a component instantiation statement that instantiates the magnitude comparitor described in Exercise 2. The data inputs are connected to signals current_position and upper_limit, the output indicating whether a < b is connected to position_ok and the remaining output is open. The propagation delay of the instance is 12 ns.

4. [❶ 13.1] Write a package declaration that defines a subtype of natural numbers representable in eight bits and a component declaration for an adder that adds values of the subtype.

5. [❶ 13.2] Suppose we have an architecture body for a digital filter, outlined as follows:

```
architecture register_transfer of digital_filter is
    . . .
    component multiplier is
        port ( . . . );
    end component multiplier;
begin
    coeff_1_multiplier : component multiplier
        port map ( . . . );
    . . .
end architecture register_transfer;
```

Write a configuration declaration that binds the multiplier component instance to a multiplier entity called fixed_point_mult from the library dsp_lib, using the architecture algorithmic.

6. [❶ 13.2] Suppose the library dsp_lib referred to in Exercise 5 includes a configuration of the fixed_point_mult entity called fixed_point_mult_std_cell. Write an alternative configuration declaration for the filter described in Exercise 5, binding the multiplier instance using the fixed_point_mult_std_cell configuration.

7. [❶ 13.2] Modify the outline of the filter architecture body described in Exercise 5 to directly instantiate the fixed_point_mult_std_cell configuration described in Exercise 6, rather than using the multiplier component.

8. [❶ 13.2] Suppose we declare and instantiate a multiplexer component in an architecture body as follows:

```
component multiplexer is
    port ( s, d0, d1 : in bit; z : out bit );
end component multiplexer;
```

```
serial_data_mux : component multiplexer
    port map ( s => serial_source_select,
                d0 => rx_data_0, d1 => rx_data_1,
                z => internal_rx_data );
```

Write a binding indication that binds the component instance to the following entity in the current working library, using the most recently analyzed architecture and
specifying a value of 3.5 ns for the propagation delay.

```
entity multiplexer is
    generic ( Tpd : delay_length := 3 ns );
    port ( s, d0, d1 : in bit; z : out bit );
end entity multiplexer;
```

9. [❶ 13.2] Draw a diagram, based on Figure 13-16 on page 316, that shows the mapping between entity ports and generics, component ports and generics and other
   values in the configured computer system model of Figure 13-15 on page 315.

10. [❶ 13.2] Suppose we have an entity nand4 with the following interface in a library
    gate_lib:

```
entity nand4 is
    generic ( Tpd_01, Tpd_10 : delay_length := 2 ns );
    port ( a, b, c, d : in bit := '1';  y : out bit );
end entity nand4;
```

We bind the entity to the component instance **gate1** described on page 317 using
the following component configuration:

```
for gate1 : nand3
    use entity get_lib.nand4(basic);
end for;
```

Write the generic and port maps that comprise the default binding indication used
in this configuration.

11. [❶ 13.3] Rewrite the component configuration information in Figure 13-15 on
    page 315 as a configuration specification for inclusion in the computer system ar-
    chitecture body.

12. [❶ 13.3] Assuming that the computer system referred to in Exercise 11 includes
    the configuration specification, write a configuration declaration that includes an
    incremental binding indication, specifying values of 4.3 ns and 3.8 ns for the entity
    generics **Tpd_01** and **Tpd_10**, respectively.

13. [❷ 13.1] Develop a structural model of a 32-bit bidirectional transceiver, imple-
    mented using a component based on the eight-bit transceiver described in Exer-
    cise 13 in Chapter 11.

14. [❷ 13.1] Develop a structural model for an eight-bit serial-in/parallel-out shift regis-
    ter, assuming you have available a four-bit serial-in/parallel-out shift register. In-
    clude a component declaration for the four-bit register, and instantiate it as re-
    quired for the eight-bit register. The four-bit register has a positive-edge-triggered
    clock input, an active-low asynchronous reset input, a serial data input and four
    parallel data outputs.

15. [❷ 13.1] Develop a package of component declarations for two-input gates and an inverter, corresponding to the logical operators in VHDL. Each component has ports of type **bit** and generic constants for rising output and falling output propagation delays.

16. [❷ 13.2] Develop a configuration declaration for the 32-bit transceiver described in Exercise 13 that binds each instance of the eight-bit transceiver component to the eight-bit transceiver entity.

17. [❷ 13.2] Develop a behavioral model of a four-bit shift register that implements the component interface described in Exercise 14. Write a configuration declaration for the eight-bit shift register, binding the component instances to the four-bit shift register entity.

18. [❷ 13.2] Suppose we wish to use an XYZ1234A serial interface controller in the microcontroller described in Figure 13-4. The entity interface for the XYZ1234A is

```
entity XYZ1234A is
    generic ( T_phi_out, T_d_z : delay_length;
              debug_trace : boolean := false );
    port ( phi1, phi2 : in std_logic;              -- 2 phase clock
           cs : in std_logic;                      -- chip select
           a : in std_logic_vector(1 downto 0);    -- address
           d : inout std_logic_vector(1 downto 0); -- data
           int_req : out std_logic;                -- interrupt
           rx_d : in std_logic;                    -- rx serial data
           tx_d : out std_logic );                 -- tx serial data
end entity XYZ1234A;
```

Write a configuration declaration that binds the serial_interface component instance to the XYZ1234A entity, using the most recently compiled architecture, setting both timing generics to 6 ns and using the default value for the debug_trace generic.

19. [❷ 13.1/13.2] Use the package described in Exercise 15 to develop a structural model of a full adder, described by the Boolean equations

$$S = (A \oplus B) \oplus C_{in}$$
$$C_{out} = A . B + (A \oplus B) . C_{in}$$

Write behavioral models of entities corresponding to each of the gate components, and a configuration declaration that binds each component instance in the full adder to the appropriate gate entity.

20. [❸ 13.2] Develop a structural model of a four-bit adder using instances of a full-adder component. Write a configuration declaration that binds each instance of the full-adder component, using the configuration declaration described in Exercise 19. For comparison, write an alternative configuration declaration that fully configures the four-bit adder hierarchy without using the configuration declaration described in Exercise 19.

21. [❸ 13.2] Develop a behavioral model of a RAM with bit-vector address, data-in and data-out ports. The size of the ports should be constrained by generics in the entity interface. Next, develop a test bench that includes a component declaration for

the RAM without the generics and with fixed-sized address and data ports. Write a configuration declaration for the test bench that binds the RAM entity to the RAM component instance, using the component local port sizes to determine values for the entity formal generics.

22. [❸ 13.3] The majority function of three inputs can be described by the Boolean equation

$$M(a, b, c) = a.b.c + a.b.\overline{c} + a.\overline{b}.c + \overline{a}.b.c$$

Develop a structural model of a three-input majority circuit, using inverter, and-gate and or-gate components with standard-logic inputs and outputs. Also develop behavioral models for the inverter and gates, including generic constants in the interfaces to specify propagation delays for rising and falling output transitions. Include configuration specifications in the structural model to bind the component instances to the entities. The configuration specifications should include estimated propagations delays of 2 ns for all gates.

Next, develop a configuration declaration for the majority circuit that includes incremental bindings to override the estimated delays with actual propagation delays as follows:

	rising-output delay	falling-output delay
inverter	1.8 ns	1.7 ns
and gate	2.3 ns	1.9 ns
or gate	2.2 ns	2.0 ns

23. [❹] Develop a suite of models of a digital stopwatch circuit. The circuit has three inputs: a 100 kHz clock, a start/stop switch input and a lap/reset switch input. The two switch inputs are normally high and are pulled low when an external push-button switch is pressed. The circuit has outputs to drive an external seven-segment display of minutes, seconds and hundredths of seconds, formatted as shown in the margin. There is a single output to drive the minutes (') and seconds (") indicators. When an output is high, the corresponding segment or indicator is visible. When the output is low, the segment or indicator is blank. The stopwatch circuit contains a time counter that count minutes, seconds and hundredths of seconds.

The stopwatch counter is initially reset to 00'00"00, with the display showing the counter time and the minute and second indicators on. In this state, pressing the start/stop button starts counting, with the display showing the counter time. Pressing the start/stop button again stops counting. Successive presses of start/stop continue or stop counting, with the display showing the counter time. If the lap/reset button is pressed while the counter is stopped and the display is showing the counter time, the counter is reset to 00'00"00. If the lap/reset button is pressed while the counter is running, the display freezes the time at which the lap/reset button was pressed, the counter continues running and the minutes and seconds indicators flash at a 1 Hz rate to indicate that the counter is still running. If the start/stop button is pressed, the counter stops, the minutes and seconds indicators stop flashing and the displayed time is unchanged. Successive presses of start/stop continue or stop counting, with the displayed time unchanged and the minutes and seconds indicators flashing when the counter is running. Pressing the lap/

reset button while the display is frozen causes it to return to displaying the current counter time, whether the counter is running or stopped.

The first model in your suite should be a behavioral model. Test your behavioral model by writing a test bench for it. You should write a configuration declaration for the test bench that binds the unit under test to the behavioral stopwatch model. Next, refine your stopwatch model to a structural design, including a control sequencer, registers, counters, decoders and other components as required. Develop behavioral models corresponding to each of these components, and write a configuration for the stopwatch that binds the behavioral models to the component instances. Revise the test-bench configuration to use the structural model, and compare its operation with that of the behavioral model. Continue this process of refinement by implementing the control sequencer as a finite-state machine with next-state logic and a state register and by implementing the other components using successively lower-level components down to the level of flipflops and gates. At each stage, develop appropriate configuration declarations to bind entities to component instances, and test the complete model using the test bench.

Generate Statements

Many digital systems can be implemented as regular iterative compositions of subsystems. Memories are a good example, being composed of a rectangular array of storage cells. Indeed, VLSI designers prefer to find such implementations, as they make it easier to produce a compact, area-efficient layout, thus reducing cost. If a design can be expressed as a repetition of some subsystem, we should be able to describe the subsystem once, then describe how it is to be repeatedly instantiated, rather than describe each instantiation individually. In this chapter, we look at the VHDL facility that allows us to generate such regular structures.

14.1 Generating Iterative Structures

We have seen how we can describe the implementation of a subsystem using concurrent statements such as processes and component instantiations. If we want to replicate a subsystem, we can use a *generate statement*. This is a concurrent statement containing further concurrent statements that are to be replicated. Generate statements are particularly useful if the number of times we want to replicate the concurrent statements is not fixed but is determined, for example, from the value of a generic constant. The syntax rule for writing iterative generate statements is

> generate_statement ⇐
>   *generate*_label :
>   **for** identifier **in** discrete_range **generate**
>   [{ block_declarative_item }
>   **begin**]
>   { concurrent_statement }
>   **end generate** [*generate*_label] ;

The generate label is required to identify the generated structure. The header of the generate statement looks very similar to that of a for loop and indeed serves a similar purpose. The discrete range specifies a set of values, and for each value, the block declarative items and concurrent statements are replicated once. Within each replication, the value from the range is given by the identifier, called the *generate parameter*. It appears as a constant, with a type that is the base type of the discrete range. We can specify the discrete range using the same notations that we used in for loops. As a reminder, here is the syntax rule for a discrete range:

> discrete_range ⇐
>   *discrete*_subtype_indication
> | *range*_attribute_name
> | simple_expression (**to** | **downto**) simple_expression

We can include declarations in the generate statement, as shown by the syntax rule. The kinds of items we can declare here are the same kinds that we can declare in the declarative part of the architecture body, including constants, types, subtypes, subprograms and signals. These items are replicated once for each copy of the set of concurrent statements and are local to that copy. Note that the syntax rule for a generate statement requires us to include the keyword **begin** if we include any declarations. However, if we have no declarations, we may omit the keyword.

EXAMPLE

We can implement a register by replicating a flipflop cell. Let us look at how to do this for a register with tristate outputs, conforming to the entity declaration shown in Figure 14-1. The generic constant **width** specifies the width of the register in bits and is used to determine the size of the data input and output ports. The **clock** port enables data to be stored in the register, and the **out_enable** port controls the tristate data output port. The architecture body implements this register in terms of a D-flipflop component and a tristate buffer for each bit.

FIGURE 14-1

```
library ieee;  use ieee.std_logic_1164.all;
entity register_tristate is
    generic ( width : positive );
    port ( clock : in std_logic;
            out_enable : in std_logic;
            data_in : in std_logic_vector(0 to width – 1);
            data_out : out std_logic_vector(0 to width – 1) );
end entity register_tristate;

------------------------------------------------------------

architecture cell_level of register_tristate is
    component D_flipflop is
        port ( clk : in std_logic;  d : in std_logic;
                q : out std_logic );
    end component D_flipflop;
    component tristate_buffer is
        port ( a : in std_logic;
                en : in std_logic;
                y : out std_logic );
    end component tristate_buffer;
begin
    cell_array : for bit_index in 0 to width – 1 generate
        signal data_unbuffered : std_logic;
    begin
        cell_storage : component D_flipflop
            port map ( clk => clock, d => data_in(bit_index),
                        q => data_unbuffered );
        cell_buffer : component tristate_buffer
            port map ( a => data_unbuffered, en => out_enable,
                        y => data_out(bit_index) );
    end generate cell_array;
end architecture cell_level;
```

An entity and architecture body for a register, based on iterative instantiation of a flipflop and tristate buffer.

The generate statement in this structural architecture body replicates the component instantiations labeled cell_storage and cell_buffer, with the number of copies being determined by width. For each copy, the generate parameter bit_index takes on successive values from 0 to width – 1. This value is used within each copy to determine which elements of the data_in and data_out ports are connected to the flipflop input and tristate buffer output. Within each copy there is also a local signal called data_unbuffered, which connects the flipflop output to the buffer input.

EXAMPLE

We can also use generate statements to describe behavioral models, in which behavioral elements implemented using process statements are replicated. Suppose we are modeling part of a graphics transformation pipeline in which a stream of points representing vertices in a scene is to be transformed by matrix multiplication. The equation describing the transformation is

$$\begin{bmatrix} p'_1 \\ p'_2 \\ p'_3 \end{bmatrix} = \begin{bmatrix} a_{11} & a_{12} & a_{13} \\ a_{21} & a_{22} & a_{23} \\ a_{31} & a_{32} & a_{33} \end{bmatrix} \begin{bmatrix} p_1 \\ p_2 \\ p_3 \end{bmatrix}$$

where $\begin{bmatrix} p_1, & p_2, & p_3 \end{bmatrix}$ is the input point to the pipeline stage, and $\begin{bmatrix} p'_1, & p'_2, & p'_3 \end{bmatrix}$ is the transformed output three clock cycles later. We can implement the transformation with three identical cells, each producing one result element. The equation is

$$p'_i = a_{i1} \cdot p_1 + a_{i2} \cdot p_2 + a_{i3} \cdot p_3, \quad i = 1, 2, 3$$

An outline of the architecture body implementing the pipeline with this stage is shown in Figure 14-2. The generate statement replicates the process statement three times, once for each element of the transformed point signal. Each copy of the process uses its value of the generate parameter i to index the appropriate elements of the point and transformation matrix signals.

FIGURE 14-2

```
architecture behavioral of graphics_engine is
    type point is array (1 to 3) of real;
    type transformation_matrix is array (1 to 3, 1 to 3) of real;
    signal p, transformed_p : point;
    signal a : transformation_matrix;
    signal clock : bit;
    . . .
begin
    transform_stage : for i in 1 to 3 generate
    begin

        cross_product_transform : process is
            variable result1, result2, result3 : real := 0.0;
        begin
            wait until clock = '1';
            transformed_p(i) <= result3;  result3 := result2;  result2 := result1;
            result1 := a(i, 1) * p(1) + a(i, 2) * p(2) + a(i, 3) * p(3);
        end process cross_product_transform;

    end generate transform_stage;

        . . .        -- other stages in the pipeline, etc
end architecture behavioral;
```

A behavioral architecture body for a graphics transformation pipeline.

If we need to describe a regular two-dimensional structure, we can use nested generate statements. Nesting of generate statements is allowed in VHDL, since a generate statement is a kind of concurrent statement, and generate statements contain concurrent statements. Usually we write nested generate statements so that the outer statement creates the rows of the structure, and the inner statement creates the elements within each row. Of course, this is purely a convention relating to the way we might draw such a regular structure graphically. However, the convention does help to design and understand such structures.

EXAMPLE

We can use nested generate statements to describe a memory array, constructed from four-bit-wide dynamic memory (DRAM) circuits. Each DRAM stores 4M words (4×2^{20} words) of four bits each. We can construct a $16M \times 32$-bit memory array by generating a 4×8 array of DRAM circuits, connected as shown in Figure 14-3. An outline of the architecture body containing the memory array is shown in Figure 14-4.

FIGURE 14-3

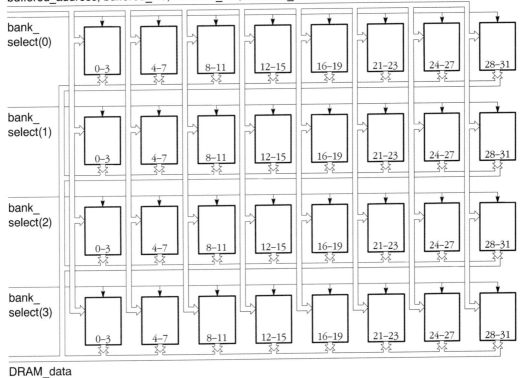

A schematic for a 16M × 32-bit memory array composed of 4M × 4-bit DRAM circuits.

FIGURE 14-4

```
architecture chip_level of memory_board is
    component DRAM is
        port ( a :  in std_logic_vector(0 to 10);
                d :  inout std_logic_vector(0 to 3);
                cs, we, ras, cas : in std_logic );
    end component DRAM;
    signal buffered_address : std_logic_vector(0 to 10);
    signal DRAM_data : std_logic_vector(0 to 31);
    signal bank_select : std_logic_vector(0 to 3);
    signal buffered_we, buffered_ras, buffered_cas : std_logic;
    . . .        -- other declarations
begin
    bank_array : for bank_index in 0 to 3 generate
    begin

        nibble_array : for nibble_index in 0 to 7 generate

            constant data_lo : natural := nibble_index * 4;
            constant data_hi : natural := nibble_index * 4 + 3;
        begin

            a_DRAM : component DRAM
                port map ( a => buffered_address,
                            d => DRAM_data(data_lo to data_hi),
                            cs => bank_select(bank_index),
                            we => buffered_we,
                            ras => buffered_ras,
                            cas => buffered_cas );

        end generate nibble_array;

    end generate bank_array;

    . . .        -- other component instances, etc
end architecture chip_level;
```

An architecture body for a memory board, using nested generate statements to create a two-dimensional array of memory chips.

VHDL-87

A generate statement may not include a declarative part or the keyword **begin** in VHDL-87. The syntax for an iterative generate statement is

```
generate_statement ⇐
    generate_label :
        for identifier in discrete_range generate
            { concurrent_statement }
        end generate [ generate_label ] ;
```

Since it is not possible to declare objects locally within a generate statement, we must declare them in the architecture body containing the generate statement. We can declare an array of objects indexed by the same range as the generate parameter. For example, the signal **data_unbuffered** declared in the generate statement in Figure 14-1 can be replaced by an array in the declarative part of the architecture body:

signal data_unbuffered : std_logic_vector(0 **to** width − 1);

Each reference to **data_unbuffered** within the generate statement is replaced by a reference to the element **data_unbuffered(bit_index)**.

14.2 Conditionally Generating Structures

In the examples in the previous section, each cell in an iterative structure was connected identically. In some designs, however, there are particular cells that need to be treated differently. This often occurs where cells are connected to their neighbors. The cells at each end do not have neighbors on both sides, but instead are connected to signals or ports in the enclosing architecture body. We can deal with these special cases within an iterative structure using a *conditional generate statement*. The syntax rule is

generate_statement ⇐
   *generate*_label :
   if *boolean*_expression **generate**
     ⟦ { block_declarative_item }
   begin ⟧
     { concurrent_statement }
   end generate ⟦ *generate*_label ⟧ ;

This is just like the iterative generate statement, except that we specify a Boolean expression instead of a range of values to control how the concurrent statements are copied in the design. If the condition is true, the declarations and statements in the generate statement are included in the design. On the other hand, if the condition is false, they are omitted. We can refer to the values of generic constants or the generate parameter of an enclosing iterative generate statement in the control expression of a conditional generate statement. The generate label is required to identify the structure that is generated if the condition is true.

EXAMPLE

We can construct a serial-to-parallel shift register from master/slave flipflop cells. The entity declaration is shown at the top of Figure 14-5. The **parallel_data** port is an **inout** port because each flipflop in the shift register takes its input from the output of the previous position, as shown in the architecture body. The architecture contains a component declaration for the flipflop, then makes multiple instantiations using an iterative generate statement. Within the iterative generate statement, a conditional generate statement is used to treat the first flipflop cell

FIGURE 14-5

```vhdl
library ieee;  use ieee.std_logic_1164.all;
entity shift_reg is
    port ( phi1, phi2 : in std_logic;
                     serial_data_in : in std_logic;
                     parallel_data : inout std_logic_vector );
end entity shift_reg;
_____

architecture cell_level of shift_reg is
    alias normalized_parallel_data :
                std_logic_vector(0 to parallel_data'length – 1) is parallel_data;
    component master_slave_flipflop is
        port ( phi1, phi2 : in std_logic;  d : in std_logic;
                q : out std_logic );
    end component master_slave_flipflop;
begin
    reg_array : for index in normalized_parallel_data'range generate
    begin
        first_cell : if index = 0 generate
        begin
            cell : component master_slave_flipflop
                port map ( phi1, phi2,
                                d => serial_data_in,
                                q => normalized_parallel_data(index) );
        end generate first_cell;
        other_cell : if index /= 0 generate
        begin
            cell : component master_slave_flipflop
                port map ( phi1, phi2,
                                d => normalized_parallel_data(index – 1),
                                q => normalized_parallel_data(index) );
        end generate other_cell;
    end generate reg_array;
end architecture cell_level;
```

An entity and architecture body for a shift register composed of flipflop cells.

differently from the other cells. The condition "index = 0" identifies this first cell, which takes its input data from the serial_data_in port. The complementary condition, "index /= 0", identifies each other cell in the structure. These cells take their input from the neighboring cell's output.

Another important use of conditional generate statements is to conditionally include or omit part of a design, usually depending on the value of a generic constant. A good example is the inclusion or otherwise of *instrumentation*: additional processes or component instances that trace or debug the operation of a design during simulation. When the design is sufficiently tested, a generic constant can be changed to exclude the instrumentation so that it does not slow down a large simulation and is not included when the design is synthesized.

EXAMPLE

Suppose we wish to measure the relative frequencies of instruction fetches, data reads and data writes made by a CPU accessing memory in a computer system. This information may be important when considering how to optimize a design to improve performance. An entity declaration for the computer system is

```
entity computer_system is
    generic ( instrumented : boolean := false );
    port ( . . . );
end entity computer_system;
```

The generic constant instrumented is used to determine whether to include the instrumentation to measure relative frequencies of each kind of memory access. An outline of the architecture body is shown in Figure 14-6. The signals ifetch_freq, write_freq and read_freq and the process access_monitor are only included in the design if the generic constant instrumented is true. The process resumes each time the CPU requests access to the memory and keeps count of the number of each kind of access, as well as the total access count. It uses these values to update the relative frequencies. We can trace these signals using our simulator to see how the relative frequencies converge over the lifetime of a simulation.

FIGURE 14-6

```
architecture block_level of computer_system is
    . . .        -- type and component declarations for cpu and memory, etc
    signal clock : bit;        -- the system clock
    signal mem_req : bit;    -- cpu access request to memory
    signal ifetch : bit;        -- indicates access is to fetch an instruction
    signal write : bit;        -- indicates access is a write
    . . .                        -- other signal declarations
begin
    . . .        -- component instances for cpu and memory, etc
    instrumentation : if instrumented generate
        signal ifetch_freq, write_freq, read_freq : real := 0.0;
    begin
        access_monitor : process is
            variable access_count, ifetch_count,
                    write_count, read_count : natural := 0;
        begin
            wait until mem_req = '1';
            if ifetch = '1' then
                ifetch_count := ifetch_count + 1;
```

(continued on page 340)

(continued from page 339)

```
            elsif write = '1' then
                write_count := write_count + 1;
            else
                read_count := read_count + 1;
            end if;
            access_count := access_count + 1;
            ifetch_freq <= real(ifetch_count) / real(access_count);
            write_freq <= real(write_count) / real(access_count);
            read_freq <= real(read_count) / real(access_count);
        end process access_monitor;
    end generate instrumentation;
end architecture block_level;
```

An instrumented architecture body for a computer system.

We can control whether the instrumentation is included or not when we write a configuration declaration for the design. To include the instrumentation, we configure an instance of the computer system as follows:

```
for system_under_test : computer_system
    use entity work.computer_system(block_level)
    generic map ( instrumented => true )
    . . .
end for;
```

To exclude the instrumentation, we change the value of the generic constant in the generic map to false.

VHDL-87

A generate statement may not include a declarative part or the keyword **begin** in VHDL-87. The syntax for a conditional generate statement is

```
generate_statement ⇐
    generate_label :
    if boolean_expression generate
        { concurrent_statement }
    end generate [ generate_label ] ;
```

Any objects required by the generate statement must be declared in the declarative part of the enclosing architecture body.

Recursive Structures

A more unusual application of conditional generate statements arises when describing recursive hardware structures, such as tree structures. We can write a description of a recursive structure using a recursive model, that is, one in which an architecture of an entity creates an instance of that same entity. We enclose the recursive instantiation in a conditional generate statement that determines when to terminate the recursion.

EXAMPLE

Clock-signal distribution can be a problem in a large integrated circuit. We typically have one clock signal that must be distributed to a very large number of components without overloading the clock drivers and without creating too much skew between different parts of the circuit. One solution is to distribute the clock signal using a fanout tree. A simplified binary fanout tree is shown in Figure 14-7. The clock signal feeds two buffers, each of which in turn feeds two buffers, and so on, until we have generated enough buffered clock signals to drive all elements of the circuit. As the diagram shows, we can think of a tree of height 3 as being constructed from two buffers feeding trees of height 2. Similarly, a tree of height 2 is two buffers feeding trees of height 1. A tree of height 1 is two buffers feeding the outputs of the fanout tree. We can think of these output connections as being degenerate trees of height 0. In general, we can say that a tree of height n consists of two buffers feeding trees of height $n-1$, where $n > 0$.

FIGURE 14-7

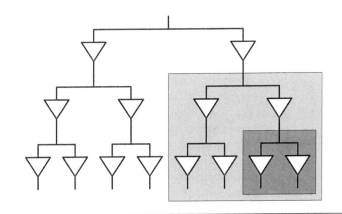

A binary fanout tree for clock distribution. The inner shaded section is a fanout tree of height 1, and the outer shaded section is a tree of height 2. The whole structure is a tree of height 3.

We can describe this structure in VHDL by starting with an entity declaration for a fanout tree that includes a generic constant **height** specifying the height of the tree, as shown in Figure 14-8. The entity has one input and 2^{height} outputs. The architecture body uses conditional generate statements that test the value of **height** to see if any subtrees are required. If **height** is zero, the output port of the fanout tree is a vector of length one. The generate statement labeled **degenerate_tree** creates a connection from the input to the single output element. Otherwise, if **height** is greater than zero, the generate statement labeled **compound_tree** creates two buffers and two subtrees of reduced height. The local signals **buffered_input_0** and **buffered_input_1** connect the buffers to the inputs of the subtrees.

FIGURE 14-8

```
library ieee;  use ieee.std_logic_1164.all;

entity fanout_tree is
    generic ( height : natural );
    port ( input : in std_logic;
            output : out std_logic_vector (0 to 2**height – 1) );
end entity fanout_tree;

——————————————————————————————————————————

architecture recursive of fanout_tree is

begin

    degenerate_tree : if height = 0 generate
    begin
        output(0) <= input;
    end generate degenerate_tree;

    compound_tree : if height > 0 generate
        signal buffered_input_0, buffered_input_1 : std_logic;
    begin

        buf_0 : entity work.buf(basic)
            port map ( a => input, y => buffered_input_0 );
        subtree_0 : entity work.fanout_tree(recursive)
            generic map ( height => height – 1 )
            port map ( input => buffered_input_0,
                        output => output(0 to 2**(height – 1) – 1) );
        buf_1 : entity work.buf(basic)
            port map ( a => input, y => buffered_input_1 );
        subtree_1 : entity work.fanout_tree(recursive)
            generic map ( height => height – 1 )
            port map ( input => buffered_input_1,
                        output => output(2**(height – 1) to 2**height – 1) );

    end generate compound_tree;

end architecture recursive;
```

An entity and architecture body for a recursive fanout tree model.

The outputs of the subtrees are of length $2^{height-1}$ and are connected to slices of the output port vector of the enclosing tree.

This compact description of a relatively complex structure is fleshed out when the design is elaborated. Suppose we instantiate a fanout tree of height 3 in a design:

```
clock_buffer_tree : entity work.fanout_tree(recursive)
    generic map ( height => 3 )
    port map ( input => unbuffered_clock,
                output => buffered_clock_array );
```

In the first stage of elaboration, height has the value 3, so the generate statement compound_tree creates the first two buffers and two instances of the fanout_tree entity with height having the value 2. In each of these instances, the generate statement compound_tree creates two more buffers and two instances of the fanout_tree entity with height having the value 1. Then, in each of these instances, the generate statement compound_tree creates a further two buffers and two instances of the fanout_tree entity with height having the value 0. In these last instances, the condition of the generate statement degenerate_tree is true, so it creates a connection directly from its input to its output. This statement is where the recursion terminates, as there are no further instantiations of the fanout_tree entity within the statement.

VHDL-87
___

Since VHDL-87 does not allow direct instantiation of design entities, descriptions of recursive structures are slightly more complex. In the architecture body, we must declare a component with the same interface as the design entity. Instead of directly instantiating the design entity, we instantiate the declared component and bind it to the design entity using a configuration specification. Note that the configuration specification must be written in the declarative region of the construct immediately enclosing the instantiated component. In our examples using VHDL-93, the recursive component instantiation statement is included in a conditional generate statement. In VHDL-87, generate statements do not include a declarative part, so we cannot include a configuration specification as part of the generate statement. Instead, we must write the component instantiation statement within a block statement that is in turn nested in the generate statement. (We describe block statements in Chapter 16.) We then write the configuration specification in the declarative part of the block statement. For example, we can rewrite the recursive fanout tree model of Figure 14-8 by declaring a component fanout_tree with the same interface as the fanout tree entity. The component instantiation statement labeled subtree_0 is rewritten as

```
block_0 : block

    for subtree_0 : fanout_tree
        use entity work.fanout_tree(recursive);
begin
    subtree_0 : fanout_tree
        generic map ( height => height – 1 )
        port map ( input => buffered_input_0,
                   output => output(0 to 2**(height – 1) – 1) );
end block block_0;
```

14.3 Configuration of Generate Statements

In this section we describe how to write configuration declarations for designs that include generate statements. If a design includes an iterative generate statement, we need to be able to identify individual cells from the iteration in order to configure them. If the design includes a conditional generate statement, we need to be able to include configuration information that is to be used only if the cell is included in the design. In order to handle these cases, we use an extended form of block configuration. We first introduced block configurations in Section 13.2. The syntax rule for the extended form is

block_configuration ⇐
   for (*architecture*_name
        ‖ *block_statement*_label
        ‖ *generate_statement*_label
              ⟦ ((discrete_range ‖ *static*_expression)) ⟧)
      { block_configuration
      ‖ **for** component_specification
         ⟦ binding_indication ; ⟧
         ⟦ block_configuration ⟧
      end for ; }
   end for ;

The new part in this rule is the alternative allowing us to configure a generate statement by writing its label. The optional part after the label is only used for iterative generate statements. This part allows us to write either an expression whose value selects a particular cell from the iterative structure or a range of values that select a collection of cells. Once we have identified the generate statement, the remaining configuration information within the block configuration specifies how the concurrent statements within the generated cells are to be configured.

Let us first apply this rule to writing configurations for conditional generate statements. In this case, we simply write the generate statement label in the block configuration and fill in the configuration information for generated component instances. If the generate statement control expression is true when the design is elaborated, the configuration information is used to bind entities to the component instances. On the other hand, if the expression is false, no instances are created, and the configuration information is ignored.

EXAMPLE

Let us return to our model of a computer system that uses a conditional generate statement to include instrumentation. Recall that the entity declaration was

   entity computer_system **is**
      generic (instrumented : boolean := false);
      port (. . .);
   end entity computer_system;

Suppose we wish to use a general purpose bus monitor component that collects statistics on bus transactions between the CPU and the memory. An outline of the revised architecture body is shown in Figure 14-9.

FIGURE 14-9

```
architecture block_level of computer_system is
        . . .       -- type and component declarations for cpu and memory, etc.
    signal clock : bit;      -- the system clock
    signal mem_req : bit;  -- cpu access request to memory
    signal ifetch : bit;      -- indicates access is to fetch an instruction
    signal write : bit;       -- indicates access is a write
        . . .                 -- other signal declarations
begin
        . . .       -- component instances for cpu and memory, etc.
    instrumentation : if instrumented generate
        use work.bus_monitor_pkg;
        signal bus_stats : bus_monitor_pkg.stats_type;
    begin
        cpu_bus_monitor : component bus_monitor_pkg.bus_monitor
            port map ( mem_req, ifetch, write, bus_stats );
    end generate instrumentation;
end architecture block_level;
```

A revised architecture body for the instrumented computer system, including an instance of a bus monitor component in the conditional generate statement.

We can write a configuration declaration for the computer system as shown in Figure 14-10. This configuration information may be used when the computer system entity is elaborated. If the value of the generic constant instrumented is true, the bus monitor is instantiated. In this case, the information in the block configuration starting with "**for** instrumentation" is used to bind an entity to the bus monitor instance. On the other hand, if instrumented is false, no instance is created, and the configuration information is ignored.

FIGURE 14-10

```
configuration architectural of computer_system is
    for block_level
        . . .       -- component configurations for cpu and memory, etc
        for instrumentation
            for cpu_bus_monitor : bus_monitor_pkg.bus_monitor
                use entity work.bus_monitor(general_purpose)
                generic map ( verbose => true, dump_stats => true );
            end for;
        end for;
    end for;
end configuration architectural;
```

A configuration declaration for the instrumented computer system.

We now turn to configurations for designs including iterative generate statements. The simplest case is a structure in which all cells are to be configured identically. In this case, we just write the generate statement label in the block configuration and include the configuration information to be applied to each cell.

EXAMPLE

In the register model in Figure 14-1 on page 333, each cell consisted of a flip-flop and a tristate buffer component. We can write a configuration declaration for this design as shown in Figure 14-11. The block configuration starting with "**for cell_array**" identifies the iterative generate statement labeled cell_array. Since there is no specification of particular cells within the generated structure, the information in the block configuration is applied to all cells.

FIGURE 14-11

```
library cell_lib;
configuration identical_cells of register_tristate is
    for cell_level
        for cell_array
            for cell_storage : D_flipflop
                use entity cell_lib.D_flipflop(synthesized);
            end for;
            for cell_buffer : tristate_buffer
                use entity cell_lib.tristate_buffer(synthesized);
            end for;
        end for;
    end for;
end configuration identical_cells;
```

A configuration declaration for a register module.

Where we have a design that includes nested generate statements to generate a two-dimensional structure, we simply nest block configurations in a configuration declaration.

EXAMPLE

The memory array described in Figure 14-4 on page 336 is implemented using two nested iterative generate statements. We can write a configuration declaration for the design as shown in Figure 14-12. The block configuration starting with "**for bank_array**" selects the memory array generated by the outer generate statement labeled bank_array. Each bank is configured identically, using the inner block configuration starting with "**for nibble_array**". This selects the generate statement that creates a bank of DRAM chips and configures each chip in the bank identically to the rest.

FIGURE 14-12

```
library chip_lib; use chip_lib.all;
configuration down_to_chips of memory_board is
    for chip_level
        for bank_array
            for nibble_array
                for a_DRAM : DRAM
                    use entity DRAM_4M_by_4(chip_function);
                end for;
            end for;
        end for;
        . . .        -- configurations of other component instances
    end for;
end configuration down_to_chips;
```

A configuration declaration for a memory array.

In some designs using iterative generate statements, there may be particular cells or groups of cells that we wish to configure differently from other cells. In these cases we can use an expression or a range of values in parentheses after the generate statement label in the block configuration. The values identify those cells to which the configuration information applies. The rules for specifying the discrete range are the same as those for specifying a discrete range in other contexts.

EXAMPLE

The shift register design shown in Figure 14-5 on page 338 is composed of cells indexed from 0 to width − 1, each of which includes an instance of a master/ slave flipflop. Suppose we wish to use an ordinary flipflop for all except the last cell of the shift register and a flipflop with high drive capacity for the last cell. A configuration declaration for the shift register that achieves this is shown in Figure 14-13.

The first of the block configurations for reg_array identifies those cells generated with index values in the range 0 to width − 2. In the first of these cells, the control condition of the inner generate statement first_cell is true and the control condition for other_cell is false. In the remaining cells, the condition for first_cell is false and the condition for other_cell is true. The two inner block configurations for first_cell and other_cell configure whichever flipflop component instance is created in each of these cells.

The second of the block configurations for reg_array singles out the cell generated with index value width − 1. This is the cell for which we wish to use a flipflop with high drive capacity. We know that in this cell the control condition for first_cell is false. Hence, we do not need to include a nested block configuration for that

FIGURE 14-13

```
library cell_lib;
configuration last_high_drive of shift_reg is
    for cell_level
        for reg_array ( 0 to parallel_data'length – 2 )
            for first_cell
                for cell : master_slave_flipflop
                    use entity cell_lib.ms_flipflop(normal_drive);
                end for;
            end for;
            for other_cell
                for cell : master_slave_flipflop
                    use entity cell_lib.ms_flipflop(normal_drive);
                end for;
            end for;
        end for;
        for reg_array ( parallel_data'length – 1 )
            for other_cell
                for cell : master_slave_flipflop
                    use entity cell_lib.ms_flipflop(high_drive);
                end for;
            end for;
        end for;
    end for;
end configuration last_high_drive;
```

A configuration declaration for a shift register.

generate statement. We only include a nested block configuration for the generate statement other_cell.

Exercises

1. [● 14.1] Draw a diagram illustrating the circuit described by the following generate statement:

   synch_delay_line : **for** stage **in** 1 **to** 4 **generate**
      delay_ff : **component** d_ff
         port map (clk => sys_clock,
                   d => delayed_data(stage – 1),
                   q => delayed_data(stage));
     end generate synch_delay_line;

2. [● 14.1] Write a generate statement that instantiates an inverter component for each element of an input bit-vector signal **data_in** to derive an inverted bit-vector output signal **data_out_n**. Use the index range of **data_in** to determine the number of inverters required, and assume that **data_out_n** has the same index range as **data_in**.

3. [● 14.2] Write conditional generate statements that connect a signal **external_clock** directly to a signal **internal_clock** if a Boolean generic constant **positive_clock** is true. If the generic is false, the statements should connect **external_clock** to **internal_clock** via an instance of an inverter component.

4. [● 14.3] Write block configurations for the generate statement shown in Exercise 1. The first flipflop (with index 1) should be bound to the entity **d_flipflop** in the library **parts_lib**, using the architecture body **low_input_load**. The remaining flipflops should be bound to the same entity, but use the architecture body **standard_input_load**.

5. [● 14.3] Write block configurations for the generate statements described in Exercise 3. The inverter component, if generated, should be bound to the entity **inverter** using the most recently analyzed architecture body in the library **parts_lib**.

6. [❷ 14.1] Develop a structural model for an *n*-bit-wide two-input multiplexer composed of single-bit-wide two-input multiplexer components. The width *n* is a generic constant in the entity interface.

7. [❷ 14.1] A first-in/first-out (FIFO) queue can be constructed from the following register components:

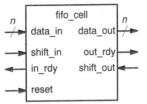

The bit width of the component is a generic constant in the component interface. The FIFO is constructed by chaining cells together and connecting their **reset** inputs in parallel. The depth of the FIFO is specified by a generic constant in the entity interface. Develop a structural model for a FIFO implemented in this manner.

8. [❷ 14.1/14.2] Develop a structural model for a binary ripple counter implemented using D-flipflops as follows. The width n is a generic constant in the entity interface.

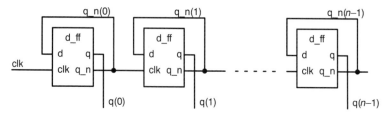

9. [❷ 14.1/14.2] Develop a structural model for an n-bit-wide ripple-carry adder. The least-significant bits are added using a half-adder component, and the remaining bits are added using full-adder components.

10. [❷ 14.3] Develop a behavioral model for a single-bit-wide two-input multiplexer. Write a configuration declaration for the n-bit-wide multiplexer described in Exercise 6, binding the behavioral implementation to each component instance.

11. [❷ 14.3] Develop a behavioral model for the D-flipflop described in Exercise 8. Write a configuration declaration for the ripple counter, binding the behavioral implementation to each D-flipflop component instance.

12. [❷ 14.3] Develop a behavioral model for a half adder and a full adder. Write a configuration declaration for the ripple-carry adder described in Exercise 9, binding the behavioral models to the component instances.

13. [❸ 14.1/14.2] Exercises 30 and 34 in Chapter 5 describe the components needed to implement a 16-bit carry-look-ahead adder. The same components can be used to implement a 64-bit carry-look-ahead adder as follows:

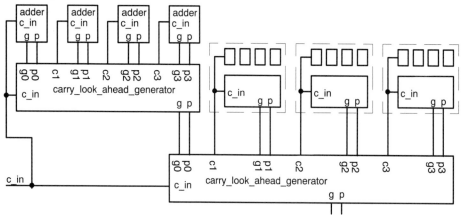

The 64-bit addition is split into four identical 16-bit groups, each implemented with a 16-bit carry-look-ahead adder. The carry-look-ahead generator is augmented to include generate and propagate outputs, calculated in the same way as those calculated by each four-bit adder. An additional carry-look-ahead generator is used to calculate the carry inputs to each 16-bit group.

Develop a structural model of a 64-bit carry-look-ahead adder using nested generate statements to describe the two-level iterative structure of the circuit.

14. [❸ 14.2] A circuit to generate the odd-parity function of an eight-bit word is implemented using a tree of exclusive-or gates as follows:

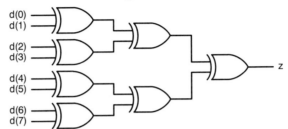

This structure can be generalized to an input word size of 2^n, implemented using a tree with n levels of gates. Develop a recursive model that describes such a parity generator circuit. The depth of the tree is a generic constant in the entity interface and is used to constrain the size of the input word.

15. [❸ 14.3] Develop a behavioral model for the FIFO cell described in Exercise 7. The cell contains storage for one n-bit word of data. When reset, the cell sets in_rdy to '1' and out_rdy to '0', indicating that it contains no data. When shift_in changes to '1', the cell latches the input data and makes it available at data_out, then sets in_rdy to '0' and out_rdy to '1', indicating that the cell contains data. When shift_out changes to '1', the cell sets in_rdy to '1' and out_rdy to '0', indicating that the cell no longer contains data. Write a configuration declaration for the FIFO queue described in Exercise 7, binding the behavioral FIFO cell model to each component instance.

16. [❹] Ward and Halstead, in their book *Computation Structures* ([13], pp. 130–134), describe a combinatorial array multiplier that multiplies two unsigned binary numbers. The multiplier consists of an array of cells, each of which contains an and gate to multiply two operand bits and a full adder to form a partial-product bit, as follows:

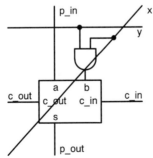

The cells are connected in the multiplier array as shown in the following diagram. Develop a structural model of an n-bit × n-bit array multiplier, in which the word length n is a generic constant in the entity interface. Write a behavioral model of the multiplier cell and a configuration declaration that binds the cell model to each cell component instance in the array multiplier. Next, refine the behavioral cell model to a gate-level model, and revise the configuration declaration to use the refined cell model.

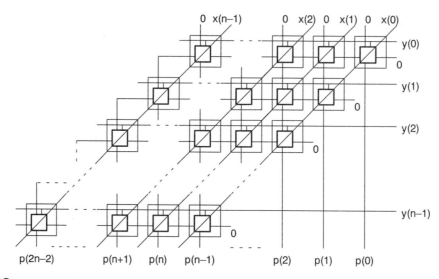

17. [❹] Weste and Eshraghian, in their book *Principles of CMOS VLSI Design: A Systems Perspective* ([14], pp. 384–407), describe a systolic array processor for dynamic time warping (DTW) pattern-matching operations used in speech recognition. Develop a model of the DTW processing element, and use it to implement the systolic array processor.

18. [❹] A hypercube multicomputer consists of a collection of 2^n processing elements (PEs) arranged at the vertices of an n-dimensional cube. Hypercubes with dimensions 1, 2, 3 and 4 are illustrated in the following diagram.

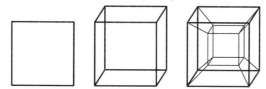

Each PE has a unique address, formed by concatenating the index (0 or 1) in each dimension to derive a binary number. Attached to each PE is a message switch with n bidirectional message channels, one in each dimension. The switches are interconnected along the edges of the hypercube. PEs exchange messages by passing them to the attached switches, which route them through the interconnections from source to destination. A message includes source and destination PE addresses, allowing the switches to determine a route for the message.

The hypercube structure can be described recursively. A hypercube of dimension 1 is simply a line from position 0 to position 1 in the first dimension. A hypercube of dimension n ($n > 1$) is composed of two sub-hypercubes of dimension $n-1$, one at position 0 in the nth dimension and the other at position 1 in the nth dimension. Each vertex in one sub-hypercube is joined to the vertex with the same address in the other sub-hypercube.

Develop a recursive structural model of an n-dimensional hypercube multicomputer, where the number of dimensions is specified by a generic constant in the entity interface. Your model should include separate component instances for the

PEs and the message switches. Also develop behavioral models for the PEs and message switches. The PEs should generate streams of test messages to different destinations to test the switch network. Each switch should implement a simple message-routing algorithm of your devising.

Case Study:
The DLX Computer System

In this, our third case study, we develop a series of models of the DLX CPU, originally described by Hennessy and Patterson [7]. We first develop a behavioral model and test it using a test bench consisting of a memory and some instrumentation. Next, we refine the model to the register-transfer level. We test this version in a test bench that compares its outputs with those of the behavioral version.

15.1 Overview of the DLX CPU

The DLX CPU was originally designed by Hennessy and Patterson [7] as a vehicle for
teaching principles of computer architecture. It is a simple reduced instruction set computer (RISC), very similar to many of the first generation of commercially available RISC
CPUs. The designers describe it as the distilled essence of these CPUs. We use it here
as the subject of a case study, showing how we might develop high-level models of
complex devices such as a CPU. We start by describing the view of the CPU as seen
by the machine language programmer and by the hardware designer interfacing the
CPU with the rest of a computer system.

DLX Registers

The DLX, like most RISC CPUs, has a relatively large number of general-purpose registers, as well as some special-purpose registers. These are all shown in Figure 15-1.
Registers r1 to r31 are general-purpose registers that may be used to hold integers
or any other 32-bit value. Register r0 is special in that it always has the value 0. Any
value written into this register is discarded. Registers f0 to f31 are 32-bit floating-point
registers. They can be used for single-precision IEEE-format floating-point numbers.
If double-precision calculation is needed, pairs of registers can be used. The most-
significant word is stored in an even-numbered register (f0, r2, ...), and the least-
significant word is stored in the next odd-numbered register (f1, f3, ...).

FIGURE 15-1

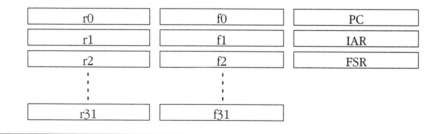

The DLX register set.

The remaining registers have special purposes and are not used to store operands.
The Program Counter (PC) holds the memory address of the next instruction to be
executed by the CPU. As we shall see, each DLX instruction is represented in one 32-bit
(four-byte) word. The DLX requires that instructions be aligned at addresses that are
a multiple of four. Hence the PC value must always be a multiple of four and is incremented by four after each instruction is fetched. The Interrupt Address Register (IAR)
is used to save the PC value when an interrupt occurs. Interrupts may result from input/
output controllers connected to the CPU or from exceptional conditions arising during
program execution. In order to simplify our model, we do not implement the interrupt
behavior of the DLX. The interested reader should refer to [7] for further information
about how the DLX handles interrupts. The Floating-point Status Register (FSR) is used
to control operation of floating-point arithmetic hardware within the CPU and to store
status information resulting from floating-point operations. Again, in the interests of

simplicity, we do not implement floating-point operations in our model. This parallels many real CPU devices in which floating-point hardware is an optional component.

DLX Instruction Set

The DLX includes instructions for transferring data to and from memory, for performing arithmetic and logical operations and for transferring control within a program. These are summarized in the following sections.

Data Transfer Instructions

The DLX instructions for transferring data are listed in Figure 15-2. The load and store instructions are the only means of transferring data between the CPU and memory. The memory address for each of these instructions is determined by adding the displacement (*disp*) to the contents of a base register (r_{s1}). The first group of instructions load a byte, a halfword (two bytes) or a word (four bytes) from memory into a destination general-purpose register r_d. The unsigned byte and halfword versions clear the most-significant bits of the destination register to '0', whereas the signed versions extend the sign of the loaded operand into the most-significant bits. The next group of instructions store the contents of a general-purpose register r_d in memory. The byte and halfword versions store from the least-significant bits of r_d.

FIGURE 15-2

Instruction	Operands	Description
lb	$r_d, disp(r_{s1})$	load byte
lbu		load byte unsigned
lh		load halfword
lhu		load halfword unsigned
lw		load word
sb	$disp(r_{s1}), r_d$	store byte
sh		store halfword
sw		store word
lf	$f_d, disp(r_{s1})$	load single float
ld		load double float
sf	$disp(r_{s1}), f_d$	store single-precision floating-point
sd		store double-precision floating-point
movi2s	s_d, r_s	move from integer register to special register
movs2i	r_d, s_s	move from special register to integer register
movf	f_d, f_s	move single float from register to register
movd	f_d, f_s	move double float from register to register
movi2fp	f_d, r_s	move from integer register to float register
movfp2i	r_d, f_s	move from float register to integer register

DLX data transfer instructions.

Following these are load and store instructions for transferring single- and double-precision floating-point values between memory and floating-point registers. In the case of double-precision operands, f_s and f_d specify the even register of the register pair.

The remaining data transfer instructions move data between registers within the CPU. The "movi2s" and "movs2i" instructions provide a means of accessing the special registers; s_d and s_s can specify the IAR or FSR. The "movf" and "movd" instructions transfer single-precision and double-precision operands between floating-point registers. Finally, the "movi2fp" and "movfp2i" instructions transfer a single word of data between a general-purpose register and a floating-point register.

Arithmetic and Logical Instructions

Figure 15-3 shows the DLX instructions for performing arithmetic operations on integer data. Integers are either unsigned or two's-complement signed values. Instructions are included to add and subtract operands in source registers (r_{s1} and r_{s2}), with the result overwriting a destination register (r_d). There are also immediate forms, in which the second operand is a value encoded in the instruction itself (*immed*). The multiplication and division instructions are different in that they are executed by the floating-point hardware of the CPU. Hence their operands are floating-point registers instead of general-purpose integer registers. Since we are not implementing floating-point operations in our model, we do not implement the multiplication and division instructions either.

FIGURE 15-3

Instruction	*Operands*	*Description*
add, addu sub, subu	r_d, r_{s1}, r_{s2}	Add signed or unsigned Subtract signed or unsigned
addi, addui subi, subui	r_d, r_{s1}, *immed*	Add signed or unsigned immediate Subtract signed or unsigned immediate
mult, multu div, divu	f_d, f_{s1}, f_{s2}	Multiply signed or unsigned Divide signed or unsigned
s*xx*, s*xx*u	r_d, r_{s1}, r_{s2}	Set if condition signed or unsigned (*xx* is one of eq, ne, lt, le, gt, ge)
s*xx*i, s*xx*ui	r_d, r_{s1}, *immed*	Set if condition signed or unsigned immediate (*xx* is one of eq, ne, lt, le, gt, ge)
lhi	r_d, *immed*	Load high immediate
nop		No operation

DLX integer arithmetic instructions.

The next two groups of instructions shown in Figure 15-3 are relational instructions, which compare their source operands. The conditions that can be tested are "eq" (equal to), "ne" (not equal to), "lt" (less than), "le" (less than or equal to), "gt" (greater than) and "ge" (greater than or equal to). If the condition is met, the destination register is set to the integer 1; otherwise it is set to zero.

The "lhi" instruction is used to load a 16-bit immediate value into the most-significant 16 bits of the destination register, clearing the least-significant 16 bits to zero. This instruction is needed since immediate operands encoded in instructions are only 16 bits. Without this instruction, it would be difficult to write a 32-bit immediate operand in a program. We can use an "lhi" to load the most-significant half of a 32-bit value and follow it with an "ori" to include the least-significant half of the value. (The "ori" instruction is shown in Figure 15-5 on page 360.) The "nop" instruction, as its name suggests, performs no operation.

The DLX instructions for performing arithmetic on floating-point operands are shown in Figure 15-4. They include versions for single-precision and double-precision operands. The conversion instructions provide a means of converting values between two's-complement integer, single-precision floating-point and double-precision floating-point representations. The last group of instructions in the table are the floating-point comparison instructions. The conditions that can be tested are the same as those for integers. However, instead of placing a result in a register, these instructions set a comparison bit in the FSR. In our model, we do not implement any of these floating-point instructions.

FIGURE 15-4

Instruction	Operands	Description
addf, addd	f_d, f_{s1}, f_{s2}	Add single or double float
subf, subd		Subtract single or double float
multf, multd		Multiply single or double float
divf, divd		Divide single or double float
cvtf2d	f_d, f_{s1}	Convert single float to double float
cvtf2i	r_d, f_{s1}	Convert single float to integer
cvtd2f	f_d, f_{s1}	Convert double float to single float
cvtd2i	r_d, f_{s1}	Convert double float to integer
cvti2f	f_d, r_{s1}	Convert integer to single float
cvti2d	f_d, r_{s1}	Convert integer to double float
*xx*f, *xx*d	f_{s1}, f_{s2}	Set FSR comparison bit if condition (*xx* is one of eq, ne, lt, le, gt, ge)

DLX floating-point arithmetic instructions.

Figure 15-5 shows the instructions for performing logical operations in the DLX CPU. The "and", "or" and "xor" instructions perform the logical operation on corresponding bits from each of the operands to generate the 32 bits of the result. The immediate versions of these instructions extend the 16-bit immediate operand to 32 bits by adding zeros to the left, in order to perform the bit-wise logical operation. The first group of shift instructions shift the value read from r_{s1} by the number of bits specified in r_{s2} and store the result in r_d. The second group shifts the value by the number of bits specified by the immediate operand.

FIGURE 15-5

Instruction	Operands	Description
and, or, xor	r_d, r_{s1}, r_{s2}	Bit-wise logical and, or, exclusive-or
andi, ori, xori	r_d, r_{s1}, *immed*	Bit-wise logical and, or, exclusive-or immediate
sll, srl, sra	r_d, r_{s1}, r_{s2}	Shift left-logical, right-logical, right-arithmetic
slli, srli, srai	r_d, r_{s1}, *immed*	Shift left-logical, right-logical, right-arithmetic immediate

DLX logical instructions.

Control Transfer Instructions

The final set of instructions provided by the DLX handle transfer of control within a program. They are shown in Figure 15-6. The branch instructions transfer control to the memory address calculated by adding the displacement (*disp*) to the PC. The "beqz" and "bnez" instructions compare a register r_{s1} with zero and branch if the condition is met. The "bfpt" and "bfpf" instructions branch if the comparison bit in the FSR is one or zero, respectively. Recall that this bit is set by the floating-point comparison instructions. Since we are not implementing floating-point operations in our DLX model, we do not implement these two instructions.

FIGURE 15-6

Instruction	Operands	Description
beqz bnez	r_{s1}, *disp*	Branch if register equal to zero Branch if register not equal to zero
bfpt bfpf	*disp*	Branch if FSR comparison bit is true Branch if FSR comparison bit is false
j jal	*disp*	Jump unconditional Jump and link unconditional
jr jalr	r_{s1}	Jump register Jump and link register
trap	*immed*	Trap to kernel
rfe		Return from exception

DLX control transfer instructions.

The next four instructions unconditionally transfer control. The "j" and "jal" instructions add the displacement to the PC to determine the target address. The "jr" and "jalr" instructions, on the other hand, use the contents of a register (r_{s1}) as the target address. The term "link" in "jal" and "jalr" means that these instructions copy the old PC value into register r31 before overwriting it with the target address. These instructions provide a means of calling subprograms, with the value written to r31 being the return address. A subprogram can return by executing a "jr" instruction with r31 as the operand register.

The final two instructions deal with exceptions and interrupts in the DLX. The "trap" instruction provides a means of transferring to the kernel of an operating system running on the CPU. The immediate operand is treated as a parameter indicating the operating system service requested by the program. In our model, we do not implement exception handling. Instead, we simply halt the CPU when a trap instruction is executed. The "rfe" instruction is intended to transfer control back to an interrupted program after an interrupt of an exception has been dealt with by the operating system. We do not implement this instruction either.

Instruction Encoding

As mentioned earlier, each DLX instruction is encoded in a 32-bit word. There are three instruction formats, I-type, R-type and J-type, shown in Figure 15-7. I-type format is generally used for arithmetic and logic instructions that have an immediate operand, and for branch instructions. In these cases, the operand or displacement is encoded in the instruction. R-type format is used for arithmetic and logic instructions that operate entirely on data in registers. J-type instructions are used for unconditional jump instructions, allowing for a larger displacement than conditional branches (26 bits as opposed to 16 bits). There are some additional cases to consider, but we deal with them as they arise when developing the behavioral CPU model.

FIGURE 15-7

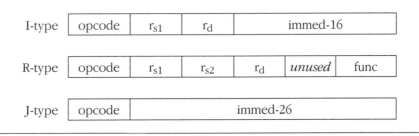

The three formats used to encode DLX instructions. The opcode specifies the operation to perform, r_{s1} and r_{s2} are source register numbers, r_d is a destination register number, func is an extension to the opcode, immed-16 is a 16-bit immediate operand and immed-26 is a 26-bit immediate operand.

DLX External Interface

The DLX CPU interfaces to the rest of the computer system via a number of external ports. These are shown in Figure 15-8. The signals phi1 and phi2 are the master clock signals that drive the CPU. They are driven with two non-overlapping clock signals, with timing shown in Figure 15-9. The reset signal is used to initialize the CPU. When reset changes to '1', the CPU aborts any activity in progress and returns all output signals to their inactive state. When reset returns to '0', the CPU resumes fetching instructions from memory address 0. The CPU uses the halt signal to indicate that it has stopped execution. In our model, the CPU stops when it executes a trap instruction. This provides us with a means of detecting when a program has completed.

FIGURE 15-8

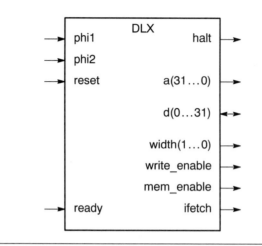

The external ports of the DLX CPU.

FIGURE 15-9

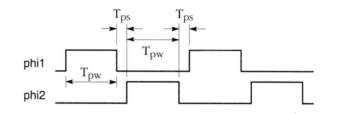

Timing for the two-phase non-overlapping master clock signals and the reset signal. These signals are used to synchronize operation of the CPU with other components of the computer system. T_{pw} is the pulse width for each clock phase, and T_{ps} is the pulse separation between phases.

The remaining ports of the CPU are its interface with the computer system's memory. The vector signal **a** is the address bus. Each address identifies a single byte of memory. In common with most computer systems, we use a descending index range for the address vector, with **a(31)** being the most-significant address bit and **a(0)** being the least-significant. The vector signal **d** is the bidirectional data bus, which transmits data to or from the memory. The DLX uses a "big-endian" addressing scheme, with the most-significant byte of a word stored at the lowest address. We remain consistent with this and use an ascending index range for **d**, with **d(0)** being the most-significant bit and **d(31)** being the least-significant. The two-element vector signal **width** specifies how much data is to be transferred. A value of b"01" indicates one byte, b"10" indicates two bytes (a halfword), b"00" indicates four bytes (a whole word) and b"11" is illegal.

FIGURE 15-10

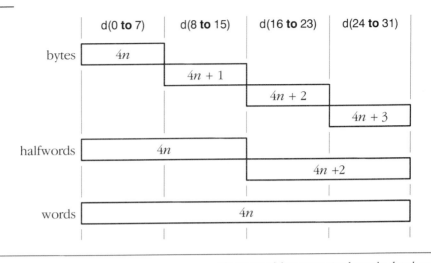

Alignment of data transmitted over the data bus d.

The DLX CPU requires that data transmitted over the data bus be aligned, as shown in Figure 15-10. A byte whose address is a multiple of four is transmitted over d(0 **to** 7). A byte whose address is one more than a multiple of four is transmitted over d(8 **to** 15), and so on. Halfwords can only be transmitted over d(0 **to** 15) if the address is a multiple of four or d(16 **to** 31) if the address is two more than a multiple of four. Halfwords based at other addresses are considered misaligned and cannot be accessed using a single load or store instruction. Similarly, whole words can only be accessed at addresses that are a multiple of four.

The signal write_enable is set to '1' to indicate a write to memory or '0' to indicate a read from memory. The signal mem_enable indicates to memory when it should perform the read or write. The memory drives ready to '1' when it has completed a write or when it has supplied data for a read. Finally, ifetch is a status signal that the CPU sets to '1' to distinguish a read to fetch an instruction from a read to fetch a data operand. This signal may be used by a bus probe when monitoring transactions on the memory bus.

The timing for a bus read operation is shown in Figure 15-11. After the rising edge of phi1, the CPU places the address on the memory address bus, sets the control signals to the required states and sets mem_enable to '1'. The memory uses this information to read the required data from memory, places it on the data bus and sets ready to '1'. The CPU tests ready on the falling edge of phi2 in each clock cycle and accepts the data when it detects ready active. It then resets mem_enable to '0'. In response, the memory stops driving the data bus and resets ready to '0'. The timing for a bus write is shown in Figure 15-12. It is similar to that for a read, except that the CPU drives the data bus with data to be written and sets write_enable to '1' instead of '0'. The memory sets ready to '1' when it has accepted the data.

FIGURE 15-11

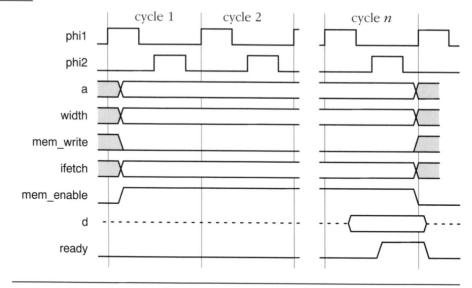

Timing for a memory read operation initiated by the CPU.

FIGURE 15-12

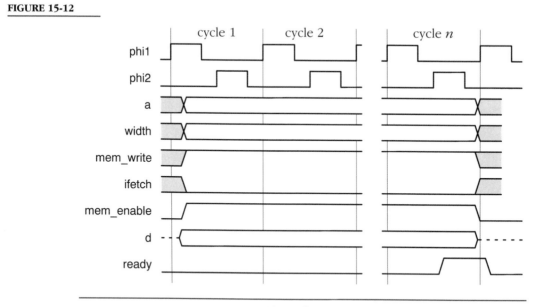

Timing for a memory write operation initiated by the CPU.

15.2 **A Behavioral Model**

Our model for the DLX CPU consists of an entity declaration and a behavioral architecture body. However, before we can write these units we need to define the types used in the external interface.

The DLX Types Package

Figure 15-13 shows a package declaration that defines the types for the CPU ports, based on the IEEE standard-logic types. The package also defines some other types that are useful in the model. The type **dlx_address** represents little-endian logic vectors used for address values. The bit-vector type **dlx_bv_address** is used within the model to represent binary versions of addresses, stripped of drive strength information. The type **dlx_word** represents big-endian logic vectors used for data values. The bit-vector type **dlx_bv_word**, like **dlx_bv_address**, is used within the model for binary data values. **Dlx_word_array** represents an array of data words and is used in the declaration of multiple output register entities. The constant **disabled_dlx_word** is the value driven by the CPU or memory onto the data bus when it is inactive. This corresponds to an inactive tristate driver. The type **dlx_mem_width** represents values driven on the CPU **width** port. The three constants define legal values for this type. Finally, **dlx_debug_control** is an

FIGURE 15-13

```vhdl
library ieee;  use ieee.std_logic_1164.all;

package dlx_types is

    -- little-endian addresses
    subtype dlx_address is std_logic_vector(31 downto 0);
    subtype dlx_bv_address is bit_vector(31 downto 0);

    -- big-endian data words
    subtype dlx_word is std_logic_vector(0 to 31);
    subtype dlx_bv_word is bit_vector(0 to 31);

    type dlx_word_array is array (natural range <>) of dlx_word;

    -- tristate bus driving value
    constant disabled_dlx_word : dlx_word := ( others => 'Z' );

    -- type for specifying data width on the data bus
    subtype dlx_mem_width is std_logic_vector(1 downto 0);

    constant dlx_mem_width_byte : dlx_mem_width := "01";
    constant dlx_mem_width_halfword : dlx_mem_width := "10";
    constant dlx_mem_width_word : dlx_mem_width := "00";

    -- type for controlling trace information generated by model
    type dlx_debug_control is
        ( none,
          msg_every_100_instructions, msg_each_instruction,
          trace_each_instruction, trace_each_step );

end package dlx_types;
```

A package declaration defining types for use in the DLX model.

enumeration type listing values that we use to control the amount of tracing information to be reported by the model. The model reports on its progress during a simulation, to help us debug the model. The values of the type are used as follows:

- none: the model does not report any information;
- msg_every_100_instructions: the model reports after every hundred instructions;
- msg_each_instruction: the model reports each time it fetches an instruction;
- trace_each_instruction: the model lists each instruction it fetches; and
- trace_each_step: the model lists each instruction it fetches and reports on each step during execution of the instruction.

The DLX Entity Declaration

Now that we have defined types for the DLX CPU's ports, we can write the entity declaration, as shown in Figure 15-14. The generic constant Tpd_clk_out specifies the propagation delay between a rising or falling clock edge and a resulting change on an output port. This is only used in the behavioral model. Once we refine the model to the register-transfer level, the delays of the components within that implementation determine the delay for the CPU. The generic constant **debug** controls the detail of reporting by the model, as described above. The ports of the entity correspond to those described in Section 15.1.

FIGURE 15-14

```
library ieee;  use ieee.std_logic_1164.all;
use work.dlx_types.all;

entity dlx is
    generic ( Tpd_clk_out : delay_length;
              debug : dlx_debug_control := none );
    port ( phi1, phi2 : in std_logic;  reset : in std_logic;
           halt : out std_logic;
           a : out dlx_address;
           d : inout dlx_word;
           width : out dlx_mem_width;  write_enable : out std_logic;
           ifetch : out std_logic;  mem_enable : out std_logic;
           ready : in std_logic );
end entity dlx;
```

An entity declaration for the DLX CPU.

The DLX Instruction Set Package

Before we embark on the description of the behavior of the DLX CPU, it is helpful to declare a package that represents the details of the DLX instruction set. We outlined the instructions and their formats in Section 15.1, but we have yet to specify encodings for opcodes. This and other information is described in the package declaration in Figure 15-15.

FIGURE 15-15

```
use work.dlx_types.all;
package dlx_instr is
    subtype dlx_opcode is bit_vector(0 to 5);
    subtype dlx_sp_func is bit_vector(0 to 5);
    subtype dlx_fp_func is bit_vector(0 to 4);
    subtype dlx_reg_addr is bit_vector(0 to 4);
    subtype dlx_immed16 is bit_vector(0 to 15);
    subtype dlx_immed26 is bit_vector(0 to 25);
    constant op_special      : dlx_opcode := B"000000";
    constant op_fparith      : dlx_opcode := B"000001";
    constant op_j            : dlx_opcode := B"000010";
    constant op_jal          : dlx_opcode := B"000011";
    constant op_beqz         : dlx_opcode := B"000100";
    . . .
    constant op_undef_3F     : dlx_opcode := B"111111";

    constant sp_func_nop      : dlx_sp_func := B"000000";
    constant sp_func_undef_01: dlx_sp_func := B"000001";
    constant sp_func_undef_02: dlx_sp_func := B"000010";
    constant sp_func_undef_03: dlx_sp_func := B"000011";
    constant sp_func_sll      : dlx_sp_func := B"000100";
    . . .
    constant sp_func_undef_3F: dlx_sp_func := B"111111";

    constant fp_func_addf     : dlx_fp_func := B"00000";
    constant fp_func_subf     : dlx_fp_func := B"00001";
    constant fp_func_multf    : dlx_fp_func := B"00010";
    constant fp_func_divf     : dlx_fp_func := B"00011";
    constant fp_func_addd     : dlx_fp_func := B"00100";
    . . .
    constant fp_func_undef_1F : dlx_fp_func := B"11111";

    subtype dlx_opcode_num is natural range 0 to 63;
    subtype dlx_sp_func_num is natural range 0 to 63;
    subtype dlx_fp_func_num is natural range 0 to 31;

    subtype instr_name is string(1 to 8);
    type opcode_name_array is array (dlx_opcode_num) of instr_name;
    type sp_func_name_array is array (dlx_sp_func_num) of instr_name;
    type fp_func_name_array is array (dlx_fp_func_num) of instr_name;

    constant opcode_names : opcode_name_array;
    constant sp_func_names : sp_func_name_array;
    constant fp_func_names : fp_func_name_array;

    subtype reg_index is natural range 0 to 31;

    constant link_reg : reg_index := 31;

    procedure disassemble ( instr : dlx_bv_word;
                            disassembled_instr : out string;  len : out positive );
end package dlx_instr;
```

A package defining the DLX instruction set and related information.

The package first declares bit-vector types for the fields in an instruction. These are followed by constants (**op_special** to **op_undef_3F**) defining the opcode values for each of the instructions in the DLX instruction set. For the sake of brevity, not all op-codes are shown here. The full set is included in the on-line models accessible to read-ers as described in the preface. The first two opcode values represent classes of instruc-tions that use R-type format. In these cases, the func field is used to specify the instruction. The first class has **op_special** as the value in the opcode field of the instruc-tion. The constants **sp_func_nop** to **sp_func_undef_3F** define the func field encodings for instructions in this class. The second class has **op_fparith** as the value in the opcode field of the instruction. For this class, the constants **fp_func_addf** to **fp_func_undef_1F** define the legal encodings for the func field. Only the rightmost five bits of the func field are used for this second class; the leftmost bit is unused.

Following these constant declarations, the package declares numeric ranges repre-senting opcode and func field values. These are used as index ranges for three constant arrays of fixed-length strings containing textual representations of the instruc-tion opcodes. For example, if we were to convert the binary opcode for the "addi" instruction to a natural number and use it to index the array **opcode_names**, we would retrieve the string **"ADDI "**. The values for the constant arrays are not defined in the package declaration. Instead, they are deferred to the package body, as we will see shortly.

Next, the type **reg_index** represents numeric values for register numbers. The constant **link_reg** is the number of the general-purpose register used in "jal" and "jalr" instructions. Finally, **disassemble** is a procedure that accepts a word representing a DLX instruction in the parameter **instr** and returns a textual representation of the instruction in the parameter **disassembled_instr**. The parameter **len** is used to indicate the actual number of characters used to represent the instruction. The remaining characters in **disassembled_instr** are not changed by the procedure. We see how the procedure is implemented when we examine the package body.

Figure 15-16 shows the package body corresponding to the declaration. The body makes use of the conversion functions **bv_to_natural** and **bv_to_integer** provided by the bit-vector arithmetic package described in Chapter 10. We assume the package has been separately analyzed and stored in a library called **bv_utilities**. The package body in Figure 15-16 includes a library clause to access the **bv_utilities** library and a use clause to import the conversion functions.

FIGURE 15-16

```
library bv_utilities;

package body dlx_instr is

    use bv_utilities.bv_arithmetic.bv_to_natural,
           bv_utilities.bv_arithmetic.bv_to_integer;

    constant opcode_names : opcode_name_array
        := ( "SPECIAL ",  "FPARITH ",  "J       ",  "JAL     ",
             "BEQZ    ",  "BNEZ    ",  "BFPT    ",  "BFPF    ",
             "ADDI    ",  "ADDUI   ",  "SUBI    ",  "SUBUI   ",
             "ANDI    ",  "ORI     ",  "XORI    ",  "LHI     ",
             "RFE     ",  "TRAP    ",  "JR      ",  "JALR    ",
             "SLLI    ",  "UNDEF_15",  "SRLI    ",  "SRAI    ",
```

```
        SEQI      ",  "SNEI      ",  "SLTI      ",  "SGTI      ",
        SLEI      ",  "SGEI      ",  "UNDEF_1E", "UNDEF_1F",
        LB        ",  "LH        ",  "UNDEF_22", "LW        ",
        LBU       ",  "LHU       ",  "LF        ",  "LD        ",
        SB        ",  "SH        ",  "UNDEF_2A", "SW        ",
        UNDEF_2C", "UNDEF_2D", "SF        ",  "SD        ",
        SEQUI     ",  "SNEUI     ",  "SLTUI     ",  "SGTUI     ",
        SLEUI     ",  "SGEUI     ",  "UNDEF_36", "UNDEF_37",
        UNDEF_38", "UNDEF_39", "UNDEF_3A", "UNDEF_3B",
        UNDEF_3C", "UNDEF_3D", "UNDEF_3E", "UNDEF_3F" );

constant sp_func_names : sp_func_name_array
    := ( "NOP       ",  "UNDEF_01", "UNDEF_02", "UNDEF_03",
         "SLL       ",  "UNDEF_05", "SRL       ",  "SRA       ",
         "UNDEF_08", "UNDEF_09", "UNDEF_0A", "UNDEF_0B",
         "UNDEF_0C", "UNDEF_0D", "UNDEF_0E", "UNDEF_0F",
         "SEQU      ",  "SNEU      ",  "SLTU      ",  "SGTU      ",
         "SLEU      ",  "SGEU      ",  "UNDEF_16", "UNDEF_17",
         "UNDEF_18", "UNDEF_19", "UNDEF_1A", "UNDEF_1B",
         "UNDEF_1C", "UNDEF_1D", "UNDEF_1E", "UNDEF_1F",
         "ADD       ",  "ADDU      ",  "SUB       ",  "SUBU      ",
         "AND       ",  "OR        ",  "XOR       ",  "UNDEF_27",
         "SEQ       ",  "SNE       ",  "SLT       ",  "SGT       ",
         "SLE       ",  "SGE       ",  "UNDEF_2E", "UNDEF_2F",
         "MOVI2S    ",  "MOVS2I    ",  "MOVF      ",  "MOVD      ",
         "MOVFP2I   ",  "MOVI2FP   ",  "UNDEF_36", "UNDEF_37",
         "UNDEF_38", "UNDEF_39", "UNDEF_3A", "UNDEF_3B",
         "UNDEF_3C", "UNDEF_3D", "UNDEF_3E", "UNDEF_3F" );

constant fp_func_names : fp_func_name_array
    := ( "ADDF      ",  "SUBF      ",  "MULTF     ",  "DIVF      ",
         "ADDD      ",  "SUBD      ",  "MULTD     ",  "DIVD      ",
         "CVTF2D    ",  "CVTF2I    ",  "CVTD2F    ",  "CVTD2I    ",
         "CVTI2F    ",  "CVTI2D    ",  "MULT      ",  "DIV       ",
         "EQF       ",  "NEF       ",  "LTF       ",  "GTF       ",
         "LEF       ",  "GEF       ",  "MULTU     ",  "DIVU      ",
         "EQD       ",  "NED       ",  "LTD       ",  "GTD       ",
         "LED       ",  "GED       ",  "UNDEF_1E", "UNDEF_1F" );

procedure disassemble ( instr : dlx_bv_word;
                        disassembled_instr : out string;  len : out positive ) is

    alias norm_disassembled_instr : string(1 to disassembled_instr'length)
        is disassembled_instr;

    alias instr_opcode : dlx_opcode is instr(0 to 5);
    alias instr_sp_func : dlx_sp_func is instr(26 to 31);
    alias instr_fp_func : dlx_fp_func is instr(27 to 31);
    alias instr_rs1 : dlx_reg_addr is instr(6 to 10);
    alias instr_rs2 : dlx_reg_addr is instr(11 to 15);
    alias instr_Itype_rd : dlx_reg_addr is instr(11 to 15);
    alias instr_Rtype_rd : dlx_reg_addr is instr(16 to 20);
```

(continued on page 370)

(continued from page 369)

```
alias instr_immed16 : dlx_immed16 is instr(16 to 31);
alias instr_immed26 : dlx_immed26 is instr(6 to 31);

variable instr_opcode_num : dlx_opcode_num;
variable instr_sp_func_num : dlx_sp_func_num;
variable instr_fp_func_num : dlx_fp_func_num;
variable rs1 : reg_index;
variable rs2 : reg_index;
variable Itype_rd : reg_index;
variable Rtype_rd : reg_index;
variable result : string(1 to 40)  -- long enough for longest instruction
            := (others => ' ');
variable index : positive range 1 to 41 := 1;  -- position for next char in result

procedure disassemble_reg ( reg : reg_index;  reg_prefix : character ) is
begin
    result(index) := reg_prefix;
    index := index + 1;
    if reg < 10 then
        result(index to index) := integer'image(reg);
        index := index + 1;
    else
        result(index to index + 1) := integer'image(reg);
        index := index + 2;
    end if;
end procedure disassemble_reg;

procedure disassemble_special_reg ( reg : reg_index ) is
begin
    case reg is
        when 0 =>
            result(index to index + 2) := "IAR";
            index := index + 3;
        when 1 =>
            result(index to index + 2) := "FSR";
            index := index + 3;
        when others =>
            disassemble_reg(reg, 'S');
    end case;
end procedure disassemble_special_reg;

procedure disassemble_integer ( int : integer ) is
    constant int_image_length : natural := integer'image(int)'length;
begin
    result(index to index + int_image_length - 1) := integer'image(int);
    index := index + int_image_length;
end procedure disassemble_integer;
begin
    instr_opcode_num := bv_to_natural(instr_opcode);
    instr_sp_func_num := bv_to_natural(instr_sp_func);
    instr_fp_func_num := bv_to_natural(instr_fp_func);
    rs1 := bv_to_natural(instr_rs1);
```

```
rs2 := bv_to_natural(instr_rs2);
Itype_rd := bv_to_natural(instr_Itype_rd);
Rtype_rd := bv_to_natural(instr_Rtype_rd);
if (instr_opcode /= op_special) and (instr_opcode /= op_fparith) then
    result(index to index + instr_name'length − 1)
        := opcode_names(instr_opcode_num);
    index := index + instr_name'length + 1;  −− include space after name
end if;
case instr_opcode is
    when op_special =>
        result(index to index + instr_name'length − 1)
            := sp_func_names(instr_sp_func_num);
        index := index + instr_name'length + 1;  −− include space after name
        case instr_sp_func is
            when sp_func_nop =>
                null;
            when sp_func_sll | sp_func_srl | sp_func_sra
                | sp_func_sequ | sp_func_sneu | sp_func_sltu
                | sp_func_sgtu | sp_func_sleu | sp_func_sgeu
                | sp_func_add | sp_func_addu | sp_func_sub | sp_func_subu
                | sp_func_and | sp_func_or | sp_func_xor
                | sp_func_seq | sp_func_sne | sp_func_slt
                | sp_func_sgt | sp_func_sle | sp_func_sge =>
                disassemble_reg(Rtype_rd, 'R');
                result(index) := ',';
                index := index + 2;  −− include space after comma
                disassemble_reg(rs1, 'R');
                result(index) := ',';
                index := index + 2;  −− include space after comma
                disassemble_reg(rs2, 'R');
            when sp_func_movi2s =>
                disassemble_special_reg(Rtype_rd);
                result(index) := ',';
                index := index + 2;  −− include space after comma
                disassemble_reg(rs1, 'R');
            . . .
            when others =>
                null;
        end case;
    when op_fparith =>
        result(index to index + instr_name'length − 1)
            := fp_func_names(instr_fp_func_num);
        index := index + instr_name'length + 1;  −− include space after name
        case instr_fp_func is
            when fp_func_addf | fp_func_subf | fp_func_multf | fp_func_divf
                | fp_func_addd | fp_func_subd | fp_func_multd | fp_func_divd
                | fp_func_mult | fp_func_div | fp_func_multu | fp_func_divu =>
                disassemble_reg(Rtype_rd, 'F');
                result(index) := ',';
```

(continued on page 372)

(continued from page 371)

```
            index := index + 2;  -- include space after comma
            disassemble_reg(rs1, 'F');
            result(index) := ',';
            index := index + 2;  -- include space after comma
            disassemble_reg(rs2, 'F');
          when fp_func_cvtf2d | fp_func_cvtd2f =>
            disassemble_reg(Rtype_rd, 'F');
            result(index) := ',';
            index := index + 2;  -- include space after comma
            disassemble_reg(rs1, 'F');
          . . .
          when others =>
              null;
          end case;
      when op_j | op_jal =>
          disassemble_integer(bv_to_integer(instr_immed26));
      when op_beqz | op_bnez =>
          disassemble_reg(rs1, 'R');
          result(index) := ',';
          index := index + 2;  -- include space after comma
          disassemble_integer(bv_to_integer(instr_immed16));
      when op_bfpt | op_bfpf =>
          disassemble_integer(bv_to_integer(instr_immed16));
      when op_slli | op_srli | op_srai =>
          disassemble_reg(Itype_rd, 'R');
          result(index) := ',';
          index := index + 2;  -- include space after comma
          disassemble_reg(rs1, 'R');
          result(index) := ',';
          index := index + 2;  -- include space after comma
          disassemble_integer(bv_to_natural(instr_immed16(11 to 15)));
      when op_addi | op_subi
          | op_seqi | op_snei | op_slti | op_sgti | op_slei | op_sgei =>
          disassemble_reg(Itype_rd, 'R');
          result(index) := ',';
          index := index + 2;  -- include space after comma
          disassemble_reg(rs1, 'R');
          result(index) := ',';
          index := index + 2;  -- include space after comma
          disassemble_integer(bv_to_integer(instr_immed16));
      . . .
      when op_lb | op_lh | op_lw | op_lbu | op_lhu | op_lf | op_ld =>
          disassemble_reg(Itype_rd, 'R');
          result(index) := ',';
          index := index + 2;  -- include space after comma
          disassemble_integer(bv_to_integer(instr_immed16));
          result(index) := '(';
          index := index + 1;
          disassemble_reg(rs1, 'R');
```

```
                    result(index) := ')';
                    index := index + 1;

            . . .

        when others =>
            null;  -- remaining opcodes have no operands to disassemble
    end case;
    if index > norm_disassembled_instr'length then
        index := norm_disassembled_instr'length;  -- limit to out parameter length
    else
        index := index - 1;  -- index points to last result character
    end if;
    norm_disassembled_instr(1 to index) := result(1 to index);
    len := index;
  end procedure disassemble;
end package body dlx_instr;
```

The body of the package that describes DLX instructions.

The package body completes the definitions of the constant arrays of opcode strings, deferred from the package declaration. We fill in the values for these arrays by writing array aggregates. At each index position in an aggregate, we write the string representing the opcode that has the index as its encoded value. We use these arrays in the implementation of the **disassemble** procedure, shown next in the package body.

The first declaration in the procedure is an alias for the string parameter, to simplify indexing the string. This is analogous to the alias we declared in the bit-vector arithmetic operations in Chapter 10. Next, the procedure declares aliases for the fields of the instruction to be disassembled, allowing us to refer to the individual fields easily. The variables after these are used to store numeric versions of instruction fields, converted from the bit vectors in the fields. The variable **result** is used to build up the disassembled instruction string. It is declared to be sufficiently long for the longest possible instruction and is initialized to a string of space characters. We use this variable instead of the procedure parameter, since the parameter may not be long enough. We check the actual length needed at the end of the procedure, rather than having to check for overflow continually throughout the procedure. The variable **index** identifies the next position in **result** in which to place a character of the disassembled instruction.

Following the variable declarations, there are three local procedures within the **disassemble** procedure. The first of these disassembles a register number, given by the parameter **reg**. This may be either a general-purpose register or a floating-point register, so the procedure has an additional parameter, **reg_prefix**, to distinguish between them. It is set to 'R' for a general-purpose register and 'F' for a floating-point register. The procedure first adds the prefix to the **result** string. It then uses the **image** attribute to derive a string representation of the register number and adds it to **result**. For register numbers between 0 and 9, the image is only one character, whereas for other registers it is two characters. The procedure advances the **index** variable by the appropriate amount in each case.

The second local procedure, **disassemble_special_reg**, adds the name of a special register to **result**. Special register 0 is the Interrupt Address Register, and special register 1 is the FP Status Register. For these cases, the abbreviated name is added to the string.

For all other numbers, our version of the DLX CPU does not define a special register. This procedure deals with these cases by disassembling them as "S2", "S3", and so on. It does so by calling the previous procedure, disassemble_reg, with the prefix parameter set to 'S'.

The third local procedure, disassemble_integer, adds the string representation of an integer to result. It also uses the image attribute to derive the string. The local constant int_image_length is set to the length of the string, and is used to determine how large a slice of result is to be written.

The body of disassemble starts by converting the fields of the instruction into numeric values, using the conversion function bv_to_natural. For all opcode values except those of special and floating-point instructions, the procedure uses the constant array opcode_names to disassemble the opcode and place the name in result. The outermost case statement then uses the opcode field to select alternatives that decode the instruction operands, depending on the instruction format. The alternatives for special and floating-point instructions use the constant tables sp_func_names and fp_func_names to disassemble the func field and add it to result. These alternatives include nested case statements, selecting further alternatives based on the func field. We have not shown all of the alternatives here. We leave completion of the omitted alternatives as an exercise for the reader.

Where an instruction has a register operand, the procedure disassemble_reg is called to disassemble the register number. For instructions that have an immediate operand or displacement, that field is converted to an integer and disassembled with disassemble_integer. The field is treated either as a signed or an unsigned integer, depending on the instruction. The procedure includes the characters comma and parentheses by inserting them into the result string and incrementing the variable index. The only action required to include a space character is to increment index, since result was initialized to spaces.

After all operands of the instruction have been disassembled into result, the procedure compares the length of the disassembled instruction with the length of the string parameter in which it is to be returned. If the parameter is too short, as much of the disassembled instruction as will fit into the parameter is returned. Otherwise the whole of the disassembled instruction is copied into the string parameter. The parameter len is set to the length of the disassembled instruction in the string parameter.

The DLX Behavioral Architecture Body

We are now in a position to write the behavioral architecture body for the DLX CPU. An outline of the architecture body is shown in Figure 15-17. It consists of a single process labeled interpreter, which implements the fetch/decode/execute loop common to nearly all basic CPUs. The process also contains variables that represent the internal registers of the CPU. We use bit-vector types for these internal registers and perform operations using the bit-vector arithmetic procedures and functions from the bv_arithmetic package.

Overview of the Interpreter

The first group of declarations in the process represent the CPU registers described in Section 15.1. The arrays reg and fp_reg represent the general-purpose and the floating-point register files, respectively. Each register is a bit vector of one word in size, indicated by the type dlx_bv_word. The variable PC represents the program counter, and the constant PC_incr is the amount by which the program counter is to be incremented after fetching each instruction. Next, the process declares IR, representing the instruction register. The aliases following it represent the fields of instructions of different formats. These aliases allow us to refer easily to the fields of an instruction in order to interpret it. The variables disassembled_instr and disassembled_instr_len are used in conjunction with the disassemble procedure described earlier to form progress messages reported by the model. The following group of variables are used to represent the register number fields of the instruction register, converted to numeric form. These are used to index the register file arrays. Next, mem_addr_reg and mem_data_reg represent the memory address and memory data registers, respectively. We use these to implement memory read and write operations within the CPU. The Boolean variable overflow represents a condition flag for the result of arithmetic operations.

FIGURE 15-17

```
library bv_utilities;  use bv_utilities.bv_arithmetic.all;
use work.dlx_instr.all;

architecture behavior of dlx is
begin
    interpreter : process is
        type reg_array is array (reg_index) of dlx_bv_word;
        variable reg : reg_array;
        variable fp_reg : reg_array;

        variable PC : dlx_bv_word;
        constant PC_incr : dlx_bv_word := X"0000_0004";

        variable IR : dlx_bv_word;
        alias IR_opcode : dlx_opcode is IR(0 to 5);
        alias IR_sp_func : dlx_sp_func is IR(26 to 31);
        alias IR_fp_func : dlx_fp_func is IR(27 to 31);
        alias IR_rs1 : dlx_reg_addr is IR(6 to 10);
        alias IR_rs2 : dlx_reg_addr is IR(11 to 15);
        alias IR_Itype_rd : dlx_reg_addr is IR(11 to 15);
        alias IR_Rtype_rd : dlx_reg_addr is IR(16 to 20);
        alias IR_immed16 : dlx_immed16 is IR(16 to 31);
        alias IR_immed26 : dlx_immed26 is IR(6 to 31);

        variable disassembled_instr : string(1 to 40);
        variable disassembled_instr_len : positive;

        variable rs1, rs2, Itype_rd, Rtype_rd : reg_index;

        variable mem_addr_reg : dlx_bv_address;
        variable mem_data_reg : dlx_bv_word;

        variable overflow : boolean;

        -- lookup table for result of set instructions
        type set_result_table is array (boolean) of dlx_bv_word;
        constant set_if : set_result_table := ( false => X"0000_0000",
                                                 true => X"0000_0001" );
```

(continued on page 376)

(continued from page 375)

```
          variable instr_count : natural;
     —— local procedures for use within the interpreter
     . . .

     begin —— interpreter
          —— reset the processor
          . . .
          wait on phi2 until falling_edge(phi2) and To_bit(reset) = '0';
          —— fetch–decode–execute loop
          while To_bit(reset) /= '1' loop
               —— fetch next instruction
               . . .

               —— increment the PC to point to the following instruction
               . . .

               —— decode the instruction
               . . .

               —— execute the instruction
               . . .

          end loop;
          —— loop is only exited when reset active:
          —— process interpreter starts again from beginning
     end process interpreter;

end architecture behavior;
```

An outline of a behavioral architecture body for the DLX CPU, containing an instruction set interpreter process.

The declaration of the constant set_if is included to simplify the interpretation of relational instructions. We return to this constant when we describe its use in interpreting the instructions. The variable instr_count is a counter for keeping track of the number of instructions fetched by the process. We use this in combination with the value of the generic constant debug to determine when to trace progress. Following the object declarations, we include declarations of local procedures for use within the interpreter. We describe them in detail later in this section.

Figure 15-17 outlines the statement part of the interpreter process. This outline serves as the framework for our implementation in the rest of this section. The process first resets the internal state of the CPU, then waits until the next falling phi2 clock edge at which reset is '0' before proceeding. The process then enters the fetch/decode/ execute loop. While the reset input remains negated, the loop reads the next instruction from memory, increments the PC, analyzes the fields of the fetched instruction and then performs the appropriate operations to execute the instruction. At strategic points within the loop, the process tests the reset input again and exits the loop if it is '1'. (The function To_bit from the std_logic_1164 package converts a standard-logic value to a bit.) When the loop is terminated, the process starts again from the top of the statement part.

Bus Read and Write Procedures

In several places within the interpreter process we need to implement bus read and write operations. Rather than writing similar sequences of statements in each place, we can abstract the operations into two local procedures within the process, one to perform a bus read and the other to perform a bus write.

The bus read procedure is shown in Figure 15-18. Its parameters are the address from which to read, the size of the data to read and a flag indicating whether the read operation is an instruction fetch or a data read. The procedure also has an **out** parameter to return the data read from memory. The body of the procedure implements the bus read protocol described in Section 15.1. It waits for the beginning of the next clock cycle, indicated by the rising edge of phi1. If at this stage the **reset** input is active, the operation is aborted and the procedure returns immediately. Otherwise, the procedure drives the CPU interface signals **a**, **width** and **ifetch** with the values passed as parameters. (The address parameter is converted from a bit-vector value to a standard-logic vector value using the function **To_X01** from the standard-logic package.) The procedure then sets the **mem_enable** signal to '1' to start the bus read operation and waits for successive falling edges of the **phi2** clock. On each falling edge, if the **reset** input is active, the operation is aborted and the procedure returns. Otherwise, if the **ready** signal from the memory is active, the procedure exits the wait loop. It tests the data supplied by the memory to verify that there are no unknown bits and converts it to

FIGURE 15-18

```
procedure bus_read ( address : in dlx_bv_address;
                     data_width : in dlx_mem_width;
                     instr_fetch : in std_logic;
                     data : out dlx_bv_word ) is
begin
    wait until rising_edge(phi1);
    if To_bit(reset) = '1' then
        return;
    end if;
    a <= To_X01(address) after Tpd_clk_out;
    width <= data_width after Tpd_clk_out;
    ifetch <= instr_fetch after Tpd_clk_out;
    mem_enable <= '1' after Tpd_clk_out;
    loop
        wait until falling_edge(phi2);
        if To_bit(reset) = '1' then
            return;
        end if;
        exit when To_bit(ready) = '1';
    end loop;
    assert not Is_X(d) report "Bus read data contains unknown bits";
    data := To_bitvector(d);
    mem_enable <= '0' after Tpd_clk_out;
end procedure bus_read;
```

The local procedure for performing a bus read operation.

bit-vector form. The procedure finally clears the mem_enable control signal to complete the bus read operation and then returns.

The bus write procedure, shown in Figure 15-19, is very similar. It has parameters for the address, data width and the data to be written. The write operation is performed similarly to a read operation, except that the write_enable signal is set to '1' instead of being maintained at '0'. Furthermore, the data value is converted to a standard-logic vector value and driven onto the data bus at the beginning of the operation. When the memory responds by setting ready to '1', the procedure drives the data bus with the value disabled_dlx_word and clears the write_enable signal to '0'.

FIGURE 15-19

```
procedure bus_write ( address : in dlx_bv_address;
                      data_width : in dlx_mem_width;
                      data : in dlx_bv_word ) is
begin
    wait until rising_edge(phi1);
    if To_bit(reset) = '1' then
        return;
    end if;
    a <= To_X01(address) after Tpd_clk_out;
    ifetch <= '0' after Tpd_clk_out;
    width <= data_width after Tpd_clk_out;
    d <= To_X01Z(data) after Tpd_clk_out;
    write_enable <= '1' after Tpd_clk_out;
    mem_enable <= '1' after Tpd_clk_out;
    loop
        wait until falling_edge(phi2);
        if To_bit(reset) = '1' then
            return;
        end if;
        exit when To_bit(ready) = '1';
    end loop;
    d <= disabled_dlx_word after Tpd_clk_out;
    write_enable <= '0' after Tpd_clk_out;
    mem_enable <= '0' after Tpd_clk_out;
end procedure bus_write;
```

The local procedure for performing a bus write operation.

Resetting the Interpreter

Figure 15-20 shows the statements that reset the interpreter before entering the loop. These statements are executed when the model is initialized, simulating a power-on reset, and when the reset input to the CPU is activated. The first four statements reset the external interface of the CPU. The data bus drivers are deactivated, the halt signal is cleared and the memory control signals write_enable and mem_enable are cleared. Next, the CPU's internal state is initialized. Register r0 is cleared to 0, the program counter is initialized to address 0 and the instruction counter is set back to 0.

FIGURE 15-20

```
-- reset the processor
d <= disabled_dlx_word;
halt <= '0';
write_enable <= '0';
mem_enable <= '0';
reg(0) := X"0000_0000";
PC := X"0000_0000";
instr_count := 0;
```

The part of the interpreter process that resets the internal state of the CPU.

Fetching an Instruction

The statements that fetch an instruction are shown in Figure 15-21. The procedure call to **bus_read** is the statement that implements the fetch operation. It uses the value of the program counter register as the address and specifies that a whole word should be read, with the **ifetch** signal set to '1'. The resulting word is stored in the instruction register. The additional statements in this group are included to aid in debugging the model and the DLX programs interpreted by the model. The first instruction increments the counter of the number of instructions fetched. Then, depending on the level of detail of reporting required and the value of the counter, a message is issued reporting the instruction count. If a message is required for each instruction fetched, it is issued at this stage. If a detailed trace is required, the instruction disassembly procedure is used to create a message to report the instruction fetched from memory. The last statement in the group waits for the start of the next clock cycle before proceeding. All operations required to interpret the fetched instruction take place in successive clock cycles, after those in which the instruction was fetched.

FIGURE 15-21

```
-- fetch next instruction
instr_count := instr_count + 1;
if debug = msg_every_100_instructions and instr_count mod 100 = 0 then
    report "instruction count = " & natural'image(instr_count);
end if;
if debug >= msg_each_instruction then
    report "fetching instruction";
end if;
bus_read( address => PC, data_width => dlx_mem_width_word,
        instr_fetch => '1', data => IR );
exit when To_bit(reset) = '1';
if debug >= trace_each_instruction then
    disassemble(IR, disassembled_instr, disassembled_instr_len);
    report disassembled_instr(1 to disassembled_instr_len);
end if;
wait until rising_edge(phi1);
```

Interpreter statements for fetching the next instruction from memory.

Incrementing the PC

After an instruction has been fetched, the CPU must increment the program counter. The statements in the interpreter that perform this operation are shown in Figure 15-22. First, if detailed tracing is required, the interpreter issues a message reporting progress to this step. It then uses the unsigned binary addition procedure from the bit-vector arithmetic package to add the increment value to the PC. No overflow indication is required, since the PC value should wrap to 0 if overflow occurs.

FIGURE 15-22

```
-- increment the PC to point to the following instruction
if debug = trace_each_step then
    report "incrementing PC";
end if;
PC := bv_addu(PC, PC_incr);
```

Statements in the interpreter that increment the PC.

Decoding the Instruction

The next step in interpreting an instruction is to decode it. In a model at a lower level of abstraction than the behavioral level, decoding involves using the opcode and operand fields in the instruction register to determine the control values and sequences needed to execute the instruction. However, since we are modeling at the behavioral level of abstraction, we can use the instruction register fields directly in subsequent steps in the interpreter. We simply take advantage of this step to convert the operand register fields in the instruction register to numeric form, as shown in Figure 15-23. This makes it easier for us to refer to registers in the register file array later in the model. The conversion is done using the bit-vector conversion functions from the bit-vector arithmetic package. If detailed tracing is required, we report a progress message at this stage.

FIGURE 15-23

```
-- decode the instruction
if debug = trace_each_step then
    report "decoding instruction";
end if;
rs1 := bv_to_natural(IR_rs1);
rs2 := bv_to_natural(IR_rs2);
Itype_rd := bv_to_natural(IR_Itype_rd);
Rtype_rd := bv_to_natural(IR_Rtype_rd);
```

Statements in the interpreter for decoding an instruction.

Executing the Instruction

The most significant part of the instruction set interpreter process is the part that actually executes instructions. This is shown in Figure 15-24. We start by issuing a progress report, if required, and clearing the overflow flag. Then we use a case statement to select which group of statements to execute, depending on the instruction opcode.

FIGURE 15-24

```
-- execute the instruction
if debug = trace_each_step then
    report "executing instruction";
end if;

overflow := false;

case IR_opcode is
    when op_special =>
        execute_op_special;
    when op_fparith =>
        execute_op_fparith;
    when op_j =>
        PC := PC + bv_sext(IR_immed26, 32);
    when op_jal =>
        reg(link_reg) := PC;
        PC := PC + bv_sext(IR_immed26, 32);
    when op_jr =>
        PC := reg(rs1);
    when op_jalr =>
        reg(link_reg) := PC;
        PC := reg(rs1);
    when op_beqz =>
        if reg(rs1) = X"0000_0000" then
            PC := PC + bv_sext(IR_immed16, 32);
        end if;
    when op_bnez =>
        if reg(rs1) /= X"0000_0000" then
            PC := PC + bv_sext(IR_immed16, 32);
        end if;
    when op_addi =>
        bv_add(reg(rs1), bv_sext(IR_immed16, 32), reg(Itype_rd), overflow);
    when op_addui =>
        bv_addu(reg(rs1), bv_zext(IR_immed16, 32), reg(Itype_rd), overflow);
    when op_subi =>
        bv_sub(reg(rs1), bv_sext(IR_immed16, 32), reg(Itype_rd), overflow);
    when op_subui =>
        bv_subu(reg(rs1), bv_zext(IR_immed16, 32), reg(Itype_rd), overflow);
    when op_slli =>
        reg(Itype_rd) := reg(rs1) sll bv_to_natural(IR_immed16(11 to 15));
    when op_srli =>
        reg(Itype_rd) := reg(rs1) srl bv_to_natural(IR_immed16(11 to 15));
    when op_srai =>
        reg(Itype_rd) := reg(rs1) sra bv_to_natural(IR_immed16(11 to 15));
    when op_andi =>
        reg(Itype_rd) := reg(rs1) and bv_zext(IR_immed16, 32);
```

(continued on page 382)

(continued from page 381)

```
        when op_ori =>
            reg(Itype_rd) := reg(rs1) or bv_zext(IR_immed16, 32);
        when op_xori =>
            reg(Itype_rd) := reg(rs1) xor bv_zext(IR_immed16, 32);
        when op_lhi =>
            reg(Itype_rd) := IR_immed16 & X"0000";
        when op_sequi =>
            reg(Itype_rd) := set_if( reg(rs1) = bv_zext(IR_immed16, 32) );
        when op_sneui =>
            reg(Itype_rd) := set_if( reg(rs1) /= bv_zext(IR_immed16, 32) );
        when op_sltui =>
            reg(Itype_rd) := set_if( reg(rs1) < bv_zext(IR_immed16, 32) );
        when op_sgtui =>
            reg(Itype_rd) := set_if( reg(rs1) > bv_zext(IR_immed16, 32) );
        when op_sleui =>
            reg(Itype_rd) := set_if( reg(rs1) <= bv_zext(IR_immed16, 32) );
        when op_sgeui =>
            reg(Itype_rd) := set_if( reg(rs1) >= bv_zext(IR_immed16, 32) );
        when op_seqi =>
            reg(Itype_rd) := set_if( reg(rs1) = bv_sext(IR_immed16, 32) );
        when op_snei =>
            reg(Itype_rd) := set_if( reg(rs1) /= bv_sext(IR_immed16, 32) );
        when op_slti =>
            reg(Itype_rd) := set_if( bv_lt(reg(rs1), bv_sext(IR_immed16, 32)) );
        when op_sgti =>
            reg(Itype_rd) := set_if( bv_gt(reg(rs1), bv_sext(IR_immed16, 32)) );
        when op_slei =>
            reg(Itype_rd) := set_if( bv_le(reg(rs1), bv_sext(IR_immed16, 32)) );
        when op_sgei =>
            reg(Itype_rd) := set_if( bv_ge(reg(rs1), bv_sext(IR_immed16, 32)) );
        when op_trap =>
            report "TRAP instruction encountered, execution halted" severity note;
            halt <= '1' after Tpd_clk_out;
            wait until To_bit(reset) = '1';
            exit;
        when op_lb =>
            execute_load(data_width => dlx_mem_width_byte, unsigned => false);
            exit when To_bit(reset) = '1';
        when op_lh =>
            execute_load(data_width => dlx_mem_width_halfword, unsigned => false);
            exit when To_bit(reset) = '1';
        when op_lw =>
            execute_load(data_width => dlx_mem_width_word, unsigned => false);
            exit when To_bit(reset) = '1';
        when op_lbu =>
            execute_load(data_width => dlx_mem_width_byte, unsigned => true);
            exit when To_bit(reset) = '1';
```

```
    when op_lhu =>
        execute_load(data_width => dlx_mem_width_halfword, unsigned => true);
        exit when To_bit(reset) = '1';
    when op_sb =>
        execute_store ( data_width => dlx_mem_width_byte );
        exit when To_bit(reset) = '1';
    when op_sh =>
        execute_store ( data_width => dlx_mem_width_halfword );
        exit when To_bit(reset) = '1';
    when op_sw =>
        execute_store ( data_width => dlx_mem_width_word );
        exit when To_bit(reset) = '1';
    when op_rfe | op_bfpt | op_bfpf | op_lf | op_ld | op_sf | op_sd =>
        report opcode_names(bv_to_natural(IR_opcode))
                & " instruction not implemented" severity warning;
    when others =>
        report "undefined instruction" severity error;
end case;
-- fix up R0 in case it was overwritten
reg(0) := X"0000_0000";

-- overflow and divide-by-zero exception handling
-- (not implemented)

if debug = trace_each_step then
    report "end of execution";
end if;
```

Interpreter statements to execute instructions.

The first alternative shown is the class of register operand instructions, with op-code value **op_special**. Since there are a number of instructions in this class, we have separated the statements to execute them into a procedure called **execute_op_special**. This simplifies the case statement alternative shown here to a simple procedure call. We return to the details of the procedure later in this section. The second alternative in the case statement handles floating-point instructions, for which the opcode value is **op_fparith**. Again, in the interest of simplifying the case statement, we have separated execution of these instructions into a procedure called **execute_op_fparith**.

We now come to the execution of the jump instructions. The first of these, with opcode value **op_j**, is an unconditional jump. We simply add the sign-extended value of the 26-bit displacement field of the instruction register to the current PC value. We use the overloaded version of the "+" operator from the bit-vector arithmetic package. Execution of the jump-and-link instruction is done similarly, except that the PC value is first copied to the link register (r31). Note that the displacement in these jump instructions is relative to the incremented value of the PC, rather than relative to the starting address of the jump instruction. Following these two instructions are the register operand versions of the jump instructions. These take the target address directly from the source register, rather than calculating it based on the PC value. The source register value is obtained by indexing the array representing the register file. The index is the numeric value corresponding to the rs1 field of the instruction register.

The next two alternatives in the case statement execute the conditional branch instructions. They each index the register file to fetch the source operand and compare it with the bit-vector value representing zero. If the test succeeds, they branch by adding the 16-bit displacement field from the instruction register to the PC value. These instructions, like the jump instructions, add the displacement to the incremented PC, rather than to the starting address of the branch instruction.

Following these are the statements to execute the add and subtract instructions with an immediate operand. In each case, the first operand is fetched by indexing the register file, and the second operand is the 16-bit immediate field of the instruction register, extended to 32 bits. For the unsigned instructions, the immediate operand is zero-extended, whereas for the signed versions, it is sign-extended. The appropriate procedure from the bit-vector arithmetic package is used to perform the operation, with the result being written to the destination register in the register file. The procedure also sets the Boolean variable **overflow** according to the result of the operation.

Following the arithmetic instructions, we have the statements to execute the immediate shift instructions. They use the five least-significant bits of the immediate field from the instruction register to specify how many places to shift the register operand. The three kinds of shift instructions are implemented using the corresponding predefined shift operations in VHDL, and the result placed in the destination register in the register file.

Next, we have the statements to execute the logical instructions that have an immediate second operand. The 16-bit immediate field from the instruction register is zero-extended to 32 bits. The required logical operation is implemented using the predefined VHDL logical operator applied to the two bit vectors.

The next case statement alternative executes the load-high-immediate instruction. It forms a 32-bit result by concatenating the 16-bit immediate value from the instruction register to a vector of sixteen '0' bits. This result is written into the destination register in the register file.

Following this alternative are the alternatives for relational instructions using an immediate operand. The 16-bit immediate field of the instruction register is extended to 32 bits—either zero-extended for unsigned comparisons or sign-extended for signed comparisons. The unsigned comparisons are performed using the predefined VHDL relational operators, whereas the signed comparisons are performed using the functions provided by the bit-vector arithmetic package. In all cases, the result is a Boolean value. The DLX instructions, however, require a bit-vector result representing the integer 1 if the comparison succeeds or 0 if it fails. The interpreter converts the Boolean value to this form by using it to index the constant array **set_if**, whose declaration is shown in Figure 15-17. The element with index **false** is the bit-vector representation of 0, and the element with index **true** is the bit-vector representation of 1. This illustrates the common technique of using a constant array as a lookup table to perform conversion operations.

We now come to the alternative that executes the trap instruction. As mentioned earlier, our model does not implement this instruction, but instead uses it to halt operation of the CPU. The interpreter issues a message to indicate that it has reached a trap instruction and sets the CPU **halt** port to '1'. It waits until the **reset** input port is activated and then exits the fetch/execute loop.

The next group of alternatives in the case statement executes the load and store instructions. Since they are relatively complex to execute, we have separated them out into separate procedures, **execute_load** and **execute_store**, that we describe later in this section. Each of the procedures aborts the load or store operation and returns immediately if the **reset** input is activated. Hence each of the case statement alternatives shown here tests the state of the **reset** input and exits the fetch/execute loop if it is '1'.

The penultimate alternative in the case statement handles instructions that are not implemented in our model. For each of these instructions, the interpreter issues a message including the opcode name. This is determined by using the numeric value of the opcode to index the array of opcode names. The last alternative handles opcode values that do not represent DLX instructions. The interpreter simply issues a message indicating that an undefined instruction has been reached.

After the case statement has been completed, the interpreter does some final "housekeeping." First, recall that register r0 in the DLX is hard-wired to the value zero and cannot be changed. In our implementation of instructions that wrote to a destination register, we did not explicitly check whether the destination was r0. Instead, our model takes the simpler approach of forcing the register back to zero after instruction execution. Next, we have included a comment in the model to indicate where the interpreter should handle exceptions that occurred during instruction execution, such as integer overflow and divide-by-zero conditions. Since our model does not implement exception handling, we have not included anything at this point. Finally, if detailed reporting of progress is required, the interpreter issues a message indicating that it has completed execution of the instruction. This completes the fetch/execute cycle.

We now return to the procedures invoked by the main case statement in the execution part of the interpreter. Figure 15-25 shows the procedure **execute_op_special**, which executes register operand instructions corresponding to the opcode value **op_special**. For these instructions, the **IR_sp_func** field of the instruction register acts as an opcode extension. The procedure body consists of a case statement with this value as the selector expression.

FIGURE 15-25

```
procedure execute_op_special is
begin
  case IR_sp_func is
    when sp_func_nop =>
      null;
    when sp_func_add =>
      bv_add(reg(rs1), reg(rs2), reg(Rtype_rd), overflow);
    when sp_func_addu =>
      bv_addu(reg(rs1), reg(rs2), reg(Rtype_rd), overflow);
    when sp_func_sub =>
      bv_sub(reg(rs1), reg(rs2), reg(Rtype_rd), overflow);
    when sp_func_subu =>
      bv_subu(reg(rs1), reg(rs2), reg(Rtype_rd), overflow);
    when sp_func_sll =>
      reg(Rtype_rd) := reg(rs1) sll bv_to_natural(reg(rs2)(27 to 31));
```

(continued on page 386)

(continued from page 385)

```
            when sp_func_srl =>
                reg(Rtype_rd) := reg(rs1) srl bv_to_natural(reg(rs2)(27 to 31));
            when sp_func_sra =>
                reg(Rtype_rd) := reg(rs1) sra bv_to_natural(reg(rs2)(27 to 31));
            when sp_func_and =>
                reg(Rtype_rd) := reg(rs1) and reg(rs2);
            when sp_func_or =>
                reg(Rtype_rd) := reg(rs1) or reg(rs2);
            when sp_func_xor =>
                reg(Rtype_rd) := reg(rs1) xor reg(rs2);
            when sp_func_sequ =>
                reg(Rtype_rd) := set_if( reg(rs1) = reg(rs2) );
            when sp_func_sneu =>
                reg(Rtype_rd) := set_if( reg(rs1) /= reg(rs2) );
            when sp_func_sltu =>
                reg(Rtype_rd) := set_if( reg(rs1) < reg(rs2) );
            when sp_func_sgtu =>
                reg(Rtype_rd) := set_if( reg(rs1) > reg(rs2) );
            when sp_func_sleu =>
                reg(Rtype_rd) := set_if( reg(rs1) <= reg(rs2) );
            when sp_func_sgeu =>
                reg(Rtype_rd) := set_if( reg(rs1) >= reg(rs2) );
            when sp_func_seq =>
                reg(Rtype_rd) := set_if( reg(rs1) = reg(rs2) );
            when sp_func_sne =>
                reg(Rtype_rd) := set_if( reg(rs1) /= reg(rs2) );
            when sp_func_slt =>
                reg(Rtype_rd) := set_if( bv_lt(reg(rs1), reg(rs2)) );
            when sp_func_sgt =>
                reg(Rtype_rd) := set_if( bv_gt(reg(rs1), reg(rs2)) );
            when sp_func_sle =>
                reg(Rtype_rd) := set_if( bv_le(reg(rs1), reg(rs2)) );
            when sp_func_sge =>
                reg(Rtype_rd) := set_if( bv_ge(reg(rs1), reg(rs2)) );
            when sp_func_movi2s | sp_func_movs2i
                 | sp_func_movf | sp_func_movd
                 | sp_func_movfp2i | sp_func_movi2fp =>
                report sp_func_names(bv_to_natural(IR_sp_func))
                        & " instruction not implemented" severity warning;
            when others =>
                report "undefined special instruction function" severity error;
        end case;
    end procedure execute_op_special;
```

The procedure that executes instructions with opcode having the value op_special.

The first alternative is the "nop" instruction. No action is required to execute this instruction, so the alternative simply includes the null statement. Following this alternative are alternatives for arithmetic, logical and relational instructions. These versions are implemented in the same way as the versions with an immediate operand, except that the second operand is fetched from the register file. No extension is needed, as the values are already 32 bits in length. The shift operations are similarly implemented, except that the second operand, specifying the number of positions by which to shift, is taken from the five least-significant bits of the register value. The remaining two alternatives in the case statement handle instructions that our model does not implement and opcode extension values that do not represent valid instructions.

The procedure execute_op_fparith, which executes floating-point instructions corresponding to the opcode value op_fparith, is shown in Figure 15-26. It also consists of a case statement, based on the value of the IR_fp_func field of the instruction register. Our model does not implement any of the instructions in this group, so the procedure simply issues a message to this effect. For values of the IR_fp_func field that do not represent valid instructions, the second alternative in the case statement procedure reports an appropriate message.

FIGURE 15-26

```
procedure execute_op_fparith is
begin
    case IR_fp_func is
        when fp_func_mult | fp_func_multu | fp_func_div | fp_func_divu
           | fp_func_addf | fp_func_subf | fp_func_multf | fp_func_divf
           | fp_func_addd | fp_func_subd | fp_func_multd | fp_func_divd
           | fp_func_cvtf2d | fp_func_cvtf2i | fp_func_cvtd2f
           | fp_func_cvtd2i | fp_func_cvti2f | fp_func_cvti2d
           | fp_func_eqf | fp_func_nef | fp_func_ltf | fp_func_gtf
           | fp_func_lef | fp_func_gef | fp_func_eqd | fp_func_ned
           | fp_func_ltd | fp_func_gtd | fp_func_led | fp_func_ged =>
           report fp_func_names(bv_to_natural(IR_fp_func))
                        & " instruction not implemented" severity warning;
        when others =>
           report "undefined floating point instruction function" severity error;
    end case;
end procedure execute_op_fparith;
```

The procedure that executes instructions with opcode having the value op_fparith.

Figure 15-27 shows the procedure execute_load, called by the interpreter to execute the different kinds of load instructions. The first parameter, data_width, specifies the amount of data to be loaded from memory: a byte, a halfword or a word. The second parameter, unsigned, specifies whether a loaded byte or halfword should be zero-extended (for unsigned load instructions) or sign-extended (for signed load instructions).

The procedure first calculates the memory address by adding the 16-bit displacement field from the instruction register and the value from the base register. It uses the version of the "+" operator from the bit-vector arithmetic package and stores the result in the variable representing the memory address register. It then performs a bus read operation using the bus_read procedure described above. The data word read from memory is placed in the variable representing the memory data register. Note

FIGURE 15-27

```
procedure execute_load ( data_width : dlx_mem_width; unsigned : boolean ) is
    variable temp : dlx_bv_word;
    -- type for least-significant two bits of address
    subtype ls_2_addr_bits is bit_vector(1 downto 0);
begin
    mem_addr_reg := reg(rs1) + bv_sext(IR_immed16, 32);
    bus_read(mem_addr_reg, data_width, '0', mem_data_reg);
    if To_bit(reset) = '1' then
        return;
    end if;
    case data_width is
        when dlx_mem_width_byte =>
            case ls_2_addr_bits'(mem_addr_reg(1 downto 0)) is
                when B"00" =>
                    temp(0 to 7) := mem_data_reg(0 to 7);
                when B"01" =>
                    temp(0 to 7) := mem_data_reg(8 to 15);
                when B"10" =>
                    temp(0 to 7) := mem_data_reg(16 to 23);
                when B"11" =>
                    temp(0 to 7) := mem_data_reg(24 to 31);
            end case;
            if unsigned then
                reg(Itype_rd) := bv_zext(temp(0 to 7), 32);
            else
                reg(Itype_rd) := bv_sext(temp(0 to 7), 32);
            end if;
        when dlx_mem_width_halfword =>
            if mem_addr_reg(1) = '0' then
                temp(0 to 15) := mem_data_reg(0 to 15);
            else
                temp(0 to 15) := mem_data_reg(16 to 31);
            end if;
            if unsigned then
                reg(Itype_rd) := bv_zext(temp(0 to 15), 32);
            else
                reg(Itype_rd) := bv_sext(temp(0 to 15), 32);
            end if;
        when dlx_mem_width_word =>
            reg(Itype_rd) := mem_data_reg;
        when others =>
            null;
    end case;
end procedure execute_load;
```

The procedure that executes load instructions.

that the **bus_read** procedure aborts the read operation if the **reset** signal is activated. The **execute_load** procedure tests whether **reset** is active, and if so, it too aborts and returns immediately. Otherwise it proceeds to extract the required amount of data from the memory data register, to write into the destination register in the register file.

For byte loads, the particular byte extracted from the register depends on the two least-significant address bits, corresponding to the alignment of data on the data bus. The type **ls_2_addr_bits** is used to qualify the case selector expression, as the type of the expression must be statically known. The extracted data is extended to 32 bits, according to the value of the **unsigned** parameter. For halfword loads, the single least-significant bit of the address is used in a similar way. It determines whether the left or the right halfword is extracted and extended. For word loads, the entire content of the memory data register is used. The case statement includes alternatives for all three cases of data size and an additional alternative for the illegal code included in the **dlx_mem_width** type. Since the procedure is never called with this illegal value, the alternative simply contains a null statement. We must nevertheless include the alternative, due to the VHDL rule requiring that all values in the type of the selector expression be covered by alternative choices in the case statement.

The procedure **execute_store**, called by the interpreter to execute store instructions, is shown in Figure 15-28. It is similar to **execute_load**. First, it calculates the address and places it in the memory address register variable. Next, it assembles the data to be written to memory. The variable representing the memory data register is initialized to all '0' bits, then the required byte, halfword or the entire register is overwritten with the byte, halfword or word to be stored. This data is fetched from the register file. Byte and halfword data is placed in the memory data register at a position determined by the least-significant address bits. Once the data has been assembled, it is written to memory using the **bus_write** procedure. We do not need to test whether **reset** is active after this procedure returns, as it is the last action in **execute_store**.

FIGURE 15-28

```
procedure execute_store ( data_width : dlx_mem_width ) is
    variable temp : dlx_bv_word;
    -- type for least–significant two bits of address
    subtype ls_2_addr_bits is bit_vector(1 downto 0);
begin
    mem_addr_reg := reg(rs1) + bv_sext(IR_immed16, 32);
    mem_data_reg := X"0000_0000";
    case data_width is
        when dlx_mem_width_byte =>
            case ls_2_addr_bits'(mem_addr_reg(1 downto 0)) is
                when B"00" =>
                    mem_data_reg(0 to 7) := reg(Itype_rd)(0 to 7);
                when B"01" =>
                    mem_data_reg(8 to 15) := reg(Itype_rd)(0 to 7);
                when B"10" =>
                    mem_data_reg(16 to 23) := reg(Itype_rd)(0 to 7);
```

(continued on page 390)

(continued from page 389)

```
                    when B"11" =>
                        mem_data_reg(24 to 31) := reg(Itype_rd)(0 to 7);
                    end case;
                when dlx_mem_width_halfword =>
                    if mem_addr_reg(1) = '0' then
                        mem_data_reg(0 to 15) := reg(Itype_rd)(0 to 15);
                    else
                        mem_data_reg(16 to 31) := reg(Itype_rd)(0 to 15);
                    end if;
                when dlx_mem_width_word =>
                    mem_data_reg := reg(Itype_rd);
                when others =>
                    null;
            end case;
            bus_write(mem_addr_reg, data_width, mem_data_reg);
        end procedure execute_store;
```

The procedure that executes store instructions.

15.3 Testing the Behavioral Model

Now that we have developed our behavioral CPU model, we can test it by writing a test-bench model. Since the function performed by the CPU is to execute a machine language program stored in memory, we can test the CPU by including a memory in the test bench. We preload the memory with a small program and monitor the ports of the CPU to verify that it is fetching and executing the program correctly. We also need to include a clock generator in the test bench to drive the clock and **reset** ports of the CPU.

The Test-Bench Clock Generator

Figure 15-29 shows the entity declaration and behavioral architecture body for the clock generator. The entity has two generic constants that are used to specify the shape of the clock waveforms. **Tpw** specifies the pulse width for each clock phase, and **Tps** specifies the pulse separation between phases, as shown in Figure 15-9 on page 362.

FIGURE 15-29

```
        library ieee;  use ieee.std_logic_1164.all;
        entity clock_gen is
            generic ( Tpw : delay_length;
                      Tps : delay_length );
            port ( phi1, phi2 : out std_logic;
                   reset : out std_logic );
        end entity clock_gen;
```

```
architecture behavior of clock_gen is
    constant clock_period : delay_length := 2 * (Tpw + Tps);
begin
    reset_driver :
        reset <= '1', '0' after 2.5 * clock_period + Tps;
    clock_driver : process is
    begin
        phi1 <= '0';
        phi2 <= '0';
        wait for clock_period / 2;
        loop
            phi1 <= '1', '0' after Tpw;
            phi2 <= '1' after clock_period / 2,
                    '0' after clock_period / 2 + Tpw;
            wait for clock_period;
        end loop;
    end process clock_driver;
end architecture behavior;
```

An entity declaration and architecture body for the clock generator used in the test bench.

The architecture body contains two processes, one to generate the **reset** signal and the other to generate the clock signals. The process **reset_driver** generates a single pulse on **reset**, starting at the beginning of a simulation and lasting until the clock has completed two cycles. The process **clock_driver** initializes the clock signals to '0', then waits for half a cycle. It then enters an infinite loop, in which it schedules the clock transitions for the next cycle and then waits for the cycle.

The Test-Bench Memory

The entity declaration for the memory to be used in the test bench is shown in Figure 15-30. The first generic constant, **mem_size**, is used to determine the amount of storage implemented within the memory. The generic constant **load_file_name** is a string that specifies a binary memory image file to be loaded into the memory when it is initialized. If we do not specify a file name, the default file name "dlx.out" is used. The remaining generic constants control the timing behavior. We design the memory to support burst data transfers as well as transfers of single words. In a burst transfer, we supply the address of the first word to be accessed and then transfer successive words from successive locations in the memory. This allows us to use the memory in extended models of computer systems that include cache memories. (See, for example, Exercise 4 at the end of this chapter.) The generic constant **Tac_first** is the access time for a single word or for the first word in a burst. **Tac_burst** is the access time for words after the first word in a burst. **Tpd_clk_out** is the propagation delay between a clock edge and a resulting output transition.

The ports of the memory entity correspond to those of the DLX CPU. They include the clock signals **phi1** and **phi2**, the address bus **a**, the bidirectional data bus **d** and the control signals **width**, **write_enable**, **mem_enable** and **ready**. The **burst** port is used to control burst transfers. When it is set to '1', the memory reads or writes successive words,

FIGURE 15-30

```
library ieee;  use ieee. std_logic_1164.all;
use work.dlx_types.all;
entity memory is
    generic ( mem_size : positive;
              Tac_first : delay_length;
              Tac_burst : delay_length;
              Tpd_clk_out : delay_length;
              load_file_name : string := "dlx.out" );
    port ( phi1, phi2 : in std_logic;
           a : in dlx_address;
           d : inout dlx_word;
           width : in dlx_mem_width;
           write_enable : in std_logic;
           burst : in std_logic := '0';
           mem_enable : in std_logic;
           ready : out std_logic );
end entity memory;
```

An entity declaration for the test-bench memory.

using the **ready** signal to indicate completion of each transfer. The **burst** port should be set to '0' during the last transfer in a burst. If **burst** is set to '0' at the start of a memory operation, a single word is transferred. The entity declaration shows that the **burst** port has a default initial value of '0', so we can simply leave it unassociated in our test bench for the DLX CPU.

A behavioral architecture body for the memory is shown in Figure 15-31. The process **mem_behavior** implements the behavior. The constant **high_address** defines the range of addresses to which the memory responds, based on the size of the memory. This constant is used to define an array type to represent the memory storage. Each element of the array is a one-word bit vector. Since we are using byte addresses to access memory, we must divide the high address bound by four to derive the index range for the array of words. Next, the process declares a variable **mem** of the array type. Since we have not yet described how to use file operations to load data, we do not initialize the memory from the file named by **load_file_name**. Instead, for this case study, we simply "preload" the memory by including an initialization expression in the variable declaration. In Chapter 18, when we cover file operations, we present an alternative architecture body that loads the memory from a file. The array aggregate we have written in the memory initialization expression contains the binary representation of the small test program shown in the comments. The program initializes register r2 to zero and then enters a loop. For each iteration, it stores the value in r2 into memory at the location labeled "counter" and then increments r2. The "snei" instruction tests whether the value in r2 is not 10, and the "bnez" instruction transfers back to the top of the loop if the test succeeded. When r2 is 10, the loop terminates, and the "trap" instruction halts execution.

FIGURE 15-31

```
library bv_utilities;

use bv_utilities.bv_arithmetic.bv_to_natural, bv_utilities.bv_arithmetic.natural_to_bv;

architecture preloaded of memory is
begin
    mem_behavior : process is
        constant high_address : natural := mem_size − 1;
        type memory_array is
            array (natural range 0 to high_address / 4) of dlx_bv_word;
        variable mem : memory_array
            := ( X"20020000",          --              addi r2, r0, 0
                 X"ac020018",       -- loop:      sw   counter(r0), r2
                 X"20420001",       --            addi r2, r2, 1
                 X"6441000a",       --            snei r1, r2, 10
                 X"1420fff0",       --            bnez r1, loop
                 X"44000000",       --            trap  0
                 X"00000000",       -- counter:   .word 0
                 others => X"00000000" );

    variable byte_address, word_address : natural;
    variable write_access : boolean;

    procedure do_write is
        subtype ls_2_bits is bit_vector(1 downto 0);
    begin
        case width is
            when dlx_mem_width_word =>
                mem(word_address) := to_bitvector(d);
            when dlx_mem_width_halfword =>
                if To_bit(a(1)) = '0' then  -- ms half word
                    mem(word_address)(0 to 15) := to_bitvector( d(0 to 15) );
                else  -- ls half word
                    mem(word_address)(16 to 31) := to_bitvector( d(16 to 31) );
                end if;
            when dlx_mem_width_byte =>
                case ls_2_bits'(To_bitvector(a(1 downto 0))) is
                    when b"00" =>
                        mem(word_address)(0 to 7) := to_bitvector( d(0 to 7) );
                    when b"01" =>
                        mem(word_address)(8 to 15) := to_bitvector( d(8 to 15) );
                    when b"10" =>
                        mem(word_address)(16 to 23) := to_bitvector( d(16 to 23) );
                    when b"11" =>
                        mem(word_address)(24 to 31) := to_bitvector( d(24 to 31) );
                end case;
            when others =>
                report "illegal width indicator in write" severity error;
        end case;
    end do_write;
```

(continued on page 394)

(continued from page 393)

```
                procedure do_read is
                begin
                    d <= To_X01( mem(word_address) );
                end do_read;

            begin
                -- initialize outputs
                d <= disabled_dlx_word;
                ready <= '0';

                -- process memory cycles
                loop
                    -- wait for a command, valid on leading edge of phi2
                    wait on phi2 until rising_edge(phi2) and To_bit(mem_enable) = '1';

                    -- decode address and perform command if selected
                    byte_address := bv_to_natural(To_bitvector(a));
                    write_access := To_bit(write_enable) = '1';
                    if byte_address <= high_address then
                        word_address := byte_address / 4;
                        if write_access then -- write cycle
                            do_write;
                            wait for Tac_first; -- write access time, 1st cycle
                        else -- read cycle
                            wait for Tac_first; -- read access time, 1st cycle
                            do_read;
                        end if;
                        -- ready synchronous with phi2
                        wait until rising_edge(phi2);
                        ready <= '1' after Tpd_clk_out;
                        wait until falling_edge(phi2);
                        ready <= '0' after Tpd_clk_out;
                        -- do subsequent cycles in burst
                        while To_bit(burst) = '1' loop
                            word_address := (word_address + 1) mod (mem_size / 4);
                            wait until rising_edge(phi2);
                            if write_access then -- write cycle
                                do_write;
                                wait for Tac_burst;  -- write access time, burst cycle
                            else -- read cycle
                                wait for Tac_burst;  -- read access time, burst cycle
                                do_read;
                            end if;
                            -- ready synchronous with phi2
                            wait until rising_edge(phi2);
                            ready <= '1' after Tpd_clk_out;
                            wait until falling_edge(phi2);
                            ready <= '0' after Tpd_clk_out;
                        end loop;
                        if not write_access then  -- was read
                            d <= disabled_dlx_word after Tpd_clk_out;
                        end if;
```

```
                        end if;
                     end loop;
                 end process mem_behavior;
            end architecture preloaded;
```

A behavioral architecture body for the memory, preloaded with a small test program.

The body of the process begins by initializing the memory output ports and then enters a loop to handle memory access cycles. The start of a cycle is indicated by the **mem_enable** port being '1' on a rising edge of **phi2**. When this is detected, the process converts the byte address input to a numeric value and determines whether the requested access is a read or write. If the address is within the memory address bounds, the memory proceeds with the access cycle. It divides the byte address by four to derive the word address to index the memory array. The input port **write_enable** indicates whether the access is a write or a read. In the case of a write, the process calls the procedure **do_write** to store the data. Note that the statements in the procedure simply implement the behavior of the memory in writing the data. They do not implement the timing. Since they are performed within a simulation cycle, no simulation time passes during their execution. Instead, the process models the timing of a write access by waiting for the access time (**Tac_first**) after the write has been performed. The process performs a read access similarly. It waits for the access time in order to model the timing behavior, then calls **do_read** to fetch the required data. In both cases, when the access is complete, the process signals that it is ready by setting the **ready** port to '1' after the next rising edge of **phi2**, then setting it back to '0' after the falling edge of **phi2**. This completes the first part of the memory access cycle.

The **burst** input port to the memory indicates whether the access cycle is to continue with the next word. If it is '1', the process increments the word address, wrapping around to zero if the address overflows the high address bound. It then repeats the operations required to implement a read or write access, but this time it waits for **Tac_burst** to model the access time. The process continues accessing successive words until **burst** changes to '0'. After the last word access, if the memory access was a read, the process disables the data output bus by assigning the value **disabled_dlx_word** to the port. This completes the entire cycle.

The procedure **do_write**, shown in the declarative part of the process, performs the operations required to store data in the memory. The word address is used as an index to determine which memory array element to update. Depending on the size of the data to be written, the procedure copies a byte, halfword or word from the data bus into the element. In the case of a word, it simply copies the entire data word into the element. In the case of a halfword, address bit **a(1)** is used to determine whether to copy the left or right halfword from the bus into the corresponding halfword of the element. In the case of a byte, the two least-significant address bits are used to determine which byte to copy. The procedure **do_read** performs the operations required to read data from the memory array. It is much simpler than **do_write**, since it does not need to deal with reading different-sized data in different ways. It simply reads the entire word, places it on the data bus port and lets the CPU select how much of the data it needs.

The Test-Bench Architecture Body and Configuration

Now that we have described the clock generator and memory, we can use them to construct the test bench for the CPU. The test-bench entity declaration and architecture body are shown in Figure 15-32. The architecture body includes component declarations corresponding to the clock generator, memory and DLX CPU entities previously described, and an instance of each of the components. Note that we do not include the generic constants in these component declarations. Instead, we use a separate configuration declaration to bind the entities to instances of the components and to fill in values for the generic constants. This is shown in Figure 15-33. For the clock generator, we specify a pulse width of 8 ns and a pulse separation of 2 ns. This corresponds to a clock period of 20 ns, or a frequency of 50 MHz. We specify a memory size of 64 Kbytes and access times of 95 ns and 35 ns for the first and subsequent accesses in a burst. The clock-to-output propagation delay for both the memory and the CPU is 2 ns. We set the **debug** generic constant of the CPU to trace_each_step so that we can trace its operation in detail.

FIGURE 15-32

```
entity dlx_test is
end entity dlx_test;

— — — — — — — — — — — — — — — — — — — — — — — — — — — — —

library ieee;  use ieee.std_logic_1164.all;

architecture bench of dlx_test is
    use work.dlx_types.all;
    component clock_gen is
        port ( phi1, phi2 : out std_logic;  reset : out std_logic );
    end component clock_gen;
    component memory is
        port ( phi1, phi2 : in std_logic;
               a : in dlx_address;
               d : inout dlx_word;
               width : in dlx_mem_width;
               write_enable : in std_logic;
               burst : in std_logic := '0';
               mem_enable : in std_logic;
               ready : out std_logic );
    end component memory;
    component dlx is
        port ( phi1, phi2 : in std_logic;  reset : in std_logic;
               halt : out std_logic;
               a : out dlx_address;
               d : inout dlx_word;
               width : out dlx_mem_width;
               write_enable : out std_logic;
               ifetch : out std_logic;
               mem_enable : out std_logic;
               ready : in std_logic );
    end component dlx;
```

```
        signal phi1, phi2, reset : std_logic;
        signal a : dlx_address;
        signal d : dlx_word;
        signal halt : std_logic;
        signal width : dlx_mem_width;
        signal write_enable, mem_enable, ifetch, ready : std_logic;
begin
    cg : component clock_gen
        port map ( phi1 => phi1, phi2 => phi2, reset => reset );

    mem : component memory
        port map ( phi1 => phi1, phi2 => phi2,
                   a => a, d => d,
                   width => width, write_enable => write_enable, burst => open,
                   mem_enable => mem_enable, ready => ready );

    proc : component dlx
        port map ( phi1 => phi1, phi2 => phi2, reset => reset, halt => halt,
                   a => a, d => d,
                   width => width, write_enable => write_enable, ifetch => ifetch,
                   mem_enable => mem_enable, ready => ready );

end architecture bench;
```

An entity declaration and architecture body for the DLX test bench.

FIGURE 15-33

```
configuration dlx_test_behavior of dlx_test is
    for bench
        for cg : clock_gen
            use entity work.clock_gen(behavior)
                generic map ( Tpw => 8 ns, Tps => 2 ns );
        end for;

        for mem : memory
            use entity work.memory(preloaded)
                generic map ( mem_size => 65536,
                              Tac_first => 95 ns, Tac_burst => 35 ns,
                              Tpd_clk_out => 2 ns );
        end for;

        for proc : dlx
            use entity work.dlx(behavior)
                generic map ( Tpd_clk_out => 2 ns, debug => trace_each_step );
        end for;

    end for;
end configuration dlx_test_behavior;
```

A configuration declaration for the test bench, using the behavioral architecture of the CPU and the preloaded architecture of the memory.

In order to execute the test bench, we need to analyze each of the design units described so far and then invoke our simulator, specifying the configuration declaration as the unit to simulate. We then use the facilities of the simulator to step through the model and to examine the test-bench signals to verify that the machine language program in the memory is correctly executed by the CPU. We do not describe the process in detail, as different simulators provide different commands and facilities for executing the model. When the model is executed using a simulator, a sequence of instruction fetches from the memory, interspersed with ten memory write operations to the address X"00000018", should be observed. The data written should be X"00000000" for the first write, X"00000001" for the next write, and so on, up to X"00000009" for the last write. Shortly after the last write, the CPU should change the halt signal to '1' and stop fetching instructions from memory. The simulation should continue, as the clock generator continues to generate clock pulses. However, there should be no further activity generated by the CPU.

Figure 15-34 shows a sample of the trace output generated by the report statements in the interpreter process when we ran the model on our simulator. Each message includes the string from the report statement, the simulation time at which the message was issued and the name of the component instance responsible for the message. We requested that the simulator continue execution until the halt signal changed to '1'. At that time, the simulator halted execution.

15.4 A Register-Transfer-Level Model

We now turn our attention to the next level of refinement of our DLX CPU model: a register-transfer-level description. At this level, the CPU is composed of registers, buses, multiplexers, an ALU and a sequential control section. Figure 15-35 shows the register-transfer-level organization of the CPU upon which we base our VHDL model. It includes a register file for the general-purpose registers, individual registers for temporary storage (Temp), the Interrupt Address Register (IAR), the Program Counter (PC), the Memory Address Register (MAR), the Memory Data Register (MDR) and the Instruction Register (IR). These all correspond to variables defined in the behavioral architecture of the CPU. The register-transfer-level CPU also contains a number of additional registers. The A and B registers are used to store values read from the register file, and the C register stores a result to be written into the register file. The S1 and S2 registers store the two source operands to be operated upon by the arithmetic and logic unit (ALU). The multiplexer at the MDR input allows the MDR to be loaded from the destination bus or the external data bus. The other multiplexer allows the memory address to be selected from the PC value or the MAR value. Finally, the two modules labeled X1 and X2 are extension modules, which extend the 16-bit or 26-bit immediate field of an instruction to 32 bits for processing by the ALU. This data path interprets DLX instructions in a sequence of steps, many of which involve ALU operations. These steps each take one complete clock cycle. During the first phase of the clock, the source operands are transferred via the S1 and S2 buses to the S1 and S2 registers, and the ALU operation commences. During the second phase, the result from the ALU is transferred via the destination bus to the destination register. This clocking scheme allows use of flow-through latches for the registers without the possibility of races aris-

FIGURE 15-34

```
** Note: fetching instruction
   Time: 68 ns   Iteration: 0  Instance:/proc
** Note: ADDI      R2, R0, 0
   Time: 188 ns   Iteration: 0  Instance:/proc
** Note: incrementing PC
   Time: 190 ns   Iteration: 1  Instance:/proc
** Note: decoding instruction
   Time: 190 ns   Iteration: 1  Instance:/proc
** Note: executing instruction
   Time: 190 ns   Iteration: 1  Instance:/proc
** Note: end of execution
   Time: 190 ns   Iteration: 1  Instance:/proc
** Note: fetching instruction
   Time: 190 ns   Iteration: 1  Instance:/proc
** Note: SW        24(R0)R2
   Time: 328 ns   Iteration: 0  Instance:/proc
...
** Note: fetching instruction
   Time: 6990 ns  Iteration: 1  Instance:/proc
** Note: TRAP      0
   Time: 7128 ns  Iteration: 0  Instance:/proc
** Note: incrementing PC
   Time: 7130 ns  Iteration: 1  Instance:/proc
** Note: decoding instruction
   Time: 7130 ns  Iteration: 1  Instance:/proc
** Note: executing instruction
   Time: 7130 ns  Iteration: 1  Instance:/proc
** Note: TRAP instruction encountered, execution halted
   Time: 7130 ns  Iteration: 1  Instance:/proc
Halt requested
```

Sample output from the test bench, generated by the report statements in the CPU model.

ing. In the final implementation, the second phase of the clock cycle can be used to pre-charge the source operand buses.

We develop our VHDL description of this implementation by first describing the data path entities and their behavioral architecture bodies. We then use them to construct the register-transfer-level architecture body of the CPU. Finally, we describe the behavioral architecture of the controller that sequences data path operations.

The Arithmetic and Logic Unit

The ALU in the CPU data path performs the operations on data needed to implement arithmetic and logical instructions. It is also used to perform address arithmetic and to align data for load and store instructions. The particular function to be performed by the ALU at any time is determined by the controller. Hence, the ALU must have an input port to select the function. We need to describe the type and allowable values for this port in a separate package, since the type and values need to be accessible both

FIGURE 15-35

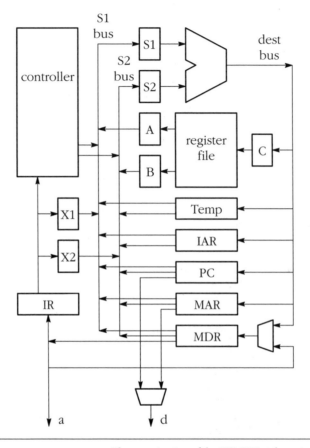

The organization of the DLX CPU at the register-transfer level.

in the ALU description and in the controller description. The package is shown in Figure 15-36. The type **alu_func** is a standard-logic vector, and the constants following it represent the encoded values for the functions performed by the ALU. The last two constants represent identity operations on each of the two ALU inputs.

The entity declaration for the ALU is shown in Figure 15-37. It has a generic constant, **Tpd**, to specify the propagation delay from input to output. The two ports **s1** and **s2** are the data inputs, and **result** is the data output. The **func** port selects the function to be performed, and the **zero, negative** and **overflow** ports are status outputs providing information about the result value.

Figure 15-38 shows the behavioral architecture body of the ALU. It contains a single process, **alu_op**, that is sensitive to changes on any of the inputs. When an input changes, the process first converts the two operands to bit-vector form using the conversion function **To_bitvector** from the standard-logic package. The local variable **temp_overflow**, representing the overflow status, is initialized to false. It is only modified by arithmetic functions, so it remains false for other functions. The process then uses the function code as the selector expression in a case statement to select the func-

FIGURE 15-36

```
library ieee;  use ieee.std_logic_1164.all;

package alu_types is

    subtype alu_func is std_logic_vector(3 downto 0);

    constant alu_add :      alu_func := "0000";
    constant alu_addu :     alu_func := "0001";
    constant alu_sub :      alu_func := "0010";
    constant alu_subu :     alu_func := "0011";
    constant alu_and :      alu_func := "0100";
    constant alu_or :       alu_func := "0101";
    constant alu_xor :      alu_func := "0110";
    constant alu_sll :      alu_func := "1000";
    constant alu_srl :      alu_func := "1001";
    constant alu_sra :      alu_func := "1010";
    constant alu_pass_s1 :alu_func := "1100";
    constant alu_pass_s2 :alu_func := "1101";

end package alu_types;
```

The package that defines the ALU function code type and allowed values.

FIGURE 15-37

```
library ieee;  use ieee.std_logic_1164.all;

use work.dlx_types.all, work.alu_types.all;

entity alu is
    generic ( Tpd : delay_length );
    port ( s1 : in dlx_word;
            s2 : in dlx_word;
            result : out dlx_word;
            func : in alu_func;
            zero, negative, overflow : out std_logic );
end entity alu;
```

An entity declaration for the ALU.

FIGURE 15-38

```
library bv_utilities;

architecture behavior of alu is
begin

    alu_op: process ( s1, s2, func ) is

        use bv_utilities.bv_arithmetic.all;

        variable bv_s1, bv_s2 : dlx_bv_word;
        variable temp_result : dlx_bv_word;
        variable temp_overflow : boolean;
```

(continued on page 402)

(continued from page 401)

```
            type boolean_to_X01_table is array (boolean) of X01;
            constant boolean_to_X01 : boolean_to_X01_table := ( '0', '1' );
        begin
            bv_s1 := To_bitvector(s1);
            bv_s2 := To_bitvector(s2);
            temp_overflow := false;
            case func is
                when alu_pass_s1 =>
                    temp_result := bv_s1;
                when alu_pass_s2 =>
                    temp_result := bv_s2;
                when alu_and =>
                    temp_result := bv_s1 and bv_s2;
                when alu_or =>
                    temp_result := bv_s1 or bv_s2;
                when alu_xor =>
                    temp_result := bv_s1 xor bv_s2;
                when alu_sll =>
                    temp_result := bv_s1 sll bv_to_natural(bv_s2(27 to 31));
                when alu_srl =>
                    temp_result := bv_s1 srl bv_to_natural(bv_s2(27 to 31));
                when alu_sra =>
                    temp_result := bv_s1 sra bv_to_natural(bv_s2(27 to 31));
                when alu_add =>
                    bv_add(bv_s1, bv_s2, temp_result, temp_overflow);
                when alu_addu =>
                    bv_addu(bv_s1, bv_s2, temp_result, temp_overflow);
                when alu_sub =>
                    bv_sub(bv_s1, bv_s2, temp_result, temp_overflow);
                when alu_subu =>
                    bv_subu(bv_s1, bv_s2, temp_result, temp_overflow);
                when others =>
                    report "illegal function code" severity error;
                    temp_result := X"0000_0000";
            end case;
            result <= To_X01(temp_result) after Tpd;
            zero <= boolean_to_X01(temp_result = X"0000_0000") after Tpd;
            negative <= To_X01(temp_result(0)) after Tpd;
            overflow <= boolean_to_X01(temp_overflow) after Tpd;
        end process alu_op;
    end architecture behavior;
```

A behavioral architecture body of the ALU.

tion to perform. For the two identity functions, the result is simply a copy of the appropriate operand. For the logical and shift functions, the predefined VHDL bit-vector
operators are used to determine the result. For the arithmetic function, the operations
provided by the bit-vector arithmetic package are used to determine the result and to

update the local overflow status variable. Note that there are a number of unused codes in the **alu_func** type. If one of these codes is selected, the process issues an error message and produces a zero result. After determining the result in bit-vector form, the process converts it to a standard-logic word for assignment to the ALU output. It also generates the status output values. The **zero** flag is set if the result is a word of all '0' bits and the **negative** flag is set if the leftmost bit of the result (the sign bit) is '1'. The **overflow** flag is determined by converting the Boolean overflow variable to a standard-logic value using a locally declared lookup table **boolean_to_X01**. We need to declare this table locally, since the standard-logic package does not provide a conversion function from **boolean** to **std_ulogic**.

The Registers

The CPU data path makes use of a number of different kinds of registers. The simplest of these is a flow-through latch. The entity declaration and behavioral architecture body are shown in Figure 15-39. The generic constant specifies the propagation delay between a change on either the data input port **d** or the control input **latch_en** and a resulting change on the data output port **q**. The architecture body consists of a concurrent signal assignment statement. It is sensitive to **d** and **latch_en**, since they are the signals included in the waveform and the condition expression. When **latch_en** is '1', any changes on **d** are copied to the output. When **latch_en** changes to '0', further changes on **d** are ignored, and the output maintains its previous value.

FIGURE 15-39

```
library ieee;  use ieee.std_logic_1164.all;
use work.dlx_types.all;
entity latch is
    generic ( Tpd : delay_length );
    port ( d : in dlx_word;
           q : out dlx_word;
           latch_en : in std_logic );
end entity latch;

------------------------------------------------------------

architecture behavior of latch is
begin
    q <= d after Tpd when To_bit(latch_en) = '1';
end architecture behavior;
```

An entity declaration and behavioral architecture body for the flow-through latch.

A number of the registers in the CPU data path have one or more outputs that can be disabled from the bus to which they are connected. We use the type **dlx_word** to implement the buses, so the registers have output ports of this type. Rather than writing different entities for each of the registers with differing numbers of outputs, we write one generic multiple-output register. The entity declaration and architecture body are shown in Figure 15-40. The generic constant **num_outputs** specifies how many output word ports the register is to have. **Tpd** is the propagation delay from an input change to the resulting output change. The first port, d, is the data input word. The port q is an array of output data words, indexed from 1 to the value of num_outputs. Each element of this port is connected to a different bus. The latch_en port controls storage of data in the register, and the out_en port controls whether the data outputs are enabled or disabled. There is an element of out_en corresponding to each element of q.

FIGURE 15-40

```
library ieee;  use ieee.std_logic_1164.all;

use work.dlx_types.all;

entity reg_multiple_out is
    generic ( num_outputs : positive;
                Tpd : delay_length );
    port ( d : in dlx_word;
            q : out dlx_word_array(1 to num_outputs);
            latch_en : in std_logic;
            out_en : in std_logic_vector(1 to num_outputs) );
end entity reg_multiple_out;

-------------------------------------------------------------

architecture behavior of reg_multiple_out is
begin
    reg: process ( d, latch_en, out_en ) is
        variable latched_value : dlx_word;
    begin
        if To_bit(latch_en) = '1' then
            latched_value := To_X01(d);
        end if;
        for index in out_en'range loop
            if To_bit(out_en(index)) = '1' then
                q(index) <= latched_value after Tpd;
            else
                q(index) <= disabled_dlx_word after Tpd;
            end if;
        end loop;
    end process reg;
end architecture behavior;
```

An entity declaration and architecture body for a generic multiple-output register.

The behavior of the register is implemented by the process reg, with a local variable latched_value to represent the storage for the data word. The process is sensitive to changes on any of its inputs. When any input changes, if the control input is '1', the current data input is stored in the local variable, with strength information stripped. Then, for each element of the output port q, if the corresponding element of the output-enable control vector is '1', the output port element is driven with the stored value. If the control element is not '1', the output port element is driven with the value disabled_dlx_word.

Two of the registers in the CPU data path, the MAR and the PC, have two outputs that may be disabled and a third that is permanently active. We could implement these registers with the **reg_multiple_out** entity, with the control input for the third output permanently set to '1'. However, this would imply additional hardware (the buffers for the third port) that is not actually needed, since the buffers would be permanently enabled. Instead, we use additional entities for the MAR and PC, based on the **reg_multiple_out** entity.

Figure 15-41 shows the entity declaration and architecture body for the first of these registers to be used for the MAR. The entity has a number of outputs determined by the generic constant **num_outputs**, plus an additional output q0 that is permanently active. The other input and output ports serve the same purpose as those of the **reg_multiple_out** entity. The architecture body is identical to that of **reg_multiple_out**, except for the addition of a signal assignment statement. Whenever the stored data word is updated, the new value is assigned to the permanently enabled port q0.

FIGURE 15-41 _____

```
library ieee;  use ieee.std_logic_1164.all;
use work.dlx_types.all;
entity reg_multiple_plus_one_out is
    generic ( num_outputs : positive;  Tpd : delay_length );
    port ( d : in dlx_word;
           q0 : out dlx_word;  q : out dlx_word_array(1 to num_outputs);
           latch_en : in std_logic;
           out_en : in std_logic_vector(1 to num_outputs) );
end entity reg_multiple_plus_one_out;

_____

architecture behavior of reg_multiple_plus_one_out is
begin
    reg: process ( d, latch_en, out_en ) is
        variable latched_value : dlx_word;
    begin
        if To_bit(latch_en) = '1' then
            latched_value := To_X01(d);
        end if;
        q0 <= latched_value after Tpd;
        for index in out_en'range loop
            if To_bit(out_en(index)) = '1' then
                q(index) <= latched_value after Tpd;
            else
                q(index) <= disabled_dlx_word after Tpd;
            end if;
        end loop;
    end process reg;
end architecture behavior;
```

An entity declaration and architecture body for a register with multiple outputs, plus an additional output that is permanently enabled.

The second register, shown in Figure 15-42, has an additional input port to reset the register to zero. This register is used for the PC, which must be reset to zero when the CPU is reset. The architecture body is based on that of the reg_multiple_plus_one_out entity. The process is sensitive to all its input signals, including reset. When resumed, if reset is '1', the process clears the variable representing the stored word to zero.

FIGURE 15-42

```
library ieee;  use ieee.std_logic_1164.all;

use work.dlx_types.all;

entity reg_multiple_plus_one_out_reset is
    generic ( num_outputs : positive;  Tpd : delay_length );
    port ( d : in dlx_word;
           q0 : out dlx_word;  q : out dlx_word_array(1 to num_outputs);
           latch_en : in std_logic;
           out_en : in std_logic_vector(1 to num_outputs);
           reset : in std_logic );
end entity reg_multiple_plus_one_out_reset;

------------------------------------------------------------

architecture behavior of reg_multiple_plus_one_out_reset is
begin
    reg: process ( d, latch_en, out_en, reset ) is
        variable latched_value : dlx_word;
    begin
        if To_bit(reset) = '1' then
            latched_value := X"0000_0000";
        elsif To_bit(latch_en) = '1' then
            latched_value := To_X01(d);
        end if;
        q0 <= latched_value after Tpd;
        for index in out_en'range loop
            if To_bit(out_en(index)) = '1' then
                q(index) <= latched_value after Tpd;
            else
                q(index) <= disabled_dlx_word after Tpd;
            end if;
        end loop;
    end process reg;
end architecture behavior;
```

An entity declaration and architecture body for a multiple output register with reset.

The Register File

The data path diagram shown in Figure 15-35 includes a register file with two read ports and one write port. The register file must have address inputs for each of these ports. The addresses are determined by the controller, based on the instruction in the

IR. At the register-transfer level of modeling, we represent the register addresses as standard-logic vectors. The package declaration shown at the top of Figure 15-43 defines a subtype for register file addresses. The subtype is a standard-logic vector, with the same index range as the bit-vector type representing register number fields in instructions. This type, dlx_reg_addr, is imported from the dlx_instr package.

FIGURE 15-43

```
library ieee;  use ieee.std_logic_1164.all;
use work.dlx_instr.dlx_reg_addr;
package reg_file_types is
    subtype reg_file_addr is std_logic_vector(dlx_reg_addr'range);
end package reg_file_types;
```

```
library ieee;  use ieee.std_logic_1164.all;
use work.dlx_types.all, work.reg_file_types.all;
entity reg_file is
    generic ( Tac : delay_length );
    port ( a1 : in reg_file_addr;
           q1 : out dlx_word;
           a2 : in reg_file_addr;
           q2 : out dlx_word;
           a3 : in reg_file_addr;
           d3 : in dlx_word;
           write_en : in std_logic );
end entity reg_file;
```

The package declaration that defines the register file address type, and the entity declaration for the register file.

The entity declaration for the register file is shown at the bottom of Figure 15-43. The generic constant Tac represents the access time for reading a word from the register file. Ports q1 and q2 are the two read ports, and d3 is the write port. Ports a1, a2 and a3 are the corresponding register addresses, and write_en is a control input indicating when the write port should store a value into the register file.

Figure 15-44 shows a behavioral architecture body for the register file. The process reg contains an array of words to implement the register file storage. It is indexed using the reg_index type, but has a lower index bound of one instead of zero. This is because register r0 in the DLX CPU does not actually represent a storage location. When read, it returns the value zero, and when written, the data is discarded. The constant all_zeros represents the value returned when r0 is read. The process is sensitive to changes on any of the inputs. It first tests whether write_en is '1', and if so, performs a write access. By performing a write before a read, the process ensures that a concurrent read of the same register returns the written data word, not the previously stored data word. Thus each location in the file acts as a flow-through register. The process performs the write by converting the address value a3 to numeric form. If the value is not zero, it is used as an index to select an element of the storage array. This element is updated

FIGURE 15-44

```
library bv_utilities;
architecture behavior of reg_file is
begin
    reg: process ( a1, a2, a3, d3, write_en ) is
        use work.dlx_instr.reg_index,
            bv_utilities.bv_arithmetic.bv_to_natural;
        constant all_zeros : dlx_word := X"0000_0000";
        type register_array is array (reg_index range 1 to 31) of dlx_word;
        variable register_file : register_array;
        variable reg_index1, reg_index2, reg_index3 : reg_index;
    begin
        -- do write first if enabled
        if To_bit(write_en) = '1' then
            reg_index3 := bv_to_natural(To_bitvector(a3));
            if reg_index3 /= 0 then
                register_file(reg_index3) := To_X01(d3);
            end if;
        end if;
        -- read port 1
        reg_index1 := bv_to_natural(To_bitvector(a1));
        if reg_index1 /= 0 then
            q1 <= register_file(reg_index1) after Tac;
        else
            q1 <= all_zeros after Tac;
        end if;
        -- read port 2
        reg_index2 := bv_to_natural(To_bitvector(a2));
        if reg_index2 /= 0 then
            q2 <= register_file(reg_index2) after Tac;
        else
            q2 <= all_zeros after Tac;
        end if;
    end process reg;
end architecture behavior;
```

A behavioral architecture body for the register file.

with the value on **d3**, stripped of strength information. After performing the write, the process updates the values on the read ports **q1** and **q2**. For each of these, the address is converted to numeric form, and if it is not zero, the addressed element of the storage array is assigned to the output port after an access delay. If the address is zero, it refers to register r0, so the value **all_zeros** is assigned to the output port.

The Multiplexer

The DLX CPU data path includes two multiplexers. An entity declaration and behavioral architecture body for the required module are shown in Figure 15-45. The generic constant **Tpd** specifies the propagation delay from the select input (**sel**) or either data input (**i0** or **i1**) to the data output (**y**). The architecture body contains a selected signal assignment statement. When the select input is '0', input **i0** is transmitted to the output; when it is '1', **i1** is transmitted to the output.

FIGURE 15-45

```
library ieee;  use ieee.std_logic_1164.all;
use work.dlx_types.all;
entity mux2 is
    generic ( Tpd : delay_length );
    port ( i0, i1 : in dlx_word;
            y : out dlx_word;
            sel : in std_logic );
end mux2;
```

```
architecture behavior of mux2 is
begin
    with To_bit(sel) select
        y <= i0 after Tpd when '0',
                i1 after Tpd when '1';
end architecture behavior;
```

An entity declaration and architecture body for the two-input multiplexer.

The Extenders

The remaining data path module to be described is the extender used to extend immediate values from the IR to 32 bits. The entity declaration is shown in Figure 15-46. The generic constant **Tpd** is the propagation delay from any input to the extended output. The input port **d** is the data word containing the field to be extended, and **q** is the 32-bit output port. If the control input **immed_size_26** is '1', the rightmost 26 bits of **d** are selected for extension; otherwise the rightmost 16 bits are selected. If **immed_unsigned** is '1', the field is treated as an unsigned binary number and zero-extended. Otherwise it is treated as a two's-complement signed number and sign-extended. Finally, the input **immed_en** controls whether the extended value is used to drive the output or the output is disabled.

Figure 15-46 also shows the behavioral architecture body for the extender module. The process **extender** is sensitive to changes on any of the inputs, and when resumed, assigns a new value to the output based on the data and control input values. The output value is derived by concatenating a bit vector to the left of the selected field from the data input. The elements of this bit vector are either all '0' for zero extension

FIGURE 15-46

```
library ieee;  use ieee.std_logic_1164.all;

use work.dlx_types.all;

entity ir_extender is
    generic ( Tpd : delay_length );
    port ( d : in dlx_word;
           q : out dlx_word;
           immed_size_26 : in std_logic;
           immed_unsigned : in std_logic;
           immed_en : in std_logic );
end entity ir_extender;

_____

use work.dlx_instr.all;

architecture behavior of ir_extender is
    subtype upper_6_bits is std_logic_vector(0 to 5);
    subtype upper_16_bits is std_logic_vector(0 to 15);
begin
    extender : process ( d, immed_en, immed_size_26, immed_unsigned ) is
    begin
        if To_bit(immed_en) = '1' then
            if To_bit(immed_size_26) = '1' then  -- 26-bit immediate
                if To_bit(immed_unsigned) = '1' then
                    q <= upper_6_bits'(others => '0') & d(6 to 31) after Tpd;
                else
                    q <= upper_6_bits'(others => d(6)) & d(6 to 31) after Tpd;
                end if;
            else -- 16-bit immediate
                if To_bit(immed_unsigned) = '1' then
                    q <= upper_16_bits'(others => '0') & d(16 to 31) after Tpd;
                else
                    q <= upper_16_bits'(others => d(16)) & d(16 to 31) after Tpd;
                end if;
            end if;
        else
            q <= disabled_dlx_word after Tpd;
        end if;
    end process extender;
end architecture behavior;
```

An entity declaration and architecture body for the immediate value extender.

or all copies of the sign bit of the data field for sign extension. The subtypes **upper_6_bits** and **upper_16_bits** are used to form bit-vector aggregates of the required length for concatenation to form a 32-bit result for assignment to the output port.

The Architecture Body

Before we describe the controller module, we present the VHDL description of the CPU data path. We need to look at this first so that we can determine which control signals are required to sequence operation of the data path. Once we have determined this set, we can define the appropriate control ports for the controller entity. Our description of the data path is based on the diagram shown in Figure 15-35 on page 400. The register-transfer-level architecture is shown in Figure 15-47. The declarative part contains component declarations corresponding to each of the data path elements previously described in this section. The components do not contain generic constants for specifying timing. These are included in a separate configuration declaration. The architecture body also declares signals corresponding to the connections shown in the data path diagram as well as additional control signals. The concurrent statement part of the architecture body consists of component instantiation statements that lay out the data path. The data input and output ports are connected using the declared signals, according to the data path diagram.

The control ports of the data path component instances are connected to the declared control signals. We determine exactly which control signals are required by listing all of the control ports of the component instances. The controller component must provide an output port for each of these control signals. It must also be connected to the IR output port and have data bus outputs for providing constant values for data path operations. Furthermore, the controller must be connected to the CPU's external control input and output ports so that it can sequence memory transfers. By combining all of these requirements, we can determine the complete set of ports for the controller component, as shown in Figure 15-47. This component is instantiated in the architecture body and connected to the control signals.

FIGURE 15-47

```
library bv_utilities;
use work.alu_types.all, work.reg_file_types.all;
architecture rtl of dlx is
    component alu is
        port ( s1 : in dlx_word;  s2 : in dlx_word;
                result : out dlx_word;
                func : in alu_func;
                zero, negative, overflow : out std_logic );
    end component alu;
    component reg_file is
        port ( a1 : in reg_file_addr;
                q1 : out dlx_word;
                a2 : in reg_file_addr;
                q2 : out dlx_word;
                a3 : in reg_file_addr;
                d3 : in dlx_word;
                write_en : in std_logic );
    end component reg_file;
```

(continued on page 412)

(continued from page 411)

```
component latch is
    port ( d : in dlx_word;
           q : out dlx_word;
           latch_en : in std_logic );
end component latch;

component ir_extender is
    port ( d : in dlx_word;
           q : out dlx_word;
           immed_size_26 : in std_logic;
           immed_unsigned : in std_logic;
           immed_en : in std_logic );
end component ir_extender;

component reg_multiple_out is
    generic ( num_outputs : positive );
    port ( d : in dlx_word;
           q : out dlx_word_array(1 to num_outputs);
           latch_en : in std_logic;
           out_en : in std_logic_vector(1 to num_outputs) );
end component reg_multiple_out;

component reg_multiple_plus_one_out is
    generic ( num_outputs : positive );
    port ( d : in dlx_word;
           q0 : out dlx_word;
           q : out dlx_word_array(1 to num_outputs);
           latch_en : in std_logic;
           out_en : in std_logic_vector(1 to num_outputs) );
end component reg_multiple_plus_one_out;

component reg_multiple_plus_one_out_reset is
    generic ( num_outputs : positive );
    port ( d : in dlx_word;
           q0 : out dlx_word;
           q : out dlx_word_array(1 to num_outputs);
           latch_en : in std_logic;
           out_en : in std_logic_vector(1 to num_outputs);
           reset : in std_logic );
end component reg_multiple_plus_one_out_reset;

component mux2 is
    port ( i0, i1 : in dlx_word;
           y : out dlx_word;
           sel : in std_logic);
end component mux2;

component controller is
    port ( phi1, phi2 : in std_logic;
           reset : in std_logic;
           halt : out std_logic;
           width : out dlx_mem_width;
           write_enable : out std_logic;
           mem_enable : out std_logic;
```

```
                                ifetch : out std_logic;
                                ready : in std_logic;
                                alu_in_latch_en : out std_logic;
                                alu_function : out alu_func;
                                alu_zero, alu_negative, alu_overflow : in std_logic;
                                reg_s1_addr, reg_s2_addr, reg_dest_addr : out reg_file_addr;
                                reg_write : out std_logic;
                                c_latch_en : out std_logic;
                                a_latch_en, a_out_en : out std_logic;
                                b_latch_en, b_out_en : out std_logic;
                                temp_latch_en, temp_out_en1, temp_out_en2 : out std_logic;
                                iar_latch_en, iar_out_en1, iar_out_en2 : out std_logic;
                                pc_latch_en, pc_out_en1, pc_out_en2 : out std_logic;
                                mar_latch_en, mar_out_en1, mar_out_en2 : out std_logic;
                                mem_addr_mux_sel : out std_logic;
                                mdr_latch_en, mdr_out_en1, mdr_out_en2, mdr_out_en3 : out std_logic;
                                mdr_mux_sel : out std_logic;
                                ir_latch_en : out std_logic;
                                ir_immed1_size_26, ir_immed2_size_26 : out std_logic;
                                ir_immed1_unsigned, ir_immed2_unsigned : out std_logic;
                                ir_immed1_en, ir_immed2_en : out std_logic;
                                current_instruction : in dlx_word;
                                mem_addr : std_logic_vector(1 downto 0);
                                const1, const2 : out dlx_word );
          end component controller;

          signal s1_bus, s2_bus : dlx_word;
          signal dest_bus : dlx_word;
          signal alu_in1, alu_in2 : dlx_word;
          signal reg_file_out1, reg_file_out2, reg_file_in : dlx_word;
          signal mdr_in : dlx_word;
          signal current_instruction : dlx_word;
          signal pc_to_mem : dlx_address;
          signal mar_to_mem : dlx_address;

          signal alu_in_latch_en : std_logic;
          signal alu_function : alu_func;
          signal alu_zero, alu_negative, alu_overflow : std_logic;
          signal reg_s1_addr, reg_s2_addr, reg_dest_addr : reg_file_addr;
          signal reg_write : std_logic;
          signal a_out_en, a_latch_en : std_logic;
          signal b_out_en, b_latch_en : std_logic;
          signal c_latch_en : std_logic;
          signal temp_out_en1, temp_out_en2, temp_latch_en : std_logic;
          signal iar_out_en1, iar_out_en2, iar_latch_en : std_logic;
          signal pc_out_en1, pc_out_en2, pc_latch_en : std_logic;
          signal mar_out_en1, mar_out_en2, mar_latch_en : std_logic;
          signal mem_addr_mux_sel : std_logic;
          signal mdr_out_en1, mdr_out_en2, mdr_out_en3, mdr_latch_en : std_logic;
          signal mdr_mux_sel : std_logic;
```

(continued on page 414)

(continued from page 413)

```vhdl
        signal ir_latch_en : std_logic;
        signal ir_immed1_size_26, ir_immed2_size_26 : std_logic;
        signal ir_immed1_unsigned, ir_immed2_unsigned : std_logic;
        signal ir_immed1_en, ir_immed2_en : std_logic;
    begin
        alu_s1_reg : component latch
            port map ( d => s1_bus, q => alu_in1, latch_en => alu_in_latch_en );
        alu_s2_reg : component latch
            port map ( d => s2_bus, q => alu_in2, latch_en => alu_in_latch_en );
        the_alu : component alu
            port map ( s1 => alu_in1, s2 => alu_in2, result => dest_bus,
                        func => alu_function,
                        zero => alu_zero, negative => alu_negative,
                        overflow => alu_overflow );
        the_reg_file : component reg_file
            port map ( a1 => reg_s1_addr, q1 => reg_file_out1,
                        a2 => reg_s2_addr, q2 => reg_file_out2,
                        a3 => reg_dest_addr, d3 => reg_file_in,
                        write_en => reg_write );
        c_reg : component latch
            port map ( d => dest_bus, q => reg_file_in, latch_en => c_latch_en );
        a_reg : component reg_multiple_out
            generic map ( num_outputs => 1 )
            port map ( d => reg_file_out1, q(1) => s1_bus,
                        latch_en => a_latch_en, out_en(1) => a_out_en );
        b_reg : component reg_multiple_out
            generic map ( num_outputs => 1 )
            port map ( d => reg_file_out2, q(1) => s2_bus,
                        latch_en => b_latch_en, out_en(1) => b_out_en );
        temp_reg : component reg_multiple_out
            generic map ( num_outputs => 2 )
            port map ( d => dest_bus, q(1) => s1_bus, q(2) => s2_bus,
                        latch_en => temp_latch_en,
                        out_en(1) => temp_out_en1, out_en(2) => temp_out_en2 );
        iar_reg : component reg_multiple_out
            generic map ( num_outputs => 2 )
            port map ( d => dest_bus, q(1) => s1_bus, q(2) => s2_bus,
                        latch_en => iar_latch_en,
                        out_en(1) => iar_out_en1, out_en(2) => iar_out_en2 );
        pc_reg : component reg_multiple_plus_one_out_reset
            generic map ( num_outputs => 2 )
            port map ( d => dest_bus, q(1) => s1_bus, q(2) => s2_bus, q0 => pc_to_mem,
                        latch_en => pc_latch_en,
                        out_en(1) => pc_out_en1, out_en(2) => pc_out_en2,
                        reset => reset );
```

```
mar_reg : component reg_multiple_plus_one_out
    generic map ( num_outputs => 2 )
    port map ( d => dest_bus, q(1) => s1_bus, q(2) => s2_bus, q0 => mar_to_mem,
               latch_en => mar_latch_en,
               out_en(1) => mar_out_en1, out_en(2) => mar_out_en2 );
mem_addr_mux : component mux2
    port map ( i0 => pc_to_mem, i1 => mar_to_mem, y => a,
               sel => mem_addr_mux_sel );
mdr_reg : component reg_multiple_out
    generic map ( num_outputs => 3 )
    port map ( d => mdr_in, q(1) => s1_bus, q(2) => s2_bus, q(3) => d,
               latch_en => mdr_latch_en,
               out_en(1) => mdr_out_en1, out_en(2) => mdr_out_en2,
               out_en(3) => mdr_out_en3 );
mdr_mux : component mux2
    port map ( i0 => dest_bus, i1 => d, y => mdr_in,
               sel => mdr_mux_sel );
instr_reg : component latch
    port map ( d => d, q => current_instruction,
               latch_en => ir_latch_en );
ir_extender1 : component ir_extender
    port map ( d => current_instruction, q => s1_bus,
               immed_size_26 => ir_immed1_size_26,
               immed_unsigned => ir_immed1_unsigned,
               immed_en => ir_immed1_en );
ir_extender2 : component ir_extender
    port map ( d => current_instruction, q => s2_bus,
               immed_size_26 => ir_immed2_size_26,
               immed_unsigned => ir_immed2_unsigned,
               immed_en => ir_immed2_en );
the_controller : component controller
    port map ( phi1 => phi1, phi2 => phi2, reset => reset, halt => halt,
               width => width, write_enable => write_enable,
               mem_enable => mem_enable,
               ifetch => ifetch, ready => ready,
               alu_in_latch_en => alu_in_latch_en, alu_function => alu_function,
               alu_zero => alu_zero, alu_negative => alu_negative,
               alu_overflow => alu_overflow,
               reg_s1_addr => reg_s1_addr, reg_s2_addr => reg_s2_addr,
               reg_dest_addr => reg_dest_addr, reg_write => reg_write,
               c_latch_en => c_latch_en,
               a_latch_en => a_latch_en, a_out_en => a_out_en,
               b_latch_en => b_latch_en, b_out_en => b_out_en,
               temp_latch_en => temp_latch_en,
               temp_out_en1 => temp_out_en1, temp_out_en2 => temp_out_en2,
               iar_latch_en => iar_latch_en,
               iar_out_en1 => iar_out_en1, iar_out_en2 => iar_out_en2,
```

(continued on page 416)

(continued from page 415)

```
                    pc_latch_en => pc_latch_en,
                    pc_out_en1 => pc_out_en1, pc_out_en2 => pc_out_en2,
                    mem_addr_mux_sel => mem_addr_mux_sel,
                    mar_latch_en => mar_latch_en,
                    mar_out_en1 => mar_out_en1, mar_out_en2 => mar_out_en2,
                    mdr_mux_sel => mdr_mux_sel, mdr_latch_en => mdr_latch_en,
                    mdr_out_en1 => mdr_out_en1, mdr_out_en2 => mdr_out_en2,
                    mdr_out_en3 => mdr_out_en3,
                    ir_latch_en => ir_latch_en,
                    ir_immed1_size_26 => ir_immed1_size_26,
                    ir_immed2_size_26 => ir_immed2_size_26,
                    ir_immed1_unsigned => ir_immed1_unsigned,
                    ir_immed2_unsigned => ir_immed2_unsigned,
                    ir_immed1_en => ir_immed1_en, ir_immed2_en => ir_immed2_en,
                    current_instruction => current_instruction,
                    mem_addr => mar_to_mem(1 downto 0),
                    const1 => s1_bus, const2 => s2_bus );

end architecture rtl;
```

A register-transfer-level architecture body for the DLX CPU.

The Controller

We are now in a position to return to the controller entity and architecture body. The entity declaration is shown in Figure 15-48. It contains exactly the same set of ports as the controller component declared in the CPU architecture body. In addition, it has two generic constants to specify timing. **Tpd_clk_ctrl** specifies the delay between a clock edge and a resulting control output change. **Tpd_clk_const** specifies the delay between a clock edge and a value being enabled onto one of the constant data output ports. The third generic constant, **debug**, is used to control the detail of trace information reported by the controller as it interprets DLX instructions.

The behavioral architecture body of the controller is outlined in Figure 15-49. The behavior is implemented by the process **sequencer**. The process declares a bit-vector word to represent the current instruction in the IR. The aliases represent the field of this instruction, either in bit-vector form (for the opcode and opcode extensions) or in standard-logic vector form (for the register number fields). The variables **result_of_set_is_1** and **branch_taken** are used for the intermediate state when sequencing relational and branch instructions. The variables **disassembled_instr**, **disassembled_instr_len** and **instr_count** are used when the process reports progress information. Following these declarations are a number of local procedures that implement various stages of instruction sequencing. We do not present all of them in our discussion, as there is much repetition of similar kinds of action. Instead, we select a few for detailed examination later in this section and leave the rest as exercises for the reader.

The body of the sequencer process is very similar in structure to that of the interpreter process in the behavioral CPU model. The difference is that the control sequencer activates control signals to cause the data path components to act on data, whereas

FIGURE 15-48

```
library ieee; use ieee.std_logic_1164.all;

use work.dlx_types.all, work.alu_types.all, work.reg_file_types.all;

entity controller is
    generic ( Tpd_clk_ctrl, Tpd_clk_const : delay_length;
                debug : dlx_debug_control := none );
    port ( phi1, phi2 : in std_logic;
            reset : in std_logic;
            halt : out std_logic;
            width : out dlx_mem_width;
            write_enable : out std_logic;
            mem_enable : out std_logic;
            ifetch : out std_logic;
            ready : in std_logic;
            alu_in_latch_en : out std_logic;
            alu_function : out alu_func;
            alu_zero, alu_negative, alu_overflow : in std_logic;
            reg_s1_addr, reg_s2_addr, reg_dest_addr : out reg_file_addr;
            reg_write : out std_logic;
            c_latch_en : out std_logic;
            a_latch_en, a_out_en : out std_logic;
            b_latch_en, b_out_en : out std_logic;
            temp_latch_en, temp_out_en1, temp_out_en2 : out std_logic;
            iar_latch_en, iar_out_en1, iar_out_en2 : out std_logic;
            pc_latch_en, pc_out_en1, pc_out_en2 : out std_logic;
            mar_latch_en, mar_out_en1, mar_out_en2 : out std_logic;
            mem_addr_mux_sel : out std_logic;
            mdr_latch_en, mdr_out_en1, mdr_out_en2, mdr_out_en3 : out std_logic;
            mdr_mux_sel : out std_logic;
            ir_latch_en : out std_logic;
            ir_immed1_size_26, ir_immed2_size_26 : out std_logic;
            ir_immed1_unsigned, ir_immed2_unsigned : out std_logic;
            ir_immed1_en, ir_immed2_en : out std_logic;
            current_instruction : in dlx_word;
            mem_addr : std_logic_vector(1 downto 0);
            const1, const2 : out dlx_word );
end entity controller;
```

An entity declaration for the controller.

the interpreter in the behavioral model acted on the data itself. The sequencer process begins by initializing the CPU external control signals and the internal data path control signal. All control signals are set to a value that causes the controlled component to become quiescent. The sequencer also disables its constant data outputs and resets the instruction counter to zero. It then waits until **reset** is '0' on a falling **phi2** clock edge before proceeding. The remainder of the sequencer process implements the fetch/ execute loop. It regularly checks the **reset** signal, and if it is set to '1', the sequencer exits the loop. The process then repeats from the beginning.

FIGURE 15-49

```
library bv_utilities;
architecture behavior of controller is
begin
    sequencer : process is
        use bv_utilities.bv_arithmetic.all, work.dlx_instr.all;
        variable current_instruction_bv : dlx_bv_word;
        alias IR_opcode : dlx_opcode is current_instruction_bv(0 to 5);
        alias IR_sp_func : dlx_sp_func is current_instruction_bv(26 to 31);
        alias IR_fp_func : dlx_fp_func is current_instruction_bv(27 to 31);
        alias IR_rs1 : reg_file_addr is current_instruction(6 to 10);
        alias IR_rs2 : reg_file_addr is current_instruction(11 to 15);
        alias IR_Itype_rd : reg_file_addr is current_instruction(11 to 15);
        alias IR_Rtype_rd : reg_file_addr is current_instruction(16 to 20);
        variable result_of_set_is_1, branch_taken : boolean;
        variable disassembled_instr : string(1 to 40);
        variable disassembled_instr_len : positive;
        variable instr_count : natural := 0;
        -- local procedures: bus_instruction_fetch, bus_data_read, bus_data_write,
        -- do_set_result, do_EX_set_unsigned, do_EX_set_signed,
        -- do_EX_arith_logic, do_EX_arith_logic_immed, do_EX_link,
        -- do_EX_lhi, do_EX_branch, do_EX_load_store,          '
        -- do_MEM_jump, do_MEM_jump_reg, do_MEM_branch,
        -- do_MEM_load, do_MEM_store, do_WB,
        -- execute_op_special, execute_op_fparith
        . . .
    begin -- sequencer
        -- initialize all control signals
        if debug > none then
            report "initializing";
        end if;
        halt <= '0' after Tpd_clk_ctrl;
        width <= dlx_mem_width_word after Tpd_clk_ctrl;
        write_enable <= '0' after Tpd_clk_ctrl;
        mem_enable <= '0' after Tpd_clk_ctrl;
        ifetch <= '0' after Tpd_clk_ctrl;
        alu_in_latch_en <= '0' after Tpd_clk_ctrl;
        alu_function <= alu_add after Tpd_clk_ctrl;
        reg_s1_addr <= B"00000" after Tpd_clk_ctrl;
        reg_s2_addr <= B"00000" after Tpd_clk_ctrl;
        reg_dest_addr <= B"00000" after Tpd_clk_ctrl;
        reg_write <= '0' after Tpd_clk_ctrl;
        c_latch_en <= '0' after Tpd_clk_ctrl;
        a_latch_en <= '0' after Tpd_clk_ctrl;
        a_out_en <= '0' after Tpd_clk_ctrl;
        b_latch_en <= '0' after Tpd_clk_ctrl;
```

```
            b_out_en <= '0' after Tpd_clk_ctrl;
            temp_latch_en <= '0' after Tpd_clk_ctrl;
            temp_out_en1 <= '0' after Tpd_clk_ctrl;
            temp_out_en2 <= '0' after Tpd_clk_ctrl;
            iar_latch_en <= '0' after Tpd_clk_ctrl;
            iar_out_en1 <= '0' after Tpd_clk_ctrl;
            iar_out_en2 <= '0' after Tpd_clk_ctrl;
            pc_latch_en <= '0' after Tpd_clk_ctrl;
            pc_out_en1 <= '0' after Tpd_clk_ctrl;
            pc_out_en2 <= '0' after Tpd_clk_ctrl;
            mar_latch_en <= '0' after Tpd_clk_ctrl;
            mar_out_en1 <= '0' after Tpd_clk_ctrl;
            mar_out_en2 <= '0' after Tpd_clk_ctrl;
            mem_addr_mux_sel <= '0' after Tpd_clk_ctrl;
            mdr_latch_en <= '0' after Tpd_clk_ctrl;
            mdr_out_en1 <= '0' after Tpd_clk_ctrl;
            mdr_out_en2 <= '0' after Tpd_clk_ctrl;
            mdr_out_en3 <= '0' after Tpd_clk_ctrl;
            mdr_mux_sel <= '0' after Tpd_clk_ctrl;
            ir_latch_en <= '0' after Tpd_clk_ctrl;
            ir_immed1_size_26 <= '0' after Tpd_clk_ctrl;
            ir_immed2_size_26 <= '0' after Tpd_clk_ctrl;
            ir_immed1_unsigned <= '0' after Tpd_clk_ctrl;
            ir_immed2_unsigned <= '0' after Tpd_clk_ctrl;
            ir_immed1_en <= '0' after Tpd_clk_ctrl;
            ir_immed2_en <= '0' after Tpd_clk_ctrl;
            const1 <= disabled_dlx_word after Tpd_clk_const;
            const2 <= disabled_dlx_word after Tpd_clk_const;

        instr_count := 0;

        wait on phi2 until falling_edge(phi2) and To_bit(reset) = '0';

        -- control loop

        loop
            exit when To_bit(reset) = '1';

            -- fetch next instruction (IF)

            wait until rising_edge(phi1);

            instr_count := instr_count + 1;
            if debug = msg_every_100_instructions
                    and instr_count mod 100 = 0 then
                report "instruction count = " & natural'image(instr_count);
            end if;

            if debug >= msg_each_instruction then
                report "fetching instruction";
            end if;

            bus_instruction_fetch;
            exit when To_bit(reset) = '1';
            current_instruction_bv := To_bitvector(current_instruction);
```

(continued on page 420)

(continued from page 419)

```
if debug >= trace_each_instruction then
    disassemble ( current_instruction_bv,
                    disassembled_instr, disassembled_instr_len);
        report disassembled_instr(1 to disassembled_instr_len);
end if;

-- instruction decode, source register read and PC increment (ID)
wait until rising_edge(phi1);

if debug = trace_each_step then
    report "decode, source register read and PC increment";
end if;

reg_s1_addr <= IR_rs1 after Tpd_clk_ctrl;
reg_s2_addr <= IR_rs2 after Tpd_clk_ctrl;
a_latch_en <= '1' after Tpd_clk_ctrl;
b_latch_en <= '1' after Tpd_clk_ctrl;

pc_out_en1 <= '1' after Tpd_clk_ctrl;
const2 <= X"0000_0004" after Tpd_clk_const;
alu_in_latch_en <= '1' after Tpd_clk_ctrl;
alu_function <= alu_addu after Tpd_clk_ctrl;

wait until falling_edge(phi1);
a_latch_en <= '0' after Tpd_clk_ctrl;
b_latch_en <= '0' after Tpd_clk_ctrl;
alu_in_latch_en <= '0' after Tpd_clk_ctrl;
pc_out_en1 <= '0' after Tpd_clk_ctrl;
const2 <= disabled_dlx_word after Tpd_clk_const;

wait until rising_edge(phi2);
pc_latch_en <= '1' after Tpd_clk_ctrl;

wait until falling_edge(phi2);
pc_latch_en <= '0' after Tpd_clk_ctrl;

-- execute instruction, (EX, MEM, WB)

if debug = trace_each_step then
    report "execute";
end if;

case IR_opcode is
    when op_special =>
        execute_op_special;
    when op_fparith =>
        execute_op_fparith;
    when op_j =>
        do_MEM_jump;
    when op_jal =>
        do_EX_link;
        do_MEM_jump;
        do_WB(To_X01(natural_to_bv(link_reg, 5)));
    when op_jr =>
        do_MEM_jump_reg;
```

```
        when op_jalr =>
            do_EX_link;
            do_MEM_jump_reg;
            do_WB(To_X01(natural_to_bv(link_reg, 5)));
        when op_beqz | op_bnez =>
            do_EX_branch;
            if branch_taken then
                do_MEM_branch;
            end if;
        when op_addi | op_subi | op_addui | op_subui
                | op_slli | op_srli | op_srai
                | op_andi | op_ori | op_xori =>
            do_EX_arith_logic_immed;
            do_WB(IR_Itype_rd);
        when op_lhi =>
            do_EX_lhi;
            do_WB(IR_Itype_rd);
        when op_sequi | op_sneui | op_sltui
                | op_sgtui | op_sleui | op_sgeui =>
            do_EX_set_unsigned(immed => true);
            do_WB(IR_Itype_rd);
        when op_seqi | op_snei | op_slti
                | op_sgti | op_slei | op_sgei =>
            do_EX_set_signed(immed => true);
            do_WB(IR_Itype_rd);
        when op_trap =>
            report "TRAP instruction encountered, execution halted"
                severity note;
            wait until rising_edge(phi1);
            halt <= '1' after Tpd_clk_ctrl;
            wait until reset = '1';
            exit;
        when op_lb | op_lh | op_lw | op_lbu | op_lhu =>
            do_EX_load_store;
            do_MEM_load;
            exit when reset = '1';
            do_WB(IR_Itype_rd);
        when op_sb | op_sh | op_sw =>
            do_EX_load_store;
            do_MEM_store;
            exit when reset = '1';
        when op_rfe | op_bfpt | op_bfpf | op_lf | op_ld | op_sf | op_sd =>
            report opcode_names(bv_to_natural(IR_opcode))
                    & " instruction not implemented" severity warning;
        when others =>
            report "undefined instruction" severity error;
    end case;

    -- overflow and divide-by-zero exception handling
    -- (not implemented)
```

(continued on page 422)

(continued from page 421)

```
            if debug = trace_each_step then
                    report "end of execution";
            end if;

        end loop;
        -- loop is only exited when reset active:
        -- process interpreter starts again from beginning
    end process sequencer;

end architecture behavior;
```

An outline of the architecture body of the controller.

The first stage in the fetch/execute loop is the *instruction fetch stage*, called the *IF stage* in [7]. The sequencer waits for the beginning of the next clock cycle, marked by a rising edge of phi1, then reports an appropriate message indicating commencement of this stage. The detail of the message depends on the value of the generic constant debug. The next instruction is fetched from memory into the IR under control of the procedure bus_instruction_fetch. We return to this procedure later in this section. When the procedure returns, the current instruction word is converted to bit-vector form in the variable current_instruction_bv.

The second stage in the fetch/execute loop, called the *ID stage* in [7], involves decoding the instruction, reading the source register values from the register file and incrementing the PC. The sequencer waits for the next clock cycle before proceeding to this stage and reports a progress message if required. As in the behavioral model of the entire CPU, the behavioral model of the sequencer need not perform any action to decode the instruction. The instruction fields can be used directly by the sequencer process when they are needed. The sequencer causes the data path to read operand registers and increment the PC. During the first phase of the clock cycle, the sequencer copies the register file addresses from the instruction fields to the address signals and enables the A and B registers to store the fetched operands. It also enables the PC register output onto the S1 bus, drives the S2 bus with the constant value 4, enables the ALU input latches and sets the ALU function control signal to cause the ALU to add its operands. At the end of the first clock phase, indicated by the falling edge of phi1, the sequencer disables the A and B registers, latching the register operands for the instruction. It also disables the ALU input latches, so that they store the PC value and the value 4. The PC value and the constant 4 are disabled from the S1 and S2 buses. During the second half of the clock cycle, the PC register input is enabled, causing it to store the incremented PC value calculated by the ALU. Then, at the end of the second phase, the PC register input is disabled again. This completes the sequencing actions required for this stage of the fetch/execute loop.

The remaining stages in the loop execute the instruction. In [7], these stages are called *EX* (ALU execution and effective address calculation), *MEM* (memory operand access) and *WB* (register write back). Depending on the instruction, some or all of these stages are required. The sequencer uses a case statement to select among different alternatives, based on the instruction opcode. For each instruction or class of instructions, the sequencer calls local procedures to control the data path operations for the required stages. For the "trap" instruction, the sequencer halts execution by setting the halt output to '1' and waiting until reset is activated. It then exits the fetch/ execute loop. For unimplemented and undefined instruction opcodes, the sequencer reports a message and takes no other action. The instruction is simply ignored. The sequencer model includes a note to indicate where statements should be placed to implement exception handling. Since our model does not handle exceptions, we do not include any instructions at this point. Instead, we simply report the end of sequencing for the current instruction and start the next iteration of the fetch/execute loop.

The actions for the case statement alternatives corresponding to the op_special and op_fparith opcodes call the procedures execute_op_special and execute_op_fparith, respectively. These are shown in Figure 15-50 and Figure 15-51, respectively. They each include further case statements using the opcode extension fields to select alternatives for the instruction subclasses.

FIGURE 15-50

```
procedure execute_op_special is
begin
    case IR_sp_func is
        when sp_func_nop =>
            null;
        when sp_func_add | sp_func_addu | sp_func_sub | sp_func_subu
            | sp_func_sll | sp_func_srl | sp_func_sra
            | sp_func_and | sp_func_or | sp_func_xor =>
            do_EX_arith_logic;
            do_WB(IR_Rtype_rd);
        when sp_func_sequ | sp_func_sneu | sp_func_sltu
            | sp_func_sgtu | sp_func_sleu | sp_func_sgeu =>
            do_EX_set_unsigned(immed => false);
            do_WB(IR_Rtype_rd);
        when sp_func_seq | sp_func_sne | sp_func_slt
            | sp_func_sgt | sp_func_sle | sp_func_sge =>
            do_EX_set_signed(immed => false);
            do_WB(IR_Rtype_rd);
        when sp_func_movi2s | sp_func_movs2i
            | sp_func_movf | sp_func_movd
            | sp_func_movfp2i | sp_func_movi2fp =>
            report sp_func_names(bv_to_natural(IR_sp_func))
                    & " instruction not implemented" severity warning;
        when others =>
            report "undefined special instruction function" severity error;
    end case;
end procedure execute_op_special;
```

The procedure that sequences instructions with opcode op_special.

FIGURE 15-51

```
procedure execute_op_fparith is
begin
    case IR_fp_func is
        when fp_func_mult | fp_func_multu | fp_func_div | fp_func_divu
           | fp_func_addf | fp_func_subf | fp_func_multf | fp_func_divf
           | fp_func_addd | fp_func_subd | fp_func_multd | fp_func_divd
           | fp_func_cvtf2d | fp_func_cvtf2i | fp_func_cvtd2f
           | fp_func_cvtd2i | fp_func_cvti2f | fp_func_cvti2d
           | fp_func_eqf | fp_func_nef | fp_func_ltf | fp_func_gtf
           | fp_func_lef | fp_func_gef | fp_func_eqd | fp_func_ned
           | fp_func_ltd | fp_func_gtd | fp_func_led | fp_func_ged =>
            report fp_func_names(bv_to_natural(IR_fp_func))
                    & " instruction not implemented" severity warning;
        when others =>
            report "undefined floating point instruction function" severity error;
    end case;
end procedure execute_op_fparith;
```

The procedure that sequences instructions with opcode op_fparith.

The Instruction Fetch Control Procedure

The first of the sequencing procedures that we examine is the procedure **bus_instruc-tion_fetch**, which sequences a bus read operation to fetch an instruction. It is shown in Figure 15-52. The procedure sets the select control signal of the memory address multiplexer to enable the PC value onto the external memory address bus. It sets the external memory control signals to indicate a transfer size of one word (width set to **dlx_mem_width_word**), an instruction fetch (ifetch set to '1') and a read operation (**write_enable** set to '0'). It sets the **mem_enable** signal to '1' to start the memory operation. The procedure then waits until the second phase of the clock cycle and enables the IR input by setting **ir_latch_en** to '1'. This allows the data returned by the memory to flow into the IR. The procedure then waits for successive falling edges of **phi2**, indicating the end of successive clock cycles. If the **reset** input is '1', the procedure aborts the memory access and returns immediately. Otherwise, if the **ready** signal from memory is '1', the procedure completes the memory access. It disables the IR control signal, capturing the instruction word supplied by the memory. It also resets **mem_en-able** to '0', completing the memory operation.

Procedures to Execute Relational Instructions

The controller sequencer includes two procedures, **do_EX_set_unsigned** and **do_EX_set_signed**, that implement the EX stage of relation instructions. We discuss only the first of these here since the other is very similar. The declaration of the first procedure is shown in Figure 15-53.

FIGURE 15-52

```
procedure bus_instruction_fetch is
begin
    -- use PC as address
    mem_addr_mux_sel <= '0' after Tpd_clk_ctrl;
    -- set up memory control signals
    width <= dlx_mem_width_word after Tpd_clk_ctrl;
    ifetch <= '1' after Tpd_clk_ctrl;
    write_enable <= '0' after Tpd_clk_ctrl;
    mem_enable <= '1' after Tpd_clk_ctrl;
    -- wait until phi2, then enable IR input
    wait until rising_edge(phi2);
    ir_latch_en <= '1' after Tpd_clk_ctrl;
    -- wait until memory is ready at end of phi2
    loop
        wait until falling_edge(phi2);
        if To_bit(reset) = '1' then
        return;
        end if;
        exit when To_bit(ready) = '1';
    end loop;
    -- disable IR input and memory control signals
    ir_latch_en <= '0' after Tpd_clk_ctrl;
    mem_enable <= '0' after Tpd_clk_ctrl;
end procedure bus_instruction_fetch;
```

The procedure that fetches an instruction from memory into the IR.

FIGURE 15-53

```
procedure do_EX_set_unsigned ( immed : boolean ) is
begin
    wait until rising_edge(phi1);
    a_out_en <= '1' after Tpd_clk_ctrl;
    if immed then
        ir_immed2_size_26 <= '0' after Tpd_clk_ctrl;
        ir_immed2_unsigned <= '1' after Tpd_clk_ctrl;
        ir_immed2_en <= '1' after Tpd_clk_ctrl;
    else
        b_out_en <= '1' after Tpd_clk_ctrl;
    end if;
    alu_in_latch_en <= '1' after Tpd_clk_ctrl;
    alu_function <= alu_subu after Tpd_clk_ctrl;

    wait until falling_edge(phi1);
    alu_in_latch_en <= '0' after Tpd_clk_ctrl;
    a_out_en <= '0' after Tpd_clk_ctrl;
```

(continued on page 426)

(continued from page 425)

```
            if immed then
                ir_immed2_en <= '0' after Tpd_clk_ctrl;
            else
                b_out_en <= '0' after Tpd_clk_ctrl;
            end if;
            wait until falling_edge(phi2);
            if immed then
                case IR_opcode is
                    when op_sequi =>
                        result_of_set_is_1 := To_bit(alu_zero) = '1';
                    when op_sneui =>
                        result_of_set_is_1 := To_bit(alu_zero) /= '1';
                    when op_sltui =>
                        result_of_set_is_1 := To_bit(alu_overflow) = '1';
                    when op_sgtui =>
                        result_of_set_is_1 := To_bit(alu_overflow) /= '1'
                                            and To_bit(alu_zero) /= '1';
                    when op_sleui =>
                        result_of_set_is_1 := To_bit(alu_overflow) = '1'
                                            or To_bit(alu_zero) = '1';
                    when op_sgeui =>
                        result_of_set_is_1 := To_bit(alu_overflow) /= '1';
                    when others =>
                        null;
                end case;
            else
                case IR_sp_func is
                    when sp_func_sequ =>
                        result_of_set_is_1 := To_bit(alu_zero) = '1';
                    when sp_func_sneu =>
                        result_of_set_is_1 := To_bit(alu_zero) /= '1';
                    when sp_func_sltu =>
                        result_of_set_is_1 := To_bit(alu_overflow) = '1';
                    when sp_func_sgtu =>
                        result_of_set_is_1 := To_bit(alu_overflow) /= '1'
                                            and To_bit(alu_zero) /= '1';
                    when sp_func_sleu =>
                        result_of_set_is_1 := To_bit(alu_overflow) = '1'
                                            or To_bit(alu_zero) = '1';
                    when sp_func_sgeu =>
                        result_of_set_is_1 := To_bit(alu_overflow) /= '1';
                    when others =>
                        null;
                end case;
            end if;
            do_set_result;
end procedure do_EX_set_unsigned;
```

The procedure that controls the EX stage of unsigned relational instructions.

The parameter **immed** indicates whether the second operand of the instruction is an immediate value or a register operand. The procedure waits until the start of the next clock cycle, then enables the A register output onto the S1 bus as the first source operand. If the second operand is an immediate value, the control signals for the extender connected to the S2 bus are activated. The signal **ir_immed2_size_26** is set to '0', indicating that the 16-bit immediate field is to be extended. The signal **ir_immed2_unsigned** is set to '1', indicating that zero extension is required. The signal **ir_immed2_en** is set to '1' to enable the extended value onto the S2 bus. If the second operand is not an immediate value, the procedure enables the B register output onto the S2 bus as the second source operand. In either case, the procedure enables the ALU input latches to accept the source operands and sets the ALU function code to cause the ALU to perform the subtraction function. The intention is that the status flags from the ALU are used to determine the relationship between the source operand values. The result of the subtraction is not used. At the end of the first phase of the clock cycle, the ALU latch-enable control signals are disabled, so that the latches store the operand values. The source operands are disabled from the source buses.

Next, the procedure waits until the end of the second phase of the clock cycle, by which time the ALU status signals have stabilized. It then uses either the instruction opcode or opcode extension to determine which relation is to be tested and sets the Boolean variable **result_of_set_is_1** to the result of the test. An equality test can be determined by examining the **alu_zero** flag from the ALU. If the operands are equal, the result of the subtraction performed by the ALU is zero. Similarly, a test for unequal operands can be determined by testing whether the **alu_zero** flag is not set. If the first operand is less than the second operand, the ALU subtraction causes an overflow. Hence the remaining inequality tests are determined by examining the **alu_overflow** and **alu_zero** flags in combination.

The relational instructions must set the destination register to the binary representation of the number 1 or 0, depending on the relation test. This final action is performed by the procedure **do_set_result**, called by **do_EX_set_unsigned**. The procedure declaration is shown in Figure 15-54. The procedure waits for the next clock cycle, then drives the S2 bus with the result to be stored in the destination register. It enables the ALU input latches and sets the function code to pass the S2 value unchanged to the result bus. At the end of the first clock phase, the procedure disables the ALU input latch and removes the result value from the S2 bus. During the second phase of the clock cycle, the procedure enables the C register input to accept the result. It disables the register at the end of the phase, by which time the result is stored in the register.

The WB stage of relation instructions is implemented by the procedure **do_WB**, shown in Figure 15-55. This procedure is called by the sequencer for any instruction that writes a result to a destination register. This includes relation instructions, as well as arithmetic, logical and load instructions. The procedure has a parameter, **Rd**, that specifies the destination register number. Depending on the instruction being executed, this parameter is set to the value from the **Itype_Rd** field or the **Rtype_Rd** field of the instruction by the caller. The procedure waits for the start of the next clock cycle, then sets the register file write port address to the destination register number and sets the **reg_write** control signal to '1'. It then allows the remainder of the clock cycle for the data to be written. After the falling edge of **phi2**, the procedure resets **reg_write** back to '0', completing the write-back stage.

FIGURE 15-54

```
procedure do_set_result is
begin
    wait until rising_edge(phi1);
    if result_of_set_is_1 then
        const2 <= X"0000_0001" after Tpd_clk_const;
    else
        const2 <= X"0000_0000" after Tpd_clk_const;
    end if;
    alu_in_latch_en <= '1' after Tpd_clk_ctrl;
    alu_function <= alu_pass_s2 after Tpd_clk_ctrl;

    wait until falling_edge(phi1);
    alu_in_latch_en <= '0' after Tpd_clk_ctrl;
    const2 <= disabled_dlx_word after Tpd_clk_const;

    wait until rising_edge(phi2);
    c_latch_en <= '1' after Tpd_clk_ctrl;

    wait until falling_edge(phi2);
    c_latch_en <= '0' after Tpd_clk_ctrl;
end procedure do_set_result;
```

The procedure that sets the destination register for relational instructions.

FIGURE 15-55

```
procedure do_WB ( Rd : reg_file_addr ) is
begin
    wait until rising_edge(phi1);
    reg_dest_addr <= Rd after Tpd_clk_ctrl;
    reg_write <= '1' after Tpd_clk_ctrl;
    wait until falling_edge(phi2);
    reg_write <= '0' after Tpd_clk_ctrl;
end procedure do_WB;
```

The procedure that sequences the write-back stage of instruction sequencing.

Procedures to Execute Arithmetic and Logic Instructions

The procedure do_EX_arith_logic, shown in Figure 15-56, sequences the EX stage of the arithmetic and logic instructions that draw both source operands from registers. The procedure waits for the start of the next clock cycle, then enables the two source operands from the A and B registers onto the S1 and S2 buses. (The source operands were stored in the A and B registers during the ID stage of the fetch/execute loop.) The procedure also enables the ALU input registers. It uses the opcode extension field to select which function the ALU should perform and sets the ALU function control signal accordingly. At the end of the first clock phase, the procedure disables the ALU input registers, storing the operand values, and disables the A and B register outputs. It then enables the C register input during the second clock phase, allowing it to capture the result from the ALU. The result is written back to the destination register in the register file by a subsequent call to the procedure do_WB, described earlier.

FIGURE 15-56

```
procedure do_EX_arith_logic is
begin
    wait until rising_edge(phi1);
    a_out_en <= '1' after Tpd_clk_ctrl;
    b_out_en <= '1' after Tpd_clk_ctrl;
    alu_in_latch_en <= '1' after Tpd_clk_ctrl;
    case IR_sp_func is
        when sp_func_add =>
            alu_function <= alu_add after Tpd_clk_ctrl;
        when sp_func_addu =>
            alu_function <= alu_addu after Tpd_clk_ctrl;
        when sp_func_sub =>
            alu_function <= alu_sub after Tpd_clk_ctrl;
        when sp_func_subu =>
            alu_function <= alu_subu after Tpd_clk_ctrl;
        when sp_func_and =>
            alu_function <= alu_and after Tpd_clk_ctrl;
        when sp_func_or =>
            alu_function <= alu_or after Tpd_clk_ctrl;
        when sp_func_xor =>
            alu_function <= alu_xor after Tpd_clk_ctrl;
        when sp_func_sll =>
            alu_function <= alu_sll after Tpd_clk_ctrl;
        when sp_func_srl =>
            alu_function <= alu_srl after Tpd_clk_ctrl;
        when sp_func_sra =>
            alu_function <= alu_sra after Tpd_clk_ctrl;
        when others =>
            null;
    end case;
    wait until falling_edge(phi1);
    alu_in_latch_en <= '0' after Tpd_clk_ctrl;
    a_out_en <= '0' after Tpd_clk_ctrl;
    b_out_en <= '0' after Tpd_clk_ctrl;
    wait until rising_edge(phi2);
    c_latch_en <= '1' after Tpd_clk_ctrl;
    wait until falling_edge(phi2);
    c_latch_en <= '0' after Tpd_clk_ctrl;
end procedure do_EX_arith_logic;
```

The procedure that sequences the EX stage of arithmetic and logic instructions.

Procedures to Execute Branch Instructions

The data path operations for branch instructions are sequenced by two procedures, do_EX_branch for the EX stage and do_MEM_branch for branch completion in the MEM stage. The declaration of do_EX_branch is shown in Figure 15-57. It controls the testing of the source register to determine whether the branch is taken. After the start of the next clock cycle, the procedure enables the A register output and the ALU input register to transfer the source register value to the ALU. It sets the ALU function control signal to cause the ALU to pass the source value through unchanged. The value itself is not used as a result. Instead, the act of passing it through the ALU causes the **alu_zero** flag to be set, depending on whether the source value is zero or not. The flag is used to determine the branch outcome. At the end of the first clock phase, the A register output and the ALU register input are disabled, latching the source value in the ALU source register. By the end of the second clock phase, the value of the **alu_zero** flag has settled. The branch opcode is used to determine whether a zero or non-zero source value should cause the branch to be taken, and the Boolean variable **branch_taken** set accordingly. This variable is subsequently used by the sequencer to determine whether to proceed to the MEM stage, to complete the branch.

FIGURE 15-57

```
procedure do_EX_branch is
begin
    wait until rising_edge(phi1);
    a_out_en <= '1' after Tpd_clk_ctrl;
    alu_in_latch_en <= '1' after Tpd_clk_ctrl;
    alu_function <= alu_pass_s1 after Tpd_clk_ctrl;

    wait until falling_edge(phi1);
    alu_in_latch_en <= '0' after Tpd_clk_ctrl;
    a_out_en <= '0' after Tpd_clk_ctrl;

    wait until falling_edge(phi2);
    if IR_opcode = op_beqz then
        branch_taken := To_bit(alu_zero) = '1';
    else
        branch_taken := To_bit(alu_zero) /= '1';
    end if;
end procedure do_EX_branch;
```

The procedure that sequences the EX stage operations for branch instructions.

If the branch is taken, the sequencer calls the procedure **do_MEM_branch**, shown in Figure 15-58. The procedure controls the addition of the 16-bit displacement field from the IR to the PC. It begins this sequence by waiting until the start of the next clock cycle then enabling the PC register output and the sign-extended displacement onto the source buses. The sign extension is done by the extender component in the data path, under control of the **ir_immed2_size_26**, **ir_immed2_unsigned** and **ir_immed2_en** signals. The procedure enables the ALU input registers and sets the ALU function to cause it to add its operands. At the end of the first clock phase, the ALU input registers are disabled, latching the source values, and the PC and extender outputs are disabled. During the second clock phase, the PC register input is enabled, allowing it to store the target address calculated by the ALU. This completes the branch instruction.

Procedures to Execute Load and Store Instructions

The procedure **do_EX_load_store**, shown in Figure 15-59, sequences calculation of the effective address for load and store instructions during the EX stage. The effective address is formed by adding the 16-bit displacement from the IR to the source register

FIGURE 15-58

```
procedure do_MEM_branch is
begin
    wait until rising_edge(phi1);
    pc_out_en1 <= '1' after Tpd_clk_ctrl;
    ir_immed2_size_26 <= '0' after Tpd_clk_ctrl;
    ir_immed2_unsigned <= '0' after Tpd_clk_ctrl;
    ir_immed2_en <= '1' after Tpd_clk_ctrl;
    alu_in_latch_en <= '1' after Tpd_clk_ctrl;
    alu_function <= alu_add after Tpd_clk_ctrl;

    wait until falling_edge(phi1);
    alu_in_latch_en <= '0' after Tpd_clk_ctrl;
    pc_out_en1 <= '0' after Tpd_clk_ctrl;
    ir_immed2_en <= '0' after Tpd_clk_ctrl;

    wait until rising_edge(phi2);
    pc_latch_en <= '1' after Tpd_clk_ctrl;

    wait until falling_edge(phi2);
    pc_latch_en <= '0' after Tpd_clk_ctrl;
end procedure do_MEM_branch;
```

The procedure that sequences branch completion in the MEM stage.

FIGURE 15-59

```
procedure do_EX_load_store is
begin
    wait until rising_edge(phi1);
    a_out_en <= '1' after Tpd_clk_ctrl;
    ir_immed2_size_26 <= '0' after Tpd_clk_ctrl;
    ir_immed2_unsigned <= '0' after Tpd_clk_ctrl;
    ir_immed2_en <= '1' after Tpd_clk_ctrl;
    alu_function <= alu_add after Tpd_clk_ctrl;
    alu_in_latch_en <= '1' after Tpd_clk_ctrl;

    wait until falling_edge(phi1);
    alu_in_latch_en <= '0' after Tpd_clk_ctrl;
    a_out_en <= '0' after Tpd_clk_ctrl;
    ir_immed2_en <= '0' after Tpd_clk_ctrl;

    wait until rising_edge(phi2);
    mar_latch_en <= '1' after Tpd_clk_ctrl;

    wait until falling_edge(phi2);
    mar_latch_en <= '0' after Tpd_clk_ctrl;
end procedure do_EX_load_store;
```

The procedure that sequences effective address calculation for load and store instructions.

operand. The procedure waits for the next clock cycle, then enables the A register output onto the S1 bus and the displacement onto the S2 bus. The A register contains the source register operand previously read from the register file. The displacement is sign-extended by the X2 extender. The procedure also enables the ALU input registers and sets the ALU function control signal to cause the ALU to add its operands. At the end of the first clock phase, the procedure disables the ALU input latches, allowing them to store the operands. It also disables the A register and X2 extender outputs from the source buses. During the second clock phase, the procedure enables the MAR input, allowing it to capture the effective address calculated by the ALU.

The memory reference for a load instruction is sequenced by the procedure do_MEM_load, shown in Figure 15-60. We leave the corresponding procedure that sequences store memory references as an exercise for the reader. The do_MEM_load procedure waits for the next clock cycle, then performs a bus read operation by calling the local procedure bus_data_read. This procedure is similar to bus_instruction_fetch, described earlier in this section. The main difference is that it causes the data to be written into the MDR instead of the IR. The size of data read is determined by the parameter to bus_read_data, which in turn is determined by the instruction opcode. If the reset signal is '1' when bus_read_data returns, the do_MEM_load procedure aborts the load instruction and returns immediately.

FIGURE 15-60

```
procedure do_MEM_load is
    subtype ls_2_addr_bits is bit_vector(1 downto 0);
begin
    wait until rising_edge(phi1);
    if IR_opcode = op_lb or IR_opcode = op_lbu then
        bus_data_read(dlx_mem_width_byte);
    elsif IR_opcode = op_lh or IR_opcode = op_lhu then
        bus_data_read(dlx_mem_width_halfword);
    else
        bus_data_read(dlx_mem_width_word);
    end if;
    if To_bit(reset) = '1' then
        return;
    end if;
    if ( (IR_opcode = op_lb or IR_opcode = op_lbu)
            and To_bitvector(mem_addr) /= "00" )
        or ( (IR_opcode = op_lh or IR_opcode = op_lhu)
            and To_bit(mem_addr(1)) /= '0' ) then
        -- first step of extension: left–justify byte or halfword –> mdr
        wait until rising_edge(phi1);
        mdr_out_en1 <= '1' after Tpd_clk_ctrl;
        if IR_opcode = op_lb or IR_opcode = op_lbu then
            case ls_2_addr_bits'(To_bitvector(mem_addr)) is
                when "00" =>
                    null;
                when "01" =>
                    const2 <= X"0000_0008" after Tpd_clk_const;
                when "10" =>
                    const2 <= X"0000_0010" after Tpd_clk_const;
                when "11" =>
                    const2 <= X"0000_0018" after Tpd_clk_const;
            end case;
```

```
        else
            const2 <= X"0000_0010" after Tpd_clk_const;
        end if;
        alu_function <= alu_sll after Tpd_clk_ctrl;
        alu_in_latch_en <= '1' after Tpd_clk_ctrl;

        wait until falling_edge(phi1);
        mdr_out_en1 <= '0' after Tpd_clk_ctrl;
        const2 <= disabled_dlx_word after Tpd_clk_const;
        alu_in_latch_en <= '0' after Tpd_clk_ctrl;

        wait until rising_edge(phi2);
        mdr_mux_sel <= '0' after Tpd_clk_ctrl;
        mdr_latch_en <= '1' after Tpd_clk_ctrl;

        wait until falling_edge(phi2);
        mdr_latch_en <= '0' after Tpd_clk_ctrl;
    end if;

    wait until rising_edge(phi1);
    mdr_out_en1 <= '1' after Tpd_clk_ctrl;
    if IR_opcode = op_lb or IR_opcode = op_lbu then
        const2 <= X"0000_0018" after Tpd_clk_const;
    elsif IR_opcode = op_lh or IR_opcode = op_lhu then
        const2 <= X"0000_0010" after Tpd_clk_const;
    else
        const2 <= X"0000_0000" after Tpd_clk_const;
    end if;
    if IR_opcode = op_lbu or IR_opcode = op_lhu then
        alu_function <= alu_srl after Tpd_clk_ctrl;
    else
        alu_function <= alu_sra after Tpd_clk_ctrl;
    end if;
    alu_in_latch_en <= '1' after Tpd_clk_ctrl;

    wait until falling_edge(phi1);
    mdr_out_en1 <= '0' after Tpd_clk_ctrl;
    const2 <= disabled_dlx_word after Tpd_clk_const;
    alu_in_latch_en <= '0' after Tpd_clk_ctrl;

    wait until rising_edge(phi2);
    c_latch_en <= '1' after Tpd_clk_ctrl;

    wait until falling_edge(phi2);
    c_latch_en <= '0' after Tpd_clk_ctrl;
end procedure do_MEM_load;
```

The procedure that sequences memory references for load instructions.

If the data read from memory is less than a word in size, it is stored in the MDR in its aligned position, depending on the least-significant bit or bits of the memory address. Furthermore, the MDR contains the other unwanted bytes read from the same word of memory. The load instruction must right-justify the byte or halfword of data and zero-extend or sign-extend it to 32 bits. We can implement this requirement by first left-shifting the byte or halfword to the leftmost position in the word. For unsigned load instructions, we then perform a logical shift right to right-justify the byte or halfword and fill the left part of the word with zero bits. For signed load instructions, we perform an arithmetic shift right to right-justify the byte or halfword and fill the left part of the word with copies of the sign bit. The **do_MEM_load** procedure sequences these steps.

First, if the instruction is a byte or halfword load and the data is not already left-justified (by virtue of its address), the procedure causes the data to be shifted left. Recall that the DLX uses "big-endian" addressing. This means that the leftmost byte of a word is stored at the lowest address. Hence if the least-significant two bits of a byte address are "00", the byte is already left-justified in the word. If bit 1 of a halfword address is '0', the halfword is already left-justified. If the data read from memory is a word in size or is already left-justified, the procedure skips this step. Otherwise it waits until the start of the next clock cycle, then enables the MDR output onto the S1 bus. It also drives a constant on the S2 bus to serve as the second operand for the shift operation, indicating how many places to shift the data. For byte load instructions, the shift amount is determined by the least-significant two bits of the memory address. If these bits are "01", the byte is offset to the right by eight bits and so must be shifted left by eight places to be left-justified. Similarly, if the address bits are "10", the byte must be shifted by 16 places, and if the address bits are "11", the byte must be shifted by 24 places. In the case of halfword load instructions, shifting is only required if bit 1 of the address is '1'. The halfword must then be shifted by 16 places. The procedure enables the ALU input registers to accept the loaded data and the shift amount and sets the ALU function code to cause it to perform the left shift. At the end of the first clock phase, the procedure disables the ALU input registers, allowing them to store the operands, and removes the operands from the source buses. During the second phase of the clock cycle, the procedure sets the MDR input multiplexer to select the result from the destination bus and enables the MDR data input.

The final step for load instructions involves right-justifying the data and moving it to the C register, from which it is subsequently written into the register file. Recall that at the start of this step, the data is either a word in size or is smaller and left-justified within the MDR word. For the sake of uniformity, if the data is a whole word, we transfer it by shifting it right zero places. The procedure performs this step by waiting for the next clock cycle, then enabling the MDR output into the S1 bus. It also drives the S2 bus with a constant value indicating how many places to shift the data. Byte data must be shifted right 24 places, halfword data by 16 places and word data by zero places. The procedure sets the ALU function code depending on the instruction opcode. For unsigned loads, the ALU must perform a logical shift right, and for signed loads it must perform an arithmetic shift right. The procedure enables the ALU input registers to accept the source operands and pass them through to the ALU. At the end of the first phase, the procedure disables the ALU input registers, causing them to store the operands, and removes the operands from the source buses. During the second clock phase, the procedure enables the C register to accept the shifted result from the ALU. This completes the sequencing for the MEM stage of load instructions.

The Configuration Declaration

One final item needed to complete our register-transfer-level model of the DLX CPU is a configuration declaration to bind the entities we have described to the component instances in the architecture body. The configuration declaration is shown in Figure 15-61. The outermost block configuration selects the architecture **rtl** of the **dlx** entity. Then, for each component instance within that architecture body, the configuration declaration includes a component configuration. The component configurations provide actual values for the generic constants used to specify propagation delay times for each of the bound entities. The component configurations for the multiple-output registers associate the value of the **num_outputs** generic of each component instance with the **num_outputs** generic of the bound entity. The component configuration for the controller associates the value of the **debug** generic constant of the enclosing **dlx** entity with the controller entity's formal generic constant.

FIGURE 15-61

```
configuration dlx_rtl of dlx is
    for rtl
        for alu_s1_reg : latch
            use entity work.latch(behavior)
                generic map ( Tpd => 2 ns );
        end for;
        for alu_s2_reg : latch
            use entity work.latch(behavior)
                generic map ( Tpd => 2 ns );
        end for;
        for the_alu : alu
            use entity work.alu(behavior)
                generic map ( Tpd => 4 ns );
        end for;
        for the_reg_file : reg_file
            use entity work.reg_file(behavior)
                generic map ( Tac => 4 ns );
        end for;
        for c_reg : latch
            use entity work.latch(behavior)
                generic map ( Tpd => 2 ns );
        end for;
        for a_reg : reg_multiple_out
            use entity work.reg_multiple_out(behavior)
                generic map ( num_outputs => num_outputs, Tpd => 2 ns );
        end for;
        for b_reg : reg_multiple_out
            use entity work.reg_multiple_out(behavior)
                generic map ( num_outputs => num_outputs, Tpd => 2 ns );
        end for;
        for temp_reg : reg_multiple_out
            use entity work.reg_multiple_out(behavior)
                generic map ( num_outputs => num_outputs, Tpd => 2 ns );
        end for;
```

(continued on page 436)

(continued from page 435)

```
            for iar_reg : reg_multiple_out
                use entity work.reg_multiple_out(behavior)
                    generic map ( num_outputs => num_outputs, Tpd => 2 ns );
            end for;

            for pc_reg :reg_multiple_plus_one_out_reset
                use entity work.reg_multiple_plus_one_out_reset(behavior)
                    generic map ( num_outputs => num_outputs, Tpd => 2 ns );
            end for;

            for mar_reg : reg_multiple_plus_one_out
                use entity work.reg_multiple_plus_one_out(behavior)
                    generic map ( num_outputs => num_outputs, Tpd => 2 ns );
            end for;

            for mem_addr_mux : mux2
                use entity work.mux2(behavior)
                    generic map ( Tpd => 1 ns );
            end for;

            for mdr_reg : reg_multiple_out
                use entity work.reg_multiple_out(behavior)
                    generic map ( num_outputs => num_outputs, Tpd => 2 ns );
            end for;

            for mdr_mux : mux2
                use entity work.mux2(behavior)
                    generic map ( Tpd => 1 ns );
            end for;

            for instr_reg : latch
                use entity work.latch(behavior)
                    generic map ( Tpd => 2 ns );
            end for;

            for ir_extender1 : ir_extender
                use entity work.ir_extender(behavior)
                    generic map ( Tpd => 2 ns );
            end for;

            for ir_extender2 : ir_extender
                use entity work.ir_extender(behavior)
                    generic map ( Tpd => 2 ns );
            end for;

            for the_controller : controller
                use entity work.controller(behavior)
                    generic map ( Tpd_clk_ctrl => 2 ns, Tpd_clk_const => 4 ns,
                                  debug => debug );
            end for;

        end for;
end configuration dlx_rtl;
```

A configuration declaration for the register-transfer-level model of the DLX CPU.

15.5 Testing the Register-Transfer-Level Model

We can test our register-transfer-level CPU model using the same test bench that we used to test the behavioral model, as described in Section 15.3. We need to modify the configuration declaration for the test bench to bind the register-transfer-level implementation to the processor component in the test bench. The revised configuration declaration is shown in Figure 15-62. In this version, the component configuration for the processor uses the configuration dlx_rtl, described in the previous section. That configuration refers to the entity work.dlx and selects the architecture rtl. We can then run our simulator, specifying the configuration dlx_test_rtl as the unit to simulate, to test the register-transfer-level model in the same way as we tested the behavioral model. The sequence of memory operations should be the same. The only observable difference should be that the CPU takes longer to execute each instruction. This is because our register-transfer-level model accurately describes the cycle-by-cycle operation of the CPU.

FIGURE 15-62

```
configuration dlx_test_rtl of dlx_test is
    for bench
        for cg : clock_gen
            use entity work.clock_gen(behavior)
                generic map ( Tpw => 8 ns, Tps => 2 ns );
        end for;
        for mem : memory
            use entity work.memory(preloaded)
                generic map ( mem_size => 65536, Tac_first => 95 ns,
                              Tac_burst => 35 ns, Tpd_clk_out => 2 ns );
        end for;
        for proc : dlx
            use configuration work.dlx_rtl
                generic map ( Tpd_clk_out => 2 ns, debug => trace_each_step );
        end for;
    end for;
end configuration dlx_test_rtl;
```

A configuration declaration for the test bench, using the register-transfer-level model for the processor component.

Another useful way of testing the register-transfer-level model is to create a test bench that runs it in parallel with the behavioral model. This new test bench automatically compares the outputs of the two models and verifies that they operate identically. While the detailed timing varies between the two models, the sequences of memory operations they generate should be identical.

Figure 15-63 shows such a test-bench architecture body. It uses the same clock generator and memory components as the previous test bench, but has two instances of the processor component, proc_behav and proc_rtl. The behavioral version is connected to the memory normally, so it controls memory read and write operations. The output signals from the register-transfer-level version are not connected to the memory. Instead, they are sensed by the process **monitor**, which compares them with the corresponding signals from the behavioral version. The memory's **ready** port is connected to the **ready** ports of both processors, so that both see acknowledgement of requested memory operations. The concurrent signal assignment statement labeled **fwd_data_from_mem_to_rtl** drives the data bus of the register-transfer-level processor with data supplied by the memory during read operations and isolates the two buses at all other times.

FIGURE 15-63

```
library ieee;  use ieee.std_logic_1164.all;
architecture verifier of dlx_test is
    use work.dlx_types.all;
    . . .        -- component declarations as in previous test bench
    signal phi1, phi2, reset : std_logic;
    signal a_behav : dlx_address;
    signal d_behav : dlx_word;
    signal halt_behav : std_logic;
    signal width_behav : dlx_mem_width;
    signal write_enable_behav, mem_enable_behav, ifetch_behav : std_logic;
    signal a_rtl : dlx_address;
    signal d_rtl : dlx_word;
    signal halt_rtl : std_logic;
    signal width_rtl : dlx_mem_width;
    signal write_enable_rtl, mem_enable_rtl, ifetch_rtl : std_logic;
    signal ready_mem : std_logic;
begin
    cg : component clock_gen
        port map ( phi1 => phi1, phi2 => phi2, reset => reset );
    mem : component memory
        port map ( phi1 => phi1, phi2 => phi2,
                   a => a_behav, d => d_behav,
                   width => width_behav, write_enable => write_enable_behav,
                   burst => open,
                   mem_enable => mem_enable_behav, ready => ready_mem );
    proc_behav : component dlx
        port map ( phi1 => phi1, phi2 => phi2, reset => reset, halt => halt_behav,
                   a => a_behav, d => d_behav,
                   width => width_behav, write_enable => write_enable_behav,
                   ifetch => ifetch_behav,
                   mem_enable => mem_enable_behav, ready => ready_mem );
    proc_rtl : component dlx
        port map ( phi1 => phi1, phi2 => phi2, reset => reset, halt => halt_rtl,
                   a => a_rtl, d => d_rtl,
                   width => width_rtl, write_enable => write_enable_rtl,
                   ifetch => ifetch_rtl,
                   mem_enable => mem_enable_rtl, ready => ready_mem );
```

```
verification_section : block is
begin
    fwd_data_from_mem_to_rtl :
        d_rtl <= d_behav when mem_enable_rtl = '1'
                                and write_enable_rtl = '0' else
            disabled_dlx_word;
    monitor : process
        variable write_command_behav : boolean;
        variable write_command_rtl : boolean;
    begin
        monitor_loop : loop
            -- wait for a command, valid on leading edge of phi2
            wait until rising_edge(phi2)
                    and mem_enable_behav = '1' and mem_enable_rtl = '1';
            -- capture the command information
            write_command_behav := write_enable_behav = '1';
            write_command_rtl := write_enable_rtl = '1';
            assert a_behav = a_rtl
                report "addresses differ";
            assert write_enable_behav = write_enable_rtl
                report "write enable states differ";
            assert ifetch_behav = ifetch_rtl
                report "instruction fetch states differ";
            assert width_behav = width_rtl
                    report "widths differ";
            if write_command_behav and write_command_rtl then
                assert d_behav = d_rtl
                    report "write data differs";
            end if;
            -- wait for the response from memory
            ready_loop : loop
                wait until falling_edge(phi2);
                exit monitor_loop when reset = '1';
                exit ready_loop when ready_mem = '1';
            end loop ready_loop;
        end loop monitor_loop;
        -- get here when reset is asserted
        wait until reset = '0';
        -- process monitor now starts again from beginning
    end process monitor;
end block verification_section;
end architecture verifier;
```

A test-bench architecture that compares the outputs of two processor instances.

The monitor process waits until both processors issue a memory request, indicated by mem_enable_behav and mem_enable_rtl both being '1' on a rising edge of phi2. The process then verifies that the two processors are requesting the same kind of memory operation at the same memory address. Furthermore, if both processes are requesting a write operation, the **monitor** process verifies that they are writing the same data value.

Figure 15-64 shows the configuration declaration for the verification test bench. The clock generator and memory component instances are bound to the behavioral implementations, as in the previous test bench. The component instance **proc_behav** is bound to the behavioral implementation of the **dlx** entity. The component instance **dlx_rtl** is bound using the configuration **dlx_rtl**, which uses the register-transfer implementation of the **dlx** entity. If we analyze all of the required design units and simulate the **dlx_test_verifier** configuration, we expect the model to run to completion without any differences reported by the **monitor** process. If differences are reported, we could resimulate with different values for the **debug** generic constants of each of the processor instances. We could then use the trace information reported by the processors to help locate the cause of the differences.

FIGURE 15-64

```
configuration dlx_test_verifier of dlx_test is
    for verifier
        for cg : clock_gen
            use entity work.clock_gen(behavior)
                generic map ( Tpw => 8 ns, Tps => 2 ns );
        end for;
        for mem : memory
            use entity work.memory(preloaded)
                generic map ( mem_size => 65536, Tac_first => 95 ns,
                              Tac_burst => 35 ns, Tpd_clk_out => 2 ns );
        end for;
        for proc_behav : dlx
            use entity work.dlx(behavior)
                generic map ( Tpd_clk_out => 2 ns, debug => none );
        end for;
        for proc_rtl : dlx
            use configuration work.dlx_rtl
                generic map ( Tpd_clk_out => 2 ns, debug => none );
        end for;
    end for;
end configuration dlx_test_verifier;
```

A configuration declaration for the verification test bench.

Exercises

1. [● 15.1/15.2] Write the 32-bit binary encoding for the following DLX instructions. (Note: The destination operand is written before source operands in DLX assembly language, and displacements in control transfer instructions are relative.)

   (a)   j   +48
   (b)   beqz   r3, +16
   (c)   sll   r2, r2, r5
   (d)   multf f3, f7, f8

2. [● 15.2] What string would be produced by the **disassemble** procedure for the bit vector X"2223002A"?

3. [● 15.4] Trace the procedure calls in the register-transfer-level controller sequencer when the CPU fetches and executes each of the following instructions (assuming **debug** has the value **none**):

   (a) jump and link
   (b) branch (not taken)
   (c) branch (taken)
   (d) add with register operands
   (e) add with an immediate operand
   (f) load byte
   (g) set unsigned with an immediate operand

4. [❸ 15.3/15.5] Develop a behavioral model of a direct-mapped write-through cache memory for inclusion in the DLX CPU test bench. The cache should use the burst-transfer protocol implemented by the memory to fetch cache lines.

5. [❸ 15.4] Complete the register-transfer-level controller by writing the missing procedures:

   bus_data_read, bus_data_write,
   do_EX_set_signed, do_EX_arith_logic_immed, do_EX_link, do_EX_lhi,
   do_MEM_jump, do_MEM_jump_reg and do_MEM_store.

6. [❹ 15.2] Extend the behavioral model of the DLX to include interrupt handling. The entity interface is extended with an additional active-low input port, **intreq_n**, which is used by external input/output controllers to request interrupts. The CPU internal state is extended with a program status register (PSR), accessed as special register 0 using movi2s and movs2i instructions. The PSR includes an Interrupt Mask (IM) bit and a Previous Interrupt Mask (PIM) bit, both initialized to '1' when the CPU is reset. The CPU tests the state of the **intreq_n** input before fetching an instruction. If the IM bit is '0' and the **intreq_n** input is low, the CPU accepts the interrupt request by copying the IM bit to the PIM bit, setting the IM bit to '1', copying the PC to the IAR and jumping to location 16. The IAR is accessed as special register 1 using movi2s and movs2i instructions. The interrupt handler returns by executing a rfe instruction, which copies the PIM bit to the IM bit and jumps to the location whose address is in the IAR.

7. [❹ 15.2] Extend the behavioral model of the DLX to include floating-point instructions. The FSR is accessed as special register 8 using movi2s and movs2i instructions. Floating-point exceptions are handled in a similar way to external interrupts, described in Exercise 6.

8. [❹ 15.2] Add paged virtual memory management unit (PVMMU) to the DLX CPU. This requires adding a supervisor mode to the CPU, controlled by a bit in the Program Status Register described in Exercise 6. Exceptions raised by the PVMMU are handled in a similar way to external interrupts, also described in Exercise 6. Control and status registers for the PVMMU are accessed as special registers using movi2s and movs2i instructions.

9. [❹ 15.4] In their book [7], Hennessy and Patterson describe a microcontroller implementation of the DLX control section. This implementation allows DLX instructions to be described using vertical micro-instructions. Develop a structural architecture body of the **controller** entity, based on Hennessy and Patterson's microcontroller.

10. [❹ 15.4] In their book [7], Hennessy and Patterson describe a pipelined implementation of the DLX CPU. Develop a structural architecture body of the DLX based on Hennessy and Patterson's design.

11. [❹ 15.5] Develop a model of a cache memory for inclusion in the DLX CPU test bench with the register-transfer-level CPU model. The cache entity interface should include generic constants to specify total cache size, line size, associativity (direct-mapped, two-way, four-way, eight-way or fully associative) and write-strategy (write-through with no write-buffer, write-through with 16-entry write-buffer or copy-back). Prepare some benchmark programs to run on the DLX, and compare their execution time with different cache organizations. (Information about compilers and assemblers for the DLX may be obtained from the author's World-Wide Web pages, described in the Preface.)

12. [❹] Develop models for I/O controllers to interface to the DLX CPU and memory. Possibilities include serial input/output UART, parallel input/output, a SCSI controller, a video frame buffer and a network interface. Use your models in a model of a computer system based around the DLX.

Guards and Blocks

In this chapter we look at a number of closely related topics. First, we discuss a new kind of resolved signal called a *guarded signal*. We see how we can disconnect drivers from such signals. Next, we introduce the idea of *blocks* in a VHDL design. We show how blocks and guarded signals work together with *guards* and *guard expressions* to cause automatic disconnection of drivers. Finally, we discuss blocks as a mechanism for describing a hierarchical structure within an architecture.

16.1 Guarded Signals and Disconnection

In Chapter 11 we saw how we can use resolved signals that include values such as 'Z' for modeling high-impedance outputs. However, if we are modeling at a higher level of abstraction, we may wish to use a more abstract type such as an integer type or a simple bit type to represent signals. In such cases, it is not appropriate to include the high-impedance state as a value, so VHDL provides us with an alternative approach, using *guarded signals*. These are resolved signals for which we can *disconnect* the drivers, that is, we can cause the drivers to stop contributing values to the resolved signal. We see why these signals are called "guarded" in the next section. First, let us look at the complete syntax rule for a signal declaration, which includes a means of declaring a signal to be guarded.

> signal_declaration ⟸
>   **signal** identifier ⟦ , ... ⟧ : subtype_indication ⟦ **register** ⟦ **bus** ⟧
>   ⟦ := expression ⟧ ;

The difference between this rule and the simplified rule we introduced earlier is the inclusion of the option to specify the signal kind as either a *register* signal or a *bus* signal. Note that a guarded signal must be a resolved signal. Hence, the subtype indication in the signal declaration must denote a resolved subtype. Some examples of declarations of guarded signals are

> **signal** interrupt_request : pulled_up bit **bus**;
>
> **signal** stored_state : resolve_state state_type **register** := init_state;

The difference between the two kinds of guarded signals lies in their behavior when all of their drivers are disconnected. A bus signal uses the resolution function to determine the signal value by passing it an empty array. The bus kind of guarded signal can be used to model a signal that is "pulled up" to some value dependent on the signal type when all drivers are disconnected. A register signal, on the other hand, keeps the resolved value that it had just before the last disconnection. The register kind of guarded signal can be used to model signals with dynamic storage, for example, signals in CMOS logic that store data as charge on transistor gates when all drivers are disconnected. Note that a signal may be neither a register nor a bus signal, in which case it is a regular (unguarded) signal, from which drivers may not be disconnected.

A process can disconnect a driver for a guarded signal by specifying a *null transaction* in a signal assignment statement. As a reminder, the syntax rule we used to introduce a signal assignment was

> signal_assignment_statement ⟸
>   ⟦ label : ⟧ name <= ⟦ delay_mechanism ⟧ waveform ;

The waveform is a sequence of transactions, that is, new values to be applied to the signal after given delays. A more complete syntax rule for waveforms includes null transactions:

> waveform ⟸
>   (*value*_expression ⟦ **after** *time*_expression ⟧
>   ⟦ **null** ⟦ **after** *time*_expression ⟧) { , ... }

This rule shows that instead of specifying a value in a transaction, we can use the keyword **null** to indicate that the driver should be disconnected after the given delay. When this null transaction matures, the driver ceases to contribute values to the resolution function used to compute the signal's value. Hence the size of the array of values passed as an argument to the resolution function is reduced by one for each driver that currently has a null transaction determining its contribution. When a driver subsequently performs a non-null transaction, it reconnects and contributes the value in the non-null transaction.

EXAMPLE

Figure 16-1 outlines an architecture body for a computer system consisting of a CPU, a memory and a DMA controller. The architecture body includes a guarded

FIGURE 16-1

```
architecture top_level of computer_system is
    function resolve_bits ( bits : bit_vector ) return bit is
        variable result : bit := '0';
    begin
        for index in bits'range loop
            result := result or bits(index);
            exit when result = '1';
        end loop;
        return result;
    end function resolve_bits;

    signal write_en : resolve_bits bit bus;
    . . .
begin
    CPU : process is
        . . .
    begin
        write_en <= '0' after Tpd;
        . . .
        loop
            wait until clock = '1';
            if hold_req = '1' then
                write_en <= null after Tpd;
                wait on clock until clock = '1' and hold_req = '0';
                write_en <= '0' after Tpd;
            end if;
            . . .
        end loop;
    end process CPU;

    . . .
end architecture top_level;
```

An outline of an architecture body for a computer system, including a guarded signal of the bus kind and a process representing the CPU that drives the signal.

signal of kind bus, **write_en**, representing a control connection to the memory. The resolution function performs the logical "or" operation of all of the contributing drivers and returns '0' if there are no drivers connected. This result ensures that the memory remains inactive when neither the CPU nor the DMA controller is driving the **write_en** control signal.

When the process representing the CPU is initialized, it drives **write_en** with the value '0'. Subsequently, when the DMA controller requests access to the memory by asserting the **hold_req** signal, the CPU schedules a null transaction on **write_en**. This transaction removes the CPU's driver from the set of drivers contributing to the resolved value of **write_en**. Later, when the DMA controller negates **hold_req**, the CPU reconnects its driver to **write_en** by scheduling a transaction with the value '0'.

EXAMPLE

Figure 16-2 shows an outline of a register-transfer-level model of a processor, in which data path elements are modeled by processes. The data path includes two register signals that represent the source operand connections to the ALU.

FIGURE 16-2

```
architecture rtl of processor is
    subtype word is bit_vector(0 to 31);
    type word_vector is array (natural range <>) of word;

    function resolve_unique ( drivers : word_vector ) return word is
    begin
        return drivers(drivers'left);
    end function resolve_unique;

    signal source1, source2 : resolve_unique word register;
    . . .
begin
    source1_reg : process (phase1, source1_reg_out_en, . . .) is
        variable stored_value : word;
    begin
        . . .
        if source1_reg_out_en = '1' and phase1 = '1' then
            source1 <= stored_value;
        else
            source1 <= null;
        end if;
    end process source1_reg;
    alu : perform_alu_op ( alu_opcode, source1, source2, destination, . . . );
    . . .
end architecture rtl;
```

An outline of an architecture body for a processor. The source operand buses are register guarded signals driven by processes during phase 1 of a clock cycle. They retain their values during phase 2.

In this design, only one process should drive each of these signals at a time. The resolution function returns the single contributing value.

The process **source1_reg** represents one of the data path elements that connects to the **source1** signal. When its output enable signal and the clock phase 1 signal are both '1', the process drives the signal with its stored value. The resolution function is passed an array of one element consisting of this driving value. It is applied to the **source1** signal and is used by the concurrent procedure call representing the ALU. At the end of the clock phase, the process disconnects from **source1** by scheduling a null transaction. Since **source1** is a register signal and all drivers are now disconnected, the resolution function is not called, and **source1** retains its value until some other driver connects. This models a real system in which the operand value is stored as electrical charge on the inputs of transistors in the ALU.

When we are dealing with guarded signals of a composite type such as an array type, it is important to note that within each driver for the signal, all elements must be connected or all must be disconnected. It is not permissible to disconnect some elements using a null transaction and leave other elements connected. The reason for this rule is that the complete composite value from each driver is passed as a contribution to the resolution function. For example, it is not possible to pass just half of a bit vector as an element in the array of values to be resolved. Thus, given a guarded bit-vector signal declared as

```
subtype word is bit_vector(0 to 31);
type word_array is array (integer range <>) of word;

function resolve_words ( words : word_array ) return word;

signal s : resolve_words word bus;
```

we may not write the following signal assignments within one process:

```
s(0 to 15) <= X"003F" after T_delay;
s(16 to 31) <= null after T_delay;
```

If the design requires that only part of a composite driver be connected at some stages during model execution, then the signal type must be a composite of individually resolved elements, rather than a resolved composite type. This is similar to the requirement we discussed in Chapter 11 on page 276.

In the above examples, we have assumed that a null transaction is scheduled after all previously scheduled transactions have been applied. We have yet to consider how null transactions are scheduled in the general case where there are still transactions pending in the driver. On page 120 in Section 5.3 we described in detail how the list of transactions previously scheduled on a driver is edited when a signal assignment is executed. In particular, when the inertial delay mechanism is used, transactions are deleted if their values differ from that of the newly scheduled transaction. For the purpose of this editing algorithm, a null transaction is deemed to have a value that is different from any value of the signal type. Successive null transactions are deemed to have the same value. So, for example, if a driver for signal **s** has transactions pending as

FIGURE 16-3

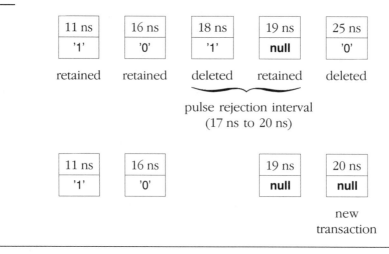

The transactions before (top) and after (bottom) an inertial delay signal assignment involving a null transaction.

shown at the top of Figure 16-3, and the following signal assignment is executed at time 10 ns:

s <= **reject** 3 ns **inertial null after** 10 ns;

the resulting list of transactions is shown at the bottom of Figure 16-3. The first two transactions are retained because they are scheduled to occur before the pulse rejection interval. The transaction at time 18 ns is deleted, as its value is different from that of the new null transaction. The transaction at 19 ns is retained because it immediately precedes the new null transaction and is deemed to have the same value. The transaction at 25 ns is deleted because it is scheduled to occur later than the new transaction.

The Driving Attribute

In addition to the 'driving_value attribute for signals that we saw in Chapter 11, VHDL also provides an attribute, 'driving, that is useful with guarded signals. It returns true if the driver in the process referring to the attribute currently has its driver connected to the signal. It returns false if the driver is disconnected. Of course, the attribute 'driving_value should not be used if the driver is disconnected, since there is no driving value in that case. An error will occur if a model tries to do this.

VHDL-87

The 'driving attribute is not provided in VHDL-87.

Guarded Ports

Throughout all the examples in this book, we have seen that the ports of an entity are treated as signals within an architecture body for that entity. Just as we can have guarded signals, so we can have guarded ports as part of an entity's interface. However, there are some important limitations that come about due to the way in which ports are resolved. The main restriction is that a guarded port can only be of the bus kind, not the register kind. A guarded port includes the keyword **bus** in its declaration. For example, given the following declarations to define a resolved subtype resolved_byte:

```
subtype byte is bit_vector(0 to 7);
type byte_array is array (integer range <>) of byte;
function resolve ( bytes : byte_array ) return byte;
subtype resolved_byte is resolve byte;
```

we can declare an entity with a guarded port q as follows:

```
entity tri_state_reg is
    port ( d : in resolved_byte;
            q : out resolved_byte bus;
            clock, out_enable : in bit );
end entity tri_state_reg;
```

Since the port q is declared to be a guarded port, a process in an architecture body for tri_state_reg can disconnect from the port by assigning a null transaction. Here is where the behavior is different from what we might first expect. Since the port is of a resolved subtype, it is resolved independently of any external signal associated with it. This means that even if all processes in the architecture for tri_state_reg are disconnected, the resolution function for the port is still invoked to determine the port's value. The port itself does not become disconnected. It continues to contribute its resolved value to the external signal associated with it. While this may seem counter-intuitive, it follows directly from the way resolved signals and ports behave in VHDL. Hence the entity tri_state_reg declared above does not in fact represent a module that can disconnect its port from an associated signal. There is no mechanism in VHDL for doing that. While some designers argue that this is a limitation of the language, there are often ways to circumvent the problem. The difficulty mainly arises when modeling at a high level of abstraction. At a lower level, we would use some multivalued logic type that includes a representation of the high-impedance state instead of using disconnection, so the problem does not arise.

EXAMPLE

Let us look more closely at the tri_state_reg module to see how we can achieve the desired effect. When using tristate logic, we only allow one output to drive a bus at a time. Our solution to the problem lies in writing the resolution function so that it returns an identity value when passed an empty array of contributing values. The identity value, when resolved with any other value, should result in the other value. For bit-vector types, we can resolve values using a logical "or" operation, which has an identity value of a bit vector comprising all '0' bits. The body of the resolution function can be written as shown in Figure 16-4. A behavioral architecture of the tri_state_reg entity can be written as shown in Figure 16-5.

While this description does not actually cause the port q to become disconnected from its associated signal in an instantiating design, it does express the intention of the designer. When the driver in reg_behavior disconnects, the resolu-

FIGURE 16-4

```
function resolve ( bytes : byte_array ) return byte is
    variable result : byte := b"0000_0000";
begin
    for index in bytes'range loop
        result := result or bytes(index);
    end loop;
    return result;
end function resolve;
```

A resolution function for a resolved bit-vector type.

FIGURE 16-5

```
architecture behavioral of tri_state_reg is
begin
    reg_behavior : process (d, clock, out_enable) is
        variable stored_byte : byte;
    begin
        if clock'event and clock = '1' then
            stored_byte := d;
        end if;
        if out_enable = '1' then
            q <= stored_byte;
        else
            q <= null;
        end if;
    end process reg_behavior;
end architecture behavioral;
```

A behavioral architecture body for a tristate register entity.

tion function is invoked with an empty array as its argument and returns the value b"0000_0000" as the resolved value for q. This value is then used as the contribution to the associated resolved signal in a design containing an instance of tri_state_reg. If this signal uses the same resolution function, the identity value returned from q will not affect the value returned by another source that is active.

Guarded Signal Parameters

In Chapter 7 we saw how we can write subprograms that have signal class parameters. We cannot, however, specify that a signal parameter be a bus signal by adding the keyword **bus** in the parameter list, as we can for ports. Instead, the subprogram uses the kind of the actual signal (bus, register or unguarded) associated with a signal parameter. A procedure can include signal assignment statements that assign null transactions to a formal parameter, but if the actual signal is not a guarded signal, the model is in error. Recall that for signal parameters of mode **out** or **inout**, when the procedure is called, it is passed a reference to the driver for the actual signal. Signal assignments within the procedure schedule transactions onto the driver for the actual signal. If the actual signal is a guarded signal, and the procedure assigns a null transaction to it, the driver that is disconnected is the one in the calling process. When the actual signal is resolved, the subprogram, acting on behalf of the process, does not contribute a value. We can take advantage of this behavior when writing high-level models that include processes that disconnect from bus signals. We can use a subprogram as an abstraction for processes, instead of using component instances.

EXAMPLE

Suppose we must write a model of a data logger that monitors two byte-wide input ports. The module includes an input register for each port. Both input registers are connected to the data bus of a small microprocessor. The data bus is a guarded signal, and each register, when enabled, connects and drives its stored value. Only one register may connect at a time. The outline of an architecture body for the data logger is shown in Figure 16-6.

FIGURE 16-6

```
architecture high_level of data_logger is
    subtype byte is bit_vector(7 downto 0);
    type byte_array is array (integer range <>) of byte;
    function resolver ( bytes : byte_array ) return byte is
    begin
        if bytes'length > 0 then
            return bytes( bytes'left );
        else
            return X"00";
        end if;
    end function resolver;
    subtype resolved_byte is resolver byte;
    procedure reg ( signal clock, out_enable : in bit;
                    signal d : in byte;  signal q : out resolved_byte ) is
        variable stored_byte : byte;
    begin
        loop
            if clock = '1' then
                stored_byte := d;
            end if;
            if out_enable = '1' then
                q <= stored_byte;
            else
                q <= null;
            end if;
            wait on clock, out_enable, d;
        end loop;
    end procedure reg;
```

(continued on page 452)

(continued from page 451)

        signal data_bus : resolved_byte **bus**;
        . . .

begin

        a_reg : reg (a_reg_clk, a_reg_read, port_a, data_bus);
        b_reg : reg (b_reg_clk, b_reg_read, port_b, data_bus);

        . . .

end architecture high_level;

An outline of a high-level architecture body of a data logger, using a procedure to encapsulate the behavior of a register process.

The procedure **reg**, activated by the concurrent procedure calls in the architecture body, encapsulates the behavior for a flow-through register with tristate outputs. In both activations, the signal **data_bus** is associated with the **out** mode signal parameter **q**. Since this signal is a guarded signal, the null signal assignment within the procedure is valid. For example, when the activation labeled **a_reg** executes the null signal assignment, the driver for **data_bus** in **a_reg** is disconnected.

VHDL-87

The VHDL-87 language definition does not disallow the keyword **bus** in the specification of a signal parameter. However, it does not specify whether the kind of signal, guarded or unguarded, is determined by the formal parameter specification or by the actual signal associated with the parameter. Implementations of VHDL-87 make different interpretations. Some require the formal parameter specification to include the keyword **bus** if the procedure includes a null signal assignment to the parameter. The actual signal associated with the parameter in a procedure call must then be a guarded signal. Other implementations follow the approach adopted in VHDL-93, prohibiting the keyword **bus** in the parameter specification and determining the kind of the parameter from the kind of the actual signal.

16.2 Blocks and Guarded Signal Assignment

In this section, we introduce the VHDL *block* statement. In their most general form, blocks provide a way of partitioning the concurrent statements within an architecture body. However, we start with a simpler form of block statement that relates to guarded signals and return to the more general form in the next section.

A *block statement* is a concurrent statement that groups together a number of inner concurrent statements. A simplified syntax rule for block statements is

```
block_statement ⇐
    block_label :
    block [ ( guard_expression ) ] [ is ]
    begin
        { concurrent_statement }
    end block [ block_label ] ;
```

The block label is required to identify the block statement. The syntax rule shows that we can write a block statement with an optional Boolean *guard expression*. If the guard expression is present, it must be surrounded by parentheses and appear after the keyword **block**. It is used to determine the value of an implicitly declared signal called **guard**. This signal is only implicitly declared if the guard expression is present. Its visibility extends over the whole of the block statement. Whenever a transaction occurs on any of the signals mentioned in the guard expression, the expression is re-evaluated and the **guard** signal is immediately updated. Since the **guard** signal has its value automatically determined, we may not include a source for it in the block. That means we may not write a signal assignment for it, nor use it as an actual signal for an output port of a component instance.

EXAMPLE

Figure 16-7 is an example of a block statement with a guard expression. Since the guard expression is present, there is a **guard** signal implicitly declared within the block. Its value is updated whenever a transaction occurs on either of the signals **reg_sel** or **read**. It is used in the conditional signal assignment statement within the block.

FIGURE 16-7

```
reg_read_selector : block ( reg_sel = '1' and read = '1' ) is
begin
    dbus <= reg0 when guard and reg_addr = '0' else
            reg1 when guard and reg_addr = '1' else
            "ZZZZZZZZ";
end block reg_read_selector;
```

An example of a block statement with a guard expression.

The main use of guard expressions in a block is to control operation of *guarded signal assignments*. These are special forms of the concurrent signal assignments described in Section 5.3. If the target of a concurrent signal assignment is a guarded signal, we must use a guarded signal assignment rather than an ordinary concurrent signal assignment. The extended syntax rules are

```
conditional_signal_assignment ⇐
    name <= [ guarded ] [ delay_mechanism ]
                { waveform when boolean_expression else }
                waveform [ when boolean_expression ] ;
```

```
selected_signal_assignment ⇐
    with expression select
        name <= [[ guarded ]] [[ delay_mechanism ]]
                { waveform when choices , }
                waveform when choices ;
```

The difference is the inclusion of the keyword **guarded** after the assignment symbol. This denotes that the signal assignment is to be executed when the guard signal
changes value. The effect depends on whether the target of the assignment is a
guarded signal or an ordinary signal. For a guarded target, if **guard** changes from true
to false, the driver for the target is disconnected using a null transaction. When **guard**
changes back to true, the assignment is executed again to reconnect the driver.

EXAMPLE

Figure 16-8 shows an outline of an architecture body for a processor node of
a multiprocessor computer. The signal address_bus is a guarded bit-vector signal.
The block labeled cache_to_address_buffer has a guard expression that is true
when the cache misses and a block needs to be replaced. The expression is evaluated whenever either cache_miss or dirty changes value, and the implicit signal
guard in the block is set to the result. If it is true, the driver in the concurrent signal
assignment statement within the block is connected. Any changes in the signals
mentioned in the statement cause a new assignment to the target signal ad-
dress_bus. When the guard signal changes to false, the driver in the assignment
is disconnected using a null transaction.

FIGURE 16-8

```
architecture dataflow of processor_node is
    signal address_bus : resolve_unique word bus;
    . . .
begin
    cache_to_address_buffer : block ( cache_miss = '1' and dirty = '1' ) is
    begin
        address_bus <= guarded
            tag_section0 & set_index & B"0000" when replace_section = '0' else
            tag_section1 & set_index & B"0000";
    end block cache_to_address_buffer;

    snoop_to_address_buffer : block ( snoop_hit = '1' and flag_update = '1' ) is
    begin
        address_bus <= guarded snoop_address(31 downto 4) & B"0000";
    end block snoop_to_address_buffer;

    . . .

end architecture dataflow;
```

*An outline of an architecture body for a processor node of a multiprocessor computer, showing parts of
the cache system that drive addresses onto the address bus.*

The block labeled snoop_to_address_buffer also has a guard expression, which is true when an external bus monitor (the "snoop") needs to update flags in the cache. The expression is evaluated when either snoop_hit or flag_update changes. The result is assigned to a separate guard signal for this block, used to control a second concurrent signal assignment statement with address_bus as the target. Assuming that the two guard expressions are mutually exclusive, only one of the drivers is connected to address_bus at a time.

If the target of a guarded signal assignment is an ordinary unguarded signal, the driver is not disconnected when guard changes to false. Instead, the assignment statement is disabled. No further transactions are scheduled for the target, despite changes that may occur on signals to which the statement is sensitive. Subsequently, when guard changes to true, the assignment is executed again and resumes normal operation.

EXAMPLE

A simple model for a transparent latch can be written using a guarded signal assignment, as shown in Figure 16-9. The architecture body uses a block statement with a guard expression that tests the state of the enable signal. When enable is '0', the guard signal is false, and the guarded signal assignment is disabled. Changes in d are ignored, so q maintains its current value. When enable changes to '1', the guarded signal assignment is enabled and copies the value of d to q. So long as enable is '1', changes in d are copied to q.

FIGURE 16-9

```
entity latch is
    generic ( width : positive );
    port ( enable : in bit;
            d : in bit_vector(0 to width – 1);
            q : out bit_vector(0 to width – 1) );
end entity latch;

----------------------------------------------------

architecture behavioral of latch is
begin
    transfer_control : block ( enable = '1' ) is
    begin
        q <= guarded d;
    end block transfer_control;
end architecture behavioral;
```

An entity and behavioral architecture body for a transparent latch.

VHDL-87

The keyword **is** may not be included in a block header in VHDL-87.

Explicit Guard Signals

In the preceding examples, the guarded signal assignment statements used the implicitly declared **guard** signal to determine whether the assignment should be executed. As an alternative, we can explicitly declare our own Boolean signal called **guard**. Provided it is visible at the position of a guarded signal assignment, it will be used to control the signal assignment. The advantage of this approach is that we can use a more complex algorithm to control the guard signal, rather than relying on a simple Boolean expression. For example, we might use a separate process to drive **guard**. Whenever **guard** is changed to false, guarded signal assignments are disabled, disconnecting any drivers for guarded signals. When **guard** is changed back to true, the assignments are reenabled.

EXAMPLE

Suppose we are modeling a computer system that includes a CPU and a DMA controller, among other modules. The DMA controller asserts the signal hold_req when it needs to use the memory address, data and control buses. The CPU completes its current operation, then disables its bus drivers before acknowledging the request. Figure 16-10 shows an outline of the computer system model, including the processes that describe the CPU. The CPU is described by a collection of processes in the block **cpu**. The address bus is driven by the guarded concurrent signal assignment labeled **cpu_address_driver**. Since the Boolean signal **guard** is visible at that point, it controls connection of the driver.

FIGURE 16-10

```
architecture abstract of computer_system is
    . . .
    signal address_bus : resolve_word word bus;
    signal hold_req : bit;
    . . .
begin
    cpu : block is
        signal guard : boolean := false;
        signal cpu_internal_address : word;
        . . .
    begin
        cpu_address_driver:
            address_bus <= guarded cpu_internal_address;
        . . .          -- other bus drivers
```

```
                    controller : process is
                       . . .
                    begin
                       . . .
                       . . .        -- determine when to disable cpu bus drivers
                       guard <= false;
                       wait on clk until hold_req = '0' and clk = '1';
                       guard <= true;  -- re–enable cpu bus drivers
                       . . .
                    end process controller;
                       . . .        -- cpu datapath processes
                    end block cpu;
                    . . .        -- blocks for DMA and other modules
                end architecture abstract;
```

An outline of a computer system model that uses an explicit guard signal to control guarded signal assignment statements representing bus drivers.

The process **controller** describes the control section of the CPU. It monitors the **hold_req** signal and determines when the guard signal should be asserted. The process then waits until the next rising clock edge after **hold_req** is negated before negating the guard signal. In this way, the CPU causes the bus drivers to be connected synchronously with the clock, rather than whenever the request signal changes.

Disconnection Specifications

One aspect of guarded signal assignments for guarded signals that we have not yet dealt with is timing. In the previous examples in this section, we have only shown zero-delay models. If we need to include delays in signal assignments, we should also include a specification of the delay associated with disconnecting a driver in a guarded signal assignment. The problem is that the null transaction that disconnects a driver in this case is not explicitly written in the model. It occurs as a result of the **guard** signal changing to false. The mechanism in VHDL that we may use if we need to specify a non-zero disconnection delay is a *disconnection specification*. The syntax rule is

disconnection_specification ⇐
    disconnect (*signal*_name { , ₀₀₀ } ‖ **others** ‖ **all**) : type_mark
    after *time*_expression ;

A disconnection specification allows us to identify a particular signal or set of signals by name and type, and to specify the delay associated with any null transactions scheduled for the signals. This delay only applies to the implicit null transactions resulting from guarded signal assignments. It does not apply to null transactions we may write explicitly using the keyword **null** in a signal assignment in a process.

A disconnection specification for a guarded signal must appear in the same list of declarations as the signal declaration for the guarded signal. So, for example, we might include the following in the declarative part of an architecture body:

```
signal memory_data_bus : resolved_word bus;
disconnect memory_data_bus : resolved_word after 3 ns;
```

We might then include the following block in the architecture body:

```
mem_write_buffer : block (mem_sel and mem_write) is
begin
    memory_data_bus <=
        guarded reject 2 ns inertial cache_data_bus after 4 ns;
end block mem_write_buffer;
```

This indicates that so long as the guard expression evaluates to true, the value of cache_data_bus will be copied to memory_data_bus with a delay of 4 ns and a pulse rejection interval of 2 ns. When the guard expression changes to false, the driver corresponding to the guarded signal assignment is disconnected with a null transaction. The delay used is 3 ns, as indicated in the disconnection specification, but the pulse rejection limit of 2 ns is still taken from the assignment statement. When the guard expression changes back to true, the assignment is executed again, scheduling a new transaction with 4 ns delay.

If we have a number of guarded signals of the same type in an architecture body, and we wish to use the same disconnection delay for all of them, we can use the **all** keyword in a disconnection specification instead of listing all of the signals. For example, if the following signal declarations are the only ones for guarded signals of type resolved_word:

```
signal source_bus_1, source_bus_2 : resolved_word bus;
signal address_bus : resolved_word bus;
```

we can specify a disconnection delay of 2 ns for all of the signals as follows:

```
disconnect all : resolved_word after 2 ns;
```

The remaining way of identifying which signals a disconnection specification applies to is with the keyword **others**. This identifies all remaining signals of a given type that are not referred to by previous disconnection specifications. For example, suppose that the signal address_bus shown above should have a disconnection delay of 3 ns instead of 2 ns. We could write the disconnection specifications for the set of signals as

```
disconnect address_bus : resolved_word after 3 ns;
```

```
disconnect others : resolved_word after 2 ns;
```

If we write a disconnection specification using the keyword **others** in an architecture body, it must appear after any other disconnection specifications referring to signals of the same type and after all declarations of signals of that type. Similarly, if we write a disconnection specification using the keyword **all**, it must be the only disconnection specification referring to signals of the given type and must appear after all declarations of signals of that type.

16.3 Using Blocks for Structural Modularity

In the previous section, we introduced block statements and showed how they may be used in conjunction with guarded signals to achieve automatic disconnection of drivers. In this section we look at the use of blocks to partition the concurrent statements within an architecture body. We can think of a block as a way of drawing a line around a collection of concurrent statements and their associated declarations, so that they can be clearly seen as a distinct aspect of a design. The full syntax rule for a block statement is as follows:

```
block_statement ⇐
    block_label :
    block ⟦ ( guard_expression ) ⟧ ⟦ is ⟧
        ⟦ generic ( generic_interface_list ) ;
        ⟦ generic map ( generic_association_list ) ; ⟧ ⟧
        ⟦ port ( port_interface_list ) ;
        ⟦ port map ( port_association_list ) ; ⟧ ⟧
        { block_declarative_item }
    begin
        { concurrent_statement }
    end block ⟦ block_label ⟧ ;
```

The block label is required to identify the block statement. The guard expression, as we saw in the previous section, may be used to control guarded signal assignments. If we are only using a block as a means of partitioning a design, we do not need to include a guard expression. The generic and port clauses allow us to define an interface to the block. We return to this shortly.

The declarative part of a block statement allows us to declare items that are local to the block. We can include the same kinds of declarations here as we can in an architecture body, for example, constant, type, subtype, signal and subprogram declarations. Items declared in a block are only visible within that block and cannot be referred to before or after it. However, items declared in the enclosing architecture body remain visible (unless hidden by a local item declared within the block).

EXAMPLE

To illustrate how blocks can be used for partitioning a design, we develop a model for a counter, including detailed pin-to-pin propagation delays and some error checking. We can specify the propagation delays as combinations of input delays before the function block and output delays after the function block, as shown in Figure 16-11. The function block implements the behavior of the counter with zero delay. The entity declaration for this counter is shown in Figure 16-12.

We can separate the delay, function and error-checking aspects of the model into separate blocks within the architecture body, as shown in Figure 16-13. The first block, input_port_delay, derives delayed versions of the input ports. These are used in the second block, functionality, the zero-delay behavioral implementation of the counter. This block consists of two concurrent signal assignment statements that together implement a finite-state machine. One statement calculates the next

FIGURE 16-11

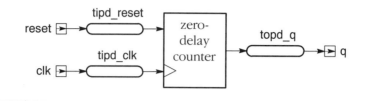

A propagation delay model for a counter.

FIGURE 16-12

```
entity counter is
    generic ( tipd_reset,              -- input prop delay on reset
              tipd_clk,                -- input prop delay on clk
              topd_q : delay_length;   -- output prop delay on q
              tsetup_reset,            -- setup: reset before clk
              thold_reset : delay_length );  -- hold time: reset after clk
    port ( reset,                      -- synchronous reset input
           clk : in bit;               -- edge triggered clock input
           q : out bit_vector );       -- counter output
end entity counter;
```

An entity declaration for the counter.

FIGURE 16-13

```
architecture detailed_timing of counter is
    signal reset_ipd,                  -- data input port delayed
           clk_ipd : bit;              -- clock input port delayed
    signal q_zd : bit_vector(q'range); -- q output with zero delay
begin
    input_port_delay : block is
    begin
        reset_ipd <= reset after tipd_reset;
        clk_ipd <= clk after tipd_clk;
    end block input_port_delay;

    functionality : block is
        function increment ( bv : bit_vector ) return bit_vector is
            variable result : bit_vector(bv'range) := bv;
            variable carry : bit := '1';
        begin
            for index in result'reverse_range loop
                result(index) := bv(index) xor carry;
                carry := bv(index) and carry;
                exit when carry = '0';
            end loop;
            return result;
        end function increment;
```

```
        signal next_count : bit_vector(q'range);
    begin
        next_count <= increment(q_zd) when reset_ipd = '0' else
                            (others => '0');
        q_zd <= next_count when clk_ipd = '1' and clk_ipd'event;
    end block functionality;

    output_port_delay : block is
    begin
        q <= q_zd after topd_q;
    end block output_port_delay;

    timing_checks : block is
    begin
        -- check setup time: reset before clk
        . . .
        -- check hold time: reset after clk
        . . .
    end block timing_checks;
end architecture detailed_timing;
```

An architecture body for the counter.

count value using the **increment** function locally declared within the block, and the other implements an edge-triggered register. The signal **next_count**, also locally declared within the block, is used to connect the two statements. The output of the state machine is used in the third block, **output_port_delay**, to apply the delay between the function block and the output port. The final block outlined in the architecture body, **timing_checks**, contains processes that verify correct setup and hold times for the **reset** signal.

Since a block contains a collection of concurrent statements, and a block statement is itself a concurrent statement, it is perfectly legal to nest blocks one inside another. The same visibility rules that we described for subprograms also apply for items declared in nested blocks. However, in practice, we would rarely write a model with nested blocks. If the design hierarchy is that complex, it is better to use separate entities and component instantiation statements to partition the design. The main reason VHDL allows complex nesting of blocks is that the block structure is used as the underlying mechanism for implementing other VHDL constructs, such as component instantiation (described in Chapter 13) and generate statements (described in Chapter 14). The language definition defines these constructs in terms of the substitution of blocks containing the contents of the architecture body being instantiated or the contents of the generate statement.

Generics and Ports in Blocks

Another aspect of block statements, also arising from their use as the underlying mechanism for component instantiation, is the possibility of including generic and port interface lists. These allow us to make explicit the interface between the block and its enclosing architecture body or enclosing block. The formal generic constants and ports can be used within the block in exactly the same way that those of an entity are used within a corresponding architecture body. The actual values for generic constants are supplied by a generic map in the block header, and the actual signals associated with the formal ports are supplied by a port map. These are all shown in the syntax rule for block statements on page 459. Since this facility is rarely used in actual model writing, we do not dwell on it beyond looking at one simple example.

EXAMPLE

The architecture body shown in Figure 16-14 contains a block, **mux**, with generic constant **width** and ports **d0**, **d1**, **y** and **sel**. The generic constant is used to constrain the size of the ports. The concurrent signal assignment statements within the block refer to the formal ports of the block and the local objects **zero**, **gated_d0** and **gated_d1**. The generic map supplies an actual value for **width**, using the constant **sig_width** declared in the enclosing architecture body. Similarly, the port map associates the actual signals **s1**, **s2**, **s3** and **sel** from the enclosing architecture body with the formal ports of the block.

FIGURE 16-14

```
architecture contrived of example_entity is
    constant sig_width : positive := 16;
    signal s1, s2, s3 : bit_vector (0 to sig_width – 1);
    signal sel : bit;
    . . .
begin
    mux : block is
        generic ( width : positive );
        generic map ( width => sig_width );
        port ( d0, d1 : in bit_vector(0 to width – 1);
               y : out bit_vector(0 to width – 1);
               sel : in bit );
        port map ( d0 => s1, d1=> s2, y => s3, sel => sel );
        constant zero : bit_vector(0 to width – 1) := ( others => '0' );
        signal gated_d0, gated_d1 : bit_vector(0 to width – 1);
    begin
        gated_d0 <= d0 when sel = '0' else zero;
        gated_d1 <= d1 when sel = '1' else zero;
        y <= gated_d0 or gated_d1;
    end block mux;

    . . .

end architecture contrived;
```

An outline of an architecture body containing a block with generic constants and ports.

Configuring Designs with Blocks

In Chapter 13 we showed how to configure a design whose hierarchy was formed by instantiating components. We configure an architecture body containing nested block statements in a similar way. When we write configuration declarations for such architecture bodies, the configuration information must mirror the block structure of the architecture body. We introduce a further level of detail in the syntax rules for configuration declarations, showing how to configure architecture bodies containing blocks.

configuration_declaration ⟸
    configuration identifier **of** *entity*_name **is**
        block_configuration
    end ⟦ **configuration** ⟧ ⟦ identifier ⟧ ;
block_configuration ⟸
    for (*architecture*_name
            ❘ *block_statement*_label)
       {   block_configuration
        ❘   **for** component_specification
            ⟦ binding_indication ; ⟧
            ⟦ block_configuration ⟧
        end for ; }
    end for ;

The difference here is that we have added a block statement label as an alternative to an architecture name at the point where we specify the region containing concurrent statements. Furthermore, we have allowed a block configuration as an alternative to component configuration information within that region. If we put these together, we can see how to write the configuration information for an architecture body containing block statements. At the top level of the configuration declaration, we write a block configuration naming the architecture body, just as we have done in all of the previous examples. Within it, however, we include block configurations that name and configure each block.

EXAMPLE

Suppose we need to write a model for an integrated circuit that takes account of propagation delays through input and output pads. The entity declaration and architecture body are shown in Figure 16-15. The architecture body is divided into blocks for input delay, function and output delay. The operation of the circuit is described structurally, as an interconnection of cells within the function block.

FIGURE 16-15

```
entity circuit is
    generic ( inpad_delay, outpad_delay : delay_length );
    port ( in1, in2, in3 : in bit;  out1, out2 : out bit );
end entity circuit;
_____

architecture with_pad_delays of circuit is
    component subcircuit is
        port ( a, b : in bit;  y1, y2 : out bit );
    end component subcircuit;

    signal delayed_in1, delayed_in2, delayed_in3 : bit;
    signal undelayed_out1, undelayed_out2 : bit;
begin
    input_delays : block is
    begin
        delayed_in1 <= in1 after inpad_delay;
        delayed_in2 <= in2 after inpad_delay;
        delayed_in3 <= in3 after inpad_delay;
    end block input_delays;

    functionality : block is
        signal intermediate : bit;
    begin
        cell1 : component subcircuit
            port map ( delayed_in1, delayed_in2, undelayed_out1, intermediate );
        cell2 : component subcircuit
            port map ( intermediate, delayed_in3, undelayed_out2, open );
    end block functionality;

    output_delays : block is
    begin
        out1 <= undelayed_out1 after outpad_delay;
        out2 <= undelayed_out2 after outpad_delay;
    end block output_delays;
end architecture with_pad_delays;
```

An entity and architecture body for a design, partitioned into separate blocks for pad delays and functionality.

A configuration declaration for this design, shown in Figure 16-16, binds the instances of the component subcircuit within the block functionality to an entity real_subcircuit with architecture basic. The block configuration starting with "**for with_pad_delays**" specifies the architecture of circuit that is being configured. Within it, the block configuration starting with "**for functionality**" specifies the configuration of the contents of the block labeled functionality. It, in turn, contains a component configuration for the two component instances. Note that there are no block configurations for the other two blocks in the design, since they do not contain any component instances. They only contain concurrent signal assignment statements, which represent leaf nodes of the design hierarchy.

FIGURE 16-16

```
configuration full of circuit is
    for with_pad_delays   -- configure the architecture
        for functionality   -- configure the block
            for all : subcircuit
                use entity work.real_subcircuit(basic);
            end for;
        end for;
    end for;
end configuration full;
```

A configuration declaration for the partitioned design.

Exercises

1. [❶ 16.1] Write signal declarations for
   - a bus-kind signal, serial_bus, of the resolved subtype wired_or_bit, and
   - a register-kind signal, d_node, of the resolved subtype unique_bit.

2. [❶ 16.1] A signal rx_bus is declared to be a bus-kind signal of type std_logic. Trace the value of the signal as transactions from the following two drivers are applied:
   - null, '0' after 10 ns, '1' after 20 ns, '0' after 30 ns, null after 40 ns
   - null, '1' after 35 ns, '0' after 45 ns, null after 55 ns

3. [❶ 16.1] Repeat Exercise 2, this time assuming rx_bus is a register-kind signal that is initialized to 'U'.

4. [❶ 16.1] Write a signal assignment statement that schedules the value 3 on an integer signal vote after 2 µs, then disconnects from the signal after 5 µs.

5. [❶ 16.1] Suppose a process contains the following signal assignment, executed at time 150 ns:

   result <= 0 **after** 10 ns, 42 **after** 20 ns, 0 **after** 100 ns, **null after** 120 ns;

   Assuming the driver for result is disconnected at time 150 ns, trace the value of result'driving resulting from the signal assignment.

6. [❶ 16.1] If the resolution function in the example on page 449 were modified to perform the logical "and" operation on the contributed values, what should the function return when called with an empty vector argument?

7. [❶ 16.2] Write a block with a guard expression that is true when a signal en is '1' or 'H'. The block should contain a guarded signal assignment that assigns an inverted version of the signal d_in to the signal q_out_n when the guard expression is true.

8. [❶ 16.2] Write disconnection specifications that specify
   - a disconnection delay of 3.5 ns for a signal **source1** of type **wired_word**,
   - a disconnection delay of 3.2 ns for other signals of type **wired_word**, and
   - a disconnection delay of 2.8 ns for all signals of type **wired_bit**.

9. [❶ 16.2] Trace the values on the signal **priority** resulting from execution of the following statements. The resolution function for the subtype **resolved_integer** selects the leftmost value from the contributing drivers or returns the value 0 if there are no contributions. Assume that no other drivers for **priority** are connected.

   ```
   signal request : integer := 0;
   signal guard : boolean := false;
   signal priority : resolved_integer bus := 0;
   disconnect priority : resolved_integer after 2 ns;
   . . .
   request <= 3 after 40 ns, 5 after 80 ns, 1 after 120 ns;
   guard <= true after 50 ns, false after 100 ns;
   priority <= guarded request after 1 ns;
   ```

10. [❶ 16.3] Write a block statement that encapsulates component instantiation statements implementing the following circuit. The signal **q_internal**, of type **bit**, should be declared local to the block.

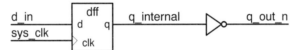

11. [❶ 16.3] Write a block configuration for the block statement described in Exercise 10, binding the flipflop component instance to an entity **d_flipflop** and architecture **basic**, and the inverter component to the entity **inverter** and architecture **basic**. The entities are in the current working library.

12. [❷ 16.1] Suppose we declare the following subtypes:

    ```
    subtype word is bit_vector(31 downto 0);
    . . .
    subtype resolved_word is bitwise_or word;
    ```

    The resolution function performs a bitwise logical "or" operation on the contributing driver values. Write a procedure that encapsulates the behavior of a tristate buffer. The procedure has input signal parameters **oe** of type **bit** and **d** of the subtype **word** and an output signal parameter **z** of type **resolved_word**. When **oe** is '1', the value of **d** is transmitted to **z**. When **oe** is '0', **z** is disconnected. Test the procedure by invoking it with a number of concurrent procedure calls in a test bench.

13. [❷ 16.2] Develop a dataflow model of a latching four-input multiplexer. The multiplexer has four data inputs, two bits of select input, and an enable input. When the enable input is high, the select inputs determine which data input is transmitted to the single data output. When the enable input is low, the value on the data output is latched.

14. [❷ 16.2] A dynamic register can be implemented in NMOS technology as follows:

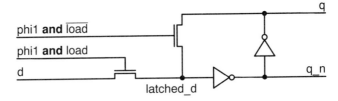

Develop a dataflow model for this form of register, using guarded signal assignments to model the pass transistors. The signals should be of a resolved subtype of bit, and the signal latched_d should be a register-kind signal.

15. [❷ 16.3] Develop a behavioral model of a three-to-eight decoder with three select inputs, an enable input and eight active-low outputs. The entity interface includes generic constants for

   • input propagation delay for the enable input,
   • input propagation delay for the select inputs, and
   • output propagation delay for the outputs.

Write the architecture body with separate blocks for input delays, function and output delays.

16. [❸ 16.1] Revise the tristate buffer procedure described in Exercise 12 to make it bidirectional. Include an additional input parameter that determines the direction of data transfer.

17. [❸ 16.1] Develop a behavioral model of a read/write memory with a bidirectional data port of the type resolved_byte, defined on page 449. The data port should be a bus-kind signal, and the model should use null signal assignments appropriately to indicate when the memory is not supplying data.

18. [❸ 16.2] A four-bit carry-look-ahead adder can be implemented in CMOS technology with a *Manchester carry chain*, shown in the following diagram:

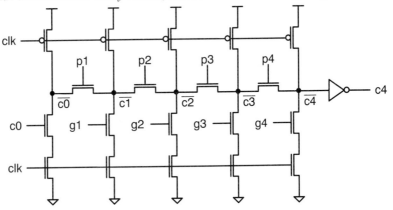

The signal c0 is the carry input, c4 is the carry output, $\overline{c0}$ to $\overline{c4}$ are active-low intermediate carry signals, g1 to g4 are carry generate signals and p1 to p4 are carry propagate signals. During the low half of a clock cycle, the intermediate carry signals are precharged to '1'. During the high half of the clock cycle, the pass transistors

controlled by the generate and propagate signals conditionally discharge the intermediate carry signals, determining their final value. The Boolean equations for
the sum, generate and propagate signals are

$$s_i = a_i \oplus b_i \oplus c_{i-1}$$
$$g_i = a_i\, b_i$$
$$p_i = a_i + b_i$$

Develop a dataflow model of a four-bit Manchester carry adder, using register-kind
signals for the internal carry signals. All signals should be of a resolved-bit type.

19. [❸ 16.2] A 4×4 barrel shifter can be constructed from pass transistors as follows:

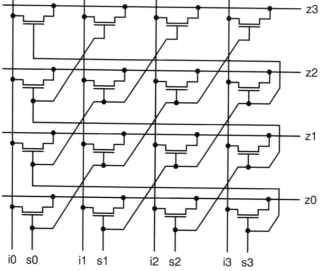

The signals i0 to i3 are the inputs, and z0 to z3 are the outputs. The control signal
s0 causes input bits to be transmitted to the outputs unshifted, s1 causes them to
be shifted by one place, s2 by two places and s3 by three places. The outputs must
be precharged to '1' on the first half of a clock cycle, then one of the control signals
activated on the second half of the clock cycle. Develop a dataflow model of the
barrel shifter, using register-kind signals for the output signals. All signals should
be of a resolved-bit type.

Access Types
and Abstract Data Types

We have seen in previous chapters how we can use variables within processes to create data that is associated with a name. We can write a variable name in a model to read its value in expressions and to update its value in variable assignment statements. In this chapter, we introduce access types as a mechanism in VHDL for creating and managing unnamed data during a simulation.

17.1 Access Types

The scalar and composite data types we are now familiar with can be used to represent either single data items or regular collections of data. However, in some applications, we need to store collections of data whose size is not known in advance. Alternatively, we may need to represent a complex set of relations between individual data objects. In these cases, simple scalar and composite types are not sufficient. Instead, we need to create data objects as they are required during a simulation and to represent the links between these data objects. We do this in VHDL using *access types*. These are similar to pointer types found in many programming languages. In VHDL, access types are used mainly in high-level behavioral models and rarely in low-level models.

We start this section with a description of access types, pointers and mechanisms for creating data objects. Then we look at the way in which these mechanisms are used to create linked data structures during a simulation.

Access Type Declarations and Allocators

We can declare an access type using a new form of type definition, given by the syntax rule

    access_type_definition ⇐ **access** subtype_indication

We can include such a type definition in a type declaration, for example:

    type natural_ptr **is access** natural;

This defines a new type, named natural_ptr, representing values that point to data objects of type natural. Values of type natural_ptr can only point to natural numbers, not to objects of any other type. In general, we can write access type declarations referring to any VHDL type except file types.

Once we have declared an access type, we can declare a variable of that type within a process or subprogram. For example, we might declare a variable of the type natural_ptr shown above:

    variable count : natural_ptr;

This declaration creates a variable, called count, that may point to a data object of type natural stored in memory. Initially, the variable has the value **null**. This is a special pointer value that does not point to any data object and is the default initial value for any access type. We can represent the null pointer variable pictorially as shown in Figure 17-1(a). The box represents the location in memory where the variable count is stored. Since it is a named variable, we can label the box with the variable name. Note that we cannot declare constants or signals of access types. Variables are the only class of object that may be of an access type.

Next, we can create a new natural number data object and set count to point to it. We do this using an *allocator*, written according to the following syntax rule:

    primary ⇐ **new** subtype_indication ∥ **new** qualified_expression

This rule shows that an allocator, written using the keyword **new**, is a kind of primary. Recall that primaries are the basis of VHDL expressions. The first form of allocator

FIGURE 17-1

(a) An access variable initialized to **null**. *(b) A data object created by an allocator expression. (c) A pointer returned by an allocator assigned to the access variable.*

creates a new data object of the specified subtype in memory, initializes it to the default initial value for the subtype and returns a pointer to it. For example, the allocator expression

    new natural

creates a natural number data object in memory and initialized to 0 (the leftmost value in the subtype **natural**). The allocator then returns a pointer to the object, as shown in Figure 17-1(b). The box represents the location in memory where the data object is stored, but since it is an unnamed object, there is no label. Instead, the arrow represents the pointer to the object. This is the only way of accessing the object.

    The next step is to assign the pointer to the access variable **count**. Since the allocator is an expression that returns the pointer value, we can write it on the right-hand side of a variable assignment statement, as follows:

    count := **new** natural;

This statement has the combined effects of creating and initializing the data object, and assigning a pointer to it to the variable **count**, as shown in Figure 17-1(c). The pointer overwrites the null pointer previously stored in **count**.

    Now that we have an access variable pointing to a data object in memory, we can use and update the value of the object, accessing it via the variable. This use of the variable is the reason for the terms "access type" and "access variable." We access the object using the keyword **all** as a suffix after the access variable name. For example, we can update the object's value as follows:

    count.**all** := 10;

and we use its value in an expression:

    if count.**all** = 0 **then**

        . . .

    end if;

    Note that we need to use the keyword **all** in this way if we wish to use the data object rather than the pointer itself. If we had written the expression "count = 0", our VHDL analyzer would report an error, since the value of **count** is a pointer, not a number, so it cannot be compared with the number 0.

    The second form of allocator, shown in the syntax rule on page 470, uses a qualified expression to specify both the subtype and the initial value for the created data object. Recall that the syntax rule for a qualified expression is

qualified expression ⇐
    type_mark ' (expression) ‖ type_mark ' aggregate

Thus, instead of writing the two statements:

```
count := new natural;
count.all := 10;
```

we could achieve the same effect with this second form of allocator:

```
count := new natural'(10);
```

The qualified expression can also take the form of an array or record aggregate. For example, if we have a record type and access type declared as

```
type stimulus_record is record
        stimulus_time : time;
        stimulus_value : bit_vector(0 to 3);
    end record stimulus_record;

type stimulus_ptr is access stimulus_record;
```

and an access variable declared as

```
variable bus_stimulus : stimulus_ptr;
```

we could create a new stimulus record data object and set **bus_stimulus** to point to it as follows:

```
bus_stimulus := new stimulus_record'( 20 ns, B"0011" );
```

The value in the allocator is a qualified record aggregate that specifies both the type of the data object (**stimulus_record**) and the value for each of the record elements.

Assignment and Equality of Access Values

Let us now look at the effect of assigning one access variable value to another access variable. Suppose we have two access variables declared as follows:

```
variable count1, count2 : natural_ptr;
```

and we create data objects and set the variables to point to them:

```
count1 := new natural'(5);
count2 := new natural'(10);
```

The variables and data objects are illustrated in Figure 17-2(a). Next, we perform the following variable assignment:

```
count2 := count1;
```

The effect of this assignment is to copy the pointer from **count1** into **count2**, making both access variables point to the same object, as shown in Figure 17-2(b). We can see that this is in fact the case by accessing the object via each of the access variables. For example, if we update the object via **count1**

```
count1.all := 20;
```

FIGURE 17-2

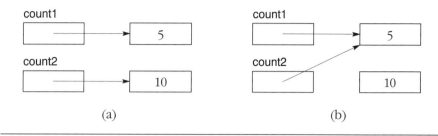

(a)   (b)

The effect of assigning one access variable to another. The two variables point to the same data object.

then the value we get via count2.**all** is 20.

Note that when we copied the pointer from count1 to count2, we overwrote the pointer to the data object 10. The object itself is still stored in memory, but count2 is no longer pointing to it. If we had previously copied the pointer before overwriting it, then we could access the object via that other copy. However, if there is no other pointer to the object, it is inaccessible. This is one of the main differences between named variables and allocated data objects. We can always access a variable by using its name, but an allocated object has no name, so we can only access it via pointers. If there are no pointers to an object, it is lost forever, even though it is still resident in the host computer's memory. We often call such inaccessible objects *garbage*. We return to the topic of dealing with unneeded objects later in this section.

Next, we look at the effect of comparing two access variables using the "=" and "/=" operators. These operators test whether the two pointers point to the same location in memory. For example, after performing the assignment

    count2 := count1;

the expression

    count1 = count2

is true, since, as Figure 17-2(b) shows, the two access variables then point to the same object. However, if we instead set count1 and count2 as follows:

    count1 := **new** natural'(30);
    count2 := **new** natural'(30);

we create two distinct data objects in memory, each storing the number 30. The variable count1 points to one of them, and count2 points to the other. In this case the result of the equality comparison is false. If we really want to test whether the data objects are equal, as opposed to testing the pointers, we write

    count1.**all** = count2.**all**

One very useful pointer comparison is the test for equality with **null**, the special pointer value that does not point to any object. For example, we might write

    if count1 /= **null then**
        count1.**all** := count1.**all** + 1;
    end if;

The test in the if statement ensures that we only access the value pointed to by count1 if there is a value to access. If count1 has the value **null**, trying to access count1.**all** results in an error.

Access Types for Records and Arrays

We have introduced access types in this section by concentrating on access types that point to scalars, in order to keep things simple. However, most models that include access types use them to point to records or arrays. Pointers to records are mainly used for building linked data structures, and pointers to arrays are used if the lengths of the arrays are not known when the model is written. In both cases, we can use a shorthand notation for referring to objects via access variables.

Let us start with records and return to the example shown earlier, in which we had types declared as

```
type stimulus_record is record
        stimulus_time : time;
        stimulus_value : bit_vector(0 to 3);
    end record stimulus_record;

type stimulus_ptr is access stimulus_record;
```

We also declared an access variable as

```
variable bus_stimulus : stimulus_ptr;
```

We have seen that we can access a record object pointed to by bus_stimulus using the notation "bus_stimulus.**all**". If we want to refer to the stimulus_time element, we could write "bus_stimulus.**all**.stimulus_time". In practice, we usually want to refer either to the pointer itself or to an element of the record, and rarely to the record as a whole. For this reason, VHDL allows us to write "bus_stimulus.stimulus_time" to refer to the record element. Whenever we select a record element name after an access variable name, we automatically follow the pointer to get to the record.

A similar shorthand notation applies when we use access variables that point to array data objects. For example, suppose we declare types as follows:

```
type coordinate is array (1 to 3) of real;
type coordinate_ptr is access coordinate;
```

and an access variable:

```
variable origin : coordinate_ptr := new coordinate'(0.0, 0.0, 0.0);
```

This last declaration creates the access variable and initializes it to point to an array object initialized with the aggregate value. We can refer to the elements of the array using the notation "origin(1)", "origin(2)" and "origin(3)", instead of having to write "origin.**all**(1)", and so on. This is similar to accessing elements of records. Whenever we write an array index after an access variable name, we automatically follow the pointer to the array.

One of the advantages of using access types that point to array objects is that we can deal with arrays of mixed lengths. This is in contrast to array variables, which have their length fixed when they are created. For example, if we create an array variable activation_times as follows:

type time_array **is array** (positive **range** <>) **of** time;
variable activation_times : time_array(1 **to** 100);

it is fixed at 100 elements for its entire lifetime. On the other hand, we can create an access type that points to data objects of an unconstrained array type, for example:

type time_array_ptr **is access** time_array;

and declare our variable to be a pointer of this type:

variable activation_times : time_array_ptr;

Since the variable points to an array object of an unconstrained type, it may point to different array objects of different lengths during the course of a simulation. However, each array object is constrained. This means that once an array object is created in memory, its length is fixed. We can create an array object using an allocator that includes a qualified aggregate, for example:

activation_times := **new** time_array'(10 us, 15 us, 40 us);

This allocator creates an array object whose length is determined from the length of the aggregate. We can update each of these elements, but we cannot change the size of the array. If we need to add two more elements, we have to create a new array object of length five, with the first three elements being a copy of the elements from the old array. This might be done as follows:

activation_times := **new** time_array'(activation_times.**all**
                                        & time_array'(70 us, 100 us));

The allocator in this assignment creates an array object whose length is determined by the result of the concatenation operation. If we want to create an array object without initializing the values, we write an allocator that names the array type and includes an index constraint. For example, to create an array object of length 10, we might write

activation_times := **new** time_array(1 **to** 10);

17.2 Linked Data Structures

Suppose we wish to store a list of values to be used to stimulate a signal during a simulation. One possible approach would be to define an array variable of stimulus values. However, a problem arises if we do not know how large to make the array. If we make it too small, we may run out of space. If we make it too large, we may waste space in the host computer's memory and run out of space for other variables. The alternative approach is to use access types and to create values only as they are needed. The values can be linked together with pointers to form an extensible data structure. There are several possible organizations for linked structures, but we look at one of the simplest, a *linked list*, as an example, showing how it is constructed and manipulated.

A linked list of values that might be used as stimuli for a signal is shown in Figure 17-3. To construct this list, we need to compose each cell from a record that

FIGURE 17-3

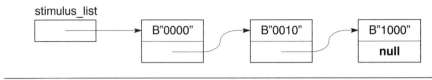

A linked list structure of stimulus records.

has one element for the stimulus value and an extra element for a pointer to the next cell in the list. This pointer must be of an access type used to access record objects. A first attempt to write the type declarations for this structure might be

type value_cell **is record**
        value : bit_vector(0 **to** 3);
        next_cell : value_ptr;
    end record value_cell;

type value_ptr **is access** value_cell;

The problem here is that the definition of **value_cell** uses the name **value_ptr** as the type of one of the elements, but **value_ptr** is not declared until after the declaration of **value_cell**. If we reverse the two type declarations, the same problem arises in the definition of **value_ptr** when it tries to use the name **value_cell**. To solve this "chicken and egg" problem, VHDL lets us write an *incomplete type declaration* for the record type. The syntax rule is

type_declaration ⇐ **type** identifier ;

An incomplete type declaration simply names the type, indicating that it will be fully defined later. Meanwhile, we can use the type name to declare access types. However, we must complete the definition of the incomplete type before the end of the declarative part in which the incomplete declaration appears. Since we can do this after the access type declaration, we can use the name of the access type within the complete type declaration. Thus, we can rewrite our circular type declarations as

type value_cell;

type value_ptr **is access** value_cell;

type value_cell **is record**
        value : bit_vector(0 **to** 3);
        next_cell : value_ptr;
    end record value_cell;

Next we can declare an access variable to point to the beginning of the list:

variable value_list : value_ptr;

This declaration creates a variable containing a null pointer, as shown in Figure 17-4(a). We can think of this as representing an empty list. Thus, if we need to determine whether a list is empty, we can test the access variable to see if it is **null**, for example:

FIGURE 17-4

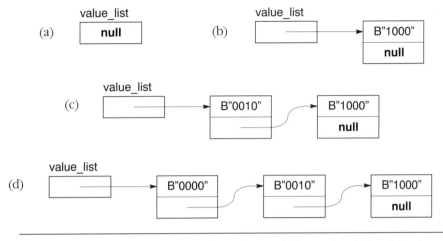

Successive stages in the creation of a list of stimulus values.

```
if value_list /= null then
    . . .        -- do something with the list
end if;
```

We can add a cell to the empty list by allocating a new record and assigning the pointer to the access variable, as follows:

```
value_list := new value_cell'( B"1000", value_list );
```

The second element in the aggregate is a copy of the pointer initially stored in **value_list**. This has the value **null**, so the result of executing the whole statement is as shown in Figure 17-4(b). The reason for using the old value of **value_list** instead of writing in the value **null** is that we can use the same form of statement to add the next cell:

```
value_list := new value_cell'( B"0010", value_list );
```

The allocator creates a new cell in memory, with the **value** element initialized to B"0010 and the **next_cell** element initialized to a copy of the pointer to the old cell. A pointer to the new cell is then returned and assigned to **value_list**, as shown in Figure 17-4(c). We can create the third cell in the same way:

```
value_list := new value_cell'( B"0000", value_list );
```

This assignment produces the final list as shown in Figure 17-4(d). Note that each cell we create is added onto the front of the list.

Now suppose we have a list of stimulus values of arbitrary length, pointed to by our access variable, and we wish to go through the list applying each value to a signal. We can write a loop to traverse the list as follows. We need to make use of a working variable, **current_stimulus**, of type **value_ptr**. The statements to perform this traversal are shown in Figure 17-5.

FIGURE 17-5

```
current_cell := value_list;
while current_cell /= null loop
    s <= current_cell.value;
    wait for 10 ns;
    current_cell := current_cell.next_cell;
end loop;
```

Statements to traverse a list of stimulus values.

FIGURE 17-6

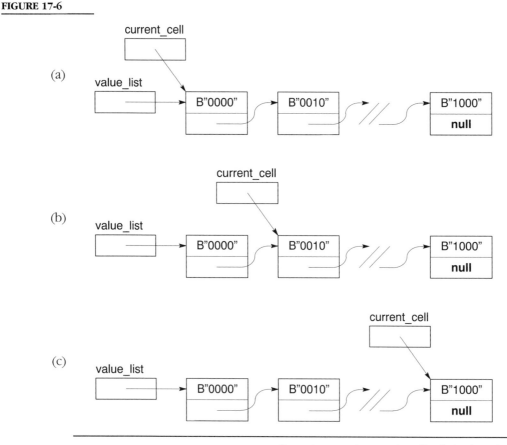

Successive stages in traversing a list of stimulus values.

The first assignment sets current_cell to point to the first cell in the list, as shown in Figure 17-6(a). The first pass through the loop uses the value element of this cell to stimulate the signal, then copies the next_cell element of the cell into the working variable. At the end of the first iteration the working variable points to the next element in the list, as shown in Figure 17-6(b). The loop repeats in this way, with current_cell being advanced from one cell to the next cell in each iteration. In the last iteration, the variable points to the last cell as shown in Figure 17-6(c). The next_cell element of this cell is **null**, and this is copied into current_cell. When the loop test is performed again it evaluates to false, and so the loop terminates.

Another operation we may wish to perform on a list is to search for a particular value. Again, we make use of a working access variable to traverse the list, checking each cell to see if its **value** element matches the value for which we are searching, as shown in Figure 17-7. The test for a null pointer in the loop condition is most important. It guards against the possibility that the sought value is not in the list. If the list terminates with the working variable equal to **null**, we know that the value was not found, and we can deal with the condition appropriately. Note that **and** operator in the loop condition is a "short circuit" operator, so the second part of the test will not proceed if current_cell is **null**, not pointing to any list cell.

FIGURE 17-7

```
current_cell := value_list;
while current_cell /= null and current_cell.value /= search_value loop
    current_cell := current_cell.next_cell;
end loop;
assert current_cell /= null
    report "search for value failed";
```

Statements to search for a value in a list of values.

The linked list data structure is just one of a number of linked data structures that we can construct using access types. Other examples include queues, trees and network structures. We come across some of these in further examples in this chapter and later in the book. However, the field of data structures is much larger than we can hope to cover in a book that focuses on hardware modeling and simulation. Fortunately, there are numerous good textbooks available that discuss data structures at length. Of these, the books that use the Ada programming language are particularly relevant, as VHDL's access types are based on those of Ada. (See, for example, [5].)

Deallocation and Storage Management

We saw earlier that if we overwrite a pointer to an unnamed data object, we can lose all means of accessing the object, making it "garbage." While this is usually not a problem, if we create too much garbage during a simulation run, the host computer may run out of memory space for allocating new objects. Some computers are able to avoid this problem by periodically scanning memory for inaccessible data and reclaiming the space they occupy, a process called *garbage collection*. However, most computers do not provide this service, so we may have to perform our own storage management.

The mechanism VHDL provides for us to do this is the implicitly defined procedure deallocate. Whenever we declare an access type, VHDL automatically provides an overloaded version of **deallocate** to handle pointers of that type. For example, if we declare an access type for pointers to objects of type T as follows:

    type T_ptr **is access** T;

we automatically get a version of **deallocate** declared as

procedure deallocate (P : **inout** T_ptr);

The purpose of this procedure is to reclaim the memory space used by the data object pointed to by the parameter P. When the procedure returns, it sets P to the null pointer, since the object is no longer stored in memory. Note that if P is **null** to start with, the procedure has no effect. Thus, there is no need to test whether a pointer is **null** before passing it to deallocate.

EXAMPLE

Suppose we wish to delete cells from our list of stimulus values, shown in the previous example. The first cell in the list is pointed to by the access variable value_list. We can delete the first cell and reclaim its storage as follows:

```
cell_to_be_deleted := value_list;
value_list := value_list.next_cell;
deallocate(cell_to_be_deleted);
```

The first statement simply copies the pointer to the first cell into the access variable cell_to_be_deleted, so that we do not lose access to it. The second statement advances the list head to the second cell. The third statement then reclaims the storage used by the first cell. Note that if we do not need to reclaim the storage for the first cell, we only need to include the second statement.

If we wish to delete the whole list, we can use a loop to repeat these statements for each cell in the list, as follows:

```
while value_list /= null loop
    cell_to_be_deleted := value_list;
    value_list := value_list.next_cell;
    deallocate(cell_to_be_deleted);
end loop;
```

This loop simply repeats the steps needed to delete the cell at the head of the list until the list is empty, indicated by value_list being **null**.

We can use deallocate to reclaim memory space, provided we are sure that no other pointer points to the object being deallocated. It is very important that we keep this condition in mind when using deallocate. If some other pointer points to an object that we deallocate, that pointer is not set to **null**. Instead, it becomes a "dangling" pointer, possibly pointing to some random piece of data in memory or not pointing to a valid memory location at all. If we try to access data via a dangling pointer, the effects are unpredictable, varying from accessing seemingly random data to crashing the simulation run. Thus, we must take the utmost care to avoid this situation when using deallocate. Furthermore, we should document such models very thoroughly, so that other designers using or modifying the models are aware of the potential problems.

17.3 Abstract Data Types Using Packages

We mentioned earlier that access types are most commonly used in high-level behavioral models of hardware systems, to create complex linked data structures. It is appropriate that we should also take a high-level view of the data structures. To do this, we introduce a term from the discipline of software engineering, *abstract data type* (ADT), and show how ADTs can be implemented in VHDL. An ADT is a data type, together with a collection of operations for creating and working with data objects of that type. In a strict implementation of an ADT, the data structure underlying the data type is not visible to users of the ADT. The operations provided are the only way of working with data objects, thus preventing incorrect use of the objects. This is the means of enforcing the abstract view of the data type. Unfortunately, VHDL does not provide a way of hiding the data structure, so we have to rely on conventions and documentation.

The most convenient way to implement an ADT in VHDL is to use a package. In the package declaration we write the VHDL type declarations that represent the underlying data structure and declare functions and procedures that perform the ADT operations. We, or other designers, can use these declarations to create data objects and perform operations on them without being concerned about the implementation details of the data structure. Any designer has plenty of other concerns to think about, so the more we can do to ease the task of system modeling, the more productive the designer will be. As implementers of the ADT, we write the details of the operations in the package body. We should make the operations as general as possible, so that we can reuse the ADT in several different designs.

EXAMPLE

Suppose we are working as part of a team designing a network communications controller. Within the behavioral model, we need to represent a buffer memory in which received bytes of data are stored. Bytes are retrieved from this buffer in the same order that they are written. This is often called a "first in, first out" (FIFO) buffer. Since memory in a real hardware system is not an infinite resource, we specify a bound on the amount of data that can be stored at once.

We write an ADT to provide types and operations for bounded buffers of bytes. The package declaration is shown in Figure 17-8. The parts of the package declaration marked as "private" are details of the concrete implementation of the bounded buffer ADT. A user of the ADT does not need to know about them. However, we need to include them in the package declaration in order to declare the type **bounded_buffer**, which is the type made public. Unfortunately, VHDL does not provide a way of hiding the types that should be private. Note that the operations **test_empty** and **test_full** are written as procedures rather than functions. We are forced to write them in this way, since function parameters must be objects of constant class, and constants may not be of an access type. Hence, we write the operations as procedures with variable class parameters of mode **in**.

The public information in the package declaration is all that is needed to write a model using bounded buffers. For example, Figure 17-9 shows a process that is part of the network receiver model, using the bounded buffer ADT. This process

FIGURE 17-8

```
package bounded_buffer_adt is
    subtype byte is bit_vector(0 to 7);
    type bounded_buffer_object;  -- private
    type bounded_buffer is access bounded_buffer_object;
    function new_bounded_buffer ( size : in positive ) return bounded_buffer;
    -- creates a bounded buffer object with 'size' bytes of storage
    procedure test_empty ( variable the_bounded_buffer : in bounded_buffer;
                           is_empty : out boolean );
    -- tests whether the bounded buffer is empty (i.e., no data to read)
    procedure test_full ( variable the_bounded_buffer : in bounded_buffer;
                          is_full : out boolean );
    -- tests whether the bounded buffer is full (i.e., no data can be written)
    procedure write ( the_bounded_buffer : inout bounded_buffer; data : in byte );
    -- if the bounded buffer is not full, writes the data
    -- if it is full, assertion violation with severity failure
    procedure read ( the_bounded_buffer : inout bounded_buffer; data : out byte );
    -- if the bounded buffer is not empty, read the first byte of data
    -- if it is empty, assertion violation with severity failure

    ------------------------------------------------------

    -- the following types are private to the ADT
    type store_array is array (natural range <>) of byte;
    type store_ptr is access store_array;
    type bounded_buffer_object is record
            byte_count : natural;
            head_index, tail_index : natural;
            store : store_ptr;
        end record bounded_buffer_object;
end package bounded_buffer_adt;
```

A package declaration for a bounded buffer ADT.

FIGURE 17-9

```
receiver : process is
    use work.bounded_buffer_adt.all;
    variable receive_buffer : bounded_buffer := new_bounded_buffer(2048);
    variable buffer_overrun, buffer_underrun : boolean;
    . . .
begin
    . . .
    test_full(receive_buffer, buffer_overrun);
    if not buffer_overrun then
        write(receive_buffer, received_byte);
    end if;
```

```
    . . .
    test_empty(receive_buffer, buffer_underrun);
    if not buffer_underrun then
        read(receive_buffer, check_byte);
    end if;
    . . .

end process receiver;
```

A process forming part of a network receiver, using the bounded buffer ADT.

FIGURE 17-10

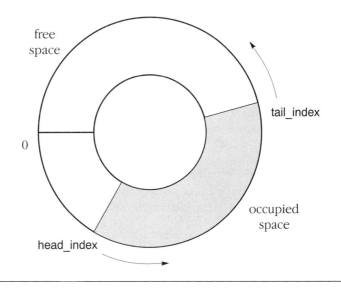

The array used to store data as a circular buffer.

makes no reference to the implementation details of the bounded buffer. It is written using only the operations provided in the public interface of the package. The advantage of separating out the bounded buffer part of the model into an ADT is that the model is more compact, easier to write and easier to understand.

We can now turn to the implementation details of the bounded buffer ADT. The converse advantage of the separation is that as the implementer of the ADT, we can concentrate on writing it as a compact, well-defined software module. We are not distracted by the code of the models that use bounded buffers. The private types in the package declaration indicate that the concrete implementation of this bounded buffer ADT is as a *circular buffer*, stored in an array of bytes, as shown in Figure 17-10. (We can think of the end of the array as being wrapped around to meet the beginning, forming a circle.) Data is stored in successive bytes in the array, starting from the first element. The record element **tail_index** contains the index of the next free position in the array, and the element **head_index** contains the index of the first available byte. Each time a new byte is written to the buffer, **tail_index** is incremented, and each time a byte is read, **head_index** is incremented. They are incremented modulo the size of the buffer, so that the space made available when bytes are read is reused for new bytes when the end of the array is reached. The record element **byte_count** keeps track of the number of bytes in the buffer, and is used to ensure that the write position does not overtake the read position, and vice versa.

The package body is shown in Figure 17-11. The function **new_bounded_buffer** allocates a new record object in memory, with the **byte_count**, **head_index** and **tail_index** elements initialized to zero. The **store** element is initialized to a pointer to an array of bytes allocated in memory. The length of this array is determined by the actual parameter passed to the function. The procedure **test_empty** simply tests whether the **byte_count** element of the record object is zero. The procedure **test_full** tests whether **byte_count** is equal to the length of the array used to store data.

FIGURE 17-11

```
package body bounded_buffer_adt is
    function new_bounded_buffer ( size : in positive ) return bounded_buffer is
    begin
        return new bounded_buffer_object'(
                            byte_count => 0, head_index => 0, tail_index => 0,
                            store => new store_array(0 to size – 1) );
    end function new_bounded_buffer;

    procedure test_empty ( variable the_bounded_buffer : in bounded_buffer;
                           is_empty : out boolean ) is
    begin
        is_empty := the_bounded_buffer.byte_count = 0;
    end procedure test_empty;

    procedure test_full ( variable the_bounded_buffer : in bounded_buffer;
                          is_full : out boolean ) is
    begin
        is_full := the_bounded_buffer.byte_count = the_bounded_buffer.store'length;
    end procedure test_full;

    procedure write ( the_bounded_buffer : inout bounded_buffer;  data : in byte ) is
        variable buffer_full : boolean;
    begin
        test_full(the_bounded_buffer, buffer_full);
        if buffer_full then
            report "write to full bounded buffer" severity failure;
        else
            the_bounded_buffer.store(the_bounded_buffer.tail_index) := data;
            the_bounded_buffer.tail_index := (the_bounded_buffer.tail_index + 1)
                                              mod the_bounded_buffer.store'length;
            the_bounded_buffer.byte_count := the_bounded_buffer.byte_count + 1;
        end if;
    end procedure write;

    procedure read ( the_bounded_buffer : inout bounded_buffer;  data : out byte ) is
        variable buffer_empty : boolean;
    begin
        test_empty(the_bounded_buffer, buffer_empty);
```

```
        if buffer_empty then
            report "read from empty bounded buffer" severity failure;
        else
            data := the_bounded_buffer.store(the_bounded_buffer.head_index);
            the_bounded_buffer.head_index := (the_bounded_buffer.head_index + 1)
                                        mod the_bounded_buffer.store'length;
            the_bounded_buffer.byte_count := the_bounded_buffer.byte_count − 1;
        end if;
    end procedure read;
end package body bounded_buffer_adt;
```

The package body for the bounded buffer ADT implementation.

The **write** procedure uses an assertion statement to test whether the buffer is full, using the ADT operation **test_full**. It then writes the data byte into the buffer at the tail position and increments the **tail_index** element of the record. The **read** procedure similarly uses an assertion statement to test whether the buffer is empty, using the ADT operation **test_empty**. It then reads the data byte from the head position of the buffer and increments the **head_index** element of the record.

The advantages of using ADTs in complex behavioral models are overwhelming, but there is one risk that must be borne. As we mentioned before, VHDL provides no way of hiding the concrete details of the data structure underlying an ADT, as the type declarations must be written in the package declaration. This means that an ADT user can make use of the information to modify the data structures without using the ADT procedures and functions. For example, if an ADT operation simply updates a record element, a user might be tempted to update the record directly and avoid the overhead of a procedure call. However, modern compilers and computers make such "optimizations" unnecessary, and the risk is that the user might inadvertently corrupt the data structure. ADTs in VHDL require that users avoid such temptations and abide by the contract expressed in the ADT interface. A small amount of self-discipline here will yield significant benefits in the modeling process.

Container ADTs

One good application of ADTs is as "container" or "collection" types. We have seen one such type when we introduced linked data structures. The linked list in that example was a collection of stimulus values. We can organize a linked structure in other ways, depending on how we need to access the objects in the collection. The significant aspect of such structures, however, is that the way we implement them is largely independent of the type of object they contain. For example, adding a new element to a list is done in the same way for a list of integers, a list of records, or lists of any other type of object. This indicates that we should look for a way to make a general-purpose list ADT that we can specialize for different types of contained objects.

Unfortunately, VHDL does not provide a mechanism for parameterizing a package with a type name, so we cannot literally write an ADT for some collection structure and fill in the type of contained object later. However, we can come close to the same effect by writing a template package for the ADT that has a placeholder where the type name for the contained object should be. Each time we need a new kind of collection, we use a text editor to make a copy of the template and fill in the placeholder.

Example: An Ordered-Collection ADT

We can create an ADT that represents an ordered collection of objects. The objects in the collection should have a key that can be used to determine their relative order. The ADT provides operations to insert new objects into a collection, to search for an object with a given key, to traverse the collection and to delete an object. First, Figure 17-12 shows the template for the package declaration defining the ADT. The identifiers in "«...»" brackets are template placeholders to be filled in when the package is specialized for a particular type of contained object. The template placeholders «element_type» and «key_type» must be replaced by the names of the element type and key type. The placeholder «key_function» must be replaced by the name of a function that takes an element as a parameter and returns its key value. The placeholder «less_than_function» must be replaced by the name of a function that compares two key values. Note that element_type and key_type may not be access types, since they are used as the types of function parameters.

FIGURE 17-12

```
package «element_type_simple_name»_ordered_collection_adt is
        -- template: fill in the placeholders to specialize for a particular type

    alias element_type is «element_type»;
    alias key_type is «key_type»;
    alias key_of is «key_function» [ element_type return key_type ];
    alias ”<” is «less_than_function» [ key_type, key_type return boolean ];

        -- types provided by the package

    type ordered_collection_object;        -- private
    type position_object;                  -- private

    type ordered_collection is access ordered_collection_object;
    type position is access position_object;

        -- operations on ordered collections

    function new_ordered_collection return ordered_collection;
        -- returns an empty ordered collection of element_type values

    procedure insert ( c : inout ordered_collection;  e : in element_type );
        -- inserts e into c in position determined by key_of(e)

    procedure get_element ( variable p : in position;  e : out element_type );
        -- returns the element value at position p in its collection

    procedure test_null_position ( variable p : in position;  is_null : out boolean );
        -- test whether p refers to no position in its collection

    procedure search ( variable c : in ordered_collection;  k : in key_type;
                            p : out position );
        -- searches for an element with key k in c, and returns the position of
        -- that element, or, if not found, a position for which test_null_position
        -- returns true
```

```
procedure find_first ( variable c : in ordered_collection;  p : out position );
-- returns the position of the first element of c

procedure advance ( p : inout position );
-- advances p to the next element in its collection,
-- or if there are no more, sets p so that test_null_position returns true

procedure delete ( p : inout position );
-- deletes the element at position p from its collection, and advances p

-- private types: pretend these are not visible

type ordered_collection_object is
    record
        element : element_type;
        next_element, prev_element : ordered_collection;
    end record ordered_collection_object;

type position_object is
    record
        the_collection : ordered_collection;
        current_element : ordered_collection;
    end record position_object;
end package «element_type_simple_name»_ordered_collection_adt;
```

A template for a package declaration for an ordered-collection ADT.

The ADT provides two types. The first, **ordered_collection**, is the actual collection type itself. The function **new_ordered_collection** returns a value of this type, representing an empty collection. We can add an element into a collection with the **insert** procedure. The second type provided by the ADT, **position**, is a type used to search for objects and to traverse a collection. Since the implementation of the collection is hidden, we are unable to access elements directly. Instead, the ADT provides the **position** type as an abstract form of index. The procedure **get_element** sets the parameter **e** to the value of the element in the collection at a given position. The procedure **test_null_position** tests whether a position value actually refers to an element or not. The procedure **search** sets the parameter **p** to a **position** value, being the position of the first element in the collection with the specified key value. If there is no such element, **p** is assigned a position value that would cause **test_null_position** to return true. The procedures **find_first** and **advance** are used to traverse a collection. We see how this is done shortly when we look at an example of a model that uses the ADT. Finally, the procedure **delete** removes an item at a given position from the collection. After the deletion, the position object refers to the element in the collection following the deleted element.

We can use this ADT to store a collection of stimulus vectors for a design under test. To do this, we must write a package defining the types and functions required by the ADT, as shown in Figure 17-13. Next, we use a text editor to replace the template placeholders in the ADT package declaration. For «element_type_simple_name», we substitute **stimulus_element**; for «element_type», we substitute **work.stimulus_types.stimulus_element**; for «key_type», we substitute **delay_length**; for «key_function», we substitute **work.stimulus_types.stimulus_key**; and for «less_than_function», we substitute

FIGURE 17-13

```
library ieee;  use ieee.std_logic_1164.all;
package stimulus_types is
    constant stimulus_vector_length : positive := 10;
    type stimulus_element is record
            application_time : delay_length;
            pattern : std_logic_vector(0 to stimulus_vector_length − 1);
        end record stimulus_element;
    function stimulus_key ( stimulus : stimulus_element ) return delay_length;
end package stimulus_types;
––––––––––––––––––––––––––––––––––––––––––––––––––––
package body stimulus_types is
    function stimulus_key ( stimulus : stimulus_element ) return delay_length is
    begin
        return stimulus.application_time;
    end function stimulus_key;
end package body stimulus_types;
```

A package declaration and body for types and functions representing stimulus information.

std.standard."<". This creates a specialized version of the ADT package called **stimu-
lus_element_ordered_collection_adt**, which defines types and operations for collections
of stimulus elements.

An outline of an architecture body that uses this specialized package is shown in
Figure 17-14. The process **stimulus_generation** declares a variable of type **or-
dered_collection**, referring to the type provided by the specialized package. The variable initially stores an empty collection. The process starts by inserting a number of
stimulus element records into the collection. In a more realistic setting, the stimulus
information would be read from a file. However, since we have not yet described file
operations in VHDL, direct insertion by the process serves to illustrate use of the insertion operation. Note that the element need not be inserted in ascending key order.
The ADT is responsible for maintaining the order of elements in the collection.

Next, the process applies the stimulus set to signals connected to the design under
test. It uses the ADT operation **find_first**, which returns a position value referring to
the first element in the collection. Since we are using the application time of each element as the key, the first element returned is the one with the earliest application time.
The process then enters a loop to traverse the entire collection in order. It tests whether
the position variable still refers to an element in the collection by using the
test_null_position operation. It uses the **get_element** operation to retrieve the element
at the next position and waits until simulation time reaches the element's application
time. After assigning the element's pattern to the test signals, it moves the position
variable to the next element in the collection using the **advance** procedure. If there
are no more elements in the collection, this procedure returns a position value that
does not refer to any element in the collection. This value causes the loop to terminate.

FIGURE 17-14

```
library ieee;  use ieee.std_logic_1164.all;
architecture initial_test of test_bench is
    use work.stimulus_types.all;
        . . .        -- component and signal declarations
begin
        . . .        -- instantiate design under test
    stimulus_generation : process is
        use work.stimulus_element_ordered_collection_adt.all;
        variable stimulus_list : ordered_collection := new_ordered_collection;
        variable next_stimulus_position : position;
        variable next_stimulus : stimulus_element;
        variable position_is_null : boolean;
    begin
        insert(stimulus_list, stimulus_element'(0 ns, "0XXXXXXXXX"));
        insert(stimulus_list, stimulus_element'(200 ns, "0000110110"));
        insert(stimulus_list, stimulus_element'(300 ns, "10001ZZZZZ"));
        insert(stimulus_list, stimulus_element'(50 ns, "1XXXXXXXXX"));
        . . .
        find_first(stimulus_list, next_stimulus_position);
        loop
            test_null_position(next_stimulus_position, position_is_null);
            exit when position_is_null;
            get_element(next_stimulus_position, next_stimulus);
            wait for next_stimulus.application_time – now;
            dut_signals <= next_stimulus.pattern;
            advance(next_stimulus_position);
        end loop;
        wait;
    end process stimulus_generation;
end architecture initial_test;
```

An architecture body that uses the ADT for collections of stimulus elements.

We can now turn to the implementation of the ordered-collection ADT. The declarations marked private in the package declaration hint that the collection is implemented using a data structure called a *doubly-linked circular list*, illustrated in Figure 17-15. Such a list consists of cells, each storing an element of the collection, a pointer to the next cell in the list and a pointer to the previous cell in the list. As Figure 17-15(a) shows, an empty collection is represented as a list with just a single cell whose pointers point back to the cell itself. This special cell is called the *list header*. Its data element does not form part of the collection, but is included so that the header cell is an object of the same type as other cells in the list. This greatly simplifies the implementation of the ADT operations. Figure 17-15(b) shows a list representing a collection into which two elements have been inserted. The next-element pointer of the last cell points back to the list header, as does the previous-element pointer of the first cell.

The ADT operations for the ordered collection are implemented in the package body shown in Figure 17-16. The function **new_ordered_collection** creates a new list cell, forming the list header for an empty collection. The **element** part of the cell is not explicitly initialized, since its value is never used. The pointer parts of the cell are set to point to the cell itself, and the pointer to the cell is returned as the function result.

FIGURE 17-15

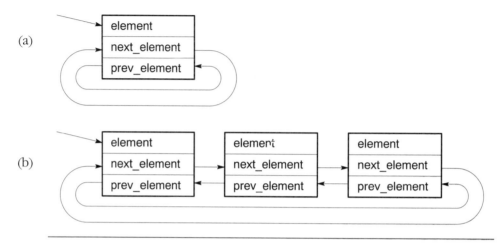

The doubly-linked circular list structure used to implement the ordered-collection ADT: (a) an empty list, consisting of just the header, and (b) a list consisting of the header and two inserted elements.

FIGURE 17-16

```
package body «element_type_simple_name»_ordered_collection_adt is
    function new_ordered_collection return ordered_collection is
        variable result : ordered_collection := new ordered_collection_object;
    begin
        result.next_element := result;  result.prev_element := result;
        return result;
    end function new_ordered_collection;

    procedure insert ( c : inout ordered_collection;  e : in element_type ) is
        variable current_element : ordered_collection := c.next_element;
        variable new_element : ordered_collection;
    begin
        while current_element /= c
            and key_of(current_element.element) < key_of(e) loop
            current_element := current_element.next_element;
        end loop;
        -- insert new element before current_element
        new_element := new ordered_collection_object'( element => e,
                                next_element => current_element,
                                prev_element => current_element.prev_element );
        new_element.next_element.prev_element := new_element;
        new_element.prev_element.next_element := new_element;
    end procedure insert;
```

```
procedure get_element ( variable p : in position;  e : out element_type ) is
begin
    e := p.current_element.element;
end procedure get_element;

procedure test_null_position ( variable p : in position;  is_null : out boolean ) is
begin
    is_null := p.current_element = p.the_collection;
end procedure test_null_position;

procedure search ( variable c : in ordered_collection;  k : in key_type;
                   p : out position ) is
    variable current_element : ordered_collection := c.next_element;
begin
    while current_element /= c and key_of(current_element.element) < k loop
        current_element := current_element.next_element;
    end loop;
    if current_element = c or k < key_of(current_element.element) then
        p := new position_object'(c, c);   -- null position
    else
        p := new position_object'(c, current_element);
    end if;
end procedure search;

procedure find_first ( variable c : in ordered_collection;  p : out position ) is
begin
    p := new position_object'(c, c.next_element);
end procedure find_first;

procedure advance ( p : inout position ) is
    variable is_null : boolean;
begin
    test_null_position(p, is_null);
    if not is_null then
        p.current_element := p.current_element.next_element;
    end if;
end procedure advance;

procedure delete ( p : inout position ) is
    variable is_null : boolean;
begin
    test_null_position(p, is_null);
    if not is_null then
        p.current_element.next_element.prev_element
            := p.current_element.prev_element;
        p.current_element.prev_element.next_element
            := p.current_element.next_element;
        p.current_element := p.current_element.next_element;
    end if;
end procedure delete;
end package body «element_type_simple_name»_ordered_collection_adt;
```

The package body for the ordered-collection ADT.

The **insert** procedure must create a new cell for the list and insert it in the appropriate position, based on the key value of the element. The procedure has a local variable, **current_element**, that is initialized to the first cell after the list header. The loop then scans from cell to cell until it returns to the header or until it reaches a cell whose element key is not less than that of the new element to be inserted. In either case, the new cell must be inserted immediately before the cell pointed to by **current_element**. The allocator creates the new cell, sets its element part to the new element value and sets its pointer parts to point to the cells on either side of the new position. The next-element pointer of the previous cell and the previous-element pointer of the next cell are then set to point to the new cell. These pointer manipulations achieve the effect of "splicing" the new cell into position in the list. Note that since the header is a cell of the same type as other list cells, we do not need to make any special cases to insert the new cell at the beginning or end of the list.

The implementation of a position object is shown in Figure 17-17. It contains two parts, one pointing to a collection and the other pointing to a cell in the linked list for that collection. The **get_element** procedure simply returns the value in the **element** part of the cell pointed to by the position object. The **test_null_position** procedure tests whether the cell pointer of the position object points to the list header of the collection. This condition is used to represent a position object that does not refer to any cell in the collection.

FIGURE 17-17

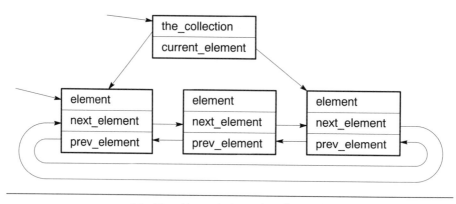

A position object, pointing to the collection list header and a cell in the list.

The **search** procedure finds a cell whose element part has the same key value as the given key and returns a position object referring to the cell. It compares key values using the "<" function provided when the package is specialized. It starts by setting a pointer variable, **current_element**, to point to the first cell after the list header. It then scans from cell to cell until it returns to the header, or until it reaches a cell whose element key is not less than the given key. If it returns to the header, or if the cell that it reaches contains an element whose key is greater than the given key, then the collection does not contain any cell matching the given key. In this case, the function returns a null position object. (Note the use of the short-circuit "or" operator in the test for this case.) Otherwise the cell reached by the function does match the given key, so the function returns a position object referring to this cell.

The procedure **find_first** returns a position object referring to the first cell after the header cell of the collection passed as a parameter. The **advance** procedure updates a position object by changing its cell pointer part to the next-element part of the cell. This change has the effect of making the position object refer to the next cell in the list.

The final procedure in the package body, **delete**, removes a cell referred to by a position object from a collection (provided the position object does, in fact, refer to a cell). The procedure uses the next-element and previous-element pointers of the cell to access the cells on either side, and updates their pointers to bypass the cell being deleted. It then updates the position object to refer to the cell following the cell being deleted. After these operations, no pointer in the structure points to the original cell any longer, so it has become garbage. If storage reclamation were an important consideration on a particular host computer system, the **delete** procedure could be modified to deallocate the cell after it has been unlinked.

VHDL-87

Since VHDL-87 does not provide aliases for non-data objects, we cannot use aliases to represent ADT template "parameters" as we have done in the example. We must replace each occurrence of an alias name in the template with the corresponding placeholder. When we edit a copy of the template to specialize the ADT, we replace these placeholders with the name of the actual type or item.

Exercises

1. [❶ 17.1] Write a type declaration for an access type that points to a character data object. Declare a variable of the type, initialized by allocating a character with the value ETX. Write a statement that changes the character value to 'A'.

2. [❶ 17.1] Identify the error in the following VHDL fragment:

   ```
   type real_ptr is access real;
   variable r : real_ptr;
   . . .
   r := new real;
   r := r + 1.0;
   ```

3. [❶ 17.1] Draw a diagram showing the pointer variables and the data objects to which they refer after execution of the following VHDL fragment:

   ```
   type int_ptr is access integer;
   variable a, b, c, d : int_ptr;
   . . .
   a := new integer'(1);  b := new integer'(2);
   c := new integer'(3);  d := new integer'(4);
   b := a; a := b;
   c.all := d.all;
   ```

4. [❶ 17.1] After execution of the fragment shown in Exercise 3, what is the value of each of the following conditions?

   a = b   c = d
   a.all = b.all   c.all = d.all

5. [❶ 17.1] Write a type declaration for an access type that points to a **string** data object. Declare a variable of the type, initialized by allocating a string of four spaces. Write a statement that changes the first character in the string to the character NUL.

6. [❶ 17.1] The following declarations define a type for complex numbers, an access type referring to the complex number type and three pointer variables:

   type complex **is record**
       re, im : real;
       end record complex;
   type complex_ptr **is access** complex;
   variable x, y, z : complex_ptr;

   Write statements that assign the complex product of the values pointed to by **x** and **y** to the data object pointed to by **z**. Refer to page 162 for a description of the steps required in complex multiplication.

7. [❶ 17.2] Write type declarations for use in constructing a linked list of message objects. Each message contains a source and destination number (both of type **natural**) and a 256-bit data field. Declare a variable to point to a list of messages, and write a statement to add to the list a message with source number 1, destination number 5 and a data field of all '0' bits.

8. [❶ 17.2] Why is the following fragment to delete the first object in a linked list incorrect?

   cell_to_be_deleted := value_list;
   deallocate(cell_to_be_deleted);
   value_list := value_list.next_cell;

9. [❶ 17.3] Suppose the variable **test_buffer** is an instance of the bounded buffer ADT described on pages 481 to 485. Write statements that fill the buffer with zero bytes.

10. [❷ 17.2] Figure 17-5 on page 478 shows statements to traverse a linked list of stimulus values and apply them to a signal. Encapsulate these statements in a procedure with the list pointer and the signal as parameters.

11. [❷ 17.2] The algorithm for traversing a list, encapsulated in a procedure as described in Exercise 10, can be expressed recursively. If the list is empty, the procedure has nothing to do, so it returns. Otherwise, the procedure applies the first stimulus value from the list, waits for the delay, then recursively calls itself with the next cell pointer as the list parameter. Thus, recursive invocation of the procedure replaces the iterative traversal of the list. Rewrite the procedure to use this recursive algorithm.

12. [❷ 17.2] Write a recursive procedure to delete all cells from a linked list pointed to by a parameter of type **value_ptr**. Hint: The procedure should call itself to delete the cells after the first cell, then delete the first cell.

13. [❸ 17.3] Develop an ADT for last-in/first-out stacks of objects. The ADT should be parameterized by the type of object and should provide operations to create a new stack, to test whether a stack is empty, to push an object onto the stack and to pop the top object from the stack and return the object's value.

14. [❸ 17.3] Develop an ADT for first-in/first-out queues of objects. The ADT should be parameterized by the type of object and maximum number of objects allowed in the queue. The operations are to create a new queue, to test whether a queue is empty or full, to add an object to the tail of a queue and to remove an object from the head of a queue and return the object's value. The queue may be implemented as a linked list, as shown in the following diagram:

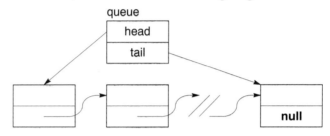

Use the ADT in a behavioral model of an eight-bit-wide FIFO, based on the behavior described in Exercises 7 and 15 in Chapter 14.

15. [❷ 17.2/17.3] Modify the implementation of the ordered-collection ADT to deallocate storage when it is no longer used. Note that the procedure **delete** is not the only place in which garbage is created.

16. [❹ 17.3] Develop an alternative implementation of the ordered-collection ADT based on a binary search tree data structure. A binary search tree is a collection of cells, each of which contains a key value, an element and pointers to a left subtree and a right subtree. All cells in the left subtree have key values that are less than that of the parent cell, and all cells in the right subtree have key values that are greater than that of the parent cell. In order to implement the position object and associated operations, the basic tree structure is augmented with pointers from each cell to its parent. Descriptions of algorithms for binary search tree operations can be found in most textbooks on data structures.

Files and Input/Output

In this chapter we look at the facilities in VHDL for file input and output. Files serve a number of purposes, one of which is to provide long-term data storage. In this context, "long-term" means beyond the lifetime of one simulation run. Files can be used to store data to be loaded into a model when it is run, or to store the results produced by a simulation. VHDL also provides specialized versions of file operations for working with text files. We show how textual input and output can be used to extend the user interface of a simulator with model-specific operations.

18.1 Files

We start our discussion of files by looking at the general-purpose mechanisms provided in VHDL for file input and output. VHDL provides sequential access to files using operations, such as "open", "close", "read" and "write", that are familiar to users of conventional programming languages.

File Declarations

A VHDL file is a class of object used to store data. Hence, as with other classes of objects, we must include file-type definitions in our models. The syntax rule for defining a file type is

file_type_definition ⇐ **file of** type_mark

A file-type definition simply specifies the type of objects to be stored in files of the given type. For example, the type declaration

type integer_file **is file of** integer;

defines **integer_file** to be a type of file that can only contain integers. A file can only contain one type of object, but that type can be almost any VHDL type, including scalar types, records and one-dimensional arrays. The only types that cannot be stored in files are multidimensional arrays, access types and other files.

Once we have defined a file type, we can then declare file objects. We do this with a new form of object declaration, described by the syntax rule

file_declaration ⇐
    file identifier { , ... } : subtype_indication
        ⟦ ⟦ **open** *file_open_kind*_expression ⟧ **is** *string*_expression ⟧ ;

A file declaration creates one or more file objects of a given file type. We can include a file declaration in any declarative part in which we can create objects, such as within architecture bodies, blocks, processes, packages and subprograms.

The optional parts of a file declaration allow us to make an association between the file object and a physical file in the host file system. If we include these parts, the file is automatically opened for access during simulation. The string after the keyword **is** is a file *logical name*, which identifies the host file to access. Since different host operating systems use different formats for naming files, many simulators provide some form of mapping between the logical name strings that we include in our models and the file names used in the host file system. For example, if we declare a file as

file lookup_table_file : integer_file **is** "lookup–values";

a simulator running under the UNIX operating system may associate the file object with a physical file named "lookup–values" in the current working directory. A different simulator, running under the MS-DOS operating system, has to associate the file object differently, since that operating system only supports files with names up to eight characters long. So it might associate the object with a physical file called "LOOKUP–V.DAT" in the current working directory.

The optional expression after the keyword **open** allows us to specify how the physical file associated with the file object should be opened. This expression must have a value of the predefined type file_open_kind, declared in the package standard. The declaration is

   type file_open_kind **is** (read_mode, write_mode, append_mode);

If we omit the open kind information from a file declaration but include the file logical name, the physical file is opened in read mode. In the rest of this section we discuss each of these modes and see how data is read and written using files opened in each of the modes.

VHDL-87

The syntax rule for file declarations in VHDL-87 is

file_declaration ⇐
     file identifier : subtype_indication **is**
          ⟦ **in** ⟧ **out** ⟧ *string*_expression ;

VHDL-87 does not provide the predefined type file_open_kind. Instead, the keywords **in** and **out** are used in file declarations to open files in read or write mode, respectively. The default is that a file is opened in read mode. Note that the VHDL-87 syntax for file declarations is not a subset of the VHDL-93 syntax. If a model includes either of the keywords **in** or **out**, it cannot be successfully analyzed with a VHDL-93 analyzer.

Reading from Files

If a file is opened in read mode, successive elements of data are read from the file using the **read** operation. Reading starts from the first element in the file, and each time an element is read the file position advances to the next element. We can use the endfile operation to determine when we have read the last element in the file. Given a file type declared as follows:

   type file_type **is file of** element_type;

the read and endfile operations are implicitly declared as

   procedure read (**file** f : file_type; value : **out** element_type);

   function endfile (**file** f : file_type) **return** boolean;

We explain subprogram file parameters later in this section.

EXAMPLE

We can use file operations to initialize the contents of a read-only memory (ROM) from a file. Figure 18-1 shows an entity declaration for a ROM that includes a generic constant to specify the name of a file from which to load the ROM contents. The architecture body for the ROM uses the file name in a file declaration, creating a file object associated with a physical file of data words. The process that

FIGURE 18-1 _____

```
library ieee;  use ieee.std_logic_1164.all;
entity ROM is
    generic ( load_file_name : string );
    port ( sel : in std_logic;
            address : in std_logic_vector;
            data : inout std_logic_vector );
end entity ROM;

————————————————————————————————————————————

architecture behavioral of ROM is
begin
    behavior : process is
        subtype word is std_logic_vector(0 to data'length – 1);
        type storage_array is
            array (natural range 0 to 2**address'length – 1) of word;
        variable storage : storage_array;
        variable index : natural;
        . . .       –– other declarations
        type load_file_type is file of word;
        file load_file : load_file_type open read_mode is load_file_name;
    begin
        –– load ROM contents from load_file
        index := 0;
        while not endfile(load_file) loop
            read(load_file, storage(index));
            index := index + 1;
        end loop;
        –– respond to ROM accesses
        loop
            . . .
        end loop;
    end process behavior;
end architecture behavioral;
```

An entity and architecture body for a ROM that reads its data from a file.

implements the behavior of the ROM loads the ROM storage array by reading successive words of data from the file, using **endfile** to determine when to stop.

In the above example, each element of the file is a standard-logic vector of a fixed length, determined by the ROM data port width. However, we are not restricted to fixed-length arrays as file elements. We may declare a file type with an unconstrained array type for the element type, for example:

type bit_vector_file **is file of** bit_vector;

The data in a file of this type is a sequence of bit vectors, each of which may be of a different length. For such a file, the **read** operation takes a slightly different form, to allow for the fact that we do not know the length of the next element until we read it. The operation is implicitly declared as

> **procedure** read (**file** f : file_type;
>   value : **out** element_type; length : **out** natural);

When we call this form of **read** operation, we supply an array variable large enough to receive the value we expect to read, and another variable to receive the actual length of the value read. For example, if we make the following declarations:

> **file** vectors : bit_vector_file **open** read_mode **is** "vectors.dat";
> **variable** next_vector : bit_vector(63 **downto** 0);
> **variable** actual_len : natural;

we can call the **read** operation as follows:

> read(vectors, next_vector, actual_len);

This allows us to read a bit vector up to 64 bits long. If the next value in the file is less than or equal to 64 bits long, it is placed in the leftmost part of next_vector, with the remaining bits being unchanged. If the value in the file is longer than 64 bits, the first 64 bits of the value are placed in next_vector, and the remaining bits are discarded. In both cases, actual_len is set to the actual length of the value in the file, whether it be shorter or longer than the length of the second argument to **read**. This allows us to test whether information has been lost. If the expression

> actual_len > next_vector'length

is true, the vector variable was not long enough to receive all of the bits.

EXAMPLE

Suppose we have designed a model for a network receiver and we wish to test it. We can generate network packets to stimulate the model by reading variable-length packets from a file. The outline of a process to do this is shown in Figure 18-2.

FIGURE 18-2

> stimulate_network : **process is**
>
>> **type** packet_file **is file of** bit_vector;
>> **file** stimulus_file : packet_file **open** read_mode **is** "test packets";
>>
>> **variable** packet : bit_vector(1 **to** 2048);
>> **variable** packet_length : natural;

(continued on page 502)

(continued from page 501)

```
begin
    while not endfile(stimulus_file) loop
        read(stimulus_file, packet, packet_length);
        if packet_length > packet'length then
            report "stimulus packet too long – ignored" severity warning;
        else
            for bit_index in 1 to packet_length loop
                wait until stimulus_clock = '1';
                stimulus_network <= not stimulus_network;
                wait until stimulus_clock = '0';
                stimulus_network <= stimulus_network xor packet(bit_index);
            end loop;
        end if;
    end loop;
    wait;  –– end of stimulation: wait forever
end process stimulate_network;
```

A process that reads network test packets from a file.

The process declares a file object, **stimulus_file**, containing variable-length bit vectors. Each file element is read into the bit-vector variable **packet**, with the length of the bit vector read from the file being stored in **packet_length**. If the bit vector in the file is longer than the bit-vector variable, the process reports the fact and ignores that stimulus packet. Otherwise, the value in **packet_length** is used to determine how many bits from **packet** should be used as data bits to stimulate the network.

Writing to Files

If a file is opened in write mode, a new empty file is created in the host computer's file system, and successive data elements are added using the **write** operation. For each file type declared, the **write** operation is implicitly declared as

procedure write (**file** f : file_type; value : **in** element_type);

One common use of output files is to save information gathered by instrumentation code. When the simulation is complete, or upon some other trigger condition, the instrumentation code can use write operations to write the data to a file for subsequent analysis.

EXAMPLE

When we are designing a new CPU instruction set, it is useful to know how frequently each instruction is used in different programs. We measure this by simulating the CPU running a program and having the CPU keep count of how often it executes each instruction. When it completes the program (for example, by reaching a halt instruction), it writes the accumulated counts to a file.

The architecture body for a CPU shown in Figure 18-3 illustrates this approach. It contains a file, instruction_counts, opened in write mode. There is also a process, interpreter, that fetches and interprets instructions. It contains an array of counters, indexed by opcode values. As the instruction interpreter process decodes each instruction, it increments the appropriate counter. When a halt instruction is executed, the interpreter stops execution and writes the counter values as successive elements in the instruction_counts file.

FIGURE 18-3

```
architecture instrumented of CPU is
    type count_file is file of natural;
    file instruction_counts : count_file open write_mode is "instructions";
begin
    interpreter : process is
        variable IR : word;
        alias opcode : byte is IR(0 to 7);
        variable opcode_number : natural;
        type counter_array is array (0 to 2**opcode'length − 1) of natural;
        variable counters : counter_array := (others => 0);
        . . .
    begin
        . . .        −− initialize the instruction set interpreter
        instruction_loop : loop
            . . .        −− fetch the next instruction into IR

            −− decode the instruction
            opcode_number := convert_to_natural(opcode);
            counters(opcode_number) := counters(opcode_number) + 1;
            . . .

            −− execute the decoded instruction
            case opcode is
                when halt_opcode => exit instruction_loop;
                . . .
            end case;
        end loop instruction_loop;

        for index in counters'range loop
            write(instruction_counts, counters(index));
        end loop;
        wait;  −− program finished, wait forever
    end process interpreter;
end architecture instrumented;
```

An architecture body for a CPU that counts instruction execution frequencies.

If an existing physical file in the host computer's file system is opened in append mode, successive data elements are added to the end of the file using the **write** operation. If there is no host file of the given name in the host file system, opening the file object in append mode creates a new file, so that data elements are written from the beginning. Append mode is used for a file that accumulates log information or simulation results over a number of simulation runs. Each run adds its data to the end of the previously accumulated data in the file.

EXAMPLE

When we are designing a cache memory to attach to a CPU, we need to measure how different cache organizations affect the miss rate, since this influences the average access time seen by the CPU. We measure the miss rate by monitoring the traffic on the buses between the CPU and cache and between the cache and main memory. At the end of a simulation run, the process monitoring the buses appends a record to a data file, storing the parameter values that determine the cache organization and the measured miss rate and average access time.

An outline of the process is shown in Figure 18-4. The process declares a record type that represents the information to be recorded for the simulation run and opens a file of records of this type in append mode. At the end of the simulation run, it creates a record value and appends it to the end of the previously existing data in the file. The record includes the values of generic constants that control the cache organization and identify the benchmark program being run, as well as the calculated values for the miss rate and average access time.

FIGURE 18-4

```
cache_monitor : process is
    type measurement_record is
        record
            cache_size, block_size, associativity : positive;
            benchmark_name : string(1 to 10);
            miss_rate : real;
            ave_access_time : delay_length;
        end record;
    type measurement_file is file of measurement_record;
    file measurements : measurement_file
        open append_mode is "cache–measurements";
    . . .
begin
    . . .
    loop
        . . .
        exit when halt = '1';
        . . .
    end loop;
```

```
write ( measurements, measurement_record'(
                    -- write values of generics for this run
                    cache_size, block_size, associativity, benchmark_name,
                    -- calculate performance metrics
                    miss_rate => real(miss_count) / real(total_accesses),
                    ave_access_time => total_delay / total_accesses ) );
    wait;

end process cache_monitor;
```

A process that measures cache performance and appends a data record to a log file.

Files Declared in Subprograms

In all of the previous examples, the file object is declared in an architecture body or a process. In these cases, the file is opened at the start of the simulation and automatically closed again at the end of the simulation. The same applies to files declared in packages. We can also declare files within subprograms, but the behavior in these cases is slightly different. The file is opened when the subprogram is called and is automatically closed again when the subprogram returns. Hence the file object, and its association with a physical file in the host file system, is purely local to the subprogram activation. So, for example, if we declare a file in a subprogram:

```
procedure write_to_file is
    file data_file : data_file_type open write_mode is "datafile";
begin
    . . .
end procedure write_to_file;
```

each time we call the procedure a new physical file is created, replacing the old one.

EXAMPLE

We can initialize the value of a constant array by calling a function that reads element values from a file. Suppose the array is of the following type, containing integer elements:

```
type integer_vector is array (integer range <>) of integer;
```

The function declaration is shown in Figure 18-5. The first parameter is the name of the file from which to read data elements, and the second parameter is the size of the array that the function should return. The function creates a file object representing a file of integer values and uses the file name parameter to open the file. It then reads values from the file into an array until it reaches the end of the file or the end of the array. It returns the array as the function result. When the function returns, the file is automatically closed. We can use this function in a constant declaration as follows:

```
constant coeffs : integer_vector := read_array("coeff-data", 16);
```

The length of the constant is determined by the result of the function.

FIGURE 18-5

```
impure function read_array ( file_name : string;  array_length : natural )
                           return integer_vector is
   type integer_file is file of integer;
   file data_file : integer_file open read_mode is file_name;
   variable result : integer_vector(1 to array_length) := (others => 0);
   variable index : integer := 1;
begin
   while not endfile(data_file) and index <= array_length loop
       read(data_file, result(index));
       index := index + 1;
   end loop;
   return result;
end function read_array;
```

A function that reads integer elements from a file and returns an array of the elements.

One important point to note about files is that we should be careful not to associate more than one VHDL file object with a single physical file in the host file system. While the language does not expressly prohibit multiple associations, it does not specify what happens when we do several reads or writes to the same physical file through different VHDL file objects. Hence the results may be unpredictable and may vary from one host to another.

This restriction may seem fairly trivial, but we may violate it inadvertently. For example, we might declare a file object in an architecture body for some entity as follows:

file log_info : log_file **open** write_mode **is** "logfile";

If our design uses multiple instances of the entity, we have multiple instances of the file object, each associated with "logfile". Possible consequences include interleaving of writes from different instances and loss of data written from all but one instance. The solution to this problem depends on the desired effect. If we intend to merge log data from all instances into one file, we should declare the file in a package. On the other hand, if we intend each instance to have its own log file, we should compute separate file logical name strings for each instance.

Explicit Open and Close Operations

The syntax rule for a file object declaration, shown on page 498, indicates that the file open mode and logical name are optional. If we include either of them, the physical file is automatically opened when the file object is created. If we omit them, the file object is created but remains unassociated with any physical file. An example of a file declaration in this form is

file lookup_table_file, result_file : integer_file;

If we declare a file object in this way, we explicitly associate it with a physical file and open the file using the **file_open** operation. Given a file type declared as follows:

        type file_type **is file of** element_type;

file_open is implicitly declared as

        procedure file_open (**file** f : file_type;
                          external_name : **in** string;
                          open_kind : **in** file_open_kind := read_mode);

The external_name and open_kind parameters serve exactly the same purpose as
the corresponding information in the optional part of a file object declaration. For example, the declaration

        file lookup_table_file : integer_file **open** read_mode **is** "lookup–values";

is equivalent to

        file lookup_table_file : integer_file;
        . . .
        file_open (lookup_table_file,
                external_name => "lookup–values", open_kind => read_mode);

The advantage of using an explicit file_open operation, as opposed to having the
file automatically opened when the file object is created, is that we can first perform
some other computation to determine how to open it. For example, we might ask the
user to type in a file name.

A problem that arises with both of the previously mentioned ways of opening a
file is that the operation may fail, causing the whole simulation to come to an abrupt
halt. We can make a model more robust by including some error checking, using a
second form of the file_open operation, implicitly declared as

        procedure file_open (status : **out** file_open_status;
                    file f : file_type;
                    external_name : **in** string;
                    open_kind : **in** file_open_kind := read_mode);

The extra parameter, status, is used to return information about the success or failure of the operation. Its type is predefined in the package standard as

        type file_open_status **is** (open_ok, status_error, name_error, mode_error);

If the file was successfully opened, the value open_ok is returned, and we can proceed with read, write and endfile operations, according to the mode. If there was a problem during the file_open operation, one of the remaining values is returned. The value
status_error indicates that the file object had previously been opened and associated
with a physical file. (This error is different from the case in which multiple file objects
are associated with the same physical file.) The value name_error is returned under
different circumstances, depending on the mode in which we attempt to open the file.
In read mode, it is returned if the named host file does not exist. In write mode, it is
returned if a file of the given name cannot be created. In append mode, it is returned
if the named file does not exist and a new file of that name cannot be created. Finally,
the value mode_error is returned from the file_open operation if the file exists but cannot
be opened in the specified mode. This error may arise if we attempt to write or append
to a file marked read-only in the host file system.

Complementing the file_open operation, VHDL also provides a file_close operation, which can be used to close a file explicitly. The operation disassociates the file object from the physical file. When a file type is declared, a corresponding version of file_close is implicitly declared as

procedure file_close (**file** f : file_type);

We can use file_open and file_close in combination, either to associate a file object with a number of different physical files in succession, or to access a particular physical file multiple times. While applying the file_close operation to a file object that is already closed has no effect, it is good style to make sure that file_open and file_close operations are always paired. We should open a file in the desired mode, perform the reads and writes required, then close the file. This discipline helps ensure that we do not inadvertently write the wrong data to the wrong file.

EXAMPLE

Suppose we wish to apply stimulus vectors from a number of different files to a model during a simulation run. We create a directory file containing a list of file names to be used as stimulus files. Our test bench model then reads the stimulus file names from this directory file, and opens the stimulus files one-by-one to read the stimulus data.

An outline of a process that reads the stimulus files is shown in Figure 18-6. The process has a string variable, file_name, into which it reads the name of the next stimulus file to be opened. Note the test to see if the actual file name is longer than this variable. This test guards against the open failing through truncation of a file name. The second form of file_open is used to open the stimulus file, using the slice of the file_name variable containing the name read from the directory. If the open fails, the stimulus file is skipped. Otherwise, the process reads the stimulus vectors from the file, then closes it. When the end of the directory is reached, all stimulus files have been read, so the process suspends.

FIGURE 18-6

```
stimulus_generator : process is
    type directory_file is file of string;
    file directory : directory_file open read_mode is "stimulus–directory";
    variable file_name : string(1 to 50);
    variable file_name_length : natural;
    variable open_status : file_open_status;

    subtype stimulus_vector is std_logic_vector(0 to 9);
    type stimulus_file is file of stimulus_vector;
    file stimuli : stimulus_file;
    variable current_stimulus : stimulus_vector;

    . . .
```

```
        begin
            file_loop : while not endfile(directory) loop
                read( directory, file_name, file_name_length );
                if file_name_length > file_name'length then
                    report "file name too long: " & file_name & "... – file skipped"
                        severity warning;
                    next file_loop;
                end if;
                file_open ( open_status, stimuli,
                            file_name(1 to file_name_length), read_mode );
                if open_status /= open_ok then
                    report file_open_status'image(open_status)
                            & " while opening file "
                            & file_name(1 to file_name_length) & " – file skipped"
                        severity warning;
                    next file_loop;
                end if;
                stimulus_loop : while not endfile(stimuli) loop
                    read(stimuli, current_stimulus);
                    ...    -- apply the stimulus
                end loop stimulus_loop;
                file_close(stimuli);
            end loop file_loop;
            wait;
        end process stimulus_generator;
```

A process that reads stimulus files, using a directory of file names.

VHDL-87

The explicit file open and close operations are not provided in VHDL-87, nor is the predefined type file_open_status.

File Parameters in Subprograms

We have seen that the file operations described above take a file object as a parameter. In general, we can include a file parameter in any subprogram we write. Files form a fourth class of parameter, along with constants, variables and signals. The syntax for a file parameter in a subprogram specification is as follows:

interface_file_declaration ⇐ **file** identifier { , ... } : subtype_indication

The file parameters in the file operations we have seen conform to this syntax rule. The subtype indication must denote a file type. When the subprogram is called, a file object of that type must be supplied as an actual parameter. This object can be a file object declared by the caller, or, if the caller is itself a subprogram, a formal file parameter of the caller. The file object is passed into the subprogram and any of the file operations can be performed on it (depending on the mode in which the file object is opened).

EXAMPLE

Suppose we need to initialize a number of two-dimensional transformation arrays of real numbers using data stored in a file. We cannot directly declare the file of array objects, as VHDL only allows us to store one-dimensional arrays in a file. Instead, we declare the file to be a file of real numbers and use a procedure to read numbers from the file into an array parameter. First, here are the declarations for the arrays and the file:

```
type transform_array is array (1 to 3, 1 to 3) of real;
variable transform1, transform2 : transform_array;

type transform_file is file of real;
file initial_transforms : transform_file
    open read_mode is "transforms.ini";
```

Next, Figure 18-7 shows the declaration of the procedure to read values into an array. It uses the **endfile** operation to test whether there is an element to read. If not, it reports the fact and returns. Otherwise, it proceeds to use the **read** operation to fetch the next element of the array.

FIGURE 18-7

```
procedure read_transform ( file f : transform_file;
                             variable transform : out transform_array ) is
begin
    for i in transform'range(1) loop
        for j in transform'range(2) loop
            if endfile(f) then
                report "unexpected end of file in read_transform – "
                    & "some array elements not read"
                    severity error;
                return;
            end if;
            read ( f, transform(i, j) );
        end loop;
    end loop;
end procedure read_transform;
```

A procedure to read values from a file into an array.

We call this procedure to read values into the two array variables as follows:

```
read_transform ( initial_transforms, transform1 );
read_transform ( initial_transforms, transform2 );
```

The file object initial_transforms remains opened between the two calls, so the second call reads values from the file beyond those read by the first call.

VHDL-87

In VHDL-87, files are of the variable class of objects. Hence file parameters in subprograms are specified as variable-class parameters. For example, the procedure **read_transform** in Figure 18-7 can be written in VHDL-87 as

procedure read_transform
             (**variable** f : **in** transform_file;
                variable transform : **out** transform_array) **is** . . .

A subprogram that reads a file parameter should declare the parameter to be of mode **in**. A subprogram that writes a file parameter should declare the parameter to be of mode **out**.

Portability of Files

We finish this section on VHDL's file facilities with a few comments about the way in which file data is stored. It is important to note that files of the types we have described store the data in some binary representation. The format is dependent on the host computer system and on the simulator being used. This fact raises the issue of portability of files between different systems. All we can expect is that a file of a given type written by one model can be read as a file of the same type in a different model, provided it is run on the same host computer using the same VHDL simulator. There is no guarantee that it can be read on a different host computer, even using the same simulator retargeted for that host, nor that it can be read on any host using a different simulator.

While this might seem to limit the use of files for storing data, in reality it does not present much of an obstacle. If we do need to transfer files between systems, we can use text files as the interchange medium. As we see in the next section, VHDL provides an extensive set of facilities for dealing with the textual representation of data. Furthermore, tools for transferring text files between different computer systems are commonplace. The other potential problem arises if we wish to use non-VHDL software tools to process files written by VHDL models. For example, we may wish to write a program in some conventional programming language to perform data analysis on a data file produced by an instrumented VHDL model. Again, we can use text files to write data in a form readable by other tools. Alternatively, we can consult the VHDL tool vendor's documentation to learn the details of the binary data representation in a file and write a program to read data in that format.

18.2 The Package Textio

The predefined package **textio** in the library **std** provides a number of useful types and operations for reading and writing text files, that is, files of character strings. In particular, it provides procedures for reading and writing textual representations of the various predefined data types provided in VHDL. These operations make it possible to write files that can be read by other software tools and transferred to other host computer systems. The package specification is shown in Figure 18-8.

FIGURE 18-8

package textio **is**

    type line **is access** string;

    type text **is file of** string;

    type side **is** (right, left); **subtype** width **is** natural;

    file input : text **open** read_mode **is** "std_input";
    file output : text **open** write_mode **is** "std_output";

    procedure readline(**file** f: text; l: **out** line);

    procedure read (L : **inout** line; value: **out** bit; good : **out** boolean);
    procedure read (L : **inout** line; value: **out** bit);

    procedure read (L : **inout** line; value: **out** bit_vector; good : **out** boolean);
    procedure read (L : **inout** line; value: **out** bit_vector);

    procedure read (L : **inout** line; value: **out** boolean; good : **out** boolean);
    procedure read (L : **inout** line; value: **out** boolean);

    procedure read (L : **inout** line; value: **out** character; good : **out** boolean);
    procedure read (L : **inout** line; value: **out** character);

    procedure read (L : **inout** line; value: **out** integer; good : **out** boolean);
    procedure read (L : **inout** line; value: **out** integer);

    procedure read (L : **inout** line; value: **out** real; good : **out** boolean);
    procedure read (L : **inout** line; value: **out** real);

    procedure read (L : **inout** line; value: **out** string; good : **out** boolean);
    procedure read (L : **inout** line; value: **out** string);

    procedure read (L : **inout** line; value: **out** time; good : **out** boolean);
    procedure read (L : **inout** line; value: **out** time);

    procedure writeline (**file** f : text; L : **inout** line);

    procedure write (L : **inout** line; value : **in** bit;
                    justified: **in** side := right; field: **in** width := 0);

    procedure write (L : **inout** line; value : **in** bit_vector;
                    justified: **in** side := right; field: **in** width := 0);

    procedure write (L : **inout** line; value : **in** boolean;
                    justified: **in** side := right; field: **in** width := 0);

    procedure write (L : **inout** line; value : **in** character;
                    justified: **in** side := right; field: **in** width := 0);

    procedure write (L : **inout** line; value : **in** integer;
                    justified: **in** side := right; field: **in** width := 0);

    procedure write (L : **inout** line; value : **in** real;
                    justified: **in** side := right; field: **in** width := 0; digits: **in** natural := 0);

    procedure write (L : **inout** line; value : **in** string;
                    justified: **in** side := right; field: **in** width := 0);

    procedure write (L : **inout** line; value : **in** time;
                    justified: **in** side := right; field: **in** width := 0; unit: **in** time := ns);

end package textio;

The textio *package.*

Input and output operations using **textio** are based on dynamic strings, accessed using pointers of the type **line**, declared in the package. We use the **readline** operation to read a complete line of text from an input file. It creates a string object in the host computer's memory and returns a pointer to the string. We then use various versions of the **read** operation to extract values of different types from the string. When we need to write text, we first use various versions of the **write** operation to form a string object in memory, then pass the string to the **writeline** operation via its pointer. The operation writes the complete line of text to the output file and resets the pointer to **null**. (The definition of **readline** in the *VHDL Language Reference Manual* specifies **out** mode for the parameter **L**. However, it also states that the procedure deallocates storage pointed to by **L** if **L** is initially not null. For deallocation to occur, the parameter must use **inout** mode. Later versions of the *VHDL Language Reference Manual* may revise the specification of **readline**.)

The reason that VHDL takes this approach to input and output is to allow multiple processes to read or write to a single file without interfering with each other. Recall that multiple processes that are resumed in the same simulation cycle execute concurrently. If processes were to write directly to the file, partial lines from different processes might be intermixed, making the output unintelligible. By having each process form a line locally, we can write each line as one atomic action. The result is an output file consisting of interleaved lines from the different processes. A similar argument applies to input. If read operations were to read directly from the file, no process would be able to read an entire line without the possibility of interference from another process also reading input. The solution is for a process to read an entire line as one atomic action and then to extract the data from the line locally.

The package **textio** declares the file type **text**, representing files of strings. The operations provided by the package act on files of this type. The package also declares the file objects **input** and **output**, respectively associated with physical files using the logical names **std_input** and **std_output**. The intention is that the host simulator associate these file objects with the standard devices used for input and output. For example, the file **input** might be associated with the workstation keyboard and the file **output** with the workstation display. A model then uses the files to interact with the user. Prompts and informational messages are displayed by writing them to **output**, and commands and data typed by the user are read from **input**.

Textio Read Operations

Let us now look at the read operations in detail. Each version of **read** has at least two parameters: a pointer to the line of text from which to read and a variable in which to store the value. The operations extract characters from the beginning of the line, looking for characters that form a textual representation of a value of the expected type. The line is modified to contain only the remaining characters, and the value represented by the extracted characters is returned.

The character version of **read** simply extracts the first character in the line and returns it. It does not look for quotation marks around the character. For example, if the line pointed to by **L** contains

a'bcd

two successive character **read** operations would return the characters 'a' and '"'.

The string version extracts enough characters to fill the actual string argument. This version of **read** does not look for double quotation marks around the string. For example, if **s** is a string variable of length five, and **L** points to the line

    fred "cat"

a read into **s** returns the string "fred ". A second read into **s** returns the string ""cat"". If the line does not contain enough characters to fill the string variable, the read operation fails. If this possibility could cause problems, we can resort to direct string manipulation of the line. So, for example, we can test the length of the line and extract fewer characters than the length of the string variable as follows:

```
if L'length < s'length then
    read(L, s(1 to L'length));
else
    read(L, s);
end if;
```

Since **L** is an access variable to a string, the 'length attribute applied to **L** returns the length of the string pointed to by **L**, provided that **L** is not **null**.

The versions of **read** for all other types of data skip over any whitespace characters in the line before the textual representation of the data. A whitespace character is a space, a non-breaking space or a horizontal tab character. These operations then extract as many characters from the line as can be used to form a valid literal of the expected type. Characters are extracted up to the first character that is not valid for a literal of that type or to the end of the line. For example, if **L** points to the line

    12   −4.27!

an integer read extracts the first two characters and returns the value 12. A subsequent read into a real variable skips the spaces, then extracts the characters up to but not including the '!' and returns the value −4.27.

For bit-vector values, the literal in the line should be a binary string without quotation marks or a base specifier (that is, just a string of '0' or '1' characters). For time values, the literal should be a number followed by a time unit, with at least one whitespace character between them.

EXAMPLE

In Chapter 15 we described a memory module in the test bench for the DLX CPU. Now that we have discussed text file operations, we look at an alternative architecture body for the memory, shown in Figure 18-9. This version loads the memory from the text file named by the generic constant **load_file_name**. Each line of the file contains an address and a data word, both formatted as eight hexadecimal digits and separated by a single space. An example of such a file is

    00000000 20020000
    00000004 ac020018
    00000008 20420001
    0000000a 6441000a

FIGURE 18-9

```vhdl
library bv_utilities;

use bv_utilities.bv_arithmetic.bv_to_natural,
    bv_utilities.bv_arithmetic.natural_to_bv,
    std.textio.all;

architecture file_loaded of memory is
begin

    mem_behavior : process is

        constant high_address : natural := mem_size − 1;

        type memory_array is
            array (natural range 0 to high_address / 4) of dlx_bv_word;

        variable mem : memory_array;

        . . .           −− other variables as in architecture preloaded

        procedure load is

            file binary_file : text open read_mode is load_file_name;
            variable L : line;
            variable ch : character;
            variable line_number : natural := 0;
            variable addr : natural;
            variable word : dlx_bv_word;

            procedure read_hex_natural ( L : inout line; n : out natural ) is
                variable result : natural := 0;
            begin
                for i in 1 to 8 loop
                    read(L, ch);
                    if '0' <= ch and ch <= '9' then
                        result := result*16 + character'pos(ch) − character'pos('0');
                    elsif 'A' <= ch and ch <= 'F' then
                        result := result*16 + character'pos(ch) − character'pos('A') + 10;
                    elsif 'a' <= ch and ch <= 'f' then
                        result := result*16 + character'pos(ch) − character'pos('a') + 10;
                    else
                        report "Format error in file " & load_file_name & " on line "
                               & integer'image(line_number) severity error;
                    end if;
                end loop;
                n := result;
            end read_hex_natural;

            procedure read_hex_word ( L : inout line; word : out dlx_bv_word ) is
                variable digit : natural;
                variable r : natural := 0;
            begin
                for i in 1 to 8 loop
                    read(L, ch);
```

(continued on page 516)

(continued from page 515)

```
                            if '0' <= ch and ch <= '9' then
                                digit := character'pos(ch) − character'pos('0');
                            elsif 'A' <= ch and ch <= 'F' then
                                digit := character'pos(ch) − character'pos('A') + 10;
                            elsif 'a' <= ch and ch <= 'f' then
                                digit := character'pos(ch) − character'pos('a') + 10;
                            else
                                report "Format error in file " & load_file_name
                                        & " on line " & integer'image(line_number)
                                        severity error;
                            end if;
                            word(r to r+3) := natural_to_bv(digit, 4);
                            r := r + 4;
                        end loop;
                    end read_hex_word;
                begin
                    while not endfile(binary_file) loop
                        readline(binary_file, L);
                        line_number := line_number + 1;
                        read_hex_natural(L, addr);
                        read(L, ch);  −− the space between addr and data
                        read_hex_word(L, word);
                        mem(addr / 4) := word;
                    end loop;
                end load;

                procedure do_write is . . .      −− as in architecture preloaded

                procedure do_read is . . .       −− as in architecture preloaded
            begin
                load;    −− read binary memory image into memory array
                . . .    −− as in architecture preloaded
            end process mem_behavior;
    end architecture file_loaded;
```

An outline of an architecture body for the memory module that loads the contents of a file.

The process in the architecture body initializes the memory by calling the procedure **load**. This procedure declares a local text file object and associates it in read mode with the physical file named by load_file_name. The procedure performs a loop that reads successive lines of the file. It uses the variable line_number to keep count of the number of lines read. The **load** procedure then calls read_hex_natural to extract the hexadecimal address, uses the character **read** operation to skip the space character and calls read_hex_word to extract the hexadecimal data word. The address and word are used to initialize an element of the memory array.

The procedure read_hex_natural first verifies that there are at least eight characters in the line pointed to by its parameter L. It then reads each character in turn, converts it to the numeric equivalent and accumulates it in the variable result. If a character is not a valid hexadecimal digit, the procedure reports the error. The procedure **read_hex_word** is similar to **read_hex_natural**. However, instead of accumulating each digit into a numeric result, **read_hex_word** converts each digit to a four-element bit vector and inserts it into the 32-bit result word. The variable **r** is used as the index at which to place the four-element bit vector.

The versions of the **read** operations in **textio** that include the third parameter, **good**, allow for graceful recovery if the next value on the input line is not a valid textual representation of a value of the expected type. In that case, they return with **good** set to false, the line unmodified and the **value** parameter undefined. For example, an integer read from a line containing

    $%@!!&

fails in this way. On the other hand, if the line does contain valid text, **good** is set to true, and the value is extracted as described above. The versions of **read** without the **good** parameter cause an error if the line contains invalid text.

EXAMPLE

Suppose we have designed a model for a thermostat system and need to test it. The thermostat has inputs connected to signals **temperature** and **setting** of type **integer** and **enable** and **heater_fail** of type **bit**. We can use a text editor to write a file that specifies input stimuli to test the thermostat. Each line of the file is formatted as follows:

    time   string   value

where *time* is the simulation time at which the stimulus is applied, *string* is a four-character string identifying one of the inputs and *value* is the value to be applied to the input. The allowed *string* values are "temp", "set ", "on " and "fail". We assume that the stimuli are sorted in increasing order of application time. A sample file in this format is

    0 ms   on   0
    2 ms   fail   0
    15 ms   temp   56
    100 ms   set   70
    1.5 sec   on   1

We write a process to interpret such a stimulus control file as shown in Figure 18-10. The process declares a file object, **control**, associated with the stimulus control file, and an access variable, **command**, to point to a command line read from the file. It also declares a number of variables to store values read from a line. The process body repeatedly reads lines from the file and extracts the fields from it using read operations. We use the forms of **read** with **good** parameters to do error checking. In this way, we make the model less sensitive to formatting errors in the control file and report useful error information when an error is detected. When the end of the command file is reached, the process suspends for the rest of the simulation.

FIGURE 18-10

```
stimulus_interpreter : process is
    use std.textio.all;
    file control : text open read_mode is "control";
    variable command : line;
    variable read_ok : boolean;
    variable next_time : time;
    variable whitespace : character;
    variable signal_id : string(1 to 4);
    variable temp_value, set_value : integer;
    variable on_value, fail_value : bit;
begin
    command_loop : while not endfile(control) loop
        readline ( control, command );

        -- read next stimulus time, and suspend until then
        read ( command, next_time, read_ok );
        if not read_ok then
            report "error reading time from line: " & command.all
                severity warning;
            next command_loop;
        end if;
        wait for next_time – now;

        -- skip whitespace
        while command'length > 0
            and ( command(command'left) = ' '        -- ordinary space
                or command(command'left) = ' '    -- non–breaking space
                or command(command'left) = HT ) loop
            read ( command, whitespace );
        end loop;

        -- read signal identifier string
        read ( command, signal_id, read_ok );
        if not read_ok then
            report "error reading signal id from line: " & command.all
                severity warning;
            next command_loop;
        end if;

        -- dispatch based on signal id
        case signal_id is
            when "temp" =>
                read ( command, temp_value, read_ok );
                if not read_ok then
                    report "error reading temperature value from line: "
                            & command.all
                        severity warning;
                    next command_loop;
                end if;
                temperature <= temp_value;
```

```
                    when "set " =>
                        . . .          -- similar to "temp"
                    when "on  " =>
                        read ( command, on_value, read_ok );
                        if not read_ok then
                            report "error reading on value from line: " & command.all
                                severity warning;
                            next command_loop;
                        end if;
                        enable <= on_value;
                    when "fail" =>
                        . . .          -- similar to "on  "
                    when others =>
                        report "invalid signal id in line: " & signal_id
                            severity warning;
                        next command_loop;
                end case;
        end loop command_loop;
        wait;
end process stimulus_interpreter;
```

A process that reads a stimulus text file to test a thermostat.

For each command line, the process first extracts the time value and suspends until simulation advances to that time. It then skips over whitespace characters in the line up to the first non-whitespace character, which should represent the signal identifier string. The process skips whitespace characters by repeatedly inspecting the first character in what remains of the command line and, if it is a whitespace character, removing it with a character read operation. Skipping whitespace in this way allows the user some flexibility in formatting the command file. The process next dispatches to different branches of a case statement depending on the signal identifier string. For each string value, the process reads a stimulus value of the appropriate type from the command line and applies it to the corresponding signal.

VHDL-87

The VHDL-87 version of the **textio** package declares an additional function:

function endline (L : **in** line) **return** boolean;

This function returns the value **true** if the string pointed to by L is empty and **false** otherwise. The same condition can be tested in VHDL-93 by evaluating the expression L'length = 0.

Textio Write Operations

We now turn to write operations, which form a line of text ready for output. Each version of **write** has two parameters, specifying the pointer to the line being formed and the value whose textual representation is to be added to the line. Subsequent parameters beyond these two are used to control the formatting of the textual representation. The **field** parameter specifies how many characters are used to represent the value. If the field is wider than necessary, space characters are used as padding. The characters representing the value are either left-justified or right-justified within the field, depending on the **justified** parameter. For example, if we write the integer 42 left-justified in a field of five characters, the string "**42**   " is added to the line. If we write the same value right-justified in a field of five characters, the string "   **42**" is added. If we specify a field width that is smaller than the minimum required to represent the value, that minimal representation is used with no space padding. Thus, writing the integer 123 with a specified field width of two characters or less results in the three-character string "**123**" being added to the line. Note that the default values for **justified** and **field** conveniently result in the minimal representation being used.

The write operations for character, string and bit-vector values write representations that do not include quotation marks or a base specifier. Bit-vector values are written in binary. For example, if we perform the following write operations to a line, L, that is initially empty:

```
write ( L, string'( "fred" ) );
write ( L, ' ' );
write ( L, bit_vector'( X"3A" ) );
```

the resulting line is

    fred 00111010

The write operation for real values has an additional parameter, **digits**, that specifies how many digits to the right of the decimal point are to be included in the textual representation of the value. For example, writing the value 3.14159 with **digits** set to 2 results in the string "**3.14**" being added to the line. If **digits** is set to 0 (the default value), the value is represented in exponential notation. For example, writing 123.4567 in this way results in the string "**1.234567e+02**" (or something similar) being added to the line.

The write operation for time values has a parameter, **unit**, that specifies the time unit to use to express the value. The output is expressed as a multiple of this unit. For example, writing the value 40 ns with **unit** set to **ps** results in the string "**40000 ps**" being added to the line. If the value to be written is not an integral multiple of the specified unit, a real literal is used in the textual representation. For example, writing the value 23 μs with **unit** set to **ms** results in the string "**0.023 ms**" being added to the line.

EXAMPLE

We can write a bus monitor process for a computer system model that creates a log file of bus activity, similar to that displayed by a bus-state analyzer monitoring real hardware. Suppose the model includes the following signals connecting the CPU with memory and I/O controllers:

```
signal address : bit_vector(15 downto 0);
signal data : resolve_bytes byte;
signal rd, wr, io : bit;                    — read, write, io/mem select
signal ready : resolve_bits bit;
```

Our monitor process is written as shown in Figure 18-11. It declares an output file **log**, of type **text**, and an access variable **trace_line**, of type **line**, for accumulating each line of output. The process is resumed when the memory or I/O controller responds to a bus read or write request. It generates a formatted line using write operations. It also keeps count of how many lines are written to the log file and includes a header line after every 60 lines of trace data. A sample log file showing how the data is formatted is

```
        Time    R/W I/M  Address           Data

      0.4 us    R   M    0000000000000000 10011110
      0.9 us    R   M    0000000000000001 00010010
        2 us    R   M    0000000000010100 11100111
      2.7 us    W   I    0000000000000111 00000000
```

FIGURE 18-11

```
bus_monitor : process is
    constant header : string(1 to 44)
        := FF & "    Time   R/W I/M  Address        Data";
    use std.textio.all;

    file log : text open write_mode is "buslog";
    variable trace_line : line;
    variable line_count : natural := 0;
begin
    if line_count mod 60 = 0 then
        write ( trace_line, header );
        writeline ( log, trace_line );
        writeline ( log, trace_line );   — empty line
    end if;
    wait until (rd = '1' or wr = '1') and ready = '1';
    write ( trace_line, now, justified => right, field => 10, unit => us );
    write ( trace_line, string'(" ") );
    if rd = '1' then
        write ( trace_line, 'R' );
    else
        write ( trace_line, 'W' );
    end if;
    write ( trace_line, string'(" ") );
    if io = '1' then
        write ( trace_line, 'I' );
    else
        write ( trace_line, 'M' );
    end if;
```

(continued on page 522)

(continued from page 521)

```
                    write ( trace_line, string'(" ") );
                    write ( trace_line, address );
                    write ( trace_line, ' ');
                    write ( trace_line, data );
                    writeline ( log, trace_line );
                    line_count := line_count + 1;
               end process bus_monitor;
```

A process that monitors a computer system bus and creates a log file of bus activity.

Reading and Writing User-Defined Types

We have seen that **textio** provides read and write operations for the predefined types. If we need to read or write values of types we declare, such as new enumeration or physical types, we use the 'image and 'value attributes to convert between the values and their textual representations. For example, if we declare an enumeration type and variable as

```
type speed_category is (stopped, slow, fast, maniacal);
variable speed : speed_category;
```

we can write a value of the type using the 'image attribute to create a string to supply to the string version of **write**:

```
write ( L, speed_category'image(speed) );
```

Reading a value of a new type we define presents more problems if we want our model to be robust in the face of invalid input. In this case, we must write VHDL code that analyzes the line of text to ensure that it contains a valid representation of a value of the expected type. If we are not so concerned with robustness, we can simply use the 'value attribute to convert the input line to a value of the expected type. For example, the statements

```
readline( input, L );
speed := speed_category'value(L.all);
```

convert an entire line of input to a value of type **speed_category**.

One final point to note about the read and write operations provided by **textio** is that they may deallocate storage used by lines of text passed to them as arguments. For example, when a read operation extracts characters from the beginning of a line, the storage for the extracted characters may be deallocated. Alternatively, the whole line may be deallocated and a new line formed from the remaining characters. The trap to be aware of is that if we copy the pointer to a line, using assignment of one value of type **line** to another, we may end up with dangling pointers after doing read or write operations. The best way to avoid problems is to avoid modifying variables of type **line** other than with read and write operations.

Exercises

1. [❶ 18.1] Write declarations to define a file of real values associated with the host file "samples.dat" and opened for reading. Write a statement to read a value from the file into a variable x.

2. [❶ 18.1] Write declarations to define a file of bit-vector values associated with the host file "/tmp/trace.tmp" and opened for writing. Write a statement to write the concatenation of the values of two signals, **addr** and **d_bus**, to the file.

3. [❶ 18.1] Write statements that attempt to open a file of integers called "waveform" for reading and report any error that results from the attempt.

4. [❶ 18.2] Suppose the next line in a text file contains the characters

    123 4.5 6789

    What is the result returned by the following **read** calls?

    ```
    readline(in_file, L);
    read(L, bit_value);      -- read a value of type bit
    read(L, int_value);      -- read a value of type integer
    read(L, real_value);     -- read a value of type real
    read(L, str_value);      -- read a value of type string(1 to 3)
    ```

5. [❶ 18.2] Write declarations and statements for a process to prompt the user to enter a number and to accept the number from the user.

6. [❶ 18.2] What string is written to the output file by the following statements:

    ```
    write(L, 3.5 us, justified => right, field => 10, unit => ns);
    write(L, ' ');
    write(L, bit_vector'(X"3C"));
    write(L, ' ');
    write(L, string'("ok"), justified => left, field => 5);
    writeline(output, L);
    ```

7. [❷ 18.1] Develop a behavioral model of a microcomputer system address decoder with the following entity interface:

    ```
    entity address_decoder is
        generic ( log_file_name : string );
        port ( address : in natural;  enable : in bit;
               ROM_sel, RAM_sel, IO_sel, int_sel : out bit );
    end entity address_decoder;
    ```

    When **enable** is '1', the decoder uses the value of **address** to determine which of the output signals to activate. The address ranges are 0 to 16#7FFF# for ROM, 16#8000# to 16#BFFF# for RAM, 16#C000# to 16#EFFF# for I/O and 16#F000# to 16#FFFF# for interrupts. The decoder should write the address to the named log file each time **enable** is activated. The log file should be a binary file rather than a text file.

8. [❷ 18.1] Write a function that may be called to initialize an array of bit-vector words. The words are of the subtype

    subtype word **is** std_logic_vector(0 **to** 15);

    The function should have two parameters, the first being the name of a file from which the words of data are read, and the second being the size of the array to return. If the file contains fewer words than required, the extra words in the array are initialized with all bits set to 'U'.

9. [❷ 18.1] Develop a procedure that writes the contents of a memory array to a file. The memory array is of the type **mem_array**, declared as

    subtype byte **is** bit_vector(7 **downto** 0);
    type mem_array **is array** (natural **range** <>) **of** byte;

    The procedure should have two parameters, one being the array whose value is to be written and the other being a file of **byte** elements into which the data is written. The procedure should assume the file has already been opened for writing.

10. [❷ 18.2] Develop a procedure that has a file name and an integer signal as parameters. The file name refers to a text file that contains a delay value and an integer on each line. The procedure should read successive lines, wait for the time specified by the delay value, then assign the integer value to the signal. When the last line has been processed, the procedure should return. Invoke the procedure using a concurrent procedure call in a test bench.

11. [❷ 18.2] Develop a procedure that logs the history of values on a bit-vector signal to a file. The procedure has two parameters, the name of a text file and a bit-vector signal. The procedure logs the initial value and the new values when events occur on the signal. Each log entry in the file should consist of the simulation time and the signal value at that time.

12. [❷ 18.2] Develop a procedure similar to that described in Exercise 11, but which logs values of a signal of type **motor_control**, declared as

    type motor_state **is** (idle, forward, reverse);
    type motor_control **is record**
            state : motor_state;
            speed : natural;
        end record motor_control;

    The **motor_control** values should be written in the format of a record aggregate using positional association.

13. [❸ 18.1] Experiment with your simulator to determine the format it uses for binary files. Write a model that creates files of various data types, and use operating system utilities (for example, hexadecimal dump utilities) to see how the data is stored. Try to develop programs in a conventional programming language to write files that can be read by VHDL models run by your simulator.

14. [❸ 18.2] A 16L2 Programmable Logic Device (PLD) is organized as follows:

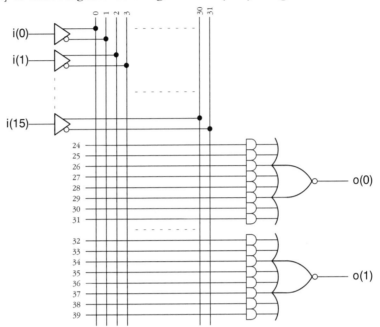

A programmable fuse connects each of the 32 column wires with each of the 16 row wires. If all fuses for a row are disconnected, the row wire floats high. A row wire is tied low by leaving all fuses in the row intact. The programming of the fuses may be specified in a fuse-map text file. It contains 16 lines, each with 32 '1' or '0' characters. A '1' corresponds to a disconnected fuse, and a '0' corresponds to an intact fuse.

Develop a behavioral model of a 16L2 PLD, with input and output ports of type **bit** and a generic constant string to specify the fuse-map file for programming an instance. The model should read the fuse-map file during initialization and use the information to perform the programmed logic function during simulation.

15. [❸ 18.2] Modify the **disassemble** procedure in the **dlx_instr** package in the DLX model suite, described in Chapter 15, to disassemble the instruction to the standard output file rather than into a string.

16. [❸ 18.2] Develop a package that provides textual read and write operations for standard-logic scalar and vector values, analogous to the operations provided for types **bit** and **bit_vector** by the **textio** package.

17. [❸ 18.2] Develop a package that provides textual read and write operations for bit-vector values in octal and hexadecimal.

18. [❹ 18.2] Develop a suite of behavioral models of programmable logic devices (PLDs) that read JEDEC format fuse-map files during initialization. Information about the JEDEC format can be found in *JEDEC Standard No. 3-A, Standard Data Transfer Format between Data Preparation System and Programmable Logic Device Programmer.*

19. [❹ 18.2] Develop a behavioral model of a ROM that reads its contents from a file in Intel hex-format.

20. [❹ 18.2] Develop a behavioral model of a ROM that reads its contents from a file in Motorola S-format.

21. [❹ 18.2] Develop a "bus functional" architecture body for the DLX CPU, described in Chapter 15. Rather than fetching and interpreting instructions, the model reads a file of commands. A "bus-transaction" command specifies a time at which a bus transaction is to be initiated by the CPU and includes the address and transaction kind (instruction fetch, read or write). The time is a delay from completion of the previous command. A "halt" command causes the model to activate the **halt** port until the next bus-transaction command is performed. An "include" command causes the model to process a subsidiary command file. Note that the subsidiary file may also contain nested include commands. When the CPU **reset** port is activated, the model terminates command processing and resets the bus signals. When **reset** is removed, the model resumes processing the command file from the beginning.

Case Study: Queuing Networks

In this final case study, we develop a suite of VHDL entities for building queuing networks. These are used to model systems at a very high level of abstraction and to gain system performance estimates before proceeding to more detailed design. Our implementation of the queuing network entities illustrates the use of abstract data types and file input/output.

19.1 Queuing Network Concepts

In all of the examples we have considered so far in this book, our main concern has been the correctness of the design. We have written models in VHDL and simulated them to verify that they correctly implement the required behavior. In our first chapter, we also mentioned performance analysis as a motivation for simulation. The requirements specification for a system often dictates that it must perform some number of operations per second or perform a task within a given amount of time. In such cases, it is important to verify that our initial high-level design meets the performance requirements. We may need to evaluate a number of alternative designs to choose one that meets the requirements with minimum cost. We would like to be able to evaluate a proposed design's performance before investing significant effort in refining it to a more detailed level.

One technique for system modeling to evaluate performance is *uninterpreted modeling* using *queuing networks*. This technique is described in many texts on computer performance analysis, including [9]. It involves modeling a system as an interconnected collection of *servers*, which process *tokens* of information. The actual data is not explicitly represented, nor is it transformed by the servers. Instead, each token just represents the presence of some data within the system. For example, a token might represent a user's job within a multiprogrammed computer system. *Queues* are used within a network to hold tokens until a server is ready to accept them. Since the data is not represented in detail, a server cannot interpret the data as it would in a behavioral model; hence the term "uninterpreted." A server merely holds a token for the amount of time it would take to process the data and then passes the token on to the rest of the system.

Figure 19-1 shows a queuing network model of a simple computer system consisting of a CPU and a disk unit. Tokens representing jobs arrive at the *source* and enter a queue waiting for service by the CPU. A job leaves the CPU, either because it has terminated or because it needs to access the disk unit. Terminated jobs are passed to the token *sink*. Jobs that need to access the disk wait in the second queue until the disk server is ready. When the disk completes the access, the job returns to the CPU queue.

FIGURE 19-1

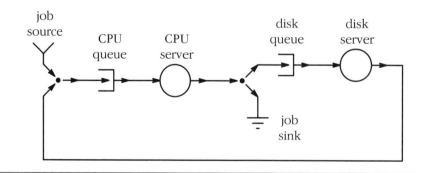

A queuing network model of a simple computer system.

Since we are interested in evaluating the performance of a system modeled as a queuing network, we need to measure the time spent by each token in the different parts of the network. The difficulty is that the processing times in the real system and the paths taken through the network depend on the actual data. We solve this difficulty by estimating the processing times and routing choices using probability distributions and using randomly generated numbers to control the flow of tokens. For example, the CPU service times in the network of Figure 19-1 might be uniformly distributed between 0 ms and 100 ms. Each time a token arrives at the CPU server, we generate a random number between 0 and 100 and hold the token for that many milliseconds. Tokens leaving the CPU server might take the path to the disk queue 95 percent of the time, or the path to the job sink 5 percent of the time. When a token arrives at this fork, we can generate a random number between 0 and 1. If the number is less than 0.95, we route the token to the disk queue; otherwise we route it to the job sink. We also need to model the creation of tokens within the network. We do this by estimating the time between arrival of new tokens as a probability distribution. Most queuing network models use an exponential distribution for inter-arrival time.

Once we have a queuing network model of a system in operation, we can evaluate various aspects of the system's performance. We can measure the throughput by counting the number of tokens processed during a simulation. We can measure the response time by looking at the time taken by tokens to proceed through the network. We can also measure the utilization of resources represented by servers by counting the proportion of the simulation time in which they are holding tokens.

19.2 Queuing Network Modules

The simple network of Figure 19-1 identifies a number of modules that we need to construct queuing networks: a token *source*, a token *sink*, a *queue*, a *server*, a *fork* and a *join*. In this section, we develop VHDL design entities to represent each of these modules. First, however, we need to provide a facility for generating random numbers according to various probability distributions. We also need to define types to represent tokens and the connections between the network modules.

Random Number Generator

Since random number generation is a generally useful facility, we develop our random number generator as a package that can be reused in a variety of contexts. We provide a way of specifying the required probability distribution for random numbers and for generating successive numbers from the distribution.

Figure 19-2 shows the package declaration for our random number generator. The type **distribution_type** identifies the different probability distributions provided by the package. For the purposes of this case study, we implement only uniform and exponential distributions. A realistic random number generator also provides a number of other distributions. The "fixed" distribution provides a sequence of numbers, each of which has a given value. This is useful in queuing networks for servers whose service time does not depend on the data represented by a token. The type **probability** consists

FIGURE 19-2

```
package random is
    type distribution_type is (fixed, uniform, exponential);
    subtype probability is real range 0.0 to 1.0;
    type probability_vector is array (positive range <>) of probability;
    type seed_type is record
            seed1, seed2 : positive;
        end record seed_type;
    type seed_array is array ( natural range <> ) of seed_type;
    constant sample_seeds : seed_array(0 to 50);
    type random_info_record is record
            seed : seed_type;
            distribution : distribution_type;
            mean : real;
            lower_bound, upper_bound : real;
        end record random_info_record;
    procedure init_fixed ( random_info : out random_info_record;
                           mean : in real );
    procedure init_uniform ( random_info : out random_info_record;
                             lower_bound, upper_bound : in real;
                             seed : in seed_type );
    procedure init_exponential ( random_info : out random_info_record;
                                 mean : in real;  seed : in seed_type );
    procedure generate_random ( random_info : inout random_info_record;
                                random_number : out real );
end package random;
```

A package declaration for the random number generator.

of real numbers between 0.0 and 1.0 representing probability values. The type **probability_vector** is an array of probability values, which we use to specify the probabilities of tokens being routed via different paths from a join module in a network.

The next type, **seed_type**, is required for our implementation of the random number generator. We generate pseudo-random sequences of numbers based on seed values provided by the model that uses the package. The model need not be concerned with the concrete representation of seeds. Instead, it should treat **seed_type** as an abstract type used only for random number generation. Our package provides a number of different initial seeds in the constant array **sample_seeds**. If we choose a different element of the array as the initial seed for each random variate, we can avoid correlation between the sequences of pseudo-random numbers.

The next type defined in the package, **random_info_record**, represents the information that describes the distribution of random numbers required by a model. It also includes the current seed value, to be used to generate the next number. Thus, a value of the **random_info_record** type represents the state of a particular sequence of random numbers. The three procedures **init_fixed**, **init_uniform** and **init_exponential** initialize a record to contain the required information for each of the three distributions provided by the package. A model must have a variable of type random_info_record for each random variate and must call one of these procedures to initialize each variable. The model then calls the procedure generate_random each time it requires a new random number.

The package body for the random number generator is shown in Figure 19-3. It makes use of the package, math_real, that provides mathematical operations on real numbers. (This package is a draft version of the real-number mathematical package being developed by the IEEE P1076.2 Working Group. See Section D.4 of Appendix D for further details.) We assume the package has been separately analyzed into the design library math. Our package body first completes the declaration of the constant sample_seeds, initializing it to an array of precomputed seed records. (For brevity, not all of the elements are shown here.) Next, the package completes the declaration of the procedures that initialize information records for random number sequences. The procedures init_uniform and init_exponential verify that the distribution parameters are legal before initializing the record.

FIGURE 19-3

```
library math;
package body random is
    use math.math_real;
    constant sample_seeds : seed_array(0 to 50)
                := (   0  => (1, 1),
                       1  => (1919456777, 2006618587),
                       2  => (928906921, 476680813),

                         . . .
                      50  => (844396720, 821616997) );
    procedure init_fixed ( random_info : out random_info_record;
                           mean : in real ) is
    begin
        random_info.distribution := fixed;
        random_info.mean := mean;
    end procedure init_fixed;
    procedure init_uniform ( random_info : out random_info_record;
                             lower_bound, upper_bound : in real;
                             seed : in seed_type ) is
    begin
        assert lower_bound <= upper_bound
            report "init_uniform: lower_bound > upper_bound" severity failure;
        random_info.distribution := uniform;
        random_info.lower_bound := lower_bound;
        random_info.upper_bound := upper_bound;
        random_info.seed := seed;
    end procedure init_uniform;
```

(continued on page 532)

(continued from page 531)

```
procedure init_exponential ( random_info : out random_info_record;
                             mean : in real;  seed : in seed_type ) is
begin
    assert mean > 0.0
        report "init_exponential: mean not positive" severity failure;
    random_info.distribution := exponential;
    random_info.mean := mean;
    random_info.seed := seed;
end procedure init_exponential;

procedure generate_uniform ( random_info : inout random_info_record;
                             random_number : out real ) is
    variable tmp : real;
begin
    math_real.uniform(random_info.seed.seed1, random_info.seed.seed2, tmp);
    random_number := random_info.lower_bound
                        + tmp * ( random_info.upper_bound
                                    – random_info.lower_bound );
end procedure generate_uniform;

procedure generate_exponential ( random_info : inout random_info_record;
                                 random_number : out real ) is
    variable tmp : real;
begin
    loop
        math_real.uniform(random_info.seed.seed1, random_info.seed.seed2, tmp);
        exit when tmp /= 0.0;
    end loop;
    random_number := – random_info.mean * math_real.log(tmp);
end procedure generate_exponential;

procedure generate_random ( random_info : inout random_info_record;
                            random_number : out real ) is
begin
    case random_info.distribution is
        when fixed =>
            random_number := random_info.mean;
        when uniform =>
            generate_uniform(random_info, random_number);
        when exponential =>
            generate_exponential(random_info, random_number);
    end case;
end procedure generate_random;
end package body random;
```

A package body for the random number generator.

At the end of the package body, the procedure **generate_random** is declared. If the random number sequence is based on a fixed distribution, the procedure returns the mean value from the information record. Otherwise it calls one of the two procedures, **generate_uniform** or **generate_exponential**, declared locally to the package. These both use the uniform random number generator provided by the math package. This operation accepts and updates the two seed elements and generates a pseudo-random number uniformly distributed between 0.0 and 1.0. The generate_uniform procedure scales the number to place it in the range specified in the information record. The generate_exponential procedure repeatedly invokes the operation until a non-zero result is produced, since it subsequently calculates the natural logarithm of the result. The logarithm of 0.0 is not defined.

A Package for Token and Arc Types

We now develop a package that declares the types for the connections between modules in a queuing network. The package declaration is shown in Figure 19-4. First, we need to declare a type to represent the tokens that flow around the network. Each token represents a unit of information, such as a job, and originates at a token source. We need to trace the flow of individual tokens. We also need to measure the time taken for a token to reach a sink, since that represents the time taken by the modeled system to process the token. Thus, the type token_type, declared by the package, includes a string and an identity number to identify the token and a time-stamp to indicate when it was created. The string is the name of the source that created the token. The number of significant characters in the string is given by the element source_name_length. The identity number is a serial number allocated by the source. The package also defines a type representing an array of tokens.

FIGURE 19-4

```
use std.textio.line;
package qsim_types is
      constant name_max_length : natural := 20;
      type token_id_type is range 0 to integer'high;
      type token_type is record
               source_name : string(1 to name_max_length);
               source_name_length : natural;
               id : token_id_type;
               creation_time : time;
          end record;
      type token_vector is array (positive range <>) of token_type;
      type arc_type is record
               transaction : boolean;   -- flips when an arc changes
               token : token_type;
          end record arc_type;
      type arc_vector is array (positive range <>) of arc_type;
      type info_detail_type is (none, summary, trace);
      procedure write ( L : inout line;  t : in token_type;
                       creation_time_unit : in time := ns );
end package qsim_types;
```

A package declaration for queuing network types.

As a first attempt, it may seem sufficient to use the type token_type for the connections between modules in a queuing network. A module could then use a wait statement to wait for a new token to arrive on an input port. The problem with this approach is that most networks of interest include feedback paths, as shown in Figure 19-5. Suppose the queue module is suspended at a wait statement, awaiting the arrival of a token on its input port. When a new token enters the loop, the join module assigns the token value to its output port. The queue module resumes in response to the event and accepts the token. Now suppose this token passes around the loop, with no other new tokens entering the loop in the meantime. The join module assigns the token value to its output. However, since the token value is the same as that for the previous assignment, the transaction on the signal does not cause an event. Hence the queue module is not resumed in response to the recurrence of the token. The result is that the token is lost.

FIGURE 19-5

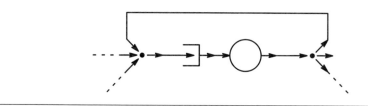

A feedback path within a queuing network.

As a second attempt, we might ensure that all modules waiting for arrival of tokens wait for transactions on their inputs, using the 'transaction attribute of their input ports. This would be sufficient for modules that have only one input, namely, the queue, server, fork and sink modules. However, the join module has a number of inputs. We would like to use an array type for the input ports, allowing us to instantiate join modules with different numbers of inputs. The problem that arises in this case is that the prefix of a 'transaction attribute must be a statically named signal. As we shall see later, the join module must detect transactions on separate elements of its input port without knowing statically how many elements there are in the array. This precludes using the 'transaction attribute to detect token arrival.

Our solution to these difficulties is to define a separate type for network *arcs* connecting modules. This type, arc_type, includes a token value as one element and a Boolean flag as another element. Each time a module assigns a token to an output, it changes the state of the flag for that output. Thus, even if the token value is the same as the previously assigned token value, the composite arc signal is assigned a different value. A module can thus wait for an event on an input port and can use the transaction flag for each element in an array of arcs to determine which element contains a new token. We see exactly how this works when we examine the implementation of each of the modules.

The remaining declarations in the qsim_types package provide control of token flow tracing within a network and report measurements made by each module. Each of the modules includes a port of type info_detail_type. When the port is assigned the value summary, the module writes a summary of measured data to an output file. When the port has the value trace, the module writes a trace message to the output file for each token that it processes. The procedure write appends a textual representation of a token to a string. It has a signature similar to those of the write procedures provided in textio and is used in the same way. Figure 19-6 shows the body of the queuing network types package, which completes the declaration of the write procedure. It uses versions of write from textio to include the token identity number, source name and creation time-stamp in the textual representation.

FIGURE 19-6

```
package body qsim_types is
    use std.textio.all;
    procedure write ( L : inout line;  t : in token_type;
                            creation_time_unit : in time := ns ) is
    begin
        write(L, string'("token "));
        write(L, natural(t.id));
        write(L, string'(" from "));
        write(L, t.source_name(1 to t.source_name_length));
        write(L, string'(" created at "));
        write(L, t.creation_time, unit => creation_time_unit);
    end write;
end package body qsim_types;
```

A package body for the queuing network types package.

The Token Source Module

Tokens in a queuing network are generated by a token *source* module. The entity declaration for a token source is shown in Figure 19-7. The generic constant name is used to identify an instance of the entity. The probability distribution for inter-arrival times is controlled by the generic constants distribution and mean_inter_arrival_time. The generic constant seed is the initial seed for the sequence of random numbers used to

FIGURE 19-7

```
use work.qsim_types.all, work.random.all;
entity source is
    generic ( name : string;
                    distribution : distribution_type;
                    mean_inter_arrival_time : delay_length;
                    seed : seed_type;
                    time_unit : delay_length := ns;
                    info_file_name : string := "info_file.dat" );
    port ( out_arc : out arc_type;
                info_detail : in info_detail_type );
end entity source;
```

An entity declaration for the token source module.

determine inter-arrival times. Each module within a network should be given a different value for **seed** to avoid correlation between their random number sequences. All times are calculated and reported in multiples of the generic constant **time_unit**. Usually, all modules within a given network would use the same value for this constant. The generic constant **info_file_name** specifies the name of the text file to be created for trace messages and statistics reported by the instance. The port **out_arc** is the connection upon which tokens are generated, and the port **info_detail** controls the reporting of information by the instance, as described earlier in this section.

The behavioral architecture body for the token source is shown in Figure 19-8. The process **token_generator** implements the behavior. The body of the process first copies the name string into the local variable **source_name**, truncating it if it is longer than **name_max_length**. This string is included in each of the tokens generated by the process. The process then opens the output file in preparation for writing trace and statistics reports. Next, the process initializes the variable that holds the random number information record. The value of the generic constant **distribution** is used to determine which initialization procedure from the package **random** to use. The random numbers are interpreted as the number of time units to wait before the next token is generated. Hence the process divides the mean inter-arrival time by the time unit value to derive the parameters for the random number distribution.

FIGURE 19-8

```
library math;
architecture behavior of source is
begin
    token_generator : process is
            variable source_name : string(1 to name_max_length) := (others => ' ');
            variable source_name_length : natural;
            variable next_token_id : token_id_type := 0;
            variable next_arrival_time : time;
            variable number_of_tokens_generated : natural := 0;
            variable inter_arrival_time : natural;   -- in time_unit
            variable sum_of_inter_arrival_times : real := 0.0;   -- in time_unit
            variable sum_of_squares_of_inter_arrival_times : real := 0.0;   --in time_unit**2

            variable random_info : random_info_record;
            variable random_number : real;

            use std.textio.all;
            file info_file : text;
            variable L : line;

            use math.math_real.sqrt;

            procedure write_summary is
                    variable measured_mean_inter_arrival_time : real
                            := sum_of_inter_arrival_times / real(number_of_tokens_generated);
                    variable measured_std_dev_of_inter_arrival_times : real
                            := sqrt ( ( sum_of_squares_of_inter_arrival_times
                                            - sum_of_inter_arrival_times**2
                                                    / real(number_of_tokens_generated) )
                                    / real( number_of_tokens_generated – 1 ) );
```

```
begin
    write(L, string'("Summary information for source "));
    write(L, name);
    write(L, string'(" up to time "));
    write(L, now, unit => time_unit);
    writeline(info_file, L);
    write(L, string'(" Inter arrival distribution: "));
    write(L, distribution_type'image(distribution));
    write(L, string'(" with mean inter arrival time of "));
    write(L, mean_inter_arrival_time, unit => time_unit);
    writeline(info_file, L);
    write(L, string'(" Number of tokens generated = "));
    write(L, natural(next_token_id));
    writeline(info_file, L);
    write(L, string'(" Mean inter arrival time = "));
    write(L, measured_mean_inter_arrival_time * time_unit, unit => time_unit);
    writeline(info_file, L);
    write(L, string'(" Standard deviation of inter arrival times = "));
    write(L, measured_std_dev_of_inter_arrival_times * time_unit,
            unit => time_unit);
    writeline(info_file, L);
    writeline(info_file, L);
end procedure write_summary;

procedure write_trace is
begin
    write(L, string'("Source "));
    write(L, name);
    write(L, string'(": at "));
    write(L, now, unit => time_unit);
    write(L, string'(" generated token "));
    write(L, natural(next_token_id));
    writeline(info_file, L);
end procedure write_trace;

begin
    if name'length > name_max_length then
        source_name := name(1 to name_max_length);
        source_name_length := name_max_length;
    else
        source_name(1 to name'length) := name;
        source_name_length := name'length;
    end if;
    file_open(info_file, info_file_name, write_mode);

    case distribution is
        when fixed =>
            init_fixed(random_info, real(mean_inter_arrival_time / time_unit));
```

(continued on page 538)

(continued from page 537)

```
                    when uniform =>
                        init_uniform( random_info,
                                    lower_bound => 0.0,
                                    upper_bound =>
                                            2.0 * real(mean_inter_arrival_time / time_unit),
                                    seed => seed );
                    when exponential =>
                        init_exponential( random_info,
                                        mean => real(mean_inter_arrival_time / time_unit),
                                        seed => seed );
                end case;
                loop
                    generate_random(random_info, random_number);
                    inter_arrival_time := natural(random_number);
                    next_arrival_time := inter_arrival_time * time_unit + now;
                    loop
                        wait on info_detail'transaction for next_arrival_time – now;
                        if info_detail'active and info_detail = summary then
                            write_summary;
                        end if;
                        exit when next_arrival_time = now;
                    end loop;
                    out_arc <= arc_type'( transaction => not out_arc.transaction'driving_value,
                                    token => token_type'( source_name =>
                                                                    source_name,
                                                        source_name_length =>
                                                                    source_name_length,
                                                        id => next_token_id,
                                                        creation_time => now ) );
                    number_of_tokens_generated := number_of_tokens_generated + 1;
                    sum_of_inter_arrival_times := sum_of_inter_arrival_times
                                                    + real(inter_arrival_time);
                    sum_of_squares_of_inter_arrival_times
                        := sum_of_squares_of_inter_arrival_times + real(inter_arrival_time) ** 2;
                    if info_detail = trace then
                        write_trace;
                    end if;
                    next_token_id := next_token_id + 1;
                end loop;
            end process token_generator;
        end architecture behavior;
```

An architecture body for the token source.

After this initialization, the process enters a loop in which it generates successive tokens. It generates a new random number and uses it to determine the absolute simulation time at which the next token should be generated (next_arrival_time). If the process were simply to wait for the inter-arrival time, it would not respond to changes on the info_detail port. Hence the process repeatedly waits either until a transaction occurs on the info_detail port or for the time interval remaining until the next token is to be generated. If the process resumes in response to a request for summary information, it calls the procedure write_summary to write the information to the output file. When the process resumes after the inter-arrival interval, it exits the inner loop and proceeds to generate the next token. It does this by assigning a new value to the output arc port. The transaction flag element is toggled to the inverse of its current value, determined using the 'driving_value attribute of the element. The new token value includes the name of the source, the next serial number and the current simulation time as a time-stamp. The process then increments the variables used to maintain statistics for tokens generated by the source. If the info_detail signal value indicates that tracing is required, the process calls write_trace to write a message to the output file. Finally, the process increments the variable holding the next token serial number.

The procedure write_summary reports measured statistics to the output file. It uses the values of the variables number_of_tokens_generated, sum_of_inter_arrival_times and sum_of_squares_of_inter_arrival_times to calculate the actual mean and standard deviation of inter-arrival times for tokens generated since the start of the simulation. The procedure uses the various versions of the write procedure and the writeline procedure from textio to form the report text. The procedure write_trace reports trace messages to the output file. Each message includes the time at which the token was generated and the identity number of the token.

The Token Sink Module

After a token is created, it flows through the modules in a queuing network until it reaches a *sink*. Arrival at a sink represents completion of processing for the information represented by the token. The lifetime of the token, from creation to arrival at the sink, represents the time taken by the system being modeled to process the information. Hence the average lifetime of all tokens arriving at a sink is a measure of the response time of the system. Our sink module accepts tokens arriving on its input and accumulates statistics about the lifetimes of the tokens. The entity declaration for the sink module is shown in Figure 19-9. The name, time_unit and info_file_name generic parameters and the info_detail port serve the same purpose as those items in the entity declaration of the source module. The in_arc port is the input for arriving tokens.

FIGURE 19-9

```
use work.qsim_types.all;
entity sink is
    generic ( name : string;
                time_unit : delay_length := ns;
                info_file_name : string := "info_file.dat" );
    port ( in_arc : in arc_type;
            info_detail : in info_detail_type );
end sink;
```

An entity declaration for the sink module.

FIGURE 19-10

```
library math;

architecture behavior of sink is
begin
    token_consumer : process is
        variable number_of_tokens_consumed : natural := 0;
        variable life_time : real;  -- in time_unit
        variable sum_of_life_times : real := 0.0;  -- in time_unit
        variable sum_of_squares_of_life_times : real := 0.0;  --in time_unit**2

        use std.textio.all;
        file info_file : text;
        variable L : line;

        use math.math_real.sqrt;

        procedure write_summary is . . .

        procedure write_trace is . . .
    begin
        file_open(info_file, info_file_name, write_mode);
        loop
            wait on info_detail'transaction, in_arc;
            if info_detail'active and info_detail = summary then
                write_summary;
            end if;
            if in_arc'event then
                number_of_tokens_consumed := number_of_tokens_consumed + 1;
                life_time := real( (now – in_arc.token.creation_time) / time_unit );
                sum_of_life_times := sum_of_life_times + life_time;
                sum_of_squares_of_life_times := sum_of_squares_of_life_times
                                                            + life_time ** 2;
                if info_detail = trace then
                    write_trace;
                end if;
            end if;
        end loop;
    end process token_consumer;
end architecture behavior;
```

An outline of the architecture body for the sink module.

The behavioral architecture body for the sink module is outlined in Figure 19-10. The process first opens the output file for trace and statistics information, then enters a loop in which it waits for information requests on the info_detail port or for tokens to arrive on the in_arc port. If a transaction occurs on info_detail, setting it to the value summary, the process calls the procedure write_summary to write the statistics information file. This procedure is similar to the procedure of the same name in the source module. When a token arrives, the process measures its lifetime by subtracting the creation time-stamp from the current simulation time. The lifetime is expressed as a multiple of the time_unit value. The process accumulates the lifetime into the variables used to maintain statistics about arriving tokens. If the info_detail signal has the value trace, the process calls write_trace to write a trace message describing the token to the output file.

The Queue Module

We now turn to the *queue* module. When a token arrives at a queue module, it enters a first-in first-out (FIFO) queue. The token at the head of the queue is released when the server associated with the queue is ready to accept the next token. This behavior has two implications for our queue module. First, we must provide a status connection between the server and the queue module so that the server can indicate when it is ready. The out_ready port of the queue entity, shown in Figure 19-11, provides this connection. Second, the implementation of the queue module must include a FIFO queue to store waiting tokens. We define an abstract data type (ADT) for FIFO queues of objects and specialize it for waiting tokens in the implementation of our queue module.

FIGURE 19-11

```
use work.qsim_types.all;

entity queue is
    generic ( name : string;
                time_unit : delay_length := ns;
                info_file_name : string := "info_file.dat" );
    port ( in_arc : in arc_type;
            out_arc : out arc_type;
            out_ready : in boolean;
            info_detail : in info_detail_type );
end entity queue;
```

An entity declaration for the queue module.

The package declaration template for the FIFO ADT is shown in Figure 19-12. This template has a placeholder, «element_type», for the type of the elements to be stored in a FIFO. The ADT provides four operations on values of FIFOs of type fifo_type. The function new_fifo creates a new empty FIFO. The procedure test_empty tests whether there are any elements in the queue. This must be a procedure rather than a function, since the concrete type used to implement FIFOs is an access type. Functions can only have parameters of class constant, and such parameters are not allowed to contain access values. Hence we declare the FIFO parameter of test_empty as an object of class variable, but with mode **in**, so that it may not be modified by the procedure. The procedure insert places an element on the tail of the FIFO queue, and the procedure remove takes the first element from the head of the FIFO queue. The private type declarations in the package declaration template show the concrete representation that we use for FIFOs. Each element is stored in a record of type fifo_entry_record. These records are joined together in a linked list. In addition, there is a header record of type fifo_record that contains pointers to the entries at the head and the tail of the list. If the FIFO is

FIGURE 19-12

```
package «element_type_simple_name»_fifo_adt is
    alias element_type is «element_type»;
    type fifo_record;
    type fifo_type is access fifo_record;
    function new_fifo return fifo_type;
    procedure test_empty ( variable fifo : in fifo_type;
                           variable is_empty : out boolean );
    procedure insert ( fifo : inout fifo_type; element : in element_type );
    procedure remove ( fifo : inout fifo_type; element : out element_type );
    -- private types
    type fifo_entry_record;
    type fifo_entry is access fifo_entry_record;
    type fifo_entry_record is record
        next_entry : fifo_entry;
        element : element_type;
      end record;
    type fifo_record is record
        head_entry, tail_entry : fifo_entry;
      end record;
end package «element_type_simple_name»_fifo_adt;
```

A package declaration template for FIFO queues of objects.

empty, these pointers are both **null**. The concrete representation of the abstract data type is a pointer to the header record.

Figure 19-13 shows the template for the FIFO ADT package body, which contains the full declarations of the ADT operations. The function new_fifo simply returns a header record with both pointers set to **null**, and the procedure test_empty tests whether the head_entry pointer of the header record is **null**. The procedure insert first creates a new fifo_entry_record object containing the element to be inserted into the FIFO. Since this record is to be added to the end of the linked list, its link pointer is set to **null**. If the FIFO is not empty, the tail_entry pointer of the header record is used to locate the entry at the tail of the linked list. The link pointer of this entry is set to point to the new entry. Otherwise, if the FIFO is empty, the new entry must become the only entry in the linked list, so the head_entry pointer of the header record is set to point to the new entry. Finally, the tail_entry pointer of the header record is set to point to the new entry, completing the insertion operation. The procedure **remove** first tests whether the FIFO is empty. If it is, the procedure reports an error message and fails. Otherwise it uses the head_entry pointer of the header record to locate the entry at the head of the FIFO and sets the result parameter to the element in this entry. It then removes this entry from the linked list by copying the link pointer to the head_entry pointer in the header record. If that pointer is **null**, the removed entry was the only entry, so the FIFO is now empty. The procedure resets the tail_entry pointer in the

FIGURE 19-13

```
package body «element_type_simple_name»_fifo_adt is
    function new_fifo return fifo_type is
    begin
        return new fifo_record'( null, null );
    end function new_fifo;

    procedure test_empty ( variable fifo : in fifo_type;
                           variable is_empty : out boolean ) is
    begin
        is_empty := fifo.head_entry = null;
    end procedure test_empty;

    procedure insert ( fifo : inout fifo_type; element : in element_type ) is
        variable new_entry : fifo_entry
                    := new fifo_entry_record'( next_entry => null,
                                               element => element );
    begin
        if fifo.tail_entry /= null then
            fifo.tail_entry.next_entry := new_entry;
        else
            fifo.head_entry := new_entry;
        end if;
        fifo.tail_entry := new_entry;
    end procedure insert;

    procedure remove ( fifo : inout fifo_type; element : out element_type ) is
        variable empty_fifo : boolean;
        variable removed_entry : fifo_entry;
    begin
        test_empty(fifo, empty_fifo);
        if empty_fifo then
            report "remove from empty fifo" severity failure;
        else
            removed_entry := fifo.head_entry;
            element := removed_entry.element;
            fifo.head_entry := removed_entry.next_entry;
            if fifo.head_entry = null then  -- fifo now empty
                fifo.tail_entry := null;
            end if;
            deallocate(removed_entry);
        end if;
    end procedure remove;
end package body «element_type_simple_name»_fifo_adt;
```

A package body template for FIFO queues of objects.

header record to **null** to reflect this fact. Finally, the procedure deallocates the storage used by the removed entry.

In order to use the FIFO ADT in our queue module, we need to define the type of the elements to be stored in a FIFO. We could simply store each token as it arrives at a queue module, in which case we could substitute work.qsim_types.token_type for the placeholder in the package declaration template. However, our queue module should keep track of the time for which each token is held in the FIFO, so that it can accumulate statistics on waiting times of tokens. We can do this by defining a new element type, as shown in Figure 19-14. The type waiting_token_type represents a token waiting in a FIFO and the time at which it was inserted into the FIFO. We create an instance of the FIFO ADT, specialized for this type, by editing the template placeholders as shown in Figure 19-15.

FIGURE 19-14

```
use work.qsim_types.all;

package queue_types is

    type waiting_token_type is record
            token : token_type;
            time_when_enqueued : time;
        end record waiting_token_type;

end package queue_types;
```

A package that defines the type of elements to be stored in queue module FIFOs.

FIGURE 19-15

```
package waiting_token_fifo_adt is

    alias element_type is work.queue_types.waiting_token_type;

    . . .

end package waiting_token_fifo_adt;
```

```
package body waiting_token_fifo_adt is

    . . .

end package body waiting_token_fifo_adt;
```

An outline of an instance of the FIFO ADT created by editing the package templates.

We can now consider the behavioral architecture body of the queue module, outlined in Figure 19-16. The queue_manager process includes a local variable waiting_token_fifo, in which it holds waiting tokens. This variable is initialized to an empty FIFO by the call to the new_fifo function. The number of tokens waiting at any time is stored in the variable current_queue_size, initialized to zero. The body of the process includes a loop, in which the process waits for a transaction on the info_detail port, the arrival of a new token or a change in the ready status of the server connected to the queue's output. When the process resumes, if a summary report is required, the process calls write_summary to generate the information. This procedure writes statistics on the waiting times of tokens that have passed through the queue since the start of simulation, as well as information about the current and the maximum queue size. If a token has arrived when the process resumes, it is inserted into the FIFO. The process creates a new element value in the variable waiting_token and passes it to the insert procedure.

It then increments the queue size variable. If the new queue size is larger than the previous maximum queue size, the process updates the maximum queue size variable. If tracing of token flow is required, the process calls **write_trace_enqueue** to write a report message to the output file.

FIGURE 19-16

```
library math;
architecture behavior of queue is
begin
    queue_manager : process is
        use work.queue_types.all, work.waiting_token_fifo_adt.all;

        variable waiting_token, head_token : waiting_token_type;
        variable waiting_token_fifo : fifo_type := new_fifo;
        variable out_token_in_transit : boolean := false;
        variable number_of_tokens_released : natural := 0;
        variable current_queue_size : natural := 0;
        variable maximum_queue_size : natural := 0;
        variable waiting_time : natural;  -- in time_unit
        variable sum_of_waiting_times : real := 0.0;  -- in time_unit
        variable sum_of_squares_of_waiting_times : real := 0.0;  --in time_unit**2

        use std.textio.all;
        file info_file : text;
        variable L : line;

        use math.math_real.sqrt;

        procedure write_summary is . . .

        procedure write_trace_enqueue is . . .

        procedure write_trace_dequeue is . . .

    begin
        file_open(info_file, info_file_name, write_mode);
        loop
            wait on info_detail'transaction, in_arc, out_ready;
            if info_detail'active and info_detail = summary then
                write_summary;
            end if;
            if in_arc'event then
                waiting_token := waiting_token_type'( token => in_arc.token,
                                                      time_when_enqueued => now );
                insert(waiting_token_fifo, waiting_token);
                current_queue_size := current_queue_size + 1;
                if current_queue_size > maximum_queue_size then
                    maximum_queue_size := current_queue_size;
                end if;
                if info_detail = trace then
                    write_trace_enqueue;
                end if;
            end if;
```

(continued on page 546)

(continued from page 545)

```
            if out_ready and current_queue_size > 0 and not out_token_in_transit then
                remove(waiting_token_fifo, head_token);
                current_queue_size := current_queue_size − 1;
                out_arc <= arc_type'(
                                    transaction => not out_arc.transaction'driving_value,
                                    token => head_token.token );
                out_token_in_transit := true;
                number_of_tokens_released := number_of_tokens_released + 1;
                waiting_time := (now − head_token.time_when_enqueued) / time_unit;
                sum_of_waiting_times := sum_of_waiting_times + real(waiting_time);
                sum_of_squares_of_waiting_times
                    := sum_of_squares_of_waiting_times + real(waiting_time) ** 2;
                if info_detail = trace then
                    write_trace_dequeue;
                end if;
            end if;
            if out_token_in_transit and not out_ready then
                out_token_in_transit := false;
            end if;
        end loop;
    end process queue_manager;
end architecture behavior;
```

An architecture body for the queue module.

The rest of the process body implements the transfer of tokens to the server associated with the queue. A token must be transferred when the out_ready port changes to true and the number of tokens in the queue is non-zero. However, this is not sufficient condition for transferring the next token. Consider the sequence of interactions that take place when the queue process assigns a new token to its output. In the next delta cycle, the new token value causes an event on the output signal, and the associated server is resumed. It accepts the token value and assigns the value false to the status signal. The queue process does not see this change until the following delta cycle, two delta cycles after it performed the original assignment. Now consider what would happen if the queue process were resumed in the intervening delta cycle. This might occur if a new token arrives on the queue input. In this delta cycle, out_ready is still true. If there is another token still in the FIFO, the queue size is still non-zero. Thus the process would remove the next token and assign it to the output port. The server would not detect the event on the signal, since it is busy serving the previous token. The second token would be lost.

The way in which we avoid this problem is by use of a Boolean state variable out_token_in_transit. The process sets this variable to true when it assigns a token to the output port, indicating that a token has been sent to the server. While this variable remains true, the process does not remove the next token from the FIFO. The process resets the variable to false when the out_ready port changes to false, indicating that the server has received the token. The fact of out_ready being false then prevents the next token from being removed while the server is serving the previous token.

When the queue process must transfer a new token to the server, it calls the **remove** procedure to remove the waiting token at the head of the FIFO and decrements the queue size variable. It composes a new value for the output port by toggling the transaction flag and assigning the waiting token to the token element. The time for which the token has waited is the difference between the time at which the token was enqueued in the FIFO and the current simulation time. This time is accumulated into the variables used to maintain statistics on waiting times. If tracing is required, the process calls the procedure **write_trace_dequeue** to write a message to the output file.

The Token Server Module

A *server* module in a queuing network represents part of the system that processes the information represented by tokens. When a token arrives at a server, the server holds the token for the time taken to process the represented information. It then passes the token on to the next module in the network and waits for another token to arrive at the server's input. Figure 19-17 shows the entity declaration for our server module. The time taken by the server to process a token is controlled by the probability distribution specified by the generic constants **distribution** and **mean_service_time**. Tokens arrive on the port **in_arc**. The port **in_ready** is a status flag indicating when the server is ready to accept the next token. A network usually includes a queue module to hold tokens until the server is ready. The **in_ready** port of the server should be connected to the **out_ready** port of the queue. Tokens leave the server via the **out_arc** port.

FIGURE 19-17

```
use work.qsim_types.all, work.random.all;
entity server is
    generic ( name : string;
              distribution : distribution_type;
              mean_service_time : time;
              seed : seed_type;
              time_unit : delay_length := ns;
              info_file_name : string := "info_file.dat" );
    port ( in_arc : in arc_type;
           in_ready : out boolean;
           out_arc : out arc_type;
           info_detail : in info_detail_type );
end entity server;
```

An entity declaration for the server module.

The behavioral architecture body for the server module is outlined in Figure 19-18. The process opens the output file and initializes its random number sequence in the same way as the source module shown earlier in this section. It also initializes the in_ready port to indicate that it is ready to accept the first token. It then enters a loop, waiting for a transaction on the **info_detail** port or the arrival of a new token on the **in_arc** port. When the process resumes, if **info_detail** has been set to **summary**, the process calls **write_summary** to write statistics to the output file. These include the number of tokens served, the mean and standard deviation of the service times and the utilization of the server (the proportion of time spent serving tokens). When a token arrives on the input, the process copies the token value into the variable **served_token** and resets the **in_ready** port to false. If tracing is required, the process calls **write_trace_service** to write a message to the output file, indicating that a token has arrived. The process then generates a random number to determine the service time and adds it to the current simulation time to determine when to release the token. The process suspends until that release time, but remains sensitive to transactions on the **info_detail** port. This is similar to the way in which the token generator module suspends while waiting for the inter-arrival time between tokens. It allows the process to respond to requests for summary information while servicing the token. When the service time has expired, the process sets the **in_ready** port to true and composes a new value to assign to the **out_arc** port. This value consists of the inverted transaction element and the released token. The process updates the variables used to accumulate statistics. Finally, if tracing is required, the process calls **write_trace_release** to write a message to the output file indicating that the token has been released.

FIGURE 19-18

```
library math;
architecture behavior of server is
begin
    service : process is
        variable served_token : token_type;
        variable release_time : time;
        variable number_of_tokens_served : natural := 0;
        variable service_time : natural;  -- in time_unit
        variable sum_of_service_times : real := 0.0;  -- in time_unit
        variable sum_of_squares_of_service_times : real := 0.0;  --in time_unit**2

        variable random_info : random_info_record;
        variable random_number : real;

        use std.textio.all;
        file info_file : text;
        variable L : line;

        use math.math_real.sqrt;

        procedure write_summary is . . .

        procedure write_trace_service is . . .

        procedure write_trace_release is . . .
    begin
        file_open(info_file, info_file_name, write_mode);

        case distribution is . . .

        in_ready <= true;
        loop
            wait on info_detail'transaction, in_arc;
            if info_detail'active and info_detail = summary then
                write_summary;
            end if;
```

```
            if in_arc'event then
                in_ready <= false;
                if info_detail = trace then
                    write_trace_service;
                end if;
                served_token := in_arc.token;
                generate_random(random_info, random_number);
                service_time := natural(random_number);
                release_time := service_time * time_unit + now;
                loop
                    wait on info_detail'transaction for release_time – now;
                    if info_detail'active and info_detail = summary then
                        write_summary;
                    end if;
                    exit when release_time = now;
                end loop;
                in_ready <= true;
                out_arc <= arc_type'(
                                transaction => not out_arc.transaction'driving_value,
                                token => served_token );
                number_of_tokens_served := number_of_tokens_served + 1;
                sum_of_service_times := sum_of_service_times + real(service_time);
                sum_of_squares_of_service_times
                    := sum_of_squares_of_service_times + real(service_time) ** 2;
                if info_detail = trace then
                    write_trace_release;
                end if;
            end if;
        end loop;
    end process service;
end architecture behavior;
```

An architecture body for the server module.

The Fork Module

In many queuing networks, tokens can flow along alternative paths to different servers. In the system being modeled, this corresponds to alternate processing operations
being performed on the information represented by the tokens. Since we do not model information content in a queuing network, we make routing decisions based on
probabilities. We use a *fork* module to choose between one of a number of paths for
each arriving token. For each output of the fork module, we specify the probability
that an arriving token takes that path. The sum of the probabilities for a given fork
module must be 1.0.

Figure 19-19 shows the entity declaration for our fork module. Tokens arrive on
the port **in_arc** and are routed to one of the elements of the vector port **out_arc**. The
generic constant **probabilities** is a vector of probability values controlling the routing
decisions. This vector must be one element shorter than the **out_arc** port. Each element
of **probabilities** specifies the probability of an arriving token being routed to the corresponding element of **out_arc**. (Elements correspond from left to right, not by index

FIGURE 19-19

```
use work.qsim_types.all, work.random.all;
entity fork is
    generic ( name : string;
              probabilities : probability_vector;
              seed : seed_type;
              time_unit : delay_length := ns;
              info_file_name : string := "info_file.dat" );
    port ( in_arc : in arc_type;
           out_arc : out arc_vector;
           info_detail : in info_detail_type );
end fork;
```

An entity declaration for the fork module.

number.) There is no element of **probabilities** corresponding to the rightmost element of **out_arc**, since the probability of a token being routed to this element is one minus the sum of the other probabilities. This is the reason behind the length constraint on the probabilities vector. Unfortunately, we cannot use a generic constant to specify the lengths of the vectors, since one of the vectors is itself a generic constant. VHDL does not allow a generic constant to be used in the same interface list as it is defined. Hence the following is illegal:

```
entity fork is   -- illegal version
    generic ( out_arc_length : positive;
              probabilities : probability_vector(1 to out_arc_length – 1); . . . );
    . . .
```

The behavioral architecture of the fork module is outlined in Figure 19-20. The process first verifies that the vector of probabilities is of the correct length. It then uses the probability vector to calculate a cumulative probability vector for subsequent use in the token routing algorithm. Each element at position i in the cumulative probability vector is the sum of the elements from the leftmost to i in the ordinary probabilities vector. To explain the routing algorithm implemented by the fork module, let us denote the number of output arcs by n, the elements of the ordinary probabilities vector by p_i ($i \in 1,\ldots,n$), and the elements of the cumulative probabilities vector by c_i ($i \in 1,\ldots,n$). Then

$$c_i = \sum_{j=1}^{i} p_j$$

When a token arrives to be routed to one of the output arcs, the routing algorithm generates a random number between 0.0 and 1.0 with uniform distribution. This number lies in the range $r_1 = [0.0, c_1)$ with probability p_1, in the range $r_i = [c_{i-1}, c_i)$ with probability p_i ($i \in 2,\ldots,n-1$) or in the range $r_n = [c_{n-1}, 1.0)$ with probability $1-c_{n-1}$. The algorithm determines which range r_k contains the random number and routes the token to output k.

After the process has initialized the cumulative probabilities vector, it initializes the random number sequence to be used by the routing algorithm and opens the output file. It then enters a loop waiting for transactions on the info_detail signal or for arrival of the next token. When info_detail is assigned the value summary, the process calls the procedure write_summary to write statistics for token routing to the output file. The statistics include a count of the tokens processed, and the relative frequencies of tokens routed to each of the output arcs.

FIGURE 19-20

```
architecture behavior of fork is
begin
    forker : process
        variable cumulative_probabilities : probability_vector(1 to probabilities'length);
        variable destination : positive range out_arc'range;
        variable probabilities_index : positive range probabilities'range;
        variable number_of_tokens_forked : natural := 0;
        type counter_array is array (positive range out_arc'range) of natural;
        variable number_forked_to_destination : counter_array := (others => 0);

        variable random_info : random_info_record;
        variable random_number : real;

        type transaction_vector is array (positive range <>) of boolean;
        variable out_arc_transaction_driving_value : transaction_vector(out_arc'range)
                        := (others => false);

        use std.textio.all;
        file info_file : text;
        variable L : line;

        procedure write_summary is . . .

        procedure write_trace is . . .
    begin
        assert probabilities'length = out_arc'length – 1
            report "incorrent number of probabilities – should be "
                    & integer'image(out_arc'length – 1) severity failure;
        cumulative_probabilities := probabilities;
        for index in 2 to cumulative_probabilities'length loop
            cumulative_probabilities(index) := cumulative_probabilities(index – 1)
                                            + cumulative_probabilities(index);
        end loop;
        init_uniform( random_info,
                    lower_bound => 0.0, upper_bound => 1.0, seed => seed );
        file_open(info_file, info_file_name, write_mode);
        loop
            wait on info_detail'transaction, in_arc;
            if info_detail'active and info_detail = summary then
                write_summary;
            end if;
```

(continued on page 552)

(continued from page 551)

```
if in_arc'event then
    generate_random(random_info, random_number);
    destination := out_arc'left;
    for index in 1 to cumulative_probabilities'length loop
        exit when random_number < cumulative_probabilities(index);
        if out_arc'ascending then
            destination := destination + 1;
        else
            destination := destination – 1;
        end if;
    end loop;
    out_arc(destination) <= arc_type'(
        transaction => not out_arc_transaction_driving_value(destination),
        token => in_arc.token );
    out_arc_transaction_driving_value(destination)
        := not out_arc_transaction_driving_value(destination);
    number_of_tokens_forked := number_of_tokens_forked + 1;
    number_forked_to_destination(destination)
        := number_forked_to_destination(destination) + 1;
    if info_detail = trace then
        write_trace;
    end if;
end if;
end loop;
end process forker;
end behavior;
```

An architecture body for the fork module.

When a token arrives on the in_arc port, the process performs the routing algorithm to select a destination arc. It generates the required random number and then locates the element in the cumulative probabilities vector corresponding to the range described above containing the number. As it scans the vector, the process also increments the variable **destination**, so that it refers to the index of the out_arc element corresponding to the element of the cumulative probabilities vector being examined. When the loop terminates, **destination** contains the index of the selected output arc. The process then assigns a new value to the selected element of the out_arc vector containing the inverse of the previous transaction flag and the new token. Note that the element of the out_arc vector is determined during the simulation, and so is not static. This means that we cannot use the 'driving_value attribute to determine the old value of the transaction flag, as we did in the modules described previously. Instead, the process in the fork module maintains a separate vector of transaction flag values called out_arc_transaction_driving_value. This vector contains an element corresponding to each element of out_arc. When the process assigns a new value to an element of out_arc, it uses the inverse of the corresponding element of the flag vector and then inverts the value in the flag vector. The process finally updates the variables used to maintain statistics of token routing and writes a trace message to the output file if required.

The Join Module

The last module in our suite is the *join* module. It accepts tokens from a number of input arcs and forwards them to a single output arc. The entity declaration is shown in Figure 19-21. The port in_arc is a vector, with each element representing an incoming path on which tokens arrive. The tokens are forwarded to the port out_arc.

FIGURE 19-21

```
use work.qsim_types.all;

entity join is
    generic ( name : string;
                time_unit : delay_length := ns;
                info_file_name : string := "info_file.dat" );
    port ( in_arc : in arc_vector;
            out_arc : out arc_type;
            info_detail : in info_detail_type );
end join;
```

An entity declaration for the join module.

The implementation of the join module is not as simple as it may at first appear. We must take account of the fact that several tokens may arrive on different inputs in the same delta cycle. We cannot simply copy them to the output as they arrive, as each would overwrite the previous one, and all but the last would be lost. Instead, we need to copy them to the output one at a time on successive delta cycles, so that the next module in the network recognizes the arrival of each new token. This introduces a further problem, in that more tokens may arrive on the inputs while we are in the process of forwarding the first set of tokens. These must be saved and subsequently forwarded.

The solution we adopt to deal with these problems requires use of a FIFO queue within the join module. When one or more tokens arrive at the join in a given delta cycle, they are inserted into the FIFO. They are then forwarded to the output on successive delta cycles, until the FIFO is emptied. Further tokens arriving during this process are simply added to the FIFO and are forwarded in later delta cycles. We can reuse the FIFO ADT that we described earlier in this section by specializing it to contain elements of type token_type. The edited templates are outlined in Figure 19-22.

The architecture body that implements this solution is outlined in Figure 19-23. The process uses the token_fifo_adt package and includes a variable token_fifo to hold tokens waiting to be forwarded. After opening the output file, the process enters a loop in which it waits for a transaction on the info_detail signal or arrival of one or more tokens on the in_arc signal. When the info_detail signal is assigned the value summary, the process calls the procedure write_summary to write statistics information to the output file. This includes a count of the number of tokens joined, and the relative frequencies of tokens arriving on the different input arcs.

FIGURE 19-22

```
package token_fifo_adt is
    alias element_type is work.qsim_types.token_type;

    . . .

end package token_fifo_adt;
```

```
package body token_fifo_adt is

    . . .

end package body token_fifo_adt;
```

An outline of an instance of the FIFO ADT specialized to contain tokens as elements.

If new tokens have arrived (indicated by a change on the in_arc composite signal), the process calls the procedure accept_new_tokens. This procedure determines which elements of the signal contain the new tokens by comparing the transaction flags in the current signal value with those of the previous signal value. (The 'last_value attribute provides the value of the entire composite signal just before the last change of any element.) For each of the in_arc elements on which a new token has arrived, the process inserts the token into the FIFO and increments the variable current_fifo_size. It also updates the variables used to maintain statistics on token arrival and writes a trace message to the output file if required. When the procedure returns, the process forwards the tokens in the FIFO to the output arc. It does this by removing the token at the head of the FIFO and assigning a new value to out_arc. The value consists of the inverse of the current transaction flag and the token to be forwarded. The process then waits until the next delta cycle before proceeding to the next token in the FIFO. When the process resumes in the next delta cycle, additional tokens may have arrived on in_arc, and there may be a new transaction on info_detail. The process deals with these cases before iterating to the next token in the FIFO. If additional tokens have arrived, the process calls accept_new_tokens to insert them into the FIFO. Eventually, when the FIFO is exhausted, the process starts again from the top of the outer loop.

FIGURE 19-23

```
architecture behavior of join is
begin
    joiner : process
        use work.token_fifo_adt.all;

        variable source : positive range in_arc'range;
        variable token_fifo : fifo_type := new_fifo;
        variable current_fifo_size : natural := 0;
        variable head_token : token_type;
        variable number_of_tokens_joined : natural := 0;
        type counter_array is array (positive range in_arc'range) of natural;
        variable number_joined_from_source : counter_array := (others => 0);
```

```vhdl
                    use std.textio.all;
                    file info_file : text;
                    variable L : line;

                    procedure write_summary is . . .

                    procedure write_trace is . .

                    procedure accept_new_tokens is
                    begin
                        for index in 1 to in_arc'length loop
                            if in_arc(index).transaction /= in_arc'last_value(index).transaction then
                                source := index;
                                insert(token_fifo, in_arc(source).token);
                                current_fifo_size := current_fifo_size + 1;
                                number_of_tokens_joined := number_of_tokens_joined + 1;
                                number_joined_from_source(source)
                                    := number_joined_from_source(source) + 1;
                                if info_detail = trace then
                                    write_trace;
                                end if;
                            end if;
                        end loop;
                    end procedure accept_new_tokens;

                begin
                    file_open(info_file, info_file_name, write_mode);
                    loop
                        wait on info_detail'transaction, in_arc;
                        if info_detail'active and info_detail = summary then
                            write_summary;
                        end if;
                        if in_arc'event then
                            accept_new_tokens;
                            while current_fifo_size > 0 loop
                                remove(token_fifo, head_token);
                                current_fifo_size := current_fifo_size - 1;
                                out_arc <= arc_type'(
                                            transaction => not out_arc.transaction'driving_value,
                                            token => head_token );
                                wait for 0 fs;  -- delta delay before next output token
                                if info_detail'active and info_detail = summary then
                                    write_summary;
                                end if;
                                if in_arc'event then
                                    accept_new_tokens;
                                end if;
                            end loop;
                        end if;
                    end loop;
                end process joiner;
        end behavior;
```

An architecture body for the join module.

19.3 A Queuing Network for a Disk System

In this section, we look at an example of a queuing network to show how the modules we have defined can be used. We model a computer system that includes a number of disks and a disk cache. The queuing network for this system is shown in Figure 19-24. Tokens representing jobs arrive at the "new_jobs" source with exponentially distributed inter-arrival time, with a mean of 50 seconds. They enter a queue awaiting service by the CPU. When they arrive at the CPU server, they are served for a period that is uniformly distributed with a mean of 50 ms. A job leaves the CPU server for one of three reasons. First, the job's CPU time quantum may have expired, in which case it returns to the CPU queue to await further service. The probability of a job taking this path is 0.5. Second, the job may have terminated, in which case it is forwarded to the job sink. The probability of a job leaving the CPU for this reason is 0.05. Third, the job may leave the CPU because it needs access to data stored on a disk. The probability of this case is 0.45.

FIGURE 19-24

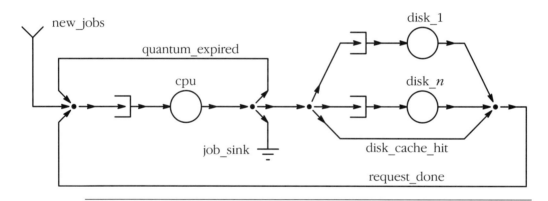

A queuing network for a disk-based computer system.

The system we are modeling includes a disk cache, which can satisfy most of the requests for disk data. If a request hits, the time taken to service the request is negligible. The requesting job simply bypasses the disk servers and returns to the CPU queue. We assume a hit rate of 0.8, but allow this parameter to be altered to investigate its effect on system performance. If a request misses in the disk cache, the job enters one of the disk queues to await service by the associated disk. We assume that accesses are spread uniformly over the n disks in the system, so the probability of a requesting job proceeding to a particular disk is $0.2/n$. We initially assume two disks in the system, but allow this to be varied to see how it affects system performance. The time taken for a disk to service a request in our model is exponentially distributed with a mean of 15 ms. When a job leaves a disk server, it returns to the CPU queue for further processing.

The entity declaration and architecture body for our queuing network model are shown in Figure 19-25. The entity has no ports, since we are modeling a closed system. The architecture body assumes that the queuing network design entities have been analyzed and placed in a design library called **qsim**. The use clause preceding the architecture body makes the design entities in the library directly visible, so that we do not need to qualify them with the library name. The constants **disk_cache_miss_rate** and **num_disks** define the parameters of the computer system that we may wish to vary between simulation runs. The constant **disk_cache_fork_probabilities** contains the probabilities that jobs leaving the CPU to access disk data are forwarded to each of the individual disks.

The statement part of the architecture body contains instances of the queuing network modules, interconnected as shown in Figure 19-24. Note that we have not specified an architecture name in the component instantiation statements. Hence the model uses the most recently analyzed architecture body for each entity at the time of elaboration. Since we only have one architecture body for each entity, this default binding is satisfactory. The signal **info_detail_control** is connected to the **info_detail** port of each instance. We can use our simulator to deposit values on this signal to control the reporting of information by each of the component instances. The statement part of the architecture body includes a generate statement to instantiate the queue and server modules for the required number of disks. The local constant **disk_index_str** is used to construct module names and file names that are unique to each instance of the generate statement. With **num_disks** set to two, the module names are "disk_queue_1", "disk_1", "disk_queue_2" and "disk_2". The file names are constructed similarly. As we mentioned in Chapter 18, we should avoid having separate file objects in different component instances referring to the same physical file. By constructing unique file names for each component instance, we have a separate physical file for each instance and avoid interleaving or losing their output.

FIGURE 19-25

```
entity disk_system is
end entity disk_system;

------------------------------------------------------------

library qsim;  use qsim.all;
architecture queue_net of disk_system is
    use qsim_types.all, random.all;
    constant disk_cache_miss_rate : real := 0.2;
    constant num_disks : positive := 2;
    constant disk_cache_fork_probabilities : probability_vector(1 to num_disks)
                := ( others => disk_cache_miss_rate / real(num_disks) );
    signal info_detail_control : info_detail_type := none;
    signal new_job, cpu_queue_in, cpu_in, cpu_out,
           quantum_expired, job_done, requesting_disk,
           disk_cache_hit, request_done : arc_type;
    signal disk_cache_miss, disk_done : arc_vector(1 to num_disks);
    signal cpu_ready : boolean;
```

(continued on page 558)

(continued from page 557)

begin

   new_jobs : **entity** source
     generic map (name => "new_jobs",
           distribution => exponential, mean_inter_arrival_time => 2 sec,
           seed => sample_seeds(1), time_unit => ms,
           info_file_name => "new_jobs.dat")
     port map (out_arc => new_job,
        info_detail => info_detail_control);

   cpu_join : **entity** join
     generic map (name => "cpu_join",
           time_unit => ms, info_file_name => "cpu_join.dat")
     port map (in_arc(1) => quantum_expired,
        in_arc(2) => new_job,
        in_arc(3) => request_done,
        out_arc => cpu_queue_in,
        info_detail => info_detail_control);

   cpu_queue : **entity** queue
     generic map (name => "cpu_queue",
           time_unit => ms, info_file_name => "cpu_queue.dat")
     port map (in_arc => cpu_queue_in,
        out_arc => cpu_in, out_ready => cpu_ready,
        info_detail => info_detail_control);

   cpu : **entity** server
     generic map (name => "cpu",
           distribution => uniform, mean_service_time => 50 ms,
           seed => sample_seeds(2), time_unit => ms,
           info_file_name => "cpu.dat")
     port map (in_arc => cpu_in, in_ready => cpu_ready,
        out_arc => cpu_out,
        info_detail => info_detail_control);

   cpu_fork : **entity** fork
     generic map (name => "cpu_fork",
           probabilities => (1 => 0.5, 2 => 0.45),
           seed => sample_seeds(3), time_unit => ms,
           info_file_name => "cpu_fork.dat")
     port map (in_arc => cpu_out,
        out_arc(1) => quantum_expired,
        out_arc(2) => requesting_disk,
        out_arc(3) => job_done,
        info_detail => info_detail_control);

   job_sink : **entity** sink
     generic map (name => "job_sink",
           time_unit => ms, info_file_name => "job_sink.dat")
     port map (in_arc => job_done,
        info_detail => info_detail_control);

   disk_cache_fork : **entity** fork
     generic map (name => "disk_cache_fork",
           probabilities => disk_cache_fork_probabilities,

```
                              seed => sample_seeds(4), time_unit => ms,
                              info_file_name => "disk_cache_fork.dat" )
          port map ( in_arc => requesting_disk,
                     out_arc(1 to num_disks) => disk_cache_miss,
                     out_arc(num_disks + 1) => disk_cache_hit,
                     info_detail => info_detail_control );
    disk_array : for disk_index in 1 to num_disks generate
        constant disk_index_str : string := integer'image(disk_index);
        signal disk_in : arc_type;
        signal disk_ready : boolean;
    begin
        disk_queue : entity queue
            generic map ( name => "disk_queue_" & disk_index_str,
                          time_unit => ms,
                          info_file_name => "disk_queue_" & disk_index_str & ".dat" )
            port map ( in_arc => disk_cache_miss(disk_index),
                       out_arc => disk_in, out_ready => disk_ready,
                       info_detail => info_detail_control );
        disk : entity server
            generic map ( name => "disk_" & disk_index_str,
                          distribution => exponential, mean_service_time => 15 ms,
                          seed => sample_seeds(4 + disk_index), time_unit => ms,
                          info_file_name => "disk_" & disk_index_str & ".dat" )
            port map ( in_arc => disk_in, in_ready => disk_ready,
                       out_arc => disk_done(disk_index),
                       info_detail => info_detail_control );
    end generate disk_array;
    disk_cache_join : entity join
        generic map ( name => "disk_cache_join",
                      time_unit => ms,
                      info_file_name => "disk_cache_join.dat" )
        port map ( in_arc(1 to num_disks) => disk_done,
                   in_arc(num_disks + 1) => disk_cache_hit,
                   out_arc => request_done,
                   info_detail => info_detail_control );
end architecture queue_net;
```

An entity declaration and architecture body for the queuing network model.

Once we have analyzed this model, we can use our simulator to run it. We do not discuss the detailed procedure involved, as this varies considerably between simulators. Instead, we simply look at the output produced by each of the modules in the queuing network. The author ran the model for 1000 seconds of simulation time and then used simulator commands to deposit the value summary on the signal info_detail_control. After a further delta cycle of simulation, the modules produced summary statistics in their output files. The output file for the job source module is shown in Figure 19-26. This shows the total number of tokens generated by the module since the start of simulation and shows the actual mean and standard deviation of inter-

FIGURE 19-26

```
Summary information for source new_jobs up to time 1000000 ms
  Inter arrival distribution: exponential with mean inter arrival
                              time of 2000 ms
  Number of tokens generated = 475
  Mean inter arrival time = 2087 ms
  Standard deviation of inter arrival times = 2051 ms
```

The summary of statistics from the job source module.

FIGURE 19-27

```
Summary information for queue cpu_queue up to time 1000000 ms
  Number of tokens currently waiting = 0
  Number of tokens released = 10367
  Maximum queue size = 10
  Mean waiting time = 60 ms
  Standard deviation of waiting times = 92 ms

Summary information for server cpu up to time 1000000 ms
  Service distribution: uniform with mean service time of 50 ms
  Number of tokens served = 10367
  Mean service time = 50 ms
  Standard deviation of service times = 29 ms
  Utilization = 0.5198
```

The summary of statistics from the CPU queue and server modules.

arrival times. The summary output listings from the CPU queue and the CPU server are shown in Figure 19-27. This shows that the most tokens waiting at one time was 10 and that the mean waiting time was 60 ms. The statistics from the server show that the utilization of the CPU was only 52 percent. We can infer that for the remaining 48 percent of the time, the CPU was idle because either there were no jobs in the system, or jobs were accessing disks. We can examine the output from the disk queues and servers, shown in Figure 19-28, to gauge their utilization. We see that the utilization for both disks is very low, presumably due to the effectiveness of the disk cache in the system. The average waiting times for jobs in the disk queues are negligible. Finally, we can examine the statistics from the job sink module, shown in Figure 19-29, to determine the average lifetimes of jobs. The number of tokens consumed is the same as the number generated by the job source. This coincidence implies that we happened to sample the statistics at a time when all of the jobs generated had run to termination. The average lifetime of tokens is approximately 2.4 seconds, which is slightly longer than the average inter-arrival time of tokens at the job source. Thus, jobs are being created at a faster rate than they are being processed. If this were to continue, we would expect the average number of jobs in the system at any instant to increase and the system to become congested.

FIGURE 19-28

```
Summary information for queue disk_queue_1 up to time 1000000 ms
  Number of tokens currently waiting = 0
  Number of tokens released = 470
  Maximum queue size = 1
  Mean waiting time = 0 ms
  Standard deviation of waiting times = 0 ms
Summary information for server disk_1 up to time 1000000 ms
  Service distribution: exponential with mean service time of 15 ms
  Number of tokens served = 470
  Mean service time = 14 ms
  Standard deviation of service times = 15 ms
  Utilization = 0.0067
Summary information for queue disk_queue_2 up to time 1000000 ms
  Number of tokens currently waiting = 0
  Number of tokens released = 458
  Maximum queue size = 1
  Mean waiting time = 0 ms
  Standard deviation of waiting times = 1 ms
Summary information for server disk_2 up to time 1000000 ms
  Service distribution: exponential with mean service time of 15 ms
  Number of tokens served = 458
  Mean service time = 16 ms
  Standard deviation of service times = 16 ms
  Utilization = 0.0072
```

Summaries of statistics from the disk queue and server modules.

FIGURE 19-29

```
Summary information for sink job_sink up to time 1000000 ms
  Number of tokens consumed = 475
  Mean life_time = 2425 ms
  Standard deviation of life_times = 3291 ms
```

The summary of statistics from the job sink module.

Exercises

1. [❶ 19.1] Devise a queuing network that represents a network interface in a computer system. Software on the system generates network packets to be transmitted. Packets are queued at the interface and transmitted in turn. After some delay, the interface receives an acknowledgement. If it is a positive acknowledgement, transmission of the packet is complete. If the acknowledgement is a negative acknowledgement, the packet is placed back in the queue for retransmission.

2. [❶ 19.2] Write declarations and statements to create and initialize a random number generator using the random package. The numbers should be uniformly distributed between 1.0 and 2.0. Write a statement that uses the generator to generate a random number in the real variable x.

3. [❷ 19.2] Create a simple queuing network that consists of just a token source connected to a token sink. Include a signal info_detail of type info_detail_type, initialized to trace and connected to the info_detail ports of the source and sink. Experiment with your simulator to see how you can change the value of info_detail to control reporting of information by the modules.

4. [❶ 19.3] Use the queuing network modules to implement the network described in Exercise 1. The packet source generates packets with a mean inter-arrival time of 100 μs, exponentially distributed. The average delay between a packet arriving at the interface for transmission and the acknowledgement being received is uniformly distributed with a mean of 70 μs. The probability that an acknowledgement is negative is 0.05.

5. [❹ 19.2/19.3] Modify the queue module to use a fixed-size queue for token storage. The maximum queue size should be an additional generic constant in the entity interface. When a token arrives at a full queue, the token is lost. The queue should maintain information about token loss. If info_detail is set to trace when a token is lost, the loss should be traced. The information provided when info_detail is set to summary should include the count and proportion of tokens lost. Use the modified queue module in the disk system network, and compare the measurements with the network using the unbounded queue.

6. [❸ 19.3] Experiment with different values of generic constants for the modules in the disk system and with different numbers of disks, to see how performance of the modeled system is affected.

Attributes and Groups

VHDL provides comprehensive facilities for expressing the behavior and structure of a design. VHDL also provides the *attribute* mechanism for annotating a model with additional information. In this chapter, we review the predefined attributes and show how to define new attributes. We also look at the group mechanism, which allows us to describe additional relationships between various items in a model.

20.1 Predefined Attributes

Throughout this book we have seen predefined attributes that are used to retrieve information about types, objects and other items within a model. In this section we summarize the previously introduced attributes and fully describe the remaining predefined attributes.

Attributes of Scalar Types

The first group of predefined attributes gives information about the values in a scalar type. These were introduced in Chapter 2 and are summarized in the following table:

FIGURE 20-1

Attribute	Type of T	Result type	Result
T'left	any scalar type or subtype	same as T	leftmost value in T
T'right	"	"	rightmost value in T
T'low	"	"	least value in T
T'high	"	"	greatest value in T
T'ascending	"	boolean	true if T is an ascending range, false otherwise
T'image(x)	"	string	a textual representation of the value x of type T
T'value(s)	"	base type of T	value in T represented by the string s
T'pos(s)	any discrete or physical type or subtype	universal integer	position number of x in T
T'val(x)	"	base type of T	value at position x in T
T'succ(x)	"	"	value at position one greater than x in T
T'pred(x)	"	"	value at position one less than x in T
T'leftof(x)	"	"	value at position one to the left of x in T
T'rightof(x)	any discrete or physical type or subtype	base type of T	value at position one to the right of x in T
T'base	any type or subtype		base type of T, for use only as prefix of another attribute

The predefined attributes giving information about values in a type.

VHDL-87

The predefined attributes 'ascending, 'image and 'value are not provided in VHDL-87.

Attributes of Array Types and Objects

The second group of predefined attributes gives information about the index values of an array object or type. These were introduced in Chapter 4 and are summarized in Figure 20-2. The prefix A in the table refers either to a constrained array type or subtype, to an array object or to a slice of an array. If A is a variable of an access type pointing an array object, the attribute refers to the array object, not the pointer value. Each of the attributes optionally takes an argument that selects one of the index dimensions of the array. The default is the first dimension. Note that if the prefix A is an alias for an array object, the attributes return information about the index values declared for the alias, not those declared for the original object.

FIGURE 20-2

Attribute	Result
A'left(n)	leftmost value in index range of dimension n
A'right(n)	rightmost value in index range of dimension n
A'low(n)	least value in index range of dimension n
A'high(n)	greatest value in index range of dimension n
A'range(n)	index range of dimension n
A'reverse_range(n)	index range of dimension n reversed in direction and bounds
A'length(n)	length of index range of dimension n
A'ascending(n)	true if index range of dimension n is ascending, false otherwise

The predefined attributes giving information about the index range of an array.

VHDL-87

The predefined attribute 'ascending is not provided in VHDL-87.

Attributes of Signals

The third group of predefined attributes gives information about signals or defines new implicit signals derived from explicitly declared signals. These attributes were introduced in Chapters 5 and 11 and are summarized in Figure 20-3. The prefix S in the table refers to any statically named signal. Three of the attributes optionally take a non-negative argument t of type time. The default is 0 fs.

FIGURE 20-3

Attribute	Result type	Result
S'delayed(t)	base type of S	implicit signal, with the same value as S, but delayed by t time units (t $\geq$ 0 ns)
S'stable(t)	boolean	implicit signal, true when no event has occurred on S for t time units, false otherwise (t $\geq$ 0 ns)
S'quiet(t)	boolean	implicit signal, true when no transaction has occurred on S for t time units, false otherwise (t $\geq$ 0 ns)
S'transaction	bit	implicit signal, changes value in simulation cycles in which a transaction occurs on S
S'event	boolean	true if an event has occurred on S in the current simulation cycle, false otherwise
S'active	boolean	true if a transaction has occurred on S in the current simulation cycle, false otherwise
S'last_event	time	time since last event occurred on S, or time'high if no event has yet occurred
S'last_active	time	time since last transaction occurred on S, or time'high if no event has yet occurred
S'last_value	base type of S	value of S before last event occurred on it
S'driving	boolean	true if the containing process is driving S (or every element of a composite signal S), or false if the containing process has disconnected its driver for S (or any element of S) with a null transaction
S'driving_value	base type of S	value contributed by driver for S in the containing process

The predefined attributes giving information about signals and values of signals.

VHDL-87

The predefined attributes 'driving and 'driving_value are not provided in VHDL-87. Note also that the 'last_value attribute for a composite signal returns the aggregate of last values for each of the scalar elements of the signal. This behavior is different from the VHDL-93 behavior, in which the attribute returns the last value of the entire composite signal.

Attributes of Named Items

The remaining predefined attributes are applied to any declared item and return a string representation of the name of the item. These attributes are summarized in Figure 20-4. The prefix X in the table refers to any declared item. If the item is an alias, the attribute returns the name of the alias itself, not the aliased item.

FIGURE 20-4

Attribute	Result
X'simple_name	a string representing the identifier, character or operator symbol defined in the declaration of the item X
X'path_name	a string describing the path through the elaborated design hierarchy, from the top-level entity or package to the item X
X'instance_name	a string similar to that produced by X'path_name, but including the names of the entity and architecture bound to each component instance in the path

The predefined attributes that provide names of declared items.

The 'simple_name attribute returns a string representation of the name of an item. For example, if a package utility_definitions in a library utilities declares a constant named word_size, the attribute

utilities.utility_definitions.word_size'simple_name

returns the string "word_size". We might ask why VHDL provides this attribute, since we need to write the simple name of the item in order to apply the attribute. It would be simpler to write the string literal directly. If nothing else, we can use the attribute to gain consistency of style in reporting item names in messages, since the 'simple_name attribute always returns a lowercase version of the name.

The 'path_name and 'instance_name attributes both return string representations of the path through the design hierarchy to an item. They are especially useful in assertion or report statements to pinpoint exactly which instance of a library unit is the source of a message. VHDL only requires that the message reported to the user by these statements indicate the name of the library unit (entity, architecture body or package) containing the statement. We can use the 'path_name or 'instance_name attribute to determine which particular instance of a process in the design hierarchy is the source of a message.

EXAMPLE

Suppose we have a design that includes numerous instances of a flipflop component bound to an entity flipflop and using an architecture behavior. Within this architecture we wish to include timing checks and report an error message if the constraints are violated. An outline of the architecture body incorporating these checks is shown in Figure 20-5. When a flipflop instance in the design detects a timing violation, it will issue an assertion violation message indicating that the problem arose in the architecture behavior of flipflop. We use the 'path_name attribute in the message string to identify which component instance bound to the flipflop entity is the one responsible for issuing the message.

FIGURE 20-5

```
architecture behavior of flipflop is
begin
    timing_check : process (clk) is
    begin
        if clk = '1' then
            assert d'last_event >= Tsetup
                report "set up violation detected in " & timing_check'path_name
                severity error;
        end if;
    end process timing_check;
    ...        -- functionality
end architecture behavior;
```

An architecture body including a process that checks for a timing constraint violation.

Unfortunately, the specification in the *VHDL Language Reference Manual (LRM)* of the values to be returned by the 'path_name and 'instance_name attributes is ill-defined. It contains some ambiguities and contradictory examples. We expect that the specification will be clarified in future versions of the standard. Meanwhile, we present one possible interpretation here.

If an item is declared in a package, both the 'path_name and 'instance_name attributes of the item return the same string, consisting of the library name, the package name and the name of the item. If the item is nested within a subprogram in the package, the string also includes the names of the containing subprogram or subprograms. The format of the string produced for an item in a package is described by the EBNF rule

package_based_path ⇐
    : *library*_logical_name : *package*_simple_name :
        { *subprogram*_simple_name : }
            〚 simple_name ∥ character_literal ∥ operator_symbol 〛

The colon characters serve as punctuation, separating elements within the path string. Note that the syntax rule for package-based paths specified in the *LRM* does not include the subprogram names shown in the syntax rule above. The examples in the manual, however, do include subprogram names, so we assume their omission in the syntax rule is an oversight.

EXAMPLE

Suppose we have a package mem_pkg stored in the library project. The package declaration is shown at the top of Figure 20-6. The 'path_name attribute applied to these items gives the following results:

FIGURE 20-6

```
package mem_pkg is
    subtype word is bit_vector(0 to 31);
    type word_array is array (natural range <>) of word;
    procedure load_array ( words : out word_array; file_name : string );
end package mem_pkg;

---------------------------------------------------

package body mem_pkg is
    procedure load_array ( words : out word_array; file_name : string ) is
        -- words'path_name = ":project:mem_pkg:load_array:words"
        use std.textio.all;
        file load_file : text open read_mode is file_name;
        -- load_file'path_name = ":project:mem_pkg:load_array:load_file"
        procedure read_line is
        -- read_line'path_name = ":project:mem_pkg:load_array:read_line:"
            variable current_line : line;
            -- current_line'path_name =
            --    ":project:mem_pkg:load_array:read_line:current_line"
        begin
            . . .
        end procedure read_line;
    begin  -- load_array
        . . .
    end procedure load_array;
end package body mem_pkg;
```

A package declaration and body, illustrating the path name attribute.

```
mem_pkg'path_name = ":project:mem_pkg:"
word'path_name = ":project:mem_pkg:word"
word_array'path_name = ":project:mem_pkg:word_array"
load_array'path_name = ":project:mem_pkg:load_array"
```

The 'instance_name attribute returns the same strings for these items. An outline of the package body is also shown in Figure 20-6. The comments indicate the values of the 'path_name attribute applied to various names within the package body. Again, the 'instance_name attribute returns the same strings as the 'path_name attribute.

If an item is declared within an entity or architecture body, the 'path_name and 'instance_name attributes return different strings depending on the structure of the elaborated design and the location of the declared item within the design hierarchy. We first look at the string returned by the 'path_name attribute, as it is the simpler of the two. The format of the string is described by the EBNF rules

instance_based_path ⇐
   : { path_instance_element : }
      ⟦ simple_name ‖ character_literal ‖ operator_symbol ⟧
path_instance_element ⇐
   *entity*_simple_name
   ‖ *component_instantiation*_label
   ‖ *block*_label
   ‖ *generate*_label ⟦ (literal) ⟧
   ‖ ⟦ *process*_label ⟧
   ‖ *subprogram*_simple_name

The string starts with the name of the topmost entity in the design and continues with the labels of any blocks, generate statements, processes and subprograms between the top and the item. If the design hierarchy includes a component instance bound to an entity and architecture body containing the item, the attribute string includes the label of the component instantiation statement. If the item is contained within an iterative generate statement, the string includes the value of the generate parameter for the particular iteration containing the item. The value is included in parentheses after the generate statement label. If the item is included in a process that has no label, the string includes an empty element in place of a process label.

The format of the string returned by the 'instance_name attribute is described by the EBNF rules

full_instance_based_path ⇐
   : { full_path_instance_element : }
      ⟦ simple_name ‖ character_literal ‖ operator_symbol ⟧
full_path_instance_element ⇐
   *entity*_simple_name (architecture_simple_name)
   ‖ *component_instantiation*_label
      @ *entity*_simple_name (architecture_simple_name)
   ‖ *block*_label
   ‖ *generate*_label ⟦ (literal) ⟧
   ‖ ⟦ *process*_label ⟧
   ‖ *subprogram*_simple_name

It is the same as that returned by 'path_name, except that the names of the entity and architecture bound to a component instance are included after the label of the component instantiation statement. Furthermore, the architecture name for the top-level design entity is also included.

EXAMPLE

We illustrate the results returned by the 'path_name and 'instance_name attributes by looking at a sample design hierarchy. The top level of the hierarchy is formed by the entity **top** and its corresponding architecture **top_arch**, declared as shown in Figure 20-7. The numbered comments in this model mark points at which various declared items are visible. The values of the 'path_name and

FIGURE 20-7

```
entity top is
end entity top;

------------------------------------------------------------

architecture top_arch of top is
    signal top_sig : . . .;                          -- 1
begin
    stimulus : process is
        variable var : . . .;                        -- 2
    begin
        . . .
    end process stimulus;
    rep_gen : for index in 0 to 7 generate
    begin
        end_gen : if index = 7 generate
            signal end_sig : . . .;                  -- 3
        begin
            . . .
        end generate end_gen;
        other_gen : if index /= 7 generate
            signal other_sig : . . .;                -- 4
        begin
            other_comp : entity work.bottom(bottom_arch)
                port map ( . . . );
        end generate other_gen;
    end generate rep_gen;
end architecture top_arch;
```

The top-level entity and architecture body of a design hierarchy.

'instance_name attributes of these items at the marked points are shown in Figure 20-8. At point 4, the string returned varies between repetitions created by the generator. Where the table shows *index* in the attribute value, the value of the generate parameter for that repetition is substituted. For example, in the repetition with the generate parameter set to 4, the result of other_sig'path_name is ":top:rep_gen(4):other_gen:other_sig".

The entity declaration and architecture body for the bottom level of the design hierarchy, instantiated in the preceding architecture body, are shown in Figure 20-9. The values of the 'path_name and 'instance_name attributes of items within this architecture at the marked points are shown in Figure 20-10. The values shown are for the instance of the architecture corresponding to the component instantiation statement in the repetition of rep_gen with index set to 4. Point 8 is within a process that has no label, so the strings returned for the item v include an empty element (two consecutive colon characters) where the process label would otherwise be.

FIGURE 20-8

Point	Item	*Item*'path_name *and item*'instance_name	
1	top	:top:	:top(top_arch):
1	top_sig	:top:top_sig	:top(top_arch):top_sig
2	stimulus	:top:stimulus:	:top(top_arch):stimulus:
2	var	:top:stimulus:var	:top(top_arch):stimulus:var
3	end_sig	:top:rep_gen(7):end_gen:end_sig :top(top_arch):rep_gen(7):end_gen:end_sig	
4	other_sig	:top:rep_gen(*index*):other_gen:other_sig :top(top_arch):rep_gen(*index*):other_gen:other_sig	

The results of applying the path and instance name attributes to the top-level design entity.

FIGURE 20-9

```
entity bottom is
    port ( . . . );
end entity bottom;
```

```
architecture bottom_arch of bottom is
    signal bot_sig : . . .;                  -- 5
    procedure proc ( . . . ) is
        variable v : . . .;                  -- 6
    begin
        . . .
    end procedure proc;
begin
    delays : block is
        constant d : integer := 1;           -- 7
    begin
        . . .
    end block delays;
    func : block is
    begin
        process is
            variable v : . . .;              -- 8
        begin
            . . .
        end process;
    end block func;
end architecture bottom_arch;
```

The bottom-level entity and architecture body of a design hierarchy.

FIGURE 20-10

Point	Item	*Item*'path_name *and item*'instance_name
5	bot_sig	:top:rep_gen(4):other_gen:other_comp:bot_sig
		:top(top_arch):rep_gen(4):other_gen:other_comp@bottom(bottom_arch):bot_sig
6	v	:top:rep_gen(4):other_gen:other_comp:proc:v
		:top(top_arch):rep_gen(4):other_gen:other_comp@bottom(bottom_arch):proc:v
7	d	:top:rep_gen(4):other_gen:other_comp:delays:d
		:top(top_arch):rep_gen(4):other_gen:other_comp@bottom(bottom_arch):delays:d
8	v	:top:rep_gen(4):other_gen:other_comp:func::v
		:top(top_arch):rep_gen(4):other_gen:other_comp@bottom(bottom_arch):func::v

The results of applying the path and instance name attributes to the bottom-level design entity.

VHDL-87

The predefined attributes 'simple_name, 'path_name and 'instance_name are not provided in VHDL-87.

VHDL-87 provides two additional attributes, 'behavior and 'structure, that can be applied to the names of architecture bodies, and that return a Boolean result. The 'behavior attribute indicates whether the architecture body is a behavioral description. It returns true if the architecture body contains no component instantiation statements. The 'structure attribute indicates whether the architecture body is a structural description. It returns true if the architecture body contains only component instantiations and passive processes. If both attributes are false, the architecture body is a mix of behavioral and structural modeling constructs.

20.2 User-Defined Attributes

The predefined attributes provide information about types, objects or other items in a VHDL model. VHDL also provides us with a way of adding additional information of our own choosing to items in our models, namely, through user-defined attributes. We can use them to add physical design information such as standard cell allocation and placements, layout constraints such as maximum wire delay and inter-wire skew or information for synthesis such as encodings for enumeration types and hints about resource allocation. In general, information of a non-structural and non-behavioral nature can be added using attributes and processed using software tools operating on the design database.

Attribute Declarations

The first step in defining an attribute is to declare the name and type of an attribute, using an *attribute declaration*. The syntax rule describing this is

attribute_declaration ⇐ **attribute** identifier : type_mark ;

An attribute declaration simply defines the identifier as representing a user-defined attribute that can take on values from the specified type. The type can be any VHDL type except an access or file type or a composite type with a subelement that is an access or file type. Some examples of attribute declarations are

```
attribute cell_name : string;
attribute pin_number : positive;
attribute max_wire_delay : delay_length;
attribute encoding : bit_vector;
```

The attribute type need not be a simple scalar. For example, we might define an attribute to represent cell placement as follows:

```
type length is range 0 to integer'high
    units
        nm;
        um = 1000 nm;
        mm = 1000 um;
        mil = 25400 nm;
    end units length;

type coordinate is record
        x, y : length;
        end record coordinate;

attribute cell_position : coordinate;
```

Attribute Specifications

Once we have defined an attribute name and type, we then use it to *decorate* items within a design. We write *attribute specifications*, nominating items that take on the attribute with particular values. The syntax rules for an attribute specification are

```
attribute_specification ⇐
    attribute identifier of entity_name_list : entity_class is expression ;

entity_name_list ⇐
    ( ( identifier ‖ character_literal ‖ operator_symbol ) [ signature ] ) { , ... }
    ‖ others
    ‖ all

entity_class ⇐
    entity          ‖ architecture     ‖ configuration   ‖ package
    ‖ procedure     ‖ function          ‖ type            ‖ subtype
    ‖ constant      ‖ signal            ‖ variable        ‖ file
    ‖ component     ‖ label             ‖ literal         ‖ units
    ‖ group
```

The first identifier in an attribute specification is the name of a previously declared attribute. The items to be decorated with this attribute are listed in the entity name list. Note that we use the term "entity" here to refer to any item in the design, not to be confused with an entity interface defined in an entity declaration. We adopt this terminology to remain consistent with the *VHDL Language Reference Manual*, since you may need to refer to it occasionally. However, we use the term as little as possible, preferring instead to refer to "items" in the design, to avoid confusion. The items to be decorated with the attribute are those named items of the particular kind specified by the "entity" class. The list of classes shown covers every kind of item we can name in a VHDL description, so we can decorate any part of a design with an attribute. Finally, the actual value for the attribute of the decorated items is the result of the expression included in the attribute specification. Here are some examples of attribute specifications using the attributes defined earlier:

> **attribute** cell_name **of** std_cell : **architecture is** "DFF_SR_QQNN";
> **attribute** pin_number **of** enable : **signal is** 14;
> **attribute** max_wire_delay **of** clk : **signal is** 50 ps;
> **attribute** encoding **of** idle_state : **literal is** b"0000";
> **attribute** cell_position **of** the_fpu : **label is** (540 um, 1200 um);

We now look at how attribute values may be specified for each of the classes of items shown in the syntax rule. For most classes of items, an attribute specification must appear in the same group of declarations as the declaration for the item being decorated. However, the first four classes shown in the syntax rule are design units that are placed in a design library as library units when analyzed. They are not declared within any enclosing declarative part. Instead, we can consider them as being declared in the context of the design library. However, this presents a problem if we wish to decorate an item of one of these classes with an attribute. For entities, architectures, configurations and packages, we solve this problem by placing the attribute specification in the declarative part of the design unit itself. For example, we decorate an architecture std_cell with the cell_name attribute as follows:

> **architecture** std_cell **of** flipflop **is**
>
> > **attribute** cell_name **of** std_cell : **architecture is** "DFF_SR_QQNN";
> >
> > . . .   *-- other declarations*
>
> **begin**
> > . . .
> **end architecture** std_cell;

In the case of packages, the attribute specification must be included in the package declaration, not the package body. For example, we can decorate a package model_utilities with the optimize attribute as follows:

> **package** model_utilities **is**
>
> > **attribute** optimize : string;
> > **attribute** optimize **of** model_utilities : **package is** "level_4";
>
> > . . .
>
> **end package** model_utilities;

When we decorate subprograms we may need to distinguish between several overloaded versions. The syntax rule on page 574 shows that we can include a signature to identify one version uniquely by specifying the types of its parameters and return value. Signatures were introduced in Chapter 9.

EXAMPLE

If we have two overloaded versions of the procedure add_with_overflow declared in a process as shown in Figure 20-11, we can decorate them using signatures in the attribute specification.

FIGURE 20-11

```
process is
    procedure add_with_overflow ( a, b : in integer;
                                   sum : out integer;
                                   overflow : out boolean ) is . . .
    procedure add_with_overflow ( a, b : in bit_vector;
                                   sum : out bit_vector;
                                   overflow : out boolean ) is . . .
    attribute built_in : string;
    attribute built_in of
        add_with_overflow [ integer, integer, integer, boolean ] : procedure is
        "int_add_overflow";
    attribute built_in of
        add_with_overflow [ bit_vector, bit_vector, bit_vector, boolean ] : procedure is
        "bit_vector_add_overflow";
begin
    . . .
end process;
```

A process using signatures in the attribute specifications for two overloaded procedures.

The syntax rule also shows that we can identify an overloaded operator by writing
the operator symbol as the function name. For example, if we declare a function to
concatenate two lists of stimulus vectors:

function "&" (a, b : stimulus_list) **return** stimulus_list;

we can decorate it with an attribute as follows:

attribute debug : string;
attribute debug **of**
    "&" [stimulus_list, stimulus_list **return** stimulus_list] : **function is**
    "source_statement_step";

The syntax rules for attribute specifications show the signature to be optional, and
indeed, we can omit it when decorating subprograms. In this case, the attribute specification applies to all subprograms with the given name declared in the same declarative
part as the attribute specification.

We can decorate a type, subtype or data objects (a constant, variable, signal or files)
by including an attribute specification after the declaration of the item. The attribute
specification must appear within the same declarative part as the declaration of the
item. For example, if we declare a resolved subtype resolved_mvl:

```
type mvl is ('X', '0', '1', 'Z');
type mvl_vector is array ( integer range <>) of mvl;
function resolve_mvl ( drivers : mvl_vector ) return mvl;

subtype resolved_mvl is resolve_mvl mvl;
```

we can decorate it as follows:

```
type builtin_types is (builtin_bit, builtin_mvl, builtin_integer);
attribute builtin : builtin_types;

attribute builtin of resolved_mvl : subtype is builtin_mvl;
```

Generics and ports in the interface of a block or entity are data objects and can be decorated with attributes. Generics are objects of constant class, and ports are objects of signal class. The interface list is included in the declarative part of the block or entity. Hence, we write attribute specifications for generics and ports in the declarative part of the block or entity. Subprogram parameters are also data objects that can be decorated with attributes. The class of each parameter is specified in the interface list of the subprogram. We write the attribute specifications for subprogram parameters in the declarative part of the subprogram.

EXAMPLE

Suppose the package **physical_attributes** declared the following attributes:

```
attribute layout_ignore : boolean;
attribute pin_number : positive;
```

We can declare an entity with decorated generics and ports as shown in Figure 20-12.

FIGURE 20-12

```
library ieee; use ieee.std_logic_1164.all;
use work.physical_attributes.all;

entity \74x138\ is
    generic ( Tpd : time );
    port ( en1, en2a_n, en2b_n : in std_logic;
        s0, s1, s2 : in std_logic;
        y0, y1, y2, y3, y4, y5, y6, y7 : out std_logic );

    attribute layout_ignore of Tpd : constant is true;

    attribute pin_number of s0 : signal is 1;
    attribute pin_number of s1 : signal is 2;
    attribute pin_number of s2 : signal is 3;
    attribute pin_number of en2a_n : signal is 4;

    . . .

end entity \74x138\;
```

An entity declaration for a 74x138 decoder, with decorated ports.

EXAMPLE

Figure 20-13 shows a procedure with three parameters of different classes. Attribute specifications for the parameters are included in the declarative part of the procedure.

FIGURE 20-13

```
procedure mem_read ( address : in natural;
                        result : out byte_vector;
                        signal memory_bus : inout ram_bus ) is
    attribute trace of address : constant is "integer/hex";
    attribute trace of result : variable is "byte/multiple/hex";
    attribute trace of memory_bus : signal is
        "custom/command=rambus.cmd";
    . . .
begin
    . . .
end procedure mem_read;
```

A procedure with decorated parameters.

We can decorate a component in a model by including an attribute specification along with the component declaration. An important point to realize is that the attribute decorates the template defined by the component declaration. It does not decorate component instances that use that template.

EXAMPLE

Figure 20-14 shows a package specification that includes a component declaration for an and gate. The package imports two attributes, graphic_symbol and graphic_style, from the package graphics_pkg in the library graphics. It decorates the component template with each of these attributes.

FIGURE 20-14

```
library ieee;  use ieee.std_logic_1164.all;
library graphics;
package gate_components is
    use graphics.graphics_pkg.graphic_symbol,
        graphics.graphics_pkg.graphic_style;
    component and2 is
        generic ( prop_delay : delay_length );
        port ( a, b : in std_logic;  y : out std_logic );
    end component and2;
```

    attribute graphic_symbol **of** and2 : **component is** "and2";
    attribute graphic_style **of** and2 : **component is** "color:default, weight:bold";

. . .

end package gate_components;

A package that declares a component and decorates it with attributes.

If we wish to decorate a component instance or any other concurrent statement with an attribute, we do so by decorating the label of the statement. The label is implicitly declared in the declarative part of the architecture or block containing the concurrent statement. Hence, we place the attribute specification in that declarative part.

EXAMPLE

We might decorate a component instance in an architecture body with an attribute describing cell placement as shown in Figure 20-15.

FIGURE 20-15

```
architecture cell_based of CPU is
    component fpu is
        port ( . . . );
    end component;
    use work.cell_attributes.all;
    attribute cell_position of the_fpu : label is ( 540 um, 1200 um );

    . . .
begin
    the_fpu : component fpu
        port map ( . . . );

    . . .
end architecture cell_based;
```

An architecture body containing a component instance whose label is decorated with an attribute.

We can decorate sequential statements within a process or a subprogram in a similar way. The syntax rules for sequential statements show that each kind of sequential statement may be labeled. We decorate a sequential statement by specifying an attribute for the label. We place the attribute specification in the declarative part of the process or subprogram containing the sequential statement.

EXAMPLE

If we wish to decorate a loop statement in a process with the attribute **synthesis_hint**, we proceed as shown in Figure 20-16.

FIGURE 20-16

```
controller : process is
    attribute synthesis_hint of control_loop : label is
        "implementation:FSM(clk)";
    . . .
begin
    . . .          -- initialization
    control_loop : loop
        wait until clk = '1';

        . . .
    end loop;
end process controller;
```

A process containing a sequential statement whose label is decorated with an attribute.

When we introduced aliases and signatures in Chapter 9, we mentioned that enumeration literals can be thought of as functions with no parameters that return values of their enumeration types. We can take the same approach when decorating enumeration literals with attributes, in order to distinguish between literals of the same name from different enumeration types.

EXAMPLE

If we have two enumeration types declared as

```
type controller_state is (idle, active, fail_safe);
type load_level is (idle, busy, overloaded);
```

we can decorate the literals of type **controller_state** as follows:

```
attribute encoding of idle [ return controller_state ] : literal is b"00";
attribute encoding of active [ return controller_state ] : literal is b"01";
attribute encoding of fail_safe [ return controller_state ] : literal is b"10";
```

The signature associated with the literal **idle** indicates that it is of type **controller_state**, not **load_level**. As with attribute specifications for subprograms, if a signature is not included for a literal, all literals of the given name declared in the same declarative part as the attribute specification are decorated with the attribute.

When we declare a physical type we introduce a primary unit name and possibly a number of secondary unit names. Each of the unit names is a declared item and so may be decorated with attributes.

EXAMPLE

Figure 20-17 shows a package interface that defines a physical type **voltage**. It also declares an attribute, **resolution**, and decorates each of the units of **voltage** with this attribute.

FIGURE 20-17

```
package voltage_defs is
    type voltage is range –2e9 to +2e9
        units nV;
            uV = 1000 nV;
            mV = 1000 uV;
            V = 1000 mV;
        end units voltage;
    attribute resolution : real;
    attribute resolution of nV : units is 1.0;
    attribute resolution of uV : units is 0.01;
    attribute resolution of mV : units is 0.01;
    attribute resolution of V : units is 0.001;
end package voltage_defs;
```

A package that declares a physical type and decorates units of the type with attributes.

The one remaining class of items that can be decorated with attributes is groups. We introduce groups in the next section and show examples of decorated groups.

If we return to the syntax rules for attribute specifications, shown on page 574, we see that we can write the keyword **others** in place of the list of names of items to be decorated. If we do so, the attribute specification applies to all items of the given class in the declarative part that are not otherwise decorated with the attribute. Such an attribute specification must be the last one in the declarative part that refers to the given attribute name and item class.

EXAMPLE

Figure 20-18 shows an architecture body in which signals are decorated with attributes specifying the maximum allowable delays due to the physical layout. The two signals **recovered_clk1** and **recovered_clk2** are explicitly decorated with the attribute value 100 ps. The remaining signals are decorated with the value 200 ps.

FIGURE 20-18

```
library ieee;  use ieee.std_logic_1164.all;
use work.timing_attributes.all;

architecture structural of sequencer is
    signal recovered_clk1, recovered_clk2 : std_logic;
    signal test_enable : std_logic;
    signal test_data : std_logic_vector(0 to 15);

    attribute max_wire_delay of recovered_clk1, recovered_clk2 : signal is 100 ps;

    attribute max_wire_delay of others : signal is 200 ps;

    . . .
begin

    . . .
end architecture structural;
```

An outline of an architecture body in which attributes are used to specify layout-based delays for signals.

The syntax rules also show that we can use the keyword **all** in place of a list of item names. In this case, all items of the given class defined in the declarative part containing the attribute specification are decorated. Such an attribute specification must be the only one in the declarative part to refer to the given attribute name and item class.

Although we can only decorate an item with one value for a given attribute name, we can decorate it with several different attributes. We simply write one attribute specification for each of the attributes decorating the item. For example, a component instance labeled mult might be decorated with several attributes as follows:

```
attribute cell_allocation of mult : label is "wallace_tree_multiplier";
attribute cell_position of mult : label is ( 1200 um, 4500 um );
attribute cell_orientation of mult : label is down;
```

If an item in a design is decorated with a user-defined attribute, we can refer to the attribute value using the same notation that we use for predefined attributes. The syntax rule for an attribute name referring to a user-defined attribute is

attribute_name ⇐ name ⟦ signature ⟧ ' identifier

If the name of the item is unambiguous, we can simply write an apostrophe and the attribute name after the item name. For example:

```
std_cell'cell_name
enable'pin_number
clk'max_wire_delay
idle_state'encoding
the_fpu'cell_position
```

In the case of attributes decorating subprograms or enumeration literals, it may be necessary to use a signature to distinguish between a number of alternative names.

For example, we might refer to attribute values of different versions of an increment function as

```
increment [ bit_vector return bit_vector ] 'built_in
increment [ std_logic_vector return std_logic_vector ] 'built_in
```

Similarly, we might refer to attribute values of enumeration literals as

```
high [ return speed_range ] 'representation
high [ return coolant_level ] 'representation
```

While it is legal VHDL to refer to attribute values such as these in expressions, it is not good design practice to use attribute values to affect the structure or behavior of the model. It is better to describe structure and behavior using the language facilities intended for that purpose and use attributes to annotate the design with other kinds of information for use by other software tools. For this reason, we do not further discuss the use of attribute values in models. Software tools that use attributes should include documentation describing the required attribute types and their usage.

In Chapter 9, we introduced aliases as a way of defining alternate names for items in a design. In most cases, referring to an item using an alias is exactly the same as referring to it using its original name. The same interpretation holds when decorating items with attributes. When we use an alias of an item in an attribute specification, it is the original object denoted by the alias that is decorated, not the alias. This is the interpretation we saw for the predefined attributes discussed in the previous section. The exceptions are the predefined attributes that return the path name of an item and those that return information about the index ranges of arrays. One restriction on decorating data objects using aliases is that we may only do so using aliases that denote whole objects, not elements or slices of records or arrays. This restriction corresponds to the restriction that an attribute must decorate a whole object. The syntax rule for an attribute specification does not provide for naming parts of objects, since we can only write a simple identifier as an object name.

One final point to mention about user-defined attributes relates to component instantiation statements and to subprogram calls. In a component instantiation statement, actual signals are associated with formal ports of an entity. If the actual signal is decorated with an attribute, the attribute information is only visible in the context of the actual signal, namely, in the architecture body in which the signal is declared. It is not carried through to the instantiated entity. For example, if we have a signal s decorated with an attribute attr, we might use it as an actual signal in a component instantiation statement:

```
c1 : entity work.e(arch)
    port map ( p => s );
```

Within the architecture body arch, we cannot refer the attribute of the signal using the notation p'attr. This notation instead refers to the attribute attr of the port p, which can only be defined in the entity declaration.

In a subprogram call an actual parameter (such as a constant, variable, signal or file) is associated with a formal parameter of the subprogram. If the actual parameter is decorated with an attribute, that attribute information is likewise not carried through to the subprogram. The decoration is purely local to the region in which the actual object is declared.

VHDL-87

The syntax rules for attribute specifications in VHDL-87 do not allow us to name a character literal as an item to be decorated. Nor may we specify the entity class **literal**, **units**, **group** or **file**. Furthermore, we may not include a signature after an item name. Hence there is no way to distinguish between overloaded subprograms or enumeration literals; all items of the given name are decorated.

The Attribute Foreign

While VHDL provides comprehensive features for modeling the structure and behavior of hardware designs, there remain some tasks for which we need to step outside of the VHDL domain. For these cases, VHDL defines the following attribute in the package std.standard:

> **attribute** foreign : string;

We can use the **foreign** attribute to decorate architectures and subprograms. When we do so, the contents of the architecture body or subprogram body are given special treatment by the simulator, using information supplied in the attribute value. VHDL does not specify what special treatment is applied, leaving that to individual vendors of VHDL tools. The language simply provides the mechanism for vendors to use to interface to non-VHDL libraries and tools. We need to consult the documentation provided with each individual VHDL tool set to find out how the **foreign** attribute is treated. Note that an implementation may restrict the class, mode and type of ports and parameters of entities and subprograms decorated with the **foreign** attribute. Such restrictions may be required to limit the data types and communications mechanisms in an interface to those that are common to the VHDL tool and the non-VHDL tools. A vendor's documentation should also describe any such restrictions.

EXAMPLE

One possible use of the **foreign** attribute is to specify some vendor-specific implementation for an architecture body, for example, an optimized implementation based on acceleration hardware. A vendor might require the architecture to be decorated with the **foreign** attribute as follows:

```
architecture accelerated of and2 is
    attribute foreign of accelerated : architecture is
        "accelerate/function:and_2in/nocheck";
begin
end architecture accelerated;
```

When a design using this architecture is elaborated, the VHDL simulator notes that the architecture is decorated with the **foreign** attribute and invokes special processing to use the accelerator, rather than elaborating the architecture in the normal way.

EXAMPLE

The **foreign** attribute might be used to specify that a subprogram is implemented in some language other than VHDL. Figure 20-19 shows a VHDL package declaring the procedure **create_window**. The package also decorates the procedure with the **foreign** attribute, specifying that the procedure is implemented in the Ada programming language. Additional information in the attribute string specifies the Ada procedure to use and describes the mapping from the VHDL procedure parameters to the Ada procedure parameters.

FIGURE 20-19

```
package display_interface is

   . . .

   procedure create_window ( size_x, size_y : natural;
                                        status : out status_type );

   attribute foreign of create_window : procedure is
         "language Ada;  with window_operations;" &
         "bind to window_operations.create_window;" &
         "parameter size_x maps to size_x : in natural;" &
         "parameter size_y maps to size_y : in natural;" &
         "parameter status maps to status : out window_operations.status_type;" &
         "others map to default";

   . . .

end package display_interface;
```

A package that declares a procedure and decorates with the foreign *attribute.*

VHDL-87

The predefined attribute 'foreign is not provided in VHDL-87. There is no standard mechanism to define foreign language interfaces.

20.3 Groups

The user-defined attribute facility discussed in the previous section allows us to annotate individual items in a design with non-structural and non-behavioral information. However, much of the additional information we may need to include can best be expressed as relationships between collections of items, rather than pertaining to individual items. For this reason VHDL provides a grouping mechanism to identify a collection of items over which some relationship holds. The information about the relationship is expressed as an attribute of the group. In this section we see how to define kinds of groups, to identify particular groups of related items and to specify attributes for particular groups.

The first stage in grouping items is to define a template for the classes of items that can be included in the group. We do this with a *group template declaration*, for which the syntax rule is

> group_template_declaration ⇐
>   **group** identifier **is** (〖 entity_class 〚 <> 〛 〗 { , ... }) ;

A group template declaration lists one or more classes of items, in order, that may constitute a group. Note that the syntax rule uses the term "entity" here in the same way as the rules for attribute specifications, namely, to refer to any kind of item in a design. We discuss the meaning of the "<>" notation shortly. An example of a group template declaration is

> **group** signal_pair **is** (**signal**, **signal**);

This defines a template for groups consisting of two signals. We can use this template to define a number of groups using *group declarations*. The syntax rule for a group declaration is

> group_declaration ⇐
>   **group** identifier : *group_template*_name
>   (〖 name ‖ character_literal 〗 { , ... }) ;

A group declaration names a template to use for the group and lists the items that are to be members of the group. Each item in the list must be of the class specified in the corresponding position in the template. For example, if we have two clock signals in a design, clk_phase1 and clk_phase2, we can group them together using the **signal_pair** template defined above by writing

> **group** clock_pair : signal_pair (clk_phase1, clk_phase2);

As we mentioned earlier, the main use of groups is as a mechanism for defining relationships between items by decorating a group of items with an attribute. We decorate a group by naming it in an attribute specification, identifying it as an item of class **group**. For example, if we have an attribute declared as

> **attribute** max_skew : time;

we can decorate the clock_pair group with this attribute as follows:

> **attribute** max_skew **of** clock_pair : **group is** 200 ps;

The decoration can be interpreted as an annotation to the design, indicating to a layout tool that the maximum permissible skew between the two signals in the group is 200 ps.

The syntax rule for a group template shows that we may write the box symbol ("<>") after an item class. In fact, we may only include such a class specification once in any template, and it must be in the last position in the list of item classes. It indicates that a group based on that template may have an indefinite number of elements of the given class (including none).

EXAMPLE

We can define a group template for a group representing component instances to be allocated to the same physical package. The members of such a group are the labels of the component instances. The group template declaration is

group component_instances **is** (**label** <>);

We can use the template to create groups of instances:

group U1 : component_instances (nand1, nand2, nand3);
group U2 : component_instances (inv1, inv2);

We can specify what kind of integrated circuit should be used for each group by defining an attribute and using it to decorate the group:

attribute IC_allocation : string;

attribute IC_allocation **of** U1 : **group is** "74LS00";
attribute IC_allocation **of** U2 : **group is** "74LS04";

An individual item in a design can belong to more than one group. We simply include its name in the declaration of each group of which it is a member.

EXAMPLE

We can use groups of signals as the basis for annotating a design entity with port-to-port timing constraints. Suppose we declare a group template port_pair and an attribute max_prop_delay in a package constraints:

group port_pair **is** (**signal**, **signal**);

attribute max_prop_delay : time;

We can then use the template to group pairs of ports of an entity and annotate them with constraint attributes, as shown in Figure 20-20. In this entity declaration, the item clock_in is a member of each of the three groups clock_to_out1, clock_to_out2 and clock_to_out3.

FIGURE 20-20

```
library ieee;  use ieee.std_logic_1164.all;
use work.constraints.port_pair, work.constraints.max_prop_delay;
entity clock_buffer is
    port ( clock_in : in std_logic;
            clock_out1, clock_out2, clock_out3 : out std_logic );
    group clock_to_out1 : port_pair ( clock_in, clock_out1 );
    group clock_to_out2 : port_pair ( clock_in, clock_out2 );
    group clock_to_out3 : port_pair ( clock_in, clock_out3 );
```

(continued on page 588)

(continued from page 587)

          attribute max_prop_delay **of** clock_to_out1 : **group is** 2 ns;
          attribute max_prop_delay **of** clock_to_out2 : **group is** 2 ns;
          attribute max_prop_delay **of** clock_to_out3 : **group is** 2 ns;
end entity clock_buffer;

An entity declaration in which group attributes are used to represent timing constraints.

VHDL-87

VHDL-87 does not allow declaration of group templates or groups.

Exercises

1. [❶ 20.1] What are the values of the following attributes of items declared within the dlx_instr package described on pages 366 to 374 of Chapter 15:

   - op_special'path_name,

   - disassemble'path_name,

   - result'path_name in the body of the procedure disassemble, and

   - int_image_length'path_name in the body of the procedure disassemble_integer.

   Assume the package is analyzed and placed in a library named dlx_lib.

2. [❶ 20.1] Suppose we instantiate the counter entity, described in the Example on page 138 of Chapter 5, in a test bench as follows:

       dut : **entity** work.counter(registered)
           port map (. . .);

   The test bench entity name is test_bench, and the architecture body name is counter_test. What are the values of the following attributes:

   - val0_reg'path_name in the architecture registered of counter,

   - bit0'path_name in the instance val1_reg of the struct architecture body of reg4, and

   - clr'path_name in the instance bit2 of the behavioral architecture body of edge_triggered_Dff, in the instance val1_reg.

   What are the values of the 'instance_name attributes of the same items?

3. [❶ 20.2] Given a physical type capacitance, declared as

       type capacitance **is range** 0 **to** integer'high
           units pF;
           end units capacitance;

   write an attribute declaration that represents a capacitive load and an attribute specification that decorates a signal d_in with a load of 3 pF.

4. [❶ 20.2] Write a physical type declaration for areas, with a primary unit of μm^2. Write an appropriate attribute declaration and specification to decorate an architecture body library_cell of an entity and3 with an area of 15 μm^2.

5. [❶ 20.2] Given an attribute declared as

   attribute optimization : string;

   decorate the following procedure with the attribute value "inline". Assume that another overloaded version of the procedure, which must not be decorated, is visible.

   procedure test_empty (list : **in** list_ptr; is_empty : **out** boolean) **is** . . .

6. [❶ 20.2] Augment the following architecture body to decorate it with the 'foreign attribute, having the value "control_unit.o control_utilities.o".

   architecture c_implementation **of** control_unit **is**
   begin
   end architecture c_implementation;

7. [❶ 20.3] Define a group template that allows two or more statement labels as members. Next, declare a group that includes the labels of the following two statements:

   step_1 : a := b * c + k;
   step_2 : n := a + 4 * j;

   Then, write an attribute specification that decorates the group with the attribute resource_allocation having the value max_sharing.

8. [❷ 20.1] Since the definition in the *VHDL LRM* of the 'path_name and instance_name attributes of items declared within packages is ambiguous, different simulators may produce different results. Construct some small examples, such as those shown in Section 20.1, and experiment with your simulator to see how it constructs values for these attributes.

9. [❷ 20.1] Develop an edge-triggered register model that includes generics for setup and hold times in its entity interface, and that reports an assertion violation if the timing constraints are not met. The message reported should include the full instance name of the entity instance in which the violation occurs.

10. [❷ 20.2] Write an entity interface that describes a 74x138 3-to-8 decoder. Include an attribute declaration and attribute specifications to decorate the ports with pin-number information for the following package:

1	s0	vcc	16
2	s1	y0_n	15
3	s2	y1_n	14
4	g2a_n	y2_n	13
5	g2b_n	y3_n	12
6	g1	y4_n	11
7	y7_n	y5_n	10
8	gnd	y6_n	9

11. [❷ 20.3] Write an entity interface for an and-or-invert gate that implements the following function:

$$z = \overline{a_1 . a_2 . a_3 + b_1 . b_2 . b_3}$$

Since the "and" function is commutative and associative, a layout tool should be able to permute the connections within each of the groups a_1, a_2, a_3 and b_1, b_2, b_3 without affecting the function performed by the circuit. Include in the entity interface of the and-or-invert gate a group template declaration and group declarations that encompass ports among which connections may be permuted.

12. [❸ 20.2] Check the documentation for your simulator to see if it makes use of the 'foreign attribute on subprograms or architecture bodies. If it does, experiment to verify that you can use the facilities it provides. For example, if the simulator uses the 'foreign attribute as a means of specifying an implementation in a non-VHDL programming language, try writing a small procedure or function in the programming language to interact with a simulation model.

13. [❹ 20.2] If your simulator allows you to call functions written in the programming language C, develop a register model that uses the graphical display libraries of your host computer system to create a pop-up window to display the register contents. Instantiate the register model in a test bench, and step through the simulation to verify that the model creates and updates the display.

21

Miscellaneous Topics

In the preceding chapters we have introduced most of the facilities provided by VHDL and shown how they may be used to model a variety of hardware systems at various levels of detail. However, there remain a few VHDL facilities that we have not yet discussed. In this chapter, we tie off these loose ends.

21.1 Buffer and Linkage Ports

When we introduced ports in Chapter 5, we identified three modes, **in**, **out** and **inout**, that control how data is passed to and from a design entity. VHDL provides two further modes, **buffer** and **linkage**. These modes may only be specified for ports of entities, blocks and components, not for generic constants or subprogram parameters.

A **buffer** mode port behaves in a similar way to an **inout** mode port, in that the port can be both read and assigned in the entity or block. The source of a **buffer** port determines the driving value of the port in the normal way. However, when the port is read, the value read is the driving value. This behavior differs from **inout** ports in that the value read for an **inout** port may be different from the driving value if the actual signal associated with the port is resolved. The behavior of a **buffer** port allows us to model a design that has a buffered output connection and internally uses the value driving the buffer. In this case we do not explicitly represent the buffer as a component, nor its input as a signal.

EXAMPLE

We can implement a counter as a string of flipflops, with each stage feeding the next. This form of counter is usually called a "ripple" counter. An entity declaration for a simple two-bit counter is shown in Figure 21-1. The corresponding architecture body drives the output ports q0 and q1 with the q outputs of the flip-flops bit0 and bit1. Ports q0 and q1 are also used as the inputs to the inverters inv0 and inv1. If q0 and q1 were declared as ports of mode **out**, we could not make these internal connections. Since we really want q0 and q1 to be outputs, we declare them to be of mode **buffer**, allowing us to read the ports internally as well as treating them as outputs.

FIGURE 21-1

```
entity count2 is
    port ( clk : in bit;  q0, q1 : buffer bit );
end entity count2;

-----------------------------------------------

architecture buffered_outputs of count2 is

    component D_flipflop is
        port ( clk, d : in bit;  q : buffer bit );
    end component D_flipflop;

    component inverter is
        port ( a : in bit;  y : out bit );
    end component inverter;

    signal q0_n, q1_n : bit;

begin
    bit0 : component D_flipflop
        port map ( clk => clk, d => q0_n, q => q0 );

    inv0 : component inverter
        port map ( a => q0, y => q0_n );
```

```
    bit1 : component D_flipflop
        port map ( clk => q0_n, d => q1_n, q => q1 );
    inv1 : component inverter
        port map ( a => q1, y => q1_n );
end architecture buffered_outputs;
```

An entity and architecture body for a two-bit ripple counter.

At first sight, buffer ports seem to be very useful. However, VHDL imposes a number of restrictions on how they may be interconnected with other ports. First, if the actual object associated with a buffer port of a component instance is a port of the enclosing entity, it must also be a buffer port. Second, if we associate a buffer port as an actual object with some formal port of a component instance, the formal port must be of mode **in**, **buffer** or **linkage**. It may not be a port of mode **out**. Thus, the D_flipflop component in Figure 21-1 has a buffer output port. Any flipflop entity bound to the flipflop instances in the counter must also have a buffer output port. Third, a buffer port can only have one source. Hence we cannot resolve a number of sources to determine the value of a buffer port. Finally, while we can associate an actual signal with a buffer port of a component instance, that port must be the only source of the signal. Thus, we cannot use a buffer port of a component as one of a number of contributors to a resolved signal. These restrictions severely limit the uses of buffer ports, so they are not commonly used in practice.

Linkage ports are provided as a means of connecting signals to foreign design entities. If the implementation of an entity is expressed in some language other than VHDL, the way in which values are generated and read within the entity may not conform to the same transaction semantics as those of VHDL. A **linkage** mode port provides the point of contact between the non-VHDL and the VHDL domains. Unless a simulator provides some additional semantics for generating and reading linkage ports, a model containing linkage ports anywhere in the hierarchy cannot be simulated.

Since the internal operation of a linkage port is not bound by the rules of VHDL, VHDL takes the safe approach and considers a linkage port connected to a signal to be both a reader and a source for the signal. Thus, if the linkage port is connected to an actual signal that is a port of an enclosing entity, the actual port cannot be of mode **in** or **out**. It must be a port of mode **inout**, **buffer** or **linkage**. One further restriction is that linkage ports may not have default expressions in their declarations.

21.2 Conversion Functions in Association Lists

In the preceding chapters, we have seen uses of association lists in generic maps, port maps and subprogram calls. An association list associates actual values and objects with formal objects. Let us now look at the full capabilities provided in association lists, shown by the following full syntax rules:

association_list ⇐ ([[formal_part =>]] actual_part) { , ... }

formal_part ⇐
    *generic*_name
    ❘ *port*_name
    ❘ *parameter*_name
    ❘ *function*_name ((*generic*_name ❘ *port*_name ❘ *parameter*_name))
    ❘ type_mark ((*generic*_name ❘ *port*_name ❘ *parameter*_name))

actual_part ⇐
    expression
    ❘ *signal*_name
    ❘ *variable*_name
    ❘ **open**
    ❘ *function*_name ((*signal*_name ❘ *variable*_name))
    ❘ type_mark ((*signal*_name ❘ *variable*_name))

The simple rules for association lists we used previously allowed us to write associations of the form "formal => actual". These new rules allow us to write associations such as

f1 (formal) => actual

formal => f2 (actual)

f1 (formal) => f2 (actual)

These associations include *conversion functions* or *type conversions*. We discussed type conversions in Chapter 2. They allow us to convert a value from one type to another closely related type. A conversion function, on the other hand, is an explicitly or implicitly declared subprogram or operation. It can be any function with one parameter and can compute its result in any way we choose.

A conversion in the actual part of an association is invoked whenever a value is passed from the actual object to the formal object. For a variable-class subprogram parameter, conversion occurs when the subprogram is called. For a signal associated with a port, conversion occurs whenever an updated signal value is passed to the port. For constant-class subprogram parameters and for generic constants, the actual values are expressions, which may directly take the form of function calls or type conversions. In these cases, the conversion is not considered to be part of the association list; instead, it is part of the expression. Conversions are not allowed in the remaining cases, namely, signal-class and file-class actual subprogram parameters.

EXAMPLE

We wish to implement a limit checker, which checks whether a signed integer is out of specified bounds. The integer and bounds are represented as standard-logic vectors of the subtype word, declared in the package project_util as

subtype word **is** std_logic_vector(31 **downto** 0);

We can use a comparison function that compares integers represented as bit vectors. The function is declared in project_util as

function "<" (bv1, bv2 : bit_vector) **return** boolean;

The entity declaration and architecure body for the limit checker are shown in Figure 21-2. The process performs the comparisons by converting the word values to bit vectors, using the conversion function word_to_bitvector. Note that we cannot use the function To_bitvector itself in the actual part of the association list, as it has two parameters, not one. Note also that the result type of the conversion function in this example must be a constrained array type in order to specify the array index range for the actual value passed to the comparison function.

FIGURE 21-2

```
library ieee;  use ieee.std_logic_1164.all;
use work.project_util.all;

entity limit_checker is
    port ( input, lower_bound, upper_bound : in word;
           out_of_bounds : out std_logic );
end entity limit_checker;
```

```
architecture behavioral of limit_checker is
    subtype bv_word is bit_vector(31 downto 0);

    function word_to_bitvector ( w : in word ) return bv_word is
    begin
        return To_bitvector ( w, xmap => '0' );
    end function word_to_bitvector;

begin
    algorithm : process (input, lower_bound, upper_bound) is
    begin
        if "<" ( bv1 => word_to_bitvector(input),
                 bv2 => word_to_bitvector(lower_bound) )
        or "<" ( bv1 => word_to_bitvector(upper_bound),
                 bv2 => word_to_bitvector(input) ) then
            out_of_bounds <= '1';
        else
            out_of_bounds <= '0';
        end if;
    end process algorithm;
end architecture behavioral;
```

An entity and architecture body for a flipflop.

A conversion can only be included in the actual part of an association if the interface object is of mode **in**, **inout** or **linkage**. If the conversion takes the form of a type conversion, it must name a subtype that has the same base type as the formal object and is closely related to the type of the actual object. If the conversion takes the form of a conversion function, the function must have only one parameter of the same type as the actual object and must return a result of the same type as the formal object. If the interface object is of an unconstrained array type, the type mark of the type conver-

sion or the result type of the conversion function must be constrained. The index range
of the type mark or function result is used as the index range of the interface object.

A conversion in the formal part of an association is invoked whenever a value is
passed from the formal object to the actual object. For a variable-class procedure parameter, conversion occurs when the procedure returns. For a signal associated with
a port, conversion occurs whenever the port drives a new value. Conversions are not
allowed for signal-class and file-class formal subprogram parameters.

EXAMPLE

Suppose a library contains the following entity, which generates a random
number at regular intervals:

```
entity random_source is
    generic ( min, max : natural;
              seed : natural;
              interval : delay_length );
    port ( number : out natural );
end entity random_source;
```

If we have a test bench including signals of type **bit**, we can use the entity to generate random stimuli. We use a conversion function to convert the numbers to bit-
vector values. An outline of the test bench is shown in Figure 21-3. The function
natural_to_bv11 has a parameter that is a natural number and returns a bit-vector
result. The architecture instantiates the random_source component, using the conversion function in the formal part of the association between the port and the
signal. Each time the component instance generates a new random number, the
function is invoked to convert it to a bit vector for assignment to stimulus_vector.

FIGURE 21-3

```
architecture random_test of test_bench is
    subtype bv11 is bit_vector(10 downto 0);
    function natural_to_bv11 ( n : natural ) return bv11 is
        variable result : bv11 := (others => '0');
        variable remaining_digits : natural := n;
    begin
        for index in result'reverse_range loop
            result(index) := bit'val(remaining_digits mod 2);
            remaining_digits := remaining_digits / 2;
            exit when remaining_digits = 0;
        end loop;
        return result;
    end function natural_to_bv11;

    signal stimulus_vector : bv11;
    . . .
```

```
begin
    stimulus_generator : entity work.random_source
        generic map ( min => 0, max => 2**10 – 1, seed => 0,
                      interval => 100 ns )
        port map ( natural_to_bv11 (number) => stimulus_vector );

    . . .

end architecture random_test;
```

An outline of a test-bench architecture body, including a random stimulus generator.

The type requirements for conversions included in the formal parts of associations mirror those of conversions in actual parts. A conversion can only be included in a formal part if the interface object is of mode **out**, **inout**, **buffer** or **linkage**. If the conversion takes the form of a type conversion, it must name a subtype that has the same base type as the actual object and is closely related to the type of the formal object. If the conversion takes the form of a conversion function, the function must have only one parameter of the same type as the formal object and must return a result of the same type as the actual object. If the interface object is of an unconstrained array type, the type mark of the type conversion or the parameter type of the conversion function must be constrained. The index range of the type mark or function parameter is used as the index range of the interface object.

Note that we can include a conversion in both the formal part and the actual part of an association if the interface object is of mode **inout** or **linkage**. The conversion on the actual side is invoked whenever a value is passed from the actual to the formal, and the conversion on the formal side is invoked whenever a value is passed from the formal to the actual.

One important use of type conversions in association lists arises when we mix arrays of unresolved and resolved elements in a model. For example, the standard-logic package declares the two types:

```
type std_ulogic_vector is array ( natural range <> ) of std_ulogic;

type std_logic_vector is array ( natural range <>) of std_logic;
```

These are two distinct types, even though the element type of std_logic_vector is a subtype of the element type of std_ulogic_vector. Thus, we cannot directly associate a std_ulogic_vector signal with a std_logic_vector port, nor a std_logic_vector port with a std_ulogic_vector signal. However, we can use type conversions or conversion functions to deal with the type mismatch.

EXAMPLE

Suppose we are developing a register-transfer-level model of a computer system. The architecture body for the processor is shown in Figure 21-4. We declare a latch component and a ROM component, both with unresolved ports. We also declare a constrained array subtype std_logic_word with resolved elements, and a number of signals of this subtype representing the internal buses of the processor.

FIGURE 21-4

```
architecture rtl of processor is
    component latch is
        generic ( width : positive );
        port ( d : in std_ulogic_vector(0 to width − 1);
               q : out std_ulogic_vector(0 to width − 1);
               . . . );
    end component latch;
    component ROM is
        port ( d_out : out std_ulogic_vector; . . . );
    end component ROM;
    subtype std_logic_word is std_logic_vector(0 to 31);
    signal source1, source2, destination : std_logic_word;
    . . .
begin
    temp_register : component latch
        generic map ( width => 32 )
        port map ( d => std_ulogic_vector(destination),
                   std_logic_vector(q) => source1, . . . );
    constant_ROM : component ROM
        port map ( std_logic_word(d_out) => source2, . . . );

    . . .

end architecture rtl;
```

An outline of a computer system model using type conversions to associate array signals with array ports.

We instantiate the latch component and associate the **destination** bus with the d port and the **source1** bus with the q port. Since the signals and the ports are of different but closely related types, we use type conversions in the association list. Although the types **std_ulogic_vector** and **std_logic_vector** are unconstrained array types, we can name them in the type conversion in this instance, since the component ports are constrained.

We also instantiate the ROM component and associate the **source2** bus with the d_out port. Here also we use a type conversion in the association list. However, the port **d_out** is of an unconstrained type. Hence we may not use the name **std_logic_vector** in the type conversion, since it, too, is unconstrained. Instead, we use the constrained subtype name **std_logic_word**. The index range of this subtype is used as the index range of the port **d_out** in the component instance.

VHDL-87

VHDL-87 does not allow type conversions in association lists, but does allow conversion functions. If we need to convert between closely related types in an association list, we can write a function that performs the type conversion and use the function as a conversion function in the association list.

21.3 Postponed Processes

VHDL provides a facility, *postponed processes*, that is useful in delta-delay models. A process is made postponed by including the keyword **postponed**, as shown by the full syntax rule for a process:

process_statement ⟸
    ⟦ *process*_label : ⟧
    ⟦ **postponed** ⟧ **process** ⟦ (*signal*_name { , ... }) ⟧ **is**
        { process_declarative_item }
    begin
        { sequential_statement }
    end ⟦ **postponed** ⟧ **process** ⟦ *process*_label ⟧ ;

The difference between a postponed process and a normal process lies in the way in which they are resumed during simulation. In our discussion of the simulation cycle in Chapter 5, we said that a normal process is triggered during a simulation cycle in which one of the signals to which it is sensitive changes value. The process then executes during that same simulation cycle. A postponed process is triggered in the same way, but may not execute in the same cycle. Instead, it waits until the last delta cycle at the current simulation time and executes after all non-postponed processes have suspended. It must wait until the non-postponed processes have suspended in order to ensure that there are no further delta cycles at the current simulation time. In addition, during initialization, a postponed process is started after all normal processes have been started and have suspended.

When we are writing models that use delta delays, we can use postponed processes to describe "steady state" behavior at each simulation time. The normal processes are executed over a series of delta delays, during which signal values are determined incrementally. Then, when all of the signals have settled to their final state at the current simulation time, the postponed processes execute, using these signal values as their input.

EXAMPLE

We can write an entity interface for a set-reset flipflop as shown in Figure 21-5. The entity declaration includes a process that verifies the outputs of the flipflop. Every implementation of the interface is required to produce complementary outputs. (The condition "now = 0 fs" is included to avoid an assertion violation during initialization.)

Figure 21-5 also shows a dataflow architecture of the flipflop. The concurrent signal assignment statements gate_1 and gate_2 model an implementation composed of cross-coupled gates. Assume that the flipflop is initally in the reset state. When s_n changes from '1' to '0', gate_1 is resumed and schedules a change on q from '0' to '1' after a delta delay. In the next simulation cycle, the change on q

FIGURE 21-5

```
entity SR_flipflop is
    port ( s_n, r_n : in bit;  q, q_n : inout bit );
begin
    postponed process (q, q_n) is
    begin
        assert now = 0 fs or q = not q_n
            report "implementation error: q /= not q_n";
    end postponed process;
end entity SR_flipflop;

_____

architecture dataflow of SR_flipflop is
begin
    gate_1 : q <= s_n nand q_n;
    gate_2 : q_n <= r_n nand q;
end architecture dataflow;
```

An entity declaration and architecture body for a set-reset flipflop.

causes **gate_2** to resume. It schedules a change on **q_n** from '1' to '0' after a delta delay. During the first delta cycle, **q** has the new value '1', but **q_n** still has its initial value of '1'. If we had made the verification process in the entity declaration a non-postponed process, it would be resumed in the first delta cycle and report an assertion violation. Since it is a postponed process, it is not resumed until the second delta cycle (the last delta cycle after the change on **s_n**), by which time **q** and **q_n** have stabilized.

It is important to note that the condition that triggers a postponed process may not obtain when the process is finally executed. For example, suppose a signal **s** is updated to the value '1', causing the following postponed process to be triggered:

```
p : postponed process is
    . . .
begin
    . . .
    wait until s = '1';
    . . .       --s may not be '1'!!
end postponed process p;
```

Because the process is postponed, it is not executed immediately. Instead, some other process may execute, assigning '0' to **s** with delta delay. This assignment causes a delta cycle during which **s** is updated to '0'. When **p** is eventually executed, it proceeds with the statements immediately after the wait statement. However, despite the appearance of the condition in the wait statement, **s** does not have the value '1' at that point.

Since each postponed process waits until the last delta cycle at a given simulation time before executing, there may be several postponed processes triggered by different conditions in different delta cycles, all waiting to execute. Since the cycle in which the postponed processes execute must be the last delta cycle at the current simulation time, the postponed processes must not schedule transactions on signals with delta delay. If they did, they would cause another delta cycle at the current simulation time, meaning that the postponed processes should not have executed. The restriction is required to avoid this paradox.

In previous chapters, we described a number of concurrent statements that are equivalent to similar sequential statements encapsulated in processes. We can write postponed versions of each of these by including the keyword **postponed** at the beginning of the statement, as shown by the following syntax rules:

concurrent_procedure_call_statement ⇐
    〚 label : 〛
    〚 **postponed** 〛 *procedure*_name 〚 (*parameter*_association_list) 〛 ;
concurrent_assertion_statement ⇐
    〚 label : 〛
    〚 **postponed** 〛 **assert** *boolean*_expression
                  〚 **report** expression 〛 〚 **severity** expression 〛 ;
concurrent_signal_assignment_statement ⇐
    〚 label : 〛 〚 **postponed** 〛 conditional_signal_assignment
   | 〚 label : 〛 〚 **postponed** 〛 selected_signal_assignment

Inclusion of the keyword **postponed** simply makes the encapsulating process a postponed process. Thus, we can rewrite the postponed process in the Example on page 600 as

postponed assert now = 0 fs **or** q = **not** q_n
    report "implementation error: q /= not q_n";

VHDL-87

Postponed processes are not provided in VHDL-87.

21.4 Shared Variables

When we introduced variables in Chapter 2, we noted that they can only be declared in processes; hence only one process can access each variable. We have also seen variables declared in subprograms, in which case they are local to the invocation of the subprogram. The reason for these restrictions is to prevent indeterminate results arising from a number of processes accessing a variable in an indeterminate order during a simulation cycle. In some circumstances, however, it is desirable to allow a number of processes to share access to a variable. Either the fact of non-determinacy may be irrelevant, or the use of shared variables may allow a more concise and understandable model. VHDL provides a mechanism for sharing variables, shown by the full syntax rule for a variable declaration:

variable_declaration ⇐
    [**shared**] **variable** identifier { , ... } : subtype_indication
        [:= expression] ;

If we include the keyword **shared** in a variable declaration, the variables defined are called shared variables and can be accessed by more than one process. We can only declare shared variables in the places in a model where we cannot declare normal variables, namely, in entity declarations and architecture bodies, in block and generate statements and in packages. For example, we might include a shared variable declaration in an architecture body as follows:

architecture instrumented **of** controller **is**

    shared variable operation_count : natural := 0;

    . . .

begin

    . . .

end architecture instrumented;

The value of a shared variable can be used in an expression in the same way as that of a normal variable. It can be updated using variable assignment statements and can be associated as an actual variable with variable-class subprogram parameters.

The inclusion of shared variables in VHDL was a contentious issue in the development of the language, and mechanisms for using them are still under development at the time of writing this book. The initial language specification for shared variables does not define the behavior of concurrent reads and writes to shared variables in the same simulation cycle. For example, difficulties can arise if reads and writes are not performed as atomic operations. It is possible that one process may write a variable (even a scalar variable) in two separate stages, and that these stages may overlap with a read performed by some other process. Hence the read may not return a predictable value, nor even a legal value for the type of the variable. Similarly, concurrent writes by two processes may result in an indeterminate or illegal value being assigned to the variable. For these reasons, the language specification deems a model to be in error if it depends on the values of shared variables accessed by more than one process during any simulation cycle.

Provided we restrict access to a shared variable to one process per simulation cycle, modeling using shared variables is safe and deterministic and is similar to using signals to communicate between processes. Access to a shared variable is serialized in simulation time by the simulation algorithm, as simulation cycles occur in a strict non-overlapping order. One such use of shared variables is in instrumenting a model. A shared variable can be used by a number of processes to accumulate information about their collective behavior. While the same effect can be achieved using a signal to hold the data, it may be better to use a variable. Conceptually, a signal represents part of the structure of a design and serves to interconnect modules in the design. Instrumentation, on the other hand, is purely an artifact of the simulation, used to observe the behavior of the system under design. The use of shared variables makes this distinction clearer.

EXAMPLE

We can use shared variables to collect information about bus usage in a model of a multiprocessor computer system. Each processor, modeled as a distinct process, is granted access to a shared bus by an arbiter process. An outline of the architecture body for the multiprocessor is shown in Figure 21-6. The instrumentation in the model consists of three shared variables, one for each kind of bus operation (instruction fetch, read and write). When each processor needs to perform a bus operation, it requests the bus from the arbiter and waits until bus access is granted. It then increments one of the shared variables, proceeds with the operation, then relinquishes the bus. The logic of the model ensures that only one process can access a shared variable in any simulation cycle, since the arbiter will only grant bus access to one process at a time.

FIGURE 21-6

```
architecture instrumented of multiprocessor is
    shared variable bus_ifetch_count,
                    bus_read_count,
                    bus_write_count : natural := 0;
    signal bus_request, bus_grant : bit_vector(0 to num_processors – 1);
    ...        -- other signal declarations
begin
    processor_array :
    for processor_id in 0 to num_processors – 1 generate
        processor : process is
            ...
        begin
            ...        -- initialize
            loop
                bus_request(processor_id) <= '1';
                wait until bus_grant(processor_id) = '1';
                bus_ifetch_count := bus_ifetch_count + 1;
                ...        -- fetch instruction
                bus_request(processor_id) <= '0';
                ...        -- decode and execute instruction
            end loop;
        end process processor;
    end generate processor_array;

    arbiter : process is
    begin
        ...
    end process arbiter;

    ...        -- other processes for memory, etc
end architecture instrumented;
```

An outline of an instrumented architecture body for a multiprocessor.

Where the logic of a design does not lead naturally to serialized access to shared variables, we need to enforce serialization explicitly. Our goal is to enforce *mutual exclusion* between accesses to shared variables from different processes. Mutual exclusion means that each access is allowed to complete without interference from other processes. When one process accesses a shared variable, it excludes accesses from other processes until the first access is complete. While it is possible to encode mutual exclusion algorithms in the current version of VHDL, we do not investigate this possibility. Instead, we await announcement of appropriate language revisions by the IEEE committee responsible for the definition of VHDL. The interested reader should refer to the sources mentioned in the Preface for further information about these language revisions.

VHDL-87

Shared variables are not provided in VHDL-87.

Exercises

1. [❶ 21.2] Suppose we wish to associate an **out** mode port of type std_logic with a signal of type bit. Why can we not use the function To_bit as a conversion function in the association?

2. [❶ 21.2] Suppose we have a gate component declared as

   component nand2 **is**
       port (a, b : **in** std_logic; y_n : **out** std_logic);
   end component nand2;

   Write a component instantiation statement that instantiates the gate, with inputs connected to signals s1 and s2 and output connected to the signal s3. All of the signals are of type bit. Use conversion functions where required.

3. [❶ 21.4] Suppose we have a shared variable declared as follows in a package instrumentation:

   shared variable multiply_counter : natural := 0;

   We have two instances, m1 and m2, of a behavioral multiplier model that includes the statement

   instrumentation.multiply_counter := instrumentation.multiply_counter + 1;

   Show how the variable may be updated incorrectly if we allow the two instances to access the variable in the same simulation cycle.

4. [❷ 21.1] Develop a structural model of an SR-flipflop constructed from nor gates as shown below. Use **buffer** mode ports for q and q_n. Use **buffer** mode ports in the entity interface of the behavioral gate models as required.

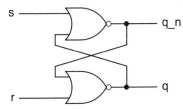

5. [❸ 21.2] Develop a behavioral model of a counter that counts from 0 to 255 with an output port of type **natural**. In a test bench, define and instantiate an eight-bit counter component. Write a configuration declaration for the test bench, binding the behavioral counter entity to the counter component instance. Use conversion functions in the binding indication as required. You may wish to use the conversion functions from the **bv_arithmetic** package described in Chapter 10. Note that a configuration declaration can use items, such as conversion functions, declared in separate packages.

6. [❸ 21.3] Exercise 17 in Chapter 11 describes a distributed priority arbiter for a shared-bus multiprocessor system. Each requester computes the minimum of all priorities. Develop a model of the minimization circuit that operates using delta delays. Include a number of instances of the minimizer in a test bench. Also include a process that verifies that the result priority is the minimum of all of the request priorities when the computation is complete.

Synthesis

Contributed by David W. Bishop
dbishop@vhdl.org

In this book we have discussed many aspects of VHDL and looked at examples of its use. One very strong motivation for using VHDL is hardware synthesis. The idea behind synthesis is to allow us to think of our design in abstract terms. We need not be so concerned about how best to implement the design in hardware logic—that is the job of the synthesis tool. It converts our abstract description into a structural description at a lower level of abstraction.

This appendix offers a brief, practical introduction to synthesis using VHDL. A full coverage of the topic warrants a complete book in its own right. We refer the interested reader to the growing number of books on hardware synthesis. References appear at the end of this book.

A.1 Synthesis Tools

We start our discussion of synthesis by comparing the capabilities of synthesis tools. They have much in common, but there are also significant differences between them. At the time of writing, there are several VHDL synthesis tools on the market, and more are about to become available. Each of these tools has its own set of commands, controls and constraint mechanisms. In order to avoid confusion, we discuss them only in general terms. Whenever there is a standard method for some task, we adopt it, even if the specification of the method is only at a preliminary stage.

Every synthesis tool must have a mechanism to constrain the output it generates. Most commonly these constraints govern speed and size; typically one is at the cost of the other. It is very important to constrain the synthesized circuit so that it will work in the final application.

Current synthesis tools work best on sequential logic; that is, they work best when synthesizing registers, not large numbers of gates. It is always best to work to a register boundary, since not only is that the logical place to break up a circuit, but it also provides an appropriate synthesis boundary. Synthesis tools typically use registers as synthesis boundaries by default.

Some of the improved synthesis tools that are becoming available can automatically place registers in a design if required. While this capability is often useful, it can sometimes be inappropriate. Sometimes we want to "hold the hand" of the synthesis tool, to make sure that it generates output in the way we want. The basic consideration is how close to the timing margins we are working. For example, if we have 20 microseconds to perform an addition, we may not care how efficient an adder is. But if we have 20 nanoseconds, we must constrain the circuit closely.

Another problem with VHDL synthesis is that there are several ways of expressing a design. For example, the four concurrent statements shown in Figure A-1 all describe an edge-triggered D-flipflop. Furthermore, different synthesis tools vary in their expectation for the expression represented by "**rising_edge(clk)**". For example, one widely used tool expects

clk'event **and** clk = '1'

and raises an error during analysis if the model contains any alternative expression. Other tools behave similarly. As an experiment, the author ran the statements in Figure A-1, with some modifications, through several synthesis tools. Only one tool was able to synthesize three out of the four statements; most could synthesize only two.

FIGURE A-1
_____

```
process (clk) is                    q <= d when rising_edge(clk) else
begin                                    q;
    if rising_edge(clk) then
        q <= d;
    end if;                          b : block ( rising_edge(clk)
end process;                                     and not clk'stable ) is
process is                          begin
begin                                   q <= guarded d;
    wait until rising_edge(clk);     end block b;
    q <= d;
end process;
```

Four equivalent models of a an edge-triggered D-flipflop.

From the point of view of expressing an algorithm, we might argue that the first of the statements in Figure A-1, a process statement with a sensitivity list, is the best. However, since not all synthesis tools are able to synthesize statements such as this, we must read the documentation for our particular tool before attempting to synthesize a design. We may need to modify our style of expression to conform to the tool's requirements.

A.2   A Synthesis Subset of VHDL

VHDL serves as a hardware description language for simulation as well as for synthesis. There are a number of constructs included in the language for simulation that cannot sensibly be synthesized into hardware. File operations, including **textio** operations, and assertion statements are good examples, since they imply the existence of a file system or a screen. Some synthesis tools allow us to specify that such operations and statements should be ignored. The specification may take the form of a command option or specially interpreted comments embedded in the model. If we are interested in portability, we should confine such operations and statements to test benches and leave them out of synthesizable sections of a model.

There are a number of VHDL constructs that are potentially synthesizable, but are not handled correctly by some synthesis tools. If we use these constructs, the synthesized hardware will produce different results from the simulated mode. For example, suppose we wish to describe a registered comparator with two data inputs, **a** and **b**, a clock input, **clk**, and a data output, **q**. The device stores the result of comparing **a** and **b** on each rising edge of **clk**. A first attempt at writing the model is shown at the left of Figure A-2. When we simulate the device, it functions correctly. Each time there is a change in **clk**, the process resumes and compares **a** and **b**. If the change in **clk** is a rising edge, the result of the comparison is assigned to the output.

FIGURE A-2

```
process (clk) is                          process (clk) is
    variable d : std_ulogic;              begin
begin                                         if rising_edge(clk) then
    if a = b then                                 if a = b then
        d := '1';                                     q <= '1';
    else                                          else
        d := '0';                                     q <= '0';
    end if;                                        end if;
    if rising_edge(clk) then               end if;
        q <= d;                        end process;
    end if;
end process;
```

Two alternate models of a registered comparator. The model on the left may not synthesize correctly, whereas the model on the right will.

When we synthesize the device from this model, we must take account of the fact that the process is resumed on both rising and falling edges of **clk**. The variable **d** is updated in both cases and is hence a function of **clk**. Some synthesis tools treat this as illegal and fail to synthesize the device. Others proceed to synthesize the device, but may not produce a correct circuit. A better description of the device is shown on the right of Figure A-2. This model accurately reflects our intention that the comparison is performed only on rising edges of **clk**. The process does not contain any unnecessary implied state.

EVSWG Synthesis Subsets

The European VHDL Synthesis Working Group is currently developing a set of guidelines for model developers aimed at achieving synthesis portability across synthesis tools from different vendors. The guidelines describe a subset of VHDL and a corresponding description style. The initial "level-0" subset aims at portability across the currently available tools. As tools evolve and are able to synthesize more complex VHDL descriptions, the EVSWG plans to develop less constrained subsets, called "level-1", "level-2" and so forth. We refer the interested reader to [3] for details of the current level-0 subset.

A.3   Tricks and Hints

In the following section, we discuss two useful approaches to writing synthesizable models: using IEEE Standard 1164 logic types and design partitioning.

Using IEEE Standard 1164 Logic Types

In Chapter 11 we introduced the IEEE standard-logic package, std_logic_1164. The package defines the unresolved type **std_ulogic** and the resolved subtype **std_logic**. If we are using tristate or bidirectional signals, we must use the **std_logic** type. Although the IEEE standard recommends use of **std_logic** for all signals, we can use **std_ulogic** if we wish to avoid inadvertently connecting two output ports to the one signal. If we inadvertently name one signal as the output from two distinct circuits, a synthesis tool will simply connect the outputs together. This may be disastrous in some logic families.

The vector versions of the standard-logic types are **std_ulogic_vector** and **std_logic_vector**. We cannot connect a port of type **std_ulogic_vector** to a signal of type **std_logic_vector**, as the two types are distinct, even though the element type of **std_logic_vector** is a subtype of the element type of **std_ulogic_vector**. However, we can use the conversion functions provided by the standard-logic package to work around the type difference. For example, given signals **sulv** and **slv** of the unresolved and resolved vector types, respectively, we can write the following assignments:

```
sulv <= To_stdulogicvector ( slv );

slv <= To_stdlogicvector ( sulv );
```

A synthesis tool treats both of these functions as feed-through wires, with no logic synthesized.

As far as a synthesis tool is concerned, the standard-logic values 'U', 'W' and 'X' all mean an unknown logic state. Even if our model checks for their occurrence, a synthesis tool will ignore them. It is best that code to be synthesized contain no checking for unknowns. If we need such tests, we should put them in the simulation test bench.

The 'Z', 'H' and 'L' standard-logic values are used by synthesis tools to imply tristate buffers, pull-ups and pull-downs. As an input to a circuit, 'H' and 'L' are treated as a '1' and '0', respectively, and 'Z' is treated as an unknown value. As an output from a synthesized circuit, 'Z' is the best way to imply a tristate buffer. For example:

```
y <= a when ena = '1' else
     'Z';
```

Occasionally we want to "pull up" the output of a tristate buffer, to provide a default value on the output signal. This may be necessary if the signal must have a valid value when it is not driven by any of the connected tristate buffers. In hardware, we would connect a resistor tied to the power supply to the output of the tristate buffer. The 'H' and 'L' standard-logic values can be used to imply this function, for example:

```
y <= a when ena = '1' else
     'H';
```

Using 'H' implies a pull-up. If we wish to have a "pull-down," we replace 'H' with 'L'.

The standard-logic value '–' is useful if supported by a synthesis tool. The value represents a "don't care" condition, which is useful in mapping logic. For example, the signal assignment

```
y <= a when x = '1' else
     b when s = '1' else
     '–';
```

expresses our intention that we don't care what value is assigned to the output y when s and x are both '0'.

Design Partitioning

One of the benefits of synthesis tools is that they can optimize the hardware synthesized from a design. They can evaluate several alternative implementations of the same circuit in order to get the best result, according to the specified constraints. Sometimes this is what we want the tool to do. At other times, if we already have a structure in mind, we don't want the tool to try alternatives. In such cases, we can partition our design into sections corresponding to our block diagram and synthesize each section separately. One approach to doing this is to use a schematic capture tool to enter the block diagram, generate a VHDL structural description with empty architecture bodies for each block and then fill in the behavior for each architecture body.

One important thing to remember when partitioning a VHDL design targeted for synthesis is that a synthesis tool logically partitions a circuit at register boundaries. Thus, if we have two separately synthesized VHDL entities, which communicate with each other without registers at the boundaries, the synthesis tool cannot combine and optimize the logic across the interface. This prevents us from achieving the best circuit that the synthesis tool can potentially create.

If our design contains a very long architecture body, synthesis of the design may be beyond the capabilities of a synthesis tool. We can deal with this by partitioning the architecture body into sub-blocks, either by using separate entity/architecture pairs for each sub-block or by using VHDL block statements. Many synthesis tools treat block statements as logical partitions, each of which can be separately synthesized.

A.4 The Draft P1076.3 Standard Synthesis Package

Every synthesis tool has its own set of VHDL utility packages that include operations commonly used in hardware models. The synthesis tool recognizes use of these operations and generates optimized output. Thus the provision of the packages not only helps us write our model but also allows us to make best use of the capabilities of the synthesis tool.

The disadvantage of using these packages is that our model is less likely to be portable to other synthesis tools. In response to this problem, several standards are being developed and adopted across the hardware synthesis industry. The first such standard to be completed was the IEEE Standard 1164 multivalued logic package.

At the time of writing, IEEE Standard 1076.3 is under development. This standard defines synthesis packages for VHDL, including packages that deal with binary numeric types. The package numeric_std represents binary digits of a number with std_logic values. The IEEE 1076.3 draft standard also includes an analogous package that represents binary digits using bit values. Some of the internal functionality of the packages may change in the adopted version of the standard, but the interfaces described here will be retained.

The numeric_std package defines two subtypes to represent binary numeric values:

```
type unsigned is array ( natural range <> ) of std_logic;
type signed is array ( natural range <> ) of std_logic;
```

These two types are used to define arithmetic operations. The first is used for unsigned arithmetic (allowing only non-negative numbers), whereas the second is used for signed arithmetic (allowing negative numbers). The package contains overloaded versions of several VHDL operators, including "+", "–", "=", that perform arithmetic operations on values of these types. It also provides conversion functions to convert between integer, unsigned and signed representations of numbers. For example, given the signals

```
signal a: integer := 0;
signal b: signed (4 downto 0);
```

we can perform the following conversion:

```
b <= To_signed ( a, b'length );
```

EXAMPLE

We can define an entity that performs signed arithmetic on integer values. It takes two non-negative numbers, adds them together and then subtracts from them another non-negative number. The entity declaration is shown in Figure A-3. The architecture body implements the arithmetic operations using the operations from the numeric_std package.

FIGURE A-3

```
library ieee;  use ieee.std_logic_1164.all;

entity add_and_sub is
    port ( a, b, c : in natural;
           y : out natural;
           ovf : out std_ulogic );
end entity add_and_sub;
```

```
library ieee;  use ieee.numeric_std.all;

architecture rtl of add_and_sub is
    signal stage2, stage3 : unsigned ( 8 downto 0 );
begin
    stage2 <= To_unsigned(a, 9) + to_unsigned(b, 9);    -- "+" from numeric_std
    stage3 <= stage2 - c;                               -- "-" from numeric_std
    y <= To_integer(stage3) ;
    ovf <= stage3(8);
end rtl;
```

An arithmetic module that uses overloaded operators from the numeric_std *package.*

The standard numeric packages also provide overloaded versions of the relational operators. These operators differ from the predefined relational operators on vectors, which simply perform left-to-right lexical comparison. The numeric operators compare the numeric values represented by the vectors. There is, however, an additional operation provided in the numeric_std package that compares the standard-logic elements of a vector. The std_match tests whether two vectors contain the same pattern of 0 and 1 values (irrespective of strength). It also ignores elements in one vector corresponding to a '–' (don't care) element in the other vector. For example, the comparison

    if std_match (b, "0–000") **then**
       . . .

tests whether b contains all '0' or 'L' values, except in the second position.

A.5   Examples—"Doing It Right"

In this section we present a series of examples that show a modeling style that can be correctly synthesized. We start with a simple gate, for example, an or gate:

    y <= a **or** b;

This is the easiest circuit to synthesize. We must remember that the predefined logical functions are overloaded for array signals. They will synthesize to an array of gates.
    Next, we show a simple multiplexer:

    y <= a **when** x = '1' **else**
        b;

Note that no process or block statement is necessary; we can simply use a concurrent signal assignment. This same statement will work just as well with array signals as it does with scalar signals. A tristate buffer, described earlier on page 610, is just a variation of the multiplexer:

```
ts <= a when x = '1' else
      'Z';
```

Note that if the library to which we are synthesizing does not include tristate buffers, the synthesizer will automatically generate a multiplexer. To extend the statement to operate with an array signal, we simply replace the 'Z' with "(others => 'Z')".

Next, Figure A-4 shows a flipflop, the most common sequential circuit element. The statements imply a flipflop with inverting and non-inverting outputs and an active high reset. We can extend the functionality of this example by placing a multiplexer in front of the flipflop, as shown in Figure A-5. Note that a combination of the previous multiplexer and flipflop examples would perform the same function. However, this example shows how we can combine the logic with the register. We can extend the example further to place more logic into the register. For example, we can specify a counter as shown in Figure A-6.

FIGURE A-4

```
ff1 : process (reset, clk) is
begin
    if reset = '1' then
        q <= '0';
    elsif rising_edge(clk) then
        q <= d;
    end if;
end process ff1;

q_n <= not q;
```

Statements representing a simple flipflop.

FIGURE A-5

```
ff2 : process (reset, clk) is
begin
    if reset = '1' then
        q <= '0';
    elsif rising_edge(clk) then
        if x = '1' then
            q <= a;
        else
            q <= b;
        end if;
    end if;
end process ff2;
```

The flipflop description, extended to include a multiplexer.

FIGURE A-6

```
constant terminal_count : integer := 2**6 – 1;
subtype counter_range is integer range 0 to terminal_count;
signal count : counter_range;
. . .
counter6 : process (reset, clk)
begin
    if reset = '0' then
        count <= 0;
    elsif rising_edge(clk) then
        if count < terminal_count then
            count <= count + 1;
        else
            count <= 0;
        end if;
    end if;
end process counter6;
```

The flipflop description, extended to form a counter.

Input/output buffers are probably one of the most difficult things to synthesize. Some synthesis vendors actually recommend that we hand-instantiate buffers to get the specific kind we want. The description shown in Figure A-7 creates a bidirectional buffer, but we should check our synthesis tool documentation or the synthesized circuit to verify the kind of buffer implied.

FIGURE A-7

```
library ieee;  use ieee.std_logic_1164.all;
entity bidir_buffer is
    port ( bidir : inout std_logic;
           ena : in std_ulogic;
           going_out : in std_ulogic;
           coming_in : out std_ulogic );
end entity bidir_buffer;

_____

architecture behavior of bidir_buffer is
begin
    bidir <= going_out when ena = '1' else
             'Z';
    coming_in <= bidir;
end architecture behavior;
```

An entity declaration and an architecture body for a bidirectional buffer.

Note that if we wish to specify a bidirectional buffer for an array signal, we must use the standard-logic conversion functions in the assignments:

```
constant hi_impedance : std_logic_vector(bidir'range) := (others => 'Z');
. . .
bidir <= To_stdlogicvector(going_out) when ena = '1' else
         hi_impedance;
coming_in <= To_stdulogicvector(bidir);
```

Finite-State Machines

We can view state equations describing finite-state machines as one of the first primitive hardware description languages. Because of their long history, synthesis techniques for state machines are well developed. A typical VHDL model for a state machine is shown in Figure A-8. Note that there are two process statements, one feeding the other. Thus, the register that is holding the current state is independent of logic that determines the next state and the outputs. This does not have to be the case, but current synthesis tools work better with the state machine specified in this way.

FIGURE A-8
_____

```
architecture rtl of entname is
    type state_type is (s0, s1, s2, s3);
    signal state, next_state : state_type;
    signal con1, con2, con3 : std_ulogic;
    signal out1, out2 : std_ulogic;
    signal clk, reset : std_ulogic;
    . . .
begin
    state_logic : process (state, con1, con2, con3) is
    begin
        case state is
            when s0 =>
                out1 <= '0';
                out2 <= '0';
                next_state <= s1;
            when s1 =>
                out1 <= '1';
                if con1 = '1' then
                    next_state <= s2;
                else
                    next_state <= s1;
                end if;
            when s2 =>
                out2 <= '1';
                next_state <= s3;
            when s3 =>
                if con2 = '0' then
                    next_state <= s3;
                elsif con3 = '0' then
                    out1 <= '0';
                    next_state <= s2;
                else
```

```
                              next_state <= s1;
                       end if;
                 end case;
           end process state_logic;

           state_register : process (clk, reset) is
           begin
                 if reset = '0' then
                       state <= s0;
                 elsif rising_edge(clk) then
                       state <= next_state;
                 end if;
           end process state_register;

           . . .

       end architecture rtl;
```

An outline of an architecture body containing a finite-state machine. The process state_logic *represents the combinatorial logic that determines the next state. The process* state_register *represents the storage for the state.*

The next problem is to encode the state. In the above example we have four states, which could be encoded using two, three or four bits. The best encoding depends on the synthesis target library, the required speed of the circuit and the circuit area available.

We can force the above state machine to use a *one hot* state encoding, in which there is one bit for each state, by modifying the state definition:

```
subtype state_type is std_ulogic_vector(3 downto 0);
constant s0 : state_type := "0001";
constant s1 : state_type := "0010";
constant s2 : state_type := "0100";
constant s3 : state_type := "1000";
```

A.6 Examples—"Doing It Wrong"

In this section we look at some examples of common mistakes made by designers writing models for synthesis. We start with the following VHDL model:

```
y <= a + b + c + d;
```

A synthesis tool will create an adder for **a** and **b**, then add the result to **c**, and then add that result to **d**. The generated circuit consists of a three-stage adder with a long propagation delay from the **a** and **b** inputs to the output. We can force the synthesizer to create a two-stage circuit by rewriting the model as follows:

```
y <= ( a + b ) + ( c + d );
```

This form tells the synthesis tool to add **a** and **b** in one adder, add **c** and **d** in another adder, then add the result together. Note that the same argument applies to gates, not just adders. For example:

```
y <= a or b or c or d;
```

can be much better synthesized if we rewrite it as

y <= (a **or** b) **or** (c **or** d);

When grouping logic in this way, it is important to remember operator associativity. For example, we may not write

y <= a **or** b **or** c **and** d;

since it is syntactically incorrect. Instead, we should write

y <= (a **or** b) **or** (c **and** d);

Another mistake to avoid is putting too much in a process statement. Typically we use process statements for flipflop and state machine synthesis, and concurrent signal assignment statements for other parts of the circuit. However, if we do add logic to a process statement, we must be very careful about the signals we include in the sensitivity list. Any process that contains synchronous logic (i.e., flipflops) should only have a clock, and perhaps a reset, in its sensitivity list. On the other hand, a process statement that contains asynchronous logic (i.e., gates) should include all the signals that are used as inputs to the process in your sensitivity list. The sensitivity list should not include any of the output signals.

As an example, consider the process shown in Figure A-9, representing synchronous logic and including a data input in the sensitivity list. Assume that there is a combinatorial feedback path from **odat** to **data**, modeled with zero propagation delay. This is a case in which the synthesized circuit may produce different results from the simulation (assuming that a tool can indeed synthesize the circuit). Note that the output **odat** changes not only on the clock but also on a change in the **data** signal. Because of the way delta delays work in VHDL, we see the expected behavior when we simulate the circuit. However, in reality, no circuit has zero delay. The synthesized circuit will produce a "glitch" on the output when **data** changes to zero. It would be better to write the model as shown in Figure A-10. This process only causes the output to be updated when the reset input is activated or when there is a rising clock edge. It conforms to the guidelines we suggested in the previous section: the logic for detecting a zero input is in front of the flipflop rather than after it.

FIGURE A-9

```
wrong_way : process ( clk25M, resetl, data )
begin
    if resetl = '0' then
        odat <= B"0000_0000";
    elsif rising_edge(clk25M) then
        odat <= data;
    elsif data = B"0000_0000" then
        odat <= B"0000_0001";
    end if;
end process wrong_way;
```

A process that includes inappropriate signals in its sensitivity list.

```
right_way : process ( clk25M, resetl )
begin
    if resetl = '0' then
        odat <= B"0000_0000";
    elsif rising_edge(clk25M) then
        if data = B"0000_0000" then
            odat <= B"0000_0001";
        else
            odat <= data;
        end if;
    end if;
end process right_way;
```

The process rewritten to conform with our synthesis guidelines.

A.7   Hand-Instantiation—"Doing It the Hard Way"

Occasionally we want to "go around" the synthesis tool to use a particular cell or macro in our target library. While this ties the model to one synthesis library, and usually to one synthesis tool, occasionally it is the only way to avoid the limitations of synthesis. Some cells that might warrant instantiation using this approach are

- a specific memory cell or ROM;
- a predesigned macro cell, such as an FFT or a microprocessor;
- a specific input/output cell; and
- a counter.

Current synthesis tools do not synthesize counters well. Typically they generate an adder with one input tied to '1' and the output connected to a register. If we need a fast counter, for example, for a clock divider, we can declare a component representing the counter cell and instantiate it in the design with a component instantiation statement.

Another component that synthesis tools do not synthesize well is memory. Typically they generate an array of D-flipflops. As an example of "going around" a tool, let us consider the Xilinx 4000 family of field-programmable gate arrays (FPGAs). These circuits are based on a static RAM cell. To include RAM in our design, we first create a component for the FPGA macro cell. A component declaration for the Xilinx 4000 RAM16X1 cell can be written as shown at the top of Figure A-11. We then use a generate statement to instantiate a number of these cells, creating our RAM array, as shown at the bottom of Figure A-11.

```
component RAM16x1 is
    port ( \a<0>\, \a<1>\, \a<2>\, \a<3>\ : in std_ulogic;
            \d\, \we\ : in std_ulogic;
            \o\ : out std_ulogic );
end component RAM16x1;
. . .
g1 : for i in 0 to 15 generate
    rama : component RAM16x1
        port map ( \a<0>\ => address(0),
                    \a<1>\ => address(1),
                    \a<2>\ => address(2),
                    \a<3>\ => address(3),
                    \d\ => raminp ( i ),
                    \we\ => write_enable,
                    \o\ => ramout ( i ) );
end generate g1;
```

A component declaration and instantiation used to specify a RAM array.

The Predefined Package Standard

The predefined types, subtypes and functions of VHDL are defined in a package called **standard**, stored in the library **std**. Each design unit in a design is automatically preceded by the following context clause:

    library std, work; **use** std.standard.**all**;

so the predefined items are directly visible in the design. The package **standard** is listed here. The comments indicate which operators are implicitly defined for each explicitly defined type. These operators are also automatically made visible in design units. The types *universal_integer* and *universal_real* are anonymous types. They cannot be referred to explicitly.

    package standard **is**

        type boolean **is** (false, true);

            −− implicitly declared for boolean operands:
            −− ”and”, ”or”, ”nand”, ”nor”, ”xor”, ”xnor”, ”not” return boolean
            −− ”=”, ”/=”, ”<”, ”<=”, ”>”, ”>=” return boolean

        type bit **is** (’0’, ’1’);

            −− implicitly declared for bit operands:
            −− ”and”, ”or”, ”nand”, ”nor”, ”xor”, ”xnor”, ”not” return bit
            −− ”=”, ”/=”, ”<”, ”<=”, ”>”, ”>=” return boolean

type character **is** (
nul,	soh,	stx,	etx,	eot,	enq,	ack,	bel,
bs,	ht,	lf,	vt,	ff,	cr,	so,	si,
dle,	dc1,	dc2,	dc3,	dc4,	nak,	syn,	etb,
can,	em,	sub,	esc,	fsp,	gsp,	rsp,	usp,
' ',	'!',	'"',	'#',	'$',	'%',	'&',	''',
'(',	')',	'*',	'+',	',',	'–',	'.',	'/',
'0',	'1',	'2',	'3',	'4',	'5',	'6',	'7',
'8',	'9',	':',	';',	'<',	'=',	'>',	'?',
'@',	'A',	'B',	'C',	'D',	'E',	'F',	'G',
'H',	'I',	'J',	'K',	'L',	'M',	'N',	'O',
'P',	'Q',	'R',	'S',	'T',	'U',	'V',	'W',
'X',	'Y',	'Z',	'[',	'\',	']',	'^',	'_',
'`',	'a',	'b',	'c',	'd',	'e',	'f',	'g',
'h',	'i',	'j',	'k',	'l',	'm',	'n',	'o',
'p',	'q',	'r',	's',	't',	'u',	'v',	'w',
'x',	'y',	'z',	'{',	'|',	'}',	'~',	del
c128,	c129,	c130,	c131,	c132,	c133,	c134,	c135,
c136,	c137,	c138,	c139,	c140,	c141,	c142,	c143,
c144,	c145,	c146,	c147,	c148,	c149,	c150,	c151,
c152,	c153,	c154,	c155,	c156,	c157,	c158,	c159,
' ',	'i',	'¢',	'£',	'¤',	'¥',	'¦',	'§'
'¨',	'©',	'ª',	'«',	'¬',	'',	'®',	'¯'
'°',	'±',	'²',	'³',	'´',	'µ',	'¶',	'·',
' ',	'¹',	'º',	'»',	'¼',	'½',	'¾',	'¿',
'À',	'Á',	'Â',	'Ã',	'Ä',	'Å',	'Æ',	'Ç',
'È',	'É',	'Ê',	'Ë',	'Ì',	'Í',	'Î',	'Ï',
'Ð',	'Ñ',	'Ò',	'Ó',	'Ô',	'Õ',	'Ö',	'×',
'Ø',	'Ù',	'Ú',	'Û',	'Ü',	'Ý',	'Þ',	'ß',
'à',	'á',	'â',	'ã',	'ä',	'å',	'æ',	'ç',
'è',	'é',	'ê',	'ë',	'ì',	'í',	'î',	'ï',
'ð',	'ñ',	'ò',	'ó',	'ô',	'õ',	'ö',	'÷',
'ø',	'ù',	'ú',	'û',	'ü',	'ý',	'þ',	'ÿ');

— implicitly declared for character operands:
— "=", "/=", "<", "<=", ">", ">=" return boolean

type severity_level **is** (note, warning, error, failure);

— implicitly declared for severity_level operands:
— "=", "/=", "<", "<=", ">", ">=" return boolean

type *universal_integer* **is range** *implementation defined*;

— implicitly declared for universal integer operands:
— "=", "/=", "<", "<=", ">", ">=" return boolean
— "**", "*", "/", "+", "–", "abs", "rem", "mod" return universal integer

type *universal_real* **is range** *implementation defined*;

— implicitly declared for universal real operands:
— "=", "/=", "<", "<=", ">", ">=" return boolean
— "**", "*", "/", "+", "–", "abs" return universal real

type integer **is range** *implementation defined*;

          −− implicitly declared for integer operands:
          −− "=", "/=", "<", "<=", ">", ">=" return boolean
          −− "**", "*", "/", "+", "−", "abs", "rem", "mod" return integer

subtype natural **is** integer **range** 0 **to** integer'high;
subtype positive **is** integer **range** 1 **to** integer'high;

type real **is range** *implementation defined*;

          −− implicitly declared for real operands:
          −− "=", "/=", "<", "<=", ">", ">=" return boolean
          −− "**", "*", "/", "+", "−", "abs" return real

type time **is range** *implementation defined*
    units
        fs;
        ps = 1000 fs;
        ns = 1000 ps;
        us = 1000 ns;
        ms = 1000 us;
        sec = 1000 ms;
        min = 60 sec;
        hr = 60 min;
    end units;

          −− implicitly declared for time operands:
          −− "=", "/=", "<", "<=", ">", ">=" return boolean
          −− "*", "+", "−", "abs" return time
          −− "/" return time or universal integer

subtype delay_length **is** time **range** 0 fs **to** time'high;

impure function now **return** delay_length;

type string **is array** (positive **range** <>) **of** character;

          −− implicitly declared for string operands:
          −− "=", "/=", "<", "<=", ">", ">=" return boolean
          −− "&" return string

type bit_vector **is array** (natural **range** <>) **of** bit;

          −− implicitly declared for bit_vector operands:
          −− "and", "or", "nand", "nor", "xor", "xnor", "not" return bit_vector
          −− "sll", "srl", "sla", "sra", "rol", "ror" return bit_vector
          −− "=", "/=", "<", "<=", ">", ">=" return boolean
          −− "&" return bit_vector

type file_open_kind **is** (read_mode, write_mode, append_mode);

          −− implicitly declared for file_open_kind operands:
          −− "=", "/=", "<", "<=", ">", ">=" return boolean

type file_open_status **is** (open_ok, status_error,
                          name_error, mode_error);

          −− implicitly declared for file_open_status operands:
          −− "=", "/=", "<", "<=", ">", ">=" return boolean

attribute foreign : string;

end package standard;

VHDL-87

The following items are not included in standard in VHDL-87: the types file_open_kind and file_open_status; the subtype delay_length; the attribute foreign; the operators **xnor**, **sll**, **srl**, **sla**, **sra**, **rol** and **ror**. The result time of the function now is time. The type character includes only the first 128 values, corresponding to the ASCII character set.

C

IEEE Standard 1164

The IEEE Standard 1164 defines types, operators and functions for detailed modeling of data in a design. It is based on a multivalued logic type, with three states (zero, one and unknown) and three driving strengths (forcing, weak and high-impedance). Forcing strength represents an active driver, such as a transistor or switch connected to a source with approximately zero impedance. Weak strength represents a resistive driver, such as a pull-up resistor or a pass transistor. High-impedance strength represents a driver that is turned off. A value driven with forcing strength dominates a value driven with weak strength, and both dominate a high-impedance driver. This multivalued logic system is augmented with values representing an uninitialized state and a "don't care" state.

The standard-logic package declaration is shown here. The examples in this book show how the operations defined in the package are used. The IEEE standard also includes a package body defining the detailed meaning of each of the operators and functions. However, simulator vendors are allowed to substitute accelerated implementations of the package rather than compiling the package body into a simulation. The IEEE standard requires the package to be in a resource library named **ieee**.

package std_logic_1164 **is**

```
    ----------------------------------------------------------------
    -- logic state system  (unresolved)
    ----------------------------------------------------------------
    type std_ulogic is ( 'U',     -- Uninitialized
                         'X',     -- Forcing  Unknown
                         '0',     -- Forcing  0
                         '1',     -- Forcing  1
                         'Z',     -- High Impedance
                         'W',     -- Weak    Unknown
                         'L',     -- Weak    0
                         'H',     -- Weak    1
                         '-'      -- Don't care
                       );
```

```
---------------------------------------------------------------
-- unconstrained array of std_ulogic for use with the resolution function
---------------------------------------------------------------

type std_ulogic_vector is array ( natural range <> ) of std_ulogic;

---------------------------------------------------------------
-- resolution function
---------------------------------------------------------------

function resolved ( s : std_ulogic_vector ) return std_ulogic;

---------------------------------------------------------------
-- *** industry standard logic type ***
---------------------------------------------------------------

subtype std_logic is resolved std_ulogic;

---------------------------------------------------------------
-- unconstrained array of std_logic for use in declaring signal arrays
---------------------------------------------------------------

type std_logic_vector is array ( natural range <> ) of std_logic;

---------------------------------------------------------------
-- common subtypes
---------------------------------------------------------------

subtype X01    is resolved std_ulogic range 'X' to '1';    -- ('X','0','1')
subtype X01Z   is resolved std_ulogic range 'X' to 'Z';    -- ('X','0','1','Z')
subtype UX01   is resolved std_ulogic range 'U' to '1';    -- ('U','X','0','1')
subtype UX01Z  is resolved std_ulogic range 'U' to 'Z';    -- ('U','X','0','1','Z')

---------------------------------------------------------------
-- overloaded logical operators
---------------------------------------------------------------

function "and"  ( l : std_ulogic; r : std_ulogic ) return UX01;
function "nand" ( l : std_ulogic; r : std_ulogic ) return UX01;
function "or"   ( l : std_ulogic; r : std_ulogic ) return UX01;
function "nor"  ( l : std_ulogic; r : std_ulogic ) return UX01;
function "xor"  ( l : std_ulogic; r : std_ulogic ) return UX01;
function "xnor" ( l : std_ulogic; r : std_ulogic ) return UX01;
function "not"  ( l : std_ulogic                 ) return UX01;

---------------------------------------------------------------
-- vectorized overloaded logical operators
---------------------------------------------------------------

function "and"  ( l, r : std_logic_vector  ) return std_logic_vector;
function "and"  ( l, r : std_ulogic_vector ) return std_ulogic_vector;

function "nand" ( l, r : std_logic_vector  ) return std_logic_vector;
function "nand" ( l, r : std_ulogic_vector ) return std_ulogic_vector;

function "or"   ( l, r : std_logic_vector  ) return std_logic_vector;
function "or"   ( l, r : std_ulogic_vector ) return std_ulogic_vector;

function "nor"  ( l, r : std_logic_vector  ) return std_logic_vector;
function "nor"  ( l, r : std_ulogic_vector ) return std_ulogic_vector;
```

```
function "xor"    ( l, r : std_logic_vector  ) return std_logic_vector;
function "xor"    ( l, r : std_ulogic_vector ) return std_ulogic_vector;

function "xnor"   ( l, r : std_logic_vector  ) return std_logic_vector;
function "xnor"   ( l, r : std_ulogic_vector ) return std_ulogic_vector;

function "not"    ( l : std_logic_vector    ) return std_logic_vector;
function "not"    ( l : std_ulogic_vector   ) return std_ulogic_vector;
```

-- *conversion functions*

```
function To_bit        ( s : std_ulogic;          xmap : bit := '0' ) return bit;
function To_bitvector  ( s : std_logic_vector ; xmap : bit := '0' ) return bit_vector;
function To_bitvector  ( s : std_ulogic_vector;xmap : bit := '0' ) return bit_vector;

function To_StdULogic        ( b : bit                   ) return std_ulogic;
function To_StdLogicVector   ( b : bit_vector            ) return std_logic_vector;
function To_StdLogicVector   ( s : std_ulogic_vector ) return std_logic_vector;
function To_StdULogicVector  ( b : bit_vector            ) return std_ulogic_vector;
function To_StdULogicVector  ( s : std_logic_vector  ) return std_ulogic_vector;
```

-- *strength strippers and type convertors*

```
function To_X01 ( s : std_logic_vector  ) return std_logic_vector;
function To_X01 ( s : std_ulogic_vector ) return std_ulogic_vector;
function To_X01 ( s : std_ulogic        ) return X01;
function To_X01 ( b : bit_vector        ) return std_logic_vector;
function To_X01 ( b : bit_vector        ) return std_ulogic_vector;
function To_X01 ( b : bit               ) return X01;

function To_X01Z ( s : std_logic_vector  ) return std_logic_vector;
function To_X01Z ( s : std_ulogic_vector ) return std_ulogic_vector;
function To_X01Z ( s : std_ulogic        ) return X01Z;
function To_X01Z ( b : bit_vector        ) return std_logic_vector;
function To_X01Z ( b : bit_vector        ) return std_ulogic_vector;
function To_X01Z ( b : bit               ) return X01Z;

function To_UX01 ( s : std_logic_vector  ) return std_logic_vector;
function To_UX01 ( s : std_ulogic_vector ) return std_ulogic_vector;
function To_UX01 ( s : std_ulogic        ) return UX01;
function To_UX01 ( b : bit_vector        ) return std_logic_vector;
function To_UX01 ( b : bit_vector        ) return std_ulogic_vector;
function To_UX01 ( b : bit               ) return UX01;
```

-- *edge detection*

```
function rising_edge ( signal s : std_ulogic ) return boolean;
function falling_edge ( signal s : std_ulogic ) return boolean;
```

```
---------------------------------------------------------
-- object contains an unknown
---------------------------------------------------------
    function Is_X ( s : std_ulogic_vector ) return  boolean;
    function Is_X ( s : std_logic_vector  ) return  boolean;
    function Is_X ( s : std_ulogic        ) return  boolean;
end std_logic_1164;
```

VHDL-87

The overloaded versions of the **xnor** operator are not included in the VHDL-87 version of the standard-logic package.

D

Related Standards

VHDL, as a hardware description language, is a fundamental tool for designing electronic circuits and systems. However, it does not stand alone. It must be part of a collection of methodologies, tools and utilities that form a complete computer-aided engineering (CAE) environment. The IEEE Design Automation Standards Committee (DASC) and other groups are actively developing standards that specify these other components of the CAE suite. In this appendix, we briefly introduce those standards that have been completed or are in progress.

The IEEE practice is to designate authorized standards development projects that are in progress with the letter 'P' followed by the standard number. Several of the projects are in this state at the time of writing. When their development work is complete and the standard is passed, the 'P' will be dropped to form the official standard number.

D.1 IEEE Std. 1029.1: WAVES

The *IEEE Standard for Waveform and Vector Exchange* (WAVES) specifies a use of VHDL to exchange stimulus/response test vector information between simulation and test environments. Because it relies purely on VHDL, it is a non-proprietary format.

A WAVES *dataset* is a collection of VHDL packages, including a *waveform generator procedure* that produces a stream of stimulus or expected response values (a *waveform)* for a unit under test. The procedure draws upon the resources of a number of predefined WAVES packages to specify the values in the waveform and the timing relationships between waveform elements. The VHDL packages in a WAVES dataset may be augmented with external files containing data in a non-VHDL format. The waveform generator procedure may read data from these files to construct the waveform. The standard defines two levels of WAVES datasets. In a Level 2 dataset, most of the sequential programming facilities are available for use in the waveform generator procedure. Thus, the procedure can perform complex algorithms to construct the waveform. In a Level 1 dataset, the kinds of computations that can be performed by the procedure are more constrained.

One of the difficulties with WAVES is that it simply defines a format for describing a waveform generator. It does not indicate how a generator is to be incorporated into a VHDL test bench to test operation of a simulation model. To address this problem, a group at Rome Laboratories of the United States Air Force has developed a WAVES-VHDL Interface. It consists of a number of packages that provide means for a VHDL test bench to connect a WAVES waveform to a unit under test, and to compare whether the responses generated by the unit under test match the expected responses. Information about the packages, sample implementations and examples of use can be found in a repository on the VIIS server, mentioned in the Preface.

D.2 IEEE P1076a: Shared Variables

In Chapter 21, we described the shared-variable facility defined by IEEE Standard 1076-1993 for VHDL-93. Shared variables were included in the language in response to user community input. However, the language design working group was not able to resolve satisfactorily the problem of synchronization of access to shared variables within a given delta cycle. Rather than delay revision of the language specification, the group decided to leave the synchronization issue undefined for VHDL-93. The P1076a Working Group is developing a revision to the language definition to specify a synchronization mechanism.

At the time of writing, the proposed mechanism is based on the idea of a *monitor*. This is a language construct that encapsulates a shared variable with access operations (procedures and functions). The only way to access the shared variable is via the operations. Furthermore, only one process may execute a monitor operation at a time, thus achieving mutually exclusive access to the shared variable. In order to include monitors in the language, some additions to the syntax rules and semantic specifications will be required. The precise form of these changes has yet to be determined.

The P1076a Working Group maintains a repository of its working reports and other information on the VIIS server, mentioned in the Preface. Readers who wish to observe progress of the project can browse this repository for information. Eventually, when the working group completes its work, a revised standard that includes the new synchronization mechanisms will be published, superseding the current standard.

D.3 IEEE P1076.1: VHDL-A — Analog Extensions to VHDL

While many electronic systems are entirely digital, there are many that include at least a small part that are analog in nature. Indeed, any system that interfaces to the "real world" must contain some analog components, such as transducers and analog/digital converters. Unfortunately, the mechanisms for describing and simulating analog circuits are quite different from those used in the digital domain. Analog modeling typically uses simultaneous or differential equations to model analog behavior, requiring iterative numerical techniques for solution. This contrasts with the programming language form of description used in VHDL to model digital behavior and the discrete event paradigm used to simulate digital systems.

The approach currently proposed by the P1076.1 Working Group is to define *natures*, which have *across* and *through* properties. A nature is used to model a particular analog domain. For example, we can define an electrical nature that has voltage as its across property and current as its through property. Other natures might include thermal nature, with temperature drop and heat flow as properties, and rotational nature, with torque and angular velocity as properties. The analog behavior of a system is specified in terms of interconnected *nodes*, at which Kirchoff conservation laws apply, and equational relations between analog *quantities*, namely, values of a given nature. The system is simulated by solving the user-specified equations subject to the conservation laws. The proposal also specifies mechanisms for interfacing between the analog and digital domains. These include predefined functions and attributes for allowing analog threshold crossings to cause digital events and for converting digital values to analog quantities.

The P1076.1 Working Group is developing standard extensions to VHDL, informally called VHDL-A, to accommodate analog modeling and simulation. The proposal is that the analog description facilities sit "side by side" with the digital facilities within the language. The current version of VHDL will be a proper subset of VHDL-A. Tool vendors who do not wish to provide analog modeling facilities will continue to conform to IEEE Std. 1076, whereas those who do offer analog facilities will specify conformance to 1076.1.

The P1076.1 Working Group maintains an e-mail mailing list. Readers interested in observing activities can be added to the mailing list by sending an e-mail message to

1076–1–request@epfl.ch

For further information, the working group secretary can be contacted at the following address:

Alain Vachoux
Swiss Federal Institute of Technology, Electronics Laboratory
LEG/C3i – Ecublens
CH–1015 Lausanne, Switzerland

E-mail: alain.vachoux@leg.de.epfl.ch

The organization Analog VHDL International (AVI) has been formed to promote adoption of VHDL-A and to act as a focus for potential VHDL-A users. AVI can be contacted at

Ian Getreu, AVI Secretary
Analogy Inc.
P. O. Box 1669
Beaverton, OR 97075–1669

E-mail: iang@analogy.com

D.4 IEEE P1076.2: Standard VHDL Language Mathematical Package

Many abstract behavioral models, particularly those that perform digital signal processing, perform mathematical operations upon data represented as real or complex numbers. While VHDL does provide a floating-point data type, it does not provide operations other than the basic arithmetic operators. In order to overcome this limitation, the P1076.2 Working Group is developing two packages of mathematical operations, one to operate on real numbers and the other to operate on complex numbers.

The proposed real math package, at the time of writing, includes

- definition of constants, including e and π;
- sign, ceiling, floor, round, min and max functions;
- a random number generator;
- square root, cube root, exponentiation, exponential and logarithm functions;
- trigonometric functions (sin, cos, etc.); and
- hyperbolic functions (sinh, cosh, etc.).

The proposed complex math function includes

- definitions of complex number types (Cartesian and polar form);
- definitions of constants for 0, 1 and j;
- absolute value, argument, negation and conjugate functions;
- square root and exponentiation functions;
- overloaded versions of basic arithmetic operators, with Cartesian, polar and real operands; and
- conversion functions.

The proposed standard includes both package declarations and package bodies. The package bodies are included to define the semantics of the operations provided. Tool vendors will be allowed to develop built-in optimized versions, provided they perform exactly the same operations. The packages will be added to the **ieee** library, along with **std_logic_1164** and other standard packages. The P1076.2 Working Group maintains a repository on the VIIS server, mentioned in the Preface. The repository contains, among other things, source files for the draft standard packages.

D.5   IEEE P1076.3: Standard VHDL Language Synthesis Package

In Appendix A we discussed the synthesis of circuits from VHDL descriptions and mentioned the proposed standard synthesis packages, **numeric_bit** and **numeric_std**. (At the time of writing, there is a possibility that the names of the packages may be changed as a result of the standards balloting process.) As well as specifying these packages, the P1076.3 Working Group is developing a standard practice for interpreting values of types **bit**, **boolean** and **std_ulogic** when synthesizing hardware. In particular, it specifies how the "metalogical" values 'U', 'X', 'W' and '–' are to be interpreted. These values are intended for use in simulation models and have no physical manifestation in a real circuit. For example, a real circuit never drives a signal with the value 'W' and never checks whether an input is in an unknown state. The proposed standard specifies how a synthesis tool should handle VHDL models that use metalogical values.

The proposed standard synthesis packages are intended for use in models that perform arithmetic operations on integer data represented in binary vector form. The packages provide

- overloaded versions of the VHDL arithmetic and relational operators,

- arithmetic shift and rotate functions,
- resizing functions (with sign extension/reduction), and
- type conversion functions.

The bit-vector package also provides edge-detection functions, analogous to those provided in **std_logic_1164** for standard-logic values. The standard-logic synthesis package provides overloaded versions of the VHDL logical operators, since the types **unsigned** and **signed** are new types declared by the package and do not inherit the functions from **std_logic_1164**. The package also provides the **std_match** function described in Appendix A.

Like other standard packages, the proposed synthesis packages are defined by package declarations and package bodies. The package bodies specify the semantics of the operations, but vendors are free to provide built-in optimized versions in their tools. The P1076.3 Working Group maintains a repository on the VIIS server, mentioned in the Preface, containing source files for the draft standard packages and other documents.

D.6 IEEE P1076.4: Timing Methodology (VITAL)

One of the most difficult aspects of designing a digital system is the timing. This is one reason why features to deal with timing are such a major part of VHDL. However, as a language, VHDL just provides basic mechanisms. It does not provide a complete methodology for specifying or testing the detailed timing behavior of a circuit. In response to this lack, a consortium of interested parties, including ASIC vendors and designers, formed an organization called the VHDL Initiative Towards ASIC Libraries (VITAL). They have developed a standard practice for including detailed timing information in VHDL models and a standard interface for back-annotation of timing data from layout tools. They have also developed a library of primitive components (gates, flipflops, registers, etc.) that conform to the methodology. The goal is to ensure that a designer is able to perform "sign-off" simulation of a design, namely, a sufficiently detailed simulation that both designer and ASIC foundry are satisfied that the fabricated ASIC will function as simulated.

The proposed VITAL standard specifies a package of types for specifying detailed pin-to-pin propagation delays and timing constraints, including maximum, minimum and nominal values. The package also provides procedures for performing timing checks. The methodology involves the designer including generic constants for timing data in entity declarations. The names and types for the generic constants are specified by the methodology, as is the way in which they should be used within architecture bodies to implement correct timing behavior and to verify timing constraints. Instead of using configuration declarations to include actual back-annotated timing data, the methodology requires simulators to read the data from files in Standard Delay File (SDF) format. The reasons for this approach are that SDF is widely used already and that reading the data in this format is faster than analyzing a VHDL version and reconfiguring the model.

At the time of writing, the VITAL specification has recently been passed over to the P1076.4 Working Group. This group will take the specification through the formal standards development and approval process, ultimately leading to a new IEEE standard. In the meantime, several VHDL tool vendors have implemented facilities in their simulators for dealing with models that conform to the proposed VITAL methodology. Like the other standards working groups, the P1076.4 Working Group maintains a repository on the VIIS server, containing source files for the draft packages and other documents.

D.7 IEEE P1076.5: VHDL Utility Library

Most organizations that use VHDL find it necessary or desirable to develop a library of packages of generally useful operations. This follows the good software engineering practice of code reuse. Since VHDL's widespread adoption, many organizations have made their utility packages freely available. However, designers often find the urge to "do it better" irresistible.

The P1076.5 Working Group has been formed to develop a utility library to add to the collection of IEEE standard packages. At the time of writing, this project has been under way for a relatively short time. To date, contributions include packages for conversions between types and for formatted input and output of different types. For example, one contribution is a text I/O package for standard-logic vectors. Other utilities that the group plans to specify include packages to support interoperability between VHDL and the Verilog hardware description language. The contributions being considered are available for perusal in the working group's repository on the VIIS server mentioned in the Preface.

D.8 IEEE P1165: EDIF Interoperability

EDIF (Electronic Design Interchange Format) is a standard that specifies a format for describing the structure and layout of integrated circuits. As its name implies, it is intended for use in communicating information between users, tools and vendors. EDIF has become quite widely used for this purpose.

The charter of the P1165 Working Group is to "recommend techniques by which relevant information migration can be achieved between VHDL and EDIF." At the time of writing, the group had only recently been established. Its first activity is to look at migration of structural connectivity information between VHDL and EDIF. Readers interested in obtaining more information about working group activities can send e-mail to the address vhdledif–info@vhdl.org. The group maintains an e-mail mailing list at the address vhdledif@vhdl.org. Requests to be added to the list should be sent to vhdledif–request@vhdl.or g.

D.9 EIA-567-A: Component Modeling and Interface Standard

The Electronic Industries Association (EIA) has developed the *VHDL Hardware Component Modeling and Interface Standard* to provide guidelines for component models. The standard addresses similar issues to those addressed by P1076.4, but with an emphasis on modeling existing hardware components rather than ASICs under development. The EIA-567-A standard specifies the form and content of an *electronic data sheet* for a hardware component, analogous to the paper data sheets provided by component manufacturers. The electronic data sheet includes an *electrical view*, a *timing view* and a *physical view*, all of which are written as VHDL packages. The data sheet also includes a VHDL simulation model that implements the component behavior, a test bench and stimulus/response test vectors, VHDL configuration declarations required to build a simulation and documentation for the model user. The electrical view specifies the signal voltage and current characteristics for each electrical connection of the component. The physical view specifies all of the pins of the physical package of the component, including power supply and electrically unconnected pins. The timing view specifies the values of timing parameters, such as setup and hold times, pulse widths and propagation delays, for minimum, nominal and maximum operating points. The standard also describes the generic constants to be included in an entity interface to specify wire delays at inputs and load delays at outputs.

The goal of the standard is to specify common modeling interfaces, conventions and simulation modes for models supplied by hardware component vendors. This will ensure that designers will be able to include models from different vendors when developing a system. At the time of writing, the standard has only recently been adopted. Hence it is too early to gauge its success in meeting these goals. Readers interested in the standard can obtain a copy from the VIIS server.

VHDL Syntax

In this appendix we present the full set of syntax rules for VHDL using the EBNF notation introduced in Chapter 1. The form of EBNF used in this book differs from that of the *VHDL Language Reference Manual* (*LRM*) in order to make the syntax rules more intelligible to the VHDL user. The *LRM* includes a separate syntax rule for each minor syntactic category. In this book, we condense the grammar into a smaller number of rules, each of which defines a larger part of the grammar. We introduce the EBNF symbols "(", ")" and "₀₀₀" as part of this simplification. Our aim is to avoid the large amount of searching required when using the LRM rules to resolve a question of grammar.

Those parts of the syntax rules that were introduced in VHDL-93 are underlined in this appendix. A VHDL-87 model may not use these features. In addition, there are some entirely new rules, introduced in VHDL-93, that have no predecessors in VHDL-87. We identify these rules individually where they occur in this appendix.

Index to Syntax Rules

E.1   Design File

design_file ⇐ design_unit { ... }

design_unit ⇐
    { library_clause ‖ use_clause }
    library_unit

library_unit ⇐
    entity_declaration | architecture_body
    | package_declaration | package_body
    | configuration_declaration

library_clause ⇐ **library** identifier { , ∘∘∘ } ;

E.2   **Library Unit Declarations**

entity_declaration ⇐
    entity identifier **is**
        ⟦ **generic** (*generic*_interface_list) ; ⟧
        ⟦ **port** (*port*_interface_list) ; ⟧
        { entity_declarative_item }
    ⟦ **begin**
        { concurrent_assertion_statement
          | *passive*_concurrent_procedure_call_statement
          | *passive*_process_statement } ⟧
    end ⟦ **entity** ⟧ ⟦ identifier ⟧ ;

entity_declarative_item ⇐
    subprogram_declaration | subprogram_body
    | type_declaration | subtype_declaration
    | constant_declaration | signal_declaration
    | *shared*_variable_declaration | file_declaration
    | alias_declaration
    | attribute_declaration | attribute_specification
    | disconnection_specification | use_clause
    | group_template_declaration | group_declaration

architecture_body ⇐
    architecture identifier **of** *entity*_name **is**
        { block_declarative_item }
    begin
        { concurrent_statement }
    end ⟦ **architecture** ⟧ ⟦ identifier ⟧ ;

configuration_declaration ⇐
    configuration identifier **of** *entity*_name **is**
        { use_clause | attribute_specification | group_declaration }
        block_configuration
    end ⟦ **configuration** ⟧ ⟦ identifier ⟧ ;

block_configuration ⇐
    for (*architecture*_name
        | *block_statement*_label
        | *generate_statement*_label 〚 ((discrete_range | *static*_expression)) 〛)
      { use_clause }
      { block_configuration
        | **for** component_specification
            〚 binding_indication ; 〛
            〚 block_configuration 〛
          end for ; }
    end for ;

package_declaration ⇐
    package identifier **is**
        { package_declarative_item }
end 〚 **package** 〛 〚 identifier 〛 ;

package_declarative_item ⇐
    subprogram_declaration
    | type_declaration | subtype_declaration
    | constant_declaration | signal_declaration
    | *shared*_variable_declaration | file_declaration
    | alias_declaration | component_declaration
    | attribute_declaration | attribute_specification
    | disconnection_specification | use_clause
    | group_template_declaration | group_declaration

package_body ⇐
    package body identifier **is**
        { package_body_declarative_item }
    end 〚 **package body** 〛 〚 identifier 〛 ;

package_body_declarative_item ⇐
    subprogram_declaration | subprogram_body
    | type_declaration | subtype_declaration
    | constant_declaration | *shared*_variable_declaration
    | file_declaration | alias_declaration
    | use_clause
    | group_template_declaration | group_declaration

E.3   Declarations and Specifications

subprogram_specification ⇐
    procedure (identifier | operator_symbol) 〚 (*parameter*_interface_list) 〛
    | 〚 **pure** | **impure** 〛
      function (identifier | operator_symbol)
           〚 (*parameter*_interface_list) 〛 **return** type_mark
subprogram_declaration ⇐ subprogram_specification ;

subprogram_body ⇐
    subprogram_specification **is**
        { subprogram_declarative_part }
    begin
        { sequential_statement }
    end ⟦ **procedure** | **function** ⟧ ⟦ identifier | operator_symbol ⟧ ;

subprogram_declarative_part ⇐
    subprogram_declaration | subprogram_body
    | type_declaration | subtype_declaration
    | constant_declaration | variable_declaration
    | file_declaration | alias_declaration
    | attribute_declaration | attribute_specification
    | use_clause
    | group_template_declaration | group_declaration

type_declaration ⇐
    type identifier **is** type_definition ;
    | **type** identifier ;

type_definition ⇐
    enumeration_type_definition | integer_type_definition
    | floating_type_definition | physical_type_definition
    | array_type_definition | record_type_definition
    | access_type_definition | file_type_definition

constant_declaration ⇐
    constant identifier { , ₒₒₒ } : subtype_indication ⟦ := expression ⟧ ;

signal_declaration ⇐
    signal identifier { , ₒₒₒ } : subtype_indication ⟦ **register** | **bus** ⟧
                    ⟦ := expression ⟧ ;

variable_declaration ⇐
    ⟦ **shared** ⟧ **variable** identifier { , ₒₒₒ } : subtype_indication ⟦ := expression ⟧ ;

file_declaration ⇐
    file identifier { , ₒₒₒ } : subtype_indication
        ⟦ ⟦ **open** *file_open_kind*_expression ⟧ **is** *string*_expression ⟧ ;

VHDL-87

The syntax for a file declaration in VHDL-87 is

file_declaration ⇐
    file identifier : subtype_indication **is** ⟦ **in** | **out** ⟧ *string*_expression ;

This difference is the only case in which VHDL-87 syntax is not a subset of VHDL-93 syntax. If a VHDL-87 model includes either of the keywords **in** or **out**, the model cannot be successfully analyzed with a VHDL-93 analyzer.

alias_declaration ⇐
    alias ⦅ identifier ⟦ character_literal ⟦ operator_symbol ⦆ ⟦: subtype_indication⟧
        is name ⟦ signature ⟧ ;

component_declaration ⇐
    component identifier ⟦ **is** ⟧
        ⟦ **generic** ⦅ *generic*_interface_list ⦆ ; ⟧
        ⟦ **port** ⦅ *port*_interface_list ⦆ ; ⟧
    end component ⟦ identifier ⟧ ;

attribute_declaration ⇐ **attribute** identifier : type_mark ;

attribute_specification ⇐
    attribute identifier **of** entity_name_list : entity_class **is** expression ;

entity_name_list ⇐
    ⦅ ⦅ identifier ⟦ character_literal ⟦ operator_symbol ⦆ ⟦ signature ⟧ ⦆ { , ₀₀₀ }
    ⟦ **others**
    ⟦ **all**

entity_class ⇐

entity	⟦ **architecture**	⟦ **configuration**	⟦ **procedure**	**function**
⟦ **package**	⟦ **type**	⟦ **subtype**	⟦ **constant**	⟦ **signal**
⟦ **variable**	⟦ **component**	⟦ **label**		
⟦ **literal**	⟦ **units**	⟦ **group**	⟦ **file**	

configuration_specification ⇐
    for component_specification binding_indication ;

component_specification ⇐
    ⦅ *instantiation*_label { , ₀₀₀ } ⟦ **others** ⟦ **all** ⦆ : *component*_name

binding_indication ⇐
    ⟦ **use** ⦅ **entity** *entity*_name ⟦ ⦅ *architecture*_identifier ⦆ ⟧
           ⟦ **configuration** *configuration*_name
           ⟦ **open** ⦆ ⟧
    ⟦ **generic map** ⦅ *generic*_association_list ⦆ ⟧
    ⟦ **port map** ⦅ *port*_association_list ⦆ ⟧

disconnection_specification ⇐
    disconnect ⦅ *signal*_name { , ₀₀₀ } ⟦ **others** ⟦ **all** ⦆ : type_mark
        after *time*_expression ;

group_template_declaration ⇐
    group identifier **is** ⦅ ⦅ entity_class ⟦ <> ⟧ ⦆ { , ₀₀₀ } ⦆ ;

group_declaration ⇐
    group identifier : *group_template*_name ⦅ ⦅ name ⟦ character_literal ⦆ { , ₀₀₀ } ⦆ ;

VHDL-87

Group template declarations and group declarations are not allowed in VHDL-87.

use_clause ⇐ **use** selected_name { , ₀₀₀ } ;

E.4   Type Definitions

enumeration_type_definition ⇐ ((identifier ‖ character_literal) { , ₀₀₀ })

integer_type_definition ⇐
    range (*range*_attribute_name
            ‖ simple_expression (**to** ‖ **downto**) simple_expression)

floating_type_definition ⇐
    range (*range*_attribute_name
            ‖ simple_expression (**to** ‖ **downto**) simple_expression)

physical_type_definition ⇐
    range (*range*_attribute_name
            ‖ simple_expression (**to** ‖ **downto**) simple_expression)
        units
            identifier ;
            { identifier = physical_literal ; }
        end units ⟦ identifier ⟧

array_type_definition ⇐
    array ((type_mark **range** <>) { , ₀₀₀ }) **of** *element*_subtype_indication
    ‖ **array** (discrete_range { , ₀₀₀ }) **of** *element*_subtype_indication

record_type_definition ⇐
    record
        (identifier { , ₀₀₀ } : subtype_indication ;)
        { ₀₀₀ }
    end record ⟦ identifier ⟧

access_type_definition ⇐ **access** subtype_indication

file_type_definition ⇐ **file of** type_mark

subtype_declaration ⇐ **subtype** identifier **is** subtype_indication ;

subtype_indication ⇐
    ⟦ *resolution_function*_name ⟧
    type_mark
        ⟦ **range** (*range*_attribute_name
                ‖ simple_expression (**to** ‖ **downto**) simple_expression)
        ‖ (discrete_range { , ₀₀₀ }) ⟧

discrete_range ⇐
    *discrete*_subtype_indication
    ‖ *range*_attribute_name
    ‖ simple_expression (**to** ‖ **downto**) simple_expression

type_mark ⇐ *type*_name ‖ *subtype*_name

E.5 Concurrent Statements

concurrent_statement ⇐
    block_statement
    ❘ process_statement
    ❘ concurrent_procedure_call_statement
    ❘ concurrent_assertion_statement
    ❘ concurrent_signal_assignment_statement
    ❘ component_instantiation_statement
    ❘ generate_statement

block_statement ⇐
    *block*_label :
    block ⟦ (*guard*_expression) ⟧ ⟦ **is** ⟧
        ⟦ **generic** (*generic*_interface_list) ;
        ⟦ **generic map** (*generic*_association_list) ; ⟧ ⟧
        ⟦ **port** (*port*_interface_list) ;
        ⟦ **port map** (*port*_association_list) ; ⟧ ⟧
        { block_declarative_item }
    begin
        { concurrent_statement }
    end block ⟦ *block*_label ⟧ ;

block_declarative_item ⇐
    subprogram_declaration   ❘ subprogram_body
    ❘ type_declaration   ❘ subtype_declaration
    ❘ constant_declaration   ❘ signal_declaration
    ❘ *shared*_variable_declaration ❘ file_declaration
    ❘ alias_declaration   ❘ component_declaration
    ❘ attribute_declaration   ❘ attribute_specification
    ❘ configuration_specification ❘ disconnection_specification
    ❘ use_clause
    ❘ group_template_declaration   ❘ group_declaration

process_statement ⇐
    ⟦ *process*_label : ⟧
    ⟦ **postponed** ⟧ **process** ⟦ (*signal*_name { , ... }) ⟧ ⟦ **is** ⟧
        { process_declarative_item }
    begin
        { sequential_statement }
    end ⟦ **postponed** ⟧ **process** ⟦ *process*_label ⟧ ;

process_declarative_item ⇐
    subprogram_declaration | subprogram_body
    | type_declaration | subtype_declaration
    | constant_declaration | variable_declaration
    | file_declaration | alias_declaration
    | attribute_declaration | attribute_specification
    | use_clause
    | group_template_declaration | group_declaration

concurrent_procedure_call_statement ⇐
    ⟦ label : ⟧
    ⟦ **postponed** ⟧ *procedure*_name ⟦ (*parameter*_association_list) ⟧ ;

concurrent_assertion_statement ⇐
    ⟦ label : ⟧
    ⟦ **postponed** ⟧ **assert** *boolean*_expression
                  ⟦ **report** expression ⟧ ⟦ **severity** expression ⟧ ;

concurrent_signal_assignment_statement ⇐
    ⟦ label : ⟧ ⟦ **postponed** ⟧ conditional_signal_assignment
    | ⟦ label : ⟧ ⟦ **postponed** ⟧ selected_signal_assignment

conditional_signal_assignment ⇐
    (name | aggregate) <=
        ⟦ **guarded** ⟧ ⟦ delay_mechanism ⟧
            { waveform **when** *boolean*_expression **else** }
            waveform ⟦ **when** *boolean*_expression ⟧ ;

selected_signal_assignment ⇐
    with expression **select**
        (name | aggregate) <=
            ⟦ **guarded** ⟧ ⟦ delay_mechanism ⟧
                { waveform **when** choices , }
                waveform **when** choices ;

component_instantiation_statement ⇐
    *instantiation*_label :
        (⟦ **component** ⟧ *component*_name
         | **entity** *entity*_name ⟦ (*architecture*_identifier) ⟧
         | **configuration** *configuration*_name)
        ⟦ **generic map** (*generic*_association_list) ⟧
        ⟦ **port map** (*port*_association_list) ⟧ ;

generate_statement ⇐
    *generate*_label :
    (**for** identifier **in** discrete_range | **if** *boolean*_expression) **generate**
        ⟦ { block_declarative_item }
    begin ⟧
        { concurrent_statement }
    end generate ⟦ *generate*_label ⟧ ;

E.6   Sequential Statements

sequential_statement ⇐
    wait_statement | assertion_statement
    | report_statement | signal_assignment_statement
    | variable_assignment_statement | procedure_call_statement
    | if_statement | case_statement
    | loop_statement | next_statement
    | exit_statement | return_statement
    | null_statement

wait_statement ⇐
    ⟦ label : ⟧ **wait** ⟦ **on** *signal*_name { , ... } ⟧
                ⟦ **until** *boolean*_expression ⟧
                ⟦ **for** *time*_expression ⟧ ;

assertion_statement ⇐
    ⟦ label : ⟧ **assert** *boolean*_expression
                ⟦ **report** expression ⟧ ⟦ **severity** expression ⟧ ;

report_statement ⇐ ⟦ label : ⟧ **report** expression ⟦ **severity** expression ⟧ ;

VHDL-87

Report statements are not allowed in VHDL-87.

---

signal_assignment_statement ⇐
    ⟦ label : ⟧ (name | aggregate) <= ⟦ delay_mechanism ⟧ waveform ;

delay_mechanism ⇐
    transport | ⟦ **reject** *time*_expression ⟧ **inertial**

waveform ⇐
    (*value*_expression ⟦ **after** *time*_expression ⟧
      | **null** ⟦ **after** *time*_expression ⟧) { , ... }
    | **unaffected**

variable_assignment_statement ⇐
    ⟦ label : ⟧ (name | aggregate) := expression ;

procedure_call_statement ⇐
    ⟦ label : ⟧ *procedure*_name ⟦ (*parameter*_association_list) ⟧ ;

if_statement ⇐
    ⟦ *if*_label : ⟧
    if *boolean*_expression **then**
        { sequential_statement }
    { **elsif** *boolean*_expression **then**
        { sequential_statement } }
    ⟦ **else**
        { sequential_statement } ⟧
    end if ⟦ *if*_label ⟧ ;
case_statement ⇐
    ⟦ *case*_label : ⟧
    case expression **is**
        (**when** choices => { sequential_statement })
        { ○○○ }
    end case ⟦ *case*_label ⟧ ;
loop_statement ⇐
    ⟦ *loop*_label : ⟧
    ⟦ **while** condition ∣ **for** identifier **in** discrete_range ⟧ **loop**
        { sequential_statement }
    end loop ⟦ *loop*_label ⟧ ;
next_statement ⇐ ⟦ label : ⟧ **next** ⟦ *loop*_label ⟧ ⟦ **when** *boolean*_expression ⟧ ;
exit_statement ⇐ ⟦ label : ⟧ **exit** ⟦ *loop*_label ⟧ ⟦ **when** *boolean*_expression ⟧ ;
return_statement ⇐ ⟦ label : ⟧ **return** ⟦ expression ⟧ ;
null_statement ⇐ ⟦ label : ⟧ **null** ;

E.7 Interfaces and Associations

interface_list ⇐
    (⟦ **constant** ⟧ identifier { , ○○○ } : ⟦ **in** ⟧ subtype_indication
                                       ⟦ := *static*_expression ⟧
    ∣ ⟦ **signal** ⟧ identifier { , ○○○ } : ⟦ mode ⟧ subtype_indication ⟦ **bus** ⟧
                                         ⟦ := *static*_expression ⟧
    ∣ ⟦ **variable** ⟧ identifier { , ○○○ } : ⟦ mode ⟧ subtype_indication
                                         ⟦ := *static*_expression ⟧
    ∣ **file** identifier { , ○○○ } : subtype_indication) { ; ○○○ }
mode ⇐ **in** ∣ **out** ∣ **inout** ∣ **buffer** ∣ **linkage**
association_list ⇐ (⟦ formal_part => ⟧ actual_part) { , ○○○ }
formal_part ⇐
    *generic*_name
    ∣ *port*_name
    ∣ *parameter*_name
    ∣ *function*_name ((*generic*_name ∣ *port*_name ∣ *parameter*_name))
    ∣ type_mark ((*generic*_name ∣ *port*_name ∣ *parameter*_name))

actual_part ⇐
    expression
    ‖ *signal*_name
    ‖ *variable*_name
    ‖ **open**
    ‖ *function*_name ((*signal*_name ‖ *variable*_name))
    ‖ type_mark ((*signal*_name ‖ *variable*_name))

E.8   Expressions

expression ⇐
    relation { **and** relation }   ‖ relation ⟦ **nand** relation ⟧
    ‖ relation { **or** relation }   ‖ relation ⟦ **nor** relation ⟧
    ‖ relation { **xor** relation }   ‖ relation { **xnor** relation }

relation ⇐ shift_expression ⟦ (= ‖ /= ‖ < ‖ <= ‖ > ‖ >=) shift_expression ⟧

VHDL-87

The syntax for a relation in VHDL-87 is

relation ⇐
    simple_expression ⟦ (= ‖ /= ‖ < ‖ <= ‖ > ‖ >=) simple_expression ⟧

shift_expression ⇐
    simple_expression ⟦ (**sll** ‖ **srl** ‖ **sla** ‖ **sra** ‖ **rol** ‖ **ror**) simple_expression ⟧

simple_expression ⇐ ⟦ + ‖ − ⟧ term { (+ ‖ − ‖ &) term }

term ⇐ factor { (* ‖ / ‖ **mod** ‖ **rem**) factor }

factor ⇐ primary ⟦ ** primary ⟧ ‖ **abs** primary ‖ **not** primary

primary ⇐
    name   ‖ literal
    ‖ aggregate   ‖ function_call
    ‖ qualified_expression   ‖ type_mark (expression)
    ‖ **new** subtype_indication   ‖ **new** qualified_expression
    ‖ (expression)

function_call ⇐ *function*_name ⟦ (*parameter*_association_list) ⟧

qualified_expression ⇐ type_mark ' (expression) ‖ type_mark ' aggregate

name ⇐
    identifier
    ‖ operator_symbol
    ‖ selected_name
    ‖ (name ‖ function_call) (expression { , ... })
    ‖ (name ‖ function_call) (discrete_range)
    ‖ attribute_name

selected_name ⇐
    (name ‖ function_call) . (identifier ‖ character_literal ‖ operator_symbol ‖ **all**)

operator_symbol ⇐ " { graphic_character } "

attribute_name ⇐ (name ‖ function_call) ⟦ signature ⟧ ' identifier ⟦ (expression) ⟧

signature ⇐ [⟦ type_mark { , ⁐ } ⟧ ⟦ **return** type_mark ⟧]

literal ⇐
    decimal_literal
    ‖ based_literal
    ‖ ⟦ decimal_literal ‖ based_literal ⟧ *unit*_name
    ‖ identifier
    ‖ character_literal
    ‖ string_literal
    ‖ bit_string_literal
    ‖ **null**

decimal_literal ⇐ integer ⟦ . integer ⟧ ⟦ E ⟦ + ⟧ integer ‖ E − integer ⟧

based_literal ⇐
    integer # based_integer ⟦ . based_integer ⟧ # ⟦ E ⟦ + ⟧ integer ‖ E − integer ⟧

integer ⇐ digit { ⟦ _ ⟧ ⁐ }

based_integer ⇐ (digit ‖ letter) { ⟦ _ ⟧ ⁐ }

character_literal ⇐ ' graphic_character '

string_literal ⇐ " { graphic_character } "

bit_string_literal ⇐ (B ‖ O ‖ X) " ⟦ (digit ‖ letter) { ⟦ _ ⟧ ⁐ } ⟧ "

aggregate ⇐ ((⟦ choices => ⟧ expression) { , ⁐ })

choices ⇐ (simple_expression ‖ discrete_range ‖ identifier ‖ **others**) { ‖ ⁐ }

label ⇐ identifier

identifier ⇐ letter { ⟦ _ ⟧ (letter ‖ digit) } ‖ \ graphic_character { ⁐ } \

Differences Between VHDL-87 and VHDL-93

In this appendix we summarize the restrictions of VHDL-87 that we mentioned throughout the book. We take the restrictive approach, rather than describing the way in which VHDL-93 is an extension of VHDL-87, since VHDL-93 is now the "official" version of the language. We expect most new models to be written in VHDL-93. Nevertheless, designers must deal with the legacy of models written before adoption of the new version of the language and with VHDL tools that have yet to be updated to handle the new version.

Lexical Differences

VHDL-87 uses the ASCII character set, rather than the full ISO character set. ASCII is a subset of the ISO character set, consisting of just the first 128 characters. This includes all of the unaccented letters, but excludes letters with diacritical marks.

VHDL-87 only allows basic identifiers, not extended identifiers. The rules for forming basic identifiers are the same as those for VHDL-93.

The following identifiers are not used as reserved words in VHDL-87. They may be used as identifiers for other purposes, although it is not advisable to do so, as this may cause difficulties in porting the models to VHDL-93.

group	**postponed**	**ror**	**sra**
impure	**pure**	**shared**	**srl**
inertial	**reject**	**sla**	**unaffected**
literal	**rol**	**sll**	**xnor**

Bit-string literals may only be used as literals for array types in which the elements are of type **bit**. The predefined type **bit_vector** is such a type. However, the standard-logic types **std_ulogic_vector** and **std_logic_vector** are not.

Syntactic Differences

The only sequential statements that may be labeled in VHDL-87 are loop statements. The remaining sequential statements, which may not be labeled, are variable assignment, signal assignment, wait, if, case, null, exit, next, assertion, procedure call and return statements.

The keyword **entity** may not be repeated at the end of an entity declaration.

The keyword **architecture** may not be repeated at the end of an architecture body.

The keyword **configuration** may not be repeated at the end of a configuration declaration.

The keyword **package** may not be repeated at the end of a package declaration.

The keywords **package body** may not be repeated at the end of a package body.

The keyword **procedure** may not be repeated at the end of a procedure declaration.

The keyword **function** may not be repeated at the end of a function declaration.

In a physical type definition, the type name may not be repeated after the keywords **end units**.

In a record type definition, the type name may not be repeated after the keywords **end record**.

The keyword **is** may not be included in the header of a block statement.

The keyword **is** may not be included in the header of a process statement.

The keyword **is** may not be included in the header of a component declaration, and the component name may not be repeated at the end of the declaration.

A generate statement may not include a declarative part or the keyword **begin**.

A component instantiation statement may not directly instantiate an entity or a configuration. It may only instantiate a declared component, but may not include the keyword **component**.

A conditional signal assignment statement may not include the keyword **else** and a condition after the last waveform in the statement.

The keyword **unaffected** may not be used in conditional and selected signal assignment statements.

An alias declaration in VHDL-87 must include a subtype indication.

The VHDL-87 syntax for file declarations is not a subset of the VHDL-93 syntax. The syntax rule in VHDL-87 is

>   file_declaration ⇐
>   **file** identifier : subtype_indication **is**
>   ⟦ **in** ⟧ **out** ⟧ *string*_expression ;

An attribute specification may not name a character literal as an item to be decorated, nor specify the entity class **literal**, **units**, **group** or **file**. An attribute specification may not include a signature after an item name.

Semantic Differences

In VHDL-87, the range specified in a slice may have the opposite direction to that of the index range of the array. In this case, the slice is a null slice.

The VHDL-87 language definition does not disallow the keyword **bus** in the specification of a signal parameter. However, it does not specify whether the kind of signal, guarded or unguarded, is determined by the formal parameter specification or by the actual signal associated with the parameter. Implementations of VHDL-87 make different interpretations. Some require the formal parameter specification to include the keyword **bus** if the procedure includes a null signal assignment to the parameter. The actual signal associated with the parameter in a procedure call must then be a guarded signal. Other implementations follow the approach adopted in VHDL-93, prohibiting the keyword **bus** in the parameter specification and determining the kind of the parameter from the kind of the actual signal.

In VHDL-87, files are of the variable class of objects. Hence file parameters in subprograms are specified as variable-class parameters. A subprogram that reads a file parameter should declare the parameter to be of mode **in**. A subprogram that writes a file parameter should declare the parameter to be of mode **out**.

Differences in the Standard Environment

The types file_open_kind and file_open_status, the subtype delay_length and the attribute foreign are not declared in std.standard. The function now returns a value of type time.

Since VHDL-87 uses the ASCII character set, the type character includes only the 128 ASCII characters.

The predefined attributes 'ascending, 'image, 'value, 'driving, 'driving_value, 'simple_name, 'path_name and 'instance_name are not provided.

The logical operator **xnor** and the shift operators **sll**, **srl**, **sla**, **sra**, **rol** and **ror** are not provided and so cannot be declared as overloaded operators. Thus, the VHDL-87 version of the standard-logic package std_logic_1164 does not define the **xnor** operator for standard-logic types.

In VHDL-87, the 'last_value attribute for a composite signal returns the aggregate of last values for each of the scalar elements of the signal, as opposed to the last value of the entire composite signal.

The VHDL-87 version of the textio package declares the function endline, which is not included in the VHDL-93 version of the package.

VHDL-93 Facilities Not in VHDL-87

VHDL-87 does not include report statements, labeled sequential statements (and hence decoration of sequential statements with attributes), postponed processes, shared variables, group templates or groups, aliases for non-data objects, declarative parts in generate statements or file open and close operations.

VHDL-87 does not allow specification of a pulse rejection interval in the delay mechanism part of a signal assignment. Transport delay can be specified using the keyword **transport**. If it is omitted, inertial delay is assumed, with a pulse rejection interval equal to the inertial delay interval.

VHDL-87 does not allow association of an expression with a port in a port map. VHDL-87 does not allow type conversions in association lists.

VHDL-87 does not allow direct instantiation of an entity or a configuration. Only declared components can be instantiated. They must be bound to design entities using configuration specifications or using component configurations in configuration declarations.

VHDL-87 does not allow incremental binding. It is an error if a design includes both a configuration specification and a component configuration for a given component instance.

Answers to Exercises

In this Appendix, we provide sample answers to the quiz-style exercises marked with the symbol "❶". Readers are encouraged to test their answers to the other, more involved, exercises by running the models on a VHDL simulator.

Chapter 1

1. Entity declaration: defines the interface to a module, in terms of its ports, their data transfer direction and their types. Behavioral architecture body: defines the function of a module in terms of an algorithm. Structural architecture body: defines an implementation of a module in terms of an interconnected composition of submodules. Process statement: encapsulates an algorithm in a behavioral description, contains sequential actions to be performed. Signal assignment statement: specifies values to be applied to signals at some later time. Port map: specifies the interconnection between signals and component instance ports in a structural architecture.

2.   apply_transform : **process is**
        begin
            d_out <= transform(d_in) **after** 200 ps;
            –– *debug_test <= transform(d_in);*
            wait on enable, d_in;
        end process apply_transform;

3. Basic identifiers: last_item. Reserved words: buffer. Invalid: prev item, value–1 and element#5 include characters that may not occur within identifiers; _control starts with an underscore; 93_999 starts with a digit; entry_ ends with an underscore.

4.   16#1#   16#22#   16#100.0#   16#0.8#

5.   12   132   44   250000   32768   0.625

6. The literal 16#23DF# is an integer expressed in base 16, whereas the literal X"23DF" is a string of 16 bits.

7.   B"111_100_111"   B"011_111_111"   B"001_011_100_101"
      B"1111_0010"   B"0000_0000_0001_0100"
      B"0000_0000_0000_0000_0000_0000_0000_0001"

Chapter 2

1.   **constant** bits_per_word : integer := 32;
      constant pi : real := 3.14159;

2.   **variable** counter : integer := 0;
      variable busy_status : boolean;
      variable temp_result : std_ulogic;

3.   counter := counter + 1;
      busy_status := true;
      temp_result := 'W';

4.   **package** misc_types **is**
           type small_int **is range** 0 **to** 255;
           type fraction **is range** –1.0 **to** +1.0;
           type current **is range** integer'low **to** integer'high
               units nA;
                   uA = 1000 nA;
                   mA = 1000 uA;
                   A = 1000 mA;
               end units;
           type colors **is** (red, yellow, green);
      end package misc_types;

5.   pulse_range'left = pulse_range'low = 1 ms
      pulse_range'right = pulse_range'high = 100 ms
      pulse_range'ascending = true
      word_index'left = 31   word_index'right = 0
      word_index'low = 0   word_index'high = 31
      word_index'ascending = false

6.   state'pos(standby) = 1   state'val(2) = active1
      state'succ(active2) is undefined   state'pred(active1) = standby
      state'leftof(off) is undefined   state'rightof(off) = standby

7.   2 * 3 + 6 / 4 = 7
      3 + –4 is syntactically incorrect
      "cat" & character'('0') = "cat0"
      true **and** x **and not** y **or** z is syntactically incorrect
      B"101110" **sll** 3= B"000101"
      B"100010" **sra** 2 & X"2C"= B"11100000111100"

Chapter 3

1. ```
   if n mod 2 = 1 then
         odd := '1';
   else
         odd := '0';
   end if;
   ```

2. ```
   if year mod 100 = 0 then
         days_in_February := 28;
   elsif year mod 4 = 0 then
         days_in_February := 29;
   else
         days_in_February := 28;
   end if;
   ```

3. ```
   case x is
         when '0' | 'L' => x := '0';
         when '1' | 'H' => x := '1';
         when others => x := 'X';
   end case;
   ```

4. ```
   case ch is
         when 'A' to 'Z' | 'a' to 'z' | 'À' to 'Ö' | 'Ø' to 'ß' | 'à' to 'ö' | 'ø' to 'ÿ' =>
               character_class := 1;
         when '0' to '9' => character_class := 2;
         when nul to usp | del | c128 to c159 => character_class := 4;
         when others => character_class := 3;
   end case;
   ```

5. ```
   loop
         wait until clk = '1';
         exit when d = '1';
   end loop;
   ```

6. ```
   sum := 1.0;
   term := 1.0;
   n := 0;
   while abs term > abs (sum / 1.0E5) loop
         n := n + 1;
         term := term * x / real(n);
         sum := sum + term;
   end loop;
   ```

7. ```
   sum := 1.0;
   term := 1.0;
   for n in 1 to 7 loop
         term := term * x / real(n);
         sum := sum + term;
   end loop;
   ```

8. ```
   assert to_X01(q) = not to_X01(q_n)
         report "flipflop outputs are not complementary";
   ```

9. Insert the statement after the comment "*-- at this point, reset = '1'*":

   ```
   report "counter is reset";
   ```

Chapter 4

1.
```
type num_vector is array (1 to 30) of integer;
variable numbers : num_vector;
. . .
sum := 0;
for i in numbers'range loop
    sum := sum + numbers(i);
end loop;
average := sum / numbers'length;
```

2.
```
type std_ulogic_to_bit_array is array (std_ulogic) of bit;
constant std_ulogic_to_bit : std_ulogic_to_bit_array
    := ( 'U' => '0', 'X' => '0', '0' => '0', '1' => '1', 'Z' => '0',
         'W' => '0', 'L' => '0', 'H' => '1', '–' => '0' );
. . .
for index in 0 to 15 loop
    v2(index) := std_ulogic_to_bit(v1(index));
end loop;
```

3.
```
type free_map_array is array (0 to 1, 0 to 79, 0 to 17) of bit;
variable free_map : free_map_array;
. . .
found := false;
for side in 0 to 1 loop
    for track in 0 to 79 loop
        for sector in 0 to 17 loop
            if free_map(side, track, sector) = '1' then
                found := true;  free_side := side;
                free_track := track;  free_sector := sector;
                exit;
            end if;
        end loop;
    end loop;
end loop;
```

4.
```
subtype std_ulogic_byte is std_ulogic_vector(7 downto 0);
constant Z_byte : std_ulogic_byte := "ZZZZZZZZ";
```

5.
```
count := 0;
for index in v'range loop
    if v(index) = '1' then
        count := count + 1;
    end if;
end loop;
```

6. Assuming the declarations
```
variable v1 : bit_vector(7 downto 0);
variable v2 : bit_vector(31 downto 0);
. . .
v2(31 downto 24) := v1;
v2 := v2 sra 24;
```

7.
```
type test_record is record
        stimulus : bit_vector(0 to 2);
```

```
                    delay : delay_length;
                    expected_response : bit_vector(0 to 7);
                end record test_record;
```

Chapter 5

1.
```
        entity lookup_ROM is
            port ( address : in lookup_index;  data : out real );

            type lookup_table is array (lookup_index) of real;
            constant lookup_data : lookup_table
                := ( real'high, 1.0, 1.0/2.0, 1.0/3.0, 1.0/4.0, . . . );

        end entity lookup_ROM;
```

2. Transactions are 'Z' at 0 ns, '0' at 10 ns, '1' at 30 ns, '1' at 55 ns, 'H' at 65 ns and 'Z' at 100 ns. The signal is active at all of these times. Events occur at each time except 55 ns, since the signal already has the value '1' at that time.

3. s'delayed(5 ns): 'Z' at 5 ns, '0' at 15 ns, '1' at 35 ns, 'H' at 70 ns, 'Z' at 105 ns. s'stable(5 ns): false at 0 ns, true at 5 ns, false at 10 ns, true at 15 ns, false at 30 ns, true at 35 ns, false at 65 ns, true at 70 ns, false at 100 ns, true at 105 ns. s'quiet(5 ns): false at 0 ns, true at 5 ns, false at 10 ns, true at 15 ns, false at 30 ns, true at 35 ns, false at 55 ns, true at 60 ns, false at 65 ns, true at 70 ns, false at 100 ns, true at 105 ns. s'transaction (assuming an initial value of '0'): '1' at 0 ns, '0' at 10 ns, '1' at 30 ns, '0' at 55 ns, '1' at 65 ns, '0' at 100 ns. At time 60 ns, s'last_event is 30 ns, s'last_active is 5 ns, and s'last_value is '0'.

4.
```
        wait on s until s = '1' and en = '1';
```

5.
```
        wait until ready = '1' for 5 ms;
```

6. The variable v1 is assigned false, since s is not updated until the next simulation cycle. The variable v2 is assigned true, since the wait statement causes the process to resume after s is updated with the value '1'.

7. At 0 ns: schedule '1' for 6 ns. At 3 ns: schedule '0' for 7 ns. At 8 ns: schedule '1' for 14 ns. At 9 ns: delete transaction scheduled for 14 ns, schedule '0' for 13 ns. The signal z takes on the values '1' at 6 ns and '0' at 7 ns. The transaction scheduled for 13 ns does not result in an event on z.

8. At 0 ns: schedule 1 for 7 ns, 23 for 9 ns, 5 for 10 ns, 23 for 12 ns and −5 for 15 ns. At 6 ns: schedule 23 for 13 ns, delete transactions scheduled for 15 ns, 10 ns and 9 ns. The signal x takes on the values 1 at 7 ns and 23 at 12 ns.

9.
```
        mux_logic : process is
        begin
            if enable = '1' and sel = '0' then
                z <= a and not b after 5 ns;
            elsif enable = '1' and sel = '1' then
                z <= x or y after 6 ns;
            else
                z <= '0' after 4 ns;
            end if;
            wait on a, b, enable, sel, x, y;
        end process mux_logic;
```

10.   **process is**
      begin
          case bit_vector'(s, r) **is**
              when "00" => **null**;
              when "01" => q <= '0';
              when "10" | "11" => q <= '1';
          end case;
          wait on s, r;
      end process;

11.   **assert** clk'last_event >= T_pw_clk
          report "interval between changes on clk is too small";

12.   bit_0 : **entity** work.ttl_74x74(basic)
          port map (pr_n => '1', d => q0_n, clk => clk, clr_n => reset,
                      q => q0, q_n => q0_n);

      bit_1 : **entity** work.ttl_74x74(basic)
          port map (pr_n => '1', d => q1_n, clk => q0_n, clr_n => reset,
                      q => q1, q_n => q1_n);

13.

14. One possible order is suggested: analyzing all entity declarations first, followed
    by all architecture bodies:

          entity edge_triggered_Dff
          entity reg4
          entity add_1
          entity buf4
          entity counter
          architecture behav of edge_triggered_Dff

architecture struct of reg4
architecture boolean_eqn of add_1
architecture basic of buf
architecture registered of counter

An alternative is

entity counter
entity buf4
entity add_1
entity reg4
architecture registered of counter
architecture basic of buf
architecture boolean_eqn of add_1
entity edge_triggered_Dff
architecture struct of reg4
architecture behav of edge_triggered_Dff

15. **library** company_lib, project_lib;
    use company_lib.in_pad, company_lib.out_pad, project_lib.**all**;

Chapter 6

1. The variables real_part_product_1, real_part_product_2, imag_part_product_1 and imag_part_product_2 are used to hold the results of the first pipeline stage computation. They are also used as the source operands for the second pipeline stage computations. If computations are performed for the first stage first, the variables are overwritten before being used for the second stage computation. The same argument applies for the variables used to hold results for subsequent stages in the pipeline.

2. Since the real part and the imaginary part of the accumulator are each restricted to the range −16.0 to +16.0, any sequence that causes either accumulator part to fall out of this range results in an overflow. An example is the sequence

   $(-1.0, 0.0) \times (-1.0, 0.0) + (-1.0, 0.0) \times (-1.0, 0.0) + \ldots$

   Each product is the complex value (1.0, 0.0), so after 16 terms, the real part of the accumulator reaches the value 16.0 and overflows.

3. The values in successive clock cycles after the first rising clock edge are shown in the following table:

Variable	Value in successive clock cycles			
input_x_real	+0.50	+0.20	+0.10	+0.10
input_x_imag	+0.50	+0.20	−0.10	−0.10
input_y_real	+0.50	+0.20	+0.10	+0.10
input_y_imag	+0.50	+0.20	+0.10	+0.10

(continued on page 662)

(continued from page 661)

Variable	Value in successive clock cycles						
real_part_product_1	?	+0.25	+0.04	+0.01	+0.01		
real_part_product_2	?	+0.25	+0.04	−0.01	−0.01		
imag_part_product_1	?	+0.25	+0.04	+0.01	+0.01		
imag_part_product_2	?	+0.25	+0.04	−0.01	−0.01		
real_product	?	?	0.00	0.00	+0.02	+0.02	
imag_product	?	?	+0.50	+0.08	0.00	0.00	
real_sum	0.00	0.00	0.00	0.00	0.00	+0.02	+0.04
imag_sum	0.00	0.00	0.00	+0.50	+0.58	+0.58	+0.58
real_accumulator_ovf	false	false	false	false	false	false	false
imag_accumulator_ovf	false	false	false	false	false	false	false

4.

Format	+0.5	−0.5
inputs	0100 . . . 0	1100 . . . 0
partial products	00100 . . . 0	11100 . . . 0
products	000100 . . . 0	111100 . . . 0
pipelined products	000100 . . . 0	111100 . . . 0
accumulated sums	00000100 . . . 0	11111100 . . . 0
outputs	0100 . . . 0	1100 . . . 0

Chapter 7

1. **constant** operand1 : **in** integer
    operand1 : integer
    constant tag : **in** bit_vector(31 **downto** 16)
    tag : bit_vector(31 **downto** 16)
    constant trace : **in** boolean := false
    trace : boolean := false

2. **variable** average : **out** real;
    average : **out** real
    variable identifier : **inout** string
    identifier : **inout** string

3. **signal** clk : **out** bit
    signal data_in : **in** std_ulogic_vector
    signal data_in : std_ulogic_vector

4. Some alternatives are

    stimulate (s, 5 ns, 3);
    stimulate (target => s, delay => 5 ns, cycles => 3);

    stimulate (s, 10 ns, 1);
    stimulate (s, 10 ns);
    stimulate (target => s, delay => 10 ns, cycles => **open**);

```
            stimulate ( target => s, cycles => open, delay => 10 ns );
            stimulate ( target => s, delay => 10 ns );

            stimulate ( s, 1 ns, 15 );
            stimulate ( target => s, delay => open, cycles => 15 );
            stimulate ( target => s, cycles => 15);
            stimulate ( s, cycles => 15);
```

5.
```
      swapper : process is
      begin
            shuffle_bytes ( ext_data, int_data, swap_control, Tpd_swap );
            wait on ext_data, swap_control;
      end process swapper;
```

6.
```
      product_size := approx_log_2(multiplicand) + approx_log_2(multiplier);
```

7.
```
      assert now <= 20 ms
            report "simulation time has exceeded 20 ms";
```

8. The third, first, none and third, respectively.

9.
```
      architecture behavioral of computer system is

            signal internal_data : bit_vector(31 downto 0);

            interpreter : process is

                  variable opcode : bit_vector(5 downto 0);

                  procedure do_write is
                        variable aligned_address : natural;
                  begin
                        . . .
                  end procedure do_write;

            begin
                  . . .
            end process interpreter;
      end architecture behavioral;
```

Chapter 8

1.
```
      package EMS_types is
            type engine_speed is range 0 to integer'high
                  units rpm;
                  end units engine_speed;
            constant peak_rpm : engine_speed := 6000 rpm;
            type gear is (first, second, third, fourth, reverse);
      end package EMS_types;

      work.EMS_types.engine_speed
      work.EMS_types.rpm                   work.EMS_types.peak_rpm
      work.EMS_types.gear                  work.EMS_types.first
      work.EMS_types.second                work.EMS_types.third
      work.EMS_types.fourth                work.EMS_types.reverse
```

2.
```
      procedure increment ( num : inout integer );
```

3.
```
      function odd ( num : integer ) return boolean;
```

4.   **constant** e : real;

5. No. The package does not contain any subprogram declarations or deferred constant declarations.

6.   **use** work.EMS_types.engine_speed;

7.   **library** DSP_lib;
       use DSP_lib.systolic_FFT, DSP_lib.DSP_types.**all**;

Chapter 9

1.   **alias** received_source **is** received_packet.source;
       alias received_dest **is** received_packet.dest;
       alias received_flags **is** received_packet.flags;
       alias received_payload **is** received_packet.payload;
       alias received_checksum **is** received_packet.checksum;

2.   **alias** received_AK **is** received_packet.flags(0);
       alias received_ACKNO : bit_vector(2 **downto** 0)
               is received_packet.flags(1 **to** 3);
       alias received_SEQNO : bit_vector(2 **downto** 0)
               is received_packet.flags(4 **to** 6);
       alias received_UD **is** received_packet.flags(7);

3.   **alias** cons **is** "&" [character, string **return** string];

       report cons (grade_char, "–grade");

Chapter 10

1.   PC := bv_addu (PC, natural_to_bv(4, PC'length));

2.   effective_address := base_address
                       + bv_sext(offset, 24) * integer_to_bv(scale_factor, 24);

Chapter 11

1. (a) '1'.
   (b) '0'.
   (c) Either '1' or '0'. The order of contributions within the array passed to the resolution function is not defined. This particular resolution function returns the leftmost non-'Z' value in the array, so the result depends on the order in which the simulator assembles the contributions.

2.   **subtype** wired_and_logic **is** wired_and tri_state_logic;
       signal synch_control : wired_and_logic := '0';

3. The initial value is 'X'. The default initial value of type MVL4, 'X', is used as the initial value of each driver of int_req. These contributions are passed to the resolution function, which returns the value 'X'.

4. No, since the operation represented by the table in the resolution function is commutative and associative, with 'Z' as its identity.

5. (a) "ZZZZ0011"

   (b) "XXXX0011"

   (c) "0011XX11"

6. "XXXXZZZZ00111100"

7. (a) '0'

   (b) '0'

   (c) 'W'

   (d) 'U'

   (e) 'X'

8.

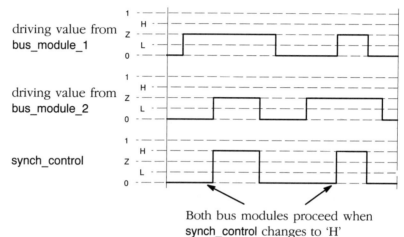

Both bus modules proceed when synch_control changes to 'H'

9. The resolution function is invoked seven times: for the Mem port, the Cache port, the CPU/Mem Section port, the Serial port, the DMA port, the I/O Section port and the Data Bus signal.

10. We cannot simply invert the value read from the port, since the value may differ from that driven by the process. Instead, we use the 'driving_value attribute:

    synch_T <= **not** synch_T'driving_value;

Chapter 12

1.   **entity** flipflop **is**
        generic (Tpw_clk_h, T_pw_clk_l : delay_length := 3 ns);
        port (clk, d : **in** bit; q, q_n : **out** bit);
    end entity flipflop;

2.   clk_gen : **entity** work.clock_generator
        generic map (period => 10 ns)
        port map (clk => master_clk);

3.   **entity** adder **is**
        generic (data_length : positive);
        port (a, b : **in** std_logic_vector(data_length − 1 **downto** 0);
            sum : **out** std_logic_vector(data_length − 1 **downto** 0));
    end entity adder;

4.   io_control_reg : **entity** work.reg
            generic map (width => 4)
            port map (d => data_out(3 **downto** 0),
                            q(0) => io_en, q(1) => io_int_en, q(2) => io_dir, q(3) => io_mode,
                            clk => io_write, reset => io_reset);

Chapter 13

1. An entity declaration uses the keyword **entity** where a component declaration uses the keyword **component**. An entity declaration is a design unit that is analyzed and placed into a design library, whereas a component declaration is simply a declaration in an architecture body or a package. An entity declaration has a declarative part and a statement part, providing part of the implementation of the interface, whereas a component declaration simply declares an interface with no implementation information. An entity declaration represents the interface of a "real" electronic circuit, whereas a component declaration represents a "virtual" or "template" interface.

2.   **component** magnitude_comparator **is**
            generic (width : positive; Tpd : delay_length);
            port (a, b : **in** std_logic_vector(width − 1 **downto** 0);
                    a_equals_b, a_less_than_b : **out** std_logic);
        end component magnitude_comparator;

3.   position_comparator : **component** magnitude_comparator
            generic map (width => current_position'length, Tpd => 12 ns)
            port map (a => current_position, b => upper_limit,
                        a_less_than_b => position_ok, a_equals_b => **open**);

4.   **package** small_number_pkg **is**
            subtype small_number **is** natural **range** 0 **to** 255;
            component adder **is**
                port (a, b : **in** small_number; s : **out** small_number);
            end component adder;
        end package small_number_pkg;

5.   **library** dsp_lib;
        configuration digital_filter_rtl **of** digital_filter **is**
            for register_transfer
                for coeff_1_multiplier : multiplier
                    use entity dsp_lib.fixed_point_mult(algorithmic);
                end for;
            end for;
        end configuration digital_filter_rtl;

6.   **library** dsp_lib;
        configuration digital_filter_std_cell **of** digital_filter **is**
            for register_transfer
                for coeff_1_multiplier : multiplier
                    use configuration dsp_lib.fixed_point_mult_std_cell;
                end for;
            end for;
        end configuration digital_filter_std_cell;

7. **library** dsp_lib;
    architecture register_transfer **of** digital_filter **is**

    . . .

    begin
        coeff_1_multiplier : **configuration** dsp_lib.fixed_point_mult_std_cell
            port map (. . .);

        . . .

    end architecture register_transfer;

8. **use entity** work.multiplexer
        generic map (Tpd => 3.5 ns);

9.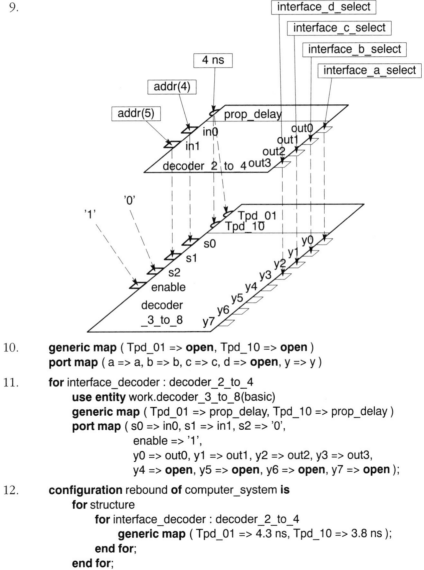

10. **generic map** (Tpd_01 => **open**, Tpd_10 => **open**)
    port map (a => a, b => b, c => c, d => **open**, y => y)

11. **for** interface_decoder : decoder_2_to_4
        use entity work.decoder_3_to_8(basic)
        generic map (Tpd_01 => prop_delay, Tpd_10 => prop_delay)
        port map (s0 => in0, s1 => in1, s2 => '0',
                    enable => '1',
                    y0 => out0, y1 => out1, y2 => out2, y3 => out3,
                    y4 => **open**, y5 => **open**, y6 => **open**, y7 => **open**);

12. **configuration** rebound **of** computer_system **is**
        for structure
            for interface_decoder : decoder_2_to_4
                generic map (Tpd_01 => 4.3 ns, Tpd_10 => 3.8 ns);
            end for;
        end for;
    end configuration rebound;

Chapter 14

1.

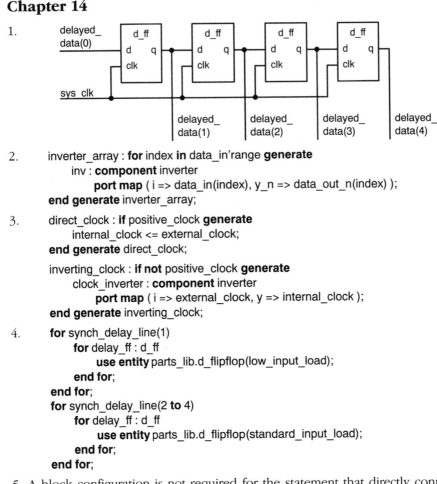

2.   inverter_array : **for** index **in** data_in'range **generate**
           inv : **component** inverter
                  port map (i => data_in(index), y_n => data_out_n(index));
           end generate inverter_array;

3.   direct_clock : **if** positive_clock **generate**
           internal_clock <= external_clock;
           end generate direct_clock;

      inverting_clock : **if not** positive_clock **generate**
           clock_inverter : **component** inverter
                  port map (i => external_clock, y => internal_clock);
           end generate inverting_clock;

4.   **for** synch_delay_line(1)
           for delay_ff : d_ff
                  use entity parts_lib.d_flipflop(low_input_load);
           end for;
      end for;
      for synch_delay_line(2 **to** 4)
           for delay_ff : d_ff
                  use entity parts_lib.d_flipflop(standard_input_load);
           end for;
      end for;

5. A block configuration is not required for the statement that directly connects the signals, since the statement does not include any component instances. The following block configuration for the statement that instantiates the inverter component is only used if the generic **positive_clock** is false when the design is elaborated:

           for inverting_clock
                  for clock_inverter : inverter
                         use entity parts_lib.inverter;
                  end for;
           end for;

Chapter 15

1. (a) X"08000030"
   (b) X"10600010"
   (c) X"00451004"
   (d) X"04E81802"

2. "ADDI   R7, R17, 42"

3. (a) sequencer calls: bus_instruction_fetch, do_EX_link,
   do_MEM_jump, do_WB

   (b) sequencer calls: bus_instruction_fetch, do_EX_branch

   (c) sequencer calls: bus_instruction_fetch, do_EX_branch, do_MEM_branch

   (d) sequencer calls: bus_instruction_fetch,
   execute_op_special, which calls: do_EX_arith_logic,
   do_WB

   (e) sequencer calls: bus_instruction_fetch,
   do_EX_arith_logic_immed, do_WB

   (f) sequencer calls: bus_instruction_fetch,
   do_EX_load_store,
   do_MEM_load, which calls bus_data_read,
   do_WB

   (g) sequencer calls: bus_instruction_fetch,
   do_EX_set_unsigned, which calls do_set_result,
   do_WB

Chapter 16

1. **signal** serial_bus : wired_or_bit **bus**;
   signal d_node : unique_bit **register**;

2. When the resolution function for a standard-logic signal is passed an empty vector, it returns the value 'Z'. Thus, the values on rx_bus are 'Z', '0' after 10 ns, '1' after 20 ns, '0' after 30 ns, 'X' after 35 ns, '1' after 40 ns, '0' after 45 ns and 'Z' after 55 ns.

3. 'U', '0' after 10 ns, '1' after 20 ns, '0' after 30 ns, 'X' after 35 ns, '1' after 40 ns, '0' after 45 ns.

4. vote <= 3 **after** 2 us, **null after** 5 us;

5. Initially false, true at 160 ns, false at 270 ns.

6. It should return the byte "1111_1111", since this is the identity value for the logical "and" operation.

7. inverting_latch : **block** (en = '1' **or** en = 'H') **is**
   begin
        q_out_n <= **guarded not** d_in;
   end block inverting_latch;

8. **disconnect** source1 : wired_word **after** 3.5 ns;
   disconnect others : wired_word **after** 3.2 ns;
   disconnect all : wired_bit **after** 2.8 ns;

9. Initially 0, 3 at 51 ns, 5 at 81 ns, 0 at 102 ns.

10.
```
inverting_ff : block is
    signal q_internal : bit;
begin
    the_dff : component dff
        port map ( clk => sys_clk, d => d_in, q => q_internal );
    the_inverter : component inverter
        port map ( i => q_internal, y => q_out_n );
end block inverting_ff;
```

11.
```
for inverting_ff
    for the_dff : dff
        use entity work.d_flipflop(basic);
    end for;
    for the_inverter : inverter
        use entity work.inverter(basic);
    end for;
end for;
```

Chapter 17

1.
```
type character_ptr is access character;
variable char : character_ptr := new character'(ETX);
. . .
char.all := 'A';
```

2. The statement "r := r + 1.0;" should be "r.all := r.all + 1.0;". The name r in the statement denotes the pointer, rather than the value pointed to. It is an error to perform an arithmetic operation on a pointer value.

3.   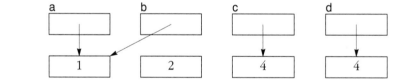

4.   a = b is true, a.**all** = b.**all** is true, c = d is false, c.**all** = d.**all** is true.

5.
```
type string_ptr is access string;
variable str : string_ptr := new string'("      ");
. . .
str(1) := NUL;
```

6.
```
z.re := x.re * y.re − x.im * y.im;
z.im := x.re * y.im + x.im * y.re;
```

7.
```
type message_cell;
type message_ptr is access message_cell;
type message_cell is record
        source, destination : natural;
        data : bit_vector(0 to 255);
        next_cell : message_ptr;
    end record message_cell;
variable message_list : message_ptr;
    . . .
```

```
message_list := new message_cell'( source => 1, destination => 5,
                                    data => (others => '0'),
                                    next_cell => message_list );
```

8. The first statement copies the pointer to the first cell to the access variable cell_to_be_deleted, and leaves value_list also pointing at that cell. The call to **deallocate** reclaims the storage and sets cell_to_be_deleted to the null pointer, but leaves value_list unchanged. The host computer system is free to reuse or remove the reclaimed storage, so the access using value_list in the third statement may not be valid.

9.
```
use work.bounded_buffer_adt.all;
. . .
loop
    test_full(test_buffer, buffer_full);
    exit when buffer_full;
    write(test_buffer, X"00");
end loop;
```

Chapter 18

1.
```
type real_file is file of real;
file sample_file : real_file open read_mode is "samples.dat";
. . .
read ( sample_file, x );
```

2.
```
type bv_file is file of bit_vector;
file trace_file : bv_file open write_mode is "/tmp/trace.tmp";
. . .
write ( trace_file, addr & d_bus );
```

3.
```
file_open ( status => waveform_status, f => waveform_file,
            external_name => "waveform", open_kind => read_mode);
assert waveform_status = open_ok
    report file_open_status'image(waveform_status)
            & " occurred opening waveform file" severity error;
```

4. The first call returns the bit value '1'. The second call returns the integer value 23. The third call returns the real value 4.5. The fourth call returns the three-character string " 67".

5.
```
use std.textio.all;
variable prompt_line, input_line : line;
variable number : integer;
. . .
write(prompt_line, string'("Enter a number:"));
writeline(output, prompt_line);
readline(input, input_line);
read(input_line, number);
```

6. "   3500 ns 00111100 ok   "

Chapter 19

1.

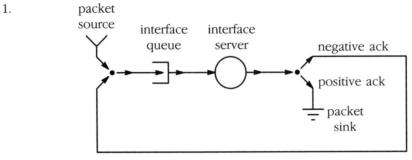

2.   **variable** random_info : random_info_record;

    . . .

    init_uniform (random_info,

                     lower_bound => 1.0, upper_bound => 2.0,

                     seed => sample_seeds(0));

    generate_random (random_info, x);

Chapter 20

1.   op_special'path_name = ":dlx_lib:dlx_instr:op_special"

    disassemble'path_name = ":dlx_lib:dlx_instr:disassemble"

    result'path_name = ":dlx_lib:dlx_instr:disassemble:result"

    int_image_length'path_name =

        ":dlx_lib:dlx_instr:disassemble"

        & ":disassemble_integer:int_image_length"

2.   val0_reg'path_name = ":test_bench:dut:val0_reg:"

    val0_reg'instance_name =

        ":test_bench(counter_test)"

        & ":dut@counter(registered):val0_reg@reg4(struct):"

    bit0'path_name = ":test_bench:dut:val1_reg:bit0"

    bit0'instance_name =

        ":test_bench(counter_test)"

        & ":dut@counter(registered):val1_reg@reg4(struct)"

        & ":bit0@edge_triggered_dff(behavioral):"

    clr'path_name = ":test_bench:dut:val1_reg:bit0:clr"

    clr'instance_name =

        ":test_bench(counter_test)"

        & ":dut@counter(registered):val1_reg@reg4(struct)"

        & ":bit0@edge_triggered_dff(behavioral):clr"

3.   **attribute** load : capacitance;

    attribute load **of** d_in : **signal is** 3 pF;

4.   **type** area **is range** 0 **to** integer'high

        units um_2;

        end units area;

    attribute cell_area : area;

    attribute cell_area **of** library_cell : architecture **is** 15 um_2;

5.   **attribute** optimization **of**
          test_empty [list_ptr, boolean] : **procedure is** "inline";

6.   **architecture** c_implementation **of** control_unit **is**
          attribute foreign **of**
               c_implementation : **architecture is**
               "control_unit.o control_utilities.o";
      begin
      end architecture c_implementation;

7.   **group** statement_set **is** (**label, label** <>);
      group steps_1_and_2 : statement_set (step_1, step_2);
      attribute resource_allocation **of** steps_1_and_2 : **group is** max_sharing;

Chapter 21

1. The function To_bit has two parameters: the value to be converted and the parameter xmap that indicates how an unknown logic level should be converted. A conversion function in an association list must have only one parameter.

2. We need to define a conversion function from std_ulogic to bit:

      function cvt_to_bit (s : std_ulogic) **return** bit **is**
      begin
          return To_bit(s);
      end function cvt_to_bit;

We can use this function and the standard-logic conversion function To_stdulogic in the association list:

      gate1 : **component** nand2
          port map (a => To_stdlogic(s1), b => To_stdlogic(s2),
               cvt_to_bit(y_n) => s3);

3. If the host computer system has multiple processors, m1 and m2 may be resumed concurrently on different processors. Suppose the variable starts with the value 0. A possible sequence of events is: m1 reads the variable and gets the value 0, m2 reads the variable and gets the value 0, m1 updates the variable with the value 1, m1 updates the variable with the value 1. Thus, the final value of the variable is 1, even though there were two increments performed.

References

[1] R. Airiau, J.-M. Bergé and V. Olive, *Circuit Synthesis with VHDL*, Kluwer, Dordrecht, The Netherlands, 1994.

[2] C. G. Bell and A. Newell, *Computer Structures: Readings and Examples*, McGraw-Hill, New York, 1971.

[3] European VHDL Synthesis Working Group, *Level-0 VHDL Synthesis Subset*, EVSWG, 1994.

[4] J. M. Feldman and C. T. Retter, *Computer Architecture: A Designer's Text Based on a Generic RISC*, McGraw-Hill, New York, 1994.

[5] M. B. Feldman, *Data Structures with Ada*, Prentice Hall, Englewood Cliffs, NJ, 1985.

[6] D. D. Gajski and R. H. Kuhn, "New VLSI Tools," *IEEE Computer*, Vol. 16, no. 12 (December 1983), pp. 11–14.

[7] J. L. Hennessy and D. A. Patterson, *Computer Architecture: A Quantitative Approach*, 2nd edition, Morgan Kaufmann, San Francisco, 1995.

[8] Institute for Electrical and Electronic Engineers, *Information Technology – Microprocessor Systems – Futurebus+ – Logical Protocol Specification*, ISO/IEC 10857, ANSI/IEEE Std. 896.1, IEEE, New York, 1994.

[9] R. Jain, *The Art of Computer System Performance Analysis: Techniques for Experimental Design, Measurement, Simulation and Modeling*, Wiley, New York, 1991.

[10] S. P. Smith and R. D. Acosta, "Value System for Switch-Level Modeling," *IEEE Design & Test of Computers*, Vol. 7, no. 3 (June 1990), pp. 33–41.

[11] I. E. Sutherland, C. E. Molnar, R. F. Sproull and J. C. Mudge, "The TRIMOSBUS," *Proceedings of the Caltech Conference on VLSI*, January 1979.

[12] A. S. Tanenbaum, *Structured Computer Organization*, 3rd edition, Prentice Hall, Englewood Cliffs, NJ, 1990.

[13] S. A. Ward and R. H. Halstead, Jr., *Computation Structures*, MIT Press, Cambridge, MA, and McGraw-Hill, New York, 1990.

[14] N. Weste and K. Eshraghian, *Principles of CMOS VLSI Design: A Systems Perspective*, Addison-Wesley, Reading, MA, 1985.

Index

Page numbers in bold face denote whole sections and subsections that address a topic.

677